WHO IS A CHRISTIAN?

Selections adapted to the seasons of the Ecclesiastical Year

FROM THE

Parochial & Plain Sermons

OF

JOHN HENRY NEWMAN

DIMENSION BOOKS INC.

PO BOX 811

DENVILLE, NJ 07834

First American Printing 1982
for
DIMENSION BOOKS INC.
Denville, New Jersey

U.S. ISBN # 0-87193-188-5

Publisher's Preface

This selection from the *Parochial and Plain Sermons,* originally published in eight volumes in 1868, follows the Maynooth edition of 1878 in which a representative number of Sermons were arranged according to the Ecclesiastical Year. The actual choice of topics was intended to emphasize Newman's own purpose, which was to bring out the fundamental Articles of the Faith and their bearing on the formation of the Christian character. This seems to have been the author's great aim from the first, under a solemn sense of responsibility "as a minister of Christ" and "as answerable for the formation of one, and one only, character in the heart of man." He tried to trace on the human heart, with a rich variety of illustrations, the features of that character and to show with deep study of our moral nature and far-reaching sympathy how faith on the basis of exact and definite doctrine develops into an expansive and enlightened love.

Judged simply as literature, the Parochial and Plain Sermons will very likely always be regarded as Newman's greatest achievement. The perfection of their themes and language remind us of great musical conceptions, their unerring balance of form and imagery combining with a sober directness in vocabulary and diction give us measure and sincerity and power and life. But these Sermons are far more than just literature. They exhibit one of the most acute theological minds of our epoch at work in developing the practical demands of daily Christian life, its attitudes and emotions and problems. What Father Przywara says of his work seems in no way an exaggeration: What St. Augustine was for the ancient world, what St. Thomas Aquinas was for the Middle Ages, that John Henry Newman is for the world today.

It is our hope that this new edition of Cardinal Newman's work will have a deep and wide influence on Christian life, and bring many readers of this selection to search out the *Parochial and Plain Sermons* in their entirety.

The title under which the book appears is our suggestion, and intended only to call the attention of many readers unfamiliar with Newman to the subject matter with which he deals and under what aspect.

CONTENTS.

a 2

SERMON I.

(ADVENT.)

Self-denial the Test of Religious Earnestness.

" Now it is high time to awake out of sleep."—ROM. xiii. 11.

BY "sleep," in this passage, St. Paul means a state of insensibility to things as they really are in God's sight. When we are asleep, we are absent from this world's action, as if we were no longer concerned in it. It goes on without us, or, if our rest be broken, and we have some slight notion of people and occurrences about us, if we hear a voice or a sentence, and see a face, yet we are unable to catch these external objects justly and truly; we make them part of our dreams, and pervert them till they have scarcely a resemblance to what they really are; and such is the state of men as regards religious truth. God is ever Almighty and All-knowing. He is on His throne in heaven, trying the reins and the hearts; and Jesus Christ, our Lord and Saviour, is on His right hand; and ten thousand Angels and Saints are ministering to Him, rapt in the contemplation of Him, or by their errands of mercy connecting this lower world with His courts above; they go to and fro, as though upon the ladder which Jacob saw. And the disclosure of this glorious invisible world is made to us principally by means of the Bible, partly by the course of nature, partly by the floating opinions of mankind, partly by the suggestions of the heart and conscience;—and all these means of information concerning it are collected and combined by the Holy Church, which heralds the news forth to the whole earth, and applies it with power to individual minds, partly by direct instruction, partly by her very form and fashion, which witnesses to them; so that the truths of religion circulate through the world almost as the

A

light of day, every corner and recess having some portion of its blessed rays. Such is the state of a Christian country. Meanwhile, how is it with those who dwell in it? The words of the text remind us of their condition. They are *asleep*. While the ministers of Christ are using the armour of light, and all things speak of Him, they "walk" not "becomingly, as in the day." Many live altogether as though the day shone not on them, but the shadows still endured; and far the greater part of them are but very faintly sensible of the great truths preached around them. They see and hear as people in a dream; they mix up the Holy Word of God with their own idle imaginings; if startled for a moment, still they soon relapse into slumber; they refuse to be awakened, and think their happiness consists in continuing as they are.

Now I do not for an instant suspect, my brethren, that you are in the sound slumber of sin. This is a miserable state, which I should hope was, on the whole, the condition of few men, at least in a place like this. But, allowing this, yet there is great reason for fearing that very many of you are not wide awake : that though your dreams are disturbed, yet dreams they are; and that the view of religion which you think to be a true one, is not that vision of the Truth which you would see were your eyes open, but such a vague, defective, extravagant picture of it as a man sees when he is asleep. At all events, however this may be, it will be useful (please God) if you ask yourselves, one by one, the question, "*How do I know* I am in the right way? *How do I know* that I have real faith, and am not in a dream?"

The circumstances of these times render it very difficult to answer this question. When the world was against Christianity it was comparatively easy. But (in one sense) the world is now *for it*. I do not mean there are not turbulent, lawless men, who would bring all things into confusion, if they could; who hate religion, and would overturn every established institution which proceeds from, or is connected with it. Doubtless there are very many such, but from such men religion has nothing to fear. The truth has ever flourished and strengthened under persecution. But what we have to fear is the opposite fact, that all the rank, and the station, and the intelligence, and the opulence of the country is professedly with religion. We have cause to fear from the very circumstance that the institutions of the country are based upon the acknowledgment of religion as true. Worthy of all honour are they who so based them! Miserable is the guilt which lies upon those who have attempted, and partly succeeded, in shaking that holy foundation! But it often happens that our most bitter are not our most dangerous enemies; on the other hand, greatest blessings are the most serious temptations to the unwary. And our danger, at present, is this, that a man's having a general character for religion, reverencing the Gospel and professing it, and to a certain point obeying it, so fully promotes his temporal interests, that it is difficult for him to make out for himself whether he really acts on faith, or from a desire of this world's advantages. It is difficult to find *tests* which may bring home the truth to his mind, and probe his heart after the manner of Him who, from His throne above, tries it with an Almighty Wisdom. It can scarcely be denied that attention to their religious duties is becoming a fashion among large portions of the community,—so large, that, to many individuals, these portions are in fact *the world.* We are, every now and then, surprised to find persons to be in the observance of family prayer, of reading Scripture, or of Holy Communion, of whom we should not have expected beforehand such a profession of faith; or we hear them avowing the high evangelical truths of the New Testament, and countenancing those who maintain them. All this brings it about, that it is our interest in this world to profess to be Christ's disciples.

And further than this, it is necessary to remark, that, in spite of this general profession of zeal for the Gospel among all respectable persons at this day, nevertheless there is reason for fearing, that it is not altogether the real Gospel that they are zealous for. Doubtless we have cause to be thankful whenever we see persons earnest in the various ways I have mentioned. Yet, somehow, after all, there is reason for being dissatisfied with the character of the religion of the day; dissatisfied, first, because oftentimes these same persons are very inconsistent;--often, for instance, talk irreverently and profanely, ridicule or slight things sacred, speak against the Holy Church, or against the blessed Saints of early times, or even against the favoured servants of God, set before us in Scripture; or *act* with the world and the worse sort of men, even when they do not speak like them; attend to them more than to the ministers of God, or are very lukewarm, lax, and unscrupulous in matters of conduct, so much so, that they seem hardly to go by principle, but by what is merely expedient and convenient. And then again, putting aside our judgment of these men as individuals, and thinking of them as well as we can (which of course it is our duty to do), yet, after all, taking merely the multitude of them as a symptom of a state of things, I own I am suspicious of any religion that is a people's religion, or an age's religion. Our Saviour says, "Narrow is the way." This, of course, must not be interpreted without great caution; yet surely the whole tenor of the Inspired Volume leads us to believe that His Truth will not be heartily received by the many, that it is against the current of human feeling and opinion, and the course of the world, and so far forth as it *is* received by a man, will be opposed by himself, *i.e.* by his old nature which remains about him, next by all others, so far forth as they have not received it. "The light shining in darkness" is the token of true religion; and, though doubtless there are seasons when a sudden enthusiasm arises in favour of the Truth (as in the history of St. John the Baptist, in whose "light" the Jews "were willing for a season to rejoice,"[1] so as even "to be baptized of him, confessing their sins "[2]), yet such a popularity of the Truth is *but* sudden, comes at once and goes at once, has no regular growth, no abiding stay. It is error alone which grows and is received heartily on a large scale. St. Paul has set up his warning against our supposing Truth will ever be heartily accepted, whatever show there may be of a general profession of it, in his last Epistle, where he tells Timothy, among other sad prophecies, that "evil men and seducers shall wax worse and worse."[3] Truth, indeed, has that power in it, that it forces men to profess it in words; but when they go on to act, instead of obeying *it*, they substitute some idol in the place of it. On these accounts, when there is much talk of religion in a country, and much congratulation that there is a general concern for it, a cautious mind will feel anxious lest some counterfeit be, in fact, honoured instead of it: lest it be the dream of man rather than the verities of God's Word, which has become popular, and lest the received form have no more of truth in it than is just necessary to recommend it to the reason and conscience:—lest, in short, it be Satan transformed into an angel of light, rather than the Light itself, which is attracting followers.

If, then, this be a time (which I suppose it is) when a general profession of religion is thought respectable and right in the virtuous and orderly classes of the community, this circumstance should not diminish your anxiety about your own state before God, but rather (I may say) increase it; for two reasons, first, because you are in danger of doing right from motives of this world; next, because you may, perchance, be cheated of the

[1] John v. 35.   [2] Matt. iii. 6.   [3] 2 Tim. iii. 13.

Truth, by some ingenuity which the world puts, like counterfeit coin, in the place of the Truth.

Some, indeed, of those who now hear me, are in situations where they are almost shielded from the world's influence, whatever it is. There are persons so happily placed as to have religious superiors, who direct them to what is good only, and who are kind to them, as well as pious towards God. This is their happiness, and they must thank God for the gift; but it is their temptation too. At least they are under one of the two temptations just mentioned; good behaviour is, in their case, not only a matter of duty, but of interest. If they obey God, they gain praise from men as well as from Him; so that it is very difficult for them to know whether they do right for conscience' sake, or for the world's sake. Thus, whether in private families, or in the world, in all the ranks of middle life, men lie under a considerable danger at this day, a more than ordinary danger, of self-deception, of being asleep while they think themselves awake.

How then shall we try ourselves? Can any tests be named which will bring certainty to our minds on the subject? No indisputable tests can be given. We cannot know for certain. We must beware of an impatience about knowing what our real state is. St. Paul himself did not know till the last days of his life (as far as we know), that he was one of God's elect who shall never perish. He said, "I know nothing by myself, yet am I not hereby justified;"[1] *i.e.* though I am not conscious to myself of neglect of duty, yet am I not therefore confident of my acceptance? Judge nothing before the time. Accordingly he says in another place, "I keep under my body, and bring it into subjection, lest that by any means, when I have preached to others, I myself should be a castaway."[2] And yet though this absolute certainty of our election unto glory be unattainable, and the desire to obtain it an impatience which ill befits sinners, nevertheless a comfortable hope, a sober and subdued belief that God has pardoned and justified us for Christ's sake (blessed be His Name!), is attainable, according to St. John's words, "If our heart condemn us not, then have we confidence toward God."[3] And the question is, How are we to attain to this, under the circumstances in which we are placed? In what does it consist?

Were we in a heathen land (as I said just now) it were easy to answer. The very profession of the Gospel would almost bring evidence of true faith, as far as we could have evidence; for such profession among Pagans is almost sure to involve per-

---

[1] 1 Cor. iv. 4.   [2] 1 Cor. ix. 27.   [3] 1 John iii. 21.

6 *Self-denial the Test*

secution. Hence it is that the Epistles are so full of expressions of joy in the Lord Jesus, and in the exulting hope of salvation. Well might they be confident who had suffered for Christ. "Tribulation worketh patience, and patience experience, and experience hope."[1] "Henceforth let no man trouble me, for I bear in my body the marks of the Lord Jesus."[2] "Always bearing about in the body the dying of the Lord Jesus; that the life also of Jesus might be made manifest in our body."[3] "Our hope of you is stedfast, knowing that as ye are partakers of the suffering, so shall ye be also of the consolation."[4] These and such like texts belong to those only who have witnessed for the truth like the early Christians. They are beyond *us*.

This is certain; yet since the nature of Christian obedience is the same in every age, it still brings with it, as it did then, an evidence of God's favour. We cannot indeed make ourselves as sure of our being in the number of God's true servants as the early Christians were, yet we may possess our degree of certainty, and by the same kind of evidence, the evidence of *self-denial.* This was the great evidence which the first disciples gave, and which we can give still. Reflect upon our Saviour's plain declarations, "Whosoever will come after Me, let him deny himself, and take up his cross and follow Me."[5] "If any man come to Me, and hate not his father and mother, and wife, and children, and brethren, and sisters, yea, and his own life also, he cannot be My disciple. And whosoever doth not bear his cross and come after Me, he cannot be My disciple."[6] "If thy hand offend thee, cut it off . . . if thy foot offend thee, cut it off . . . if thine eye offend thee, pluck it out : . . . it is better for thee to enter into life maimed . . . halt . . . with one eye than to be cast into hell."[7]

Now without attempting to explain perfectly such passages as these, which doubtless cannot be understood without a fulness of grace which is possessed by very few men, yet at least we learn thus much from them, that a rigorous self-denial is a chief duty, nay, that it may be considered the test whether we are Christ's disciples, whether we are living in a mere dream, which we mistake for Christian faith and obedience, or are really and truly awake, alive, living in the day, on our road heavenwards. The early Christians went through self-denials in their very profession of the Gospel ; *what are our self-denials*, now that the

[1] Rom. v. 3, 4.   [2] Gal. vi. 17.   [3] 2 Cor. iv. 10.
[4] 2 Cor. i. 7.   [5] Mark viii. 34.   [6] Luke xiv. 26, 27.
[7] Mark ix. 43-47.

profession of the Gospel is not a self-denial? In what sense do *we* fulfil the words of Christ? have we any distinct notion what is meant by the words "taking up our cross"? in what way are we acting, in which we should not act, supposing the Bible and the Church were unknown to this country, and religion, as existing among us, was *merely* a fashion of this world? What are we doing, which we have reason to trust is done for Christ's sake who bought us?

You know well enough that works are said to be the fruits and evidence of faith. That faith is said to be dead which has them not. Now what works have we to show of such a kind as to give us "confidence," so that we may "not be ashamed before Him at His coming"?[1]

In answering this question I observe, first of all, that, according to Scripture, the self-denial which is the test of our faith must be daily. "If any man will come after Me, let him deny himself, and take up his cross *daily*, and follow Me."[2] It is thus St. Luke records our Saviour's words. Accordingly, it seems that Christian obedience does not consist merely in a few occasional efforts, a few accidental good deeds, or certain seasons of repentance, prayer, and activity; a mistake, which minds of a certain class are very apt to fall into. This is the kind of obedience which constitutes what the world calls a great man, *i.e.* a man who has some noble points, and every now and then acts heroically, so as to astonish and subdue the minds of beholders, but who in private life has no abiding personal religion, who does not regulate his thoughts, words, and deeds, according to the law of God. Again, the word *daily* implies, that the self-denial which is pleasing to Christ consists in little things. This is plain, for opportunity for great self-denials does not come every day. Thus to take up the Cross of Christ is no great action done once for all, it consists in the continual practice of small duties which are distasteful to us.

If, then, a person asks how he is to know whether he is dreaming on in the world's slumber, or is really awake and alive unto God, let him first fix his mind upon some one or other of his besetting infirmities. Every one who is at all in the habit of examining himself, must be conscious of such within him. Many men have more than one, all of us have some one or other; and in resisting and overcoming such, self-denial has its first employment. One man is indolent and fond of amusement, another man is passionate or ill-tempered, another is vain, another

[1] 1 John ii. 28.   [2] Luke ix. 23.

has little control over his tongue ; others are weak, and cannot resist the ridicule of thoughtless companions ; others are tormented with bad passions, of which they are ashamed, yet are overcome.   Now let every one consider what his weak point is ; in that is his trial.   His trial is not in those things which are easy to him, but in that one thing, in those several things, whatever they are, in which to do his duty is against his nature.   Never think yourself safe because you do your duty in ninety-nine points ; it is the hundredth which is to be the ground of your self-denial, which must evidence, or rather instance and realize your faith.   It is in reference to this you must watch and pray ; pray continually for God's grace to help you, and watch with fear and trembling lest you fall.   Other men may not know what these weak points of your character are, they may mistake them.   But you may know them ; you may know them by *their* guesses and hints, and your own observation, and the light of the Spirit of God.   And oh, that you may have strength to wrestle with them and overcome them !   Oh, that you may have the wisdom to care little for the world's religion, or the praise you get from the world, and your agreement with what clever men, or powerful men, or many men, make the standard of religion, compared with the secret consciousness that you are obeying God in little things as well as great, in the hundredth duty as well as in the ninety-nine !   Oh, that you may (as it were) sweep the house diligently to discover what you lack of the *full* measure of obedience !   for be quite sure, that this apparently small defect will influence your whole spirit and judgment in all things.   Be quite sure that your judgment of persons, and of events, and of actions, and of doctrines, and your spirit towards God and man, your faith in the high truths of the Gospel, and your knowledge of your duty, all depend in a strange way on this strict endeavour to observe the whole law, on this self-denial in those little things in which obedience *is* a self-denial.   Be not content with a warmth of faith carrying you over many obstacles even in your obedience, forcing you past the fear of men, and the usages of society, and the persuasions of interest ; exult not in your experience of God's past mercies, and your assurance of what He has already done for your soul, if you are conscious you have neglected the one thing needful, the " one thing " which " thou lackest,"—daily self-denial.

But, besides this, there are other modes of self-denial to try your faith and sincerity, which it may be right just to mention. It may so happen that the sin you are most liable to, is not

called forth every day. For instance : anger and passion are
irresistible perhaps when they come upon you, but it is only
at times that you are provoked, and then you are off your
guard ; so that the occasion is over, and you have failed, before
you were well aware of its coming. It is right then almost to
find out for yourself daily self-denials ; and this because our Lord
bids you take up your cross daily, and because it proves your
earnestness, and because by doing so you strengthen your general
power of self-mastery, and come to have such an habitual command of yourself, as will be a defence ready prepared when the
season of temptation comes. Rise up then in the morning with
the purpose that (please God) the day shall not pass without its
self-denial, with a self-denial in innocent pleasures and tastes, if
none occurs to mortify sin. Let your very rising from your
bed be a self-denial ; let your meals be self-denials. Determine
to yield to others in things indifferent, to go out of your way in
small matters, to inconvenience yourself (so that no direct duty
suffers by it), rather than you should not meet with your daily
discipline. This was the Psalmist's method, who was, as it were,
"punished all day long, and chastened every morning."[1] It
was St. Paul's method, who "kept under," or bruised "his body,
and brought it into subjection."[2] This is one great end of fasting. A man says to himself, "How am I to know I am in
earnest ?" I would suggest to him, Make some sacrifice, do
some distasteful thing, which you are not actually obliged to do
(so that it be lawful), to bring home to your mind that in fact
you do love your Saviour, that you do hate sin, that you do hate
your sinful nature, that you have put aside the present world.
Thus you will have an evidence (to a certain point) that you are
not using mere words. It is easy to make professions, easy to
say fine things in speech or in writing, easy to astonish men with
truths which they do not know, and sentiments which rise
above human nature. "But thou, O servant of God, flee these
things, and follow after righteousness, godliness, faith, love,
patience, meekness." Let not your words run on ; force every
one of them into action as it goes, and thus, cleansing yourself
from all pollution of the flesh and spirit, perfect holiness in the
fear of God. In dreams we sometimes move our arms to see if
we are awake or not, and so we are awakened. This is the way
to keep your heart awake also. Try yourself daily in little deeds,
to prove that your faith is more than a deceit.

I am aware all this is a hard doctrine ; hard to those even who

---

[1] Psalm lxxiii. 14.   [2] 1 Cor. ix. 27.

assent to it, and can describe it most accurately. There are such imperfections, such inconsistencies in the heart and life of even the better sort of men, that continual repentance must ever go hand in hand with our endeavours to obey. Much we need the grace of Christ's blood to wash us from the guilt we daily incur; much need we the aid of His promised Spirit! And surely He will grant all the riches of His mercy to His true servants; but as surely He will vouchsafe to none of us the power to believe in Him, and the blessedness of being one with Him, who are not as earnest in obeying Him as if salvation depended on themselves.

SERMON II.

(ADVENT.)

Divine Calls.

"And the Lord came, and stood, and called as at other times, Samuel, Samuel. Then Samuel answered, Speak; for Thy servant heareth."—
1 SAM. iii. 10.

IN the narrative of which these words form part, we have a remarkable instance of a Divine call, and the manner in which it is our duty to meet it. Samuel was from a child brought to the house of the Lord; and in due time he was called to a sacred office, and made a prophet. He was called, and he forthwith answered the call. God said, "Samuel, Samuel." He did not understand at first who called, and what was meant; but on going to Eli he learned who spoke, and what his answer should be. So when God called again, he said, "Speak, Lord; for Thy servant heareth." Here is prompt obedience.

Very different in its circumstances was St. Paul's call, but resembling Samuel's in this respect, that, when God called, he, too, promptly obeyed. When St. Paul heard the voice from heaven, he said at once, trembling and astonished, "Lord, what wilt Thou have me to do?"[1] This same obedient temper of his is stated or implied in the two accounts which he himself gives of his miraculous conversion. In the 22nd chapter he says, "And I said, What shall I do, Lord?" And in the 26th, after telling King Agrippa what the Divine Speaker said to him, he adds what comes to the same thing, "Whereupon, O King Agrippa, *I was not disobedient* unto the heavenly vision." Such is the account given us in St. Paul's case of that first step in God's gracious dealings with him, which ended in his eternal salvation.

[1] Acts ix. 6.

"Whom He did foreknow, He also did predestinate;"[1]—"whom He did predestinate, them He also called"—here was the first act which took place in time—"and whom He called, them He also justified; and whom He justified, them He also glorified." Such is the Divine series of mercies; and you see that it was prompt obedience on St. Paul's part which carried on the first act of Divine grace into the second, which knit together the first mercy to the second. "Whom He called, them He also justified." St. Paul was called when Christ appeared to him in the way; he was justified when Ananias came to baptize him: and it was prompt obedience which led him from his call to his baptism. "Lord, what wilt Thou have me to do?" The answer was, "Arise, and go into Damascus; and there it shall be told thee of all things which are appointed for thee to do."[2] And when he came to Damascus, Ananias was sent to him by the same Lord who had appeared to him; and he reminded St. Paul of this when he came to him. The Lord had appeared for his call; the Lord appeared for his justification.

This, then, is the lesson taught us by St. Paul's conversion, promptly to obey the call. If we do obey it, to God be the glory, for He it is works in us. If we do not obey, to ourselves be all the shame, for sin and unbelief work in us. Such being the state of the case, let us take care to act accordingly,—being exceedingly alarmed lest we should *not* obey God's voice when He calls us, yet not taking praise or credit to ourselves if we *do* obey it. This has been the temper of all saints from the beginning—working out their salvation with fear and trembling, yet ascribing the work to Him who wrought in them to will and do of His good pleasure; obeying the call, and giving thanks to Him who calls, to Him who fulfils in them their calling. So much on the pattern afforded us by St. Paul.

Very different in its circumstances was Samuel's call, when a child in the temple, yet resembling St. Paul's in this particular, —that for our instruction the circumstance of his obedience to it is brought out prominently even in the words put into his mouth by Eli in the text. Eli taught him what to say, when called by the Divine voice. Accordingly, when "the Lord came, and stood, and called as at other times, Samuel, Samuel, then Samuel answered, Speak, Lord; for Thy servant heareth."

Such, again, is the temper of mind expressed by holy David in the 27th Psalm, "When Thou saidst, Seek ye My face, my heart said unto Thee, Thy face, Lord, will I seek."

[1] Rom. viii. 29.   [2] Acts xxii. 10.

And this temper, which in the above instances is illustrated in words spoken, is in the case of many other Saints in Scripture shown in word and deed; and, on the other hand, is illustrated negatively by being neglected in the case of others therein mentioned, who might have entered into life, and did not.

For instance, we read of the Apostles, that "Jesus, walking by the sea of Galilee, saw two brethren, Simon called Peter, and Andrew his brother, casting a net into the sea; for they were fishers. And He saith unto them, Follow Me, and I will make you fishers of men. *And* they *straightway* left their nets and followed Him."[1] Again; when He saw James and John with their father Zebedee, "He *called* them; and they *immediately left the ship, and their father,* and *followed* Him." And so of St. Matthew at the receipt of custom, "He said unto him, Follow Me; and he left all, rose up, and followed Him."

Again, we are told in St. John's Gospel, "Jesus would go forth into Galilee, and findeth Philip, and saith unto him, *Follow* Me." Again, "Philip findeth Nathanael," and in like manner says to him, "Come and see." "Jesus saw Nathanael coming unto Him, and saith of him, Behold an Israelite indeed, in whom is no guile."

On the other hand, the young ruler shrunk from the call, and found it a hard saying, "If thou wilt be perfect, go and sell that thou hast, and give to the poor, and thou shalt have treasure in heaven; and come, and follow Me. But when the young man heard that saying, he went away sorrowful, for he had great possessions."[2] Others who seemed to waver, or rather who asked for some little delay from human feeling, were rebuked for want of promptitude in their obedience;—for time stays for no one; the word of call is spoken and is gone; if we do not seize the moment, it is lost. Christ was on His road heavenward. He walked by the sea of Galilee;[3] He "passed forth;"[4] He "passed by;"[5] He did not stop; all men must join Him, or He would be calling on others beyond them.[6] "He said to another, Follow Me. But he said, Lord, suffer me first to go and bury my father. Jesus said unto him, Let the dead bury their dead: but go thou and preach the kingdom of God. And another also said, Lord, I will follow Thee: but let me first go bid them farewell, which are at home at my house. And Jesus said unto him, No man, having put his hand to the plough, and looking back, is fit for the kingdom of God."[7]

[1] Matt. iv. 18-20. [2] Matt. xix. 21, 22. [3] Matt. iv. 18.
[4] Matt. ix. 9. [5] Mark ii. 14. [6] Matt. xx. 6, 7.
[7] Luke ix. 59-62.

Not unlike these last instances are the circumstances of the call of the great prophet Elisha, though he does not seem to have incurred blame from Elijah for his lingering on the thoughts of what he was leaving. "He found Elisha, the son of Shaphat, who was ploughing . . . Elijah passed by him, and cast his mantle over him." He did not stay; he passed on, and Elisha was obliged to run after him. "And he left the oxen, and ran after Elijah, and said, Let me, I pray thee, kiss my father and my mother, and then I will follow thee." This the prophet allowed him to do, and after that "he arose and followed Elijah, and ministered unto him."

Or once more consider the circumstances of the call of Abraham, the father of all who believe. He was called from his father's house, but was not told whither. St. Paul was bid go to Damascus, and there he was to receive further directions. In like manner Abraham left his home for a land "that I *will* show thee,"[1] says Almighty God. Accordingly he went out, "not knowing whither he went." "Abram departed as the Lord had spoken unto him."

Such are the instances of Divine calls in Scripture, and their characteristic is this: to require instant obedience, and next to call us we know not to what; to call us on in the darkness. Faith alone can obey them.

But it may be urged, How does this concern us now? We were all called to serve God in infancy, before we could obey or disobey; we found ourselves called when reason began to dawn; we have been called to a state of salvation, we have been living as God's servants and children, all through our time of trial, having been brought into it in infancy through Holy Baptism, by the act of our parents. Calling is not a thing future with us, but a thing past.

This is true in a very sufficient sense; and yet it is true also that the passages of Scripture which I have been quoting do apply to us still,—do concern us, and may warn and guide us in many important ways; as a few words will show.

For in truth we are not called once only, but many times; all through our life Christ is calling us. He called us first in Baptism; but afterwards also; whether we obey His voice or not, He graciously calls us still. If we fall from our Baptism, He calls us to repent; if we are striving to fulfil our calling, He calls us on from grace to grace, and from holiness to holiness, while life is given us. Abraham was called from his home,

[1] Gen. xii. 1.

Peter from his nets, Matthew from his office, Elisha from his farm, Nathanael from his retreat ; we are all in course of calling, on and on, from one thing to another, having no resting-place, but mounting towards our eternal rest, and obeying one command only to have another put upon us. He calls us again and again, in order to justify us again and again,—and again and again, and more and more, to sanctify and glorify us.

It were well if we understood this ; but we are slow to master the great truth, that Christ is, as it were, walking among us, and by His hand, or eye, or voice, bidding us follow Him. We do not understand that His call is a thing which takes place now. We think it took place in the Apostles' days ; but we do not believe in it, we do not look out for it in our own case. We have not eyes to see the Lord ; far different from the beloved Apostle, who knew Christ even when the rest of the disciples knew Him not. When He stood on the shore after His resurrection, and bade them cast the net into the sea, " that disciple whom Jesus loved saith unto Peter, It is the Lord."[1]

Now what I mean is this : that they who are living religiously, have from time to time truths they did not know before, or had no need to consider, brought before them forcibly ; truths which involve duties, which are in fact precepts, and claim obedience. In this and such like ways Christ calls us now. There is nothing miraculous or extraordinary in His dealings with us. He works through our natural faculties and circumstances of life. Still what happens to us in providence is in all essential respects what His voice was to those whom He addressed when on earth : whether He commands by a visible presence, or by a voice, or by our consciences, it matters not, so that we feel it to be a command. If it is a command, it may be obeyed or disobeyed ; it may be accepted as Samuel or St. Paul accepted it, or put aside after the manner of the young man who had great possessions.

And these Divine calls are commonly, from the nature of the case, sudden now, and as indefinite and obscure in their consequences as in former times. The accidents and events of life are, as is obvious, one special way in which the calls I speak of come to us ; and they, as we all know, are in their very nature, and as the word accident implies, sudden and unexpected. A man is going on as usual ; he comes home one day, and finds a letter, or a message, or a person, whereby a sudden trial comes on him, which, if met religiously, will be the means of advancing him to a higher state of religious excellence, which at present

[1] John xxi. 7.

he as little comprehends as the unspeakable words heard by St.
Paul in paradise. By a trial we commonly mean, a something
which, if encountered well, will confirm a man in his present way;
but I am speaking of something more than this; of what will
not only confirm him, but raise him into a high state of knowledge and holiness. Many persons will find it very striking, on
looking back on their past lives, to observe what different notions
they entertained at different periods, of what Divine truth was,
what was the way of pleasing God, and what things were allowable or not, what excellence was, and what happiness. I do
not scruple to say, that these differences may be as great as that
which may be supposed to have existed between St. Peter's state
of mind when quietly fishing on the lake, or Elisha's when
driving his oxen, and that new state of mind of each of them
when called to be Apostle or Prophet. Elisha and St. Peter
indeed were also called to a new mode of life; that I am not
speaking of. I am not speaking of cases when persons change
their condition, their place in society, their pursuit, and the like;
I am supposing them to remain pretty much the same as before
in outward circumstances; but I say that many a man is conscious to himself of having undergone inwardly great changes of
view as to what truth is and what happiness. Nor, again, am I
speaking of changes so great, that a man reverses his former
opinions and conduct. He may be able to see that there is a connection between the two; that his former has led to his latter;
and yet he may feel that after all they differ in kind; that he
has got into a new world of thought, and measures things and
persons by a different rule.

Nothing, indeed, is more wonderful and strange than the
different views which different persons take of the same subject.
Take any single fact, event, or existing thing which meets us in
the world; what various remarks will be made on it by different
persons! For instance, consider the different lights in which
any single action, of a striking nature, is viewed by different
persons; or consider the view of wealth or a wealthy man, taken
by this or that class in the community; what different feelings
does it excite—envy, or respect, or ridicule, or angry opposition,
or indifference, or fear and compassion; here are states of mind
in which different parties may regard it. These are broad
differences; others are quite as real, though more subtle.
Religion, for instance, may be reverenced by the soldier, the man
of literature, the trader, the statesman, and the theologian; yet
how very distinct their modes of reverencing it, and how separate

the standard which each sets up in his mind! Well, all these various modes of viewing things cannot one and all be the best mode, even were they all good modes; but this even is not the case. Some are contrary to others; some are bad. But even of those that are on the whole good, some are but in part good, some are imperfect, some have much bad mixed with them; and only one is best. Only one is the truth and the perfect truth; and which that is, none know but those who are in possession of it, if even they. But God knows which it is; and towards that one and only Truth He is leading us forward. He is leading forward His redeemed, He is training His elect, one and all, to the one perfect knowledge and obedience of Christ; not, however, without their co-operation, but by means of calls which they are to obey, and which if they do not obey, they lose place, and fall behind in their heavenly course. He leads them forward from strength to strength, and from glory to glory, up the steps of the ladder whose top reacheth to heaven. We pass from one state of knowledge to another; we are introduced into a higher region from a lower, by listening to Christ's call and obeying it.

Perhaps it may be the loss of some dear friend or relative through which the call comes to us; which shows us the vanity of things below, and prompts us to make God our sole stay. We through grace do so in a way we never did before; and in the course of years, when we look back on our life, we find that that sad event has brought us into a new state of faith and judgment, and that we are as though other men from what we were. We thought, before it took place, that we were serving God, and so we were in a measure; but we find that, whatever our present infirmities may be, and however far we be still from the highest state of illumination, then at least we were serving the world under the show and the belief of serving God.

Or again, perhaps something occurs to force us to take a part for God or against Him. The world requires of us some sacrifice which we see we ought not to grant to it. Some tempting offer is made us; or some reproach or discredit threatened us; or we have to determine and avow what is truth and what is error. We are enabled to act as God would have us act; and we do so in much fear and perplexity. We do not see our way clearly; we do not see what is to follow from what we have done, and how it bears upon our general conduct and opinions: yet perhaps it has the most important bearings. That little deed, suddenly exacted of us, almost suddenly resolved on and executed, may be as though a gate into the second or third heaven—an entrance into a higher

B

state of holiness, and into a truer view of things than we have hitherto taken.

Or again, we get acquainted with some one whom God employs to bring before us a number of truths which were closed on us before; and we but half understand them, and but half approve of them; and yet God seems to speak in them, and Scripture to confirm them. This is a case which not unfrequently occurs, and it involves a call "to follow on to know the Lord."[1]

Or again, we may be in the practice of reading Scripture carefully, and trying to serve God, and its sense may, as if suddenly, break upon us, in a way it never did before. Some thought may suggest itself to us, which is a key to a great deal in Scripture, or which suggests a great many other thoughts. A new light may be thrown on the precepts of our Lord and His Apostles. We may be able to enter into the manner of life of the early Christians, as recorded in Scripture, which before was hidden from us, and into the simple maxims on which Scripture bases it. We may be led to understand that it is very different from the life which men live now. Now knowledge is a call to action : an insight into the way of perfection is a call to perfection.

Once more, it may so happen that we find ourselves, how or why we cannot tell, much more able to obey God in certain respects than heretofore. Our minds are so strangely constituted, it is impossible to say whether it is from the growth of habit suddenly showing itself, or from an unusual gift of Divine grace poured into our hearts, but so it is; let our temptation be to sloth, or irresolution, or worldly anxiety, or pride, or to other more base and miserable sins, we may suddenly find ourselves possessed of a power of self-command which we had not before. Or again, we may have a resolution grow on us to serve God more strictly in His house and in private than heretofore. This is a call to higher things; let us beware lest we receive the grace of God in vain. Let us beware of lapsing back; let us avoid temptation. Let us strive by quietness and caution to cherish the feeble flame, and shelter it from the storms of this world. God may be bringing us into a higher world of religious truth; let us work with Him.

To conclude. Nothing is more certain in matter of fact, than that some men do feel themselves called to high duties and works, to which others are not called. Why this is we do not know; whether it be that those who are not called, forfeit the call from having failed in former trials, or have been called and have not followed; or that though God gives baptismal grace to all, yet

[1] Hosea vi. 3.

He really does call some men by His free grace to higher things than others. But so it is; this man sees sights which that man does not see, has a larger faith, a more ardent love, and a more spiritual understanding. No one has any leave to take another's lower standard of holiness for his own. It is nothing to us what others are. If God calls us to greater renunciation of the world, and exacts a sacrifice of our hopes and fears, this is our gain, this is a mark of His love for us, this is a thing to be rejoiced in. Such thoughts, when properly entertained, have no tendency to puff us up; for if the prospect is noble, yet the risk is more fearful. While we pursue high excellence, we walk among precipices, and a fall is easy. Hence the Apostle says, "Work out your own salvation with fear and trembling, for it is God that worketh in you."[1] Again, the more men aim at high things, the more sensitive perception they have of their own short-comings; and this again is adapted to humble them especially. We need not fear spiritual pride, then, in following Christ's call, if we follow it as men in earnest. Earnestness has no time to compare itself with the state of other men; earnestness has too vivid a feeling of its own infirmities to be elated at itself. Earnestness is simply set on doing God's will. It simply says, "Speak, Lord, for Thy servant heareth;" "Lord, what wilt Thou have me to do?" Oh that we had more of this spirit! Oh that we could take that simple view of things, as to feel that the one thing which lies before us is to please God! What gain is it to please the world, to please the great, nay, even to please those whom we love, compared with this? What gain is it to be applauded, admired, courted, followed, compared with this one aim, of not being disobedient to a heavenly vision? What can this world offer comparable with that insight into spiritual things, that keen faith, that heavenly peace, that high sanctity, that ever-lasting righteousness, that hope of glory, which they have who in sincerity love and follow our Lord Jesus Christ?

Let us beg and pray Him day by day to reveal Himself to our souls more fully; to quicken our senses; to give us sight and hearing, taste and touch of the world to come; so to work within us that we may sincerely say, "Thou shalt guide me with Thy counsel, and after that receive me to glory. Whom have I in heaven but Thee? and there is none upon earth that I desire in comparison of Thee: my flesh and my heart faileth; but God is the strength of my heart, and my portion for ever."

[1] Phil. ii. 12, 13.

SERMON III.

(ADVENT.)

The Ventures of Faith.

" They say unto Him, We are able."—MATT. xx. **22.**

THESE words of the holy Apostles James and John were in reply to a very solemn question addressed to them by their Divine Master. They coveted, with a noble ambition, though as yet unpractised in the highest wisdom, untaught in the holiest truth,—they coveted to sit beside Him on His Throne of Glory. They would be content with nothing short of that special gift which He had come to grant to His elect, which He shortly after died to purchase for them, and which He offers to us. They ask the gift of eternal life ; and He in answer told them, not that they should have it (though for them it was really reserved), but He reminded them what they *must venture for it :* " Are ye able to drink of the cup that I shall drink of, and to be baptized with the baptism that I am baptized with ? They say unto Him, We are able." Here then a great lesson is impressed upon us, that our duty as Christians lies in this, in making ventures for eternal life without the absolute certainty of success.

Success and reward everlasting they will have who persevere unto the end. Doubt we cannot, that the ventures of all Christ's servants must be returned to them at the Last Day with abundant increase. This is a true saying,—He returns far more than we lend to Him, and without fail. But I am speaking of individuals, of ourselves one by one. No one among us knows for certain that he himself will persevere ; yet every one among us, to give himself even a chance of success at all, must make a venture. As regards individuals, then, it is quite true, that all of us must for certain make ventures for heaven, yet without the certainty of success through them. This, indeed, is the very meaning of the word "venture;" for that is a strange venture which has nothing in it of fear, risk, danger, anxiety, uncertainty. Yes, so it certainly is; and in this consists the excellence and nobleness of *faith;* this is the very reason why *faith* is singled out from other graces, and honoured as the especial means of our justification, because its presence implies that we have the heart to make a venture.

St. Paul sufficiently sets this before us in the eleventh chapter of his Epistle to the Hebrews, which opens with a definition of faith, and after that, gives us examples of it, as if to guard against any possibility of mistake. After quoting the text, "The just shall live by faith," and thereby showing clearly that he is speaking of what he treats in his Epistle to the Romans as *justifying* faith, he continues, "Now faith is the substance," that is, the realizing, "of things hoped for, the evidence," that is, the ground of proof, "of things not seen." It is in its very essence the making present what is unseen; the acting upon the mere prospect of it, as if it really were possessed; the venturing upon it, the staking present ease, happiness, or other good, upon the chance of the future. And hence in another epistle he says pointedly, "If in this life only we have hope in Christ, we are of all men most miserable."[1] If the dead are not raised, we have indeed made a most signal miscalculation in the choice of life, and are altogether at fault. And what is true of the main doctrine itself, is true also of our individual interest in it. This he shows us in his Epistle to the Hebrews, by the instance of the ancient Saints, who thus risked their present happiness on the chance of future. Abraham "went out, not knowing whither he went." He and the rest died "not having received the promises, but having seen them afar off, and were persuaded of them, and embraced them, and confessed that they were strangers and pilgrims on the earth." Such was the faith of the Patriarchs: and in the text the youthful Apostles, with an untaught but generous simplicity, lay claim to the same. Little as they knew what they said in its fulness, yet their words were anyhow expressive of their hidden hearts, prophetic of their future conduct. They say unto Him, "We are able." They pledge themselves as if unawares, and are caught by One mightier than they, and, as it were, craftily made captive. But, in truth, their unsuspicious pledge was, after all, heartily made, though they knew not what they promised; and so was accepted. "Are ye able to

[1] 1 Cor. xv. 19.

drink of **My** cup, and be baptized with My baptism? **They say** unto Him, We are able." He in answer, without promising them heaven, graciously said, "Ye *shall* drink indeed of My cup, and be baptized with the baptism that I am baptized with."

Our Lord appears to act after the same manner towards St. Peter: He accepted his office of service, yet warned him how little he himself understood it. The zealous Apostle wished to follow his Lord at once: but He answered, "Whither I go thou canst not follow Me now, but thou shalt follow Me afterwards."[1] At another time He claimed the promise already made to Him; He said, "Follow thou Me;" and at the same time explained it, "Verily, verily, I say unto thee, When thou wast young, thou girdedst thyself, and walkedst whither thou wouldest: but when thou shalt be old, thou shalt stretch forth thy hands, and another shall gird thee, and carry thee whither thou wouldest not."[2]

Such were the ventures made in faith, and in uncertainty, by Apostles. Our Saviour, in a passage of St. Luke's Gospel, binds upon us all the necessity of deliberately doing the like: "Which of you, intending to build a tower, sitteth not down first and counteth the cost, whether he have sufficient to finish it? Lest haply, after he hath laid the foundation, and is not able to finish it, all that behold it begin to mock him, saying, This man began to build, and is not able to finish." And then He presently adds, "So likewise, whosoever he be of you that forsaketh not all that he hath, he cannot be My disciple,"[3] thus warning us of the full sacrifice we must make. We give up our all to Him; and He is to claim this or that, or grant us somewhat of it for a season, according to His good pleasure. On the other hand, the case of the rich young man, who went away sorrowful when our Lord bade him give up his all and follow Him, is an instance of one who had *not* faith to make the venture of this world for the next upon His word.

If then faith be the essence of a Christian life, and if it be what I have now described, it follows that our duty lies in risking upon Christ's word what we have for what we have not; and doing so in a noble, generous way, not indeed rashly or lightly, still without knowing accurately what we are doing, not knowing either what we give up, nor again what we shall gain; uncertain about our reward, uncertain about our extent of sacrifice, in all respects leaning, waiting upon Him, trusting in Him to fulfil His promise, trusting in Him to enable us to fulfil our

---

[1] John xiii. 36.   [2] John xxi. 18-22.   [3] Luke xiv. 28-33.

own vows, and so in all respects proceeding without carefulness
or anxiety about the future.

Now I dare say that what I have said as yet seems plain and
unexceptionable to most of those who hear me; yet surely, when
I proceed to draw the practical inference which immediately
follows, there are those who in their secret hearts, if not in open
avowal, will draw back.   Men allow us ministers of Christ to
proceed in our preaching, while we confine ourselves to general
truths, until they see that they themselves are implicated in
them, and have to act upon them; and then they suddenly come
to a stand; they collect themselves and draw back, and say,
" They do not see *this*—or do not admit *that* "—and though they
are quite unable to say *why* that should not follow from what
they already allow, which we show *must* follow, still they persist
in saying, that they do not see that it does follow; and they
look about for excuses, and they say we carry things too far, and
that we are extravagant, and that we ought to limit and modify
what we say, that we do not take into account times, and seasons,
and the like.   This is what they pretend; and well has it been
said, " Where there is a will there is a way; " for there is no truth,
however overpoweringly clear, but men may escape from it by
shutting their eyes; there is no duty, however urgent, but they
may find ten thousand good reasons against it, in their own case.
And they are sure to say we carry things too far, when we carry
them home to themselves.

This sad infirmity of men, called Christians, is exemplified in
the subject immediately before us.   Who does not at once
admit that faith consists in venturing on Christ's word without
seeing?   Yet in spite of this, may it not be seriously questioned,
whether men in general, even those of the better sort, venture
anything upon His truth at all?

Consider for an instant.   Let every one who hears me ask
himself the question, what stake has *he* in the truth of Christ's
promise?   How would he be a whit the worse off, supposing
(which is impossible), but, supposing it to fail?   We know what
it is to have a stake in any venture of this world.   We venture
our property in plans which promise a return; in plans which we
trust, which we have faith in.   What have we ventured for Christ?
What have we given to Him on a belief of His promise?   The
Apostle said, that he and his brethren would be of all men most
miserable, if the dead were not raised.   Can we in any degree
apply this to ourselves?   We think, perhaps, at present, we have
some hope of heaven.   Well, *this* we should lose, of course; but

after all, how should we be worse off as to our *present* condition ?
A trader, who has embarked some property in a speculation which
fails, not only loses his prospect of gain, but somewhat of his own,
which he ventured with the *hope* of the gain. This is the
question, What have *we* ventured ? I really fear, when we come
to examine, it will be found that there is nothing we resolve,
nothing we do, nothing we do not do, nothing we avoid, nothing
we choose, nothing we give up, nothing we pursue, which we
should not resolve, and do, and not do, and avoid, and choose,
and give up, and pursue, if Christ had not died, and heaven were
not promised us. I really fear that most men called Christians,
whatever they may profess, whatever they may think they feel,
whatever warmth and illumination and love they may claim as
their own, yet would go on almost as they do, neither much better
nor much worse, if they believed Christianity to be a fable.
When young, they indulge their lusts, or at least pursue the
world's vanities ; as time goes on, they get into a fair way of
business, or other mode of making money ; then they marry and
settle ; and their interest coinciding with their duty, they seem to
be, and think themselves, respectable and religious men ; they
grow attached to things as they are ; they begin to have a zeal
against vice and error ; and they follow after peace with all men.
Such conduct, indeed, as far as it goes, is right and praiseworthy.
Only I say, it has not necessarily anything to do with religion at
all ; there is nothing in it which is any proof of the presence of
religious principle in those who adopt it ; there is nothing they
would not do still, though they had nothing to gain from it, except
what they gain from it now. They do gain something now, they
do gratify their present wishes, they are quiet and orderly, because
it is their interest and taste to be so ; but they *venture* nothing,
they risk, they sacrifice, they abandon nothing on the faith of
Christ's word.

For instance : St. Barnabas had a property in Cyprus ; he gave
it up for the poor of Christ. Here is an intelligible sacrifice. He
did something he would not have done, unless the Gospel were
true. It is plain, if the Gospel turned out a fable (which God
forbid, but if so), he would have taken his line most unskilfully ;
he would be in a great mistake, and would have suffered a loss.
He would be like a merchant whose vessels were wrecked, or whose
correspondents had failed. Man has confidence in man, he trusts
to the credit of his neighbour ; but Christians do not risk largely
upon their Saviour's word, and this is the one thing they have to
do. Christ tells us Himself, "Make to yourselves friends of the

mammon of unrighteousness; that, when ye fail, they may receive you into everlasting habitations; "[1] *i.e.* buy an interest in the next world with that wealth which this world uses unrighteously; feed the hungry, clothe the naked, relieve the sick, and it shall turn to "bags that wax not old, a treasure in the heavens that faileth not."[2] Thus almsdeeds, I say, are an intelligible *venture*, and an evidence of faith.

So again the man who, when his prospects in the world are good, gives up the promise of wealth or of eminence, in order to be nearer Christ, to have a place in His temple, to have more opportunity for prayer and praise, he makes a sacrifice.

Or he who, from a noble striving after perfection, puts off the desire of worldly comforts, and is, like Daniel or St. Paul, in much labour and business, yet with a solitary heart, he too ventures something upon the certainty of the world to come.

Or he who, after falling into sin, repents in deed as well as in word; puts some yoke upon his shoulder; subjects himself to punishment; is severe upon his flesh; denies himself innocent pleasures; or puts himself to public shame,—he too shows that his faith is the realizing of things hoped for, the warrant of things not seen.

Or again, he who only gets himself to pray against those things which the many seek after, and to embrace what the heart naturally shrinks from; he who, when God's will seems to tend towards worldly ill, while he deprecates it, yet prevails on himself to say heartily, "Thy will be done;" he, even, is not without his sacrifice. Or he who, being in prospect of wealth, honestly prays God that he may never be rich; or he who is in prospect of station, and earnestly prays that he may never have it; or he who has friends or kindred, and acquiesces with an entire heart in their removal while it is yet doubtful, who can say, "Take them away, if it be Thy will; to Thee I give them up, to Thee I commit them," who is willing to be taken at his word; he too risks somewhat, and is accepted.

Such a one is taken at his word, while he understands not, perhaps, what he says; but he is accepted, as meaning somewhat, and risking much. Generous hearts, like James and John, or Peter, often speak largely and confidently beforehand of what they will do for Christ, not insincerely, yet ignorantly; and for their sincerity's sake they are taken at their word as a reward, though they have yet to learn how serious that word is. "They say unto Him, We are able;"—and the vow is recorded

[1] Luke xvi. 9.   [2] Luke xii. 33.

in heaven. This is the case of all of us at many seasons. First, at Confirmation; when we promise what was promised for us at Baptism, yet without being able to understand how much we promise, but rather trusting to God gradually to reveal it, and to give us strength according to our day. So again they who enter Holy Orders promise they know not what, engage themselves they know not how deeply, debar themselves of the world's ways they know not how intimately, find perchance they must cut off from them the right hand, sacrifice the desire of their eyes and the stirring of their hearts at the foot of the Cross, while they thought, in their simplicity, they were but choosing the quiet, easy life of "plain men dwelling in tents." And so again, in various ways, the circumstances of the times cause men at certain seasons to take this path or that, for religion's sake. They know not whither they are being carried; they see not the end of their course; they know no more than this, that it is right to do what they are now doing; and they hear a whisper within them, which assures them, as it did the two holy brothers, that whatever their present conduct involves in time to come, they shall, through God's grace, be equal to it. Those blessed Apostles said, "We are able;" and in truth they were enabled to do and suffer as they had said. St. James was given strength to be stedfast unto death, the death of martyrdom, being slain with the sword in Jerusalem. St. John, his brother, had still more to bear, dying last of the Apostles, as St. James first. He had to bear bereavement, first of his brother, then of the other Apostles. He had to bear a length of years in loneliness, exile, and weakness. He had to experience the dreariness of being solitary, when those whom he loved had been summoned away. He had to live in his own thoughts, without familiar friend, with those only about him who belonged to a younger generation. Of him were demanded by his gracious Lord, as pledges of his faith, all his eye loved and his heart held converse with. He was as a man moving his goods into a far country, who at intervals and by portions sends them before him, till his present abode is wellnigh unfurnished. He sent forward his friends on their journey, while he stayed himself behind, that there might be those in heaven to have thoughts of him, to look out for him, and receive him when his Lord should call. He sent before him, also, other still more voluntary pledges and ventures of his faith,—a self-denying walk, a zealous maintenance of the truth, fasting and prayers, labours of love, a virgin life, buffetings from the heathen, persecution, and banishment. Well might so great a Saint say, at the end of his days, "Come, Lord Jesus!"

as those who are weary of the night, and wait for the morning. All his thoughts, all his contemplations, desires, and hopes, were stored in the invisible world ; and death, when it came, brought back to him the sight of what he had worshipped, what he had loved, what he had held intercourse with, in years long passed away. Then, when again brought into the presence of what he had lost, how would remembrance revive, and familiar thoughts long buried come to life. Who shall dare to describe the blessedness of those who find all their pledges safe returned to them, all their ventures abundantly and beyond measure satisfied ?

Alas that we, my brethren, have not more of this high and unearthly spirit ! How is it that we are so contented with things as they are,—that we are so willing to be let alone, and to enjoy this life,—that we make such excuses, if any one presses on us the necessity of something higher, the duty of bearing the Cross, if we would earn the Crown, of the Lord Jesus Christ ?

I repeat it : what are our ventures and risks upon the truth of His word ? for He says expressly, " Every one that hath forsaken houses, or brethren, or sisters, or father, or mother, or wife, or children, or lands, for My Name's sake, shall receive an hundred-fold, and shall inherit everlasting life. But many that are first shall be last ; and the last shall be first." [1]

[1] Matt. xix. 29, 30.

SERMON IV.

(ADVENT.)

Watching.

" *Take ye heed, watch and pray ; for ye know not when the time is.*"
—MARK xiii. 33.

OUR Saviour gave this warning when He was leaving this
world,—leaving it, that is, as far as His visible presence is
concerned. He looked forward to the many hundred years which
were to pass before He came again. He knew His own purpose
and His Father's purpose gradually to leave the world to itself,
gradually to withdraw from it the tokens of His gracious presence.
He contemplated, as contemplating all things, the neglect of Him
which would spread even among His professed followers ; the
daring disobedience, and the loud words, which would be ventured
against Him and His Father by many whom He had regenerated :
and the coldness, cowardice, and tolerance of error which would
be displayed by others, who did not go so far as to speak or to
act against Him. He foresaw the state of the world and the
Church as we see it this day, when His prolonged absence has
made it practically thought that He never will come back in
visible presence : and in the text He mercifully whispers into
our ears, not to trust in what we see, not to share in that general
unbelief, not to be carried away by the world, but to " take heed,
watch,[1] pray," and look out for His coming.

Surely this gracious warning should be ever in our thoughts,
being so precise, so solemn, so earnest. He foretold His first
coming, yet He took His Church by surprise when He came ;
much more will He come suddenly the second time, and overtake men, now that He has not measured out the interval before

---

[1] ἀγρυπνεῖτε.

it, as then He did, but left our watchfulness to the keeping of faith and love.

Let us then consider this most serious question, which concerns every one of us so nearly ;—What it is to *watch* for Christ. He says, " *Watch* ye therefore, for ye know not when the Master of the house cometh ; at even, or at midnight, or at the cock-crowing, or in the morning ; lest coming suddenly He find you sleeping. And what I say unto you, I say unto all, *Watch.*"[1] And again, "If the goodman of the house had known what hour the thief would come, he would have *watched,* and not have suffered his house to be broken through."[2] A like warning is given elsewhere both by our Lord and by His Apostles. For instance ; we have the parable of the Ten Virgins, five of whom were wise and five foolish ; on whom the bridegroom, after tarrying, came suddenly, and five were found without oil. On which our Lord says, " *Watch* therefore, for ye know neither the day nor the hour wherein the Son of Man cometh."[3] Again He says, "Take heed to yourselves, lest at any time your hearts be overcharged with surfeiting and drunkenness, and cares of this life, and so that day come upon you unawares ; for as a snare shall it come on all them that dwell on the face of the whole earth. *Watch* ye therefore, and pray always, that ye may be accounted worthy to escape all these things that shall come to pass, and to stand before the Son of Man."[4] In like manner He upbraided Peter thus : "Simon, sleepest thou ? couldest not thou *watch* one hour ?"[5]

In like manner St. Paul in his Epistle to the Romans : "Now it is high time to awake out of sleep. . . . The night is far spent, the day is at hand."[6] Again, " *Watch* ye, stand fast in the faith, quit you like men, be strong."[7] "Be strong in the Lord, and in the power of His might ; put on the whole armour of God, that ye may be able to stand against the wiles of the devil ; . . . that ye may be able to withstand in the evil day, and having done all to stand."[8] "Let us not sleep as do others, but let us *watch* and be sober."[9] In like manner St. Peter : "The end of all things is at hand ; be ye therefore sober, and *watch* unto prayer." "Be sober, be *vigilant,* because your adversary the devil, as a roaring lion, walketh about seeking whom he may devour."[10] And St. John : "Behold I come as a thief ; blessed is he that *watcheth* and keepeth his garments."[11]

---

[1] Mark xiii. 35-37, γρηγορεῖτε.   [2] Luke xii. 39.   [3] Matt. xxv. 13.
[4] Luke xxi. 36.   [5] Mark xiv. 37.   [6] Rom. xiii. 11, 12.
[7] 1 Cor. xvi. 13.   [8] Eph. vi. 10-13.   [9] 1 Thess. v. 6.
[10] 1 Pet. iv. 7, νήψατε, v. 8.   [11] Rev. xvi. 15.

Now I consider this word *watching*, first used by our Lord, then by the favoured Disciple, then by the two great Apostles, Peter and Paul, is a remarkable word; remarkable because the idea is not so obvious as might appear at first sight, and next because they all inculcate it. We are not simply to believe, but to watch; not simply to love, but to watch; not simply to obey, but to watch; to watch for what? for that great event, Christ's coming. Whether then we consider what is the obvious meaning of the word, or the Object towards which it directs us, we seem to see a special duty enjoined on us, such as does not naturally come into our minds. Most of us have a general idea what is meant by believing, fearing, loving, and obeying; but perhaps we do not contemplate or apprehend what is meant by watching.

And I conceive it is one of the main points, which, in a practical way, will be found to separate the true and perfect servants of God from the multitude called Christians; from those who are, I do not say false and reprobate, but who are such that we cannot speak much about them, nor can form any notion what will become of them. And in saying this, do not understand me as saying, which I do not, that we can tell for certain who are the perfect, and who the double-minded or incomplete Christians; or that those who discourse and insist upon these subjects are necessarily on the right side of the line. I am but speaking of two *characters*, the true and consistent character, and the inconsistent; and these I say will be found in no slight degree discriminated and distinguished by this one mark,—true Christians, whoever they are, watch, and inconsistent Christians do not. Now what is watching?

I conceive it may be explained as follows :—Do you know the feeling in matters of this life, of expecting a friend, expecting him to come, and he delays? Do you know what it is to be in unpleasant company, and to wish for the time to pass away, and the hour strike when you may be at liberty? Do you know what it is to be in anxiety lest something should happen which may happen or may not, or to be in suspense about some important event, which makes your heart beat when you are reminded of it, and of which you think the first thing in the morning? Do you know what it is to have a friend in a distant country, to expect news of him, and to wonder from day to day what he is now doing, and whether he is well? Do you know what it is so to live upon a person who is present with you, that your eyes follow his, that you read his soul, that you see all its changes in his countenance, that you anticipate his wishes, that you smile in his smile, and are sad in his sadness, and are downcast when he is vexed, and rejoice in his successes? To watch for Christ is a feeling such as all these; as far as feelings of this world are fit to shadow out those of another.

He watches for Christ, who has a sensitive, eager, apprehensive mind; who is awake, alive, quick-sighted, zealous in seeking and honouring Him; who looks out for Him in all that happens, and who would not be surprised, who would not be over-agitated or overwhelmed, if he found that He was coming at once.

And he watches *with* Christ, who, while he looks on to the future, looks back on the past, and does not so contemplate what his Saviour has purchased for him, as to forget what He has suffered for him. He watches with Christ, who ever commemorates and renews in his own person Christ's Cross and Agony, and gladly takes up that mantle of affliction which Christ wore here, and left behind Him when He ascended. And hence in the Epistles, often as the inspired writers show their desire for His second coming, as often do they show their memory of His first, and never lose sight of His Crucifixion in His Resurrection. Thus if St. Paul reminds the Romans that they "wait for the redemption of the body" at the Last Day, he also says, "If so be that we *suffer with Him*, that we may be also glorified together." If he speaks to the Corinthians of "waiting for the coming of our Lord Jesus Christ," he also speaks of "always bearing about in the body the *dying* of the Lord Jesus, *that* the life also of Jesus might be made manifest in our body." If to the Philippians of "the power of His resurrection," he adds at once "*and the fellow-ship of His sufferings*, being made conformable unto His death." If he consoles the Colossians with the hope "when Christ shall appear," of their "appearing with Him in glory," he has already declared that he "*fills up that which remains of the afflictions of Christ* in his flesh for His body's sake, which is the Church."[1] Thus the thought of what Christ is must not obliterate from the mind the thought of what He was; and faith is always sorrowing with Him while it rejoices. And the same union of opposite thoughts is impressed on us in Holy Communion, in which we see Christ's death and resurrection together, at one and the same time; we commemorate the one, we rejoice in the other; we make an offering, and we gain a blessing.

This then is to watch; to be detached from what is present, and to live in what is unseen; to live in the thought of Christ

[1] Rom. viii. 17-23.   1 Cor. i. 7.   2 Cor. iv. 10.   Phil. iii. 10.   Col. iii. 4; i. 24.

as He came once, and as He will come again; to desire His
second coming, from our affectionate and grateful remembrance
of His first. And this it is, in which we shall find that men in
general are wanting. They are indeed without faith and love
also; but at least they profess to have these graces, nor is it easy
to convince them that they have not. For they consider they
have faith, if they do but own that the Bible came from God, or
that they trust wholly in Christ for salvation; and they consider
they have love if they obey some of the most obvious of God's
commandments. Love and faith they think they have; but
surely they do not even fancy that they watch. What is meant
by watching, and how it is a duty, they have no definite idea;
and thus it accidentally happens that watching is a suitable test
of a Christian, in that it is that particular property of faith and
love, which, essential as it is, men of this world do not even profess; that particular property which is the life or energy of
faith and love, the way in which faith and love, if genuine, show
themselves.

It is easy to exemplify what I mean, from the experience
which we all have of life. Many men indeed are open revilers
of religion, or at least openly disobey its laws; but let us consider those who are of a more sober and conscientious cast of
mind. They have a number of good qualities, and are in a
certain sense and up to a certain point religious; but they do
not watch. Their notion of religion is briefly this: loving God
indeed, but loving this world too; not only doing their *duty*,
but finding their chief and highest *good*, in that state of life to
which it has pleased God to call them, resting in it, taking it as
their portion. They serve God, and they seek Him; but they
look on the present world as if it were the eternal, not a mere
temporary, scene of their duties and privileges, and never contemplate the prospect of being separated from it. It is not that
they forget God, or do not live by principle, or forget that the
goods of this world are His gift; but they love them for their
own sake more than for the sake of the Giver, and reckon on their
remaining, as if they had that permanence which their duties and
religious privileges have. They do not understand that they
are called to be strangers and pilgrims upon the earth, and that
their worldly lot and worldly goods are a sort of accident of
their existence, and that they really have no property, though
human law guarantees property to them. Accordingly, they set
their heart upon their goods, be they great or little, not without
a sense of religion the while, but still idolatrously. *This* is their

fault,—an identifying God with this world, and therefore an idolatry towards this world; and so they are rid of the trouble of looking out for their God, for they think they have found Him in the goods of this world. While, then, they are really praiseworthy in many parts of their conduct, benevolent, charitable, kind, neighbourly, and useful in their generation, nay, constant perhaps in the ordinary religious duties which custom has established, and while they display much right and amiable feeling, and much correctness in opinion, and are even in the way to improve in character and conduct as time goes on, correct much that is amiss, gain greater command over themselves, mature in judgment, and are much looked up to in consequence; yet still it is plain that they love this world, would be loth to leave it, and wish to have more of its good things. They like wealth, and distinction, and credit, and influence. They may improve in conduct, but not in aims; they advance, but they do not mount; they are moving on a low level, and were they to move on for centuries, would never rise above the atmosphere of this world. "I will stand upon my watch, and set me upon the tower, and will watch to see what He will say unto me, and what I shall answer when I am reproved."[1] This is the temper of mind which they have not; and when we reflect how rarely it *is* found among professing Christians, we shall see why our Lord is so urgent in enforcing it;—as if He said, "I am not warning you, My followers, against open apostasy; that will not be; but I foresee that very few will keep awake and watch while I am away. Blessed are the servants who do so; few will open to Me *immediately,* when I knock. They will have something to do first; they will have to get ready. They will have to recover from the surprise and confusion which overtake them on the first news of My coming, and will need time to collect themselves, and summon about them their better thoughts and affections. They feel themselves very well off as they are; and wish to serve God as they are. They are satisfied to remain on earth; they do not wish to move; they do not wish to change."

Without denying, then, to these persons the praise of many religious habits and practices, I would say that they want the tender and sensitive heart which hangs on the thought of Christ, and lives in His love. The breath of the world has a peculiar power in what may be called rusting the soul. The mirror within them, instead of reflecting back the Son of God their Saviour, has become dim and discoloured; and hence, though

[1] Hab. ii. 1.

c

(to use a common expression) they have a good deal of good *in* them, it is only *in* them, it is not through them, around them, and upon them. An evil crust is *on* them : they think with the world ; they are full of the world's notions and modes of speaking ; they appeal to the world, and have a sort of reverence for what the world will say. There is a want of naturalness, simplicity, and childlike teachableness in them. It is difficult to touch them, or (what may be called) get at them, and to persuade them to a straightforward course in religion. They start off when you least expect it : they have reservations, make distinctions, take exceptions, indulge in refinements, in questions where there are really but two sides, a right and a wrong. Their religious feelings do not flow forth easily, at times when they ought to flow ; either they are diffident, and can say nothing, or else they are affected and strained in their mode of conversing. And as a rust preys upon metal and eats into it, so does this worldly spirit penetrate more and more deeply into the soul which once admits it. And this is one great end, as it would appear, of afflictions, viz. to rub away and clear off these outward defilements, and to keep the soul in a measure of its baptismal purity and brightness.

Now, it cannot surely be doubted that multitudes in the Church are such as I have been describing, and that they would not, could not, at once welcome our Lord on His coming. We cannot, indeed, apply what has been said to this or that individual ; but on the whole, viewing the multitude, one cannot be mistaken. There may be exceptions ; but after all conceivable deductions, a large body must remain thus double-minded, thus attempting to unite things incompatible. This we might be sure of, though Christ had said nothing on the subject ; but it is a most affecting and solemn thought, that He has actually called our attention to this very danger, the danger of a worldly religiousness, for so it may be called, though it *is* religiousness ; this mixture of religion and unbelief, which serves God indeed, but loves the fashions, the distinctions, the pleasures, the comforts of this life,—which feels a satisfaction in being prosperous in circumstances, likes pomps and vanities, is particular about food, raiment, house, furniture, and domestic matters, courts great people, and aims at having a position in society. He warns His disciples of the danger of having their minds drawn off from the thought of Him, by whatever cause ; He warns them against *all* excitements, *all* allurements of this world ; He solemnly warns them that the world will not be prepared for

His coming, and tenderly intreats of them not to take their portion with the world. He warns them by the instance of the rich man whose soul was required, of the servant who ate and drank, and of the foolish virgins. When He comes, they will one and all want time; their head will be confused, their eyes will swim, their tongue falter, their limbs totter, as men who are suddenly awakened. They will not all at once collect their senses and faculties. O fearful thought! the bridal train is sweeping by,—Angels are there,—the just made perfect are there,—little children, and holy teachers, and white-robed saints, and martyrs washed in blood; the marriage of the Lamb is come, and His wife hath made herself ready. She has already attired herself : while we have been sleeping, she has been robing; she has been adding jewel to jewel, and grace to grace; she has been gathering in her chosen ones, one by one, and has been exercising them in holiness, and purifying them for her Lord; and now her marriage hour is come. The holy Jerusalem is descending, and a loud voice proclaims, "Behold, the bridegroom cometh; go ye out to meet Him!" but we, alas! are but dazzled with the blaze of light, and neither welcome the sound, nor obey it,—and all for what? what shall we have gained then? what will this world have then done for us? wretched, deceiving world! which will then be burned up, unable not only to profit us, but to save itself. Miserable hour, indeed, will that be, when the full consciousness breaks on us of what we will not believe now, viz. that we *are* at present serving the world. We trifle with our conscience now; we deceive our better judgment; we repel the hints of those who tell us that we are joining ourselves to this perishing world. We *will* taste a little of its pleasures, and follow its ways, and think it no harm, so that we do not altogether neglect religion. I mean, we allow ourselves to covet what we have not, to boast in what we have, to look down on those who have less; or we allow ourselves to profess what we do not try to practise, to argue for the sake of victory, and to debate when we should be obeying; and we pride ourselves on our reasoning powers, and think ourselves enlightened, and despise those who had less to say for themselves, and set forth and defend our own theories; or we are over-anxious, fretful, and careworn about worldly matters, spiteful, envious, jealous, discontented, and evil-natured : in one or other way we take our portion with this world, and we will not believe that we do. We obstinately refuse to believe it; we know we are not altogether irreligious, and we persuade ourselves that we are religious. We learn to think it is possible to be too religious; we have taught ourselves that there is nothing high or deep in religion, no great exercise of our affections, no great food for our thoughts, no great work for our exertions. We go on in a self-satisfied or a self-conceited way, not looking out of ourselves, not standing like soldiers on the watch on the dark night; but we kindle our own fire, and delight ourselves in the sparks of it. This is our state, or something like this, and the Day will declare it; the Day is at hand, and the Day will search our hearts, and bring it home even to ourselves, that we have been cheating ourselves with words, and have not served Christ, as the Redeemer of the soul claims, but with a meagre, partial, worldly service, and without really contemplating Him who is above and apart from this world.

Year passes after year silently; Christ's coming is ever nearer than it was. O that, as He comes nearer earth, we may approach nearer heaven! O my brethren, pray Him to give you the heart to seek Him in sincerity. Pray Him to make you in earnest. You have one work only, to bear your cross after Him. Resolve in His strength to do so. Resolve to be no longer beguiled by "shadows of religion," by words, or by disputings, or by notions, or by high professions, or by excuses, or by the world's promises or threats. Pray Him to give you what Scripture calls "an honest and good heart," or "a perfect heart," and, without waiting, begin at once to obey Him with the best heart you have. Any obedience is better than none,—any profession which is disjoined from obedience, is a mere pretence and deceit. Any religion which does not bring you nearer to God is of the world. You have to seek His face; obedience is the only way of seeking Him. All your duties are obediences. If you are to believe the truths He has revealed, to regulate yourselves by His precepts, to be frequent in His ordinances, to adhere to His Church and people, why is it, except because *He* has bid you? and to do what He bids is to obey Him, and to obey Him is to approach Him. Every act of obedience is an approach,—an approach to Him who is not far off, though He seems so, but close behind this visible screen of things which hides Him from us. He is behind this material framework; earth and sky are but a veil going between Him and us; the day will come when He will rend that veil, and show Himself to us. And then, according as we have waited for Him, will He recompense us. If we have forgotten Him, He will not know us; but "blessed are those servants whom the Lord, when He cometh, shall find watching. . . . . He shall gird Him-

self, and make them sit down to meat, and will come forth and
serve them.   And if He shall come in the second watch, or come
in the third watch, and find them so, blessed are those servants."[1]
May this be the portion of every one of us !   It is hard to attain
it ; but it is woeful to fail.   Life is short ; death is certain ; and
the world to come is everlasting.

[1] Luke xii. 37, 28.

SERMON V.

(CHRISTMAS DAY.)

Religious Joy.

"*And the angel said unto them, Fear not: for, behold, I bring you good tidings of great joy, which shall be to all people. For unto you is born this day in the city of David a Saviour, which is Christ the Lord.*"—
LUKE ii. 10, 11.

THERE are two principal lessons which we are taught on the great Festival which we this day celebrate, lowliness and joy. This surely is a day, of all others, in which is set before us the heavenly excellence and the acceptableness in God's sight of that state which most men have, or may have, allotted to them, humble or private life, and cheerfulness in it. If we consult the writings of historians, philosophers, and poets of this world, we shall be led to think great men happy; we shall be led to fix our minds and hearts upon high or conspicuous stations, strange adventures, powerful talents to cope with them, memorable struggles, and great destinies. We shall consider that the highest course of life is the mere pursuit, not the enjoyment, of good.

But when we think of this day's Festival, and what we commemorate upon it, a new and very different scene opens upon us. First, we are reminded that though this life must ever be a life of toil and effort, yet that, properly speaking, we have not to seek our highest good. It is found, it is brought near us, in the descent of the Son of God from His Father's bosom to this world. It is stored up among us on earth. No longer need men of ardent minds weary themselves in the pursuit of what they fancy may be chief goods; no longer have they to wander about and encounter peril in quest of that unknown blessedness to which their hearts naturally aspire, as they did in heathen times. The text speaks to them and to all, "Unto you," it says, "is born this day in the city of David a Saviour, which is Christ the Lord."

Nor, again, need we go in quest of any of those things which this vain world calls great and noble. Christ altogether dishonoured what the world esteems, when He took on Himself a rank and station which the world despises. No lot could be more humble and more ordinary than that which the Son of God chose for Himself.

So that we have on the Feast of the Nativity these two lessons —instead of anxiety within and despondence without, instead of a weary search after great things,—to be cheerful and joyful; and, again, to be so in the midst of those obscure and ordinary circumstances of life which the world passes over and thinks scorn of.

Let us consider this more at length, as contained in the gracious narrative of which the text is part.

1. First, what do we read just before the text? that there were certain shepherds keeping watch over their flock by night, and Angels appeared to them. Why should the heavenly hosts appear to these shepherds? What was it in them which attracted the attention of the Angels and the Lord of Angels? Were these shepherds learned, distinguished, or powerful? Were they especially known for piety and gifts? Nothing is said to make us think so. Faith, we may safely say, they had, or some of them, for to him that hath more shall be given; but there is nothing to show that they were holier and more enlightened than other good men of the time, who waited for the consolation of Israel. Nay, there is no reason to suppose that they were better than the common run of men in their circumstances, simple, and fearing God, but without any great advances in piety, or any very formed habits of religion. Why then were they chosen? for their poverty's sake and obscurity. Almighty God looks with a sort of especial love, or (as we may term it) affection, upon the lowly. Perhaps it is that man, a fallen, dependent, and destitute creature, is more in his proper place when he is in lowly circumstances, and that power and riches, though unavoidable in the case of some, are unnatural appendages to man, as such. Just as there are trades and callings which are unbecoming, though requisite; and while we profit by them, and honour those the more who engage in them, yet we feel we are glad that they are not ours; as we feel grateful and respectful towards a soldiers' profession, yet do not affect it; so in God's sight greatness is less acceptable than obscurity. It becomes us less.

The shepherds, then, were chosen on account of their lowliness to be the first to hear of the Lord's nativity, a secret which none of the princes of this world knew.

And what a contrast is presented to us when we take into account who were our Lord's messengers to them! The Angels who excel in strength, these did His bidding towards the shepherds. Here the highest and the lowest of God's rational creatures are brought together. A set of poor men, engaged in a life of hardship, exposed at that very time to the cold and darkness of the night, watching their flocks, with the view of scaring away beasts of prey or robbers; they—when they are thinking of nothing but earthly things, counting over the tale of their sheep, keeping their dogs by their side, and listening to the noises over the plain, considering the weather and watching for the day—suddenly are met by far other visitants than they conceived. We know the contracted range of thought, the minute and ordinary objects, or rather the one or two objects, to and fro again and again without variety, which engage the minds of men exposed to such a life of heat, cold, and wet, hunger and nakedness, hardship and servitude. They cease to care much for anything, but go on in a sort of mechanical way, without heart, and still more without reflection.

To men so circumstanced the Angel appeared, to open their minds, and to teach them not to be downcast and in bondage because they were low in the world. He appeared as if to show them that God had chosen the poor in this world to be heirs of His kingdom, and so to do honour to their lot. "Fear not," he said; "for, behold, I bring you good tidings of great joy, which shall be to all people. For unto you is born this day in the city of David a Saviour, which is Christ the Lord."

2. And now comes a second lesson, which I have said may be gained from the Festival. The Angel honoured a humble lot by his very appearing to the shepherds; next he taught it to be joyful by his message. He disclosed good tidings so much above this world as to equalize high and low, rich and poor, one with another. He said, "Fear not." This is a mode of address frequent in Scripture, as you may have observed, as if man needed some such assurance to support him, especially in God's presence. The Angel said, "Fear not," when he saw the alarm which his presence caused among the shepherds. Even a lesser wonder would have reasonably startled them. Therefore the Angel said, "Fear not." We are naturally afraid of any messenger from the other world, for we have an uneasy conscience

when left to ourselves, and think that his coming forebodes evil.
Besides, we so little realize the unseen world, that were Angel or
spirit to present himself before us we should be startled by reason
of our unbelief, a truth being brought home to our minds which
we never apprehended before. So for one or other reason the
shepherds were sore afraid when the glory of the Lord shone
round about them. And the Angel said, "Fear not." A little
religion makes us afraid; when a little light is poured in upon
the conscience, there is a darkness visible; nothing but sights of
woe and terror; the glory of God alarms while it shines around.
His holiness, the range and difficulties of His commandments, the
greatness of His power, the faithfulness of His word, frighten the
sinner, and men seeing him afraid, think religion has made him
so, whereas he is not yet religious at all. They call him religious,
when he is merely conscience-stricken. But religion itself, far
from inculcating alarm and terror, says, in the words of the
Angel, "Fear not;" for such is His mercy, while Almighty God
has poured about us His glory, yet it is a consolatory glory, for
it is the light of His glory in the Face of Jesus Christ.[1] Thus
the heavenly herald tempered the too dazzling brightness of the
Gospel on that first Christmas. The glory of God at first
alarmed the shepherds, so he added the tidings of good, to
work in them a more wholesome and happy temper. Then they
rejoiced.

"Fear not," said the Angel; "for, behold, I bring you good
tidings of great joy, which shall be to all people. For unto you
is born this day in the city of David a Saviour, which is Christ
the Lord." And then, when he had finished his announcement,
"suddenly there was with the Angel a multitude of the heavenly
host praising God, and saying, Glory to God in the highest, and
on earth peace, good will toward men." Such were the words
which the blessed Spirits who minister to Christ and His Saints,
spoke on that gracious night to the shepherds, to rouse them out
of their cold and famished mood into great joy; to teach them
that they were objects of God's love as much as the greatest of
men on earth; nay more so, for to them first He had imparted
the news of what that night was happening. His Son was then
born into the world. Such events are told to friends and in-
timates, to those whom we love, to those who will sympathize
with us, not to strangers. How could Almighty God be more
gracious, and show His favour more impressively to the lowly
and the friendless, than by hastening (if I may use the term) to

[1] 2 Cor. iv. 6.

confide the great, the joyful secret to the shepherds keeping watch over their sheep by night?

The Angel then gave the first lesson of mingled humility and joyfulness; but an infinitely greater one was behind in the event itself, to which he directed the shepherds, in that birth itself of the Holy Child Jesus. This he intimated in these words: "Ye shall find the babe wrapped in swaddling-clothes, lying in a manger." Doubtless, when they heard the Lord's Christ was born into the world, they would look for Him in kings' palaces. They would not be able to fancy that He had become one of themselves, or that they might approach Him; therefore the Angel thus warned them where to find Him, not only as a sign, but as a lesson also.

"The shepherds said one to another, Let us now go even unto Bethlehem, and see this thing which is come to pass, which the Lord hath made known to us." Let us too go with them, to contemplate that second and greater miracle to which the Angel directed them, the Nativity of Christ. St. Luke says of the Blessed Virgin, "She brought forth her first-born Son, and wrapped Him in swaddling-clothes, and laid Him in a manger." What a wonderful sign is this to all the world, and therefore the Angel repeated it to the shepherds: "Ye shall find the babe wrapped in swaddling-clothes, lying in a manger." The God of heaven and earth, the Divine Word, who had been in glory with the Eternal Father from the beginning, He was at this time born into this world of sin as a little infant. He, as at this time, lay in His mother's arms, to all appearance helpless and powerless, and was wrapped by Mary in an infant's bands, and laid to sleep in a manger. The Son of God Most High, who created the worlds, became flesh, though remaining what He was before. He became flesh as truly as if He had ceased to be what He was, and had actually been changed into flesh. He submitted to be the offspring of Mary, to be taken up in the hands of a mortal, to have a mother's eye fixed upon Him, and to be cherished at a mother's bosom. A daughter of man became the Mother of God —to her, indeed, an unspeakable gift of grace; but in Him what condescension! What an emptying of His glory to become man! and not only a helpless infant, though that were humiliation enough, but to inherit all the infirmities and imperfections of our nature which were possible to a sinless soul. What were His thoughts, if we may venture to use such language or admit such a reflection concerning the Infinite, when human feelings, human sorrows, human wants, first became His? What a mystery is there from first to last in the Son of God becoming man ! Yet in proportion to the mystery is the grace and mercy of it; and as is the grace, so is the greatness of the fruit of it.

Let us steadily contemplate the mystery, and say whether any consequence is too great to follow from so marvellous a dispensation ; any mystery so great, any grace so overpowering, as that which is already manifested in the incarnation and death of the Eternal Son. Were we told that the effect of it would be to make us as Seraphim, that we were to ascend as high as He descended low—would that startle us after the Angel's news to the shepherds ? And this indeed is the effect of it, so far as such words may be spoken without impiety. Men we remain, but not mere men, but gifted with a measure of all those perfections which Christ has in fulness, partaking each in his own degree of His Divine Nature so fully, that the only reason (so to speak) why His saints are not really like Him, is that it is impossible —that He is the Creator, and they His creatures; yet still so, that they are all but Divine, all that they can be made without violating the incommunicable majesty of the Most High. Surely in proportion to His glory is His power of glorifying ; so that to say that through Him we shall be made *all but* gods—though it is to say, that we are infinitely below the adorable Creator—still is to say, and truly, that we shall be higher than every other being in the world ; higher than Angels or Archangels, Cherubim or Seraphim—that is, not here, or in ourselves, but in heaven and in Christ :—Christ, already the first fruits of our race, God and man, having ascended high above all creatures, and we through His grace tending to the same high blessedness, having the earnest of His glory given here, and (if we be found faithful) the fulness of it hereafter.

If all these things be so, surely the lesson of joy which the Incarnation gives us is as impressive as the lesson of humility. St. Paul gives us the one lesson in his Epistle to the Philippians : "Let this mind be in you, which was also in Christ Jesus : who, being in the form of God, thought it not robbery to be equal with God : but made Himself of no reputation, and took upon Him the form of a servant, and was made in the likeness of men :"[1] and St. Peter gives us the lesson of joyfulness : "Whom having not seen, ye love ; in whom, though now ye see Him not, yet believing, ye rejoice with joy unspeakable, and full of glory : receiving the end of your faith, even the salvation of your souls."

Take these thoughts with you, my brethren, to your homes on

[1] Phil. ii. 5-7.   1 Pet. i. 8, 9.

this festive day; let them be with you in your family and social meetings. It is a day of joy: it is good to be joyful—it is wrong to be otherwise. For one day we may put off the burden of our polluted consciences, and rejoice in the perfections of our Saviour Christ, without thinking of ourselves, without thinking of our own miserable uncleanness; but contemplating His glory, His righteousness, His purity, His majesty, His overflowing love. We may rejoice in the Lord, and in all His creatures see Him. We may enjoy His temporal bounty, and partake the pleasant things of earth with Him in our thoughts; we may rejoice in our friends for His sake, loving them most especially because He has loved them.

"God has not appointed us unto wrath, but to obtain salvation through our Lord Jesus Christ, who died for us, that whether we wake or sleep, we should live together with Him." Let us seek the grace of a cheerful heart, an even temper, sweetness, gentleness, and brightness of mind, as walking in His light, and by His grace. Let us pray Him to give us the spirit of ever-abundant, ever-springing love, which overpowers and sweeps away the vexations of life by its own richness and strength, and which above all things unites us to Him who is the fountain and the centre of all mercy, loving-kindness, and joy.

SERMON VI.

(NEW YEAR'S SUNDAY.)

The Lapse of Time.

" Whatsoever thy hand findeth to do, do it with thy might; for there is no work, nor device, nor knowledge, nor wisdom, in the grave, whither thou goest."—ECCLES. ix. 10.

SOLOMON'S advice that we should do whatever our hand findeth to do with our might, naturally directs our thoughts to that great work in which all others are included, which will outlive all other works, and for which alone we really are placed here below—the salvation of our souls. And the consideration of this great work, which must be done with all our might, and completed before the grave, whither we go, presents itself to our minds with especial force at the commencement of a new year. We are now entering on a fresh stage of our life's journey; we know well how it will end, and we see where we shall stop in the evening, though we do not see the road. And we know in what our business lies while we travel, and that it is important for us to do it with our "might; for there is no work, nor device, nor knowledge, nor wisdom, in the grave." This is so plain, that nothing need be said in order to convince us that it is true. We know it well; the very complaint which numbers commonly make when told of it, is that they know it already, that it is nothing new, that they have no need to be told, and that it is tiresome to hear the same thing said over and over again, and impertinent in the person who repeats it. Yes; thus it is that sinners silence their conscience, by quarrelling with those who appeal to it; they defend themselves, if it may be called a defence, by pleading that they already know what they should do and do not; that they know perfectly well that they are living at a distance from God, and are in peril of eternal ruin; that they know they are making themselves children of Satan, and denying the Lord that bought them, and want no one to tell them so. Thus they witness against themselves.

However, though we already know well enough that we have much to do before we die, yet (if we will but attend) it may be of use to hear the fact dwelt upon; because by thinking over it steadily and seriously, we may possibly, through God's grace, gain some deep conviction of it; whereas, while we keep to general terms, and confess that this life is important and is short, in the mere summary way in which men commonly confess it, we have, properly speaking, no knowledge of that great truth at all.

Consider, then, what it is to die; "there is no work, device, knowledge, or wisdom, in the grave." Death puts an end absolutely and irrevocably to all our plans and works, and it is inevitable. The Psalmist speaks to "high and low, rich and poor, one with another." "No man can deliver his brother, nor make agreement unto God for him." Even "wise men die, as well as the ignorant and foolish, and leave their riches for other."[1] Difficult as we may find it to bring it home to ourselves, to realize it, yet as surely as we are here assembled together, so surely will every one of us, sooner or later, one by one, be stretched on the bed of death. We naturally shrink from the thought of death, and of its attendant circumstances; but all that is hateful and fearful about it will be fulfilled in our case, one by one. But all this is nothing compared with the conse-quences implied in it. Death stops us; it stops our race. Men are engaged about their work, or about their pleasure; they are in the city, or the field; anyhow they are stopped; their deeds are suddenly gathered in—a reckoning is made—all is sealed up till the great Day. What a change is this! In the words used familiarly in speaking of the dead, they are no more. They were full of schemes and projects; whether in a greater or humbler rank, they had their hopes and fears, their prospects, their pursuits, their rivalries; all these are now come to an end. One builds a house, and its roof is not finished; another buys merchandise, and it is not yet sold. And all their virtues and pleasing qualities which endeared them to their friends are, as far as this world is concerned, vanished. Where are they who were so active, so sanguine, so generous? the amiable, the modest, and the kind? We were told that they were dead; they suddenly disappeared;

[1] Ps. xlix. 2-10.

that is all we know about it. They were silently taken from us; they are not met in the seat of the elders, nor in the assemblies of the people; in the mixed concourse of men, nor in the domestic retirement which they prized. As Scripture describes it, "the wind has passed over them, and they are gone, and their place shall know them no more." And they have burst the many ties which held them; they were parents, brothers, sisters, children, and friends; but the bond of kindred is broken, and the silver cord of love is loosed. They have been followed by the vehement grief of tears, and the long sorrow of aching hearts; but they make no return, they answer not; they do not even satisfy our wish to know that they sorrow for us as we for them. We talk about them thenceforth as if they were persons we do not know; we talk about them as third persons; whereas they used to be always with us, and every other thought which was within us was shared by them. Or perhaps, if our grief is too deep, we do not mention their names at all. And their possessions, too, all fall to others. The world goes on without them; it forgets them. Yes, so it is; the world contrives to forget that men have souls, it looks upon them all as mere parts of some great visible system. This continues to move on; to this the world ascribes a sort of life and personality. When one or other of its members die, it considers them only as falling out of the system, and as come to nought. For a minute, perhaps, it thinks of them in sorrow, then leaves them—leaves them for ever. It keeps its eye on things seen and temporal. Truly whenever a man dies, rich or poor, an immortal soul passes to judgment; but somehow we read of the deaths of persons we have seen or heard of, and this reflection never comes across us. Thus does the world really cast off men's souls, and recognizing only their bodies, it makes it appear as if "that which befalleth the sons of men befalleth beasts, even one thing befalleth them, as the one dieth so dieth the other; yea, they have all one breath, so that a man hath no pre-eminence over a beast, for all is vanity."[1]

But let us follow the course of a soul thus casting off the world, and cast off by it. It goes forth as a stranger on a journey. Man seems to die and to be no more, when he is but quitting us, and is really beginning to live. Then he sees sights which before it did not even enter into his mind to conceive, and the world is even less to him than he to the world. Just now he was lying on the bed of sickness, but in that moment of death

[1] Eccles. iii. 19.

what an awful change has come over him! What a crisis for
him! There is stillness in the room that lately held him;
nothing is doing there, for he is gone, he now belongs to others;
he now belongs entirely to the Lord who bought him; to Him he
returns; but whether to be lodged safely in His place of hope, or
to be imprisoned against the great Day, that is another matter,
that depends on the deeds done in the body, whether good or
evil. And now what are his thoughts? How infinitely important now appears the value of time, now when it is nothing
to him! Nothing; for though he spend centuries waiting for
Christ, he cannot now alter his state from bad to good, or from
good to bad. What he dieth that he must be for ever; as the
tree falleth so must it lie. This is the comfort of the true
servant of God, and the misery of the transgressor. His lot is
cast once and for all, and he can but wait in hope or in dread.
Men on their deathbeds have declared that no one could form a
right idea of the value of time till he came to die; but if this
has truth in it, how much more truly can it be said after death!
What an estimate shall we form of time while we are waiting for
judgment! Yes, it is we—all this, I repeat, belongs to us most
intimately. It is not to be looked at as a picture, as a man
might read a light book in a leisure hour. *We* must die, the
youngest, the healthiest, the most thoughtless; *we* must be thus
unnaturally torn in two, soul from body; and only united again
to be made more thoroughly happy or to be miserable for ever.

Such is death considered in its inevitable necessity, and its unspeakable importance—nor can we ensure to ourselves any certain
interval before its coming. The time may be long; but it may
also be short. It is plain, a man may die any day; all we can
say is, that it is unlikely that he will die. But of this, at least,
we are certain, that, come it sooner or later, death is continually
on the move towards us. We are ever nearer and nearer to it.
Every morning we rise we are nearer that grave in which there
is no work, nor device, than we were. We are now nearer the
grave than when we entered this church. Thus life is ever
crumbling away under us. What should we say to a man who
was placed on some precipitous ground, which was ever-crumb-
ling under his feet, and affording less and less secure footing, yet
was careless about it? Or what should we say to one who
suffered some precious liquor to run from its receptacle into the
thoroughfare of men, without a thought to stop it? who carelessly looked on and saw the waste of it becoming greater and
greater every minute? But what treasure can equal time? It is

the seed of eternity : yet we suffer ourselves to go on, year after year, hardly using it at all in God's service, or thinking it enough to give Him at most a tithe or a seventh of it, while we strenuously and heartily sow to the flesh, that from the flesh we may reap corruption. We try how little we can safely give to religion, instead of having the grace to give abundantly. "Rivers of water run down mine eyes, because men keep not Thy law;" so says the holy Psalmist. Doubtless an inspired prophet saw far more clearly than we can see, the madness of men in squandering that treasure upon sin, which is meant to buy their chief good ;—but if so, what must this madness appear in God's sight! What an inveterate malignant evil is it in the hearts of the sons of men, that thus leads them to sit down to eat, and drink, and rise up to play, when time is hurrying on and judgment coming? We have been told what He thinks of man's unbelief, though we cannot enter into the depths of His thoughts. He showed it to us in act and deed, as far as we could receive it, when He even sent His only-begotten Son into the world as at this time, to redeem us from the world,—which, most surely, was not lightly done ; and we also learn His thoughts about it from the words of that most merciful Son,—which most surely were not lightly spoken, "The wicked," He says, "shall go into everlasting punishment."

Oh that there were such a heart in us that we would fear God and keep His commandments always! But it is of no use to speak ; men know their duty—they will not do it. They say they do not need or wish to be told it, that it is an intrusion, and a rudeness, to tell them of death and judgment. So must it be,—and we, who have to speak to them, must submit to this. Speak we must, as an act of duty to God, whether they will hear or not, and then must leave our words as a witness. Other means for rousing them we have none. We speak from Christ our gracious Lord, their Redeemer, who has already pardoned them freely, yet they will not follow Him with a true heart; and what can be done more?

Another year is now opening upon us ; it speaks to the thoughtful, and is heard by those, who have expectant ears, and watch for Christ's coming. The former year is gone, it is dead, there it lies in the grave of past time, not to decay however, and be forgotten, but kept in the view of God's omniscience, with all its sins and errors irrevocably written, till, at length, it will be raised again to testify about us at the last day ; and who among us can bear the thought of his own doings, in the course of it?—all that he has said and done, all that has been conceived within his mind, or been acted on, and all that he has not said and done, which it was a duty to say or do. What a dreary prospect seems to be before us, when we reflect that we have the solemn word of truth pledged to us, in the last and most awful revelation, which God has made to us about the future, that in that day the books will be opened, "and another book opened, which is the book of life, and the dead judged out of those things which were written in the books according to their works"![1] What would a man give, any one of us, who has any real insight into his polluted and miserable state—what would he give to tear away some of the leaves there preserved! For how heinous are the sins therein written! Think of the multitude of sins done by us since we first knew the difference between right and wrong. We have forgotten them, but there we might read them clearly recorded. Well may holy David exclaim, "Remember not the sins of my youth nor my transgressions, according to Thy mercy remember Thou me." Conceive, too, the multitude of sins which have so grown into us as to become part of us, and in which we now live, not knowing, or but partially knowing, that they are sins; habits of pride, self-reliance, self-conceit, sullenness, impurity, sloth, selfishness, worldliness. The history of all these, their beginnings and their growth, is recorded in those dreadful books; and when we look forward to the future, how many sins shall we have committed by this time next year,—though we try ever so much to know our duty, and overcome ourselves! Nay, or rather shall we have the opportunity of obeying or disobeying God for a year longer? Who knows whether by that time our account may not be closed for ever?

"Remember me, O Lord, when Thou comest into Thy king-dom."[2] Such was the prayer of the penitent thief on the cross, such must be our prayer. Who can do us any good but He, who shall also be our Judge? When shocking thoughts about ourselves come across us and afflict us, "Remember me," this is all we have to say. We have "no work, nor device, nor know-ledge, nor wisdom" of our own, to better ourselves withal. We can say nothing to God in defence of ourselves,—we can but acknowledge that we are grievous sinners, and addressing Him as suppliants, merely beg Him to bear us in mind in mercy, for His Son's sake to do us some favour, not according to our deserts, but for the love of Christ. The more we try to serve Him here, the better; but after all, so far do we fall short of what we

[1] Rev. xx. 12. [2] Luke xxiii. 42.

should be, that if we had but what we are in ourselves to rely upon, wretched are we,—and we are forced out of ourselves by the very necessity of our condition. To whom should we go? Who can do us any good, but He who was born into this world for our regeneration, was bruised for our iniquities, and rose again for our justification? Even though we have served Him from our youth up, though after His pattern we have grown, as far as mere man can grow, in wisdom as we grew in stature, though we ever have had tender hearts, and a mortified will, and a conscientious temper, and an obedient spirit; yet, at the very best, how much have we left undone, how much done, which ought to be otherwise! What He can do for our nature, in the way of sanctifying it, we know indeed in a measure; we know in the case of His saints; and we certainly do not know the limit of His carrying forward in those objects of His special favour the work of purification, and renewal through His Spirit. But for ourselves, we know full well that much as we may have attempted, we have done very little, that our very best service is nothing worth,—and the more we attempt, the more clearly we shall see how little we have hitherto attempted.

Those whom Christ saves are they who at once attempt to save themselves, yet despair of saving themselves; who aim to do all, and confess they do nought; who are all love, and all fear; who are the most holy, and yet confess themselves the most sinful; who ever seek to please Him, yet feel they never can; who are full of good works, yet of works of penance. All this seems a contradiction to the natural man, but it is not so to those whom Christ enlightens. They understand in proportion to their illumination, that it is possible to work out their salvation, yet to have it wrought out for them, to fear and tremble at the thought of judgment, yet to rejoice always in the Lord, and hope and pray for His coming.

SERMON VII.

(EPIPHANY.)

Remembrance of Past Mercies.

" I am not worthy of the least of all the mercies, and of all the truth, which Thou hast showed unto Thy servant."—GEN. xxxii. 10.

THE spirit of humble thankfulness for past mercies which these words imply, is a grace to which we are especially called in the Gospel. Jacob, who spoke them, knew not of those great and wonderful acts of love with which God has since visited the race of man. But though he might not know the depths of God's counsels, he knew himself so far as to know that he was worthy of no good thing at all, and he knew also that Almighty God had shown him great mercies and great truth: mercies, in that He had done for him good things, whereas he had deserved evil; and truth, in that He had made him promises, and had been faithful to them. In consequence, he overflowed with gratitude when he looked back upon the past; marvelling at the contrast between what he was in himself and what God had been to him.

Such thankfulness, I say, is eminently a Christian grace, and is enjoined on us in the New Testament. For instance, we are exhorted to be "thankful," and to let "the Word of Christ dwell in us richly in all wisdom; teaching and admonishing one another in psalms and hymns and spiritual songs, singing with grace in our hearts to the Lord."

Elsewhere we are told to "speak to ourselves in psalms and hymns and spiritual songs, singing and making melody in our heart to the Lord: giving thanks always for all things unto God and the Father, in the Name of our Lord Jesus Christ."

Again: "Be careful for nothing: but in every thing by prayer and supplication, with thanksgiving, let your requests be made known unto God."

Again : " In every thing give thanks : for this is the will of God in Christ Jesus concerning you."[1]

The Apostle, who writes all this, was himself an especial pattern of a thankful spirit : " Rejoice in the Lord alway," he says ; "and again I say, Rejoice." "I have learned, in whatsoever state I am, therewith to be content. I have all and abound ; I am full." Again : "I thank Christ Jesus our Lord, who hath enabled me, for that He counted me faithful, putting me into the ministry ; who was before a blasphemer and a persecutor, and injurious. But I obtained mercy, because I did it ignorantly in unbelief. And the grace of our Lord was exceeding abundant, with faith and love which is in Christ Jesus."[2]   O great Apostle ! how could it be otherwise, considering what he had been and what he was,— transformed from an enemy to a friend, from a blind Pharisee to an inspired preacher ?   And yet there is another Saint, besides the patriarch Jacob, who is his fellow in this excellent grace,— like them, distinguished by great vicissitudes of life, and by the adoring love and the tenderness of heart with which he looked back upon the past—I mean " David, the son of Jesse, the man who was raised up on high, the anointed of the God of Jacob, and the sweet Psalmist of Israel."[3]

The Book of Psalms is full of instances of David's thankful spirit, which I need not cite here, as we are all so well acquainted with them.   I will but refer to his thanksgiving, when he set apart the precious materials for the building of the Temple, as it occurs at the end of the First Book of Chronicles ; when he rejoiced so greatly, because he and his people had the heart to offer freely to God, and thanked God for his very thankfulness.   " David, the king, . . rejoiced with great joy ; wherefore David blessed the Lord before all the congregation ; and David said, Blessed be Thou, Lord God of Israel, our Father, for ever and ever. . . . Both riches and honour come of Thee, and Thou reignest over all ; and in Thine hand is power and might, and in Thine hand it is to make great, and to give strength unto all.   Now, therefore, our God, we thank Thee, and praise Thy glorious Name.   But who am I, and what is my people, that we should be able to offer so willingly after this sort ? for all things come of Thee, and of Thine own have we given Thee."[4]

---

[1] Col. iii. 15, 16.   Eph. v. 19, 20.   Phil. iv. 6.   1 Thess. v. 18.
[2] Phil. iv. 4, 11, 18.   1 Tim. i. 12-14.
[3] 2 Sam. xxiii. 1.   [4] 1 Chron. xxix. 9-14.

Such was the thankful spirit of David, looking back upon the past, wondering and rejoicing at the way in which his Almighty Protector had led him on, and at the works He had enabled him to do ; and praising and glorifying Him for His mercy and truth. David, then, Jacob, and St. Paul, may be considered the three great patterns of thankfulness, which are set before us in Scripture ;—saints, all of whom were peculiarly the creation of God's grace, and whose very life and breath it was humbly and adoringly to meditate upon the contrast between what, in different ways, they had been, and what they were. A perishing wanderer had unexpectedly become a patriarch; a shepherd, a king ; and a persecutor, an apostle: each had been chosen, at God's inscrutable pleasure, to fulfil a great purpose, and each, while he did his utmost to fulfil it, kept praising God that he was made His instrument. Of the first it was said, " Jacob have I loved, but Esau have I hated ; " of the second, that " He refused the tabernacle of Joseph, and chose not the tribe of Ephraim, but chose the tribe of Judah, even the hill of Sion, which He loved : He chose David also His servant, and took him away from the sheepfolds." And St. Paul says of himself, " Last of all, He was seen of me also, as of one born out of due time." [1]

These thoughts naturally come over the mind at this season, when we are engaged in celebrating God's grace in making us His children, by the incarnation of His only-begotten Son, the greatest and most wonderful of all His mercies. And to the Patriarch Jacob our minds are now particularly turned, by the First Lessons for this day,[2] taken from the Prophet Isaiah, in which the Church is addressed and comforted under the name of Jacob. Let us then, in this season of thankfulness, and at the beginning of a new year, take a brief view of the character of this Patriarch ; and though David and Isaiah be the prophets of grace, and St. Paul its special herald and chief pattern, yet, if we wish to see an actual specimen of a habit of thankfulness occupied in the remembrance of God's mercies, I think we shall not be wrong in betaking ourselves to Jacob.

Jacob's distinguishing grace then, as I think it may be called, was a habit of affectionate musing upon God's providences towards him in times past, and of overflowing thankfulness for them. Not that he had not other graces also, but this seems to have been his distinguishing grace. All good men have in their measure all graces ; for He, by whom they have any, does not give one apart

---

[1] Rom. ix. 13.   Ps. lxxviii. 68-71.   1 Cor. xv. 8.
[2] Second Sunday after Christmas.

from the whole: He gives the root, and the root puts forth branches. But since time, and circumstances, and their own use of the gift, and their own disposition and character, have much influence on the mode of its manifestation, so it happens that each good man has his own distinguishing grace, apart from the rest, his own particular hue and fragrance and fashion, as a flower may have. As, then, there are numberless flowers on the earth, all of them flowers, and so far like each other; and all springing from the same earth, and nourished by the same air and dew, and none without beauty; and yet some are more beautiful than others; and of those which are beautiful, some excel in colour, and others in sweetness, and others in form; and then, again, those which are sweet have such perfect sweetness, yet so distinct, that we do not know how to compare them together, or to say which is the sweeter: so is it with souls filled and nurtured by God's secret grace. Abraham, for instance, Jacob's forefather, was the pattern of faith. This is insisted on in Scripture, and it is not here necessary to show that he was so. It will be sufficient to say that he left his country at God's word; and, at the same word, took up the knife to slay his own son. Abraham seems to have had something very noble and magnanimous about him. He could realize and make present to him things unseen. He followed God in the dark as promptly, as firmly, with as cheerful a heart, and bold a stepping, as if he were in broad daylight. There is something very great in this; and, therefore, St. Paul calls Abraham *our* father, the father of Christians as well as of Jews. For we are especially bound to walk by faith, not by sight; and are blessed in faith, and justified by faith, as was faithful Abraham. Now (if I may say it, with due reverence to the memory of that favoured servant of God, in whose praise I am now speaking) that faith in which Abraham excelled was not Jacob's characteristic excellence. Not that he had not faith, and great faith, else he would not have been so dear to God. His buying the birthright and gaining the blessing from Esau were proofs of faith. Esau saw nothing or little precious in them,—he was profane; easily parted with the one, and had no high ideas of the other. However, Jacob's faith, earnest and vigorous as it was, was not like Abraham's. Abraham kept his affections loose from everything earthly, and was ready at God's word to slay his only son. Jacob had many sons, and may we not even say that he indulged them overmuch? Even as regards Joseph, whom he so deservedly loved, beautiful and touching as his love of him is, yet there is a great contrast between his feelings towards the "son of his old age" and those of Abraham towards Isaac, the unexpected offspring of his hundredth year,—nor only such, but his long-promised only son, with whom were the promises. Again : Abraham left his country,—so did Jacob ; but Abraham, at God's word,—Jacob, from necessity on the threat of Esau. Abraham, from the first, felt that God was his portion and his inheritance, and, in a great and generous spirit, he freely gave up all he had, being sure that he should find what was more excellent in doing so. But Jacob, in spite of his really living by faith, wished (if we may so say), as one passage of his history shows, to see before he fully believed. When he was escaping from Esau and came to Bethel, and God appeared to him in a dream and gave him promises, but not yet the performance of them,—what did he do ? Did he simply accept them ? He says, " *If* God will be with me, and will keep me in this way that I go, and will give me bread to eat, and raiment to put on, so that I come again to my father's house in peace, *then* shall the Lord be my God."[1] He makes his obedience, in some sense, depend on a condition ; and although we must not, and need not, take the words as if he meant that he would not serve God *till* and *unless* He did for him what He had promised, yet they seem to show a fear and anxiety, gentle indeed, and subdued, and very human (and therefore the more interesting and winning in the eyes of us common men, who read his words), yet an anxiety which Abraham had not. We feel Jacob to be more like ourselves than Abraham was.

What, then, was Jacob's distinguishing grace, as faith was Abraham's ? I have already said it : I suppose, thankfulness. Abraham appears ever to have been looking forward in *hope*,— Jacob looking back in *memory :* the one rejoicing in the future, the other in the past ; the one setting his affections on the future, the other on the past ; the one making his way towards the promises, the other musing over their fulfilment. Not that Abraham did not look back also, and Jacob, as he says on his deathbed, did not " wait for the salvation " of God ; but this was the difference between them, Abraham was a hero, Jacob " a plain man, dwelling in tents."

Jacob seems to have had a gentle, tender, affectionate, timid mind—easily frightened, easily agitated, loving God so much that he feared to lose Him, and, like St. Thomas perhaps, anxious for sight and possession from earnest and longing desire of them. Were it not for faith, love would become impatient, and thus Jacob desired to possess, not from cold incredulity or hardness of heart,

---

[1] Gen. xxviii. 20, 21.

but from such a loving impatience. Such men are easily down-cast, and must be treated kindly; they soon despond, they shrink from the world, for they feel its rudeness, which bolder natures do not. Neither Abraham nor Jacob loved the world. But Abraham did not fear, did not feel it. Jacob felt and winced, as being wounded by it. You recollect his touching complaints, "All these things are against me!"—"Then shall ye bring down my grey hairs with sorrow to the grave."—"If I am bereaved of my children, I am bereaved." Again, elsewhere we are told, "All his sons and all his daughters rose up to comfort him, but he refused to be comforted." At another time, "Jacob's heart fainted, for he believed them not." Again, "The spirit of Jacob their father revived." [1] You see what a childlike, sensitive, sweet mind he had. Accordingly, as I have said, his happiness lay, not in looking forward to the hope, but backwards upon the experience, of God's mercies towards him. He delighted lovingly to trace, and gratefully to acknowledge, what had been given, leaving the future to itself.

For instance, when coming to meet Esau, he brings before God in prayer, in words of which the text is part, what He had already done for him, recounting His past favours with great and humble joy in the midst of his present anxiety. "O God of my father Abraham," he says, "and God of my father Isaac, the Lord which saidst unto me, Return unto thy country, and to thy kindred, and I will deal well with thee: I am not worthy of the least of all the mercies, and of all the truth, *which Thou hast showed unto Thy servant; for with my staff I passed over this Jordan, and now I am become two bands.*" Again, after he had returned to his own land, he proceeded to fulfil the promise he had made to consecrate Bethel as a house of God, "Let us arise, and go up to Bethel; and I will make there an altar unto God, *who answered me in the day of my distress, and was with me in the way which I went.*" Again, to Pharaoh, still dwelling on the past: "The days of the years of my pilgrimage are an hundred and thirty years; few and evil have the days of the years of my life been," he means, in themselves, and as separate from God's favour, "and have not attained unto the days of the years of the life of my fathers, in the days of their pilgrimage." Again, when he was approaching his end, he says to Joseph, "God Almighty *appeared unto me* at Luz," that is, Bethel, "in the land of Canaan, and blessed me." Again, still looking back, "As for me, when I came from Padan, Rachel died by me in the land of Canaan, in the way, when yet

[1] Gen. xlii. 36, 38; xliii. 14; xxxvii. 35; xlv. 26, 27.

there was but a little way to come to Ephrath; and I buried her there in the way of Ephrath." Again, his blessing upon Ephraim and Manasseh : "God, before whom my fathers Abraham and Isaac did walk, *the God which fed me all my life long unto this day,* the Angel which redeemed me from all evil, bless the lads." Again he looks back on the land of promise, though in the plentifulness of Egypt : "Behold, I die, but God shall be with you, and bring you again unto the land of your fathers." And when he gives command about his burial, he says : "I am to be gathered unto my people ; bury me with my fathers in the cave that is in the field of Ephron the Hittite." He gives orders to be buried with his fathers ; this was natural, but observe, he goes on to *enlarge* on the subject, after his special manner : "There they buried Abraham and Sarah his wife ; there they buried Isaac and Rebekah his wife ; and *there I buried Leah.*" And further on, when he speaks of waiting for God's salvation, which is an act of hope, he so words it as at the same time to dwell upon the past : "I *have* waited," he says, that is, all my life long, "I have waited for Thy salvation, O Lord."[1] Such was Jacob, living in memory rather than in hope, counting times, recording seasons, keeping days ; having his history by heart, and his past life in his hand ; and as if to carry on his mind into that of his descendants, it was enjoined upon them, that once a year every Israelite should appear before God with a basket of fruit of the earth, and call to mind what God had done for him and his father Jacob, and express his thankfulness for it. "A Syrian ready to perish was my father," he had to say, meaning Jacob ; "and he went down into Egypt, and sojourned there, and became a nation, great, mighty, and populous. . . . And the Lord brought us forth out of Egypt with an outstretched arm, and with great terribleness, and with signs, and with wonders ; and hath brought us into this land . . . that floweth with milk and honey. And now, behold, I have brought the first-fruits of the land, which Thou, O Lord, hast given me."[2]

Well were it for us, if we had the character of mind instanced in Jacob, and enjoined on his descendants ; the temper of dependence upon God's providence, and thankfulness under it, and careful memory of all He has done for us. It would be well if we were in the habit of looking at all we have as God's gift, undeservedly given, and day by day continued to us solely by His

[1] Gen. xxxii. 9, 10 ; xxxv. 3 ; xlvii. 9 ; xlviii. 3, 7, 15, 16, 21 ; xlix. 29-31, 18.   [2] Deut. xxvi. 5-10.

mercy. He gave; He may take away. He gave us all we have, life, health, strength, reason, enjoyment, the light of conscience; whatever we have good and holy within us; whatever faith we have; whatever of a renewed will; whatever love towards Him; whatever power over ourselves; whatever prospect of heaven. He gave us relatives, friends, education, training, knowledge, the Bible, the Church. All comes from Him. He gave; He may take away. Did He take away, we should be called on to follow Job's pattern, and be resigned : "The Lord gave, and the Lord hath taken away. Blessed be the Name of the Lord."[1] While He continues His blessings, we should follow David and Jacob, by living in constant praise and thanksgiving, and in offering up to Him of His own.

We are not our own, any more than what we possess is our own. We did not make ourselves; we cannot be supreme over ourselves. We cannot be our own masters. We are God's property by creation, by redemption, by regeneration. He has a triple claim upon us. Is it not our happiness thus to view the matter? Is it any happiness, or any comfort, to consider that we *are* our own? It may be thought so by the young and prosperous. These may think it a great thing to have everything, as they suppose, their own way,—to depend on no one,—to have to think of nothing out of sight,—to be without the irksomeness of continual acknowledgment, continual prayer, continual reference of what they do to the will of another. But as time goes on, they, as all men, will find that independence was not made for man—that it is an unnatural state—may do for a while, but will not carry us on safely to the end. No, we are creatures; and, as being such, we have two duties, to be resigned and to be thankful.

Let us then view God's providences towards us more religiously than we have hitherto done. Let us try to gain a truer view of what we are, and where we are, in His kingdom. Let us humbly and reverently attempt to trace His guiding hand in the years which we have hitherto lived. Let us thankfully commemorate the many mercies He has vouchsafed to us in time past, the many sins He has not remembered, the many dangers He has averted, the many prayers He has answered, the many mistakes He has corrected, the many warnings, the many lessons, the much light, the abounding comfort which He has from time to time given. Let us dwell upon times and seasons, times of trouble, times of joy, times of trial, times of refreshment. How

[1] Job i. 21.

did He cherish us as children! How did He guide us in that dangerous time when the mind began to think for itself, and the heart to open to the world! How did He with His sweet discipline restrain our passions, mortify our hopes, calm our fears, enliven our heavinesses, sweeten our desolateness, and strengthen our infirmities! How did He gently guide us towards the strait gate! how did He allure us along His everlasting way, in spite of its strictness, in spite of its loneliness, in spite of the dim twilight in which it lay! He has been all things to us. He has been, as He was to Abraham, Isaac, and Jacob, our God, our shield, and great reward, promising and performing, day by day. "Hitherto hath He helped us." "He hath been mindful of us, and He will bless us." He has not made us for nought; He has brought us thus far, in order to bring us further, in order to bring us on to the end. He will never leave us nor forsake us; so that we may boldly say, "The Lord is my Helper; I will not fear what flesh can do unto me." We may "cast all our care upon Him, who careth for us." What is it to us how our future path lies, if it be but His path? What is it to us whither it leads us, so that in the end it leads to Him? What is it to us what He puts upon us, so that He enables us to undergo it with a pure conscience, a true heart, not desiring anything of this world in comparison of Him? What is it to us what terror befalls us, if He be but at hand to protect and strengthen us? "Thou, Israel," He says, "art My servant Jacob, whom I have chosen, the seed of Abraham My friend." "Fear not, thou worm Jacob, and ye men of Israel; I will help thee, saith the Lord, and thy Redeemer, the Holy One of Israel." "Thus saith the Lord that created thee, O Jacob, and He that formed thee, O Israel, Fear not; for I have redeemed thee, I have called thee by thy name; thou art Mine. When thou passest through the waters, I will be with thee; and through the rivers, they shall not overflow thee; when thou walkest through the fire, thou shalt not be burned; neither shall the flame kindle upon thee. For I am the Lord thy God, the Holy One of Israel, thy Saviour." [1]

[1] Isa. xli. 8, 14; xliii. 1-3.

SERMON VIII.

(EPIPHANY.)

Equanimity.

" Rejoice in the Lord alway, and again I say, Rejoice."—PHIL. iv. 4.

IN other parts of Scripture the prospect of Christ's coming
is made a reason for solemn fear and awe, and a call for
watching and prayer, but in the verses connected with the text a
distinct view of the Christian character is set before us, and
distinct duties urged on us. "The Lord is at hand," and what
then? why, if so, we must "rejoice in the Lord;" we must be conspicuous for "moderation;" we must be "careful for nothing;"
we must seek from God's bounty, and not from man, whatever we
need; we must abound in "thanksgiving;" and we must cherish,
or rather we must pray for, and we shall receive from above, "the
peace of God which passeth all understanding," to "keep our
hearts and minds through Christ Jesus."

Now this is a view of the Christian character definite and complete enough to admit of commenting on,—and it may be useful
to show that the thought of Christ's coming not only leads to fear,
but to a calm and cheerful frame of mind.

Nothing perhaps is more remarkable than that an Apostle,—a
man of toil and blood, a man combating with powers unseen, and
a spectacle for men and Angels, and much more that St. Paul,
a man whose natural temper was so zealous, so severe, and so
vehement,—I say, nothing is more striking and significant than
that St. Paul should have given us this view of what a Christian
should be. It would be nothing wonderful, it *is* nothing wonderful, that writers in a day like this should speak of peace, quiet,
sobriety, and cheerfulness, as being the tone of mind that becomes
a Christian; but considering that St. Paul was by birth a Jew,

and by education a Pharisee, that he wrote at a time when, if at any time, Christians were in lively and incessant agitation of mind; when persecution and rumours of persecution abounded; when all things seemed in commotion around them; when there was nothing fixed; when there were no churches to soothe them, no course of worship to sober them, no homes to refresh them; and, again, considering that the Gospel is full of high and noble, and what may be called even romantic, principles and motives, and deep mysteries;—and, further, considering the very topic which the Apostle combines with his admonitions is that awful subject, the coming of Christ;—it is well worthy of notice, that, in such a time, under such a covenant, and with such a prospect, he should draw a picture of the Christian character as free from excitement and effort, as full of repose, as still and as equable, as if the great Apostle wrote in some monastery of the desert or some country parsonage. Here surely is the finger of God; here is the evidence of supernatural influences, making the mind of man independent of circumstances! This is the thought that first suggests itself; and the second is this, how deep and refined is the true Christian spirit!—how difficult to enter into, how vast to embrace, how impossible to exhaust! Who would expect such composure and equanimity from the fervent Apostle of the Gentiles? We know St. Paul could do great things; could suffer and achieve, could preach and confess, could be high and could be low: but we might have thought that all this was the limit and the perfection of the Christian temper, as he viewed it; and that no room was left him for the feelings which the text and following verses lead us to ascribe to him.

And yet he who "laboured more abundantly than all" his brethren, is also a pattern of simplicity, meekness, cheerfulness, thankfulness, and serenity of mind. These tempers were especially characteristic of St. Paul, and are much insisted on in his Epistles. For instance: "Mind not high things, but condescend to men of low estate. Be not wise in your own conceits. . . . Provide things honest in the sight of all men. If it be possible, as much as lieth in you, live peaceably with all men." He enjoins, that "the aged men be sober, grave, temperate, sound in faith, in charity, in patience." "The aged women likewise, . . . not false accusers, not given to much wine, teachers of good things, that they may teach the young women to be sober, to love their husbands, to love their children, to be discreet, chaste, keepers at home, good, obedient to their own husbands." And "young men" to be "sober-minded." And it is remarkable that he ends this exhortation with urging the same reason as is given in the verse after the text: "looking for that blessed hope, and the glorious appearing of our great God and Saviour Jesus Christ." In like manner, he says, that Christ's ministers must show "uncorruptness in doctrine, gravity, sincerity, sound speech that cannot be condemned;" that they must be "blameless, not self-willed, not soon angry; . . . lovers of good men, sober, just, holy, temperate."[1] All this is the description of what seems almost an ordinary character; I mean, it is so staid, so quiet, so unambitious, so homely. It displays so little of what is striking or extraordinary. It is so negligent of this world, so unexcited, so single-minded.

It is observable, too, that it was foretold as the peculiarity of Gospel times by the Prophet Isaiah: "The work of righteousness shall be peace; and the effect of righteousness, quietness and assurance for ever. And My people shall dwell in a peaceable habitation, and in sure dwellings, and in quiet resting-places."[2]

Now then let us consider more particularly what is this state of mind, and what the grounds of it. These seem to be as follows: The Lord is at hand; this is not your rest; this is not your abiding-place. Act then as persons who are in a dwelling not their own; who are not in their own home; who have not their own goods and furniture about them; who, accordingly, make shift and put up with anything that comes to hand, and do not make a point of things being the best of their kind. "But this I say, brethren, the time is short." What matters it what we eat, what we drink, how we are clothed, where we lodge, what is thought of us, what becomes of us, since we are not at home? It is felt every day, even as regards this world, that when we leave home for a while we are unsettled. This, then, is the kind of feeling which a belief in Christ's coming will create within us. It is not worth while establishing ourselves here; it is not worth while spending time and thought on such an object. We shall hardly have got settled when we shall have to move.

This being apparently the general drift of the passage, let us next enter into the particular portions of it.

1. "Be careful for nothing," he says, or, as St. Peter, "casting all your care upon Him," or, as He Himself, "Take no thought" or care "for the morrow, for the morrow will take thought for the things of itself."[3] This of course is the state of mind which is directly consequent on the belief that "the Lord is at hand." Who would care for any loss or gain to-day, if he knew for certain

---

[1] Rom. xii. 16-18. Titus ii. 2-13 ; i. 7, 8.
[2] Isa. xxxii. 17, 18. [3] 1 Peter v. 7. Matt. vi. 34.

that Christ would show Himself to-morrow? no one. Well, then, the true Christian feels as he would feel did he know for certain that Christ would be here to-morrow. For he knows for certain that at least Christ will come to him when he dies; and faith anticipates his death, and makes it just as if that distant day, if it *be* distant, were past and over. One time or another Christ will come, for certain: and when He once *has* come, it matters not what length of time there was before He came;—however long that period may be, it has an end. Judgment is coming, whether it comes sooner or later, and the Christian realizes that it is coming; that is, time does not enter into his calculation, or interfere with his view of things. When men expect to carry out their plans and projects, then they care for them; when they know these will come to nought, they give them over, or become indifferent to them.

So, again, it is with all forebodings, anxieties, mortifications, griefs, resentments of this world. "The time is short." It has sometimes been well suggested, as a mode of calming the mind when set upon an object, or much vexed or angered at some occurrence, what will you feel about all this a year hence? It is very plain that matters which agitate us most extremely now, will then interest us not at all; that objects about which we have intense hope and fear now, will then be to us nothing more than things which happen at the other end of the earth. So will it be with all human hopes, fears, pleasures, pains, jealousies, disappointments, successes, when the last day is come. They will have no life in them; they will be as the faded flowers of a banquet, which do but mock us. Or when we lie on the bed of death, what will it avail us to have been rich, or great, or fortunate, or honoured, or influential? All things will then be vanity. Well, what this world will be understood by all to be then, such is it felt to be by the Christian now. He looks at things as he then will look at them, with an uninterested and dispassionate eye, and is neither pained much nor pleased much at the accidents of life, because they are accidents.

2. Another part of the character under review is, what our translation calls moderation: "Let your moderation be known unto all men," or, as it may be more exactly rendered, your consideration, fairness, or equitableness. St. Paul makes it a part of a Christian character to have a reputation for candour, dispassionateness, tenderness towards others. The truth is, as soon and in proportion as a person believes that Christ is coming, and recognises his own position as a stranger on earth, who has but

hired a lodging in it for a season, he will feel indifferent to the course of human affairs. He will be able to look on, instead of taking a part in them. They will be nothing to him. He will be able to criticise them, and pass judgment on them, without partiality This is what is meant by "our moderation" being acknowledged by all men. Those who have strong interests one way or the other, cannot be dispassionate observers and candid judges. They are partisans; they defend one set of people, and attack another. They are prejudiced against those who differ from them, or who thwart them. They cannot make allowances, or show sympathy for them. But the Christian has no keen expectations, no acute mortifications. He is fair, equitable, considerate towards all men, because he has no temptation to be otherwise. He has no violence, no animosity, no bigotry, no party feeling. He knows that his Lord and Saviour must triumph; he knows that He will one day come from heaven, no one can say how soon. Knowing then the end to which all things tend, he cares less for the road which is to lead to it. When we read a book of fiction we are much excited with the course of the narrative till we know how things will turn out; but when we do the interest ceases. So is it with the Christian. He knows Christ's battle will last till the end; that Christ's cause will triumph in the end; that His Church will last till He comes. He knows what is truth and what is error, where is safety and where is danger; and all this clear knowledge enables him to make concessions, to own difficulties, to do justice to the erring, to acknowledge their good points, to be content with such countenance, greater or less, as he himself receives from others. He does not fear; fear it is that makes men bigots, tyrants, and zealots; but for the Christian, it is his privilege, as he is beyond hopes and fears, suspense and jealousy, so also to be patient, cool, discriminating, and impartial;—so much so, that this very fairness marks his character in the eyes of the world, is "known unto all men."

3. Joy and gladness are also characteristics of him, according to the exhortation in the text, "Rejoice in the Lord alway," and this in spite of the fear and awe which the thought of the Last Day ought to produce in him. It is by means of these strong contrasts that Scripture brings out to us what is the real meaning of its separate portions. If we had been told merely to fear, we should have mistaken a slavish dread, or the gloom of despair, for godly fear; and if we had been told merely to rejoice, we should perhaps have mistaken a rude freedom and familiarity for joy; but when we are told both to fear and to rejoice, we gain

thus much at first sight, that our joy is not to be irreverent, nor our fear to be desponding; that though both feelings are to remain, neither is to be what it would be by itself. This is what we gain at once by such contrasts. I do not say that this makes it at all easier to combine the separate duties to which they relate; that is a further and higher work; but thus much we gain at once, a better knowledge of those separate duties themselves. And now I am speaking about the duty of rejoicing, and I say, that whatever be the duty of fearing greatly and trembling greatly at the thought of the Day of Judgment, and of course it is a great duty, yet the command so to do cannot reverse the command to rejoice; it can only so far interfere with it as to explain what is meant by rejoicing. It is as clear a duty to rejoice in the prospect of Christ's coming, as if we were not told to fear it. The duty of fearing does but perfect our joy; that joy alone is true Christian joy, which is informed and quickened by fear, and made thereby sober and reverent.

How joy and fear can be reconciled words cannot show. Act and deed alone can show how. Let a man try both to fear and to rejoice, as Christ and His Apostles tell him, and in time he will learn how; but when he has learned, he will be as little able to explain how it is he does both as he was before. He will seem inconsistent, and may easily be proved to be so, to the satisfaction of irreligious men, as Scripture is called inconsistent. He becomes the paradox which Scripture enjoins. This is variously fulfilled in the case of men of advanced holiness. They are accused of the most opposite faults; of being proud, and of being mean; of being over-simple, and being crafty; of having too strict, and, at the same time, too lax a conscience; of being unsocial, and yet being worldly; of being too literal in explaining Scripture, and yet of adding to Scripture, and superseding Scripture. Men of the world, or men of inferior religiousness, cannot understand them, and are fond of criticising those who, in seeming to be inconsistent, are but like Scripture teaching.

But to return to the case of joy and fear. It may be objected, that at least those who fall into sin, or who have in times past sinned grievously, cannot have this pleasant and cheerful temper which St. Paul enjoins. I grant it. But what is this but saying that St. Paul enjoins us *not* to fall into sin? When St. Paul warns us against sadness and heaviness, of course he warns us against those things which make men sad and heavy; and therefore especially against sin, which is an especial enemy of joyfulness. It is not that sorrowing for sin is wrong when we *have sinned,* but the *sinning* is wrong which causes the sorrowing. When a person has sinned he cannot do anything better than sorrow. He ought to sorrow; and so far as he does sorrow, he is certainly *not* in the perfect Christian state; but it is his sin that has forfeited it. And yet even here sorrow is not inconsistent with rejoicing. For there are few men who are really in earnest in their sorrow, but after a time may be conscious that they are so; and, when man knows himself to be in earnest, he knows that God looks mercifully upon him; and this gives him sufficient reason for rejoicing, even though fear remains. St. Peter could appeal to Christ, "Lord, Thou knowest all things; Thou knowest that I love Thee." We of course cannot appeal so unreservedly—still we can timidly appeal—we can say that we humbly trust that, whatever be the measure of our past sins, and whatever of our present self-denial, yet at bottom we do wish and strive to give up the world and to follow Christ; and in proportion as this sense of sincerity is strong upon our minds, in the same degree shall we rejoice in the Lord, even while we fear.

4. Once more, peace is part of this same temper also. "The peace of God," says the Apostle, "which passeth all understanding, shall keep your hearts and minds through Christ Jesus." There are many things in the Gospel to alarm us, many to agitate us, many to transport us, but the end and issue of all these is *peace.* "Glory to God in the highest, and on earth peace." It may be asked indeed whether warfare, perplexity, and uncertainty be not the condition of the Christian here below; whether St. Paul himself does not say that he has "the care," or the anxiety, "of all the churches," and whether he does not plainly evince and avow in his Epistles to the Galatians and Corinthians much distress of mind? "Without were fightings, within fears." [1] I grant it; he certainly shows at times much agitation of mind; but consider this. Did you ever look at an expanse of water and observe the ripples on the surface? Do you think that disturbance penetrates below it? Nay; you have seen or heard of fearful tempests on the sea; scenes of horror and distress, which are in no respect a fit type of an Apostle's tears or sighings about his flock. Yet even these violent commotions do not reach into the depths. The foundations of the ocean, the vast realms of water which girdle the earth, are as tranquil and as silent in the storm as in a calm. So is it with the souls of holy men. They have a well of peace springing up within them unfathomable; and though the accidents of the hour may make them seem

[1] 2 Cor. vii. 5.

agitated, yet in their hearts they are not so. Even angels joy over sinners repentant, and, as we may therefore suppose, grieve over sinners impenitent,—yet who shall say that they have not perfect peace? Even Almighty God Himself deigns to speak of His being grieved, and angry, and rejoicing,—yet is He not the Unchangeable? And in like manner, to compare human things with divine, St. Paul had perfect peace, as being stayed in soul on God, though the trials of life might vex him.

For, as I have said, the Christian has a deep, silent, hidden peace which the world sees not,—like some well in a retired and shady place, difficult of access. He is the greater part of his time by himself, and when he is in solitude, that is his real state. What he is when left to himself and to his God, that is his true life. He can bear himself; he can (as it were) joy in himself, for it is the grace of God within him, it is the presence of the Eternal Comforter, in which he joys. He can bear, he finds it pleasant, to be with himself at all times,—"never less alone than when alone." He can lay his head on his pillow at night, and own in God's sight, with overflowing heart, that he wants nothing,—that he "is full and abounds,"—that God has been all things to him, and that nothing is not his which God could give him. More thankfulness, more holiness, more of heaven he needs indeed, but the thought that he can have more is not a thought of trouble, but of joy. It does not interfere with his peace to know that he may grow nearer God. Such is the Christian's peace, when, with a single heart and the Cross in his eye, he addresses and commends himself to Him with whom the night is as clear as the day. St. Paul says that "the peace of God shall *keep* our hearts and minds." By "keep" is meant "guard," or "garrison," our hearts; so as to keep out enemies. And he says, our "hearts and minds" in contrast to what the world sees of us. Many hard things may be said of the Christian, and done against him, but he has a secret preservative or charm, and minds them not.

These are some few suggestions on that character of mind which becomes the followers of Him who was once "born of a pure Virgin," and who bids them as "new-born babes desire the sincere milk of the Word, that they may grow thereby." The Christian is cheerful, easy, kind, gentle, courteous, candid, unassuming; has no pretence, no affectation, no ambition, no singularity; because he has neither hope nor fear about this world. He is serious, sober, discreet, grave, moderate, mild, with so little that is unusual or striking in his bearing, that he may easily be taken at first sight for an ordinary man. There are persons who think religion consists in ecstasies, or in set speeches;—he is not of those. And it must be confessed, on the other hand, that there is a commonplace state of mind which does show itself calm, composed, and candid, yet is very far from the true Christian temper. In this day especially it is very easy for men to be benevolent, liberal, and dispassionate. It costs nothing to be dispassionate when you feel nothing, to be cheerful when you have nothing to fear, to be generous or liberal when what you give is not your own, and to be benevolent and considerate when you have no principles and no opinions. Men nowadays are moderate and equitable, not because the Lord is at hand, but because they do not feel that He is coming. Quietness is a grace, not in itself, only when it is grafted on the stem of faith, zeal, self-abasement, and diligence.

May it be our blessedness, as years go on, to add one grace to another, and advance upward, step by step, neither neglecting the lower after attaining the higher, nor aiming at the higher before attaining the lower. The first grace is faith, the last is love; first comes zeal, afterwards comes loving-kindness; first comes humiliation, then comes peace; first comes diligence, then comes resignation. May we learn to mature all graces in us;—fearing and trembling, watching and repenting, because Christ is coming; joyful, thankful, and careless of the future, because He is come.

SERMON IX.

The Immortality of the Soul.

" What shall a man give in exchange for his soul?"—MATT. xvi. 26.

I SUPPOSE there is no tolerably informed Christian but considers he has a correct notion of the difference between our
religion and the paganism which it supplanted. Every one, if
asked what it is we have gained by the Gospel, will promptly
answer, that we have gained the knowledge of our immortality,
of our having souls which will live for ever; that the heathen
did not know this, but that Christ taught it, and that His disciples know it. Every one will say, and say truly, that this was
the great and solemn doctrine which gave the Gospel a claim to
be heard when first preached, which arrested the thoughtless
multitudes who were busied in the pleasures and pursuits of this
life, awed them with the vision of the life to come, and sobered
them till they turned to God with a true heart. It will be said,
and said truly, that this doctrine of a future life was the doctrine
which broke the power and the fascination of paganism. The
poor benighted heathen were engaged in all the frivolities and
absurdities of a false ritual, which had obscured the light of
nature. They knew God, but they forsook Him for the inven-
tions of men; they made protectors and guardians for themselves;
and had " gods many and lords many." [1] They had their profane worship, their gaudy processions, their indulgent creed,
their easy observances, their sensual festivities, their childish
extravagances, such as might suitably be the religion of beings
who were to live for seventy or eighty years, and then die once
for all, never to live again. " Let us eat and drink, for to-morrow

[1] 1 Cor. viii. 5.

we die," was their doctrine and their rule of life. "To-morrow we die;"—this the Holy Apostles admitted. They taught so far *as* the heathen; "To-morrow we die;" but then they added, "And after death *the judgment;*"—judgment upon the eternal soul, which lives in spite of the death of the body. And this was the truth, which awakened men to the necessity of having a better and deeper religion than that which had spread over the earth, when Christ came,—which so wrought upon them that they left that old false worship of theirs, and it fell. Yes! though throned in all the power of the world, a sight such as eye had never before seen, though supported by the great and the many, the magnificence of kings and the stubbornness of people, it fell. Its ruins remain scattered over the face of the earth; the shattered works of its great upholder, that fierce enemy of God, the Pagan Roman Empire. Those ruins are found even among ourselves, and show how marvellously great was its power, and therefore how much more powerful was that which broke its power; and this was the doctrine of the immortality of the soul. So entire is the revolution which is produced among men wherever this high truth is really received.

I have said that every one of us is able fluently to speak of this doctrine, and is aware that the knowledge of it forms the fundamental difference between our state and that of the heathen. And yet, in spite of our being able to speak about it and our "form of knowledge"[1] (as St. Paul terms it), there seems scarcely room to doubt, that the greater number of those who are called Christians in no true sense realize it in their own minds at all. Indeed, it is a very difficult thing to bring home to us, and to feel that we have souls; and there cannot be a more fatal mistake than to suppose we see what the doctrine means as soon as we can use the words which signify it. So great a thing is it to understand that we have souls, that the knowing it, taken in connection with its results, is all one with *being serious, i.e.* truly religious. To discern our immortality is necessarily connected with fear and trembling and repentance in the case of every Christian. Who is there but would be sobered by an actual sight of the flames of hell fire and the souls therein hopelessly enclosed? Would not all his thoughts be drawn to that awful sight, so that he would stand still, gazing fixedly upon it, and forgetting everything else; seeing nothing else, hearing nothing, engrossed with the contemplation of it; and when the sight was withdrawn, still having it fixed in his memory, so that

[1] Rom. ii. 20.

he would be henceforth dead to the pleasures and employments of this world, considered in themselves, thinking of them only in their reference to that fearful vision? This would be the over-powering effect of such a disclosure, whether it actually led a man to repentance or not. And thus absorbed in the thought of the life to come are they who really and heartily receive the words of Christ and His Apostles. Yet to this state of mind, and therefore to this true knowledge, the multitude of men called Christians are certainly strangers; a thick veil is drawn over their eyes; and in spite of their being able to talk of the doctrine, they are as if they never had heard of it. They go on just as the heathen did of old: they eat, they drink; or they amuse themselves in vanities, and live in the world, without fear and without sorrow, just as if God had not declared that their conduct in this life would decide their destiny in the next; just as if they either had no souls, or had nothing or little to do with the saving of them, which was the creed of the heathen.

Now let us consider what it is to bring home to ourselves that we have souls, and in what the especial difficulty of it lies; for this may be of use to us in our attempt to realize that awful truth.

We are from our birth apparently dependent on things about us. We see and feel that we could not live or go forward without the aid of man. To a child this world is everything: he seems to him-self a part of this world,—a part of this world in the same sense in which a branch is part of a tree; he has little notion of his own separate and independent existence, that is, he has no just idea he has a soul. And if he goes through life with his notions un-changed, he has no just notion, even to the end of life, that he has a soul. He views himself merely in his connection with this world, which is his all; he looks to this world for his good as to an idol; and when he tries to look beyond this life, he is able to discern nothing in prospect, because he has no idea of anything, nor can fancy anything, *but* this life. And if he is obliged to fancy something, he fancies this life over again; just as the heathen, when they reflected on those traditions of another life, which were floating among them, could but fancy the happiness of the blessed to consist in the enjoyment of the sun, and the sky, and the earth, as before, only as if these were to be more splendid than they are now.

To understand that we have souls, is to feel our separation from things visible, our independence of them, our distinct existence in ourselves, our individuality, our power of acting for ourselves this way or that way, our accountableness for what we do. These are the great truths which lie wrapped up indeed even in a child's mind, and which God's grace can unfold there in spite of the influence of the external world; but at first this outward world prevails. We look off from self to the things around us, and forget ourselves in them. Such is our state,—a depending for support on the reeds which are no stay, and overlooking our real strength,—at the time when God begins His process of reclaiming us to a truer view of our place in His great system of providence. And when He visits us, then in a little while there is a stirring within us. The unprofitableness and feebleness of the things of this world are forced upon our minds; they promise but cannot perform, they disappoint us. Or, if they do perform what they promise, still (so it is) they do not satisfy us. We still crave for something, we do not well know what; but we are sure it is something which the world has not given us. And then its changes are so many, so sudden, so silent, so continual. It never leaves changing; it goes on to change, till we are quite sick at heart :— then it is that our reliance on it is broken. It is plain we cannot continue to depend upon it unless we keep pace with it and go on changing too; but this we cannot do. We feel that, while it changes, we are one and the same; and thus, under God's blessing, we come to have some glimpse of the meaning of our independence of things temporal, and our immortality. And should it so happen that misfortunes come upon us (as they often do), then still more are we led to understand the nothingness of this world ; then still more are we led to distrust it, and are weaned from the love of it, till at length it floats before our eyes merely as some idle veil, which, notwithstanding its many tints, cannot hide the view of what is beyond it ;—and we begin, by degrees, to perceive that there are but two beings in the whole universe, our own soul, and the God who made it.

Sublime, unlooked-for doctrine, yet most true! To every one of us there are but two beings in the whole world, himself and God; for, as to this outward scene, its pleasures and pursuits, its honours and cares, its contrivances, its personages, its kingdoms, its multitude of busy slaves, what are they to us? nothing—no more than a show :—"The world passeth away and the lust thereof." And as to those others nearer to us, who are not to be classed with the vain world, I mean our friends and relations, whom we are right in loving, these, too, after all, are nothing to us here. They cannot really help or profit us; we see them, and they act upon us, only (as it were) at a distance, through the medium of sense; they cannot get at our souls; they cannot enter into our thoughts, or really be companions to us. In the next world it will, through God's mercy, be otherwise; but here we enjoy, not their presence, but the anticipation of what one day shall be; so that, after all, they vanish before the clear vision we have, first, of our own existence, next of the presence of the great God in us and over us, as our Governor and Judge, who dwells in us by our conscience, which is His representative.

And now consider what a revolution will take place in the mind that is not utterly reprobate, in proportion as it realizes this relation between itself and the Most High God. We never in this life can fully understand what is meant by our living for ever, but we can understand what is meant by this world's *not* living for ever, by its dying never to rise again. And learning this, we learn that we owe it no service, no allegiance; it has no claim over us, and can do us no material good nor harm. On the other hand, the law of God written on our hearts bids us serve Him, and partly tells us how to serve Him, and Scripture completes the precepts which nature began. And both Scripture and conscience tell us we are answerable for what we do, and that God is a righteous Judge; and, above all, our Saviour, as our visible Lord God, takes the place of the world as the Only-begotten of the Father, having shown Himself openly, that we may not say that God is hidden. And thus a man is drawn forward by all manner of powerful influences to turn from things temporal to things eternal, to deny himself, to take up his cross and follow Christ. For there are Christ's awful threats and warnings to make him serious, His precepts to attract and elevate him, His promises to cheer him, His gracious deeds and sufferings to humble him to the dust, and to bind his heart once and for ever in gratitude to Him who is so surpassing in mercy. All these things act upon him; and, as truly as St. Matthew rose from the receipt of custom when Christ called, heedless what bystanders would say of him, so they who, through grace, obey the secret voice of God, move onward contrary to the world's way, and careless what mankind may say of them, as understanding that they have souls, which is the one thing they have to care about.

I am well aware that there are indiscreet teachers gone forth into the world, who use language such as I have used, but mean something very different. Such are they who deny the grace of baptism, and think that a man is converted to God all at once. But I have no need now to mention the difference between their teaching and that of Scripture. Whatever their peculiar errors are, so far as they say that we are by nature blind and sinful, and must, through God's grace, and our own endeavours, learn that we have souls and rise to a new life, severing ourselves from the world that is, and walking by faith in what is unseen and future, so far they say true, for they speak the words of Scripture; which says, " Awake thou that sleepest, and arise from the dead, and Christ shall give thee light. See then that ye walk circumspectly, not as fools, but as wise, redeeming the time, because the days are evil. Wherefore be ye not unwise, but understanding what the will of the Lord is." [1]

Let us, then, seriously question ourselves, and beg of God grace to do so honestly, whether we are loosened from the world; or whether, living as dependent on it, and not on the Eternal Author of our being, we are in fact taking our portion with this perishing outward scene, and ignorant of our having souls. I know very well that such thoughts are distasteful to the minds of men in general. Doubtless many a one there is, who, on hearing doctrines such as I have been insisting on, says in his heart, that religion is thus made gloomy and repulsive; that he would attend to a teacher who spoke in a less severe way; and that in fact Christianity was not intended to be a dark burdensome law, but a religion of cheerfulness and joy. This is what young people think, though they do not express it in this argumentative form. They view a strict life as something offensive and hateful; they turn from the notion of it. And then, as they get older and see more of the world, they learn to defend their opinion, and express it more or less in the way in which I have just put it. They hate and oppose the truth, as it were upon principle; and the more they are told that they have souls, the more resolved they are to live as if they had not souls. But let us take it as a clear point from the first, and not to be disputed, that religion must ever be difficult to those who neglect it. All things that we have to learn are difficult at first; and our duties to God, and to man for His sake, are peculiarly difficult, because they call upon us to take up a new life, and quit the love of this world for the next. It cannot be avoided; we must fear and be in sorrow before we can rejoice. The Gospel must be a burden before it comforts and brings us peace. No one can have his heart cut away from the natural objects of its love without pain during the process and throbbings afterwards. This is plain from the nature of the case; and, however true it be, that this or that teacher may be harsh and repulsive, yet he cannot materially alter things. Religion is in itself at first a weariness to the worldly mind, and it requires

[1] Eph. v. 14-17.

an effort and a self-denial in every one who honestly determines to be religious.

But there are other persons who are far more hopeful than those I have been speaking of, who, when they hear repentance and newness of life urged on them, are frightened at the thought of the greatness of the work; they are disheartened at being told to do so much. Now let it be well understood, that to realize our own individual accountableness and immortality, of which I have been speaking, is not required of them all at once. I never said a person was not in a hopeful way who did not thus fully discern the world's vanity and the worth of his soul. But a man is truly in a very desperate way who does not wish, who does not try, to discern and feel all this. I want a man on the one hand to confess his immortality with his lips, and on the other to live as if he tried to understand his own words, and then he is in the way of salvation; he is in the way towards heaven, even though he has not yet fully emancipated himself from the fetters of this world. Indeed none of us (of course) are entirely loosened from this world. We all use words, in speaking of our duties, higher and fuller than we really understand. No one entirely realizes what is meant by his having a soul; even the best of men is but in a state of progress towards the simple truth; and the most weak and ignorant of those who seek after it cannot but be in progress. And therefore no one need be alarmed at hearing that he has much to do before he arrives at a right view of his own condition in God's sight, *i.e.* at *faith;* for we all have much to do, and the great point is, are we willing to do it?

Oh that there were such an heart in us, to put aside this visible world, to desire to look at it as a mere screen between us and God, and to think of Him who has entered in beyond the veil, and who is watching us, trying us, yes, and blessing, and influencing, and encouraging us towards good, day by day! Yet, alas, how do we suffer the mere varying circumstances of every day to sway us! How difficult it is to remain firm and in one mind under the seductions or terrors of the world! We feel variously according to the place, time, and people we are with. We are serious on Sunday, and we sin deliberately on Monday. We rise in the morning with remorse at our offences and resolutions of amendment, yet before night we have transgressed again. The mere change of society puts us into a new frame of mind; nor do we sufficiently understand this great weakness of ours, or seek for strength where alone it can be found, in the Unchangeable God. What will be our thoughts in that day, when at length this outward world drops away altogether, and we find ourselves where we ever have been, in His presence, with Christ standing at His right hand!

On the contrary, what a blessed discovery is it to those who make it, that this world is but vanity and without substance; and that really they are ever in their Saviour's presence. This is a thought which it is scarcely right to enlarge upon in a mixed congregation, where there may be some who have not given their hearts to God; for why should the privileges of the true Christian be disclosed to mankind at large, and sacred subjects, which are his peculiar treasure, be made common to the careless liver? He knows his blessedness, and needs not another to tell it him. He knows in whom he has believed; and in the hour of danger or trouble he knows what is meant by that peace, which Christ did not explain when He gave it to His Apostles, but merely said it was not as the world could give.

"Thou wilt keep him in perfect peace whose mind is stayed on Thee; because he trusteth in Thee. Trust ye in the Lord for ever: for in the Lord Jehovah is everlasting strength."[1]

[1] Isa. xxvi. 3, 4.

SERMON X.

(EPIPHANY.)

Christian Manhood.

" When I was a child, I spake as a child, I understood as a child, I thought as a child; but when I became a man, I put away childish things."—
I COR. xiii. 11.

WHEN our Lord was going to leave the world and return to His Father, He called His disciples *orphans;* children, as it were, whom He had been rearing, who were still unable to direct themselves, and who were soon to lose their Protector; but He said, "I will not leave you comfortless orphans, I will come to you;"[1] meaning to say, He would come again to them in the power of His Holy Spirit, who should be their present all-sufficient Guide, though He Himself was away. And we know, from the sacred history, that when the Holy Spirit came, they ceased to be the defenceless children they had been before. He breathed into them a divine life, and gifted them with spiritual manhood, or *perfection,* as it is called in Scripture. From that time forth they put away childish things: they spake, they understood, they thought, as those who had been taught to govern themselves; and who, having "an unction from the Holy One, knew all things."

That such a change was wrought in the Apostles, according to Christ's promise, is evident from comparing their conduct *before* the Day of Pentecost, when the Holy Spirit descended on them, and *after.* I need not enlarge on their wonderful firmness and zeal in their Master's cause afterwards. On the other hand, it is plain from the Gospels, that before the Holy Ghost came down, that is, while Christ was still with them, they were as helpless and ignorant as children; had no clear notion what they ought to seek

[1] John xiv. 18.

after, and how ; and were carried astray by their accidental feelings and their long-cherished prejudices.—What was it but to act the child, to ask how many times a fellow-Christian should offend against us, and we forgive him, as St. Peter did ? or to ask to see the Father, with St. Philip ? or to propose to build tabernacles on the mount, as if they were not to return to the troubles of the world ? or to dispute who should be the greatest?[1] or to look for Christ's restoring at that time the temporal kingdom to Israel?[2] Natural as such views were in the case of half-instructed Jews, they were evidently unworthy of those whom Christ had made His, that He might "present them perfect" before the throne of God.

Yet the first disciples of Christ at least put off their vanities once for all, when the Spirit came upon them ; but as to ourselves, the Spirit has long since been poured upon us, even from our earliest years ; yet it is a serious question, whether multitudes of us, even of those among us who make a profession of religion, are even so far advanced in a knowledge of the Truth as the Apostles were before the Day of Pentecost. It may be a profitable employment to-day to consider this question, as suggested by the text,— to inquire how far we have proceeded in putting off such childish things as are inconsistent with a manly, honest profession of the Gospel.

Now, observe, I am not inquiring whether we are plainly living in sin, in wilful disobedience ; nor even whether we are yielding through thoughtlessness to sinful practices and habits. The con- dition of those who act against their conscience, or who act without conscience, that is, lightly and carelessly, is far indeed from bear- ing any resemblance to that of the Apostles in the years of their early discipleship. I am supposing you, my brethren, to be on the whole followers of Christ, to profess to obey Him ; and I address you as those who seem to themselves to have a fair hope of salvation. I am directing your attention, not to your sins, not to those faults and failings which you know to be such, and are trying to conquer, as being confessedly evil in themselves, but to such of your views, wishes, and tastes as resemble those which the Apostles cherished, true believers though they were, before they attained their manhood in the Gospel : and I ask, how far you have dismissed these from your minds as vain and trifling; that is, how far you have made what St. Paul in the text seems to consider the first step in the true spiritual course of a Christian, on whom the Holy Ghost has descended.

1. For example, Let us consider our love of the pleasures of

[1] Matt. xvii. 4 ; xviii. 1 ; xx. 20   John xiv. 8.   [2] Acts i. 6.

life. I am willing to allow there is an innocent love of the world, innocent in itself. God made the world, and has sanctioned the general form of human society, and has given us abundant pleasures in it; I do not say *lasting* pleasures, but still, while they are present, really pleasures. It is natural that the young should look with hope to the prospect before them. They cannot help forming schemes what they will do when they come into active life, or what they would wish to be had they their choice. They indulge themselves in fancyings about the future, which they know at the time cannot come true. At other times they confine themselves to what is possible; and then their hearts burn while they dream of quiet happiness, domestic comfort, independence. Or, with bolder views, they push forward their fortunes into public life, and indulge ambitious hopes. They fancy themselves rising in the world, distinguished, courted, admired ; securing influence over others, and rewarded with high station. James and John had such a dream when they besought Christ that they might sit at His side in the most honourable places in His kingdom.

Now such dreams can hardly be called sinful in themselves, and without reference to the particular case ; for the gifts of wealth, power, and influence, and much more of domestic comfort, come from God, and may be religiously improved. But, though not directly censurable, they are *childish :* childish either in themselves, or at least when cherished and indulged ; childish in a Christian, who has infinitely higher views to engross his mind ; and, as being childish, excusable only in the young. They *are* an offence when retained as life goes on ; but in the young we may regard them after the pattern of our Saviour's judgment upon the young man who was rich and noble. He is said to have "loved him ; " pitying (that is) and not harshly denouncing the anticipations which he had formed of happiness from wealth and power, yet withal not concealing from him the sacrifice of all these which he must make, "if he would be perfect," that is, a man, and not a mere child in the Gospel.

2. But there are other childish views and habits besides, which must be put off while we take on ourselves the full profession of a Christian ; and these, not so free from intrinsic guilt as those which have been already noticed ;—such as the love of display, greediness of the world's praise, and the love of the comforts and luxuries of life. These, though wrong tempers of mind, still I do not now call by their hardest names, because I would lead persons. if I could, rather to turn away from them as unworthy a

Christian, with a sort of contempt, outgrowing them as they grow in grace, and laying them aside as a matter of course, while they are gradually learning to "set their affections on things above, not on things of the earth."

Children have evil tempers and idle ways which we do not deign to speak seriously of. Not that we, in any degree, approve them or endure them on their own account ; nay, we punish some of them ; but we bear them *in* children, and look for their disappearing as the mind becomes more mature. And so in religious matters there are many habits and views which we bear with in the unformed Christian, but which we account disgraceful and contemptible should they survive that time when a man's character may be supposed to be settled. Love of display is one of these ; whether we are vain of our abilities, or our acquirements, or our wealth, or our personal appearance ; whether we discover our weakness in talking much, or in love of managing, or again in love of dress. Vanity, indeed, and conceit are always disagreeable, for the reason that they interfere with the comfort of other persons, and vex them ; but I am here observing, that they are *in themselves* odious, when discerned in those who enjoy the full privileges of the Church, and are by profession men in Christ Jesus, odious from their inconsistency with Christian faith and earnestness.

And so with respect to the love of worldly comforts and luxuries (which, unhappily, often grows upon us rather than disappears, as we get old), whether or not it be natural in youth, at least, it is (if I may so say) *shocking* in those who profess to be "perfect," if we would estimate things aright ; and this from its great incongruity with the spirit of the Gospel. Is it not something beyond measure strange and monstrous (if we could train our hearts to possess a right judgment in all things) to profess that our treasure is not here, but in heaven with Him who is ascended thither, and to own that we have a cross to bear after Him, who first suffered before He triumphed ; and yet to set ourselves *deliberately* to study our own comfort as some great and sufficient end, to go much out of our way to promote it, to sacrifice anything considerable to guard it, and to be downcast at the prospect of the loss of it ? Is it possible for a true son of the Church militant, while "the ark, and Israel, and Judah abide in tents," and the "servants of his Lord are encamped in the open field," to "eat and drink" securely, to wrap himself in the furniture of wealth, to feed his eyes with the "pride of life," and complete for himself the measure of this world's elegancies ?

F

Again, all timidity, irresolution, fear of ridicule, weakness of purpose, such as the Apostles showed when they deserted Christ, and Peter especially when he denied Him, are to be numbered among the tempers of mind which are childish as well as sinful; which we must learn to despise,—to be ashamed at ourselves if we are influenced by them, and, instead of thinking the conquest of them a great thing, to account it as one of the very first steps towards being but an ordinary true believer; just as the Apostles, in spite of their former discipleship, only commenced (surely) their Christian course at the Day of Pentecost, and then took to themselves a good measure of faith, boldness, zeal, and self-mastery, not as some great proficiency and as a boast, but as the very condition of their being Christians at all, as the elements of spiritual life, as a mere outfitting, and a small attainment indeed in that extended course of sanctification through which the Blessed Spirit is willing to lead every Christian.

Now in this last remark I have given a chief reason for dwelling on the subject before us. It is very common for Christians to make much of what are but petty services; first to place the very substance of religious obedience in a few meagre observances, or particular moral precepts which are easily complied with, and which they think fit to call giving up the world; and then to make a great vaunting about their having done what, in truth, every one who is not a mere child in Christ ought to be able to do, to congratulate themselves upon their success, ostentatiously to return thanks for it, to condemn others who do not happen to move exactly along the very same line of minute practices in detail which they have adopted, and in consequence to forget that, after all, by such poor obedience, right though it be, still they have not approached even to a distant view of that point in their Christian course, at which they may consider themselves, in St. Paul's words, to have "attained" a sure hope of salvation; just as little children, when they first have strength to move their limbs, triumph in every exertion of their newly-acquired power, as in some great victory. To put off idle hopes of earthly good, to be sick of flattery and the world's praise, to see the emptiness of temporal greatness, and to be watchful against self-indulgence, —these are but the beginnings of religion; these are but the preparation of heart which religious earnestness implies; without a good share of them, how can a Christian move a step? How could Abraham, when called of God, have even set out from his native place, unless he had left off to think much of this world, and cared not for its ridicule? Surely these attainments are but our first manly robe, showing that childhood is gone; and, if we feel the love and fear of the world still active within our hearts, deeply must we be humbled, yes, and alarmed; and humbled even though but the traces remain of former weaknesses. But even if otherwise, what thank have we? See what the Apostles were, by way of contrast, and then you will see what is the true life of the Spirit, the substance and full fruit of holiness. To love our brethren with a resolution which no obstacles can overcome, so as almost to consent to an anathema on ourselves, if so be we may save those who hate us,—to labour in God's cause against hope, and in the midst of sufferings,—to read the events of life, as they occur, by the interpretation which Scripture gives them, and that, not as if the language were strange to us, but to do it promptly, —to perform all our relative daily duties most watchfully,—to check every evil thought, and bring the whole mind into captivity to the law of Christ,—to be patient, cheerful, forgiving, meek, honest, and true,—to persevere in this good work till death, making fresh and fresh advances towards perfection—and after all, even to the end, to confess ourselves unprofitable servants, nay, to feel ourselves corrupt and sinful creatures, who (with all our proficiency) would still be lost unless God bestowed on us His mercy in Christ;—these are some of the difficult realities of religious obedience, which we must pursue, and which the Apostles in high measure attained, and which we may well bless God's holy Name, if He enables us to make our own.

Let us then take it for granted, as a truth which cannot be gainsaid, that to break with the world, and make religion our first concern, is only to cease to be children; and, again, that in consequence, those Christians who have come to mature years, and yet do not even so much as this, are "in the presence of the angels of God" an odious and unnatural spectacle, a mockery of Christianity. I do not say what such men are in God's sight, and what are their prospects for the next world, for that is a fearful thought,—and we ought to be influenced by motives far higher than that mere slavish dread of future punishment to which such a consideration would lead us.

But here some one may ask, whether I am not speaking severely in urging so many sacrifices at the beginning of true Christian obedience. In conclusion, then, I observe, in the first place, that I have not said a word against the moderate and thankful enjoyment of this life's goods, *when* they actually come in our way; but against the wishing earnestly for them, seeking them, and preferring them to God's righteousness, which is commonly done.

Further, I am not excluding from the company of Christians all who cannot at once make up their minds thus vigorously to reject the world, when its goods are dangerous, inexpedient, or unsuitable; but excluding them from the company of mature, manly Christians. Doubtless our Lord deals gently with us. He has put His two Sacraments apart from each other. Baptism first admits us to His favour; the Holy Eucharist brings us among His perfect ones. He has put from fourteen to twenty years between them, in the ordinary course of things, that we may have time to count the cost, and make our decision calmly. Only there must be no standing still,—there cannot be; time goes slowly, yet surely, from birth to the age of manhood, and in like manner, our minds, though slowly formed to love Christ, must still be forming. It is when men are mature in years, and yet are "children in understanding," then they are intolerable, because they have exceeded their season, and are out of place. Then it is that ambitious thoughts, trifling pursuits and amusements, passionate wishes and keen hopes, and the love of display, are directly sinful, because they are by that time deliberate sins. While they were children, "they spake as children, understood, thought as children;" but when they became men, "it was high time to awake out of sleep," and "put away childish things." And if they have continued children instead of "having their senses exercised to discriminate between the excellent and the base," alas! what deep repentance must be theirs, before they can know what true peace is!—what self-reproach and sharp self-discipline, before their eyes can be opened to see effectually those truths which are "spiritually discerned!"

So much on the case of those who neglect to grow betimes into the hope of their calling. As to the young themselves, it is plain that nothing I have said can give encouragement to them to acquiesce in their present incomplete devotion of themselves to God, because it will be as much as they can do, even with their best efforts, to make their growth of wisdom and of stature keep pace with each other. And if there be any one who, as thinking the enjoyments of youth must soon be relinquished, deliberately resolves to make the most of them before the duties of manhood come upon him, such a one, in doing so, is rendering it impossible for him to give them up when he is called to do so. As for those who allow themselves in what, even in youth, is clearly sinful,— the deliberate neglect of prayer, profaneness, riotous living, or other immorality,—the case of such persons has not even entered into my mind, when I spoke of youthful thoughtlessness. They, of course, have no "inheritance in the kingdom of Christ and of God."

But if there be those among us, and such there well may be, who, like the young ruler, "worshipping Christ," and "loved" by Him, and obeying His commandments from their youth up, yet cannot but be "sorrowful" at the thought of giving up their pleasant visions, their childish idolatries, and their bright hopes of earthly happiness, such I bid be of good cheer, and take courage. What is it your Saviour requires of you more than will also be exacted from you by that hard and evil master, who desires your ruin? Christ bids you give up the world; but will not, at any rate, the world soon give up you? Can you keep it by being its slave? Will not he, whose creature of temptation it is, the prince of the world, take it from you, whatever he at present promises? What does your Lord require of you, but to look at all things as they really are, to account them merely as His instruments, and to believe that good is good because He wills it, that He can bless as easily by hard stone as by bread, in the desert as in the fruitful field, if we have faith in Him who gives us the true bread from heaven? Daniel and his friends were princes of the royal house of David; they were "children well-favoured, and skilful in all wisdom, cunning in knowledge, and understanding science;"[1] yet they had faith to refuse even the literal meat and drink given them, because it was an idol's sacrifice, and God sustained them without it. For ten days of trial they lived on pulse and water; yet "at the end," says the sacred record, "their countenances appeared fairer and fatter in flesh than all the children which did eat the portion of the king's meat." Doubt not, then, His power to bring you through any difficulties, who gives you the command to encounter them. He has showed you the way; He gave up the home of His mother Mary to "be about His Father's business," and now He but bids you take up after Him the cross which He bore for you, and "fill up what is wanting of His afflictions in your flesh." Be not afraid,—it is but a pang now and then, and a struggle; a covenant with your eyes, and a fasting in the wilderness, some calm habitual watchfulness, and the hearty effort to obey, and all will be well. Be not afraid. He is most gracious, and will bring you on by little and little. He does not show you whither He is leading you; you might be frightened did you see the whole prospect at once. Sufficient for the day is its own evil. Follow His plan; look not on anxiously; look down at your present footing "lest it be turned out of the way," but speculate not about the future. I can well believe that you have hopes now, which you cannot give up, and even which support

[1] Dan. i. 4.

you in your present course. Be it so; whether they will be fulfilled, or not, is in His hand.   He may be pleased to grant the
desires of your heart; if so, thank Him for His mercy; only be
sure that all will be for your highest good, and "as thy days, so
shall thy strength be.   There is none like unto the God of Jeshu-
run, who rideth upon the heaven in thy help, and in His excellency
on the sky.   The Eternal God is thy refuge, and underneath are
the everlasting arms." [1]   He knows no variableness, neither shadow
of turning; and when we outgrow our childhood, we but approach,
however feebly, to His likeness, who has no youth nor age, who
has no passions, no hopes, nor fears, but who loves truth, purity,
and mercy, and who is supremely blessed, because He is supremely
holy.

Lastly, while we thus think of Him, let us not forget to be up
and doing.   Let us beware of indulging a mere barren faith and
love, which dreams instead of working, and is fastidious when it
should be hardy.   This is only spiritual childhood in another
form; for the Holy Ghost is the Author of active good works,
and leads us to the observance of all lowly deeds of ordinary
obedience as the most pleasing sacrifice to God.

[1] Deut. xxxiii. 25-27.

SERMON XI.

(EPIPHANY.)

Sincerity and Hypocrisy.

*" If there be first a willing mind, it is accepted according to that a man hath,
and not according to that he hath not."*—2 COR. viii. 12.

MEN may be divided into two great classes, those who profess
religious obedience, and those who do not; and of those
who do profess to be religious, there are again those who perform
as well as profess, and those who do not. And thus on the whole
there are three classes of men in the world, open sinners, consistent
Christians, and between the two (as speaking with the one, and
more or less acting with the other), professing Christians, or, as
they are sometimes called, nominal Christians. Now the distinction between open sinners and consistent Christians is so clear, that
there is no mistaking it, for they agree in nothing; they neither
profess the same things nor practise the same. But the difference
between professing Christians and true Christians is not so clear,
for this reason, that true Christians, however consistent they are,
yet do sin, as being not yet perfect; and so far as they sin, are
inconsistent, and this is all that professing Christians are. What
then, it may be asked, is the real difference between true and
professing Christians, since both the one and the other profess
more than they practise? Again, if you put the question to one of
the latter class, however inconsistent his life may be, yet he will
be sure to say that he wishes he was better; that he is sorry for
his sins; that the flesh is weak; that he cannot overcome it; that
God alone can overcome it; that he trusts God will, and that he
prays to Him to enable him to do it. There is no form of words
conceivable which a mere professing Christian cannot use,—nay,
more, there appears to be no sentiment which he cannot feel,—as

well as the true Christian, and at first sight apparently with the same justice. He *seems* just in the very position of the true Christian, only perhaps behind him ; not *so* consistent, not advanced so much ; still, on the same line. Both confess to a struggle within them ; both sin, both are sorry ; what then is the difference between them ?

There are many differences ; but, before going on to mention that one to which I shall confine my attention, I would have you observe that I am speaking of differences in God's sight. Of course, we men may after all be unable altogether, and often are unable, to see differences between those who, nevertheless, are on different sides of the line of life. Nor may we judge anything absolutely before the time, whereas God "searcheth the hearts." He alone, "who searcheth the hearts," "knoweth what is the mind of the Spirit." We do not even know ourselves absolutely. "Yea, I judge not mine own self," says St. Paul, "but He that judgeth me is the Lord." God alone can unerringly discern between sincerity and insincerity, between the hypocrite and the man of perfect heart. I do not, of course, mean that we can form no judgment at all upon ourselves, or that it is not useful to do so ; but here I will chiefly insist upon the point of *doctrine*, viz. how does the true Christian differ in God's sight from the insincere and double-minded?—leaving any practical application which it admits to be incidentally brought out in the course of my remarks.

Now the real difference between the true and the professing Christian seems to be given us in the text : "If there be a willing mind, it is accepted." St. Paul is speaking of almsgiving ; but what he says seems to apply generally. He is laying down a principle, which applies of course in many distinct cases, though he uses it with reference to one in particular. An honest, unaffected *desire* of doing right is the test of God's true servants. On the other hand, a double mind, a pursuing other ends besides the truth, and in consequence an inconsistency in conduct, and a half-consciousness (to say the least) of inconsistency, and a feeling of the necessity of defending oneself to oneself, and to God, and to the world ; in a word, hypocrisy ; these are the signs of the merely professed Christian. Now I am going to give some instances of this distinction in Scripture and in fact.

For instance. The two great Christian graces are faith and love. Now, how are these characterized in Scripture ?—By their being honest or single-minded. Thus St. Paul, in one place, speaks of "the end of the commandment being love ; " what love?—"love *out of a pure heart*," he proceeds, "and of a *good conscience ; "* and still further, "and of faith,"—what kind of faith ?—"faith *unfeigned ;*" or, as it may be more literally translated, "unhypocritical faith ;" for so the word means in Greek. Again, elsewhere he speaks of his "calling to remembrance the *unfeigned* faith" which dwelt in Timothy, and in his mother and grandmother before him; that is, literally, "unhypocritical faith." Again, he speaks of the Apostles approving themselves as the ministers of God, "by kindness, by the Holy Ghost, by love *unfeigned,*" or, more literally, "unhypocritical love." Again, as to love towards man. "Let love be *without dissimulation,*" or, more literally, as in the other cases, "let love be unhypocritical." In like manner, St. Peter speaks of Christians "having purified their souls in obeying the truth through the Spirit unto unhypocritical love of the brethren." And in like manner, St. James speaks of "the wisdom that is from above, being first *pure* . . ." and, presently, "without partiality, and *without hypocrisy.*"[1] Surely it is very remarkable that three Apostles, writing on different subjects and occasions, should each of them thus speak about whether faith or love as without hypocrisy.

A true Christian, then, may almost be defined as one who has a ruling sense of God's presence within him. As none but justified persons have that privilege, so none but the justified have that practical perception of it. A true Christian, or one who is in a state of acceptance with God, is he who, in such sense, has faith in Him, as to live in the thought that He is present with him,— present not externally, not in nature merely, or in providence, but in his innermost heart, or in his *conscience.* A man is justified whose conscience is illuminated by God, so that he habitually realizes that all his thoughts, all the first springs of his moral life, all his motives and his wishes, are open to Almighty God. Not as if he was not aware that there is very much in him impure and corrupt, but he wishes that all that is in him should be bare to God. He believes that it is so, and he even joys to think that it is so, in spite of his fear and shame at its being so. He alone admits Christ into the shrine of his heart; whereas others wish, in some way or other, to be by themselves, to have a home, a chamber, a tribunal, a throne, a self where God is not,—a home within them which is not a temple, a chamber which is not a confessional, a tribunal without a judge, a throne without a king; —that self may be king and judge; and that the Creator may rather be dealt with and approached as though a second party, instead of His being that true and better self, of which self itself should be but an instrument and minister.

[1] 2 Cor. vi. 6.   Rom. xii. 9.   1 Pet. i. 22.   James iii. 17.

Scripture tells us that God the Word, who died for us and rose again, and now lives for us, and saves us, is "quick and powerful, and sharper than any two-edged sword, piercing even to the dividing asunder of soul and spirit, and of the joints and marrow, and a discerner of the thoughts and intents of the heart. Neither is there any creature that is not manifest in His sight; but all things are naked and opened unto the eyes of Him with whom we have to do."[1] Now the true Christian realizes this; and what is the consequence?—Why, that he enthrones the Son of God in his conscience, refers to Him as a sovereign authority, and uses no reasoning with Him. He does not reason, but he says, "Thou God seest me." He feels that God is too near him to allow of argument, self-defence, excuse, or objection. He appeals in matters of duty, not to his own reason, but to God Himself, whom with the eyes of faith he sees, and whom he makes the Judge; not to any fancied fitness, or any preconceived notion, or any abstract principle, or any tangible experience.

The Book of Psalms continually instances this temper of profound, simple, open-hearted confidence in God. "O Lord, Thou hast searched me out and known me. Thou knowest my down-sitting and mine uprising. Thou understandest my thoughts long before. . . . There is not a word in my tongue but Thou knowest it altogether." "My soul hangeth upon Thee. Thy right hand hath upholden me." "When I wake up, I am present with Thee." "Into Thy hands I commend my spirit, for Thou hast redeemed me, O Lord, Thou God of Truth." "Commit thy way unto the Lord, and put thy trust in Him, and He shall bring it to pass. He shall make thy righteousness as clear as the light, and thy just dealing as the noonday." "Against Thee only have I sinned, and done this evil in Thy sight." "Hear the right, O Lord, consider my complaint, and hearken unto my prayer that goeth not out of feigned lips. Let my sentence come forth from Thy presence, and let Thine eyes look upon the thing that is equal. Thou hast proved and visited mine heart in the night season. Thou hast tried me, and shalt find no wickedness in me; for I am utterly purposed that my mouth shall not offend." Once more, "Thou shalt guide me with Thy counsel, and after that receive me with glory. Whom have I in heaven but Thee? and there is none upon earth that I desire in comparison of Thee. My flesh and my heart faileth, but God is the strength of mine heart and my portion for ever."[2]

[1] Heb. iv. 12, 13.
[2] Ps. cxxxix. 1, 2, 4; lxiii. 8; xxxi. 5; xxxvii. 5, 6; li. 4; xvii. 1-3; lxxiii. 24-26.

Or, again, consider the following passage in St. John's First Epistle : "If our heart condemn us, God is greater than our heart and knoweth all things. Beloved, if our heart condemn us not, then have we confidence towards God." And in connection with this, the following from the same Epistle : "God is Light, and in Him is no darkness at all. If we say that we have fellowship with Him, and walk in darkness, we lie, and do not the truth. . . . If we confess our sins, He is faithful and just to forgive us our sins, and to cleanse us from all unrighteousness." Again, "The darkness is past, and the true light now shineth." Again, "Hereby we know that He abideth in us, by the Spirit which He hath given us." And again, "He that believeth on the Son of God hath the witness in himself." And, in the same connection, consider St. Paul's statement, that "the Spirit itself beareth witness with our spirit, that we are the children of God." [1]

And now, on the other hand, let us contrast such a temper of mind which loves to walk in the light with that of the merely professing Christian, or, in Scripture language, of the *hypocrite*. Such are they who have two ends which they pursue, religion *and* the world ; and hence St. James calls them "double-minded." Hence, too, our Lord, speaking of the Pharisees who were hypocrites, says, "Ye cannot serve God *and* mammon." [2] A double-minded man, then, as having two ends in view, dare not come to God, lest he should be discovered ; for "all things that are reproved are made manifest by the light." [3] Thus, whereas the Prodigal Son "rose and came to his father," on the contrary, Adam hid himself among the trees of the garden. It was not simple dread of God, but dread joined to an unwillingness to be restored to God. He had a secret in his heart which he kept from God. He felt towards God—as it would seem, or at least his descendants so feel—as one man often feels towards another in the intercourse of life. You sometimes say of a man, "He is friendly, or courteous, or respectful, or considerate, or communicative ; but, after all, there is something, perhaps without his knowing it, in the background. He professes to be agreed with me ; he almost displays his agreement ; he says he pursues the same objects as I ; but still I do not know him, I do not make progress with him, I have no confidence in him, I do not know him better than the first time I saw him." Such is the way in which the double-minded approach the Most High,—they have a something private, a hidden self at bottom. They look on them

---

[1] 1 John iii. 20, 21 ; i. 5-9 ; ii. 8 ; iii. 24 ; v. 10. Rom. viii. 16.
[2] Luke xvi. 13.   [3] Ephes. v. 13.

selves, as it were, as independent parties, treating with Almighty God as one of their fellows. Hence, so far from seeking God, they hardly like to be sought by Him. They would rather keep their position and stand where they are,—on earth, and so make terms with God in heaven; whereas, "he that doeth truth cometh to the light, that his deeds may be made manifest that they are wrought in God."[1]

This being the case, there being in the estimation of the double-minded man two parties, God and self, it follows (as I have said) that reasoning and argument is the mode in which he approaches his Saviour and Judge; and that for two reasons,—first, because he will not *give* himself up to God, but stands upon his rights and appeals to his notions of fitness : and next, because he has some secret misgiving after all that he is dishonest, or some consciousness that he may appear so to others ; and therefore he goes about to fortify his position, to explain his conduct, or to excuse himself.

Some such argument or excuse had the unprofitable servant when called before his Lord. The other servants said, " Lord, Thy pound hath gained ten, " or "five pounds." They said no more ; nothing more was necessary ; the case spoke for itself. But the unprofitable servant did not dare leave his conduct to tell its own tale at God's judgment-seat; he said not merely, "Lord, I have kept Thy pound laid up in a napkin : " he appealed, as it were, to the reasonableness of his conduct against his Maker : he felt he must make out a case, and he went on to attempt it. He trusted not his interests to the Eternal and All-perfect Reason of God, before whom he stood, but entrenched himself in his own.

Again :—when our Lord said to the scribe, who had answered Him that eternal life was to be gained by loving God and his neighbour, " Thou hast answered right," this ought to have been enough. But his object was not to please God, but to exalt himself. And therefore he went on to make an objection. "But he, willing to *justify himself*, said unto Jesus, And who is my neighbour ? " whereas they only are justified in God's judgment who give up the notion of justifying themselves by word or deed, who start with the confession that they are unjust, and who come to God, not upon their own merits, but for His mercy.

Again : we have the same arguing and insincere spirit exposed in the conduct of the Pharisees when they asked Christ for the authority on which He acted. They said, " By what authority doest Thou these things ? " This might be the question of sincere

[1] John iii. 21.

inquirers or mere objectors, of faith or of hypocrisy. Observe how our Lord detects it. He asked them about St. John's baptism; meaning to say, that if they acknowledged St. John, they must acknowledge Himself, of whom St. John spake. They, unwilling to submit to Christ as a teacher and Lord, preferred to deny John to going on to acknowledge Him. Yet, on the other hand, they dare not openly deny the Baptist, because of the people; so, between hatred of our Lord and dread of the people, they would give no answer at all. "They *reasoned* among themselves," we are told. In consequence, our Lord left them to their reasonings; He refused to tell them what, had they reasoned sincerely, they might learn for themselves.

What is seen in the Gospels had taken place from the beginning. Our first parents were as ready with excuses as their posterity when Christ came. First, Adam says, "I hid myself, for I was afraid;" though fear and shame were not the sole or chief reasons why he fled, but an incipient hatred, if it may be said, of his Maker. Again, he says, "The woman whom Thou gavest me, . . . she gave me of the tree." And the woman says, "The serpent beguiled me." They did not honestly surrender themselves to their offended God, but had something to say in their behalf. Again, Cain says, when asked where his brother was, whom he had murdered, "Am I my brother's keeper?"

Balaam, again, is a most conspicuous instance of a double mind, or of hypocrisy. He has a plausible reason for whatever he does; he can so skilfully defend himself, that to this day he looks like a good man, and his conduct and fortunes are a perplexity to many minds. But it is one thing to have good excuses, another to have good motives. He had not the love of the truth, the love of God, in his heart; he was covetous of worldly goods; and, therefore, all his excuses only avail to mark him as double-minded.

Again :—Saul is another very remarkable instance of a man acting for his own ends, and yet having plausible *reasons* for what he did. He offered sacrifice on one occasion, not having a commission; this was a sin; yet what was his excuse?—a very fair one. Samuel had promised to come to offer the sacrifice, and did not. Saul waited some days, the people grew discouraged, his army fell off, and the enemy was at hand,—so, as he says, he "*forced* himself." [1]

Such is the conduct of insincere men in difficulty. Perhaps their difficulty may be a real one; but in this they differ from the sincere :—the latter seek God *in* their difficulty, feeling that He only who imposes it can remove it; but insincere men do not like to go to God; and to them the difficulty is only so much gain, for it gives them an apparent reason, a sort of excuse, for not going by God's rule, but for deciding in their own way. Thus Saul took his own course; thus Jeroboam, when in a difficulty, put up calves of gold and instituted a new worship without Divine command. Whereas, when Hezekiah was in trouble, he took the letter of Sennacherib, "and went up into the house of the Lord, and spread it before the Lord." [1] And when St. Peter was sinking in the water, he cried out to Christ, "Lord, save me." [2] And in like manner holy David, after he had sinned in numbering the people, and was told to choose between three punishments offered him, showed the same honest and simple-hearted devotion in choosing that of the three which might be the most exactly called falling into the Lord's hands. If he must suffer, let the Lord chastise him.—"I am in a great strait," he says; "let us fall now into the hands of the Lord; for His mercies are great; and let me not fall into the hand of man." [3]

Great, then, is the difference between sincere and insincere Christians, however like their words may be to each other; and it is needless to say, that what I have shown in a few examples, might be instanced again and again from every part of Scripture, particularly from the history of the Jews, as contained in the Prophets. All men, even after the gift of God's grace, sin: God's true servants profess and sin,—sin, and are sorry; and hypocrites profess and sin,—sin and are sorry. Thus the two parties look like each other. But the Word of God discriminates one from the other by this test,—that Christ dwells in the conscience of one, not of the other; that the one opens his heart to God, the other does not; the one views Almighty God only as an accidental guest, the other as Lord and owner of all that he is; the one admits Him as if for a night, or some stated season, the other gives himself over to God, and considers himself God's servant and instrument now and for ever. Not more different is the intimacy of friends from mere acquaintance; not more different is it to know a person in society, to be courteous and obliging to him, to interchange civilities, from opening one's heart to another, admitting him into it, seeing into his, loving him, and living in him;— than the external worship of the hypocrite, from the inward devotion of true faith; approaching God with the lips, from believing on Him with the heart; so opening to the Spirit that He opens to us, from so living to self as to exclude the light of heaven.

Now, as to applying what I have been showing from Scripture

[1] Isa. xxxvii. 14.   [2] Matt. xiv. 30.   [3] 2 Sam. xxiv. 14.

to ourselves, this shall here be left, my brethren, to the consciences of each of us, and a few words will suffice to do this. Do you, then, habitually thus unlock your hearts and subject your thoughts to Almighty God? Are you living in this conviction of His Presence, and have you this special witness that that Presence is really set up within you unto your salvation, viz. that you live in the sense of it? Do you believe, and act on the belief, that His light penetrates and shines through your heart, as the sun's beams through a room? You know how things look when the sun's beams are on it,—the very air then appears full of impurities, which, before it came out, were not seen. So is it with our souls. We are full of stains and corruptions, we see them not, they are like the air before the sun shines ; but though we see them not, God sees them : He pervades us as the sunbeam. Our souls, in His view, are full of things which offend, things which must be repented of, forgiven, and put away. He, in the words of the Psalmist, "has set our misdeeds before Him, our secret sins in the light of His countenance."[1] This is most true, though it be not at all welcome doctrine to many. We cannot hide ourselves from Him ; and our wisdom, as our duty, lies in embracing this truth, acquiescing in it, and acting upon it. Let us then beg Him to teach us the Mystery of His Presence in us, that, by acknowledging it, we may thereby possess it fruitfully. Let us confess it in faith, that we may possess it unto justification. Let us so own it as to set Him before us in everything. "I have set God always before me," says the Psalmist, "for He is on my right hand, therefore I shall not fall."[2] Let us, in all circumstances, thus regard Him. Whether we have sinned, let us not dare keep from Him, but with the prodigal son, rise and go to Him. Or, if we are conscious of nothing, still let us not boast in ourselves or justify ourselves, but feel that "He who judgeth us is the Lord." In all circumstances, of joy or sorrow, hope or fear, let us aim at having Him in our inmost heart ; let us have no secret apart from Him. Let us acknowledge Him as enthroned within us at the very springs of thought and affection. Let us submit ourselves to His guidance and sovereign direction ; let us come to Him that He may forgive us, cleanse us, change us, guide us, and save us.

This is the true life of saints. This is to have the Spirit witnessing with our spirits that we are sons of God. Such a faith alone will sustain the terrors of the Last Day ; such a faith alone will be proof against those fierce flames which are to surround the Judge, when He comes with His holy angels to separate between "those who serve God, and those who serve Him not."[3]

[1] Ps. xc. 8.   [2] Ps. xvi. 8.   [3] Mal. iii. 18.

SERMON XII.

Christian Sympathy.

" For verily He took not on Him the nature of angels, but He took on Him the seed of Abraham."—HEB. ii. 16.

WE are all of one nature, because we are sons of Adam; we are all of one nature, because we are brethren of Christ. Our old nature is common to us all, and so is our new nature. And because our old nature is one and the same, therefore is it that our new nature is one and the same. Christ could not have taken the nature of every one of us unless every one of us had the same nature already. He could not have become our Brother unless we were all brethren already; He could not have made us His brethren unless by becoming our Brother; so that our brotherhood in the first man is the means towards our brotherhood in the Second.

I do not mean to limit the benefits of Christ's atoning death, or to dare to say that it may not effect ends infinite in number and extent beyond those expressly recorded. But still so far is plain, that it is by taking our nature that He has done for us what He has done for none else; that, by taking the nature of angels, He would not have done for us what He has done; that it is not only the humiliation of the Son of God, but His humiliation in our nature, which is our life. He might have humbled Himself in other natures besides human nature; but it was decreed that "the Word" should be "made flesh." "Forasmuch as the children are partakers of flesh and blood, He also Himself likewise took part of the same." And, as the text says, "He took not hold of angels, but He took hold of the seed of Abraham."

And since His taking on Him our nature is a necessary condition of His imparting to us those great benefits which have accrued to us from His death, therefore, as I have said, it was necessary that we should, one and all, have the same original nature, in order to be redeemed by Him; for, in order to be redeemed, we must all have that nature which He the Redeemer took. Had our natures been different, He would have redeemed one and not another. Such a common nature we have, as being one and all children of one man, Adam; and thus the history of our fall is connected with the history of our recovery.

Christ then took our nature when He would redeem it; He redeemed it by making it suffer in His own Person; He purified it by making it pure in His own Person. He first sanctified it in Himself, made it righteous, made it acceptable to God, submitted it to an expiatory passion, and then He imparted it to us. He took it, consecrated it, broke it, and said, "Take, and divide it among yourselves."

And moreover, He raised the condition of human nature by submitting it to trial and temptation; that what it failed to do in Adam, it might be able to do in Him. Or, in other words, which it becomes us rather to use, He condescended, by an ineffable mercy, to be tried and tempted in it; so that, whereas He was God from everlasting, as the Only-begotten of the Father, He took on Him the thoughts, affections, and infirmities of man, thereby, through the fulness of His Divine Nature, to raise those thoughts and affections, and destroy those infirmities, that so, by God's becoming man, men, through brotherhood with Him, might in the end become as gods.

There is not a feeling, not a passion, not a wish, not an infirmity, which we have, which did not belong to that manhood which He assumed, except such as is of the nature of sin. There was not a trial or temptation which befalls us, but was, in kind at least, presented before Him, except that He had nothing within Him sympathizing with that which came to Him from without. He said upon His last and greatest trial, "The Prince of this world cometh and hath nothing in Me;" yet at the same time we are mercifully assured that "we have not a High Priest which cannot be touched with the feeling of our infirmities, but" one who "was in all points tempted like as we are, yet without sin." And again, "In that He Himself hath suffered being tempted, He is able to succour them that are tempted." [1]

But what I would to-day draw attention to is the thought with which I began, viz. the comfort vouchsafed to us in being able to

[1] Heb. iv. 15; ii. 18.

contemplate Him whom the Apostle calls " the Man Christ Jesus," the Son of God in our flesh. I mean, the thought of Him, " the beginning of the creation of God," "the firstborn of every creature," binds us together by a sympathy with one another, as much greater than that of mere nature, as Christ is greater than Adam. We were brethren, as being of one nature with him, who was " of the earth, earthy ; " we are now brethren, as being of one nature with " the Lord from heaven." All those common feelings, which we have by birth, are far more intimately common to us, now that we have obtained the second birth. Our hopes and fears, likes and dislikes, pleasures and pains, have been moulded upon one model, have been wrought into one image, blended and combined unto " the measure of the stature of the fulness of Christ." What they become, who have partaken of " the Living Bread, which came down from heaven," the first converts showed, of whom it is said that they " had all things common ; " that " the multitude of them that believed were of one heart and of one soul ; " as having " one body, and one Spirit, one hope, one Lord, one Faith, one Baptism, one God and Father of all." [1] Yes, and one thing needful ; one narrow way ; one business on earth ; one and the same enemy ; the same dangers ; the same temptations ; the same afflictions ; the same course of life ; the same death ; the same resurrection ; the same judgment. All these things being the same, and the new nature being the same, and from the Same, no wonder that Christians can sympathize with each other, even as by the power of Christ sympathizing in and with each of them.

Nay, and further, they sympathize together in those respects too in which Christ has not, could not have, gone before them ; I mean, in their common sins. This is the difference between Christ's temptation and ours : His temptations were without sin, but ours with sin. Temptation with us almost certainly involves sin. We sin, almost spontaneously, in spite of His grace. I do not mean, God forbid, that His grace is not sufficient to subdue all sin in us ; or that, as we come more and more under its influence, we are not less and less exposed to the involuntary impression of temptation, and much less exposed to voluntary sin ; but that so it is, our evil nature remains in us in spite of that new nature which the touch of Christ communicates to us ; we have still earthly principles in our souls, though we have heavenly ones, and these so sympathize with temptation, that, as a mirror reflects promptly and of necessity what is presented to it.

[1] Acts ii. 44 ; iv. 32.   Eph. iv. 4-6.

so the body of death which infects us, when the temptations of this world assail it,—when honour, pomp, glory, the world's praise, power, ease, indulgence, sensual pleasure, revenge are offered to it,—involuntarily responds to them, and sins—sins because it *is* sin; sins before the better mind can control it, because it exists, because its life is sin; sins *till* it is utterly subdued and expelled from the soul by the gradual growth of holiness and the power of the Spirit. Of all this, Christ had nothing. He was "born of a pure Virgin," the immaculate Lamb of God; and though He was tempted, yet it was by what was good in the world's offers, though unseasonable and unsuitable, and not by what was evil in them. He overcame what it had been unbecoming to yield to, while He felt the temptation. He overcame also what was sinful, but He felt no temptation to it.

And yet it stands to reason, that though His temptations differed from ours in this main respect, yet His presence in us makes us sympathize one with another, even in our sins and faults, in a way which is impossible without it; because, whereas the grace in us is common to us all, the sins against that grace are common to us all also. We have the same gifts to sin against, and therefore the same powers, the same responsibilities, the same fears, the same struggles, the same guilt, the same repentance, and such as none can have but we. The Christian is one and the same wherever found; as in Christ, who is perfect, so in himself, who is training towards perfection; as in that righteousness which is imputed to him in fulness, so in that righteousness which is imparted to him only in its measure, and not yet in fulness.

This is a consideration full of comfort, but of which commonly we do not avail ourselves as we might. It is one comfortable thought, and the highest of all, that Christ, who is on the right hand of God exalted, has felt all that we feel, sin excepted; but it is very comfortable also, that the new and spiritual man, which He creates in us, or creates us into,—that is, the Christian, as he is naturally found everywhere,—has everywhere the same temptations, and the same feelings under them, whether innocent or sinful; so that, as we are all bound together in our Head, so are we bound together, as members of one body, in that body, and believe, obey, sin, and repent, all in common.

I do not wish to state this too strongly. Doubtless there are very many differences between Christian and Christian. Though their nature is the same, and their general duties, hindrances, helps, privileges, and rewards the same, yet certainly there are great differences of character, and peculiarities belonging either

to individuals or to classes. High and low, rich and poor, Jew
and Gentile, man and woman, bond and free, learned and unlearned, though equal in the Gospel, do in many respects differ,
so that descriptions of what passes in the mind of one will often
appear strange and new to the other. Their temptations differ,
and their diseases of mind. And the difference becomes far
greater, by the difficulty persons have of expressing exactly what
they mean, so that they convey wrong ideas to one another, and
offend and repel those who really do feel what they feel, though
they would express themselves otherwise.

Again, of course there is this great difference between Christians,
that some are penitents, and some have never fallen away since
they were brought near to God; some have fallen for a time, and
grievously; others for long years, yet perhaps only in lesser
matters. These circumstances will make real differences between
Christian and Christian, so as sometimes even to remove the
possibility of sympathy almost altogether. Sin certainly does contrive this victory in some cases, to hinder us being even fellows
in misery; it separates us while it seduces, and, being the broad
way, has different lesser tracks marked out upon it.

But still, after all such exceptions, I consider that Christians,
certainly those who are in the same outward circumstances, are
very much more like each other in their temptations, inward
diseases, and methods of cure, than they at all imagine. Persons
think themselves isolated in the world; they think no one ever
felt as they feel. They do not dare to expose their feelings, lest
they should find that no one understands them. And thus they
suffer to wither and decay what was destined in God's purpose to
adorn the Church's paradise with beauty and sweetness. Their
"mouth is not opened," as the Apostle speaks, nor their "heart
enlarged;" they are "straitened" in themselves, and deny themselves the means they possess of at once imparting instruction and
gaining comfort.

Nay, instead of speaking out their own thoughts, they suffer
the world's opinion to hang upon them as a load, or the influence
of some system of religion which is in vogue. It very frequently
happens that ten thousand people all say what not any one of
them feels, but each says it because every one else says it, and
each fears not to say it lest he should incur the censure of all the
rest. Such are very commonly what are called the opinions of
the age. They are bad principles or doctrines, or false notions or
views, which live in the mouths of men, and have their strength
in their public recognition. Of course by proud men, or blind,

or carnal, or worldly, these opinions which I speak of are really felt and entered into; for they are the natural growth of their own evil hearts. But very frequently the same are set forth, and heralded, and circulated, and become current opinions among vast multitudes of men who do not feel them. These multitudes, however, are obliged to receive them by what is called the force of public opinion; the careless, of course, carelessly, but the better sort superstitiously. Thus ways of speech come in, and modes of thought quite alien to the minds of those who give in to them, who feel them to be unreal, unnatural, and uncongenial to themselves, but consider themselves obliged, often from the most religious principles, not to confess their feelings about them. They dare not say, they dare not even realize to themselves their own judgments. Thus it is that the world cuts off the intercourse between soul and soul, and substitutes idols of its own for the one true Image of Christ, in and through which only souls can sympathize. Their best thoughts are stifled, and when by chance they hear them put forth elsewhere, as may sometimes be the case, they feel as it were conscious and guilty, as if some one were revealing something against them, and they shrink from the sound as from a temptation, as something pleasing indeed but forbidden. Such is the power of false creeds to fetter the mind and bring it into captivity; false views of things, of facts, of doctrines, are imposed on it tyrannically, and men live and die in bondage who were destined to rise to the stature of the fulness of Christ. Such, for example, I consider to be, among many instances, the interpretation which is popularly received among us at present of the doctrinal portion of St. Paul's Epistles, an interpretation which has troubled large portions of the Church for a long three hundred years.

But, I repeat, we are much more like each other, even in our sins, than we fancy. I do not of course mean to say that we are one and all at the same point in our Christian course, or have one and all had the same religious history in times past; but that, even taking a man who has never fallen from grace, and one who has fallen most grievously and repented, even they will be found to be very much more like each other in their view of themselves, in their temptations, and feelings upon those temptations, than they might fancy beforehand. This we see most strikingly instanced when holy men set about to describe their real state. Even bad men at once cry out, "This is just our case," and argue from it that there is no difference between bad and good. They impute all their own sins to the holiest of men, as making their own lives a sort of comment upon the text which his words furnish, and appealing to the appositeness of their own interpretation in proof of its correctness. And I suppose it cannot be denied, concerning all of us, that we are generally surprised to hear the strong language which good men use of themselves, as if such confessions showed them to be more like ourselves, and much less holy than we had fancied them to be. And on the other hand, I suppose, any man of tolerably correct life, whatever his positive advancement in grace, will seldom read accounts of notoriously bad men, in which their ways and feelings are described, without being shocked to find that these more or less cast a meaning upon his own heart, and bring out into light and colour lines and shapes of thought within him, which, till then, were almost invisible. Now this does not show that bad and good men are on a level, but it shows this, that they are of the same nature. It shows that the one has within him in tendency what the other has brought out into actual existence; so that the good has nothing to boast of over the bad, and while what is good in him is from God's grace, there is an abundance left, which marks him as being beyond all doubt of one blood with those sons of Adam who are still far from Christ their Redeemer. And if this is true of bad and good, much more is it true in the case of which I am speaking, that is, of good men one with another; of penitents and the upright. They understand each other far more than might at first have been supposed. And whereas their sense of the heinousness of sin rises with their own purity, those who are holiest will speak of themselves in the same terms as impure persons use about themselves; so that Christians, though they really differ much, yet as regards the power of sympathizing with each other will be found to be on a level. The one is not too high or the other too low. They have common ground; and as they have one faith and hope, and one Spirit, so also they have one and the same circle of temptations, and one and the same confession.

It were well if we understood all this. Perhaps the reason why the standard of holiness among us is so low, why our attainments are so poor, our view of the truth so dim, our belief so unreal, our general notions so artificial and external, is this, that we dare not trust each other with the secret of our hearts. We have each the same secret, and we keep it to ourselves, and we fear that, as a cause of estrangement, which really would be a bond of union. We do not probe the wounds of our nature thoroughly; we do not lay the foundation of our religious profession in the ground of our inner man; we make clean the outside of things; we are amiable and friendly to each other in words and deeds, but our love is not enlarged, our bowels of affection are straitened, and we fear to let the intercourse begin at the root; and, in consequence, our religion, viewed as a social system, is hollow. The presence of Christ is not in it.

To conclude. If it be awful to tell to another in our own way what we are, what will be the awfulness of that Day when the secrets of all hearts shall be disclosed! Let us ever bear this in mind when we fear that others should know what we are really, —whether we are right or wrong in hiding our sins now, it is a vain notion if we suppose they will always be hidden. The Day shall declare it; the Lord will come in Judgment; He "will bring to light the hidden things of darkness, and will make manifest the counsels of the hearts."[1] With this thought before us, surely it is a little thing whether or not man knows us here. *Then* will be knowledge without sympathy: then will be shame with everlasting contempt. Now, though there be shame, there is comfort and a soothing relief; though there be awe, it is greater on the side of him who hears than of him who makes avowal.

[1] 1 Cor. iv. 5.

SERMON XIII.

(SEPTUAGESIMA.)

Present Blessings.

" I have all, and abound : I am full."—PHIL. iv. 18.

SUCH is St. Paul's confession concerning his temporal condition, even in the midst of his trials. Those trials brought with them spiritual benefits ; but, even as regarded this world, he felt he had cause for joy and thankfulness, in spite of sorrows, pains, labours, and self-denials. He did not look on this life with bitterness, complain of it morosely, or refuse to enjoy it ; he was not soured, as the children of men often are, by his trials ; but he felt, that if he had troubles in this world, he had blessings also ; and he did not reject these, but made much of them. "I have all, and abound : I am full," he says. And, elsewhere, he tells us, that "every creature of God is good," and that "godliness is profitable unto all things, having the promise of the life that now is, and of that which is to come." [1]

Gloom is no Christian temper ; that repentance is not real which has not love in it ; that self-chastisement is not acceptable which is not sweetened by faith and cheerfulness. We must live in sunshine even when we sorrow ; we must live in God's presence, we must not shut ourselves up in our own hearts, even when we are reckoning up our past sins.

These thoughts are suitable on this day, when we first catch a sight, as it were, of the Forty Days of Lent. If God then gives us grace to repent, it is well ; if He enables us to chasten heart and body, to Him be praise ; and for that very reason, while we do so, we must not cease rejoicing in Him. All through Lent we must rejoice while we afflict ourselves. Though "many be called,

[1] 1 Tim. iv. 4, 8.

but few chosen;" though all run in the race, but "one receiveth the prize;" though we must "so run that we may obtain;" though we must be "temperate in all things," and "keep under our body and bring it into subjection, lest we be castaways;" yet through God alone we can do this; and while He is with us, we cannot but be joyful; for His absence only is a cause for sorrow. The Three Holy Children are said to have stood up in the midst of the fire, and to have called on all the works of God to rejoice with them; on sun and moon, stars of heaven, nights and days, showers and dew, frost and cold, lightnings and clouds, mountains and hills, green things upon the earth, seas and floods, fowls of the air, beasts and cattle, and children of men,—to praise and bless the Lord, and magnify Him for ever. We have no such trial as theirs; we have no such awful suspense as theirs when they entered the burning fiery furnace; we attempt for the most part what we know; we begin what we think we can go through. We can neither instance their faith nor equal their rejoicing; yet we can imitate them so far as to look abroad into this fair world, which God made "very good," while we mourn over the evil which Adam brought into it; to hold communion with what we see there, while we seek Him who is invisible; to admire it, while we abstain from it; to acknowledge God's love, while we deprecate His wrath; to confess that, many as are our sins, His grace is greater. Our sins are more in number than the hairs of our head; yet even the hairs of our head are all numbered by Him. He counts our sins, and, as He counts, so can He forgive; for that reckoning, great though it be, comes to an end; but His mercies fail not, and His Son's merits are infinite.

Let us, then, on this day, dwell upon a thought, which it will be a duty to carry with us through Lent, the thought of the blessings and mercies of which our present life is made up. St. Paul said that he had all, and abounded, and was full; and this in a day of persecution. Surely, if we have but religious hearts and eyes, we too must confess that our daily and hourly blessings in this life are not less than his. Let us recount some of them.

1. First, then, we ought to bless and praise God that we have the gift of life. By this I mean, not merely that we live, but for those blessings which are included in the notion of our living. He has made life in its very nature to imply the existence of certain blessings which are themselves a happiness, and which bring it to pass that, in spite of all evils, life in itself, except in rare cases, cannot be otherwise than desirable. We cannot live without the means of life; without the means of life we should die; and the

means of life are means of pleasure. It might have so been
ordered that life could not have been sustained without the use
of such means as were indifferent, neither pleasurable nor painful,
—or of means which were even painful; as in the case of illness
or disease, when we actually find that we cannot preserve it without painful remedies. Now, supposing the ordinary ways of
preserving it had been what are now but extraordinary: supposing
food were medicine; supposing wounds or blows imparted health
and strength. But it is not so. On the contrary, life consists in
things pleasant; it is sustained by blessings. And, moreover,
the Gospel, by a solemn grant, guarantees these things to us.
After the Flood God Almighty condescended to promise that
there never should be such a flood again; that seed-time and
harvest should not fail. He ratified the stability of nature by
His own Word, and by that Word it is upheld. And in like
manner He has, in a special way, guaranteed to us in the Gospel
that law of nature whereby good and pleasant gifts are included
in our idea of life, and life becomes a blessing. Did He so will,
He might sustain us Christians, not by bread only, but by every
word that proceedeth out of His mouth. But He has not done
so. He has pledged to us those ordinary means of sustenance
which we naturally like: "bread shall be given us; our water
shall be sure;" "all these things shall be added unto us." He
has not indeed promised us what the world calls its great prizes;
He has not promised us those goods, so called, of which the goodness depends on the imagination; He has not promised us large
estates, magnificent domains, houses like palaces, sumptuous furniture, retainers and servants, chariots and horses, rank, name, credit,
popularity, power, the deference of others, the indulgence of our
wills, luxuries, sensual enjoyments. These, on the contrary, He
denies us; and withal, He declares that, specious and inviting
as they are, really they are evil. But still He has promised that
this shall be His rule,—that thus shall it be fulfilled to us as His
ordinary providence, viz. that life shall not be a burden to us,
but a blessing, and shall contain more to comfort than to afflict.
And giving us as much as this, He bids us be satisfied with it;
He bids us confess that we "have all" when we have so much;
that we "abound" when we have enough; He promises us food,
raiment, and lodging; and He bids us, "having food and raiment,
therewith to be content." [1] He bids us be content with those
gifts, and withal unsolicitous about them; tranquil, secure, and
confident, because He has promised them; He bids us be sure

[1] 1 Tim. vi. 8.

that we shall have so much, and not be disappointed that it is no more. Such is His merciful consideration of us; He does not separate us from this world, though He calls us out of it; He does not reject our old nature when He gives us a new one; He does but redeem it from the curse, and purify it from the infection which came through Adam, and is none of His. He especially blesses the creation to our use, though we be regenerate. "Every creature of God," says the Apostle, "is good, and nothing to be refused, if it be received with thanksgiving, for it is sanctified by the word of God and prayer." [1] He does not bid us renounce the creation, but associates us with the most beautiful portions of it. He likens us to the flowers with which He has ornamented the earth, and to the birds that live solitary under heaven, and makes them the type of a Christian. He denies us Solomon's regal magnificence, to unite us to the lilies of the field and the fowls of the air. "Take no thought for your life, what ye shall eat, or what ye shall drink; nor yet for your body, what ye shall put on. Is not the life more than meat, and the body than raiment? Behold the fowls of the air: for they sow not, neither do they reap, nor gather into barns; yet your heavenly Father feedeth them. Are ye not much better than they? . . . And why take ye thought for raiment? Consider the lilies of the field, how they grow; they toil not, neither do they spin; and yet I say unto you, that even Solomon in all his glory was not arrayed like one of these." [2]

Here then, surely, is a matter for joy and thankfulness at all seasons, and not the least at times when, with a religious forbearance, and according to the will of the Giver, not from thanklessness, but from prudence, we, for a while, more or less withhold from ourselves His good gifts. Then, of all times, when we think it right to suspend our use of the means of life, so far as may not hurt that life, His gift, and to prove how pleasant is the using them by the pain of abstaining from them,—now especially, my brethren, in the weeks in prospect, when we shall be called on to try ourselves, as far as may be, by hunger, or cold, or watching, or seclusion, that we may be brought nearer to God,—let us now thank God that He has not put us into an evil world, or subjected us to a cruel master, but has given us a continual record of His own perfections in all that lies around us. Alas! it will be otherwise hereafter with those whom God puts out of His sight for ever. Their world will be evil; their life will be death; their rulers will be the devil and his angels; flames of fire and the lake

[1] 1 Tim. iv. 4. 5.   [2] Matt. vi. 25-29.

of brimstone will be their meat and drink ; the heaven above them will be brass; their earth will be dust and ashes; the blood in their veins will be as molten lead.   Fearful thought ! which it is not right to do more than glance at.   Let us utter it and pass by. Rather it is for us to rejoice that we are still in the light of His countenance, on His good earth, and under His warm sun.   Let us thank Him that He gives us the fruits of the earth in their season ; that He gives us "food out of the earth, and wine that maketh glad the heart of man, and oil to make him a cheerful countenance, and bread to strengthen man's heart." [1]   Thus was it with our fathers of old time ; thus is it with us now.   After Abraham had fought with the kings, Melchizedek brought forth bread and wine to refresh him.   The angels who visited him made themselves men, and ate of the calf which he dressed for them.   Isaac blessed Jacob after the savoury meat.   Joseph's brethren ate and drank, and were merry with him.   The seventy elders went up Mount Sinai with Moses, Aaron, Nadab, and Abihu, and they saw God, and moreover "did eat and drink."   David, after his repentance, had "bread set before him, and he did eat." When Elijah went for his life, and requested that he might die, "an angel touched him, and said unto him, Arise and eat;" and he did eat and drink, once and twice, and lay down to sleep between his meals; and when he arose, he "went in the strength of that meat forty days and forty nights unto Horeb the mount of God."   St. Paul also, after his conversion and baptism, "received meat and was strengthened." [2]

2. Again, what a great blessing is that gift of which I have just spoken in Elijah's case, the gift of sleep ! Almighty God does not suffer us to be miserable for a long while together even when He afflicts us ; but He breaks our trial into portions ; takes us out of this world ever and anon, and gives us a holyday-time, like children at school, in an unknown and mysterious country.

All this then must be borne in mind in reflecting on those solemn and sobering truths concerning the Christian's calling, which it is necessary often to insist upon.   It is often said, and truly, that the Christian is born to trouble,—that sorrow is the rule with him, and pleasure the exception.   But when this is said, it is with reference to seasons, circumstances, events, such things as are adventitious and additional to the gift of life itself.   The Christian's *lot* is one of sorrow, but as the regenerate *life* with

[1] Ps. civ. 14, 15.
[2] Gen. xiv. 18 ; xviii. 8 ; xxvii. 25 ; xliii. 34.   Exod. xxiv. 11 2 Sam. xii. 20.   1 Kings xix. 5-8.   Acts ix. 19.

him is happiness, so is the gift of natural life also. We live, therefore we are happy; *upon* this life of ours come joys and sorrows; and in proportion as we are favourites of God, it is sorrow that comes, not joy. Still after all considered in ourselves, that we live; that God breathes in us; that we exist in Him; that we think and act; that we have the means of life; that we have food, and sleep, and raiment, and lodging; and that we are not lonely, but in God's Church, and are sure of brethren by the very token of our having a Father which is in heaven; so far, rejoicing is the very condition of our being, and all pain is little more than external, not reaching to our inmost heart. So far all men almost are on a level, seasons of sickness excepted. Even delicate health and feebleness of life does not preclude these pleasures. And as to seasons of sickness, or even long and habitual pain or disease, the good Lord can compensate for them in His own way by extraordinary supplies of grace, as in early times He made even the torments of Christians in persecution literally pleasant to them. He who so ordered it, that even the red-hot iron did feel pleasant to the martyrs after a while, cannot fail of means to support His servants when life becomes a burden. But, generally speaking, it is a happiness, and that to all ranks. High and low, rich and poor, have the same refreshment in their pilgrimage. Hunger is as pleasantly appeased by the low as by the high, on coarse fare as on delicate. Sleep is equally the comfort and recruiting of rich and poor. We eat, drink, and sleep whether we are in sorrow or in joy, in anxiety or in hope. Our natural life is the type of our spiritual life, and thus, in a literal as well as higher sense, we may bless Him "who saveth our life from destruction, and crowneth us with mercy and loving-kindness; who satisfieth our mouth with good things, making us young and lusty as an eagle." [1]

3. Now, again, consider the blessings which we have in Christian brotherhood. In the beginning, woman was made that man might not be alone, but might have a help meet for him; and our Lord promised that all who gave up this world and this world's kindred for Him should "receive manifold more in this present time, houses, and brethren, and sisters, and mothers, and children, and lands, with persecutions." [2] You see He mentions the troubles of Christians, which were their lot *as* Christians; but still these did not interfere with the prior law of their very nature, that they should not be friendless. As food and raiment are necessary conditions of life, society is an inseparable adjunct of it. God does

---

[1] Ps. ciii. 4, 5. 　　　　[2] Mark x. 30.

not take away food and raiment when He gives grace, nor does
He take away brotherhood.   He removes from the world to put
into the Church.   Religion without a Church is as unnatural as
life without food and raiment.   He began our life anew, but He
built it up upon the same foundations ; and as He did not strip us
of our body when He made us Christians, neither did He of social
ties.   Christ finds us in the double tabernacle, of a house of flesh
and a house of brethren, and He sanctifies both, not pulls them
down.   Our first life is in ourselves ; our second in our friends.
They whom God forces to part with their near of kin for His
sake find brethren in the spirit at their side.   They who remain
solitary for His sake have children in the spirit raised up to them.
How should we thank God for this great benefit ! Now especially,
when we are soon to retire, more or less, into ourselves, and to
refrain from our ordinary intercourse with one another, let us
acknowledge the blessing, whether of the holy marriage bond, or
of family affection, or of the love of friends, which He so boun-
teously bestows.   He gives, He takes away ; blessed be His Name.
But He takes away to give again, and He withdraws one blessing
to restore fourfold.   Abraham offered his only son, and received
Him back again at the angel's voice.   Isaac "took Rebekah, and
she became his wife, and he loved her ; and Isaac was comforted
after his mother's death."   Jacob lost Joseph, and found him
governor of Egypt.   Job lost all his children, yet his end was
more blessed than his beginning.   We too, through God's mercy,
whether we be young or old, whether we have many friends or few,
if we be Christ's, shall all along our pilgrimage find those in whom
we may live, who will love us and whom we may love, who will
aid us and help us forward, and comfort us, and close our eyes.
For His love is a secret gift, which, unseen by the world, binds
together those in whom it lives, and makes them live and
sympathize in one another.

4. Again, let us bless and praise God for the present peace of
the Church, and the freedom of speech and action which He has
vouchsafed to us.   There have been times when to be a Christian
was to be an outcast and a criminal, when to profess the faith of
the saints would have subjected us to bonds and imprisonment.
Let us thank God that at present we have nothing to fear, but
may serve Him zealously, "no man forbidding" us.   No thanks
indeed to the world, which has given us this peace, not from any
love to the Church or the Truth, but from selfish and ungodly
principles of its own ; but great thanks to God, who has made use
of the world, and has overruled its course of opinion to our benefit.

We have large and noble churches to worship in; we may go freely to worship when we will; we may enjoy the advice of those who know better than ourselves; we may speak our mind one to another; we may move about freely; we may hold intercourse with whom we will; we may write what we will, explaining, defending, recommending, spreading the truth, without suffering or inconvenience. This is the blessing which we pray for in our Collects; and wonderfully has God granted it for very many years past. We pray daily that God would "give peace in our time." We pray three times a week that "those evils, which the craft and subtilty of the devil or man worketh against us, be brought to nought;" and "that, being hurt by no persecutions, we may evermore give thanks unto God in His Holy Church." We pray yearly that "the course of this world may be so peaceably ordered by His governance, that His Church may joyfully serve Him in all godly quietness;" and that He may "keep His household, the Church, in continual godliness, that through His protection it may be free from all adversities, and devoutly given to serve Him in good works, to the glory of His Name." Now all this is most wonderfully fulfilled to us at this day,—praised be His great mercy! You will ask, perhaps, whether too much prosperity is not undesirable for the Church?—It is so; but I am speaking, not of the Church, but of ourselves as individuals: what is dangerous to the body may be a blessing to the separate members. As to ourselves, one by one, God has His own secret chastisements for us, which, if He loves us, He will apply when we need them; but, if we know how to use the blessing duly, it is, I say, a great gift, that we are allowed to serve God with such freedom and in such peace as are now vouchsafed us. Great mercy indeed, which we forget because we are used to it; which many prophets and righteous men in the first ages of the Gospel had not, yet which we have had from our youth up. We from our youth up have lived in peace; with no persecution, no terror, no hindrance in serving God. The utmost we have had to endure is what is almost too trifling for a Christian to mention,—cold looks, or contempt, or ridicule from those who have not the heart themselves to attempt the narrow way.

5. Lastly, and very briefly, my brethren, let us remind ourselves of our own privileges here in this place. How great is our privilege, my brethren!—every one of us enjoys the great privilege of daily Worship and weekly Communion. This great privilege God has given to me and to you,—let us enjoy it while we have it. Not any one of us knows how long it may be his own. Perhaps

there is no one among us all who can reckon upon it for a continuance. Perhaps, or rather probably, it is a bright spot in our lives. Perhaps we shall look upon these days or years, time hence; and then reflect, when all is over, how pleasant they were; how pleasant to come, day after day, quietly and calmly, to kneel before our Maker,—week after week, to meet our Lord and Saviour. How soothing will then be the remembrance of His past gifts! we shall remember how we got up early in the morning, and how all things, light or darkness, sun or air, cold or freshness, breathed of Him,—of Him, the Lord of glory, who stood over us, and came down upon us, and gave Himself to us, and poured forth milk and honey for our sustenance, though we saw him not. Surely we have all, and abound : we are full.

SERMON XIV.

(SEXAGESIMA.)

Endurance, the Christian's Portion.

"All these things are against me."—GEN. xlii. 36.

SO spoke the Patriarch Jacob when Joseph had been made
away with, Simeon was detained in Egypt, Benjamin
threatened, and his remaining sons suspected by him and dis-
trusted; when out of doors, nay, at his door, was a grievous
famine, enemies or strangers round about, evil in prospect, and in
the past a number of sad remembrances to pain, not to cheer
him,—the dreadful misconduct of his own family and its consequences, and, further back, the wrath of Esau, his separation
from his father's house, his wanderings, and his ill-usage by
Laban. From his youth upwards he had been full of sorrows,
and he bore them with a troubled mind. His first words are,
"If God will be with me . . . then shall the Lord be my God."
His next, "Deliver me, I pray Thee." His next, "Ye have
troubled me." His next, "I will go down into the grave unto my
son mourning." His next, "All these things are against me."
And his next, "Few and evil have the days of the years of my
life been."[1] Blow after blow, stroke after stroke, trouble came
like hail. That one hailstone falls is a proof, not that no more
will come, but that others are coming surely; when we feel the
first, we say, "It *begins* to hail,"—we do not argue that it is over,
but that it is to come. Thus was it with Jacob: the storm
muttered around him, and heavy drops fell while he was in his
father's house; it drove him abroad. It did not therefore cease
because he was out in it : it did not end because it had begun.

[1] Gen. xxviii. 20, 21 ; xxxii. 11 ; xxxiv. 30 ; xxxvii. 35 ; xlii. 36 ;
xlvii. 9.

H

Rather, it continued, because it had begun; its beginning marked its presence; it began upon a law, which was extended over him in manhood also and old age, as in early youth. It was his calling to be in the storm : it was his very life to be a pilgrimage; it was the very thread of the days of his years to be few and evil.

And what Jacob was all his life, that was his son Joseph at least in the early part of it; for thirteen years, from seventeen to thirty, he was in trouble far greater than Jacob's ;—in captivity, in slavery, in prison, in bonds so tight that the iron is said to have entered into his soul. And what Joseph was in the beginning of life, such was Abraham, his forefather, in the latter half of it. For seventy-five years he lived in his "father's house;" but henceforward he was a wanderer. Thus did Almighty God, by the instance of the patriarchs of His ancient people, remind that people themselves that this world was not their rest; thus did He foreshadow that condition of life, which is not only a lesson, but a pattern to us of our very state of life, "if we live godly in Christ Jesus."[1] He Himself, the Lord Incarnate, chose only to sojourn on earth ; He had not where to lay His head. " Let us go forth, therefore, unto Him without the camp, bearing His reproach, for here we have no continuing city, but we seek one to come."[2] In Jacob is prefigured the Christian. He said, "All these things are against me ; " and what he said in a sort of dejection of mind that must the Christian say, not in dejection, not sorrowfully, or passionately, or in complaint, or in impatience, but calmly, as if confessing a doctrine. " All these things are against me ; " but it is my portion; they are against me, that I may fight against them and overcome them. If there were no enemy, there could be no conflict; were there no trouble, there could be no faith ; were there no trial, there could be no love; were there no fear, there could be no hope. Hope, faith, and love are weapons, and weapons imply foes and encounters ; and, relying on my weapons, I will glory in my suffering, being "persuaded that neither death, nor life, nor angels, nor principalities, nor powers, nor things present, nor things to come, nor height, nor depth, nor any other creature, shall be able to separate us from the love of God which is in Christ Jesus our Lord."[3]

That trouble and sorrow are in some especial sense the lot of the Christian, is plain from such passages of Scripture as the following :—For instance, St. Paul and St. Barnabas remind the

[1] 2 Tim. iii. 12.   [2] Heb. xiii. 13, 14.

[3] Rom. viii. 38. 39.

disciples "that we must through much tribulation enter into the kingdom of God." Again, St. Paul says, "If so be that we suffer with Him, that we may be also glorified together." Again, "If we suffer, we shall also reign with Him." Again, "Yea, and all that will live godly in Christ Jesus, shall suffer persecution." Again, St. Peter, "If, when ye do well, and suffer for it, ye take it patiently, this is acceptable with God; for even hereunto were ye called." And our Saviour declares that those who have given up the relations of this world "for His sake and the Gospel's" shall receive "an hundred-fold" now, "with persecutions." And St. Paul speaks in his own case of his "perils" by sea and land, from friend and foe, without and within him, of the body and of the soul. Yet he adds, "I will glory of the things which concern mine infirmities." [1]

To passages, however, like these, it is natural to object that they do not apply to the present time; that they apply to a time of persecution, which is past and over; and that men enter the kingdom now, without the afflictions which it once involved. What we see, it may be said, is a disproof of so sad and severe a doctrine. In this age, and in this country, the Church surely is in peace; rights are secured to it, and privileges added. Christians now, to say the very least, have liberty of person and property; they live without disquietude, and they die happily. Nay, they have much more than mere toleration, they have possession of the whole country; there are none but Christians in it; and if they suffer persecution, it must be (as it were) self-inflicted from the hands of each other. Christianity is the law of the land; its ministry is a profession, its offices are honours, its name a recommendation. So far from Christians being in trial because they are Christians, those who are not Christians, infidels and profligates, it is they who are under persecution. Under disabilities indeed these are, and justly; but it would be as true to say that Christians are justly in trouble, as to say that they are in trouble at all. What confessorship is there in a man's putting himself in the front of the Christian fight when that front is a benefice or a dignity? Rulers of the Church were aforetime marks for the persecutor; now they are but forced into temporal rank and power. Aforetime, the cross was in the inventory of holy treasures handed down from bishop to bishop; but now what self-denial is there in the apostolate, what bitterness in Christ's cup, what marks of the Lord Jesus in the touch of His Hand,

[1] Acts xiv. 22. Rom. viii. 17. 2 Tim. ii. 12; iii. 12. 1 Pet. ii. 20. Matt. xix. 29. Mark x. 30. 2 Cor. xi. 30.

what searching keenness in His sacred Breath? Of old time, indeed, as the Spirit forthwith drave Him into the wilderness to be tempted of the devil, so they, also, who received the Almighty Comforter, in any of His high gifts, were at once among the wild beasts of Ephesus, or amid the surges of the sea; but there are no such visible proofs now of the triumphs of God's grace, humbling the individual, while using him for heavenly purposes.

This is what objectors may say; and, in corroboration, they may tell us to look at the feelings of the world towards the Church and its sacred offices, and to judge for ourselves whether they have not the common sense of mankind with them. For is not the ministry of the Church what is called an easy profession? Do we not see it undertaken by those who love quiet, or who are unfit for business; by those who are less keen, less active-minded, less venturous than others? Does it not lead rather to a land of Canaan, as of old time, than to the narrow rugged way and the thorny couch of the Gospel? Has it not fair pastures, and pleasant resting-places, and calm refreshing streams, and milk and honey flowing, according to the promise of the Old Covenant, rather than that baptism and that draught which is the glory of the New? Facts then, it will be said, refute such notions of the suffering character of the Christian Church. It suffered at first,—suffering was the price of its triumphing; and since that, it has ceased to suffer. It is as truly in peace now as it was truly in suffering then;—one might as well deny that it did suffer, as that it is in peace; and to apply texts which speak of what it was then to what it is now, is unreal, offends some hearers, and excites ridicule in others. This is what may be said.

Yet is it so indeed? Let us look into the Bible again. Are we to go by faith or by sight?—for surely, whatever conclusions follow from what we see, these cannot undo what is written. What is written remains; and if sight is against it, we must suppose that there is some way of solving the difficulty, though we may not see how; and we will try, as well as we can, to solve it in the case before us.

Let us, I say, consider the words of Scripture again. Surely, if endurance be not in some sense or other the portion of Christians, the whole New Testament itself has but a temporary meaning; for it is all built upon this doctrine as a groundwork. If "the present distress,"[1] of which St. Paul speaks, does not denote the ordinary state of the Christian Church, the New Testament is scarcely written for us, but must be remodelled before it can be

[1] 1 Cor. vii. 26.

made apply. There are men of the world in this day who are attempting to supersede the precepts of Christ about almsgiving and the maintenance of the poor. We are accustomed to object that they contravene Scripture. Again, we hear of men drawing up a Church government for themselves, or omitting Sacraments, or modifying doctrines. We say they do not read Scripture rightly. They answer, perhaps, that Scripture commands or countenances many things which are not binding on us eighteen hundred years after. They consider that the management of the poor, the form of the Church, the power of the State over it, the nature of its faith, or the choice of its ordinances, are not points on which we need rigidly keep to Scripture; that times have changed. This is what they say; and can we find fault with them if we ourselves allow that the New Testament is a dead letter in another most essential part of it? Is it strange that they should think that the world may now tyrannize over the Church, when we allow that the Church may now indulge in the world? Surely they do but make a fair bargain with us; both they and we put aside Scripture, and then agree together, we to live in ease, and they to rule. We have taken the world's pay, and must not grudge its yoke. Independence surely is not the Church's privilege unless hardship is her portion.

Well, and perhaps affliction, hardship, distress, ill-usage, evil report, are her portion, both promised and bestowed, though at first sight they may seem not to be. What proof is there that temporal happiness was the gift of the Law, which will not avail for temporal adversity being that of the Gospel? You say the Jews had the promise of this world. True. But look at their history. Is that promise fulfilled on its surface? Had they not long periods of captivity, war, famine, pestilence, weakness, internal division? Look at their history as a whole. Is it not very like other histories? Had not their power a beginning, a progress, and an end? Did they not pass through those successive stages which other states pass through? What prosperity had they, to go by appearances, which other states had not? What trouble had other states which they were spared? If, then, the face of things be taken to prove that the Christian Church is not born to trouble, would it not also prove that the Jewish Church was not allotted prosperity? And if, in spite of appearances, we yet say that the Israelites had special temporal blessings, why may we not, in spite of the appearance, say that Christians have special temporal trials?

You will say, perhaps, that the Jewish promise was suspended on a condition, the condition of obedience, and that the Jews forfeited the reward, because they did not merit it. True; let it be so. And what hinders, in like manner, if Christians are in prosperity, not in adversity, that it is because they too have forfeited the promise and privilege of affliction by disobedience? And what hinders that, as in spite of the sins of the people, the Jewish Church still in some sufficient sense did obtain the temporal promise; so, in like manner, in spite of the sins of the multitude of Christians, the Christian Church as a whole, and her true children in particular, may partake in the promise of distress?

It is very difficult then to argue from what we see, and there are many ways in which what is written may be fulfilled in spite, or by means, of it. All that clearly can be pointed out is the word of promise. It was said of Israel: "He loved the people; all His saints are in Thy hand; and they sat down at Thy feet; every one shall receive of Thy words. . . . Let Reuben live and not die; and let not his men be few. . . . Hear, Lord, the voice of Judah, and bring him unto his people. Let his hands be sufficient for him, and be Thou an help to him from his enemies." And of Levi: "Let Thy Thummim and Thy Urim be upon Thy Holy One. . . . Bless, Lord, his substance, and accept the work of his hands: smite through the loins of them that rise against him, and of them that hate him, that they rise not again." And of Benjamin: "The Beloved of the Lord shall dwell in safety by Him." And of Joseph: "Blessed of the Lord be his land, for the precious things of heaven, for the dew, and for the deep that coucheth beneath, and for the precious things brought forth by the sun, and for the precious things brought forth by the moon, and for the chief things of the ancient mountains, and for the precious things of the lasting hills, and for the precious things of the earth, and the fulness thereof." And of Zebulun: "Rejoice, Zebulun; in thy going out; and, Issachar, in thy tents . . . they shall suck of the abundance of the seas, and of treasures hid in the sand." And, "Blessed be he that enlargeth Gad; he dwelleth as a lion, and teareth the arm with the crown of the head." And, "O Naphtali, satisfied with favour, and full of the blessing of the Lord, possess thou the west and the south." And, "Let Asher be blessed with children; thy shoes shall be iron and brass; and as thy days, so shall thy strength be." And of all of them together it was said, "Israel shall dwell in safety alone; the fountain of Jacob shall be upon a land of corn and wine; and his heavens shall drop down dew."[1] These were the bright and

[1] Deut. xxxiii.

pleasant things promised to the first people of God, in the plains of Moab, on their entering into the land. And now in turn, what did the second and greater Prophet of the Church declare, when He was set upon the mount, with the people around Him, and published His covenant of grace. " He opened His mouth and said, Blessed are the poor in spirit, for theirs is the kingdom of heaven. Blessed are they that mourn, for they shall be comforted. Blessed are the meek. . . . Blessed are they which do hunger and thirst after righteousness. . . . Blessed are the merciful. . . . Blessed are the pure in heart. . . . Blessed are the peacemakers." And lastly, " Blessed are ye when men shall revile you and persecute you, and shall say all manner of evil against you falsely for My sake. Rejoice, and be exceeding glad ; for great is your reward in heaven ; for so persecuted they the prophets which were before you." And by contrast, He added, " But woe unto you that are rich, for ye have received your consolation. Woe unto you that are full, for ye shall hunger. Woe unto you that laugh now, for ye shall mourn and weep. Woe unto you when all men shall speak well of you, for so did their fathers unto the false prophets."[1]

At another time He spoke thus : " Sell that ye have, and give alms." " If thou wilt be perfect, go and sell that thou hast, and give to the poor." " It is easier for a camel to go through the eye of a needle, than for a rich man to enter into the kingdom of God." " Whosoever will be chief among you, let him be your servant." " If any man will come after Me, let him deny himself, and take up his cross, and follow Me." And, in a word, the doctrine of the Gospel, and the principle of it, is thus briefly stated by the Apostle in the words of the Wise Man: " Whom the Lord loveth He chasteneth, and scourgeth every son whom He receiveth. If ye endure chastening, God dealeth with you as with sons. . . . If ye be without chastisement, *whereof all are partakers*, then are ye bastards, and not sons."[2] Can words speak it plainer, that, as certainly as temporal prosperity is the gift of the Law, so also are hardship and distress the gift of the Gospel ?

Take up thy portion, then, Christian soul, and weigh it well, and learn to love it. Thou wilt find, if thou art Christ's, in spite of what the world fancies, that after all, even at this day, endurance, in a special sense, *is* the lot of those who offer themselves to be servants of the King of sorrows. There is an inward world which none see but those who belong to it ; and though the out-

---

[1] Matt. v. 2-12. Luke vi. 24-26.
[2] Luke xii. 33. Matt. xix. 21, 24 ; xx. 27 ; xvi. 24. Heb. xii. 6-8.

side robe be many-coloured, like Joseph's coat, inside it is lined with camel's hair, or sackcloth, fitting those who desire to be one with Him who fared hardly in the wilderness, in the mountain, and on the sea. There is an inward world into which they enter who come near to Christ, though to men in general they seem the same as before. They hold the same place as before in the world's society; their employments are the same, their ways, their comings-in and goings-out. If they were high in rank, they are still high; if they were in active life, they are still active; if they were wealthy, they still have wealth. They have still great friends, powerful connections, ample resources, fair name in the world's eye; but if they have drunk of Christ's cup, and tasted the bread of His Table in sincerity, it is not with them as in time past. A change has come over them, unknown indeed to themselves, except in its effects, but they have a portion in destinies to which other men are strangers, and, as having destinies, they have conflicts also. They drank what looked like a draught of this world, but it associated them in hopes and fears, trials and purposes, above this world. They came as for a blessing, and they have found a work. They are soldiers in Christ's army; they fight against "things that are seen," and they have "all these things against them." To their surprise, as time goes on, they find that their lot is changed. They find that in one shape or other adversity happens to them. If they refuse to afflict themselves, God afflicts them. One blow falls, they are startled; it passes over, it is well; they expect nothing more. Another comes; they wonder; "Why is this?" they ask; they think that the first should be their security against the second; they bear it, however; and it passes too. Then a third comes; they almost murmur; they have not yet mastered the great doctrine that endurance is their portion. O simple soul, is it not the law of thy being to endure since thou camest to Christ? Why camest thou but to endure? Why didst thou taste His heavenly feast, but that it might work in thee? Why didst thou kneel beneath His hand, but that He might leave on thee the print of His wounds? Why wonder then that one sorrow does not buy off the next? Does one drop of rain absorb the second? Does the storm cease because it has begun? Understand thy place in God's kingdom, and rejoice, not complain, that in thy day thou hast thy lot with Prophets and Apostles. Envy not the gay and thriving world. Religious persons ask, "Why are we so marked out for crosses? Others get on in the world; others are prosperous; their schemes turn out well, and their families settle happily; there is no anxiety, no bereavement among

them, while the world fights against us." This is what they sometimes say, though with some exaggeration certainly, for almost all
men, sooner or later, have their troubles, and Christians, as well
as others, have their continual comforts. But what then, be it
ever so true ? If so, it is but what was foretold long ago, and even
under the Law fulfilled in its degree. "They have children at
their desire, and leave the rest of their substance for their babes."
"They are in no peril of death, but are lusty and strong. They
come in no misfortune like other folk, neither are they plagued
like other men. . . . Their eyes swell with fatness, they do even
what they lust. . . . Lo, these are the ungodly, these prosper in
the world, and these have riches in possession." Such is the
portion, such the punishment of those who forsake their God.
"Verily, I say unto you, They have their reward."[1]

When, then, my brethren, it is objected that times are changed
since the Gospel was first preached, and that what Scripture says
of the lot of Christians does not apply to us, make answer, that
the Church of Christ doubtless is in high estate everywhere, and
so must be, for it is written, "I will give Thee the heathen for
Thine inheritance, and the utmost parts of the earth for Thy
possession." Yet that while she maintains her ground, she ever
suffers *in* maintaining it; she has to fight the good fight, in order
to maintain it : she fights and she suffers, in proportion as she plays
her part well ; and if she is without suffering, it is because she is
slumbering. Her doctrines and precepts never can be palatable
to the world ; and if the world does not persecute, it is because
she does not preach. And so of her individual members : they in
their own way suffer ; not after her manner, perhaps, nor for the
same reason, nor in the same degree, but more or less, as being
under the law of suffering which Christ began. Judge not then
by outward appearance ; think not that His servants are in ease
and security because things look smooth, else you will be startled,
perhaps, and offended, when suffering falls upon you. Temporal
blessings, indeed, He gives to you and to all men in abundance ;
"He maketh His sun to rise upon the just and unjust ;" but in
your case it will be "houses and brethren and lands, with persecutions." Judge not by appearance, but be sure that, even when
things seem to brighten and smile upon God's true servants, there
is much within to try them, though you see it not. Of old time
they wore clothing of hair and sackcloth under rich robes. Men
do not observe this custom nowadays ; but be quite sure still,
that there are as many sharp distresses underneath the visible garb

[1] Ps. xvii. 15 ; lxxiii. 4-12. Matt. vi. 5.

of things, as if they did.   Many a secret ailment or scarcely observed infirmity exercises him who has it better than thorns or knotted cord.   Many a silent grief, lying like lead within the breast, or like cold ice upon the heart.   Many a sad secret, which a man dare not tell lest he should find no sympathy.   Many a laden conscience, laden because the owner of it has turned to Christ, and which he would not have felt had he kept from Him. Many an apprehension for the future, which cannot be spoken ; many a bereavement which has robbed the world's gifts of their pleasant savour, and leads the heart but to sigh at the sight of them.   No ; never while the Church lasts, will the words of old Jacob be reversed,—all things here are against us but God ; but if God be for us, who can really be against us ?   If He is in the midst of us, how shall we be moved ?   If Christ has died and risen again, what death can come upon us, though we be made to die daily ? what sorrow, pain, humiliation, trial, but must end as His has ended, in a continual resurrection into His new world, and in a nearer and nearer approach to Him ?   He pronounced a blessing over His Apostles, and they have scattered it far and wide all over the earth unto this day.   It runs as follows : " Peace I leave with you, My peace I give unto you ; not as the world giveth, give I unto you."   " These things I have spoken unto you, that in Me ye might have peace.   In the world ye shall have tribu lation ; but be of good cheer, I have overcome the world." [1]

[1] John xiv. 27 ; xvi. 33.

SERMON XV.

(QUINQUAGESIMA.)

Love, the One Thing needful.

*' Though I speak with the tongues of men and of angels, and have not charity,
I am become as sounding brass, or a tinkling cymbal."*—I COR. xiii. 1.

I SUPPOSE the greater number of persons who try to live
Christian lives, and who observe themselves with any care,
are dissatisfied with their own state on this point, viz. that, whatever their religious attainments may be, yet they feel that their
motive is not the highest;—that the love of God, and of man for
His sake, is not their ruling principle. They may do much, nay,
if it so happen, they may suffer much; but they have little reason
to think that they love much, that they do and suffer for love's
sake. I do not mean that they thus express themselves exactly,
but that they are dissatisfied with themselves, and that when this
dissatisfaction is examined into, it will be found ultimately to
come to this, though they will give different accounts of it. They
may call themselves cold, or hard-hearted, or fickle, or double-
minded, or doubting, or dim-sighted, or weak in resolve, but they
mean pretty much the same thing, that their affections do not
rest on Almighty God as their great Object. And this will be
found to be the complaint of religious men among ourselves, not
less than others; their reason and their heart not going together;
their reason tending heavenwards, and their heart earthwards.

I will now make some remarks on the defect I have described,
as thinking that the careful consideration of it may serve as one
step towards its removal.

Love, and love only, is the fulfilling of the Law, and they only are
in God's favour in whom the righteousness of the Law is fulfilled.
This we know full well; yet, alas! at the same time, we cannot

deny that whatever good thing we have to show, whether activity, or patience, or faith, or fruitfulness in good works, love to God and man is not ours, or, at least, in very scanty measure; not at all proportionately to our apparent attainments. Now, to enlarge upon this.

In the first place, love clearly does not consist merely in great sacrifices. We can take no comfort to ourselves that we are God's own merely on the ground of great deeds or great sufferings. The greatest sacrifices without love would be nothing worth, and that they are great does not necessarily prove they are done with love. St. Paul emphatically assures us that his acceptance with God did not stand in any of those high endowments, which strike us in him at first sight, and which, did we actually see him, doubtless would so much draw us to him. One of his highest gifts, for instance, was his spiritual knowledge. He shared, and felt the sinfulness and infirmities of human nature; he had a deep insight into the glories of God's grace, such as no natural man can have. He had an awful sense of the realities of heaven, and of the mysteries revealed. He could have answered ten thousand questions on theological subjects, on all those points about which the Church has disputed since his time, and which we now long to ask him. He was a man whom one could not come near without going away from him wiser than one came : a fount of knowledge and wisdom ever full, ever approachable, ever flowing, from which all who came in faith gained a measure of the gifts which God had lodged in him. His presence inspired resolution, confidence, and zeal, as one who was the keeper of secrets, and the revealer of the whole counsel of God; and who by look, and word, and deed encompassed, as it were, his brethren with God's mercies and judgments, spread abroad and reared aloft the divine system of doctrine and precept, and seated himself and them securely in the midst of it. Such was this great servant of Christ and Teacher of the Gentiles; yet he says, " Though I speak with the tongues of men and of angels, though I have the gift of prophecy, and understand all mysteries, and all knowledge, and have not charity, I am become as sounding brass, or a tinkling cymbal. . . . I am nothing." Spiritual discernment, an insight into the Gospel covenant, is no evidence of love.

Another distinguishing mark of his character, as viewed in Scripture, is his faith, a prompt, decisive, simple assent to God's word, a deadness to motives of earth, a firm hold of the truths of the unseen world, and keenness in following them out; yet he says of his faith also, " Though I have all faith, so that I could

remove mountains, and have not charity, I am nothing." Faith
is no necessary evidence of love.

A tender consideration of the temporal wants of his brethren
is another striking feature of his character, as it is a special
characteristic of every true Christian; yet he says, "Though I
bestow all my goods to feed the poor, and have not charity, it
profiteth me nothing." Self-denying almsgiving is no necessary
evidence of love.

Once more. He, if any man, had the spirit of a martyr; yet
he implies that even martyrdom, viewed in itself, is no passport
into the heavenly kingdom. "Though I give my body to be
burned, and have not charity, it profiteth me nothing." Martyrdom is no necessary evidence of love.

I do not say that at this day we have many specimens or much
opportunity of such high deeds and attainments; but in our degree
we certainly may follow St. Paul in them,—in spiritual discernment, in faith, in works of mercy, and in confessorship. We may,
we ought to follow him. Yet though we do, still, it may be, we
are not possessed of the one thing needful, of the spirit of love,
or in a very poor measure; and this is what serious men feel in
their own case.

Let us leave these sublimer matters, and proceed to the humbler
and continual duties of daily life; and let us see whether these
too may not be performed with considerable exactness, yet with
deficient love. Surely they may; and serious men complain of
themselves here, even more than when they are exercised on
greater subjects. Our Lord says, "If ye love Me, keep My commandments;" but they feel that though they are, to a certain
point, keeping God's commandments, yet love is not proportionate,
does not keep pace, with their obedience; that obedience springs
from some source short of love. This they perceive; they feel
themselves to be hollow; a fair outside, without a spirit within it.

I mean as follows:—It is possible to obey, not from love towards God and man, but from a sort of conscientiousness short of
love; from some notion of acting up to a *law;* that is, more from
the fear of God than from love of Him. Surely this is what, in
one shape or other, we see daily on all sides of us; the case of
men living to the world, yet not without a certain sense of religion,
which acts as a restraint on them. They pursue ends of this
world, but not to the full; they are checked, and go a certain way
only, because they dare not go further. This external restraint
acts with various degrees of strength on various persons. They
all live to this world, and act from the love of it; they all allow

their love of the world a certain range; but, at some particular point, which is often quite arbitrary, this man stops, and that man stops. Each stops at a different point in the course of the world, and thinks every one else profane who goes further, and superstitious who does not go so far,—laughs at the latter, is shocked at the former. And hence those few who are miserable enough to have rid themselves of all scruples, look with great contempt on such of their companions as have any, be those scruples more or less, as being inconsistent and absurd. They scoff at the principle of mere fear as a capricious and fanciful principle; proceeding on no rule, and having no evidence of its authority, no claim on our respect; as a weakness in our nature, rather than an essential portion of that nature, viewed in its perfection and entireness. And this being all the notion which their experience gives them of religion, as not knowing really religious men, they think of religion only as a principle which interferes with our enjoyments unintelligibly and irrationally. Man is made to love. So far is plain. They see that clearly and truly; but religion, as far as they conceive of it, is a system destitute of objects of love; a system of fear. It repels and forbids, and thus seems to destroy the proper function of man, or, in other words, to be unnatural. And it is true that this sort of fear of God, or rather slavish dread, as it may more truly be called, *is* unnatural; but then it is not religion, which really consists, not in the mere fear of God, but in His love; or if it be religion, it is but the religion of devils, who believe and tremble; or of idolaters, whom devils have seduced, and whose worship is superstition,—the attempt to appease beings whom they love not; and, in a word, the religion of the children of this world, who would, if possible, serve God and Mammon, and, whereas religion consists of love *and* fear, give to God their fear, and to Mammon their love.

And what takes place so generally in the world at large, this, I say, serious men will feel as happening, in its degree, in their own case. They will understand that even strict obedience is no evidence of fervent love, and they will lament to perceive that they obey God far more than they love Him. They will recollect the instance of Balaam, who was even exemplary in his obedience, yet had not love; and the thought will come over them as a perplexity, what proof they have that they are not, after all, deceiving themselves, and thinking themselves religious when they are not. They will indeed be conscious to themselves of the sacrifice they make of their own wishes and pursuits to the will of God; but they are conscious also that they sacrifice **them** because they know they *ought* to do so, not simply from love of God. And they ask, almost in a kind of despair, How are we to learn, not merely to obey, but to love ?

They say, How are we to fulfil St. Paul's words, " The life which I now live in the flesh I live by the faith of the Son of God, who loved me, and gave Himself for me "? And this would seem an especial difficulty in the case of those who live among men, whose duties lie amid the engagements of this world's business, whose thoughts, affections, exertions, are directed towards things which they see, things present and temporal. In their case it seems to be a great thing, even if their *rule* of life is a heavenly one, if they *act* according to God's will ; but how can they hope that heavenly Objects should fill their heart when there is no room left for them ? how shall things absent displace things present, things unseen the things that are visible ? Thus they seem to be reduced, as if by a sort of necessity, to that state, which I just now described as the state of men of the world, that of having their hearts set on the world, and being only restrained outwardly by religious rules.

To proceed. Generally speaking, men will be able to bring against themselves positive charges of want of love, more unsatisfactory still. I suppose most men, or at least a great number of men, have to lament over their hardness of heart, which, when analyzed, will be found to be nothing else but the absence of love. I mean that hardness which, for instance, makes us unable to repent as we wish. No repentance is truly such without love ; it is love which gives it its efficacy in God's sight. Without love there may be remorse, regret, self-reproach, self-condemnation, but there is not saving penitence. There may be conviction of the reason, but not conversion of the heart. Now, I say, a great many men lament in themselves this want of love in repenting ; they are hard-hearted ; they are deeply conscious of their sins ; they abhor them ; and yet they can take as lively interest in what goes on around them as if they had no such consciousness ; or they mourn this minute, and the next are quite impenetrable. Or, though, as they think and believe, they fear God's anger, and are full of confusion at themselves, yet they find (to their surprise, I may say) that they cannot abstain from any indulgence ever so trivial, which would be (as their reason tells them) a natural way of showing sorrow. They eat and drink with as good a heart as if they had no distress upon their minds ; they find no difficulty in entering into any of the recreations or secular employments which come in their way. They sleep as soundly ; and, in spite of their grief, perhaps find it most difficult to persuade themselves to rise early to pray for pardon. These are signs of want of love.

Or, again, without reference to the case of penitence, they have a general indisposition towards prayer and other exercises of devotion. They find it most difficult to get themselves to pray; most difficult, too, to rouse their minds to attend to their prayers. At very best they do but feel satisfaction in devotion *while* they are engaged in it. Then perhaps they find a real pleasure in it, and wonder they can ever find it irksome; yet if any chance throws them out of their habitual exercises, they find it most difficult to return to them. They do not like them well enough to seek them *from* liking them. They are kept in them by habit, by regularity in observing them; not by love. When the regular course is broken, there is no inward principle to act at once in repairing the mischief. In wounds of the body, nature works towards a recovery, and, left to itself, would recover; but we have no spiritual principle strong and healthy enough to set religious matters right in us when they have got disordered, and to supply for us the absence of rule and custom. Here, again is obedience, more or less mechanical, or without love.

Again:—a like absence of love is shown in our proneness to be taken up and engrossed with trifles. Why is it that we are so open to the power of excitement? why is it that we are looking out for novelties? why is it that we complain of want of variety in a religious life? why that we cannot bear to go on in an ordinary round of duties year after year? why is it that lowly duties, such as condescending to men of low estate, are distasteful and irksome? why is it that we need powerful preaching, or interesting and touching books, in order to keep our thoughts and feelings on God? why is it that our faith is so dispirited and weakened by hearing casual objections urged against the doctrine of Christ? why is it that we are so impatient that objections should be answered? why are we so afraid of worldly events, or the opinions of men? why do we so dread their censure or ridicule? —Clearly because we are deficient in love. He who loves cares little for anything else. The world may go as it will; he sees and hears it not, for his thoughts are drawn another way; he is solicitous mainly to walk with God, and to be found with God; and is in perfect peace because he is stayed in Him.

And here we have an additional proof how weak our love is; viz. when we consider how little adequate our professed principles are found to be to support us in affliction. I suppose it often happens to men to feel this when some reverse or unexpected distress comes upon them. They indeed most especially will feel it, of course, who have let their words, nay their thoughts, much outrun their hearts ; but numbers will feel it too, who have tried to make their reason and affections keep pace with each other. We are told of the righteous man, that " he will not be afraid of any evil tidings, for his heart standeth fast, and believeth in the Lord. His heart is established, and will not shrink." [1] Such must be the case of every one who realizes his own words, when he talks of the shortness of life, the wearisomeness of the world, and the security of heaven. Yet how cold and dreary do all such topics prove when a man comes into trouble ? and why, except that he has been after all set upon things visible, not on God, while he has been speaking of things invisible ? There has been much profession and little love.

These are some of the proofs which are continually brought home to us, if we attend to ourselves, of our want of love to God; and they will readily suggest others to us. If I must, before concluding, remark upon the mode of overcoming the evil, I must say plainly this, that, fanciful though it may appear at first sight to say so, the comforts of life are the main cause of it ; and, much as we may lament and struggle against it, till we learn to dispense with them in good measure, we shall not overcome it. Till we, in a certain sense, detach ourselves from our bodies, our minds will not be in a state to receive divine impressions, and to exert heavenly aspirations. A smooth and easy life, an uninterrupted enjoyment of the goods of Providence, full meals, soft raiment, well-furnished homes, the pleasures of sense, the feeling of security, the consciousness of wealth,—these, and the like, if we are not careful, choke up all the avenues of the soul, through which the light and breath of heaven might come to us. A hard life is, alas ! no certain method of becoming spiritually minded, but it is one out of the means by which Almighty God makes us so. We must, at least at seasons, defraud ourselves of nature if we would not be defrauded of grace. If we attempt to force our minds into a loving and devotional temper, without this preparation, it is too plain what will follow,—the grossness and coarseness, the affectation, the effeminacy, the unreality, the presumption, the hollowness (suffer me, my brethren, while I say plainly, but seriously, what I mean), in a word, what Scripture calls the Hypocrisy, which we see around us ; that state of mind in which the reason, seeing what we should be, and the conscience enjoining it, and the heart being unequal to it, some or other pretence is set up.

[1] Ps. cxii. 7, 8.

by way of compromise, that men may say, " Peace, peace, when there is no peace."

And next, after enjoining this habitual preparation of heart, let me bid you cherish, what otherwise it were shocking to attempt, a constant sense of the love of your Lord and Saviour in dying on the cross for you. " The love of Christ," says the Apostle, " constraineth us ; " not that gratitude leads to love where there is no sympathy (for, as all know, we often reproach ourselves with not loving persons who yet have loved us), but where hearts are in their degree renewed after Christ's image, there, under His grace, gratitude to Him will increase our love of Him, and we shall rejoice in that goodness which has been so good to us. Here, again, self-discipline will be necessary. It makes the heart tender as well as reverent. Christ showed His love in deed, not in word, and you will be touched by the thought of His cross far more by bearing it after Him than by glowing accounts of it. All the modes by which you bring it before you must be simple and severe ; " excellency of speech," or " enticing words," to use St. Paul's language, is the worst way of any. Think of the Cross when you rise and when you lie down, when you go out and when you come in, when you eat and when you walk and when you converse, when you buy and when you sell, when you labour and when you rest, consecrating and sealing all your doings with this one mental action, the thought of the Crucified. Do not talk of it to others ; be silent, like the penitent woman, who showed her love in deep subdued acts. She " stood at His feet behind Him weeping, and began to wash His feet with tears, and did wipe them with the hairs of her head, and kissed His feet, and anointed them with the ointment." And Christ said of her, " Her sins, which are many, are forgiven her, for she loved much ; but to whom little is forgiven, the same loveth little." [1]

And, further, let us dwell often upon those His manifold mercies to us and to our brethren, which are the consequence of His coming upon earth ; His adorable counsels, as manifested in our personal election,—how it is that we are called and others not ; the wonders of His grace towards us from our infancy until now ; the gifts He has given us ; the aid He has vouchsafed ; the answers He has accorded to our prayers. And, further, let us, as far as we have the opportunity, meditate upon His dealings with His Church from age to age ; on His faithfulness to His promises, and the mysterious mode of their fulfilment ; how He has ever led His people forward safely and prosperously on the whole amid

[1] Luke vii. 38, 47.

so many enemies; what unexpected events have worked His
purposes; how evil has been changed into good; how His sacred
truth has ever been preserved unimpaired; how saints have been
brought on to their perfection in the darkest times. And, further,
let us muse over the deep gifts and powers lodged in the Church :
what thoughts do His ordinances raise in the believing mind !—
what wonder, what awe, what transport, when duly dwelt upon !

It is by such deeds and such thoughts that our services, our
repentings, our prayers, our intercourse with men, will become
instinct with the spirit of love. Then we do everything thankfully and joyfully, when we are temples of Christ, with His Image
set up in us. Then it is that we mix with the world without
loving it, for our affections are given to another. We can bear to
look on the world's beauty, for we have no heart for it. We are
not disturbed at its frowns, for we live not in its smiles. We
rejoice in the House of Prayer, because He is there "whom our
soul loveth." We can condescend to the poor and lowly, for they
are the presence of Him who is Invisible. We are patient in
bereavement, adversity, or pain, for they are Christ's tokens.

Thus let us enter the Forty Days of Lent now approaching.
For Forty Days we seek after love by means of fasting. May we
find it more and more, the older we grow, till death comes and
gives us the sight of Him who is at once its Object and its
Author.

SERMON XVI.

(LENT.)

The Individuality of the Soul.

" The spirit shall return unto God, who gave it."—ECCLES. **xii. 7**.

HERE we are told that upon death the spirit of man returns to God. The sacred writer is not speaking of good men only, or of God's chosen people, but of men generally. In the case of all men, the soul, when severed from the body, returns to God. God gave it: He made it, He sent it into the body, and He upholds it there; He upholds it in distinct existence wherever it is. It animates the body while life lasts; it returns again, it relapses into the unseen state upon death. Let us steadily contemplate this truth, which at first sight we may fancy we altogether enter into. The point to be considered is this, that every soul of man which is or has been on earth, has a separate existence; and that, in eternity, not in time merely,—in the unseen world, not merely in this,—not only during its mortal life, but ever from the hour of its creation, whether joined to a body of flesh or not.

Nothing is more difficult than to realize that every man has a distinct soul, that every one of all the millions who live or have lived, is as whole and independent a being in himself as if there were no one else in the whole world but he. To explain what I mean: do you think that a commander of an army realizes it when he sends a body of men on some dangerous service? I am not speaking as if he were wrong in so sending them; I only ask in matter of fact, does he, think you, commonly understand that each of those poor men has a soul, a soul as dear to himself, as precious in its nature, as his own? Or does he not rather look on the body of men collectively, as one mass, as parts of a whole, as but the wheels or springs of some great machine, to which he assigns the individuality, not to each soul that goes to make it up?

This instance will show what I mean, and how open we all lie to the remark, that we do not understand the doctrine of the distinct individuality of the human soul. We class men in masses, as we might connect the stones of a building. Consider our common way of regarding history, politics, commerce, and the like, and you will own that I speak truly. We generalize, and lay down laws, and then contemplate these creations of our own minds, and act upon and towards them, as if they were the real things, dropping what are more truly such. Take another instance: when we talk of national greatness, what does it mean? Why, it really means that a certain distinct definite number of immortal individual beings happen for a few years to be in circumstances to act together and one upon another, in such a way as to be able to act upon the world at large, to gain an ascendency over the world, to gain power and wealth, and to look like one, and to be talked of and to be looked up to as one. They seem for a short time to be some one thing: and we, from our habit of living by sight, regard them as one, and drop the notion of their being anything else. And when this one dies and that one dies, we forget that it is the passage of separate immortal beings into an unseen state, that the whole which appears is but appearance, and that the component parts are the realities. No, we think nothing of this; but though fresh and fresh men die, and fresh and fresh men are born, so that the whole is ever shifting, yet we forget all that drop away, and are insensible to all that are added; and we still think that this whole which we call the nation, is one and the same, and that the individuals who come and go, exist only in it and for it, and are but as the grains of a heap or the leaves of a tree.

Or again, survey some populous town: crowds are pouring through the streets; some on foot, some in carriages; while the shops are full, and the houses too, could we see into them. Every part of it is full of life. Hence we gain a general idea of splendour, magnificence, opulence, and energy. But what is the truth? why, that every being in that great concourse is his own centre, and all things about him are but shades, but a "vain shadow," in which he "walketh and disquieteth himself in vain." He has his own hopes and fears, desires, judgments, and aims; he is everything to himself, and no one else is really anything. No one outside of him can really touch him, can touch his soul, his immortality;

he must live with himself for ever.   He has a depth within him unfathomable, an infinite abyss of existence; and the scene in which he bears part for the moment is but like a gleam of sunshine upon its surface.

Again : when we read history, we meet with accounts of great slaughters and massacres, great pestilences, famines, conflagrations, and so on; and here again we are accustomed in an especial way to regard collections of people as if individual units. We cannot understand that a multitude is a collection of immortal souls.

I say immortal souls : each of those multitudes, not only *had* while he was upon earth, but *has* a soul, which did in its own time but return to God who gave it, and not perish, and which now lives unto Him.   All those millions upon millions of human beings who ever trod the earth and saw the sun successively, are at this very moment in existence all together.   This, I think, you will grant we do not duly realize.   All those Canaanites, whom the children of Israel slew, every one of them is somewhere in the universe, now at this moment, where God has assigned him a place.   We read, "They utterly destroyed all that was in" Jericho, "young and old."   Again, as to Ai : "So it was that all that fell that day, both of men and women, were twelve thousand." Again, " Joshua took Makkedah, Libnah, Lachish, Eglon, Hebron, Debir, and smote them with the edge of the sword, and utterly destroyed all the souls that were therein."[1]   Every one of those souls still lives.   They had their separate thoughts and feelings when on earth, they have them now.   They had their likings and pursuits ; they gained what they thought good and enjoyed it ; and they still somewhere or other live, and what they then did in the flesh surely has its influence upon their present destiny.   They live, reserved for a day which is to come, when all nations shall stand before God.

But why should I speak of the devoted nations of Canaan, when Scripture speaks of a wider, more comprehensive judgment, and in one place appears to hint at the present state of awful waiting in which they are who were involved in it?   What an overwhelming judgment was the Flood !   all human beings on the earth but eight were cut off by it.   That old world of souls still lives, though its material tabernacle was drowned.   Scripture, I say, signifies this; obscurely indeed, yet still, as it appears, certainly.   St. Peter speaks of "the spirits in prison," that is, *then* in prison, who had been " disobedient," " when once the long-

[1] Jos. vi. viii. x.

suffering of God waited in the days of Noah." [1] Those many, many souls, who were violently expelled from their bodies by the waters of the deluge, were alive two thousand years afterwards, when St. Peter wrote. Surely they are alive still.

And so of all the other multitudes we anywhere read of.—All the Jews who perished in the siege of Jerusalem still live ; Sennacherib's army still lives ; Sennacherib himself still lives ; all the persecutors of the Church that ever were, are still alive. The kings of Babylon are still alive ; they are still, as they are described by the prophet, weak indeed now, and in "hell beneath," but having an account to give, and waiting for the day of summons. All who have ever gained a name in the world, all the mighty men of war that ever were, all the great statesmen, all the crafty counsellors, all the scheming aspirants, all the reckless adventurers, all the covetous traders, all the proud voluptuaries, are still in being, though helpless and unprofitable. Balaam, Saul, Joab, Ahithophel, good and bad, wise and ignorant, rich and poor, each has his separate place, each dwells by himself in that sphere of light or darkness, which he has provided for himself here. What a view this sheds upon history ! We are accustomed to read it as a tale or a fiction, and we forget that it concerns immortal beings, who cannot be swept away, who are what they were, however this earth may change.

And so again all the names we see written on monuments in churches or churchyards, all the writers whose names and works we see in libraries, all the workmen who raised the great buildings, far and near, which are the wonder of the world, they are all in God's remembrance, they all live.

It is the same with those whom we ourselves have seen, who now are departed. I do not now speak of those whom we have known and loved. These we cannot forget ; we cannot rid our memory of them : but I speak of all whom we have *ever* seen ; it is also true that they live. Where we know not, but live they do. We may recollect when children, perhaps, once seeing a certain person ; and it is almost like a dream to us now that we did. It seems like an accident which goes and is all over, like some creature of the moment, which has no existence beyond it. The rain falls, and the wind blows ; and showers and storms have no existence beyond the time when we felt them ; they are nothing in themselves. But if we have but once seen any child of Adam, we have seen an immortal soul. It has not passed away as a breeze or sunshine, but it lives ; it lives at this moment in one

[1] 1 Pet. iii. 20.

of those many places, whether of bliss or misery, in which all souls are reserved until the end.

Or again, let us call to mind those whom we knew a little better, though not intimately :—all who died suddenly or before their time, all whom we have seen in high health and spirits, all whom we have seen in circumstances which in any way brought out their characters, and gave them some place in our memories. They are gone from our sight, but they all live still, each with his own thoughts ; they are waiting for the judgment.

I think we shall see that these thoughts concerning others are not familiar to us ; yet no one can say they are not just. And I think too that the thoughts concerning others, which *are* familiar to us, are not those which become believers in the Gospel ; whereas these which I have been tracing do become us, as tending to make us think less of this world, with its hopes and fears, its plans, successes, and enjoyments.

Moreover, every one of all the souls which have ever been on earth is, as I have already implied, in one of two spiritual states, so distinct from one another, that the one is the subject of God's favour, and the other under His wrath ; the one on the way to eternal happiness, the other to eternal misery. This is true of the dead, and is true of the living also. All are tending one way or the other ; there is no middle or neutral state for any one ; though as far as the sight of the external world goes, all men seem to be in a middle state common to one and all. Yet, much as men look the same, and impossible as it is for us to say where each man stands in God's sight, there are two, and but two classes of men, and these have characters and destinies as far apart in their tendencies as light and darkness : this is the case even of those who are in the body, and it is much more true of those who have passed into the unseen state.

No thought of course is more overpowering than that every one who lives or has lived is destined for endless bliss or torment. It is far too vast for us to realize. But what especially increases the mind's confusion when it attempts to do so, is just this very thing which I have been mentioning, that there are but these two states, that every individual among us is either in one or the other,—that the states in which we individually are placed are so unspeakably contrary to each other, while we look so like each other. It is certainly quite beyond our understandings, that all we should now be living together as relatives, friends, associates, neighbours ; that we should be familiar or intimate with each other, that there should be among us a general intercourse, circulation of thought, interchange of good offices, the action of mind upon mind, and will upon will, and conduct upon conduct, and yet after all that there should be a bottomless gulf between us, running among us invisibly, and cutting us off into two parties;—not indeed a gulf impassable here, God be praised!—not impassable till we pass into the next world, still really existing, so that every person we meet is in God's unerring eye either on the one side or the other, and, did He please to take him hence at once, would find himself either in paradise or in the place of torment. Our Lord observes this concerning the Day of Judgment, "Two women shall be grinding at the mill; the one shall be taken, and the other left. Two men shall be in the field; the one shall be taken, and the other left."

What makes this thought still more solemn, is that we have reason to suppose that souls on the wrong side of the line are far more numerous than those on the right. It is wrong to speculate; but it is safe to be alarmed. This much we know, that Christ says expressly, "Many are called few are chosen;" "Broad is the way that leadeth to destruction, and many there be who go in thereat;" whereas "narrow is the way that leadeth to life, and few there be who find it."

If then it is difficult, as I have said it is, to realize that all who ever lived still live, it is as difficult at least to believe that they are in a state either of eternal rest or eternal woe; that all whom we have known and who are gone, are, and that we who still live, were we now to die, should then at once be either in the one state or the other. Nay, I will say more : when we think seriously on the subject, it is almost impossible to comprehend, I do not say that a great number, but that any person whom we see before us, however unsatisfactory appearances may be, is really under God's displeasure, and in a state of reprobation. So hard is it to live by faith ! People feel it to be a difficulty to have to admit certain other doctrines of the Church, which are more or less contrary to sight. For instance, they say as an argument against regeneration in Baptism, "Is it possible that all who have been baptized can have been born again, considering what lives they lead?" They make the evidence of sight tell against a doctrine which demands their faith. Yet, after all, is there anything more startling, more difficult to believe, than that any one person, whom we see, however sinful his life, is at present under God's eternal wrath, and would incur it if he were to die at once, and will incur it unless he repents ? This is what we cannot bring ourselves to believe. All we commonly allow is, that certain

persons are what we call "in *danger* of hell." Now, if by using
this cautious phrase we mean merely to express that irreligious
men may repent before death, or that men may seem to be
irreligious to us who are not so, and therefore that it is safer to
speak of men being in danger of God's wrath than actually under
it; so far is well. But we are in error if we mean, as is often
the case, to deny thereby that irreligious men, as such, whether
man can ascertain them or not, are at this very time not only in
danger, but actually under the power of God's wrath. Healthy
men in a sickly country may be said to be in danger of sickness;
soldiers in a battle are in danger of wounds; but irreligious men
not only hazard, but do lie under God's eternal curse; and when
we see an irreligious man, we see one who is under it, only we
speak guardedly, both as hoping that he may repent, and as feeling that we may be mistaken. But whether or not men may be
what they seem, or whether or not they are to change, certain it
is that every one who dies, passes at once into one or other of two
states; and if he dies unsanctified and unreconciled to God, into
a state of eternal misery.

How little the world at large realizes this, is shown by the
conduct of surviving friends after a loss. Let a person who is
taken away have been ever so notorious a sinner, ever so confirmed
a drunkard, ever so neglectful of Christian ordinances, and though
they have no reason for supposing anything hopeful was going
on in his mind, yet they will generally be found to believe that he
has gone to heaven; they will confidently talk of his being at
peace, of his pains being at an end, of his happy release, and the
like. They enlarge on these subjects; whereas their duty lies in
keeping silence, waiting in trembling hope, and being resigned.
Now, why is it they speak and think in this manner? Apparently
because they cannot conceive it possible that he or that they
should be lost. Even the worst men have qualities which endear
them to those who come near them. They have human affections
in some shape or other. Even the witch of Endor showed a
sympathy and kindness towards her guest which move us.
Human feelings cannot exist in hell, and we cannot bring ourselves
to think that they are subjects of hell who have them. And for
this reason men cannot admit the bare possibility of another being
lost; they reject the idea, and therefore, when a man dies, they
conclude, as the only alternative, that he must be in Abraham's
bosom; and they boldly say so, and they catch at some half
sentence which he said during his illness, when he was calmer or

weaker, or at the ease with which he died, in confirmation of their belief.

And if it is difficult to believe that there are any persons among us at this moment in a state of spiritual death, how shall we understand, what perchance is the case, that there are many such, perhaps multitudes? how shall we persuade ourselves of the great truth that, in spite of outward appearances, human society, as we find it, is but a part of an invisible world, and is really divided into but two companies, the sons of God and the children of the wicked one; that some souls are ministered unto by angels, others led captive by devils; that some are "fellow-citizens of the saints," and of the invisible "household of God," and others companions of those His enemies in time past, who now are waiting in prison for the judgment.

How blessed would it be if we really understood this! What a change it would produce in our thoughts, unless we were utterly reprobate, to understand what and where we are,—accountable beings on their trial, with God for their friend and the devil for their enemy, and advanced a certain way on their road either to heaven or to hell. No truths indeed, ever so awful, ever so fully brought home to the mind, will change it, if the love of God and of holiness be not there; but none among us, as we may humbly trust, is in this reprobate state. One wishes to think that no one has so done despite to the Spirit of grace, and so sinned against the Blood of the Covenant, as to have nothing of his regenerate nature left to him; no one among us, but, if he shut his eyes to the external world, and opened them to the world within him, contemplated his real state and prospects, and called to mind his past life, would be brought to repentance and amendment. Endeavour then, my brethren, to realize that you have souls, and pray God to enable you to do so. Endeavour to disengage your thoughts and opinions from the things that are seen; look at things as God looks at them, and judge of them as He judges. Pass a very few years, and you will actually experience what as yet you are called on to believe. There will be no need of the effort of mind to which I invite you when you have passed into the unseen state. There will be no need of shutting your eyes to this world when this world has vanished from you, and you have nothing before you but the throne of God, and the slow but continual movements about it in preparation of the judgment. In that interval, when you are in that vast receptacle of disembodied souls, what will be your thoughts about the world which you have left ! how poor will then seem to you its highest aims, how faint its keenest pleasures, compared with the eternal aims, the infinite pleasures, of which you will at length feel your souls to be capable ! O my brethren, let this thought be upon you day by day, especially when you are tempted to sin. Avoid sin as a serpent ; it looks and promises well ; it bites afterwards. It is dreadful in memory, dreadful even on earth ; but in that awful period, when the fever of life is over, and you are waiting in silence for the judgment, with nothing to distract your thoughts, who can say how dreadful may be the memory of sins done in the body ? Then the very apprehension of their punishment, when Christ shall suddenly visit, will doubtless outweigh a thousand-fold the gratification, such as it was, which you felt in committing them ; and if so, what will be the proportion between it and that punishment, if after all it be actually inflicted ? Let us lay to heart our Saviour's own most merciful words, " Be not afraid," He says, " of them that kill the body, and after that have no more that they can do. But I will forewarn you, whom ye shall fear. Fear Him, which, after He hath killed, hath power to cast into hell. Yea, I say unto you, Fear Him."

SERMON XVII.

(LENT.)

Life the Season of Repentance.

" And when Esau heard the words of his father, he cried with a great and exceeding bitter cry, and said unto his father, Bless me, even me also, O my father."—GEN. xxvii. 34.

I SUPPOSE no one can read this chapter without feeling some pity for Esau. He had expected that his father would give him his blessing, but his brother was beforehand with him and got the blessing instead. He did not know what had happened, and he came in to his father to be blessed, without any suspicion that he was not to be blessed. His father, full of amazement and distress, told him, that without knowing it, for he was blind and could not see, he had already given the blessing to his brother Jacob, and he could not recall it. On hearing this, Esau burst out into "a great and exceeding bitter cry," as the text expresses it. All his hopes were disappointed in a moment. He had built much upon this blessing. For Esau, when he was young, had committed a very great sin against God. He was his father's firstborn, and in those times, as now among the rich and noble, it was a great thing to be the eldest in a family. In Esau's case these privileges were the greater, for they were the direct gift of God. Esau, as being the eldest born of his father Isaac, inherited certain rights and privileges which Isaac, the long-expected heir of Abraham, had received from Abraham. Now Esau's sin, when he was a young man, had been this—he parted with his birthright to his younger brother Jacob. He thought lightly of God's great gift. How little he thought of it is plain by the price he took for it. Esau had been hunting, and he came home tired and faint. Jacob, who had remained at home, had some pottage ;

and Esau begged for some of it.   Jacob knew the worth of the
birthright, though Esau did not; he had faith to discern it.   So,
when Esau asked for pottage, he said he would give it to Esau in
exchange for his birthright; and Esau, caring nothing for the
birthright, sold it to Jacob for the mess of food.   This was a
great sin, as being a contempt of a special gift of God, a gift,
which, after his father Isaac, no one in the whole world had but he.

Time went on.   Esau got older; and understood more than
before the value of the gift which he had thus profanely surrendered.   Doubtless he would fain have got it back again if
he could; but that was impossible.   Under these circumstances,
as we find in the chapter which has been read in the course of
to-day's service, his father proposed to give him his solemn blessing before he died.   Now this blessing in those times carried great
weight with it, as being of the nature of a prophecy, and it had
been from the first divinely intended for Jacob; Esau had no
right to it, but he thought that in this way he should in a certain
sense get back his birthright, or what would stand in its place.
He had parted with it easily, and he expected to regain it easily.
Observe, he showed no repentance for what he had done, no self-
reproach; he had no fear that God would punish him.   He only
regretted his loss, without humbling himself; and he determined
to retrace his steps as quickly and quietly as he could.   He went
to hunt for venison, and dress it as savoury meat for his father,
as his father bade him.   And having got all ready, he came with
it and stood before his father.   Then was it that he learned, to
his misery, that God's gifts are not thus lightly to be treated; he
had sold, he could not recover.   He had hoped to have had his
father's blessing, but Jacob had received it instead.   He had
thought to regain God's favour, not by fasting and prayer, but
by savoury meat, by feasting and making merry.

Such seems, on the whole, St. Paul's account of the matter, in
his Epistle to the Hebrews.   After having given examples of
faith, he bids his Christian brethren beware lest there should be
any one among them like Esau, whom he calls a "profane
person;" as having thought and acted with so little of real
perception of things unseen; "looking diligently," he says, "lest
any man fail of the grace of God; lest there be any fornicator, or
profane person, as Esau, who for one morsel of meat sold his
birthright.   For ye know how that afterwards, when he would
have inherited the blessing, he was rejected; for he found no
place of repentance, though he sought it carefully with tears." [1]

[1] Heb. xii. 15-17.

This then is the meaning of Esau's great and bitter cry, which at first sight we are disposed to pity. It is the cry of one who has rejected God, and God in turn has rejected him. It is the cry of one who has trifled with God's mercies, and then sought to regain them when it was all too late. It is the cry of one who has not heeded the warning, "See that ye receive not the grace of God in vain," and who has "come short of the grace of God." [1] It is the cry predicted by the wise man, "Then shall they call upon Me, but I will not answer; they shall seek Me early, but they shall not find Me." [2] That subtilty and keenness of his brother Jacob, by which he got before him, and took the kingdom of heaven by violence, was God's act; it was God's providence punishing Esau for former sin. Esau had sinned; he had forfeited his birthright, and he could not get it back. That cry of his, what was it like? it was like the entreaty of the five foolish virgins when the door was shut, "Lord, Lord, open to us; but He answered and said, Verily, I say unto you, I know you not." [3] It was like "the weeping and gnashing of teeth" of lost souls. Yes, surely, a great and bitter cry it well might be. Well may they weep and cry, as they will most largely, who have received God's grace and done despite to it.

The mournful history then which I have been reviewing, is a description of one who was first profane and then presumptuous. Esau was profane in selling his birthright, he was presumptuous in claiming the blessing. Afterwards, indeed, he did repent, but when it was too late. And I fear such as Esau was of old time, such are too many Christians now. They despise God's blessings when they are young, and strong, and healthy; then, when they get old, or weak, or sick, they do not think of repenting, but they think they may take and enjoy the privileges of the Gospel as a matter of course, as if the sins of former years went for nothing. And then, perhaps, death comes upon them; and then after death, when it is too late, they would fain repent. Then they utter a great, bitter, and piercing cry to God; and when they see happy souls ascending towards heaven in the fulness of Gospel blessings, they say to their offended God, "Bless me, even me also, O my Father."

Is it not, I say, quite a common case for men and for women to neglect religion in their best days? They have been baptized, they have been taught their duty, they have been taught to pray, they know their Creed, their conscience has been enlightened, they have opportunity to come to Church. This is their birthright,

---

[1] 2 Cor. vi. 1.   [2] Prov. i. 28.   [3] Matt. xxv. 11, 12.

the privileges of their birth of water and of the Spirit; but they sell it, as Esau did.   They are tempted by Satan with some bribe of this world. and they give up their birthright in exchange for what is sure to perish, and to make them perish with it.   Esau was tempted by the mess of pottage which he saw in Jacob's hands. Satan arrested the eyes of his lust, and he gazed on the pottage, as Eve gazed on the fruit of the tree of knowledge of good and evil.   Adam and Eve sold their birthright for the fruit of a tree— that was their bargain.   Esau sold his for a mess of lentils—that was his.   And men nowadays often sell theirs, not indeed for anything so simple as fruit or herbs, but for some evil gain or other, which at the time they think worth purchasing at any price; perhaps for the enjoyment of some particular sin, or more commonly for the indulgence of general carelessness and spiritual sloth, because they do not like a strict life, and have no heart for God's service.   And thus they are profane persons, for they despise the great gift of God.

And then, when all is done and over, and their souls sold to Satan, they never seem to understand that they *have* parted with their birthright.   They think that they stand just where they did, before they followed the world, the flesh, and the devil; they take for granted that when they choose to become more decent, or more religious, they have all their privileges just as before.   Like Samson, they propose to go out as at other times before, and shake themselves.   And like Esau, instead of repenting for the loss of the birthright, they come, as a matter of course, for the blessing. Esau went out to hunt for venison gaily, and promptly brought it to his father.   His spirits were high, his voice was cheerful. It did not strike him that God was angry with him for what had passed years ago.   He thought he was as sure of the blessing as if he had *not* sold the birthright.

And then, alas! the truth flashed upon him; he uttered a great and bitter cry when it was too late.   It would have been well had he uttered it before he came for the blessing, not after it. He repented when it was too late—it had been well if he had repented in time.   So I say of persons who have in any way sinned. It is good for them not to forget that they have sinned. It is good that they should lament and deplore their past sins. Depend upon it, they will wail over them in the next world, if they wail not here.   Which is better, to utter a bitter cry now or then?—then, when the blessing of eternal life is refused them by the just Judge at the last day, or now, in order that they may gain it?   Let us be wise enough to have our agony in this world, not in the next. If we humble ourselves now, God will pardon us then. We cannot escape punishment, here or hereafter; we must take our choice, whether to suffer and mourn a little now, or much then.

Would you see how a penitent should come to God? turn to the parable of the Prodigal Son. He, too, had squandered away his birthright, as Esau did. He, too, came for the blessing, like Esau. Yes; but how differently he came! he came with deep confession and self-abasement. He said, "Father, I have sinned against heaven and before thee, and am no more worthy to be called thy son: make me as one of thy hired servants:" but Esau said, "Let my father arise, and eat of his son's venison, that thy soul may bless me." The one came for a son's privileges, the other for a servant's drudgery. The one killed and dressed his venison with his own hand, and enjoyed it not; for the other the fatted calf was prepared, and the ring for his hand, and shoes for his feet, and the best robe, and there was music and dancing.

These are thoughts, I need hardly say, especially suited to this season. From the earliest times down to this day, these weeks before Easter have been set apart every year for the particular remembrance and confession of our sins. From the first age downward, not a year has passed but Christians have been exhorted to reflect how far they have let go their birthright, as a preparation for their claiming the blessing. At Christmas we are born again with Christ; at Easter we keep the Eucharistic Feast. In Lent, by penance, we join the two great sacraments together. Are you, my brethren, prepared to say,—is there any single Christian alive who will dare to profess,—that he has not in greater or less degree sinned against God's free mercies as bestowed on him in Baptism without, or rather against his deserts? Who will say that he has so improved his birthright that the blessing is his fit reward, without either sin to confess, or wrath to deprecate? See, then, the Church offers you this season for the purpose. "Now is the accepted time, now the day of salvation." Now it is that, God being your helper, you are to attempt to throw off from you the heavy burden of past transgression, to reconcile yourselves to Him who has once already imparted to you His atoning merits, and you have profaned them.

And be sure of this: that if He has any love for you, if He sees aught of good in your soul, *He* will afflict you, if you will not afflict yourselves. He will not let you escape. He has ten thousand ways of purging those whom He has chosen from the dross and alloy with which the fine gold is defaced. He can bring diseases on you, or can visit you with misfortunes, or take away your friends, or oppress your minds with darkness, or refuse you strength to bear up against pain when it comes upon you. He can inflict on you a lingering and painful death. He can make "the bitterness of death pass" not. We, indeed, cannot decide in the case of others, when trouble is a punishment, and when not; yet this we know, that all sin brings affliction. We have no means of judging others, but we may judge ourselves. Let us judge ourselves, that we be not judged. Let us afflict ourselves, that God may not afflict us. Let us come before Him with our best offerings, that He may forgive us.

Such advice is especially suitable to an age like this, when there is an effort on all hands to multiply comforts, and to get rid of the daily inconveniences and distresses of life. Alas! my brethren, how do you know, if you avail yourselves of the luxuries of this world without restraint, but that you are only postponing, and increasing by postponing, an inevitable chastisement? How do you know, but that, if you will not satisfy the debt of daily sin now, it will hereafter come upon you with interest? See whether this is not a thought which would spoil that enjoyment which even religious persons are apt to take in this world's goods, if they would but admit it. It is said that we ought to enjoy this life as the gift of God. Easy circumstances are generally thought a special happiness; it is thought a great point to get rid of annoyance or discomfort of mind and body; it is thought allowable and suitable to make use of all means available for making life pleasant. We desire, and confess we desire, to make time pass agreeably, and to live in the sunshine. All things harsh and austere are carefully put aside. We shrink from the rude lap of earth, and the embrace of the elements, and we build ourselves houses in which the flesh may enjoy its lust, and the eye its pride. We aim at having all things at our will. Cold, and hunger, and hard lodging, and ill usage, and humble offices, and mean appearance, are all considered serious evils. And thus year follows year, to-morrow as to-day, till we think that this, our artificial life, is our natural state, and must and ever will be. But, O ye sons and daughters of men, what if this fair weather but ensure the storm afterwards? what if it be, that the nearer you attain to making yourselves as gods on earth now, the greater pain lies before you in time to come, or even (if it must be said), the more certain becomes your ruin when time is at an end? Come down, then, from your high chambers at this season to avert what else may be. Sinners as ye are, act at least like the prosperous heathen, who threw his choicest trinket into the water, that he might propitiate fortune. Let not the year go round and round without a break and interruption in its circle of pleasures. Give back some of God's gifts to God, that you may safely enjoy the rest. Fast, or watch, or abound in alms, or be instant in prayer, or deny yourselves society, or pleasant books, or easy clothing, or take on you some irksome task or employment; do one or other, or some, or all of these, unless you say that you have never sinned, and may go like Esau with a light heart to take your crown. Ever bear in mind that Day which will reveal all things, and will test all things "so as by fire," and which will bring us into judgment ere it lodges us in heaven.

And for those who have in any grievous way sinned or neglected God, I recommend such persons never to forget they *have* sinned; if they forget it not, God in mercy *will* forget it. I recommend them every day, morning and evening, to fall on their knees, and say, "Lord, forgive me my past sins." I recommend them to pray God to visit their sins in this world rather than in the next. I recommend them to go over their dreadful sins in their minds (unless, alas! it makes them sin afresh to do so), and to confess them to God again and again with great shame, and to entreat His pardon. I recommend them to look on all pain and sorrow which comes on them as a *punishment* for what they once were; and to take it patiently on that account, nay, joyfully, as giving them a hope that God *is* punishing them here instead of hereafter. If they have committed sins of uncleanness, and are now in narrow circumstances, or have undutiful children, let them take their present distress as God's merciful punishment. If they have lived to the world, and now have worldly anxieties, these anxieties are God's punishment. If they have led intemperate lives, and now are afflicted by any malady, this is God's punishment. Let them not cease to pray, under all circumstances, that God will pardon them, and give them back what they have lost. And thus, by God's grace, it shall be restored to them, and Esau's great and bitter cry never shall be theirs.

SERMON XVIII.

(LENT.)

Bodily Suffering.

" I fill up that which is behind of the afflictions of Christ in my flesh for
His body's sake, which is the Church."—COLOS. i. 24.

OUR Lord and Saviour Jesus Christ came by blood as well as by water, not only as a Fount of grace and truth—the source of spiritual light, joy, and salvation—but as a combatant with sin and Satan, who was "consecrated through suffering." He was, as prophecy had marked Him out, "red in His apparel, and His garments like Him that treadeth in the wine-fat;" or, in the words of the Apostle, "He was clothed with a vesture dipped in blood." It was the untold sufferings of the Eternal Word in our nature, His body dislocated and torn, His blood poured out, His soul violently separated by a painful death, which has put away from us the wrath of Him whose love sent Him for that very purpose. This only was our Atonement; no one shared in the work. He "trod the wine-press alone, and of the people there was none with Him." When lifted up upon the cursed tree, He fought with all the hosts of evil, and conquered by suffering.

Thus, in a most mysterious way, all that is needful for this sinful world, the life of our souls, the regeneration of our nature, all that is most joyful and glorious, hope, light, peace, spiritual freedom, holy influences, religious knowledge and strength, all flow from a fount of blood. A work of blood is our salvation; and we, as we would be saved, must draw near and gaze upon it in faith, and accept it as the way to heaven. We must take Him, who thus suffered, as our guide; we must embrace His sacred feet, and follow Him. No wonder, then, should we receive on ourselves some drops of the sacred agony which bedewed His garments ; no wonder, should we be sprinkled with the sorrows which He bore in expiation of our sins !

And so it has ever been in very deed ; to approach Him has been, from the first, to be partaker, more or less, in His sufferings ; I do not say in the case of every individual who believes in Him, but as regards the more conspicuous, the more favoured, His choice instruments, and His most active servants ; that is, it has been the lot of the Church, on the whole, and of those, on the whole, who had been most like Him, as rulers, intercessors, and teachers of the Church. He, indeed, alone meritoriously ; they, because they have been near Him. Thus, immediately upon His birth, He brought the sword upon the infants of His own age at Bethlehem. His very shadow, cast upon a city, where He did not abide, was stained with blood. His Blessed Mother had not clasped Him to her breast for many weeks ere she was warned of the penalty of that fearful privilege : " Yea, a sword shall pierce through thy own soul also." [1]   Virtue went out of Him ; but the water and the blood flowed together as afterwards from His pierced side. From among the infants He took up in His arms to bless, is said to have gone forth a chief martyr of the generation after Him. Most of His Apostles passed through lifelong sufferings to a violent death. In particular, when the favoured brothers, James and John, came to Him with a request that they might sit beside Him in His kingdom, He plainly stated this connection between nearness to Him and affliction. " Are ye able," He said, " to drink of the cup that I shall drink of, and to be baptized with the baptism that I am baptized with ? " [2]   As if He said, " Ye cannot have the sacraments of grace without the painful figures of them. The Cross, when imprinted on your foreheads, will draw blood. You shall receive, indeed, the baptism of the Spirit, and the cup of My communion, but it shall be with the attendant pledges of My cup of agony, and My baptism of blood." Elsewhere He speaks the same language to all who would partake the benefits of His death and passion : " Whosoever doth not bear his cross, and come after Me, cannot be My disciple." [3]

Accordingly, His Apostles frequently remind us of this necessary, though mysterious appointment, and bid us " think it not strange concerning the fiery trial which is to try us, as though some strange thing happened unto us, but to rejoice in having communion with the sufferings of Christ." [4]   St. Paul teaches us

[1] Luke ii. 35.
[3] Luke xiv. 27.
[2] Matt. xx. 22.
[4] 1 Pet. iv. 12, 13.

the same lesson in the text, in which he speaks of taking up the remnant of Christ's sorrows, as some precious mantle dropped from the Cross, and wearing it for His sake. " I rejoice in my sufferings for you, and fill up in my flesh what remains of the afflictions of Christ for His body's sake, that is, the Church." [1] And though he is speaking especially of persecution and other sufferings borne in the cause of the Gospel, yet it is our great privilege, as Scripture tells us, that all pain and trouble, borne in faith and patience, will be accounted as marks of Christ, grace-tokens from the absent Saviour, and will be accepted and rewarded for His sake at the last day. It declares generally, " When thou passest through the waters, I will be with thee; and through the rivers, they shall not overflow thee : when thou walkest through the fire, thou shalt not be burned ; neither shall the flame kindle upon thee." " Our light affliction, which is but for a moment, worketh for us a far more exceeding and eternal weight of glory." [2]

Thus the Gospel, which has shed light in so many ways upon the state of this world, has aided especially our view of the *sufferings* to which human nature is subjected; turning a punishment into a privilege, in the case of all pain, and especially of bodily pain, which is the most mysterious of all. Sorrow, anxiety, and disappointment are more or less connected with sin and sinners; but bodily pain is involuntary for the most part, stretching over the world by some external irresistible law, reaching to children who have never actually sinned, and to the brute animals, who are strangers to Adam's nature, while in its manifestations it is far more piteous and distressing than any other suffering. It is the lot of all of us, sooner or later; and that, perhaps in a measure which it would be appalling and wrong to anticipate, whether from disease, or from the casualties of life. And all of us at length must die ; and death is generally ushered in by disease, and ends in that separation of soul and body, which itself may, in some cases, involve peculiar pain.

Worldly men put such thoughts aside as gloomy; they can neither deny nor avert the prospect before them ; and they are wise, on their own principles, not to embitter the present by anticipating it. But Christians may bear to look at it without undue apprehension; for this very infliction, which most touches the heart and imagination, has (as I have said) been invested by Almighty God with a new and comfortable light, as being the medium of His choicest mercies towards us. Pain is no longer

---

[1] Vide also 2 Cor. iv. 10.   [2] Isa. xliii. 2 ; 2 Cor. iv. 17.

a curse, a necessary evil to be undergone with a dry submission or passive endurance—it may be considered even as a blessing of the Gospel, and being a blessing, admits of being met well or ill. In the way of nature, indeed, it seems to shut out the notion of duty, as if so masterful a discipline from without superseded the necessity or opportunity of self-mastery; but now that "Christ hath suffered in the flesh," we are bound "to arm ourselves with the same mind," and to obey, as He did, amid suffering.

In what follows, I shall remark briefly, first, on the natural effect of pain upon the mind; and next, upon the remedies and correctives of that effect which the knowledge of the Gospel supplies.

1. Now, as to its effect upon the mind, let it be well understood that it has no sanctifying influence in itself. Bad men are made worse by it. This should be borne in mind, lest we deceive ourselves; for sometimes we speak (at least the poor often so speak) as though present hardship and suffering were in some sense a ground of confidence in themselves as to our future prospects, whether as expiating our sins or bringing our hearts nearer to God. Nay, even the more religious among us may be misled to think that pain makes them better than it really does; for the effect of it at length, on any but very proud or ungovernable tempers, is to cause a languor and composure of mind, which looks like resignation, while it necessarily throws our reason upon the especial *thought* of God, our only stay in such times of trial. Doubtless it does really benefit the Christian, and in no scanty measure; and he may thank God who thus blesses it; only let him be cautious of *measuring* his spiritual state by the particular exercise of faith and love in his heart at the time, especially if that exercise be limited to the affections themselves, and have no opportunity of showing itself in works. St. Paul speaks of chastisement "yielding *afterwards* the peaceable fruit of righteousness,"[1] formed indeed and ripened at the moment, but manifested in due season. This may be the real fruit of the suffering of a deathbed, even though it may not have time to show itself to others before the Christian departs hence. Surely we may humbly hope that it perfects habits hitherto but partially formed, and blends the several graces of the Spirit more entirely. Such is the issue of it in *established* Christians;—but it *may* possibly effect nothing so blessed. Nay, in the case of those who have followed Christ with but a half heart, it may be a trial too strong for their feebleness, and may overpower them. This is a

---

[1] Heb. xii. 11.

dreadful reflection for those who put off the day of repentance. Well does our Church pray for us: "Suffer us not, at our last hour, for any pains of death to fall from Thee!" As for unbelievers, we know how it affects them, from such serious passages of Scripture as the following: "They gnawed their tongues for pain, and blasphemed the God of heaven because of their pains and their sores, and repented not of their deeds." [1]

Nay, I would go so far as to say, not only that pain does not commonly improve us, but that without care it has a strong tendency to do our souls harm, viz. by making us selfish; an effect produced even when it does us good in other ways. Weak health, for instance, instead of opening the heart, often makes a man supremely careful of his bodily ease and wellbeing. Men find an excuse in their infirmities for some extraordinary attention to their comforts; they consider they may fairly consult, on all occasions, their own convenience rather than that of another. They indulge their wayward wishes, allow themselves in indolence when they really might exert themselves, and think they may be fretful because they are weak. They become querulous, self-willed, fastidious, and egotistical. Bystanders, indeed, should be very cautious of thinking any particular sufferer to be thus minded, because, after all, sick people have a multitude of feelings which they cannot explain to any one else, and are often in the right in those matters in which they appear to others most fanciful or unreasonable. Yet this does not interfere with the correctness of my remark on the whole.

Take another instance under very different circumstances. If bodily suffering can be presented under distinct aspects, it is in the lassitude of a sickbed and in the hardships of the soldier's life. Yet of the latter we find selfishness almost a proverbial characteristic. Surely the life of soldiers on service is a very school of generosity and self-neglect, if rightly understood, and is used as such by the noble and high-principled; yet here, a low and carnal mind, instead of profiting by its advantages, will yield to the temptation of referring everything that befalls it to its own comfort and profit,—to secure its own interests, will become enshrined within it as its main duty, and with the greater plausibility, inasmuch as there is a sense in which it may really be so accounted. Others (it will suggest) must take care of themselves; it is a folly and weakness to think of them; there are but few chances of safety; the many must suffer, some unto death; it is wisdom to struggle for life and comfort, and to

[1] Rev. xvi. 10, 11.

dismiss the thought of others. Alas! instances occur, every now and then in the experience of life, which show that such thoughts and feelings are not peculiar to any one class of men, but are the actuating principles of the multitude. If an alarm of danger be given amid a crowd, the general eagerness for safety leads men to act towards each other with utter unconcern, if not with frantic cruelty. There are stories told of companies of men finding themselves at sea with scanty provisions, and of the shocking deeds which followed, when each was struggling to preserve his own life.

The natural effect, then, of pain and fear, is to individualize us in our own minds, to fix our thoughts on ourselves, to make us selfish. It is through pain, chiefly, that we realize to ourselves, even our bodily organs ; a frame entirely without painful sensations is (as it were) one whole without parts, and prefigures that future spiritual body which shall be the portion of the saints. And to this we most approximate in our youth, when we are not sensible that we are compacted of gross terrestrial matter, as advancing years convince us. The young reflect little upon themselves ; they gaze around them, and live out of doors, and say they have souls, little understanding their words. "They rejoice in their youth." This, then, is the effect of suffering, that it arrests us : that it puts, as it were, a finger upon us to ascertain for us our own individuality. But it does no more than this ; if such a warning does not lead us through the stirrings of our conscience heavenwards, it does but imprison us in ourselves and make us selfish.

2. Here, then, it is that the Gospel finds us ; heirs to a visitation, which, sooner or later, comes upon us, turning our thoughts from outward objects, and so tempting us to idolize self, to the dishonour of that God whom we ought to worship, and the neglect of man whom we should love as ourselves. Thus it finds us, and it obviates this danger, not by removing pain, but by giving it new associations. Pain, which by nature leads us only to ourselves, carries on the Christian mind from the thought of self to the contemplation of Christ, His passion, His merits, and His pattern ; and, thence, further to that united company of sufferers who follow Him and "are what He is in this world." He is the great Object of our faith ; and, while we gaze upon Him, we learn to forget ourselves.

Surely that is not the most fearful and hateful of evils, here below, however trying to the flesh, which Christ underwent voluntarily. No one chooses evil for its own sake, but for the greater good wrought out through it. He underwent it as for ends greater than the immediate removal of it, "not grudgingly or of necessity," but cheerfully doing God's will, as the Gospel history sets before us. When His time was come, we are told, "He steadfastly set His face to go to Jerusalem." His disciples said, "Master, the Jews of late sought to stone Thee, and goest Thou thither again?" but He persisted. Again, He said to Judas, "That thou doest, do quickly." He proceeded to the garden beyond Cedron, though Judas knew the place; and when the band of officers came to seize Him, "He went forth, and said unto them, I am He." [1] And with what calmness and majesty did He bear His sufferings, when they came upon Him, though by His agony in the garden He showed He fully felt their keenness! The Psalmist, in his prediction of them, says, "I am poured out like water, and all my bones are out of joint; my heart is like wax, it is melted;" [2] describing, as it would seem, that sinking of spirit and enfeebling of nerve which severe pain causes. Yet, in the midst of distress which seemed to preclude the opportunity of obedience, He was "about His Father's business," even more diligently than when in His childhood He asked questions of the doctors in the Temple; not thinking to be merely passive under the trial, but accounting it as if a great occasion for a noble and severe surrender of Himself to His Father's will. Thus He "learned obedience by the things that He suffered." Consider the deep and serene compassion which led Him to pray for those who crucified Him; His solicitous care of His Mother; and His pardoning words addressed to the robber who suffered with Him. And so, when He said, "It is finished," He showed that He was still contemplating, with a clear intellect, "the travail of His soul, and was satisfied;" and in the solemn surrender of Himself into His Father's hand, He showed where His mind rested in the midst of its darkness. Even when He seemed to be thinking of Himself, and said, "I thirst," He really was regarding the words of prophecy, and was bent on vindicating, to the very letter, the divine announcements concerning Him. Thus, upon the Cross itself, we discern in Him the mercy of a Messenger from heaven, the love and grace of a Saviour, the dutifulness of a Son, the faith of a created nature, and the zeal of a servant of God. His mind was stayed upon His Father's sovereign will and infinite perfections, yet could pass, without effort, to the claim of filial duty, or the need of an individual sinner. Six out of His seven last words were words of faith and

---

[1] Luke ix. 51; John xi. 8; xiii. 27; xviii. 2, 4, 5.   [2] Ps. xxii. 14.

love. For one instant a horrible dread overwhelmed Him, when He seemed to ask why God had forsaken Him. Doubtless "that voice was for our sakes;" as when He made mention of His thirst; and, like the other, was taken from inspired prophecy. Perhaps it was intended to set before us an example of a special trial to which human nature is subject, whatever was the real and inscrutable manner of it in Him, who was all along supported by an inherent Divinity; I mean the trial of sharp agony, hurrying the mind on to vague terrors and strange inexplicable thoughts; and is, therefore, graciously recorded for our benefit, in the history of His death, "who was tempted in all points like as we are, yet without sin."[1]

Such, then, were our Lord's sufferings, voluntarily undergone, and ennobled by an active obedience; themselves the centre of our hopes and worship, yet borne without thought of self, towards God and for man. And who, among us, habitually dwells upon them, but is led, without deliberate purpose, by the very warmth of gratitude and adoring love, to attempt bearing his own inferior trials in the same heavenly mind? Who does not see that to bear pain well is to meet it courageously, not to shrink or waver, but to pray for God's help, then to look at it steadfastly, to summon what nerve we have of mind and body, to receive its attack, and to bear up against it (while strength is given us) as against some visible enemy in close combat? Who will not acknowledge that, when sent to us, we must make its presence (as it were) our own voluntary act, by the cheerful and ready concurrence of our own will with the will of God? Nay, who is there but must own that with Christ's sufferings before us, pain and tribulation are, after all, not only the most blessed, but even the most congruous attendants upon those who are called to inherit the benefit of them? Most congruous, I say, not as though necessary, but as most natural and befitting, harmonizing most fully with the main Object in the group of sacred wonders on which the Church is called to gaze. Who, on the other hand, does not at least perceive that all the glare and gaudiness of this world, its excitements, its keenly-pursued goods, its successes and its transports, its pomps and its luxuries, are not in character with that pale and solemn scene which faith must ever have in its eye? What Christian will not own that to "reign as kings," and to be "full," is not his calling; so as to derive comfort in the hour of sickness, or bereavement, or other affliction, from the thought that he is now in his own place, if he be Christ's, in his

[1] Heb. iv. 15

true home, the sepulchre in which his Lord was laid? So deeply have His saints felt this, that when times were peaceful, and the Church was in safety, they could not rest in the lap of ease, and have secured to themselves hardnesses, lest the world should corrupt them. They could not bear to see the much-enduring Paul adding to his necessary tribulations a self-inflicted chastisement of the flesh, and yet allow themselves to live delicately, and fare sumptuously every day. They saw the image of Christ reflected in tears and blood, in the glorious company of the Apostles, the goodly fellowship of the Prophets, and the noble army of Martyrs; they read in prophecy of the doom of the Church, as "a woman fed by God in the wilderness," [1] and her witnesses as "clothed in sackcloth;" and they could not believe that they were meant for nothing more than to enjoy the pleasures of this life, however innocent and moderate might be their use of them. Without deciding about their neighbours, they felt themselves called to higher things; their own sense of the duty became the sanction and witness of it. They considered that God, at least, would afflict them in His love, if they spared themselves ever so much. The thorn in the flesh, the buffetings of Satan, the bereavement of their eyes, these were their portion; and, in common prudence, were there no higher thought, they could not live out of time and measure with these expected visitations. With no superstitious alarms, or cowardly imaginations, or senseless hurrying into difficulty or trial, but calmly and in faith, they surrendered themselves into His hands, who had told them in His inspired Word that affliction was to be their familiar food; till at length they gained such distaste for the luxuries of life as to be impatient of them from their very fulness of grace.

Even in these days, when the "fine gold has become dim," such has been the mind of those we most revere.[2] But such was it especially in primitive times. It was the temper, too, of those Apostles who were removed, more than their brethren, from the world's buffetings; as if the prospect of suffering afterwards were no ground of dispensation for a present self-inflicted discipline, but rather demanded it. St. James the Less was Bishop of Jerusalem, and was highly venerated for his uprightness by the unbelieving Jews among whom he lived unmolested.

---

[1] Vide Rev. xii. 6; xi. 3.

[2] "It is a most miserable state for a man to have everything according to his desire, and quietly to enjoy the pleasures of life. There needs no more to expose him to eternal misery."—BISHOP WILSON, *Sacra Privata,* *Wednesday.*

We are told that he drank no wine nor strong drink, nor did he eat any animal food, nor indulge in the luxury of the bath. "So often was he in the Temple on his knees, that they were thin and hard by his continual supplication."[1] Thus he kept his "loins girded about, and his lamp burning," for the blessed martyrdom which was to end his course. Could it be otherwise? How could the great Apostle, sitting at home by his Lord's decree, "nourish his heart," as he calls it, "as for the slaughter"? How could he eat, and drink, and live as other men, when "the Ark, and Israel, and Judah were in tents," encamped in the open fields, and one by one God's chosen warriors were falling before the brief triumph of Satan! How could he be "delicate on the earth, and wanton," when Paul and Barnabas, Peter, too, and John were in stripes and prisons, in labours and perils, in hunger and thirst, in cold and nakedness! Stephen had led the army of martyrs in Jerusalem itself, which was his own post of service. James, the brother of John, had followed him in the same city; he first of the Apostles tasting our Lord's cup, who had unwittingly asked to drink it. And if this was the feeling of the Apostles when in temporary safety, why is it not ours, who altogether live at ease, except that we have not faith enough to realize what is past? Could we see the Cross upon Calvary, and the list of sufferers who resisted unto blood in the times that followed it, is it possible that we should feel surprise when pain overtook us, or impatience at its continuance? Is it strange though we are smitten by ever so new a plague? Is it grievous that the Cross presses on one nerve or limb ever so many years till hope of relief is gone? Is it, indeed, not possible with the Apostle to rejoice in "bearing in our body the marks of the Lord Jesus"? And much more, can we, for very shame's sake, suffer ourselves to be troubled at what is but ordinary pain, to be irritated or saddened, made gloomy or anxious by inconveniences which never could surprise or unsettle those who had studied and understood their place as servants of a crucified Lord?

Let us, then, determine with cheerful hearts to sacrifice unto the Lord our God our comforts and pleasures, however innocent, when He calls for them, whether for the purposes of His Church, or in His own inscrutable Providence. Let us lend to Him a few short hours of present ease, and we shall receive our own with abundant usury in the day of His coming. There is a Treasury in heaven stored with such offerings as the natural man abhors; with sighs and tears, wounds and blood, torture and death.

EUSEB. *Hist.* ii. 23.

The martyrs first began the contribution, and we all may follow them; all of us, for every suffering, great or little, may, like the widow's mite, be sacrificed in faith to Him who sent it. Christ gave us the words of consecration when He for an ensample said, "Thy will be done." Henceforth, as the Apostle speaks, we may "glory in tribulation," as the seed of future glory.

Meanwhile, let us never forget in all we suffer, that, properly speaking, our own sin is the cause of it, and it is only by Christ's mercy that we are allowed to range ourselves at His side. We who are children of wrath, are made through Him children of grace; and our pains—which are in themselves but foretastes of hell—are changed by the sprinkling of His blood into a preparation for heaven.

SERMON XIX.

(LENT.)

Tears of Christ at the Grave of Lazarus.

"Jesus said, Where have ye laid him? They said unto Him, Lord, come and see. Jesus wept. Then said the Jews, Behold how He loved him."
—JOHN xi. 34-36.

ON first reading these words the question naturally arises in the mind, *Why* did our Lord weep at the grave of Lazarus? He knew He had power to raise him, why should He act the part of those who sorrow for the dead? In attempting any answer to this inquiry, we should ever remember that the thoughts of our Saviour's mind are far beyond our comprehension. Hardly do we enter into the feelings and meaning of men like ourselves, who are gifted with any special talent; even human philosophers or poets are obscure from the depth of their conceptions. What then must be the marvellous abyss of love and understanding in Him who, though partaker of our nature, is the Son of God?

This, indeed, is evident, as a matter of fact, on the face of the Scripture record, as any one may see who will take the trouble to inspect it. It is not, for instance, the text alone which raises a question; but the whole narrative in which it occurs exhibits our Saviour's conduct in various lights, which it is difficult for weak creatures, such as we are, properly to blend together.

When He first received the news of Lazarus's illness, "He abode two days still in the same place where He was." Then telling His disciples that Lazarus was dead, He said He was "glad for their sake that He was not there;" and said that He would "go and awaken him out of sleep." Then, when He was come to Bethany, where Lazarus dwelt, He was so moved by the sorrow of the Jews, that "He groaned in the spirit and was troubled." Lastly, in spite of His perturbation and weeping, presently He raised Lazarus.

I say, it is remarkable that such difficulties as these should lie on the face of Scripture, quite independently of those arising from the comparison of the texts in question with the doctrine of His divine nature. We know, indeed, there are insuperable mysteries involved in the union of His divine with His human attributes, which seem incompatible with each other; for instance, how He should be ever-blessed, and yet weep—all-knowing, yet apparently ignorant; but, without entering into the consideration of the mysteries of faith, commonly so called, it is worth inquiring whether the very surface of the sacred history does not contain seeming inconsistencies, of a nature to prepare us for such other difficulties as may lie from a deeper comparison of history with doctrine.

As another instance of the discrepancy I speak of, consider our Saviour's words according to the received versions, "Sleep on now, and take your rest;" and immediately after, "Rise, let us be going."[1]

So again, "He that hath no sword, let him sell his garment and buy one;" then follows, "Lord, behold, here are two swords. And He said, It is enough;" lastly, when Peter used his sword, "Put up again thy sword into his place: for all they that take the sword shall perish with the sword."[2]

I am not saying that we cannot possibly remove any part of the seeming opposition between such passages, but only that on the whole there is quite enough in the narrative to show that He who speaks is not one whose thoughts it is easy to get possession of; that it is no light matter to put one's self, even in part, into the position of His mind, and to state under what feelings and motives He said this or that; in a word, I wish to impress upon you, that our Saviour's words are not of a nature to be heard once and no more, but that to understand them we must feed upon them, and live in them, as if by little and little growing into their meaning.

It would be well if we understood the necessity of this more than we do. It is very much the fashion at present to regard the Saviour of the world in an irreverent and unreal way—as a mere idea or vision; to speak of Him so narrowly and unfruitfully, as if we only knew of His name; though Scripture has set Him before us in His actual sojourn on earth, in His gestures, words, and deeds, in order that we may have that on which to

[1] Matt. xxvi. 45, 46.   [2] Luke xxii. 36, 38; Matt. xxvi. 52.

fix our eyes. And till we learn to do this, to leave off vague statements about His love, His willingness to receive the sinner, His imparting repentance and spiritual aid, and the like, and view Him in His particular and actual works, set before us in Scripture, surely we have not derived from the Gospels that very benefit which they are intended to convey. Nay, we are in some danger, perhaps, even as regards our faith; for, it is to be feared, while the thought of Christ is but a creation of our minds, it may gradually be changed or fade away, it may become defective or perverted; whereas, when we contemplate Christ as manifested in the Gospels, the Christ who exists therein, external to our own imaginings, and who is as really a living being, and sojourned on earth as truly as any of us, then we shall at length believe in Him with a conviction, a confidence, and an entireness, which can no more be annihilated than the belief in our senses. It is impossible for a Christian mind to meditate on the Gospels without feeling, beyond all manner of doubt, that He who is the subject of them is God; but it is very possible to speak in a vague way of His love towards us, and to use the name of Christ, yet not at all to realize that He is the Living Son of the Father, or to have any anchor for our faith within us, so as to be fortified against the risk of future defection.

I will say a few words then under this impression, and with the reverent thoughts before me with which I began, by way of comment on our Saviour's weeping at Lazarus's grave; or, rather, I will suggest what each of you may, please God, improve for himself.

What led our Lord to weep over the dead, who could at a word restore him, nay, had it in purpose so to do?

1. First of all, as the context informs us, He wept from very sympathy with the grief of others. "When Jesus saw Mary weeping, and the Jews also weeping which came with her, He groaned in the spirit, and was troubled." It is the very nature of compassion or sympathy, as the word implies, to "rejoice with those who rejoice, and weep with those who weep." We know it is so with men; and God tells us He also is compassionate, and full of tender mercy. Yet we do not well know what this means, for how can God rejoice or grieve? By the very perfection of His nature Almighty God cannot show sympathy, at least to the comprehension of beings of such limited minds as ours. He, indeed, is hid from us; but if we were allowed to see Him, how could we discern in the Eternal and Unchangeable signs of sympathy? Words and works of sympathy He does display to

L

us; but it is the very sight of sympathy in another that affects and comforts the sufferer more even than the fruits of it. Now we cannot see God's sympathy; and the Son of God, though feeling for us as great compassion as His Father, did not show it to us while He remained in His Father's bosom. But when He took flesh and appeared on earth, He showed us the Godhead in a new manifestation. He invested Himself with a new set of attributes, those of our flesh, taking into Him a human soul and body, in order that thoughts, feelings, affections, might be His, which could respond to ours and certify to us His tender mercy. When, then, our Saviour weeps from sympathy at Mary's tears, let us not say it is the love of a man overcome by natural feeling. It is the love of God, the bowels of compassion of the Almighty and Eternal, condescending to show it as we are capable of receiving it, in the form of human nature.

Jesus wept, therefore, not merely from the deep thoughts of His understanding, but from spontaneous tenderness; from the gentleness and mercy, the encompassing loving-kindness and exuberant fostering affection of the Son of God for His own work, the race of man. Their tears touched Him at once, as their miseries had brought Him down from heaven. His ear was open to them, and the sound of weeping went at once to His heart.

2. But next, we may suppose (if it is allowable to conjecture), that His pity, thus spontaneously excited, was led forward to dwell on the various circumstances in man's condition which excite pity. It was awakened, and began to look around upon the miseries of the world. What was it He saw? He saw visibly displayed the *victory of death;* a mourning multitude—everything present which might waken sorrow except him who was the chief object of it. He was not—a stone marked the place where he lay. Martha and Mary, whom He had known and loved in their brother's company, now solitary, approached Him, first one and then the other, in far other mood and circumstance than heretofore—in deep affliction! in faith indeed and resignation, yet, apparently, with somewhat of a tender complaint: " Lord, if Thou hadst been here, my brother had not died." Such has been the judgment passed, or the doubt raised, concerning Him, in the breast of the creature in every age. Men have seen sin and misery around them, and, whether in faith or unbelief, have said, " If Thou hadst been here," if Thou hadst interfered, it might have been otherwise. Here, then, was the Creator surrounded by the works of His hands, who adored Him indeed, yet seemed to ask why He suffered what He Himself had

made so to be marred. Here was the Creator of the world at a scene of death, seeing the issue of His gracious handiwork. Would not He revert in thought to the hour of creation, when He went forth from the bosom of the Father to bring all things into existence? There had been a day when He had looked upon the work of His love, and seen that it was "very good." Whence had the good been turned to evil, the fine gold become dim? "An enemy had done this." Why it was allowed, and how achieved, was a secret with Him; a secret from all who were about Him, as it is a secret to us at this day. Here He had incommunicable thoughts with His Eternal Father. He would not tell them why it was; He chose another course for taking away their doubts and complaints. "He opened not His mouth," but He wrought wondrously. What He has done for all believers, revealing His atoning death yet not explaining it, this He did for Martha and Mary also, proceeding to the grave in silence, to raise their brother, while they complained that he had been allowed to die.

Here then, I say, were abundant sources for His grief (if we may be permitted to trace them), in the contrast between Adam, in the day in which he was created, innocent and immortal, and man as the devil had made him, full of the poison of sin and the breath of the grave; and again, in the timid complaint of His sorrowing friends that that change had been permitted. And though He was about to turn back the scene of sorrow into joy again, yet, after all, Lazarus one day must die again—He was but delaying the fulfilment of His own decree. A stone lay upon him now; and, though he was raised from the grave, yet, by His own inscrutable law, one day he must lie down again in it. It was a respite, not a resurrection.

3. Here I have suggested another thought which admits of being dwelt upon. Christ was come to do a deed of mercy, and it was a secret in His own breast. All the love which He felt for Lazarus was a secret from others. He was conscious to Himself He loved him; but none could tell but He how earnest that affection was. Peter, when his love for Christ was doubted, found a relief in an appeal to Himself: "Lord, Thou knowest all things: Thou knowest that I love Thee."[1] But Christ had no earthly friend who could be His confidant in this matter; and, as His thoughts turned on Lazarus, and His heart yearned towards him, was He not in Joseph's case, who not in grief, but from the very fulness of his soul, and his desolateness in a heathen land, when

[1] John xxi. 17.

his brethren stood before him, "sought where to weep," as if his own tears were his best companions, and had in them a sympathy to soothe that pain which none could share? Was He not in the case of a parent hanging over an infant, and weeping upon it, from the very thought of its helplessness and insensibility to the love poured out upon it? But the parent weeps from the feeling of her weakness to defend it; knowing that what is now a child must grow up and take its own course, and (whether for earthly or heavenly good) must depend, not on her, but on the Creator and on itself. Christ's was a different contemplation; yet attended with its own peculiar emotion. I mean the feeling that He *had* power to raise up Lazarus. Joseph wept, as having a secret, not only of the past, but of the future ;—of good in store as well as of evil done—of good which it was in his own power to confer. And our Lord and Saviour knew that, while all seemed so dreary and hopeless, in spite of the tears and laments of his friends, in spite of the corpse four days old, of the grave and the stone which was upon it, He had a spell which could overcome death, and He was about to use it. Is there any time more affecting than when you are about to break good news to a friend who has been stricken down by tidings of ill ?

4. Alas ! there were other thoughts still to call forth His tears. This marvellous benefit to the forlorn sisters, how was it to be attained ? at His own cost. Joseph knew he could bring joy to his brethren, but at no sacrifice of his own. Christ was bringing life to the dead by His own death. His disciples would have dissuaded Him from going into Judea, *lest* the Jews should kill Him. Their apprehension was fulfilled. He went to raise Lazarus, and the fame of that miracle was the immediate cause of His seizure and crucifixion. This He knew beforehand, He saw the prospect before Him; He saw Lazarus raised ; the supper in Martha's house ; Lazarus sitting at table ; joy on all sides of Him ; Mary honouring her Lord on this festive occasion by the outpouring of the very costly ointment upon His feet ; the Jews crowding not only to see Him, but Lazarus also ; His triumphant entry into Jerusalem ; the multitude shouting Hosanna ; the people testifying to the raising of Lazarus ; the Greeks, who had come up to worship at the feast, earnest to see Him ; the children joining in the general joy ; and then the Pharisees plotting against Him, Judas betraying Him, His friends deserting Him, and the cross receiving Him. These things doubtless, among a multitude of thoughts unspeakable, passed over His mind. He felt that Lazarus was wakening to life at His own sacrifice ; that

He was descending into the grave which Lazarus left. He felt that Lazarus was to live and He to die; the appearance of things was to be reversed; the feast was to be kept in Martha's house, but the last passover of sorrow remained for Him. And He knew that this reverse was altogether voluntary with Him. He had come down from His Father's bosom to be an Atonement of blood for all sin, and thereby to raise all believers from the grave, as He was then about to raise Lazarus; and to raise them, not for a time, but for eternity; and now the sharp trial lay before Him, through which He was to "open the kingdom of heaven to all believers." Contemplating then the fulness of His purpose while now going about a single act of mercy, He said to Martha, "I am the Resurrection and the Life: he that believeth in Me, though he were dead, yet shall he live, and whosoever liveth and believeth in Me, shall never die."

Let us take to ourselves these comfortable thoughts, both in the contemplation of our own death, or upon the death of our friends. Wherever faith in Christ is, there is Christ Himself. He said to Martha, "Believest thou this?" Wherever there is a heart to answer, "Lord, I believe," there Christ is present. There our Lord vouchsafes to stand, though unseen—whether over the bed of death or over the grave; whether we ourselves are sinking or those who are dear to us. Blessed be His Name! nothing can rob us of this consolation: we will be as certain, through His grace, that He is standing over us in love, as though we saw Him. We will not, after our experience of Lazarus's history, doubt an instant that He is thoughtful about us. He knows the beginnings of our illness, though He keeps at a distance. He knows when to remain away and when to draw near. He notes down the advances of it, and the stages. He tells truly when His friend Lazarus is sick and when he sleeps. We all have experience of this in the narrative before us, and henceforth, so be it! will never complain at the course of His providence. Only, we will beg of Him an increase of faith;—a more lively perception of the curse under which the world lies, and of our own personal demerits, a more understanding view of the mystery of His Cross, a more devout and implicit reliance on the virtue of it, and a more confident persuasion that He will never put upon us more than we can bear, never afflict His brethren with any woe except for their own highest benefit.

SERMON XX.

(LENT.)

Christ's Privations a Meditation for Christians.

*" Ye know the grace of our Lord Jesus Christ, that, though He was rich,
yet for your sakes He became poor, that ye through His poverty might
be rich."*—2 Cor. viii. 9.

AS time goes on, and Easter draws nearer, we are called upon
not only to mourn over our sins, but especially over the
various sufferings which Christ our Lord and Saviour underwent
on account of them. Why is it, my brethren, that we have so
little feeling on the matter as we commonly have? Why is it
that we are used to let the season come and go just like any other
season, not thinking more of Christ than at other times, or, at
least, not feeling more? Am I not right in saying that this is
the case? and if so, have I not cause for asking why it is the
case? We are not moved when we hear of the bitter passion
of Jesus Christ, the Son of God, for us. We neither bewail our
sins which caused it, nor have any sympathy with it. We do not
suffer *with* Him. If we come to church, we hear, and then we
go away again; not distressed at all; or if distressed, only for the
moment. And many do not come to church at all; and to them,
of course, this holy and solemn time is like other times. They
eat, and drink, and sleep, and rise up, and go about their business
and their pleasure, just as usual. They do not carry the thought
of Him who died for them along with them,—with them
wherever they are,—with them "whether they eat, or drink, or
whatever they do." They in no sense "live," to use St. Paul's
words, "by the faith of the Son of God, who loved them and
gave Himself for them."

This, alas! cannot be denied. Yet, if it be so, that the Son of

God came down from heaven, put aside His glory, and submitted to be despised, cruelly treated, and put to death by His own creatures,—by those whom He had made, and whom He had preserved up to that day, and was then upholding in life and being,—is it reasonable that so great an event should not move us? Does it not stand to reason that we must be in a very irreligious state of mind, unless we have some little gratitude, some little sympathy, some little love, some little awe, some little self-reproach, some little self-abasement, some little repentance, some little desire of amendment, in consequence of what He has done and suffered for us? Or, rather, may not so great a Benefactor demand of us some overflowing gratitude, keen sympathy, fervent love, profound awe, bitter self-reproach, earnest repentance, eager desire and longing after a new heart? Who can deny all this? Why then, O my brethren, is it not so? why are things with us as they are? Alas! I sorrowfully foretell that time will go on, and Passion-tide, Good Friday, and Easter Day will pass by, and the weeks after it, and many of you will be just what you were—not at all nearer heaven, not at all nearer Christ in your hearts and lives, not impressed lastingly or savingly with the thought of His mercies and your own sins and demerits.

But why is this? why do you so little understand the Gospel of your salvation? why are your eyes so dim, and your ears so hard of hearing? why have you so little faith? so little of heaven in your hearts? For this one reason, my brethren, if I must express my meaning in one word, because you so little *meditate.* You do not meditate, and therefore you are not impressed.

What is meditating on Christ? it is simply this, thinking habitually and constantly of Him and of His deeds and sufferings. It is to have Him before our minds as One whom we may contemplate, worship, and address when we rise up, when we lie down, when we eat and drink, when we are at home and abroad, when we are working, or walking, or at rest, when we are alone, and again when we are in company; this is meditating. And by this, and nothing short of this, will our hearts come to feel as they ought. We have stony hearts, hearts as hard as the highways; the history of Christ makes no impression on them. And yet, if we would be saved, we must have tender, sensitive, living hearts; our hearts must be broken, must be broken up like ground, and dug, and watered, and tended, and cultivated, till they become as gardens, gardens of Eden, acceptable to our God, gardens in which the Lord God may walk and dwell; filled, not with briers and thorns, but with all sweet-smelling and useful plants, with heavenly trees and flowers. The dry and barren waste must burst forth into springs of living water. This change must take place in our hearts if we would be saved; in a word, we must have what we have not by nature, faith, and love; and how is this to be effected, under God's grace, but by godly and practical meditation through the day?

St. Peter describes what I mean, when he says, speaking of Christ, "Whom having not seen ye love: in whom, though now ye see Him not, yet believing, ye rejoice with joy unspeakable and full of glory."[1]

Christ is gone away; He is not seen; we never saw Him, we only read and hear of Him. It is an old saying, "Out of sight, out of mind." Be sure, so it *will* be, so it *must* be with us, as regards our blessed Saviour, unless we make continual efforts all through the day to think of Him, His love, His precepts, His gifts, and His promises. We must recall to mind what we read in the Gospels and in holy books about Him; we must bring before us what we have heard in church; we must pray God to enable us to do so, to bless the doing so, and to make us do so in a simple-minded, sincere, and reverential spirit. In a word, we must meditate, for all this is meditation; and this even the most unlearned person can do, and will do, if he has a will to do it.

Now of such meditation, or thinking over Christ's deeds and sufferings, I will say two things; the first of which would be too plain to mention, except that, did I not mention it, I might seem to forget it, whereas I grant it. It is this: that such meditation is not at all pleasant at first. I know it; people will find it at first very irksome, and their minds will gladly slip away to other subjects. True: but consider, if Christ thought your salvation worth the great sacrifice of voluntary sufferings for you, should not you think (what is your own concern) your own salvation worth the slight sacrifice of learning to meditate upon those sufferings? Can a less thing be asked of you, than, when He has done the work, that you should only have to believe in it and accept it?

And my second remark is this: that it is only by slow degrees that meditation is able to soften our hard hearts, and that the history of Christ's trials and sorrows really moves us. It is not once thinking of Christ or twice thinking of Christ that will do it. It is by going on quietly and steadily, with the thought of Him in our mind's eye, that by little and little we shall gain

[1] 1 Pet. i. 8.

something of warmth, light, life, and love. We shall not perceive ourselves changing. It will be like the unfolding of the leaves in spring. You do not see them grow; you cannot, by watching, detect it. But every day, as it passes, has done something for them; and you are able, perhaps, every morning to say that they are more advanced than yesterday. So is it with our souls; not indeed every morning, but at certain periods, we are able to see that we are more alive and religious than we were, though during the interval we were not conscious that we were advancing.

Now, then, as if by way of specimen, I will say a few words upon the voluntary self-abasement of Christ, to suggest to you thoughts, which you ought, indeed, to bear about you at all times, but especially at this most holy season of the year; thoughts which will in their poor measure (please God) prepare you for seeing Christ in heaven, and, in the meanwhile, will prepare you for seeing Him in His Easter Festival. Easter Day comes but once a year; it is short, like other days. O that we may make much of it, that we may make the most of it, that we may enjoy it! O that it may not pass over like other days, and leave us no fragrance after it to remind us of it!

Come then, my brethren, at this time, before the solemn days are present, and let us review some of the privations of the Son of God made man, which should be your meditation through these holy weeks.

And, chiefly, He seems to speak to the poor. He came in *poverty*. St. Paul says, in the text, " Ye know the grace of our Lord Jesus Christ, that though He was rich, yet for your sakes He became poor, that ye through His poverty might be rich." Let not the poor suppose that their hardships are their own only, and that no one else ever felt them. The Most High God, God the Son, who had reigned with the Father from everlasting, supremely blessed, He, ever He, became a poor man, and suffered the hardships of the poor. What are their hardships? I suppose such as these :—that they have bad lodging, bad clothing, not enough to eat, or of a poor kind, that they have few pleasures or amusements, that they are despised, that they are dependent upon others for their living, and that they have no prospects for the future. Now how was it with Christ, the Son of the Living God? Where was He born? In a stable. I suppose not many men suffer an indignity so great; born, not in quiet and comfort, but amid the brute cattle; and what was His first cradle, if I may so call it? a manger. Such were the beginnings of His earthly life; nor did His condition mend as life went on. He says on one occasion, "Foxes have holes, and birds of the air have nests, but the Son of Man hath not where to lay His head."[1] He had no home. He was, when He began to preach, what would now be called with contempt a vagrant. There are persons who are obliged to sleep where they can; such, in good measure, seems to have been our blessed Lord. We hear of Martha who was hospitable to Him, and of others; but, though little is told us, He seems, from what *is* told, to have lived a rougher life than any village peasant. He was forty days in the wilderness: where do you think He slept then? in caves of the rock. And who were His companions then? worse companions even than those He was born among. He was born in a cave; He passed forty nights in a cave; but on His birth, at least, they were tame beasts whom He was among, the ox and the ass. But during His forty days' temptation He "was with the wild beasts." Those caverns in the wilderness are filled with fierce and poisonous creatures. There Christ slept; and doubtless, but for His Father's unseen arm and His own sanctity, they would have fallen upon Him.

Again, cold is another hardship which sensibly afflicts us. This, too, Christ endured. He remained whole nights in prayer upon the mountains. He rose before day and went into solitary places to pray. He was on the sea at night.

Heat is a suffering which does not afflict us much in our country, but is very formidable in the Eastern parts, where our Saviour lived. Men keep at home when the sun is high, lest it should harm them; yet we read of His sitting down on Jacob's well at mid-day, being wearied with His journey.

Observe this also, to which I have already referred. He was constantly journeying during His ministry, and journeying on foot. Once He rode into Jerusalem, to fulfil a prophecy.

Again, He endured hunger and thirst. He was athirst at the well, and asked the Samaritan woman to give Him water to drink. He was hungry in the wilderness, when He fasted forty days. At another time, when actively engaged in His works of mercy, He and His disciples had no time to eat bread.[2] And, indeed, wandering about as He did, He seldom could have been certain of a meal. And what was the kind of food He lived on? He was much in the neighbourhood of an inland sea or lake, called the Sea of Gennesaret, or Tiberias, and He and His Apostles lived on bread and fish; as spare a diet as poor men have now, or

[1] Luke ix. 58.   [2] Mark vi. 31.

sparer. We hear, on one well-known occasion, of five barley loaves and two small fishes. After His resurrection He provided for His Apostles—"a fire, and fish laid thereon, and bread;"[1] as it would seem, their usual fare.

Yet it deserves notice that, in spite of this penury, He and His were in the custom of giving something to the poor notwithstanding. They did not allow themselves to make the most even of the little they had. When the traitor Judas rose up and went out to betray Him, and Jesus spoke to him, some of the Apostles thought that He was giving directions about alms to the poor; this shows His practice.

And He was, as need scarcely be added, quite dependent on others. Sometimes rich men entertained Him. Sometimes, as I have said, pious persons ministered to Him of their substance.[2] He lived, in His own blessed words, like the ravens, whom God feeds, or like the grass of the field, which God clothes.

Need I add that He had few pleasures, few recreations? it is hardly in place to speak on such a topic in the case of One who came from God, and who had other thoughts and ways than we have. Yet there are innocent enjoyments which God gives us here to counterbalance the troubles of life; our Lord was exposed to the trouble, and might have taken also its compensation. But He refrained. It has been observed, that He is never spoken of as mirthful; we often read of His sighing, groaning, and weeping. He was "a man of sorrows and acquainted with grief."

Now let us proceed to other greater sufferings, which He took on Himself when He became poor. Contempt, hatred, and persecution from the world was one of these. Even in His infancy Mary had to flee with Him into Egypt to hinder Herod from killing Him. When He returned, it was not safe to dwell in Judea, and He was brought up at Nazareth, a place of evil name, where the holy Virgin had been when Gabriel the angel came to her. I need not say how He was set at nought and persecuted by the Pharisees and priests when He began to preach, and had again and again to flee for His life, which they were bent on taking.

Another great suffering from which our Lord did not withdraw Himself, was what in our case we call bereavement, the loss of relations or friends by death. This, indeed, it was not easy for Him to sustain, who had but one earthly near relation, and so few friends; but even this affliction he tasted for our sakes. Lazarus was His friend, and He lost Him. He knew, indeed,

---

[1] John xxi. 9.   [2] Luke viii. 3.

that He could restore him, and He did. Yet still He bitterly lamented him, for whatever reason, so that the Jews said, "Behold how He loved him." But a greater and truer bereavement, as far as we dare speak of it, was His original act of humiliation itself, in leaving His heavenly glory and coming down on earth. This, of course, is a great mystery to us from beginning to end; still, He certainly vouchsafes to speak, through His Apostle, of His "emptying Himself" of His glory; so that we may fairly and reverently consider it as an unspeakable and wondrous bereavement, which He underwent, in being for the time, as it were, disinherited, and made in the likeness of sinful flesh.

But all these were but the beginning of sorrows with Him; to see their fulness we must look on to His passion. In the anguish which He then endured, we see all His other sorrows concentrated and exceeded; though I shall say little of it now, when His "time is not yet come."

But I will observe thus much; first, what is very wonderful and awful, the overwhelming fear He had of His sufferings before they came. This shows how great they were; but it would seem besides this, as if He had decreed to go through all trials for us, and, among them, the trial of fear. He says, "Now is My soul troubled, and what shall I say? Father, save Me from this hour; but for this cause came I unto this hour." And when the hour came, this terror formed the beginning of His sufferings, and caused His agony and bloody sweat. He prayed, "O My Father, if it be possible, let this cup pass from Me; nevertheless, not My will, but Thine, be done." St. Luke adds: "And being in an agony, He prayed more earnestly, and His sweat was as it were great drops of blood falling down to the ground."[1]

Next, He was betrayed to death by one of His own friends. What a bitter stroke was this! He was lonely enough without this: but in this last trial, one of the twelve Apostles, His own familiar friend, betrayed Him, and the others forsook Him and fled; though St. Peter and St. John afterwards recovered heart a little, and followed Him. Yet soon St. Peter himself incurred a worse sin, by denying Him thrice. How affectionately He felt towards them, and how He drew towards them with a natural movement of heart upon the approach of His trial, though they disappointed Him, is plain from the words He used towards them at His Last Supper: "He said unto them, With desire I have desired to eat this passover with you before I suffer."[2]

[1] John xii. 27.   Matt. xxvi. 39.   Luke xxii. 44.   [2] Luke xxii. 15.

Soon after this His sufferings began; and both in soul and in body was this Holy and Blessed Saviour, the Son of God, and Lord of life, given over to the malice of the great enemy of God and man. Job was given over to Satan in the Old Testament, but within prescribed limits; first, the Evil One was not allowed to touch his person, and afterwards, though his person, yet not his life. But Satan had power to triumph, or what he thought was triumphing, over the life of Christ, who confesses to His persecutors, "This is your hour, and the power of darkness." [1] His head was crowned and torn with thorns, and bruised with staves; His face was defiled with spitting; His shoulders were weighed down with the heavy cross; His back was rent and gashed with scourges; His hands and feet gored through with nails; His side, by way of contumely, wounded with the spear; His mouth parched with intolerable thirst; and His soul so bedarkened, that He cried out, "My God, My God, why hast Thou forsaken Me?" [2] And thus He hung upon the Cross for six hours, His whole body one wound, exposed almost naked to the eyes of men, "despising the shame," [3] and railed at, taunted, and cursed by all who saw Him. Surely to Him alone, in their fulness, apply the prophet's words: "Is it nothing to you, all ye that pass by? behold, and see if there be any sorrow like unto My sorrow, which is done unto Me, wherewith the Lord hath afflicted Me in the day of His fierce anger." [4]

How little are our sorrows to these! how little is our pain, our hardships, our persecutions, compared with those which Christ voluntarily undertook for us! If He, the Sinless, underwent these, what wonder is it that we sinners should endure, if it so be, the hundredth part of them? How base and miserable are we for understanding them so little, for being so little impressed by them! Alas! if we felt them as we ought, of course they would be to us, at seasons such as that now coming, far worse than what the death of a friend is, or his painful illness. We should not be able at such times to take pleasure in this world; we should lose our enjoyment of things of earth; we should lose our appetite, and be sick at heart, and only as a matter of duty eat, and drink, and go about our work. The holy season on which we shall soon enter would be a week of mourning, as when a dead body is in a house. We cannot, indeed, thus feel, merely because we wish and ought so to feel. We cannot force ourselves into so feeling. I do not exhort this man or that so to feel, since

[1] Luke xxii. 53.   [2] Matt. xxvii. 46.
[3] Heb. xii. 2.   [4] Lam. i. 12.

it is not in his power. We cannot work ourselves up into such feelings; or, if we can, it is better we should not, because it *is* a working up, which is bad. Deep feeling is but the natural or necessary attendant on a holy heart. But though we cannot at our will thus feel, and at once, we can go the way thus to feel. We can grow in grace till we thus feel. And, meanwhile, we can observe such an outward abstinence from the innocent pleasures and comforts of life, as may prepare us for thus feeling; such an abstinence as we should spontaneously observe if we did thus feel. We may meditate upon Christ's sufferings; and by this meditation we *shall* gradually, as time goes on, be brought to these deep feelings. We may pray God to do for us what we cannot do for ourselves, to *make* us feel; to give us the spirit of gratitude, love, reverence, self-abasement, godly fear, repentance, holiness, and lively faith.

SERMON XXI.

(LENT.)

The Cross of Christ the Measure of the World.

" And I, if I be lifted up from the earth, will draw all men unto Me."—
JOHN xii. 32.

A GREAT number of men live and die without reflecting at all upon the state of things in which they find themselves. They take things as they come, and follow their inclinations as far as they have the opportunity. They are guided mainly by pleasure and pain, not by reason, principle, or conscience ; and they do not attempt to *interpret* this world, to determine what it means, or to reduce what they see and feel to system. But when persons, either from thoughtfulness of mind, or from intellectual activity, begin to contemplate the visible state of things into which they are born, then forthwith they find it a maze and a perplexity. It is a riddle which they cannot solve. It seems full of contradictions and without a drift. Why it is, and what it is to issue in, and how it is what it is, and how we come to be introduced into it, and what is our destiny, are all mysteries.

In this difficulty, some have formed one philosophy of life, and others another. Men have thought they had found the key, by means of which they might read what is so obscure. Ten thousand things come before us one after another in the course of life, and what are we to think of them ? what colour are we to give them ? Are we to look at all things in a gay and mirthful way ? or in a melancholy way ? in a desponding or a hopeful way ? Are we to make light of life altogether, or to treat the whole subject seriously ? Are we to make greatest things of little consequence, or least things of great consequence ? Are we to keep in mind what is past and gone, or are we look on to the future, or are we to be absorbed in what is present? *How* are we to look at things? this is the question which all persons of observation ask themselves, and answer each in his own way. They wish to think by rule; by something within them, which may harmonize and adjust what is without them. Such is the need felt by reflective minds. Now, let me ask, what *is* the real key, what is the Christian interpretation of this world? What is given us by revelation to estimate and measure this world by? The event of this season,—the Crucifixion of the Son of God.

It is the death of the Eternal Word of God made flesh, which is our great lesson how to think and how to speak of this world. His Cross has put its due value upon everything which we see, upon all fortunes, all advantages, all ranks, all dignities, all pleasures; upon the lust of the flesh, and the lust of the eyes, and the pride of life. It has set a price upon the excitements, the rivalries, the hopes, the fears, the desires, the efforts, the triumphs of mortal man. It has given a meaning to the various, shifting course, the trials, the temptations, the sufferings, of his earthly state. It has brought together and made consistent all that seemed discordant and aimless. It has taught us how to live, how to use this world, what to expect, what to desire, what to hope. It is the tone into which all the strains of this world's music are ultimately to be resolved.

Look around, and see what the world presents of high and low. Go to the court of princes. See the treasure and skill of all nations brought together to honour a child of man. Observe the prostration of the many before the few. Consider the form and ceremonial, the pomp, the state, the circumstance; and the vainglory. Do you wish to know the worth of it all? look at the Cross of Christ.

Go to the political world: see nation jealous of nation, trade rivalling trade, armies and fleets matched against each other. Survey the various ranks of the community, its parties and their contests, the strivings of the ambitious, the intrigues of the crafty. What is the end of all this turmoil? the grave. What is the measure? the Cross.

Go, again, to the world of intellect and science: consider the wonderful discoveries which the human mind is making, the variety of arts to which its discoveries give rise, the all but miracles by which it shows its power; and next, the pride and confidence of reason, and the absorbing devotion of thought to transitory objects, which is the consequence. Would you form a right judgment of all this? look at the Cross.

Again : look at misery, look at poverty and destitution, look at oppression and captivity ; go where food is scanty, and lodging unhealthy. Consider pain and suffering, diseases long or violent, all that is frightful and revolting. Would you know how to rate all these? gaze upon the Cross.

Thus in the Cross, and Him who hung upon it, all things meet ; all things subserve it, all things need it. It is their centre and their interpretation. For He was lifted up upon it, that He might draw all men and all things unto Him.

But it will be said, that the view which the Cross of Christ imparts to us of human life and of the world, is not that which we should take, if left to ourselves ; that it is not an obvious view ; that if we look at things on their surface, they are far more bright and sunny than they appear when viewed in the light which this season casts upon them. The world seems made for the enjoyment of just such a being as man, and man is put into it. He has the *capacity* of enjoyment, and the world supplies the *means.* How natural this, what a simple as well as pleasant philosophy, yet how different from that of the Cross ! The doctrine of the Cross, it may be said, disarranges two parts of a system which seem made for each other; it severs the fruit from the eater, the enjoyment from the enjoyer. How does this solve a problem? does it not rather itself create one?

I answer, first, that whatever force this objection may have, surely it is merely a repetition of that which Eve felt and Satan urged in Eden ; for did not the woman see that the forbidden tree was "good for food," and "a tree to be *desired*"? Well, then, is it wonderful that we too, the descendants of the first pair, should still be in a world where there is a forbidden fruit, and that our trials should lie in being within reach of it, and our happiness in abstaining from it? The world, at first sight, appears *made* for pleasure, and the vision of Christ's Cross is a solemn and sorrowful sight interfering with this appearance. Be it so ; but why may it not be our duty to abstain from enjoyment notwithstanding, if it was a duty even in Eden?

But again : it is but a superficial view of things to say that this life is made for pleasure and happiness. To those who look under the surface, it tells a very different tale. The doctrine of the Cross does but teach, though infinitely more forcibly, still after all it does but teach the very same lesson which this world teaches to those who live long in it, who have much experience in it, who know it. The world is sweet to the lips, but bitter to the taste. It pleases at first, but not at last. It looks gay on the

M

outside, but evil and misery lie concealed within. When a man has passed a certain number of years in it, he cries out with the Preacher, " Vanity of vanities, all is vanity." Nay, if he has not religion for his guide, he will be forced to go further, and say, " All is vanity and vexation of spirit ; " all is disappointment ; all is sorrow ; all is pain. The sore judgments of God upon sin are concealed within it, and force a man to grieve whether he will or no. Therefore the doctrine of the Cross of Christ does but anticipate for us our experience of the world. It is true, it bids us grieve for our sins in the midst of all that smiles and glitters around us ; but if we will not heed it, we shall at length be forced to grieve for them from undergoing their fearful punishment. If we will not acknowledge that this world has been made miserable by sin, from the sight of Him on whom our sins were laid, we shall experience it to be miserable by the recoil of those sins upon ourselves.

It may be granted, then, that the doctrine of the Cross is not on the surface of the world. The surface of things is bright only, and the Cross is sorrowful ; it is a hidden doctrine ; it lies under a veil ; it at first sight startles us, and we are tempted to revolt from it. Like St. Peter, we cry out, " Be it far from Thee, Lord ; this shall not be unto Thee."[1] And yet it is a true doctrine ; for truth is not on the surface of things, but in the depths.

And as the doctrine of the Cross, though it be the true interpretation of this world, is not prominently manifested in it, upon its surface, but is concealed ; so again, when received into the faithful heart, there it abides as a living principle, but deep, and hidden from observation. Religious men, in the words of Scripture, "live by the faith of the Son of God, who loved them and gave Himself for them : "[2] but they do not tell this to all men ; they leave others to find it out as they may. Our Lord's own command to His disciples was, that when they fast, they should "anoint their head and wash their face."[3] Thus they are bound not to make a display, but ever to be content to look outwardly different from what they are really inwardly. They are to carry a cheerful countenance with them, and to control and regulate their feelings, that those feelings, by not being expended on the surface, may retire deep into their hearts and there live. And thus " Jesus Christ and He crucified " is, as the Apostle tells us, " a hidden wisdom ; "—hidden in the world, which seems at first sight to speak a far other doctrine,—and hidden in the faithful soul, which to persons at a distance, or to chance beholders,

---

[1] Matt. xvi. 22. [2] Gal. ii. 20. [3] Matt. vi. 17.

seems to be living but an ordinary life, while really it is in secret holding communion with Him who was "manifested in the flesh," "crucified through weakness," "justified in the Spirit, seen of angels, and received up into glory."

This being the case, the great and awful doctrine of the Cross of Christ, which we now commemorate, may fitly be called, in the language of figure, the *heart* of religion. The heart may be considered as the seat of life; it is the principle of motion, heat, and activity; from it the blood goes to and fro to the extreme parts of the body. It sustains the man in his powers and faculties; it enables the brain to think; and when it is touched, man dies. And in like manner the sacred doctrine of Christ's atoning Sacrifice is the vital principle on which the Christian lives, and without which Christianity is not. Without it no other doctrine is held profitably; to believe in Christ's divinity, or in His manhood, or in the Holy Trinity, or in a judgment to come, or in the resurrection of the dead, is an untrue belief, not Christian faith, unless we receive also the doctrine of Christ's sacrifice. On the other hand, to receive it presupposes the reception of other high truths of the Gospel besides; it involves the belief in Christ's true divinity, in His true incarnation, and in man's sinful state by nature; and it prepares the way to belief in the sacred Eucharistic feast, in which He who was once crucified is ever given to our souls and bodies, verily and indeed, in His Body and in His Blood. But again, the heart is hidden from view; it is carefully and securely guarded; it is not like the eye set in the forehead, commanding all, and seen of all: and so in like manner the sacred doctrine of the atoning Sacrifice is not one to be talked of, but to be lived upon; not to be put forth irreverently, but to be adored secretly; not to be used as a necessary instrument in the conversion of the ungodly, or for the satisfaction of reasoners of this world, but to be unfolded to the docile and obedient; to young children, whom the world has not corrupted; to the sorrowful, who need comfort; to the sincere and earnest, who need a rule of life; to the innocent, who need warning; and to the established, who have earned the knowledge of it.

One more remark I shall make, and then conclude. It must not be supposed, because the doctrine of the Cross makes us sad, that therefore the Gospel is a sad religion. The Psalmist says, "They that sow in tears shall reap in joy;" and our Lord says, "They that mourn shall be comforted." Let no one go away with the impression that the Gospel makes us take a gloomy view of the world and of life. It hinders us indeed from taking a superficial view, and finding a vain transitory joy in what we see; but it forbids our immediate enjoyment, only to grant enjoyment in truth and fulness afterwards. It only forbids us to *begin* with enjoyment. It only says, If you begin with pleasure, you will end with pain. It bids us begin with the Cross of Christ, and in that Cross we shall at first find sorrow, but in a while peace and comfort will rise out of that sorrow. That Cross will lead us to mourning, repentance, humiliation, prayer, fasting; we shall sorrow for our sins, we shall sorrow with Christ's sufferings; but all this sorrow will only issue, nay, will be undergone in a happiness far greater than the enjoyment which the world gives,—though careless worldly minds indeed will not believe this, ridicule the notion of it, because they never have tasted it, and consider it a mere matter of words, which religious persons think it decent and proper to use, and try to believe themselves, and to get others to believe, but which no one really feels. This is what they think; but our Saviour said to His disciples, "Ye now therefore have sorrow, but I will see you again, and your heart shall rejoice, and your joy no man taketh from you." . . . "Peace I leave with you; My peace I give unto you; not as the world giveth, give I unto you." And St. Paul says, "The natural man receiveth not the things of the Spirit of God; for they are foolishness unto him; neither can he know them, because they are spiritually discerned." "Eye hath not seen, nor ear heard, neither have entered into the heart of man, the things which God hath prepared for them that love Him." [1] And thus the Cross of Christ, as telling us of our redemption as well as of His sufferings, wounds us indeed, but so wounds as to heal also.

And thus, too, all that is bright and beautiful, even on the surface of this world, though it has no substance, and may not suitably be enjoyed for its own sake, yet is a figure and promise of that true joy which issues out of the Atonement. It is a promise beforehand of what is to be: it is a shadow, raising hope because the substance is to follow, but not to be rashly taken instead of the substance. And it is God's usual mode of dealing with us, in mercy to send the shadow before the substance, that we may take comfort in what is to be, before it comes. Thus our Lord before His Passion rode into Jerusalem in triumph, with the multitudes crying Hosanna, and strewing His road with palm branches and their garments. This was but a vain and hollow pageant, nor did our Lord take pleasure in it. It was a shadow which stayed not, but flitted away. It could not be more than a

[1] John xvi. 22; xiv. 27. 1 Cor. ii. 9, 14.

shadow, for the Passion had not been undergone by which His true triumph was wrought out. He could not enter into His glory before He had first suffered. He could not take pleasure in this semblance of it, knowing that it was unreal. Yet that first shadowy triumph was the omen and presage of the true victory to come, when He had overcome the sharpness of death. And we commemorate this figurative triumph on the last Sunday in Lent, to cheer us in the sorrow of the week that follows, and to remind us of the true joy which comes with Easter Day.

And so, too, as regards this world, with all its enjoyments, yet disappointments. Let us not trust it; let us not give our hearts to it; let us not begin with it. Let us begin with faith; let us begin with Christ; let us begin with His Cross and the humiliation to which it leads. Let us first be drawn to Him who is lifted up, that so He may, with Himself, freely give us all things. Let us "seek first the kingdom of God and His righteousness," and then all those things of this world "will be added to us." They alone are able truly to enjoy this world, who begin with the world unseen. They alone enjoy it, who have first abstained from it. They alone can truly feast, who have first fasted; they alone are able to use the world, who have learned not to abuse it; they alone inherit it, who take it as a shadow of the world to come. and who for that world to come relinquish it.

SERMON XXII.

The Crucifixion.

" He was oppressed, and He was afflicted, yet He opened not His mouth ;
He is brought as a lamb to the slaughter, and as a sheep before he?
shearers is dumb, so He openeth not His mouth."—ISA. liii. 7.

ST. PETER makes it almost a description of a Christian, that
he loves Him whom he has not seen ; speaking of Christ,
he says, " Whom having not seen, ye love ; in whom, though now
ye see Him not, yet believing, ye rejoice with joy unspeakable
and full of glory." Again he speaks of " tasting that the Lord is
gracious." [1] Unless we have a true love of Christ, we are not
His true disciples ; and we cannot love Him unless we have heart-
felt gratitude to Him ; and we cannot duly feel gratitude, unless
we feel keenly what He suffered for us. I say it seems to us
impossible, under the circumstances of the case, that any one can
have attained to the love of Christ, who feels no distress, no
misery, at the thought of His bitter pains, and no self-reproach at
having through his own sins had a share in causing them.

I know quite well, and wish you, my brethren, never to forget,
that feeling is not enough ; that it is not enough merely to feel
and nothing more ; that to feel grief for Christ's sufferings, and
yet not to go on to obey Him, is not true love, but a mockery.
True love both feels right and acts right ; but at the same time
as warm feelings without religious conduct are a kind of hypocrisy, so, on the other hand, right conduct, when unattended with
deep feelings, is at best a very imperfect sort of religion. And
at this time of year [2] especially are we called upon to raise our
hearts to Christ, and to have keen feelings and piercing thoughts

[1] 1 Pet. i. 8 ; ii. 3.   [2] Passion-tide.

of sorrow and shame, of compunction and of gratitude, of love and tender affection and horror and anguish, at the review of those awful sufferings whereby our salvation has been• purchased.

Let us pray God to give us *all* graces; and while, in the first place, we pray that He would make us holy, really holy, let us also pray Him to give us the *beauty* of holiness, which consists in tender and eager affection towards our Lord and Saviour; which is, in the case of the Christian, what beauty of person is to the outward man, so that through God's mercy our souls may have, not strength and health only, but a sort of bloom and comeliness; and that as we grow older in body, we may, year by year, grow more youthful in spirit.

You will ask, *how* are we to learn to feel pain and anguish at the thought of Christ's sufferings? I answer, *by* thinking of them, that is, by *dwelling* on the thought. This, through God's mercy, is in the power of every one. No one who will but solemnly think over the history of those sufferings, as drawn out for us in the Gospels, but will gradually gain, through God's grace, a sense of them, will in a measure realize them, will in a measure be as if he saw them, will feel towards them as being not merely a tale written in a book, but as a true history, as a series of events which took place. It is indeed a great mercy that this duty which I speak of, though so high, is notwithstanding so level with the powers of all classes of persons, learned and unlearned, if they wish to perform it. Any one can think of Christ's sufferings, if he will; and knows well what to think about. "It is not in heaven that thou shouldst say, Who shall go up for us to heaven and bring it to us, that we may hear it and do it? Neither is it beyond the sea that thou shouldst say, Who shall go over the sea for us? . . . but the word is very nigh unto thee;" very nigh, for it is in the four Gospels, which, at this day at least, are open to all men. All men may read or hear the Gospels, and in knowing them, they will know all that is necessary to be known in order to feel aright; they will know all that any one knows, all that has been told us, all that the greatest saints have ever had to make them full of love and sacred fear.

Now, then, let me make one or two reflections by way of stirring up your hearts and making you mourn over Christ's sufferings, as you are called to do at this season.

1. First, as to these sufferings you will observe that our Lord is called a lamb in the text; that is, He was as defenceless, and as innocent, as a lamb is. Since then Scripture compares Him

to this inoffensive and unprotected animal, we may without presumption or irreverence take the image as a means of conveying to our minds those feelings which our Lord's sufferings should excite in us. I mean, consider how very horrible it is to read the accounts which sometimes meet us of cruelties exercised on brute animals. Does it not sometimes make us shudder to hear tell of them, or to read them in some chance publication which we take up? At one time it is the wanton deed of barbarous and angry owners who ill-treat their cattle, or beasts of burden; and at another, it is the cold-blooded and calculating act of men of science, who make experiments on brute animals, perhaps merely from a sort of curiosity. I do not like to go into particulars, for many reasons; but one of those instances which we read of as happening in this day, and which seems more shocking than the rest, is, when the poor dumb victim is fastened against a wall, pierced, gashed, and so left to linger out its life. Now do you not see that I have a reason for saying this, and am not using these distressing words for nothing? For what was this but the very cruelty inflicted upon our Lord? He was gashed with the scourge, pierced through hands and feet, and so fastened to the Cross, and there left, and that as a spectacle. Now what is it moves our very hearts, and sickens us so much at cruelty shown to poor brutes? I suppose this first, that they have done no harm; next, that they have no power whatever of resistance; it is the cowardice and tyranny of which they are the victims which makes their sufferings so especially touching. For instance, if they were dangerous animals, take the case of wild beasts at large, able not only to defend themselves, but even to attack us; much as we might dislike to hear of their wounds and agony, yet our feelings would be of a very different kind; but there is something so very dreadful, so satanic in tormenting those who never have harmed us, and who cannot defend themselves, who are utterly in our power, who have weapons neither of offence nor defence, that none but very hardened persons can endure the thought of it. Now this was just our Saviour's case: He had laid aside His glory, He had (as it were) disbanded His legions of angels, He came on earth without arms, except the arms of truth, meekness, and righteousness, and committed Himself to the world in perfect innocence and sinlessness, and in utter helplessness, as the Lamb of God. In the words of St. Peter, "Who did no sin, neither was guile found in His mouth; who, when He was reviled, reviled not again; when He suffered, He threatened not; but committed Himself to Him that judgeth righteously."[1] Think then, my brethren, of your feelings at cruelty practised upon brute animals, and you will gain one sort of feeling which the history of Christ's Cross and Passion ought to excite within you. And let me add, this is in all cases one good use to which you may turn any accounts you read of wanton and unfeeling acts shown towards the inferior animals; let them remind you, as a picture, of Christ's sufferings. He who is higher than the angels, deigned to humble Himself even to the state of the brute creation, as the Psalm says, "I am a worm, and no man; a very scorn of men, and the outcast of the people."[2]

2. Take another example, and you will see the same thing still more strikingly. How overpowered should we be, nay not at the sight only, but at the very hearing of cruelties shown to a little child, and why so? for the same two reasons, because it was so innocent, and because it was so unable to defend itself. I do not like to go into the details of such cruelty, they would be so heart-rending. What if wicked men took and crucified a young child? What if they deliberately seized its poor little frame, and stretched out its arms, nailed them to a cross bar of wood, drove a stake through its two feet, and fastened them to a beam, and so left it to die? It is almost too shocking to say; perhaps, you will actually say it *is* too shocking, and ought not to be said. O my brethren, you feel the horror of this, and yet you can bear to read of Christ's sufferings without horror; for what is that little child's agony to His? and which deserved it more? which is the more innocent? which the holier? was He not gentler, sweeter, meeker, more tender, more loving, than any little child? Why are you shocked at the one, why are you not shocked at the other?

Or take another instance, not so shocking in its circumstances, yet introducing us to another distinction, in which Christ's Passion exceeds that of any innocent sufferers, such as I have supposed. When Joseph was sent by his father to his brethren on a message of love, they, when they saw him, said, "Behold, this dreamer cometh; come now, therefore, and let us slay him."[3] They did not kill him, however, but they put him in a pit in spite of the anguish of his soul, and sold him as a slave to the Ishmaelites, and he was taken down into a foreign country, where he had no friends. Now this was most cruel and most cowardly in the sons of Jacob; and what is so especially shocking in it is, that Joseph was not only innocent and defenceless, their younger brother whom they ought to have protected, but besides that, he was so confiding and loving, that he need not have come to them,

---

[1] 1 Pet. ii. 22, 23. [2] Ps. xxii. 6. [3] Gen. xxxvii. 19, 20.

that he would not at all have been in their power, *except* for his desire to do them service. Now, whom does this history remind us of but of Him concerning whom the Master of the vineyard said, on sending Him to the husbandmen, "They will reverence My Son"?[1] "But when the husbandmen saw the Son, they said among themselves, This is the Heir, come, let us kill Him, and let us seize on His inheritance. And they caught Him, and cast Him out of the vineyard, and slew Him." Here, then, is an additional circumstance of cruelty to affect us in Christ's history, such as is suggested in Joseph's, but which no instance of a brute animal's or of a child's sufferings can have; our Lord was not only guiltless and defenceless, but He had come among His persecutors in love.

3. And now, instead of taking the case of the young, innocent, and confiding, let us take another instance which will present to us our Lord's Passion under another aspect. Let us suppose that some aged and venerable person whom we have known as long as we could recollect anything, and loved and reverenced, suppose such a one, who had often done us kindnesses, who had taught us, who had given us good advice, who had encouraged us, smiled on us, comforted us in trouble, whom we knew to be very good and religious, very holy, full of wisdom, full of heaven, with grey hairs and awful countenance, waiting for Almighty God's summons to leave this world for a better place; suppose, I say, such a one whom we have ourselves known, and whose memory is dear to us, rudely seized by fierce men, stripped naked in public, insulted, driven about here and there, made a laughing-stock, struck, spit on, dressed up in other clothes in ridicule, then severely scourged on the back, then laden with some heavy load till he could carry it no longer, pulled and dragged about, and at last exposed with all his wounds to the gaze of a rude multitude who came and jeered him, what would be our feelings? Let us in our mind think of this person or that, and consider how we should be overwhelmed and pierced through and through by such a hideous occurrence.

But what is all this to the suffering of the holy Jesus, which we bear to read of as a matter of course! Only think of Him, when in His wounded state, and without garment on, He had to creep up the ladder, as He could, which led Him up the Cross high enough for His murderers to nail Him to it; and consider *who* it was that was in that misery. Or again, view Him dying, hour after hour bleeding to death; and how? in peace? no; with

[1] Matt. xxi. 37-39.

His arms stretched out, and His face exposed to view, and any one who pleased coming and staring at Him, mocking Him, and watching the gradual ebbing of His strength, and the approach of death. These are some of the appalling details which the Gospels contain, and surely they were not recorded for nothing; but that we might dwell on them.

Do you think that those who saw these things had much heart for eating or drinking or enjoying themselves? On the contrary, we are told that even "the people who came together to that sight, smote their breasts and returned." [1] If these were the feelings of the people, what were St. John's feelings, or St. Mary Magdalene's, or St. Mary's, our Lord's blessed mother? Do we desire to be of this company? do we desire, according to His own promise, to be rather blessed than the womb that bare Him, and the paps that He sucked? do we desire to be as His brother, and sister, and mother? [2] Then, surely, ought we to have some portion of that mother's sorrow! When He was on the Cross and she stood by, then, according to Simeon's prophecy, "a sword pierced through her soul." [3] What is the use of our keeping the memory of His Cross and Passion, unless we lament and are in sorrow with her? I can understand people who do not keep Good Friday at all; they are indeed very ungrateful, but I know what they mean; I understand them. But I do not understand at all, I do not at all see what men mean who *do* profess to keep it, yet do not sorrow, or at least try to sorrow. Such a spirit of grief and lamentation is expressly mentioned in Scripture as a characteristic of those who turn to Christ. If then *we* do not sorrow, have *we* turned to Him? "I will pour upon the house of David," says the merciful Saviour Himself, before He came on earth, speaking of what was to come, "upon the inhabitants of Jerusalem, the spirit of grace and of supplications; and they shall look upon Me whom they have pierced. and they shall *mourn* for Him, as one mourneth for his only son, and shall be in bitterness for Him, as one that is in bitterness for his firstborn." [4]

One thing I will add :—if there be persons here present who are conscious to themselves that they do not feel the grief which this season should cause them, who feel now as they do at other times, let them consider with themselves whether perhaps this defect does not arise from their having neglected to come to church, whether during this season or at other times, as often as they might. Our feelings are not in our own power; God alone

---

[1] Luke xxiii. 48.
[2] Matt. xii. 46, etc.
[3] Luke ii. 35.
[4] Zech. xii. 10.

can rule our feelings; God alone can make us sorrow, when we would but cannot sorrow; but *will* He, if we have not diligently sought Him according to our opportunities in this house of grace? I speak of those who might come to prayers more frequently, and do not. I know well that many cannot come. I speak of those who can, if they will. Even if they come as often as they are able, I know well they will not be *satisfied* with their own feelings; they will be conscious even then that they ought to grieve more than they do; of course none of us feels the great event of this day as he ought, and therefore we all *ought* to be dissatisfied with ourselves. However, if this is not our own fault, we need not be out of heart, for God will mercifully lead us forward in His own time; but if it arises from our not coming to prayers here as often as we might, then our coldness and deadness *are* our own fault, and I beg you all to consider that that fault is not a slight one. It is said in the Book of Revelation, "Behold He cometh with clouds; and every eye shall see Him, and they also which pierced Him: and all kindreds of the earth shall wail because of Him." [1] We, my brethren, every one of us, shall one day rise from our graves, and see Jesus Christ; we shall see Him who hung on the Cross, we shall see His wounds, we shall see the marks in His hands, and in His feet, and in His side. Do we wish to be of those, then, who wail and lament, or of those who rejoice? If we would not lament at the sight of Him then, we must lament at the thought of Him now. Let us prepare to meet our God; let us come into His Presence whenever we can; let us try to fancy as if we saw the Cross and Him upon it; let us draw near to it; let us beg Him to look on us as He did on the penitent thief, and let us say to Him, "Lord, remember me when Thou comest in Thy kingdom." [2]

Let this be added to the prayer, my brethren, with which you are about to leave this church. After I have given the blessing, you will say to yourselves a short prayer. Well; fancy you see Jesus Christ on the Cross, and say to Him with the penitent thief, "Lord, remember me when Thou comest in Thy kingdom;" that is, "Remember me, Lord, in mercy, remember not my sins, but Thine own Cross; remember Thine own sufferings, remember that Thou sufferedst for me, a sinner; remember in the last day that I, during my lifetime, felt Thy sufferings, that I suffered on my cross by Thy side. Remember me then, and make me remember Thee now."

[1] Rev. i. 7.   [2] Luke xxiii. 42.

SERMON XXIII.

(EASTER DAY.)

Keeping Fast and Festival.

"A time to weep, and a time to laugh : a time to mourn, and a time to dance."—ECCLES. iii. 4.

AT Christmas we joy with the natural, unmixed joy of children, but at Easter our joy is highly wrought and refined in its character. It is not the spontaneous and unartificial outbreak which the news of Redemption might occasion, but it is thoughtful; it has a long history before it, and has run through a long course of feelings before it becomes what it is. It is a last feeling and not a first. St. Paul describes its nature and its formation when he says, "Tribulation worketh patience, and patience experience, and experience hope ; and hope maketh not ashamed, because the love of God is shed abroad in our hearts by the Holy Ghost which is given unto us." [1] And the prophet Isaiah, when he says, "They joy before Thee according to the joy in harvest, and as men rejoice when they divide the spoil." [2] Or as it was fulfilled in the case of our Lord Himself, who, as being the Captain of our salvation, was made perfect through sufferings. Accordingly, Christmas Day is ushered in with a time of awful expectation only, but Easter Day with the long fast of Lent, and the rigours of the Holy Week just past : and it springs out and (as it were) is born of Good Friday.

On such a day, then, from the very intensity of joy which Christians ought to feel, and the trial which they have gone through, they will often be disposed to say little. Rather, like sick people convalescent, when the crisis is past, the illness over, but strength not yet come, they will go forth to the light of day

[1] Rom. v. 3-5.   [2] Isa. ix. 3.

and the freshness of the air, and silently sit down with great delight under the shadow of that Tree, whose fruit is sweet to their taste. They are disposed rather to muse and be at peace than to use many words; for their joy has been so much the child of sorrow, is of so transmuted and complex a nature, so bound up with painful memories and sad associations, that though it is a joy only the greater from the contrast, it is not, cannot be, as if it had never been sorrow.

And in this too the feeling at Easter is not unlike the revulsion of mind on a recovery from sickness, that in sickness also there is much happens to us that is strange, much that we must feebly comprehend and vaguely follow after. For in sickness the mind wanders from things that are seen into the unknown world, it turns back into itself, and is in company with mysteries; it is brought into contact with objects which it cannot describe, which it cannot ascertain. It sees the skirts of powers and providences beyond this world, and is at least more alive, if not more exposed to the invisible influences, bad and good, which are its portion in this state of trial. And afterwards it has recollections which are painful, recollections of distress, of which it cannot recall the reasons, of pursuits without an object, and gleams of relief without continuance. And what is all this but a parallel feeling to that, with which the Christian has gone through the contemplations put before his faith in the week just passed, which are to him as a fearful harrowing dream, of which the spell is now broken? The subjects, indeed, which have been brought before him are no dream, but a reality,—his Saviour's sufferings, his own misery and sin. But, alas! to him at best they are but a dream, because, from lack of faith and of spiritual discernment, he understands them so imperfectly. They have been to him a dream, because only at moments his heart has caught a vivid glimpse of what was continually before his reason,—because the impression it made upon him was irregular, shifting, and transitory,—because even when he contemplated steadily his Saviour's sufferings, he did not, could not understand the deep reasons of them, or the meaning of his Saviour's words,—because what most forcibly affected him came through his irrational nature, was not of the mind but of the flesh, not of the scenes of sorrow which the lessons and Gospels record, but of his own discomfort of body, which he has been bound, as far as health allows, to make sympathize with the history of those sufferings which are his salvation. And thus I say his disquiet during the week has been like that of a bad dream, restless and dreary; he has felt he ought to be very sorry, and could not say why,—could not master his grief, could no, realize his fears, but was as children are, who wonder, weep, and are silent, when they see their parents in sorrow, from a feeling that there is something wrong, though they cannot say what.

And therefore now, though it is over, he cannot so shake off at once what has been, as to enter fully into what is. Christ indeed, though He suffered and died, yet rose again vigorously on the third day, having loosed the pains of death : but we cannot accomplish in our contemplation of Him, what He accomplished really ; for He was the Holy One, and we are sinners. We have the languor and oppression of our old selves upon us, though we be new ; and therefore we must beg Him who is the Prince of Life, the Life itself, to carry us forth into His new world, for we cannot walk thither, and seat us down whence, like Moses, we may see the land, and meditate upon its beauty !

And yet, though the long season of sorrow which ushers in this blessed day, in some sense sobers and quells the keenness of our enjoyment, yet without such preparatory season, let us be sure we shall not rejoice at all. None rejoice in Easter-tide less than those who have not grieved in Lent. This is what is seen in the world at large. To them, one season is the same as another, and they take no account of any. Feast-day and fast-day, holy tide and other tide, are one and the same to them. Hence they do not realize the next world at all. To them the Gospels are but like another history ; a course of events which took place eighteen hundred years since. They do not make our Saviour's life and death present to them : they do not transport themselves back to the time of His sojourn on earth. They do not act over again, and celebrate His history, in their own observance ; and the consequence is, that they feel no interest in it. They have neither faith nor love towards it ; it has no hold on them. They do not form their estimate of things upon it ; they do not hold it as a sort of practical principle in their heart. This is the case not only with the world at large, but too often with men who have the Name of Christ in their mouths. They think they believe in Him, yet when trial comes, or in the daily conduct of life, they are unable to act upon the principles which they profess : and why ? because they have thought to dispense with the religious ordinances, the course of service, and the round of sacred seasons of the Church, and have considered it a simpler and more spiritual religion, not to act religiously except when called to it by extraordinary trial or temptation ; because they have thought that. since it is the Christian's duty to rejoice evermore, they would rejoice better if they never sorrowed and never travailed with righteousness. On the contrary, let us be sure that, as previous humiliation sobers our joy, it alone secures it to us. Our Saviour says, "Blessed are they that mourn, for they shall be comforted;" and what is true hereafter, is true here. Unless we have mourned, in the weeks that are gone, we shall not rejoice in the season now commencing. It is often said, and truly, that providential affliction brings a man nearer to God. What is the observance of holy seasons but such a means of grace?

This too must be said concerning the connection of fasts and feasts in our religious service, viz. that that sobriety in feasting which previous fasting causes, is itself much to be prized, and especially worth securing. For in this does Christian mirth differ from worldly, that it is subdued; and how shall it be subdued except that the past keeps its hold upon us, and while it warns and sobers us, actually indisposes and tames our flesh against indulgence? In the world feasting comes first and fasting afterwards; men first glut themselves, and then loathe their excesses; they take their fill of good, and then suffer; they are rich that they may be poor; they laugh that they may weep; they rise that they may fall. But in the Church of God it is reversed; the poor *shall* be rich, the lowly shall be exalted, those that sow in tears shall reap in joy, those that mourn shall be comforted, those that suffer with Christ shall reign with Him; even as Christ (in our Church's words) "went not up to joy, but first He suffered pain. He entered not into His glory before He was crucified. So truly our way to eternal joy is to suffer here with Christ, and our door to enter into eternal life is gladly to die with Christ, that we may rise again from death, and dwell with Him in everlasting life." [1] And what is true of the general course of our redemption is, I say, fulfilled also in the yearly and other commemorations of it. Our festivals are preceded by humiliation, that we may keep them duly; not boisterously or fanatically, but in a refined, subdued, chastised spirit, which is the true rejoicing in the Lord.

In such a spirit let us endeavour to celebrate this most holy of all festivals, this continued festal season, which lasts for fifty days, whereas Lent is forty, as if to show that where sin abounded, there much more has grace abounded. Such indeed seems the tone of mind which took possession of the Apostles when certified of the Resurrection; and while they waited for,

_____
[1] Visitation of the sick.

or when they had the sight of their risen Lord. If we consider, we shall find the accounts of that season in the Gospels, marked with much of pensiveness and tender and joyful melancholy; the sweet and pleasant frame of those who have gone through pain, and out of pain receive pleasure. Whether we read the account of St. Mary Magdalen weeping at the sepulchre, seeing Jesus and knowing Him not, recognising His voice, attempting to embrace His feet, and then sinking into silent awe and delight, till she rose and hastened to tell the perplexed Apostles;—or turn to that solemn meeting, which was the third, when He stood on the shore and addressed His disciples, and Peter plunged into the water, and then with the rest was awed into silence and durst not speak, but only obeyed His command, and ate of the fish in silence, and so remained in the presence of One in whom they joyed, whom they loved, as He knew, more than all things, till He broke silence by asking Peter if he loved Him :—or lastly, consider the time when He appeared unto a great number of disciples on the mountain in Galilee, and all worshipped Him, but some doubted :—who does not see that their festival was such as I have been describing it, a holy, tender, reverent, manly joy, not *so* manly as to be rude, not *so* tender as to be effeminate, but (as if) an angel's mood, the mingled offering of all that is best and highest in man's and woman's nature brought together,—St. Mary Magdalen and St. Peter blended into St. John? And here perhaps we learn a lesson from the deep silence which Scripture observes concerning the Blessed Virgin [1] after the Resurrection; as if she, who was too pure and holy a flower to be more than seen here on earth, even during the season of her Son's humiliation, was altogether drawn by the Angels within the veil on His Resurrection, and had her joy in Paradise with Gabriel, who had been the first to honour her, and with those elder saints who arose after the Resurrection, appeared in the Holy City, and then vanished away.

May we partake in such calm and heavenly joy; and, while we pray for it, recollecting the while that we are still on earth, and our duties in this world, let us never forget that, while our love must be silent, our faith must be vigorous and lively. Let us never forget that in proportion as our love is "rooted and grounded" in the next world, our faith must branch forth like a fruitful tree into this. The calmer our hearts, the more active be our lives; the more tranquil we are, the more busy; the more resigned, the more zealous; the more unruffled, the more fervent.

[1] *Vide* Christian Year. Fourth Sunday in Lent.

N

This is one of the many paradoxes in the world's judgment of him, which the Christian realizes in himself. Christ is risen; He is risen from the dead. We may well cry out, "Alleluia, the Lord Omnipotent reigneth." He has crushed all the power of the enemy under His feet. He has gone upon the lion and the adder. He has stopped the lion's mouth for us His people, and has bruised the serpent's head. There is nothing impossible to us now, if we do but enter into the fulness of our privileges, the wondrous power of our gifts. The thing cannot be named in heaven or earth within the limits of truth and obedience which we cannot do through Christ; the petition cannot be named which may not be accorded to us for His Name's sake. For, we who have risen with Him from the grave, stand in His might, and are allowed to use His weapons. His infinite influence with the Father is ours,—not always to use, for perhaps in this or that effort we make, or petition we prefer, it would not be good for us; but so far ours, so fully ours, that when we ask and do things according to His will, we are really possessed of a power with God, and do prevail :—so that little as we may know when and when not, we are continually possessed of heavenly weapons, we are continually touching the springs of the most wonderful providences in heaven and earth; and by the Name, and the Sign, and the Blood of the Son of God, we are able to make devils tremble and saints rejoice. Such are the arms which faith uses, small in appearance, yet "not carnal, but mighty through God to the pulling down of strongholds;"[1] despised by the world, what seems a mere word, or a mere symbol, or mere bread and wine; but God has chosen the weak things of the world to confound the mighty, and foolish things of the world to confound the wise; and as all things spring from small beginnings, from seeds and elements invisible or insignificant, so when God would renew the race of man, and reverse the course of human life and earthly affairs, He chose cheap things for the rudiments of His work, and bade us believe that He *could* work through them, and He would do so. As then we Christians discern in Him, when He came on earth, not the carpenter's son, but the Eternal Word Incarnate, as we see beauty in Him in whom the world saw no form or comeliness, as we discern in that death an Atonement for sin in which the world saw nothing but a malefactor's sentence; so let us believe with full persuasion that all that He has bequeathed to us has power from Him. Let us accept His ordinances, and His creed, and His precepts; and let us stand

---

[1] 2 Cor. x. 4.

upright with an undaunted faith, resolute, with faces like flint, to serve Him in and through them; to inflict them upon the world without misgiving, without wavering, without anxiety; being sure that He who saved us from hell through a Body of flesh which the world insulted, tortured, and triumphed over, much more can now apply the benefits of His Passion through ordinances which the world has lacerated and now mocks.

This then, my brethren, be our spirit on this day. God rested from His labours on the seventh day, yet He worketh evermore. Christ entered into His rest, yet He too ever works. We too, if it may be said, in adoring and lowly imitation of what is infinite, while we rest in Christ and rejoice in His shadow, let us too beware of sloth and cowardice, but serve Him with steadfast eyes yet active hands; that we may be truly His in our hearts, as we were made His by Baptism,—as we are made His continually, by the recurring celebration of His purifying fasts and holy feasts.

SERMON XXIV.

(EASTER TIDE.)

Witnesses of the Resurrection.

"Him God raised up the third day, and showed Him openly; not to all the
people, but unto witnesses chosen before of God, even to us, who did eat
and drink with Him after He rose from the dead."—ACTS x. 40, 41.

IT might have been expected that, on our Saviour's rising again
from the dead, He would have shown Himself to very great
numbers of people, and especially to those who crucified Him;
whereas we know from the history that, far from this being the
case, He showed Himself only to chosen witnesses, chiefly His
immediate followers; and St. Peter avows this in the text. This
seems at first sight strange. We are apt to fancy the resurrection
of Christ as some striking visible display of His glory, such as
God vouchsafed from time to time to the Israelites in Moses' day;
and considering it in the light of a public triumph, we are led to
imagine the confusion and terror which would have overwhelmed
His murderers, had He presented Himself alive before *them*.
Now, thus to reason, is to conceive Christ's kingdom of *this*
world, which it is not; and to suppose that then Christ came to
judge the world, whereas that judgment will not be till the last
day, when in very deed those wicked men *shall* "look on Him
whom they have pierced."

But even without insisting upon the spiritual nature of Christ's
kingdom, which seems to be the direct reason why Christ did not
show Himself to all the Jews after His resurrection, other distinct
reasons may be given, instructive too. And one of these I will
now set before you.

This is the question, "Why did not our Saviour show Himself
after His resurrection to all the people? why only to witnesses

chosen before of God?" and this is my answer: "Because this was the most effectual means of propagating His religion through the world."

After His resurrection, He said to His disciples, "Go, convert all nations:"[1] this was His especial charge. If, then, there are grounds for thinking that, by showing Himself to a few rather than to many, He was more surely advancing this great object, the propagation of the Gospel, this is a sufficient reason for our Lord's having so ordained; and let us thankfully receive His dispensation as He has given it.

1. Now consider what would have been the probable effect of a public exhibition of His resurrection. Let us suppose that our Saviour had shown Himself as openly as before He suffered; preaching in the Temple and in the streets of the city; traversing the land with His Apostles, and with multitudes following to see the miracles which He did. What would have been the effect of this? Of course, what it had already been. His former miracles had not effectually moved the body of the people; and, doubtless, this miracle too would have left them as it found them, or worse than before. They might have been more startled at the time; but why should this amazement last? When the man taken with a palsy was suddenly restored at His word, the multitude were all amazed, and glorified God, and were filled with fear, saying, "We have seen strange things to-day."[2] What *could* they have said and felt more than this, when "one rose from the dead"? In truth, this is the way of the mass of mankind in all ages, to be influenced by sudden fears, sudden contrition, sudden earnestness, sudden resolves, which disappear as suddenly. Nothing is done effectually through untrained human nature; and such is ever the condition of the multitude. Unstable as water, it cannot excel. One day it cried Hosanna; the next, Crucify Him. And, had our Lord appeared to them *after* they had crucified Him, of course they would have shouted Hosanna once more; and when He had ascended out of sight, then again they would have persecuted His followers. Besides, the miracle of the resurrection was much more exposed to the cavils of unbelief than others which our Lord had displayed; than that, for instance, of feeding the multitudes in the wilderness. Had our Lord appeared in public, yet few could have touched Him, and certified themselves it was He Himself. Few, comparatively, in a great multitude could so have seen Him both before and after His death, as to be adequate witnesses of the reality of the miracle. It would have been open to the greater

[1] Matt. xxviii. 19.   [2] Luke v. 26.

number of them still to deny that He *was* risen. This is the very feeling St. Matthew records. When He appeared on a mountain in Galilee to His Apostles and others, as it would seem (perhaps the five hundred brethren mentioned by St. Paul), "*some doubted*" whether it were He. How could it be otherwise? these had no means of ascertaining that they really saw *Him* who had been crucified, dead, and buried. Others, admitting it was Jesus, would have denied that He ever died. Not having seen Him dead on the cross, they might have pretended He was taken down thence before life was extinct, and so restored. This supposition would be a sufficient excuse to those who *wished* not to believe. And the more ignorant part would fancy they had seen a *spirit* without flesh and bones as man has. They would have resolved the miracle into a magical illusion, as the Pharisees had done before, when they ascribed His works to Beelzebub; and would have been rendered no better or more religious by the sight of Him than the common people are nowadays by tales of apparitions and witches.

Surely so it would have been; the chief priests would not have been moved at all; and the populace, however they had been moved at the time, would not have been lastingly moved, not practically moved, not so moved as to proclaim to the world what they had heard and seen, as to preach the Gospel. This is the point to be kept in view : and consider that the very reason *why* Christ showed Himself at all was in order to raise up *witnesses* to His resurrection, ministers of His Word, founders of His Church ; and how in the nature of things could a populace ever become such?

2. Now, on the other hand, let us contemplate the means which His Divine Wisdom actually adopted with a view of making His resurrection subservient to the propagation of His Gospel.—He showed Himself openly, not to all the people, but unto witnesses chosen before of God. It is, indeed, a *general* characteristic of the course of His providence to make the few the channels of His blessings to the many; but in the instance we are contemplating, a few were selected, because only a few *could* (humanly speaking) be made instruments. As I have already said, to be witnesses of His resurrection it was requisite to have known our Lord intimately before His death. This was the case with the Apostles ; but this was not enough. It was necessary they should be certain it was He Himself, the very same whom they before knew. You recollect how He urged them to handle Him, and be sure that they could testify to His rising

again. This is intimated in the text also : "Witnesses chosen before of God, even to us who did eat and drink with Him after He rose from the dead." Nor were they required merely to know Him, but the thought of Him was to be stamped upon their minds as the one master-spring of their whole course of life for the future. But men are not easily wrought upon to be faithful advocates of any cause. Not only is the multitude fickle : but the best men, unless urged, tutored, disciplined to their work, give way ; untrained nature has no principles.

It would seem, then, that our Lord gave His attention to a few, because, if the few be gained, the many will follow. To these few He showed Himself again and again. These He restored, comforted, warned, inspired. He formed them unto Himself, that they might show forth His praise. This His gracious procedure is opened to us in the first words of the Book of the Acts : "To the Apostles whom He had chosen He showed Himself alive after His Passion by many infallible proofs ; being seen of them forty days, and speaking of the things pertaining to the kingdom of God." Consider, then, if we may state the alternative reverently, *which* of the two seems the more likely way, even according to a human wisdom, of forming preachers of the Gospel to all nations,—the exhibition of the Resurrection to the Jewish people generally, or this intimate private certifying of it to a few ? And remember that, as far as we can understand, the two procedures were inconsistent with each other ; for that period of preparatory prayer, meditation, and instruction, which the Apostles passed under our Lord's visible presence for forty days, was to them what it could not have been, had they been following Him from place to place in public, supposing there had been an object in this, and mixing in the busy crowds of the world.

3. I have already suggested, what is too obvious almost to insist upon, that in making a select few the ministers of His mercy to mankind at large, our Lord was but acting according to the general course of His providence. It is plain every great change is effected by the few, not by the many ; by the resolute, undaunted, zealous few. True it is that societies sometimes fall to pieces by their own corruption, which is in one sense a change without special instruments chosen or allowed by God ; but this is a dissolution, not a work. Doubtless, much may be *undone* by the many, but nothing is *done* except by those who are specially trained for action. In the midst of the famine Jacob's sons stood looking one upon another, but did nothing. One or two men, of small outward pretensions, but with their hearts in their work,

these do great things.   These are prepared, not by sudden excitement, or by vague general belief in the truth of their cause, but
by deeply impressed, often repeated instruction; and since it
stands to reason that it is easier to teach a few than a great
number, it is plain such men always will be few.   Such as these
spread the knowledge of Christ's resurrection over the idolatrous
world.   Well they answered the teaching of their Lord and
Master.   Their success sufficiently approves to us His wisdom in
showing Himself to them, not to all the people.

4.   Remember, too, this further reason why the witnesses of the
Resurrection were few in number; viz. because they were on the
side of *Truth*.   If the witnesses were to be such as really loved
and obeyed the Truth, there *could not* be many chosen.   Christ's
cause was the cause of light and religion, therefore His advocates
and ministers were necessarily few.   It is an old proverb (which
even the heathen admitted) that "the many are bad."   Christ
did not confide His Gospel to the many; had He done so, we
may even say, that it would have been at first sight a presumption
against its coming from God.   What was the chief work of His
whole ministry, but that of choosing and separating *from* the
multitude those who should be fit recipients of His Truth?   As
He went the round of the country again and again, through
Galilee and Judea, He tried the spirits of men the while; and
rejecting the baser sort who "honoured Him with their lips while
their hearts were far from Him," He specially chose twelve.
The many He put aside for a while as an adulterous and sinful
generation, intending to make one last experiment on the mass
when the Spirit should come.   But His twelve He brought near
to Himself at once, and taught them.   Then He sifted them, and
one fell away; the eleven escaped as though by fire.   *For* these
eleven especially He rose again; He visited *them* and taught *them*
for forty days; for in *them* He saw the fruit of the "travail of
His soul and was satisfied;" in them "He saw His seed, He
prolonged His days, and the pleasure of the Lord prospered in
His hand."   These were His witnesses, for they had the love of
the Truth in their hearts.   "I have chosen you," He says to
them, "and ordained you, that ye should go and bring forth fruit,
and that your fruit should remain." [1]

So much then in answer to the question, Why did not Christ
show Himself to the whole Jewish people after His resurrection?
I ask in reply, What would have been the use of it? a mere
passing triumph over sinners whose judgment is reserved for the

[1] John xv. 16.

next world. On the other hand, such a procedure would have interfered with, nay, defeated, the real object of His rising again, the propagation of His Gospel through the world by *means of His own intimate friends* and followers. And further, this preference of the few to the many seems to have been necessary from the nature of man, since all great works are effected, not by a multitude, but by the deep-seated resolution of a few;—nay, necessary too from man's depravity, for, alas ! popular favour is hardly to be expected for the cause of Truth. And our Lord's instruments were few, if for no other reason, yet at least for this, because more were not to be found, because there were but few faithful Israelites without guile in Israel according to the flesh.

Now, let us observe how much matter, both for warning and comfort, is supplied by this view. We learn from the picture of the *infant* Church what that Church has been ever since, that is, as far as man can understand it. Many are called, few are chosen. We learn to reflect on the great danger there is, lest we be not in the *number* of the chosen, and are warned to "watch and pray that we enter not into temptation," to "work out our salvation with fear and trembling," to seek God's mercy in His Holy Church, and to pray to Him ever that He would "fulfil in us the good pleasure of His will," and complete what He once began.

But, besides this, we are comforted too ; we are comforted, as many of us as are living humbly in the fear of God. Who those secret ones are, who in the bosom of the visible Church live as saints fulfilling their calling, God only knows. We are in the dark about it. We may indeed know much about ourselves, and we may form somewhat of a judgment about those with whom we are well acquainted. But of the general body of Christians we know little or nothing. It is our duty to consider them as Christians, to take them as we find them, and to love them ; and it is no concern of ours to debate about their state in God's sight. Without, however, entering into this question concerning God's secret counsels, let us receive this truth before us for a practical purpose ; that is, I speak to *all who* are conscious to themselves that they wish and try to serve God, whatever their progress in religion be, and whether or not they dare apply to themselves, or in whatever degree, the title of Christian in its most sacred sense. All who obey the Truth are on the side of the Truth, and the Truth will prevail. Few in number but strong in the Spirit, despised by the world, yet making way while they suffered, the twelve Apostles overturned the power of darkness, and established the Christian Church. And let all "who love the Lord Jesus Christ in sincerity" be quite sure, that weak though they seem, and solitary, yet the "foolishness of God is wiser than men, and the weakness of God is stronger than men." The many are "deceitful," and the worldly-wise are "vain;" but he "that feareth the Lord, the same shall be praised." The most excellent gifts of the intellect last but for a season. Eloquence and wit, shrewdness and dexterity, these plead a cause well and propagate it quickly, but it dies with them. It has no root in the hearts of men, and lives not out a generation. It is the consolation of the despised Truth, that its works endure. Its words are few, but they live. Abel's faith to this day "yet speaketh."[1] The blood of the martyrs is the seed of the Church. "Fret not thyself" then "because of evildoers, neither be thou envious against the workers of iniquity. For they shall soon be cut down like the grass, and wither as the green herb. Trust in the Lord and do good . . . delight thyself also in Him, and He shall give thee the desires of thy heart; commit thy way unto the Lord, trust also in Him, and He shall bring it to pass. . . . He shall bring forth thy righteousness as the light, and thy judgment as the noonday. . . . A little that a righteous man hath is better than the riches of *many* wicked. For the arms of the wicked shall be broken, but the Lord upholdeth the righteous. . . . I have seen the wicked in great power, and spreading himself like a green bay-tree: yet he passed away, and, lo! he was not; yea, I sought him, and he could not be found." [2] The heathen world made much ado when the Apostles preached the Resurrection. They and their associates were sent out as lambs among wolves; but they prevailed.

We, too, though we are not witnesses of Christ's actual resurrection, are so spiritually. By a heart awake from the dead, and by affections set on heaven, we can as truly and without figure witness that Christ liveth, as they did. He that believeth on the Son of God hath the witness in himself. Truth bears witness by itself to its Divine Author. He who obeys God conscientiously, and lives holily, forces all about him to believe and tremble before the unseen power of Christ. To the world indeed at large he witnesses not; for few can see him near enough to be moved by his manner of living. But to his neighbours he manifests the Truth in proportion to their knowledge of him; and some of them, through God's blessing, catch the holy flame, cherish it, and in their turn transmit it. And thus in a dark

[1] Heb. xi. 4.   [2] Ps. xxxvii. 1-6, 16, 17, 35, 36.

world Truth still makes way in spite of the darkness, passing from hand to hand. And thus it keeps its station in high places, acknowledged as the creed of nations, the multitude of which are ignorant, the while, on what it rests, how it came there, how it keeps its ground; and despising it, think it easy to dislodge it. But "the Lord reigneth." He is risen from the dead, "His throne is established of old; He is from everlasting. The floods have lifted up their voice, the floods lift up their waves. The Lord on high is mightier than the noise of many waters, yea, than the mighty waves of the sea. His testimonies are very sure; holiness becometh His house for ever." [1]

Let these be our thoughts whenever the prevalence of error leads us to despond. When St. Peter's disciple, Ignatius, was brought before the Roman emperor, he called himself Theophorus; and when the emperor asked the feeble old man why he so called himself, Ignatius said it was because he carried Christ in his breast. He witnessed there was but One God, who made heaven, earth, and sea, and all that is in them, and One Lord Jesus Christ, His Only-begotten Son, "whose kingdom," he added, "be my portion!" The emperor asked, "His kingdom, say you, who was crucified under Pilate?" "His," answered the saint, "who crucified my sin in me, and who has put all the fraud and malice of Satan under the feet of those who carry Him in their hearts: as it is written, 'I dwell in them and walk in them.'"

Ignatius was one against many, as St. Peter had been before him; and was put to death as the Apostle had been:—but he handed on the Truth in his day. At length we have received it. Weak though we be, and solitary, God forbid we should not in our turn hand it on; glorifying Him by our lives, and in all our words and works witnessing Christ's passion, death, and resurrection!

[1] Ps. xciii. 2-5.

SERMON XXV.

(EASTER TIDE.)

A Particular Providence as Revealed in the Gospel.

" Thou God seest me."—GEN. xvi. 13.

WHEN Hagar fled into the wilderness from the face of her mistress, she was visited by an angel, who sent her back; but, together with this implied reproof of her impatience, he gave her a word of promise to encourage and console her. In the mixture of humbling and cheerful thoughts thus wrought in her, she recognised the presence of her Maker and Lord, who ever comes to His servants in a twofold aspect, severe because He is holy, yet soothing as abounding in mercy. In consequence, she called the Name of the Lord that spake unto her, "Thou God seest me."

Such was the condition of man before Christ came, favoured with some occasional notices of God's regard for individuals, but, for the most part, instructed merely in His general Providence, as seen in the course of human affairs. In this respect even the Law was deficient, though it abounded in proofs that God was a living, all-seeing, all-recompensing God. It was deficient, in comparison of the Gospel, in evidence of the really-existing relation between each soul of man and its Maker, independently of everything else in the world. Of Moses, indeed, it is said, that "the Lord spake unto him *face to face*, as a man speaketh unto his friend." [1] But this was an especial privilege vouchsafed to him only and some others, as to Hagar, who records it in the text, not to all the people. But, under the New Covenant, this distinct regard, vouchsafed by Almighty God to every one of us, is clearly revealed. It was foretold of the Christian Church: "*All* thy children shall be taught of the Lord; and great shall be the peace

[1] Exod. xxxiii. 11.

of thy children." [1] When the Eternal Son came on earth in our flesh, men saw their invisible Maker and Judge. He showed Himself no longer through the mere powers of nature, or the maze of human affairs, but in our own likeness to Him. "God, who commanded the light to shine out of darkness, hath shined in our hearts, to give the light of the knowledge of the glory of God in the face of Jesus Christ;" [2] that is, in a sensible form, as a really existing individual being. And, at the same time, He forthwith began to speak to *us* as individuals. He, on the one hand, addressed each of us on the other. Thus it was in some sense a revelation face to face.

This is the subject on which I propose now to make a few remarks. And first, let me observe, it is very difficult, in spite of the revelation made us in the Gospel, to master the idea of this particular providence of God. If we allow ourselves to float down the current of the world, living as other men, gathering up our notions of religion here and there, as it may be, we have little or no true comprehension of a particular Providence. We conceive that Almighty God works on a large plan; but we cannot realize the wonderful truth that He sees and thinks of individuals. We cannot believe He is really present everywhere, that He is wherever we are, though unseen. For instance, we can understand, or think we understand, that He was present on Mount Sinai, or within the Jewish Temple, or that He clave the ground under Dathan and Abiram. But we do not in any sufficient sense believe that He is in like manner "about *our* path, and about *our* bed, and spieth out all *our* ways." [3] We cannot bring ourselves to get fast hold of the solemn fact, that He sees what is going on among ourselves at this moment; that this man falls and that man is exalted, at His silent, invisible appointment. We use, indeed, the prayers of the Church, and intercede, not only for all conditions of men, but for the King and the Nobility, and the Court of Parliament, and so on, down to individual sick people in our own parish; yet in spite of all this, we do not bring home to our minds the truth of His omniscience. We know He is in heaven, and forget that He is also on earth. This is the reason why the multitude of men are so profane. They use light words; they scoff at religion; they allow themselves to be lukewarm and indifferent; they take the part of wicked men; they push forward wicked measures; they defend injustice, or cruelty, or sacrilege, or infidelity; because they have no grasp of a truth, which nevertheless they have no intention to deny, that God sees

---

[1] Isa. liv. 13.   [2] 2 Cor. iv. 6.   [3] Ps. cxxxix. 2.

them.   There is, indeed, a self-will, and self-deceit, which would
sin on even in God's visible presence.   This was the sin of
Balaam, who took part with the enemies of Israel for reward;
and of Zimri, the son of Salu, a prince of the Simeonites, on
whom Phinehas did judgment; and such the sin of Saul, of Judas,
of Ananias and Sapphira.   Alas! doubtless such is the sin of
many a man now in England, unless human nature is other than
it was aforetime; alas! such a sin is in a measure our own from
time to time, as any one may know for certain who is used to
self-examination.   Yet, over and above this, certainly there is also
a great deal of profane sinning from our *forgetting*, not comprehending that we are in God's presence; not comprehending, or (in
other words) believing, that He sees and hears and notes down
everything we do.

This, again, is often the state in which persons find themselves
on falling into trouble.   The world fails them, and they despair,
because they do not realize to themselves the loving-kindness and
the presence of God.   They find no comfort in a truth which to
them is not a substance but an opinion.   Therefore it was that
Hagar, when visited in the wilderness by the angel, called the
Name of the Lord that spake unto her, "Thou God seest me!"
It came as a new truth to her that, amid her trouble and her
waywardness, the eye of God was upon her.   The case is the
same now.   Men talk in a general way of the goodness of God,
His benevolence, compassion, and long-suffering; but they think
of it as of a flood pouring itself out all through the world, as the
light of the sun, not as the continually repeated action of an
intelligent and living Mind, contemplating whom it visits and
intending what it effects.   Accordingly, when they come into
trouble, they can but say, "It is all for the best—God is good,"
and the like; and this does but fall as cold comfort upon them,
and does not lessen their sorrow, because they have not accustomed
their minds to feel that He is a merciful God, regarding them
individually, and not a mere universal Providence acting by
general laws.   And then, perhaps, all of a sudden the true notion
breaks on them, as it did upon Hagar.   Some especial Providence,
amid their infliction, runs right into their heart, and brings it
close home to them, in a way they never experienced before, that
God sees them.   And then, surprised at this, which is a something quite new to them, they go into the other extreme, in proportion to their former apathy, and are led to think that they
are especial objects of God's love, more than all other men.
Instead of taking what has happened to them as an evidence of

His particular Providence over all, as revealed in Scripture, they still will not believe a jot or tittle more than they see; and, while discovering He loves them individually, they do not advance one step, on that account, to the general truth, that He loves other men individually also. Now, had they been all along in the practice of studying Scripture, they would have been saved from both errors—their first, which was blindness to a particular Providence altogether—their second, which was a narrow-minded limiting of it to themselves, as if the world at large were rejected and reprobate; for Scripture represents this privilege as the portion of all men one by one.

I suppose it is scarcely necessary to prove to those who have allowed their minds to dwell on the Gospels, that the peculiar character of our Lord's goodness, as displayed therein, is its tenderness and its considerateness. These qualities are the very perfection of kindness between man and man; but, from the very extent and complication of the world's system, and from its Maker being invisible, our imagination scarcely succeeds in attributing them to Him, even when our reason is convinced, and we wish to believe accordingly. His Providence manifests itself in general laws, it moves forward upon the lines of truth and justice; it has no respect of persons, rewarding the good and punishing the bad, not as individuals, but according to their character. How shall He who is Most Holy direct His love to this man or that for the sake of each, contemplating us one by one, without infringing on His own perfections? Or even were the Supreme Being a God of unmixed benevolence, how, even then, shall the thought of Him come home to our minds with that constraining power which the kindness of a human friend exerts over us? The greatest acknowledgment we can make of the kindness of a superior, is to say that he acts as if he were personally interested in us. The mass of benevolent men are kind and generous, because it is their way to be so, irrespectively of the person whom they benefit. Natural temper, a flow of spirits, or a turn of good fortune, opens the heart, which pours itself out profusely on friend and enemy. They scatter benefits as they move along. Now, at first sight, it is difficult to see how our idea of Almighty God can be divested of these earthly notions, either that His goodness is imperfect, or that it is fated and necessary; and wonderful indeed, and adorable is the condescension by which He has met our infirmity. He has met and aided it in that same Dispensation by which He redeemed our souls. In order that we may understand that in spite of His mysterious perfections He has a separate knowledge and regard for individuals, He has taken upon Him the thoughts and feelings of our own nature, which we all understand *is* capable of such personal attachments. By becoming man, He has cut short the perplexities and the discussions of our reason on the subject, as if He would grant our objections for argument's sake, and supersede them by taking our own ground.

The most winning property of our Saviour's mercy (if it is right so to speak of it) is its dependence on time and place, person and circumstance; in other words, its tender discrimination. It regards and consults for each individual as he comes before it. It is called forth by some as it is not by others, it cannot (if I may say so) manifest itself to every object alike; it has its particular shade and mode of feeling for each; and on some men it so bestows itself, as if He depended for His own happiness on their wellbeing. This might be illustrated, as is often done, by our Lord's tender behaviour towards Lazarus and his sisters, or His tears over Jerusalem; or by His conduct towards St. Peter, before and after his denial of Him, or towards St. Thomas when he doubted, or by His love of His mother, or of St. John. But I will direct your attention rather to His treatment of the traitor Judas; both because it is not so commonly referred to, and also because, if there was a being in the whole world whom one might suppose to be cast out of His presence as hateful and reprobate, it was he whom He foresaw would betray Him. Yet we shall find that even this wretched man was followed and encompassed by His serene though grave regard till the very hour he betrayed Him.

Judas was in darkness and hated the light, and "went to his own place;" yet he found it, not by the mere force of certain natural principles working out their inevitable results—by some unfeeling fate, which sentences the wicked to hell—but by a Judge who surveys him from head to foot, who searches him through and through, to see if there is any ray of hope, any latent spark of faith; who pleads with him again and again, and, at length abandoning him, mourns over him the while with the wounded affection of a friend rather than the severity of the Judge of the whole earth. For instance, first a startling warning a year before his trial. "Have not I chosen you twelve, and one of you is a devil?" Then, when the time was come, the lowest act of abasement towards one who was soon to betray Him, and to suffer the unquenchable fire. "He riseth from supper, and . . . poureth water into a bason, and began to wash the disciples' feet,"[1] and

[1] John vi. 70; xiii. 4, 5.

Judas in the number. Then a second warning at the same time, or rather a sorrowful lament spoken as if to Himself, "Ye are not all clean." Then openly, "Verily, verily, I say unto you, that one of you shall betray Me." "The Son of Man goeth as it is written of Him; but woe unto that man by whom the Son of Man is betrayed! it had been good for that man if he had not been born. Then Judas, which betrayed Him, answered and said, Master, is it I? He said unto him, Thou hast said." Lastly, when He was actually betrayed by him, "Friend, wherefore art thou come?" "Judas" (He addresses him by name), "betrayest thou the Son of Man with a kiss?"[1] I am not attempting to reconcile His divine foreknowledge with this special and prolonged anxiety, this personal feeling towards Judas; but wish you only to dwell upon the latter, in order to observe what is given us by the revelation of Almighty God in the Gospels, viz. an acquaintance with His providential regard for *individuals*, making His sun to rise on the evil as well as on the good. And, in like manner doubtless, at the last day, the wicked and impenitent shall be condemned, not in a mass, but one by one—one by one, appearing each in his own turn before the righteous Judge, standing under the full glory of His countenance, carefully weighed in the balance and found wanting, dealt with, not indeed with a weak and wavering purpose, where God's justice claims satisfaction, yet, at the same time, with all the circumstantial solicitude and awful care of one who would fain make, if He could, the fruit of His Passion more numerous than it is.

This solemn reflection may be further enforced by considering our Lord's behaviour towards strangers who came to Him. Judas was His friend; but *we* have never seen Him. How will He look, and how does He look upon us? Let His manner in the Gospels towards the multitude of men assure us. All-holy, Almighty as He is, and has shown Himself to be, yet in the midst of His Divine Majesty, He could display a tender interest in all who approached Him; as if He could not cast His eyes on any of His creatures without the overflowing affection of a parent for his child, regarding it with a full satisfaction, and simply desiring its happiness and highest good. Thus, when the rich young man came to him, it is said, "And Jesus beholding him, *loved him*, and said unto him, One thing thou lackest." When the Pharisees asked a sign, "He sighed deeply in His Spirit." At another time, "He looked round about on them"— as if on every one, to see if here or there perchance there might

[1] Matt. xxvi. 24, 25, 50. Luke xxii. 48.

be an exception to the general unbelief, and to condemn, one by one, those who were guilty[1]—"He looked round about on them with anger, being grieved for the hardness of their hearts." Again, when a leper came to Him, He did not simply heal him, but, "moved with compassion, He put forth His hand."[2]

How gracious is this revelation of God's particular providence to those who seek Him! how gracious to those who have discovered that this world is but vanity, and who are solitary and isolated in themselves, whatever shadows of power and happiness surround them! The multitude, indeed, go on without these thoughts, either from insensibility, as not understanding their own wants, or changing from one idol to another, as each successively fails. But men of keener hearts would be overpowered by despondency, and would even loathe existence, did they suppose themselves under the mere operation of fixed laws, powerless to excite the pity or the attention of Him who has appointed them. What should they do especially, who are cast among persons unable to enter into their feelings, and thus strangers to them, though by long custom ever so much friends! or who have perplexities of mind they cannot explain to themselves, much less remove, and no one to help them; or who have affections and aspirations pent up within them, because they have not met with objects to which to devote them; or who are misunderstood by those around them, and find they have no words to set themselves right with them, or no principles in common by way of appeal; or who seem to themselves to be without place or purpose in the world, or to be in the way of others; or who have to follow their own sense of duty without advisers or supporters, nay, to resist the wishes and solicitations of superiors or relatives; or who have the burden of some painful secret, or of some incommunicable solitary grief! In all such cases the Gospel narrative supplies our very need, not simply presenting to us an unchangeable Creator to rely upon, but a compassionate Guardian, a discriminating Judge and Helper.

God beholds thee individually, whoever thou art. He "calls thee by thy name." He sees thee, and understands thee, as He made thee. He knows what is in thee, all thy own peculiar feelings and thoughts, thy dispositions and likings, thy strength and thy weakness. He views thee in thy day of rejoicing and thy day of sorrow. He sympathizes in thy hopes and thy

---

[1] Mark x. 21; viii. 12; iii. 5.
[2] *Vide* also Matt. xix 26. Luke xxii. 61. Mark iii. 34: i. 41.

temptations. He interests Himself in all thy anxieties and remembrances, all the risings and fallings of thy spirit. He has numbered the very hairs of thy head and the cubits of thy stature. He compasses thee round and bears thee in His arms; He takes thee up and sets thee down. He notes thy very countenance, whether smiling or in tears, whether healthful or sickly. He looks tenderly upon thy hands and thy feet; He hears thy voice, the beating of thy heart, and thy very breathing. Thou dost not love thyself better than He loves thee. Thou canst not shrink from pain more than He dislikes thy bearing it; and if He puts it on thee, it is as thou wilt put it on thyself, if thou art wise, for a greater good afterwards. Thou art not only His creature (though for the very sparrows He has a care, and pitied the "much cattle" of Nineveh), thou art man redeemed and sanctified, His adopted son, favoured with a portion of that glory and blessedness which flows from Him everlastingly unto the Only-begotten. Thou art chosen to be His, even above thy fellows who dwell in the east and south. Thou wast one of those for whom Christ offered up His last prayer, and sealed it with His precious blood. What a thought is this, a thought almost too great for our faith ! Scarce can we refrain from acting Sarah's part, when we bring it before us, so as to "laugh" from amazement and perplexity. What is man, what are we, what am I, that the Son of God should be so mindful of me ? What am I, that He should have raised me from almost a devil's nature to that of an angel's ? that He should have changed my soul's original constitution, new-made me, who from my youth up have been a transgressor, and should Himself dwell personally in this very heart of mine, making me His temple ? What am I, that God the Holy Ghost should enter into me, and draw up my thoughts heavenward "with plaints unutterable" ?

These are the meditations which come upon the Christian to console him while he is with Christ upon the holy mount. And, when he descends to his daily duties, they are still his inward strength, though he is not allowed to tell the vision to those around him. They make his countenance to shine, make him cheerful, collected, serene, and firm in the midst of all temptation, persecution, or bereavement. And with such thoughts before us, how base and miserable does the world appear in all its pursuits and doctrines ! How truly miserable does it seem to seek good from the creature ; to covet station, wealth, or credit; to choose for ourselves, in fancy, this or that mode of life ; to affect the manners and fashions of the great : to spend our time in follies ;

to be discontented, quarrelsome, jealous or envious, censorious or resentful; fond of unprofitable talk, and eager for the news of the day; busy about public matters which concern us not; hot in the cause of this or that interest or party; or set upon gain; or devoted to the increase of barren knowledge! And at the end of our days, when flesh and heart fail, what will be our consolation, though we have made ourselves rich, or have served an office, or been the first man among our equals, or have depressed a rival, or managed things our own way, or have settled splendidly, or have been intimate with the great, or have fared sumptuously, or have gained a name! Say, even if we obtain that which lasts longest, a place in history, yet, after all, what ashes shall we have eaten for bread! and, in that awful hour, when death is in sight, will He, whose eye is now so loving towards us, and whose hand falls on us so gently, will He acknowledge us any more? or, if He still speaks, will His voice have any power to stir us? rather will it not repel us, as it did Judas, by the very tenderness with which it would invite us to Him?

Let us then endeavour, by His grace, rightly to understand where we stand, and what He is towards us; most tender and pitiful, yet, for all His pity, not passing by the breadth of a single hair the eternal lines of truth, holiness, and justice; He who can condemn to the woe everlasting, though He weeps and laments beforehand, and who, when once the sentence of condemnation has gone forth, will wipe out altogether the remembrance of us, "and know us not." The tares were "bound in bundles" for the burning, indiscriminately, promiscuously, contemptuously. "Let us then fear, lest a promise being left us of entering into His rest, any of us should seem to come short of it."

SERMON XXVI.

(EASTER-TIDE.)

Christ Manifested in Remembrance.

"He shall glorify Me."—JOHN xvi. 14.

WHEN our Lord was leaving His Apostles, and they were sorrowful, He consoled them by the promise of another Guide and Teacher, on whom they might rely instead of Him, and who should be more to them even than He had been. He promised them the Third Person in the Ever-blessed Trinity, the Holy Ghost, the Spirit of Himself and of His Father, who should come invisibly, and with the greater power and comfort, inasmuch as He was invisible ; so that His presence would be more real and efficacious by how much it was more secret and inscrutable. At the same time this new and most gracious Comforter, while bringing a higher blessedness, would not in any degree obscure or hide what had gone before. Though He did more for the Apostles than Christ had done, He would not throw into the shade and supersede Him whom He succeeded. How could that be ? who could come greater or holier than the Son of God ? who could obscure the Lord of glory ? how could the Holy Ghost, who was one with the Son, and the Spirit proceeding from the Son, do otherwise than manifest the Son, while manifesting Himself ? how could He fail to illuminate the mercies and perfections of Him whose death upon the Cross opened a way for Himself, the Holy Ghost, to be gracious to man also ? Accordingly, though it was expedient that the Son should go away, in order that the Comforter might come, we did not lose the sight of the Son in the presence of the Comforter. On the contrary, Christ expressly announced to the Apostles concerning Him, in the words of the text, " He shall glorify Me."

Now these words lead us first to consider in what special way the Holy Ghost gives glory to the Son of God; and next to inquire whether there is not in this appointment some trace of a general law of Divine Providence, which is observed, as in Scripture, so in the world's affairs.

The special way in which God the Holy Ghost gave glory to God the Son, seems to have been His revealing Him as the Only-begotten Son of the Father, who had appeared as the Son of Man. Our Saviour said most plainly that He was the Son of God; but it is one thing to declare the whole truth, another to receive it. Our Saviour said all that need be said, but His Apostles understood Him not. Nay, when they made confession, and that in faith, and by the secret grace of God, and therefore acceptably to Christ, still they understood not fully what they said. St. Peter acknowledged Him as the Christ, the Son of God. So did the centurion who was present at His crucifixion. Did that centurion, when he said, "Truly, this was the Son of God," understand his own words? Surely not. Nor did St. Peter, though he spoke, not through flesh and blood, but by the revelation of the Father. Had he understood, could he so soon after, when our Lord spoke of His passion which lay before Him, have presumed to "take Him, and begin to rebuke Him"? Certainly he did not understand that our Lord, as being the Son of God, was not the creature of God, but the Eternal Word, the Only-begotten Son of the Father, one with Him in substance, distinct in Person.

And when we look into our Saviour's conduct in the days of His flesh, we find that He purposely concealed that knowledge, which yet He gave; as if intending it should be enjoyed, but not at once; as if His words were to stand, but to wait awhile for their interpretation; as if reserving them for His coming who at once was to bring Christ and His words into the light. Thus when the young ruler came to Him, and said, "Good Master," He showed Himself more desirous of correcting him than of revealing Himself, desirous rather to make him weigh his words than Himself to accept them. At another time, when He had so far disclosed Himself that the Jews accused Him of blasphemy, in that He, being a man, made Himself God, far from repeating and insisting on the Sacred Truth which they rejected, He invalidated the terms in which He had conveyed it, by intimating that even the prophets of the Old Testament were called gods as well as He. And when He stood before Pilate, He refused to bear witness to Himself, or say what He was, or whence He came.

Thus He was among them " as he that serveth." Apparently, it was not till after His resurrection, and especially after His ascension, when the Holy Ghost descended, that the Apostles understood who had been with them. When all was over they knew it, not at the time.

Now here we see, I think, the trace of a general principle, which comes before us again and again both in Scripture and in the world, that God's presence is not discerned at the time when it is upon us, but afterwards, when we look back upon what is gone and over.

Our Saviour's history itself will supply instances in evidence of the existence of this remarkable law.

St. Philip, for instance, when he asked to see the Almighty Father, little understood the privilege he had already so long enjoyed; accordingly, our Lord answered, " Have I been so long time with you, and yet hast thou not known Me, Philip ?"

Again, on another occasion, He said to St. Peter, " What I do thou knowest not now, but thou shalt know hereafter." [1] Again, " These things understood not His disciples at the first; but when Jesus was glorified, then remembered they that these things were written of Him, and that they had done these things unto Him." [2]

And in like manner, while He talked with the two disciples going to Emmaus, their eyes were holden that they did not know Him. When they recognised Him, at once He vanished out of their sight. *Then* " they said one to another, Did not our heart burn within us while He talked with us by the way ?" [3]

Such too are the following, taken from the Old Testament. Jacob, when he fled from his brother, " lighted upon a certain place, and tarried there all night, because the sun was set." In his sleep he saw the vision of angels, and the Lord above them. Accordingly, when he awaked out of his sleep, he said, " Surely the Lord is in this place, and I knew it not. And he was afraid, and said, How dreadful is this place ! This is none other but the house of God, and this is the gate of heaven." [4]

Again, after wrestling all night with the Angel, not knowing who it was, and asking after His Name, then at length " Jacob called the name of the place Peniel; for I have seen God face to face, and my life is preserved." [5]

So again, after the Angel had departed from Gideon, who had treated Him like a man, then, and not till then, he discovered who

---

[1] John xiii. 7.   [2] John xii. 16.   [3] Luke xxiv. 32.
[4] Gen. xxviii. 11-17.   [5] Gen. xxxii. 30.

had been with him, and he said, "Alas, O Lord God; for because I have seen an Angel of the Lord face to face." [1]

And so in like manner, after the Angel had departed from Manoah and his wife, then, and not till then, they discovered Him. Then they "fell on their faces to the ground. . . . And Manoah said unto his wife, We shall surely die, because we have seen God." [2]

Such is God's rule in Scripture, to dispense His blessings silently and secretly; so that we do not discern them at the time, except by faith, afterwards only. Of which, as I have said, we have two special instances in the very outline of the Gospel history; the mission of our Saviour, who was not understood till afterwards to be the Son of God Most High, and the mission of the Holy Ghost, which was still more laden with spiritual benefits, and is still more secret. Flesh and blood could not discern the Son of God, even when He wrought visible miracles; the natural man still less discerns the things of the Spirit of God; yet in the next world all shall be condemned, for not believing here what it was never given them to see. Thus the presence of God is like His glory as it appeared to Moses; He said, "Thou canst not see my face . . . and live;" but He passed by, and Moses saw that glory, as it retired, which he might not see in front, or in passing; he saw it, and he acknowledged it, and "made haste and bowed his head toward the earth, and worshipped." [3]

Now consider how parallel this is to what takes place in the providences of daily life. Events happen to us pleasant or painful; we do not know at the time the meaning of them, we do not see God's hand in them. If indeed we have faith, we confess what we do not see, and take all that happens as His; but whether we will accept it in faith or not, certainly there is no other way of accepting it. We see nothing. We see not why things come, or whither they tend. Jacob cried out on one occasion, "All these things are against me;" [4] certainly so they seemed to be. One son made away with by the rest, another in prison in a foreign land, a third demanded: "me have ye bereaved of my children; Joseph is not, and Simeon is not, and ye will take Benjamin away: all these things are against me." Yet all these things were working for good. Or pursue the fortunes of the favourite and holy youth who was the first taken from him; sold by his brethren to strangers, carried into Egypt, tempted by a very perilous temptation, overcoming it but not rewarded, thrown into prison, the iron

[1] Judges vi 22.   [2] Judges xiii. 20, 22.
[3] Exod. xxxiii. 20; xxxiv. 8.   [4] Gen. xlii. 36.

entering into his soul, waiting there till the Lord should be gracious, and "look down from heaven;" but waiting—why? and how long? It is said again and again in the sacred narrative, "The Lord was with Joseph;" but do you think he saw at the time any tokens of God? any tokens, except so far as by faith he realized them, in faith he saw them? His faith was its own reward; which to the eye of reason was no reward at all, for faith forsooth did but judge of things by that standard which it had originally set up, and pronounce that Joseph was happy because he ought to be so. Thus, though the Lord was with him, apparently all things were against him. Yet afterwards he saw what was so mysterious at the time;—"God did send me before you," he said to his brethren, "to preserve life. . . . It was not you that sent me hither, but God; and He hath made me a father to Pharaoh, and lord of all his house, and a ruler throughout all the land of Egypt."

Wonderful providence indeed, which is so silent, yet so efficacious, so constant, so unerring! This is what baffles the power of Satan. He cannot discern the hand of God in what goes on; and though he would fain meet it and encounter it, in his mad and blasphemous rebellion against heaven, he cannot find it. Crafty and penetrating as he is, yet his thousand eyes and his many instruments avail him nothing against the majestic serene silence, the holy imperturbable calm which reigns through the providences of God. Crafty and experienced as he is, he appears like a child or a fool, like one made sport of, whose daily bread is but failure and mockery, before the deep and secret wisdom of the Divine counsels. He makes a guess here, or does a bold act there, but all in the dark. He knew not of Gabriel's coming, and the miraculous conception of the Virgin,[1] or what was meant by that Holy Thing which was to be born being called the Son of God. He tried to kill Him, and he made martyrs of the innocent children; he tempted the Lord of all with hunger and with ambitious prospects; he sifted the Apostles, and got none but one, who already bore his own name, and had been already given over as a devil. He rose against his God in his full strength, in the hour and power of darkness, and then he seemed to conquer; but with his utmost effort, and as his greatest achievement, he did no more than "whatsoever Thy hand and Thy counsel determined before to be done."[2] He brought into the world the very salvation which he feared and hated. He accomplished the Atonement of that world whose misery He was plotting. Wonderfully silent,

---

[1] *Vide* Ignat. ad Eph. 19.   [2] Acts iv. 28.

yet resistless course of God's providence! "Verily, Thou art a God that hidest Thyself, O God of Israel, the Saviour;" and if even devils, sagacious as they are, spirits by nature and experienced in evil, cannot detect His hand, while He works, how can we hope to see it except by that way which the devils cannot take, by a loving faith? how can we see it except afterwards as a reward to our faith, beholding the cloud of glory in the distance, which when present was too rare and impalpable for mortal sense?

And so, again, in a number of other occurrences, not striking, not grievous, not pleasant, but ordinary, we are able afterwards to discern that He has been with us, and, like Moses, to worship Him. Let a person who trusts he is on the whole serving God acceptably, look back upon his past life, and he will find how critical were moments and acts, which at the time seemed the most indifferent : as for instance, the school he was sent to as a child, the occasion of his falling in with those persons who have most benefited him, the accidents which determined his calling or prospects whatever they were. God's hand is ever over His own, and He leads them forward by a way they know not of. The utmost they can do is to believe, what they cannot see now, what they shall see hereafter ; and as believing, to act together with God towards it.

And hence perchance it is, that years that are past bear in retrospect so much of fragrance with them, though at the time perhaps we saw little in them to take pleasure in ; or rather we did not, could not realize that we *were* receiving pleasure, though we received it. We received pleasure, because we were in the presence of God, but we knew it not ; we knew not what we received ; we did not bring home to ourselves or reflect upon the pleasure we were receiving ; but afterwards, when enjoyment is past, reflection comes in. We feel at the time ; we recognise and reason afterwards. Such, I say, is the sweetness and softness with which days long passed away fall upon the memory, and strike us. The most ordinary years, when we seemed to be living for nothing, these shine forth to us in their very regularity and orderly course. What was sameness at the time, is now stability ; what was dulness, is now a soothing calm ; what seemed unprofitable, has now its treasure in itself ; what was but monotony, is now harmony ; all is pleasing and comfortable, and we regard it all with affection. Nay, even sorrowful times (which at first sight is wonderful) are thus softened and illuminated afterwards : yet why should they not be so, since then, more than at other times, our Lord is present, when He seems leaving His own to desolateness and orphanhood? The planting of Christ's Cross in the heart is sharp and trying; but the stately tree rears itself aloft, and has fair branches and rich fruit, and is good to look upon. And if all this be true, even of sad or of ordinary times, much more does it hold good of seasons of religious obedience and comfort.

Such are the feelings with which men often look back on their childhood, when any accident brings it vividly before them. Some relic or token of that early time, some spot, or some book, or a word, or a scent, or a sound, brings them back in memory to the first years of their discipleship, and they then see, what they could not know at the time, that God's presence went up with them and gave them rest. Nay, even now perhaps they are unable to discern fully what it was which made that time so bright and glorious. They are full of tender, affectionate thoughts towards those first years, but they do not know why. They think it is those very years which they yearn after, whereas it is the presence of God which, as they now see, was then over them, which attracts them. They think that they regret the past, when they are but longing after the future. It is not that they would be children again, but that they would be angels and would see God; they would be immortal beings, crowned with amaranth, robed in white, and with palms in their hands, before His throne.

What happens in the fortunes of individuals happens also to the Church. Its pleasant times are pleasant in memory. We cannot know who are great and who are little, what times are serious and what are their effects, till afterwards. Then we make much of the abode, and the goings-out and the comings-in of those who in their day lived familiarly with us, and seemed like other men. Then we gather up the recollection of what they did here, and what they said there. Then their persecutors, however powerful, are not known or spoken of, except by way of setting off *their* achievements and triumphs in the Gospel. "Kings of the earth, and the great men, and rich men, and the chief captains, and the mighty men," who in their day so magnified themselves, so ravaged and deformed the Church, that it could not be seen except by faith, then are found in nowise to have infringed the continuity of its outlines, which shine out clear and glorious, and even more delicate and tender for the very attempt to obliterate them. It needs very little study of history to prove how really this is the case; how little schism and divisions, and disorders and troubles, and fears and persecutions, and scatterings and threatenings interfere with the glory of Christ Mystical, as looked upon afterwards, though at the time they almost hid it. Great saints, great events, great privileges, like the everlasting mountains, grow as we recede from them.

And it is a sort of instinct, felt by the multitude, that they really are in possession of that which they neither see nor in faith accept, which (as some have remarked) makes them so unwilling just at the last moment to give up those privileges which they have so long possessed without valuing or using. Sometimes at the last moment, when mercies are about to be withdrawn, when it is too late, or all but too late, a feeling comes over them that something precious is going from them. They seem to hear the sound of arms, and the voices in the Temple saying, " Let us depart hence ; " and they attempt to retain what they cannot see ; —penitents, when the day of grace is over.

Once more : every one of us surely must have experienced this general feeling most strongly, at one time or other, as regards the sacraments and ordinances of the Church. At the time, we cannot realize, we can but believe that Christ is with us ; but after an interval a sweetness breathes from them, as from His garments " of myrrh, aloes, and cassia." Such is the memory of many a Holy Communion in Church, of Holy Communions solemnized at a sickbed, of Baptisms assisted in, of Confirmation, of Marriage, of Ordination ; nay, services which at the time we could not enjoy, from sickness, from agitation, from restlessness, —services which at the time, in spite of our belief in their blessedness, yet troubled our wayward hearts, — services which we were tempted to think long, feared beforehand, nay, and wished over when they were performing (alas ! that we should be so blind and dead to our highest good), yet afterwards are full of God. We come, like Jacob, in the dark, and lie down with a stone for our pillow ; but when we rise again, and call to mind what has passed, we recollect we have seen a vision of angels, and the Lord manifested through them, and we are led to cry out, " How dreadful is this place ! This is *none other* than the house of God, and this is the gate of heaven."

To conclude. Let us profit by what every day and hour teaches us as it flies. What is dark while it is meeting us, reflects the Sun of Righteousness when it is past. Let us profit by this in future, so far as this, to have *faith in what* we cannot see. The world seems to go on as usual. There is nothing of heaven in the face of society ; in the news of the day there is nothing of heaven ; in the faces of the many, or of the great, or of the rich, or of the busy, there is nothing of heaven ; in the words of the eloquent, or the deeds of the powerful, or the counsels of the wise, or the resolves of the lordly, or the pomps of the wealthy, there is nothing of heaven. And yet the Ever-blessed Spirit of God is here; the Presence of the Eternal Son, ten times more glorious, more powerful than when He trod the earth in our flesh, is with us. Let us ever bear in mind this divine truth,—the more secret God's hand is, the more powerful —the more silent, the more awful. We are under the awful ministration of the Spirit, against whom whoso speaks hazards more than can be reckoned up ; whom whoso grieves loses more of blessing and glory than can be fathomed. The Lord was with Joseph, and the Lord was with David, and the Lord, in the days of His flesh, was with His Apostles; but now, He is with us in the Spirit. And inasmuch as the Divine Spirit is more than flesh and blood ; inasmuch as the risen and glorified Saviour is more powerful than when He was in the form of a servant; inas-much as the Eternal Word, spiritualizing His own manhood, has more of virtue for us, and grace, and blessing, and life, than when concealed in it, and subject to temptation and pain ; inas-much as faith is more blessed than sight; by so much more are we now more highly privileged, have more title to be called kings and priests unto God, even than the disciples who saw and touched Him. He who glorified Christ imparts Him thus glorified to us. If He could work miracles in the days of His flesh, how much more can He work miracles now ? and if His visible miracles were full of power, how much more His miracles invisible ? Let us beg of Him grace wherewith to enter into the depth of our privileges,—to enjoy what we possess,—to believe in, to use, to improve, to glory in our present gifts as " members of Christ, children of God, and inheritors of the kingdom of heaven."

SERMON XXVII.

(EASTER-TIDE.)

The Invisible World.

" While we look not at the things which are seen, but at the things which are not seen ; for the things which are seen are temporal, but the things which are not seen are eternal."—2 COR. iv. 18.

THERE are two worlds, " the visible and the invisible," as the Creed speaks,—the world we see, and the world we do not see ; and the world which we do not see as really exists as the world we do see. It really exists, though we see it not. The world that we see we know to exist, *because* we see it. We have but to lift up our eyes and look around us, and we have proof of it : our eyes tell us. We see the sun, moon and stars, earth and sky, hills and valleys, woods and plains, seas and rivers. And again, we see men, and the works of men. We see cities, and stately buildings, and their inhabitants ; men running to and fro, and busying themselves to provide for themselves and their families, or to accomplish great designs, or for the very business' sake. All that meets our eyes forms one world. It is an immense world ; it reaches to the stars. Thousands on thousands of years might we speed up the sky, and though we were swifter than the light itself, we should not reach them all. They are at distances from us greater than any that is assignable. So high, so wide, so deep is the world ; and yet it also comes near and close to us. It is everywhere ; and it seems to leave no room for any other world.

And yet in spite of this universal world which we see, there is another world, quite as far-spreading, quite as close to us, and more wonderful ; another world all around us, though we see it not, and more wonderful than the world we see, for this reason if for no other, that we do not see it. All around us are number-less objects, coming and going, watching, working, or waiting, which we see not : this is that other world, which the eyes reach not unto, but faith only.

Let us dwell upon this thought. We are born into a world of sense; that is, of the real things which lie round about us, one great department comes to us, accosts us, through our bodily organs, our eyes, ears, and fingers. We feel, hear, and see them; and we know they exist, because we do thus perceive them. Things innumerable lie about us, animate and inanimate ; but one particular class of these innumerable things is thus brought home to us through our senses. And moreover, while they act upon us, they make their presence known. We are sensible of them at the time, we are conscious that we perceive them. We not only see, but know that we see them ; we not only hold intercourse, but know that we do. We are among men, and we know that we are. We feel cold and hunger ; we know what sensible things remove them. We eat, drink, clothe ourselves, dwell in houses, converse and act with others, and perform the duties of social life ; and we feel vividly that we are doing so, while we do so. Such is our relation towards one part of the innumerable beings which lie around us. They act upon us, and we know it ; and we act upon them in turn, and know we do.

But all this does not interfere with the existence of that other world which I speak of, acting upon us, yet not impressing us with the consciousness that it does so. It may as really be present and exert an influence as that which reveals itself to us. And that such a world there is, Scripture tells us. Do you ask what it is, and what it contains ? I will not say that all that belongs to it is vastly more important than what we see, for among things visible are our fellow-men, and nothing created is more precious and noble than a son of man. But still, taking the things which we see altogether, and the things we do not see altogether, the world we do not see is on the whole a much higher world than that which we do see. For, first of all, He is there who is above all beings, who has created all, before whom they all are as nothing, and with whom nothing can be compared. Almighty God, we know, exists more really and absolutely than any of those fellow-men whose existence is conveyed to us through the senses ; yet we see Him not, hear Him not, we do but "feel after Him," yet without finding Him. It appears, then, that the things which are seen are but a part, and but a secondary part of the beings about us, were it only on this ground, that Almighty

God, the Being of beings, is not in their number, but among "the things which are not seen." Once, and once only, for thirty-three years, has He condescended to become one of the beings which are seen, when He, the Second Person of the Ever-blessed Trinity, was, by an unspeakable mercy, born of the Virgin Mary into this sensible world. And then He was seen, heard, handled; He ate, He drank, He slept, He conversed, He went about, He acted as other men: but excepting this brief period, His presence has never been perceptible; He has never made us conscious of His existence by means of our senses. He came, and He retired beyond the veil: and to us individually, it is as if He had never shown Himself; we have as little sensible experience of His presence. Yet "He liveth evermore."

And in that other world are the souls also of the dead. They too, when they depart hence, do not cease to exist, but they retire from this visible scene of things; or, in other words, they cease to act towards us and before us *through our senses.* They live as they lived before; but that outward frame, through which they were able to hold communion with other men, is in some way, we know not how, separated from them, and dries away and shrivels up as leaves may drop off a tree. They remain, but without the usual means of approach towards us, and correspondence with us. As when a man loses his voice or hand, he still exists as before, but cannot any longer talk or write, or otherwise hold intercourse with us; so when he loses not voice and hand only, but his whole frame, or is said to die, there is nothing to show that he is gone, but we have lost our means of apprehending him.

Again: Angels also are inhabitants of the world invisible, and concerning them much more is told us than concerning the souls of the faithful departed, because the latter "rest from their labours;" but the Angels are actively employed among us in the Church. They are said to be "ministering spirits, sent forth to minister for them who shall be heirs of salvation."[1] No Christian is so humble but he has Angels to attend on him, if he lives by faith and love. Though they are so great, so glorious, so pure, so wonderful, that the very sight of them (if we were allowed to see them) would strike us to the earth, as it did the prophet Daniel, holy and righteous as he was; yet they are our "fellow-servants" and our fellow-workers, and they carefully watch over and defend even the humblest of us, if we be Christ's. That they form a part of our unseen world, appears from the vision

[1] Heb. i. 14.

seen by the patriarch Jacob. We are told that when he fled
from his brother Esau, "he lighted upon a certain place, and
tarried there all night, because the sun had set ; and he took of
the stones of that place, and put them for his pillows, and lay
down in that place to sleep."[1] How little did he think that
there was anything very wonderful in this spot ! It looked like
any other spot. It was a lone, uncomfortable place: there was no
house there : night was coming on ; and he had to sleep upon the
bare rock. Yet how different was the truth ! He saw but the
world that is seen; he saw not the world that is not seen; yet the
world that is not seen was there. It was there, though it did
not at once make known its presence, but needed to be super-
naturally displayed to him. He saw it in his sleep. "He
dreamed, and behold, a ladder set up on the earth, and the top of
it reached up to heaven ; and behold, the Angels of God ascending and descending on it. And behold, the Lord stood above
it." This was the other world. Now, let this be observed.
Persons commonly speak as if the other world did not exist now,
but would after death. No: it exists now, though we see it not.
It is among us and around us. Jacob was shown this in his
dream. Angels were all about him, though he knew it not.
And what Jacob saw in his sleep, that Elisha's servant saw as if
with his eyes ; and the shepherds, at the time of the Nativity,
not only saw, but heard. They heard the voices of those
blessed spirits who praise God day and night, and whom we, in
our lower state of being, are allowed to copy and assist.

We are then in a world of spirits, as well as in a world of
sense, and we hold communion with it, and take part in it,
though we are not conscious of doing so. If this seems strange
to any one, let him reflect that we are undeniably taking part in
a third world, which we do indeed see, but about which we do
not know more than about the Angelic hosts—the world of brute
animals. Can anything be more marvellous or startling, unless
we were used to it, than that we should have a race of beings
about us whom we do but see, and as little know their state, or
can describe their interests, or their destiny, as we can tell of the
inhabitants of the sun and moon ? It is indeed a very overpowering thought, when we get to fix our minds on it, that we
familiarly use, I may say hold intercourse with creatures who are
as much strangers to us, as mysterious, as if they were the fabul-
ous, unearthly beings, more powerful than man, and yet his slaves,
which Eastern superstitions have invented. We have more real

[1] Gen. xxviii. 11.

knowledge about the Angels than about the brutes. They have apparently passions, habits, and a certain accountableness, but all is mystery about them. We do not know whether they can sin or not, whether they are under punishment, whether they are to live after this life. We inflict very great sufferings on a portion of them, and they in turn, every now and then, seem to retaliate upon us, as if by a wonderful law. We depend upon them in various important ways; we use their labour, we eat their flesh. This however relates to such of them as come near us : cast your thoughts abroad on the whole number of them, large and small, in vast forests, or in the water, or in the air; and then say whether the presence of such countless multitudes, so various in their natures, so strange and wild in their shapes, living on the earth without ascertainable object, is not as mysterious as anything which Scripture says about the Angels? Is it not plain to our senses that there is a world inferior to us in the scale of beings, with which we are connected without understanding what it is? and is it difficult to faith to admit the word of Scripture concerning our connection with a world superior to us?

When, indeed, persons feel it so difficult to conceive the existence among us of the world of spirits, because they are not aware of it, they should recollect how many worlds all at once are in fact contained in human society itself. We speak of the political world, the scientific, the learned, the literary, the religious world; and suitably : for men are so closely united with some men, and so divided from others, they have such distinct objects of pursuit one from another, and such distinct principles and engagements in consequence, that in one and the same place there exist together a number of circles or (as they may be called) worlds, made up of visible men, but themselves invisible, unknown, nay, unintelligible to each other. Men move about in the common paths of life, and look the same ; but there is little community of feeling between them ; each knows little about what goes on in any other sphere than his own ; and a stranger coming into any neighbourhood would, according to his own pursuits or acquaintances, go away with an utterly distinct or a reverse impression of it, viewed as a whole. Or again, leave for a while the political and commercial excitement of some large city, and take refuge in a secluded village ; and there, in the absence of news of the day, consider the mode of life and habits of mind, the employments and views of its inhabitants; and say whether the world, when regarded in its separate portions, is not more unlike itself than it is unlike the world of Angels which Scripture places in the midst of it?

The world of spirits then, though unseen, is present; present, not future, not distant. It is not above the sky, it is not beyond the grave; it is now and here; the kingdom of God is among us. Of this the text speaks. "We look," says St. Paul, "not at the things which are seen, but at the things which are not seen; for the things which are seen are temporal, but the things which are not seen are eternal." You see he regarded it as a practical truth, which was to influence our conduct. Not only does he speak of the world invisible, but of the duty of "looking at" it; not only does he contrast the things of time with it, but says that their belonging to time is a reason, not for looking at, but for looking off them. Eternity was not distant because it reached to the future; nor the unseen state without its influence on us, because it was impalpable. In like manner, he says in another Epistle, "Our conversation is in heaven." And again, "God hath raised us up together, and made us sit together in heavenly places in Christ Jesus." And again, "Your life is hid with Christ in God." And to the same purport are St. Peter's words, "Whom having not seen, ye love; in whom, though now ye see Him not, yet believing, ye rejoice with joy unspeakable and full of glory." And again, St. Paul speaking of the Apostles, "We are made a spectacle unto the world, and to Angels, and to men." And again in words already quoted, he speaks of the Angels as "ministering spirits sent forth to minister for them who shall be heirs of salvation."[1]

Such is the hidden kingdom of God; and, as it is now hidden, so in due season it shall be revealed. Men think that they are lords of the world, and may do as they will. They think this earth their property, and its movements in their power; whereas it has other lords besides them, and is the scene of a higher conflict than they are capable of conceiving. It contains Christ's little ones whom they despise, and His Angels whom they disbelieve; and these at length shall take possession of it and be manifested. At present, "all things," to appearance, "continue as they were from the beginning of the creation;" and scoffers ask, "Where is the promise of His coming?" but at the appointed time there will be a "manifestation of the sons of God," and the hidden saints "shall shine out as the sun in the kingdom of their Father." When the Angels appeared to the shepherds it was a sudden appearance,—"*suddenly* there was with the Angel a multitude of the heavenly host." How

[1] Phil. iii. 20. Eph. ii. 6. Col. iii. 3. 1 Pet. i. 8. 1 Cor. iv. 9 Heb. i. 14.

wonderful a sight ! The night had before that seemed just like any other night ; as the evening on which Jacob saw the vision seemed like any other evening. They were keeping watch over their sheep ; they were watching the night as it passed. The stars moved on,—it was midnight. They had no idea of such a thing when the Angel appeared. Such are the power and virtue hidden in things which are seen, and at God's will they are manifested. They were manifested for a moment to Jacob, for a moment to Elisha's servant, for a moment to the shepherds. They will be manifested for ever when Christ comes at the Last Day "in the glory of His Father with the holy Angels." Then this world will fade away and the other world will shine forth.

Let these be your thoughts, my brethren, especially in the spring season, when the whole face of nature is so rich and beautiful. Once only in the year, yet once, does the world which we see show forth its hidden powers, and in a manner manifest itself. Then the leaves come out, and the blossoms on the fruit-trees and flowers ; and the grass and corn spring up. There is a sudden rush and burst outwardly of that hidden life which God has lodged in the material world. Well, that shows you, as by a sample, what it can do at God's command, when He gives the word. This earth, which now buds forth in leaves and blossoms, will one day burst forth into a new world of light and glory, in which we shall see Saints and Angels dwelling. Who would think, except from his experience of former springs all through his life, who could conceive two or three months before, that it was possible that the face of nature, which then seemed so life-less, should become so splendid and varied ? How different is a tree, how different is a prospect, when leaves are on it and off it ! How unlikely it would seem, before the event, that the dry and naked branches should suddenly be clothed with what is so bright and so refreshing ! Yet in God's good time leaves come on the trees. The season may delay, but come it will at last. So it is with the coming of that Eternal Spring, for which all Christians are waiting. Come it will, though it delay ; yet though it tarry, let us wait for it, "because it will surely come, it will not tarry." Therefore we say day by day, " Thy kingdom come ;" which means,—O Lord, show Thyself; manifest Thyself; Thou that sittest between the cherubim, show Thyself; stir up Thy strength and come and help us. The earth that we see does not satisfy us ; it is but a beginning ; it is but a promise of something beyond it ; even when it is gayest, with all its blossoms on, and shows most touchingly what lies hid in it, yet it is not enough. We know much more lies hid in it than we see. A world of saints and Angels, a glorious world, the palace of God, the mountain of the Lord of Hosts, the heavenly Jerusalem, the throne of God and Christ—all these wonders, everlasting, all-precious, mysterious, and incomprehensible, lie hid in what we see. What we see is the outward shell of an eternal kingdom ; and on that kingdom we fix the eyes of our faith. Shine forth, O Lord, as when on Thy Nativity Thine Angels visited the shepherds; let Thy glory blossom forth as bloom and foliage on the trees ; change with Thy mighty power this visible world into that diviner world, which as yet we see not ; destroy what we see, that it may pass and be transformed into what we believe. Bright as is the sun, and the sky, and the clouds; green as are the leaves and the fields ; sweet as is the singing of the birds ; we know that they are not all, and we will not take up with a part for the whole. They proceed from a centre of love and goodness, which is God Himself ; but they are not His fulness ; they speak of heaven, but they are not heaven; they are but as stray beams and dim reflections of His Image; they are but crumbs from the table. We are looking for the coming of the day of God, when all this outward world, fair though it be, shall perish ; when the heavens shall be burnt, and the earth melt away. We can bear the loss, for we know it will be but the removing of a veil. We know that to remove the world which is seen, will be the manifestation of the world which is not seen. We know that what we see is as a screen hiding from us God and Christ, and His Saints and Angels. And we earnestly desire and pray for the dissolution of all that we see, from our longing after that which we do not see.

O blessed they indeed who are destined for the sight of those wonders in which they now stand, at which they now look, but which they do not recognise ! Blessed they who shall at length behold what as yet mortal eye hath not seen and faith only enjoys ! Those wonderful things of the new world are even now as they shall be then. They are immortal and eternal; and the souls who shall then be made conscious of them, will see them in their calmness and their majesty where they ever have been. But who can express the surprise and rapture which will come upon those who then at last apprehend them for the first time, and to whose perceptions they are new ! Who can imagine by a stretch of fancy the feelings of those who, having died in faith, wake up to enjoyment ! The life then begun, we know, will last for ever ; yet surely if memory be to us then what it is now, that will be a day much to be observed unto the Lord through all the ages of eternity.   We may increase indeed for ever in knowledge and in love, still that first waking from the dead, the day at once of our birth and our espousals, will ever be endeared and hallowed in our thoughts.   When we find ourselves after long rest gifted with fresh powers, vigorous with the seed of eternal life within us, able to love God as we wish, conscious that all trouble, sorrow, pain, anxiety, bereavement, is over for ever, blessed in the full affection of those earthly friends whom we loved so poorly, and could protect so feebly, while they were with us in the flesh, and above all, visited by the immediate visible ineffable Presence of God Almighty, with his Only-begotten Son our Lord Jesus Christ, and His Coequal, Coeternal Spirit, that great sight in which is the fulness of joy and pleasure for evermore,—what deep, incommunicable, unimaginable thoughts will be then upon us ! what depths will be stirred up within us ! what secret harmonies awakened, of which human nature seemed incapable !   Earthly words are indeed all worthless to minister to such high anticipations.   Let us close our eyes and keep silence.

"All flesh is grass, and all the goodliness thereof is as the flower of the field.   The grass withereth, the flower fadeth, because the Spirit of the Lord bloweth upon it : surely the people is grass.   The grass withereth, the flower fadeth ; but the word of our God shall stand for ever." [1]

[1] Isa. xl. 6-8.

SERMON XXVIII.

(EASTER TIDE.)

Waiting for Christ.

"He who testifieth these things saith, Surely I come quickly. Amen.
Even so, come, Lord Jesus."—REV. xxii. 20.

WHEN our Lord was going away, He said He would quickly come again ; yet knowing that by "quickly" He did not mean what would be at first sight understood by the word, He added, "suddenly," or "as a thief." "Behold I come as a thief; blessed is he that watcheth, and keepeth his garments."[1] Had His coming been soon, in our sense of the word, it could not well have been sudden. Servants who are bid to wait for their master's return from an entertainment, could not, one should think, be overtaken by that return. It was because to us His coming would not *seem* soon, that it *was* sudden. What you expect to come, you wait for; what fails to come, you give up; while, then, Christ said that His coming would be soon, yet by saying it would be sudden, He said that to us it would seem long.

Yet though to us He seems to delay, yet He has declared that His coming is speedy, He has bid us ever look out for His coming; and His first followers, as the Epistles show us, *were* ever looking out for it. Surely it is our duty to look out for it, as likely to come immediately, though hitherto for near two thousand years the Church has been looking out in vain.

Is it not something significant that, in the last book of Scripture, which more than any other implies a long continuance to the Christian Church,—that there we should have such express and repeated assurances that Christ's coming would be speedy? Even in the last chapter we are told it three times. "Be-

[1] Rev. xvi. 15.

hold I come quickly, blessed is he that keepeth the sayings of the prophecy of this book." "Behold I come quickly, and My reward is with Me." And again, in the text, "He that testifieth these things, saith, Surely I come quickly." Such is the announcement; and, in consequence, we are commanded to be ever looking out for the great day, to "wait for His Son from heaven;"[1] to "look for and haste unto the coming of the day of God."[2]

It is true, indeed, that in one place St. Paul cautions his brethren against expecting the immediate coming of Christ; but he does not say more than that Christ will send a sign immediately before His coming,—a certain dreadful enemy of the truth,—which is to be followed by Himself at once, and therefore does not stand in our way, or prevent eager eyes from looking out for Him. And, in truth, St. Paul seems rather to be warning his brethren against being disappointed if Christ did not come, than hindering them from expecting Him.

Now it may be objected that this is a kind of paradox; how is it possible, it may be asked, ever to be expecting what has so long been delayed? What has been so long coming may be longer still. It was possible, indeed, for the early Christians, who had no experience of the long period which the Church was to remain on earth, to look out for Christ; but we cannot help using our reason: there are no more grounds to expect Christ now than at those many former times when, as the event showed, He did not come. Christians have ever been expecting the last day, and ever meeting with disappointment. They have seen what they thought symptoms of His coming, and peculiarities in their own times, which a little more knowledge of the world, a more enlarged experience, would have shown them to be common to all times. They have ever been frightened without good reason, fretting in their narrow minds, and building on their superstitious fancies. What age of the world has there been in which people did not think the Day of Judgment coming? Such expectation has but evidenced and fostered indolence and superstition; it is to be considered as a mere weakness.

Now I shall attempt to say something in answer to this objection.

1. And first, considered as an objection to a habit of continual waiting (to use the common phrase), it proves too much. If it is consistently followed up, no age ought ever to expect the day of Christ; the age in which He shall come (whenever it is) ought

[1] 1 Thess. i. 10.   [2] 2 Pet. iii. 12.

not to expect Him;—which is the very thing He has warned us against. He nowhere warns us against what is contemptuously called superstition; but He expressly warns us against high-minded security. If it be true that Christians have expected Him when He did not come, it is quite as true that when He does come the world will not expect Him. If it be true that Christians have fancied signs of His coming when there were none, it is equally true that the world will not see the signs of His coming when they are present. His signs are not so plain but you have to search for them; not so plain but you may be mistaken *in* your search; and your choice lies between the risk of thinking you see what is not, and of not seeing what is. True it is, that many times, many ages, have Christians been mistaken in thinking they discerned Christ's coming; but better a thousand times think Him coming when He is not than once think Him not coming when He is. Such is the difference between Scripture and the world; judging by Scripture, you would ever be expecting Christ; judging by the world, you would never expect Him. Now He must come one day, sooner or later. Worldly men have their scoff at our failure of discernment now; but whose will be the want of discernment, whose the triumph then? And what does Christ think of their present scoff? He expressly warns us, by His Apostle, of scoffers, who shall say, "Where is the promise of His coming? for since the fathers fell asleep, all things continue as they were from the beginning of the creation. . . . But, beloved," continues St. Peter, "be not ignorant of this one thing, that one day is with the Lord as a thousand years, and a thousand years as one day."[1]

It should be recollected, too, that the enemies of Christ have ever been expecting the downfall of His religion, age after age; and I do not see why the one expectation is more unreasonable than the other; indeed they illustrate each other. So it is, undeterred by the failure of former anticipations, unbelievers are ever expecting that the Church and the religion of the Church are coming to an end. They thought so in the last century. They think so now. They ever think the light of truth is going out, and that their hour of victory is come. Now, I repeat, I do not see why it is reasonable to expect the overthrow of religion still, after so many failures; and yet unreasonable, because of previous disappointments, to expect the coming of Christ. Nay, Christians at least, over and above the aspect of things, can point to an express promise of Christ, that He will one day come:

---

[1] 2 Pet. iii. 4, 8.

whereas unbelievers, I suppose, do not profess any grounds at all
for expecting their own triumph, except the signs of the times.
They are sanguine, because they seem so strong, and the Church
of God seems so weak; yet they have not enlarged their minds
enough by the contemplation of past history to know that such
apparent strength on the one side, and such apparent weakness
on the other, has ever been the state of the world and the Church;
and that this has ever been one chief or rather the main reason,
why Christians have expected the immediate end of all things,
because the prospects of religion *were* so gloomy. So that, in
fact, Christians and unbelievers have taken precisely the same
view of the facts of the case; only they have drawn distinct conclusions from them, according to their creed. The Christian has
said, " All looks so full of tumult, that the world is coming to an
end;" and the unbeliever has said, " All is so full of tumult,
that the Church is coming to an end;" and there is nothing,
surely, more superstitious in the one opinion than in the other.

Now when Christians and unbelievers thus unite in expecting
substantially the same thing, though they view it differently,
according to their respective modes of thought, there cannot be
anything very extravagant in the expectation itself; there must
be something ever present in the world which warrants it. And
I hold this to be the case. Ever since Christianity came into
the world, it has been, in one sense, going out of it. It is so
uncongenial to the human mind, it is so spiritual, and man is so
earthly, it is apparently so defenceless, and has so many strong
enemies, so many false friends, that every age, as it comes, may
be called "the last time." It has made great conquests, and
done great works; but still it has done all, as the Apostle says of
himself, " in weakness, and in fear, and in much trembling."[1]
How it is that it is always failing, yet always continuing, God
only knows who wills it,—but so it is; and it is no paradox to
say, on the one hand, that it has lasted eighteen hundred years,
that it may last many years more, and yet that it draws to an
end, nay, is likely to end any day. And God would have us
give our minds and hearts to the latter side of the alternative,
to open them to impressions *from* this side, viz. that the end is
coming;—it being a wholesome thing to live as if *that* will come
in our day which may come any day.

It was different during the ages before Christ came. The
Saviour was to come. He was to bring perfection, and religion
was to grow *towards* that perfection. There was a system of

[1] 1 Cor. ii. 3.

successive revelations going on, first one and then another; each prophet in his turn adding to the store of Divine truth, and gradually tending towards the full Gospel. Time was measured out for believing minds before Christ came by the word of prophecy; so that He never could be expected in any age before the "fulness of time" in which He came. The chosen people were not bidden to expect Him at once; but after a sojourning in Canaan, and a captivity in Egypt, and a wandering in the wilderness, and judges, and kings, and prophets, at length seventy long weeks were determined to introduce Him into the world. Thus His delay was, as I may say, *recognised* then; and, *during* His delay, other doctrines, other rules, were given to fill the interval. But when once the Christ had come, as the Son over His own house, and with His perfect Gospel, nothing remained but to gather in His saints. No higher Priest could come,—no truer doctrine. The Light and Life of men had appeared, and had suffered, and had risen again; and nothing more was left to do. Earth had had its most solemn event, and seen its most august sight; and therefore it was the last time. And hence, though time intervene between Christ's first and second coming, it is not *recognised* (as I may say) in the Gospel scheme, but is, as it were, an accident. For so it was, that up to Christ's coming in the flesh, the course of things ran straight towards that end, nearing it by every step; but now, under the Gospel, that course has (if I may so speak) altered its direction, as regards His second coming, and runs, not towards the end, but along it, and on the brink of it; and is at all times equally near that great event, which, did it run towards, it would at once run into. Christ, then, is ever at our doors; as near eighteen hundred years ago as now, and not nearer now than then; and not nearer when He comes than now. When He says that He will come soon, "soon" is not a word of time, but of natural order. This present state of things, "the present distress" as St. Paul calls it, is ever *close upon* the next world, and resolves itself into it. As when a man is given over, he may die any moment, yet lingers; as an implement of war may any moment explode, and must at some time; as we listen for a clock to strike, and at length it surprises us; as a crumbling arch hangs, we know not how, and is not safe to pass under; so creeps on this feeble weary world, and one day, before we know where we are, it will end.

And here I may observe in passing, on the light thus thrown upon the doctrine, that Christ is the sole Priest under the Gospel, or that the Apostles ever sit on twelve thrones, judging the twelve tribes of Israel, or that Christ is with them always, even unto the end of the world. Do you not see the force of these expressions? The Jewish covenant, indeed, had "sundry times," which were ordered "in divers manners;" it had a long array of priests and a various history; one part of the series holier than another, and nearer heaven. But when Christ had come, suffered, and ascended, He was henceforth ever near us, ever at hand, even though He was not actually returned, ever scarcely gone, ever all but come back. He is the only Ruler and Priest in His Church, dispensing gifts, and has appointed none to supersede Him, because He is departed only for a brief season. Aaron took the place of Christ, and had a priesthood of his own; but Christ's priests have no priesthood but His. They are merely His shadows and organs, they are His outward signs; and what they do, He does; when they baptize, He is baptizing; when they bless, He is blessing. He is in all acts of His Church, and one of its acts is not more truly His act than another, for all are His. Thus we are, in all times of the Gospel, brought close to His Cross. We stand, as it were, under it, and receive its blessings fresh from it; only that since, historically speaking, time has gone on, and the Holy One is away, certain outward forms are necessary, by way of bringing us again under His shadow; and we enjoy those blessings through a mystery, or sacramentally, in order to enjoy them really. All this witnesses to the duty both of remembering and of looking out for Christ, teaching us to neglect the present, to rely on no plans, to form no expectations for the future, but so to live in faith, as if He had not left us, so in hope, as if He had returned to us. We must try to live as if the Apostles were living, and we must try to muse upon our Lord's life in the Gospels, not as a history, but as if a recollection.

2. This leads me to remark upon a second aspect under which the objection in question may be urged; viz. that this waiting for Christ is not only extravagant in its very idea, but becomes a superstition and weakness whenever carried into effect. The mind, intent upon the thought of an awful visitation close at hand, begins to fancy signs of it in the natural and moral world, and mistakes the ordinary events of God's providence for miracles. Thus Christians are brought into bondage, and substitute for the Gospel a fond religion, in which imagination takes the place of faith, and things visible and earthly take the place of Scripture. This is the objection; yet the text, on the other hand, while it sanctions the expectation, in the words "Surely I come quickly,"

surely sanctions the temper of waiting also, by adding, "Amen, even so, come, Lord Jesus."

I observe, then, that though Christians might be mistaken in what they took to be signs of Christ's coming, yet they were not wrong in their state of mind; they were not mistaken in looking out, and that for Christ. Whether credulous or not, they only acted as one acts towards some person beloved, or revered, or admired on earth. Consider the mode in which loyal persons look up to a good prince; you will find stories current, up and down the country, in his favour; people delight in believing that they have fallen in with tokens of his beneficence, nobleness, and paternal kindness. Many of these reports are false, yet others are true, and, on the whole, we should not think highly of that man who, instead of being touched at this mutual sympathy between sovereign and people, occupied himself merely in carping at what he called their credulity, and sifting the accuracy of this or that particular story. A great thing, truly, after all, to be able to detect a few misstatements, and to expose a few fictions, and to be without a heart! And forsooth, on the other hand, a sad deficiency in that people, I suppose, merely to be right on the whole, not in every particular, and to have the heart right! Who would envy such a man's knowledge? who would not rather have that people's ignorance? And, in like manner, I had rather be he who, from love of Christ and want of science, thinks some strange sight in the sky, comet or meteor, to be the sign of His coming, than the man who, from more knowledge and from lack of love, laughs at the mistake.

Before now, religious persons have taken appearances in the heaven for signs of Christ's coming, which do not now frighten us at all. Granted, but what then? let us consider the state of the case. Of old time it was not *known* generally that certain heavenly bodies moved and appeared at *fixed* times and by a rule; now it is known; that is, now men are *accustomed* to see them, then they were not accustomed. We know as little now as then *how* they come, or why; but then men were startled when they saw them, because they were strange, and now they are not strange, and therefore men are not startled. But how was it therefore absurd and ridiculous (for so it is that persons nowadays talk), why was it a foolish fond thing in a man to be impressed by what was rare and strange? Take a parallel case: travelling is common now, it was not common formerly. In consequence, we now travel without any serious emotion at parting from our friends; but then, because it was uncommon, even when risks were the same and the absence as long, persons did not go from home without much preparation, many prayers, and much leave-taking. I do not see anything very censurable in being more impressed at uncommon things than at common.

And you will observe, that in the case of which I am speaking, persons who are looking out for Christ are not only, *in that* they look out, acting in obedience to Him, but are looking out—in their very *way* of looking out, through the very signs through which they look out—in obedience to Him. Always since the first, Christians have been looking out for Christ *in* the signs of the natural and moral world. If they have been poor and un-educated, strange sights in the sky, or tremblings of the ground, storms, failure of harvest, or disease, or anything monstrous and unnatural, has made them think that He was at hand. If they were in a way to take a view of the social and political world, then the troubles of states—wars, revolutions, and the like—have been additional circumstances which served to impress them, and kept their hearts awake for Christ. Now all these are nothing else but those very things which He Himself has told us to dwell upon, and has given us as signs of His coming. "There shall be signs," He says, "in the sun, and in the moon, and in the stars ; and upon the earth distress of nations, with perplexity, the sea and the waves roaring ; men's hearts failing them for fear, and for looking after those things which are coming on the earth ; for the powers of heaven shall be shaken. . . . And when these things begin to come to pass, then look up and lift up your heads, for your redemption draweth nigh."[1] One day the lights of heaven *will* be signs ; one day the affairs of nations also *will* be signs ; why, then, is it superstitious to *look* towards them? It is not. We may be wrong in the particulars we rest upon, and may show our ignorance in doing so ; but there is nothing ridiculous or contemptible in our ignorance, and there is much that is religious in our watching. It is better to be wrong in our watching than not to watch at all.

Nor does it follow that Christians were wrong, even in their particular anticipations, though Christ did not come, whereas they said they saw His signs. Perhaps they *were* His signs, and He withdrew them again. Is there no such thing as countermand-ing? Do not skilful men in matters of this world sometimes form anticipations which turn out wrong, and yet we say that they *ought* to have been right? The sky threatens and then clears again. Or some military leader orders his men forward, and

[1] Luke xxi. 25. 26, 28.

then for some reason recalls them; shall we say that informants were wrong who brought the news that he was moving? Well, in one sense Christ is ever moving forward, ever checking the armies of heaven. Signs of the white horses are ever appearing, ever vanishing. "Clouds return after the rain;" and His servants are not wrong in pointing to them, and saying that the weather is breaking, though it does not break, for it is ever unsettled.

And another thing should be observed, that though Christians have ever been expecting Christ, ever pointing to His signs, they have never said that He was come. They have but said that He was just coming, *all but* come. And so He was and is. Enthusiasts, sectaries, wild presumptuous men, *they* have said that He was *actually* come, or they have pointed out the exact year and day in which He would come. Not so His humble followers. They have neither announced nor sought Him, either in the desert or in the secret chambers, nor have they attempted to determine "the times and seasons which the Father has put in His own power." They have but waited; when He actually comes, they will not mistake Him; and before then, they pronounce nothing. They do but see His forerunners.

Surely there can be no great harm, and nothing very ridiculous, where men are religious, in thus thinking the events of their day more than ordinary, in fancying that the world's matters are winding up, and that events are thickening for a final visitation; for, let it be observed, Scripture sanctions us in interpreting *all* that we see in the world in a religious sense, and as if all things were tokens and revelations of Christ, His Providence, and will. I mean that if this lower world, which seems to go on in its own way, independently of Him, governed by fixed laws or swayed by lawless hearts, will, nevertheless, one day in an awful way, herald His coming to judge it, surely it is not impossible that the same world, both in its physical order and its temporal course, speaks of Him also in other manners. At first, indeed, one might argue that this world did but speak a language contrary to Him; that in Scripture it is described as opposed to God, to truth, to faith, to heaven; that it is said to be a deceitful veil, misrepresenting things, and keeping the soul from God. How then, it may be asked, can this world have upon it tokens of His presence, or bring us near to Him? Yet certainly so it is, that in spite of the world's evil, after all, He is in it and speaks through it, though not loudly. When He came in the flesh "He was in the world, and the world was made by Him, and the world knew Him not." Nor did He strive nor cry, nor lift up His voice in the streets.

So it is now. He still is here; He still whispers to us, He still makes signs to us. But His voice is so low, and the world's din is so loud, and His signs are so covert, and the world is so restless, that it is difficult to determine when He addresses us, and what He says. Religious men cannot but feel, in various ways, that His Providence is guiding them and blessing them personally, on the whole; yet when they attempt to put their finger upon the times and places, the traces of His presence disappear. Who is there, for instance, but has been favoured with answers to prayer, such that, at the time, he has felt he never could again be unbelieving? Who has not had strange coincidences in his course of life which brought before him, in an overpowering way, the hand of God? Who has not had thoughts come upon him with a sort of mysterious force for his warning or his direction? And some persons, perhaps, experience stranger things still. Wonderful providences have before now been brought about by means of dreams; or in other still more unusual ways Almighty God has at times interposed. And then, again, things which come before our eyes, in such wise take the form of types and omens of things moral or future, that the spirit within us cannot but reach forward and presage what it is not told from what it sees. And sometimes these presages are remarkably fulfilled in the event. And then, again, the fortunes of men are so singularly various, as if a law of success and prosperity embraced a certain number, and a contrary law others. All this being so, and the vastness and mystery of the world being borne in upon us, we may well begin to think that there is nothing here below but, for what we know, has a connection with everything else; the most distant events may yet be united, the meanest and highest may be parts of one; and God may be teaching us and offering us knowledge of His ways, if we will but open our eyes, in all the ordinary matters of the day. This is what thoughtful persons come to believe, and they begin to have a sort of faith in the Divine meaning of the accidents (as they are called) of life, and a readiness to take impressions from them, which may easily become excessive, and which, whether excessive or not, is sure to be ridiculed by the world at large as superstition. Yet, considering Scripture tells us that the very hairs of our head are all numbered by God, that all things are ours, and that all things work together for our good, it does certainly encourage us in thus looking out for His presence in everything that happens, however trivial, and in holding that to religious ears even the bad world prophesies of Him.

Yet, I say, this religious waiting upon God through the day, which is so like that spirit of watching which is under consideration, is just as open to objection and scoffing from the world. God does not so speak to us through the occurrences of life, that you can persuade others that He speaks. He does not act upon such explicit laws, that you can speak of them with certainty. He gives us sufficient tokens of Himself to raise our minds in awe towards Him; but He seems so frequently to undo what He has done, and to suffer counterfeits of His tokens, that a conviction of His wonder-working presence can but exist in the individual himself. It is not a truth that can be taught and recognised in the face of men; it is not of a nature to be urged upon the world at large, nay, even on religious persons, as a principle. God gives us enough to make us inquire and hope; not enough to make us insist and argue.

I have all along been speaking of thoughtful and conscientious persons; those who do their duty, and who study Scripture. It is quite certain that this regard to outward occurrences does become superstition, when it is found in men of irreligious lives, or of slender knowledge of Scripture. The great and chief revelation which God has made us of His will is from Christ by His Apostles. They have given us a knowledge of the truth; they have sent forth heavenly principles and doctrines into the world; they have accompanied that revealed truth by Divine sacraments, which convey to the heart what otherwise would be a mere outward and barren knowledge; and they have told us to practise what we know, and obey what we are taught, that the Word of Christ may be formed and dwell in us. They have been inspired, moreover, to write Holy Scriptures for our learning and comfort; and in those Scriptures we find the history of this world interpreted for us by a heavenly rule. When, then, a man, thus formed and fortified within, with these living principles in his heart, with this firm hold and sight of things invisible, with likings, opinions, views, aims, moulded upon God's revealed law, looks abroad into the world, he does not come to the world for a revelation,—he has one already. He does not take his religion from the world, nor does he set an overvalue upon the tokens and presages which he sees there. But far different is the case when a man is not thus enlightened and informed by revealed truth. Then he is but a prey, he becomes the slave, of the occurrences and events, the sights and sounds, the omens and prodigies, which meet him in the world, natural and moral. His religion is a bondage to things perishable, an idolatry of the creature, and is, in the worst sense of the word, superstition. Hence it is a common remark, that irreligious men are most open to superstition. For they have a misgiving that there is something great and Divine somewhere : and since they have it not within them, they have no difficulty in believing that it is anywhere else, wherever men pretend to the possession of it. Thus you find in history men in high place practising unlawful arts, consulting professed wizards, or giving heed to astrology. Others have had their lucky and unlucky days ; others have been the sport of dreams, or of other idle fancies. And you have had others bowing themselves down to idols. For they have had no principle, no root in themselves. They have been ignorant, too, of Scripture, in which God has most mercifully removed the veil off a portion of this world's history, in order that we may see *how* He works. Scripture is the key by which we are given to interpret the world; but they who have it not roam amid the shadows of the world, and interpret things at random.

The same want of inward religious principle is shown in the light, senseless way in which so many adopt wrong forms of religious profession. He who has the light of Christ within him, hears the voice of enthusiastic, mistaken, self-willed, or hypocritical men, calling him to follow them, without being moved. But when a man is conscious he is a wilful sinner, and not at peace with God, when his own heart is against him and he has no principle, no stay within him, then he is the prey of the first person who comes to him with strong language, and bids him believe in him. Hence you find numbers running eagerly after men who profess to work miracles, or who denounce the Church as apostate, or who maintain that none are saved but those who agree with themselves, or any one who, without any warrant of his being right, speaks confidently. Hence the multitude is so open to sudden alarms. You hear of their rushing out of a city in numbers at some idle prediction that the Day of Judgment is coming. Hence so many, in the private and lower ranks of life, are so full of small superstitions, which are too minute to mention; all because they have not the light of truth burning in their heart.

But the true Christian is not of these. To him apply St. Paul's words, "All things are lawful unto me, but all things are not expedient; all things are lawful for me, but I will not be brought under the power of any." [1] He knows how to "use this world as not abusing it." He *depends* on nothing in this world. He trusts not *its* sights against the revealed Word. "Thou wilt keep him in perfect peace whose mind is stayed on Thee, because

[1] 1 Cor. vi. 12.

he trusteth in Thee." Such is the promise made to him. And if he looks out into the world to seek, it is not to seek what he does not know, but what he does. He does not seek a Lord and Saviour. He has "found the Messias" long since; and he is looking out for *Him.* His Lord Himself has *bid* him look for Him in the signs of the world, and therefore he looks out. His Lord Himself has shown him, in the Old Testament, how He, the Lord of Glory, condescends to humble Himself to the things of heaven and earth. He knows that God's angels are about the earth. He knows that once they were even used to come in human shape. He knows that the Son of God, ere now, has come on earth. He knows that He promised to His Church the presence of a miraculous agency, and has never recalled His promise. Again, he reads, in the Book of the Revelation, quite enough, not to show him what is coming, but to show him that now, as heretofore, a secret supernatural system is going on *under* this visible scene. And therefore he looks out for Christ, for His present providences, and for His coming; and though often deceived in his expectation, and fancying wonderful things are coming on the earth, when they still delay, he uses, and comforts him with the prophet's words, "I will stand upon my watch, and set me upon the tower, and will watch to see what He will say unto me, and what I shall answer when I am reproved. And the Lord answered me. . . . The vision is yet for an appointed time, but at the end it shall speak and not lie; though it tarry, wait for it, because it will surely come, it will not tarry. Behold, his soul, which is lifted up, is not upright in him; but the just shall live by his faith." [1]

[1] Hab. ii. 1-4.

SERMON XXIX.

(ASCENSION.)

Warfare the Condition of Victory

" And they worshipped Him, and returned to Jerusalem with great joy: and were continually in the Temple, praising and blessing God. Amen."—
LUKE xxiv. 52, 53.

FOR forty days after His resurrection did our Saviour Christ endure to remain below, at a distance from the glory which He had purchased. The glory was now His, He might have entered into it. Had He not had enough of earth? what should detain Him here, instead of returning to the Father, and taking possession of His throne? He delayed in order to comfort and instruct those who had forsaken Him in the hour of trial. A time had just passed when their faith had all but failed, even while they had His pattern before their eyes; and a time, or rather a long period was in prospect, when heavier trials far were to come upon them, yet He was to be withdrawn. They hitherto understood not that suffering is the path to glory, and that none sit down upon Christ's throne, who do not first overcome, as He overcame. He stayed to impress upon them this lesson, lest they should still misunderstand the Gospel, and fail a second time. "Ought not Christ," He said, "to suffer these things, and to enter into His glory?" And having taught them fully, after forty days, at length He rose above the troubles of this world. He rose above the atmosphere of sin, sorrow, and remorse, which broods over it. He entered into the region of peace and joy, into the pure light, the dwelling-place of angels, the courts of the Most High, through which resound continually the chants of blessed spirits and the praises of the seraphim. There He entered, leaving His brethren in due season to come after Him, by the light of His example and the grace of His Spirit.

Yet, though forty days was a long season for Him to stay, it was but a short while for the Apostles to have Him among them. What feeling must have been theirs, when He parted from them? So late found, so early lost again. Hardly recognised, and then snatched away. The history of the two disciples at Emmaus was a figure or picture of the condition of the eleven. Their eyes were holden that they should not know Him, while He talked with them for three years; then suddenly they were opened, and He forthwith vanished away. So had it been, I say, with all of them. "Have I been so long time with you, and yet hast thou not known Me, Philip?" [1] had already been His expostulation with one of them. They had not known Him all through His ministry. Peter, indeed, had confessed Him to be the Christ, the Son of the Living God; but even he showed inconsistency and change of mind in his comprehension of this great truth. They did not understand at that time who and what He was. But after His resurrection it was otherwise: Thomas touched His hands and His side, and said, "My Lord and my God;" in like manner, they all began to know Him; at length they recognised Him as the Living Bread which came down from heaven, and was the Life of the world. But hardly had they recognised Him, when He withdrew Himself once for all from their sight, never to see them again, or to be seen by them on earth; never to visit earth again, till He comes at the last day to receive all saints unto Himself, and to take them to their rest. "So, then, after the Lord had spoken unto them, He was received up into heaven, and sat on the right hand of God." [2] Late found, early lost. This, perhaps, was the Apostles' first feeling on His parting from them. And the like often happens here below. We understand our blessings just when about to forfeit them; prospects are most hopeful just when they are to be hopelessly clouded. Years upon years we have had great privileges, the light of truth, the presence of holy men, opportunities of religious improvement, kind and tender parents. Yet we knew not, or thought not of our happiness; we valued not our gift; and then it is taken away, just when we have begun to value it.

What a time must that forty days have been, during which, while He taught them, all His past teaching must have risen in their minds, and their thoughts then must have recurred in over-powering contrast to their thoughts now. His manner of life, His ministry, His discourses, His parables, His miracles, His meekness, gravity, incomprehensible majesty, the mystery of His grief

[1] John xiv. 9.   [2] Mark xvi. 19.

and joy; the agony, the scourge, the cross, the crown of thorns, the spear, the tomb; their despair, their unbelief, their perplexity, their amazement, their sudden transport, their triumph,—all this was in their minds; and surely not the least at that awful hour, when He led His breathless followers out to Bethany, on the fortieth day. "He led them out as far as to Bethany, and He lifted up His hands and blessed them. And it came to pass, while He blessed them, He was parted from them and carried up into heaven." [1] Surely all His history, all His dealings with them, came before them, gathered up in that moment. Then, as they gazed upon that dread Divine countenance and that heavenly form, every thought and feeling which they ever had had about Him came upon them at once. He had gone through His work; theirs was to come, their work and their sufferings. He was leaving them just at the most critical time. When Elijah went up, Elisha said, "My father, my father, the chariot of Israel and the horsemen thereof." With a like feeling might the Apostles now gaze up into heaven, as if with the hope of arresting His ascent. Their Lord and their God, the light of their eyes, the stay of their hearts, the guide of their feet, was taken away. "My beloved had withdrawn Himself and was gone. My soul failed when He spake; I sought Him, but I could not find Him; I called Him, but He gave me no answer." [2] Well might they use the Church's words as now, "We beseech Thee, leave us not comfortless." O Thou who wast so gentle and familiar with us, who didst converse with us by the way, and sit at meat with us, and didst enter the vessel with us, and teach us on the Mount, and bear the malice of the Pharisees, and feast with Martha, and raise Lazarus, art Thou gone, and shall we see Thee no more? Yet so it was determined: privileges they were to have, but not the same; and their thoughts henceforth were to be of another kind than heretofore. It was in vain wishing back what was past and over. They were but told, as they gazed, "This same Jesus, which is taken up from you into heaven, shall so come in like manner as ye have seen Him go into heaven."

Such are some of the feelings which the Apostles may have experienced on our Lord's Ascension; but these are after all but human and ordinary, and of a kind which all of us can enter into; but other than these were sovereign with them at that solemn time, for upon the glorious Ascension of their Lord, "they worshipped Him," says the text, "and returned to Jerusalem with *great joy,* and were continually in the Temple praising and

[1] Luke xxiv. 50. 51.   [2] Cant. v. 6.

blessing God." Now how was it, that when nature would have wept, the Apostles rejoiced? When Mary came to the sepulchre and found not our Lord's body, she stood without at the sepulchre weeping, and the angels said unto her, as Christ said after them, "Woman, why weepest thou?"[1] Yet, on our Saviour's departure forty days afterwards, when the Angels would reprove the Apostles, they did but say, "Why stand ye gazing up into heaven?" There was no sorrow in the Apostles, in spite of their loss, in spite of the prospect before them, but "great joy," and "continual praise and blessing." May we venture to surmise that this rejoicing was the high temper of the brave and noble-minded, who have faced danger in idea and are prepared for it? Moses brought out of Egypt a timid nation, and in the space of forty years trained it to be full of valour for the task of conquering the promised land; Christ in forty days trains His Apostles to be bold and patient instead of cowards. "They mourned and wept" at the beginning of the season, but at the end they are full of courage for the good fight; their spirits mount high with their Lord, and when He is received out of their sight, and their own trial begins, "they return to Jerusalem with great joy, and are continually in the Temple, praising and blessing God."

For Christ surely had taught them what it was to have their treasure in heaven; and they rejoiced, not that their Lord was gone, but that their hearts had gone with Him. Their hearts were no longer on earth, they were risen aloft. When he died on the Cross, they knew not whither He was gone. Before He was seized, they had said to Him, "Lord, whither goest Thou? Lord, we know not whither Thou goest?" They could but follow Him to the grave and there mourn, for they knew no better; but now they saw Him ascend on high, and in spirit they ascended with Him. Mary wept at the grave because she thought enemies had taken Him away, and she knew not where they had laid Him. "Where your treasure is, there will your heart be also."[2] Mary had no heart left to her, for her treasure was lost; but the Apostles were continually in the Temple, praising and blessing God, for their hearts were in heaven, or, in St. Paul's words, they "were dead, and their life was hid with Christ in God."

Strengthened, then, with this knowledge, they were able to face those trials which Christ had first undergone Himself, and had foretold as their portion. "Whither I go," He had said to St. Peter, "thou canst not follow Me now, but thou shalt follow Me afterwards." And He told them, "They shall put you out

[1] John xx. 15.   [2] Matt. vi. 21.

of the synagogues, yea, the time cometh, that whosoever killeth you will think that he doeth God service."[1]   That time was now coming, and they were able to rejoice in what so troubled them forty days before.   For they understood the promise, "To him that overcometh, will I grant to sit with Me in My throne, even as I also overcame, and am set down with My Father in His Throne."[2]

It will be well if we take this lesson to ourselves, and learn that great truth which the Apostles shrank from at first, but at length rejoiced in.   Christ suffered, and entered into joy; so did they, in their measure, after Him.   And in our measure, so do we.   It is written, that "through much tribulation we must enter into the kingdom of God."   God has all things in His own hands.   He can spare, He can inflict : He often spares (may He spare us still !), but He often tries us,—in one way or another He tries every one.   At some time or other of the life of every one there is pain, and sorrow, and trouble.   So it is; and the sooner perhaps we can look upon it as a law of our Christian condition the better.   One generation comes, and then another. They issue forth and succeed like leaves in spring; and in all this law is observable.   They are tried, and then they triumph ; they are humbled, and then are exalted; they overcome the world, and then they sit down on Christ's throne.

Hence St. Peter, who at first was in such amazement and trouble at his Lord's afflictions, bids us not look on suffering as a strange thing, "as though some strange thing happened to us, but *rejoice*, inasmuch as we are *partakers* of Christ's sufferings; that when His glory shall be revealed, we may be glad also with exceeding joy."   Again, St. Paul says, "We glory in tribulations, knowing that tribulation worketh patience."   And again, "If so be we suffer with Him, that we may be also glorified together."   And again, "If we suffer, we shall also reign with Him."   And St. John, "The world knoweth us not, because it knew Him not."   "We know that when He shall appear, we shall be like Him, for we shall see Him as He is."[3]   What is here said of persecution will apply of course to all trials, and much more to those lesser trials which are the utmost which Christians have commonly to endure now.   Yet I suppose it is a long time before any one of us recognises and understands that his own state on earth is in one shape or other a state of trial and sorrow; and that if he has intervals of external peace, this

---

[1] John xvi. 2.   [2] Rev. iii. 21.
[3] 1 Pet. iv. 12, 13.   Rom. v. 3.   2 Tim. ii. 12.   1 John iii. 1, 2.

is all gain, and more than he has a right to expect. Yet how different must the state of the Church appear to beings who can contemplate it as a whole, who have contemplated it for ages,— as the Angels ! We know what experience does for us in this world. Men get to see and understand the course of things, and by what rules it proceeds ; and they can foretell what will happen, and they are not surprised at what does happen. They take the history of things as a matter of course. They are not startled that things happen in one way, not in another ; it is the rule. Night comes after day ; winter after summer ; cold, frost, and snow, in their season. Certain illnesses have their times of recurrence, or visit at certain ages. All things go through a process,—they have a beginning and an end. Grown men know this, but it is otherwise with children. To them everything that they see is strange and surprising. They by turns feel wonder, admiration, or fear at everything that happens ; they do not know whether it will happen again or not ; and they know nothing of the regular operation of causes, or the connection of those effects which result from one and the same cause. And so too as regards the state of our souls under the covenant of mercy ; the heavenly hosts, who see what is going on upon earth, well understand, even from having seen it often, what is the course of a soul travelling from hell to heaven. They have seen, again and again, in numberless instances, that suffering is the path to peace ; that they that sow in tears shall reap in joy ; and that what was true of Christ is fulfilled in a measure in His followers.

Let us try to accustom ourselves to this view of the subject. The whole Church, all elect souls, each in its turn, is called to this necessary work. Once it was the turn of others, and now it is our turn. Once it was the Apostles' turn. It was St. Paul's turn once. He had all cares on him all at once ; covered from head to foot with cares, as Job with sores. And, as if all this were not enough, he had a thorn in the flesh added,—some personal discomfort ever with him. Yet he did his part well,— he was as a strong and bold wrestler in his day, and at the close of it was able to say, "I have fought a good fight, I have finished my course, I have kept the faith." [1] And after him, the excellent of the earth, the white-robed army of Martyrs, and the cheerful company of Confessors, each in his turn, each in his day, have likewise played the man. And so down to this very time, when faith has wellnigh failed, first one and then another have

[1] 2 Tim. iv. 7.

been called out to exhibit before the Great King. It is as though all of us were allowed to stand around His throne at once, and He called on first this man, and then that, to take up the chant by himself, each in his turn having to repeat the melody which his brethren have before gone through. Or as if we held a solemn dance to His honour in the courts of heaven, and each had by himself to perform some one and the same solemn and graceful movement at a signal given. Or as if it were some trial of strength, or of agility, and, while the ring of bystanders beheld and applauded, we in succession, one by one, were actors in the pageant. Such is our state;—angels are looking on,—Christ has gone before,—Christ has given us an example, that we may follow His steps. He went through far more, infinitely more, than we can be called to suffer. Our brethren have gone through much more; and they seem to encourage us by their success, and to sympathize in our essay. Now it is our turn; and all ministering spirits keep silence and look on. O let not your foot slip, or your eye be false, or your ear dull, or your attention flagging! Be not dispirited; be not afraid; keep a good heart; be bold; draw not back;—you will be carried through. Whatever troubles come on you, of mind, body, or estate; from within or from without; from chance or from intent; from friends or foes;—whatever your trouble be, though you be lonely, O children of a heavenly Father, be not afraid! quit you like men in your day; and when it is over, Christ will receive you to Himself, and your heart shall rejoice, and your joy no man taketh from you.

Christ is already in that place of peace, which is all in all. He is on the right hand of God. He is hidden in the brightness of the radiance which issues from the everlasting throne. He is in the very abyss of peace, where there is no voice of tumult or distress, but a deep stillness,—stillness, that greatest and most awful of all goods which we can fancy,—that most perfect of joys, the utter, profound, ineffable tranquillity of the Divine Essence. He has entered into His rest.

O how great a good will it be, if, when this troublesome life is over, we in our turn also enter into that same rest,—if the time shall one day come, when we shall enter into His tabernacle above, and hide ourselves under the shadow of His wings; if we shall be in the number of those blessed dead who die in the Lord, and rest from their labour. Here we are tossing upon the sea, and the wind is contrary. All through the day we are tried and tempted in various ways. We cannot think, speak, or act, but infirmity and sin are at hand. But in the unseen world, where Christ has entered, all is peace. There is the eternal throne, and a rainbow round about it, like unto an emerald; and in the midst of the throne the Lamb that has been slain, and has redeemed many people by His blood : and round about the throne four-and-twenty seats for as many elders, all clothed in white raiment, and crowns of gold upon their heads. And four living beings full of eyes before and behind. And seven Angels standing before God, and doing His pleasure unto the ends of the earth. And the Seraphim above. And withal, a great multitude which no man can number, of all nations, and kindreds, and people, and tongues, clothed with white robes, and palms in their hands. "These are they which came out of great tribulation, and have washed their robes and made them white in the blood of the Lamb."[1] "They shall hunger no more, neither thirst any more; neither shall the sun light on them, nor any heat." "There is no more death, neither sorrow nor crying, neither any more pain; for the former things are passed away."[2] Nor any more sin; nor any more guilt; no more remorse; no more punishment; no more penitence; no more trial; no infirmity to depress us; no affection to mislead us; no passion to transport us; no prejudice to blind us; no sloth, no pride, no envy, no strife; but the light of God's countenance, and a pure river of water of life, clear as crystal, proceeding out of the throne. That is our *home;* here we are but on pilgrimage, and Christ is calling us home. He calls us to His many mansions, which He has prepared. And the Spirit and the Bride call us too, and all things will be ready for us by the time of our coming. "Seeing then that we have a great High Priest that has passed into the heavens, Jesus the Son of God, let us hold fast our profession;" seeing we have "so great a cloud of witnesses, let us lay aside every weight;" "let us labour to enter into our rest;" "let us come boldly unto the Throne of Grace, that we may obtain mercy, and find grace to help in time of need."[3]

[1] Rev vii. 14. [2] Rev. xxi. 4. [3] Heb. iv. 11, 14, 16; xii. 1.

SERMON XXX.

(SUNDAY AFTER ASCENSION.)

Rising with Christ.

" If ye then be risen with Christ, seek those things which are above, where Christ sitteth on the right hand of God. Set your affection on things above, not on things on the earth. For ye are dead, and your life is hid with Christ in God."—COL. iii. 1-3.

BEFORE Holy Communion we are exhorted to "lift up our hearts;" we answer, "We lift them up unto the Lord,"—unto the Lord, that is, who is ascended on high; to Him who is not here, but has risen, appeared to His Apostles, and retired out of sight. To that ascended and unseen Saviour, who has overcome death, and opened the kingdom of heaven to all believers, this day and all days, but especially at this season, when we commemorate His Resurrection and Ascension, are we bound to rise in spirit after His pattern. Far otherwise, alas! is it with the many: they are hindered, nay, possessed and absorbed by this world, and they cannot rise because they have no wings. Prayer and fasting have been called the wings of the soul, and they who neither fast nor pray, cannot follow Christ. They cannot lift up their hearts to Him. They have no treasure above, but their treasure, and their heart, and their faculties are all upon the earth; the earth is their portion, and not heaven.

Great, then, is the contrast between the many, and those holy and blessed souls (and may we be in their company!) who rise with Christ, and set their affection on things above, not on things on the earth. The one are in light and peace, the others form the crowd who are thronging and hurrying along the broad way "which leadeth to destruction;" who are in tumult, warfare, anxiety, and bitterness, or, at least, in coldness and barrenness of mind; or, at best, in but a short-lived merriment, hollow and restless; or altogether blind to the future. This is the case of the many; they walk without aim or object, they live irreligiously, or in lukewarmness, yet have nothing to say in their defence. They follow whatever strikes them and pleases them; they indulge their natural tastes. They do not think of forming their tastes and principles, and of rising higher than they are, but they sink and debase themselves to their most earthly feelings and most sensual inclinations, because these happen to be the most powerful. On the contrary, holy souls take a separate course; they have risen with Christ, and they are like persons who have climbed a mountain and are reposing at the top. All is noise and tumult, mist and darkness at its foot; but on the mountain's top it is so very still, so very calm and serene, so pure, so clear, so bright, so heavenly, that to their sensations it is as if the din of earth did not sound below, and shadows and gloom were nowhere to be found.

And, indeed, the mountain's top is a frequent image in Scripture, under which the Almighty Spirit speaks to us of our calling in Christ. Thus, for instance, it was prophesied of the Christian Church, "that the mountain of the Lord's House should be established in the top of the mountains . . . and many people should go and say, Come ye, and let us go up to the mountain of the Lord." And, in like manner, the Temple built by Solomon was upon a high place; doubtless, among other reasons, which at first sight seem of an opposite nature, by way of showing us that religion consists in retiring from the world, and rising towards heaven. "He chose the tribe of Judah," says the Psalmist, "even the hill of Sion which He loved. And there He built His Temple on high."[1] I do not mean, of course, that a man can be religious who neglects his duties of this world; but that there is an inner and truer life in religious men, beyond the life and conversation which others see, or, in the words of the text, their "life is hid with Christ in God." Christ, indeed, Himself worketh hitherto, as His Father worketh, and He bids us also "work while it is day;" yet, for all this, it is true that the Father and the Son are invisible, that They have an ineffable union with each other, and are not in any dependence upon the mortal concerns of this world; and so we, in our finite measure, must live after Their Divine pattern, holding communion with Them, as if we were at the top of the mount, while we perform our duties towards that sinful and irreligious world which lies at the foot of it.

[1] Isa. ii. 2, 3. Ps. lxxviii. 69, 70.

The history of Moses affords us another instance of this lifting up of the heart to God, and that, too, represented to us under the same image. He went up to the mount for forty days, and there he saw visions. And observe, he remained all this time without eating bread or drinking water. That miraculous fast was a lesson to us, how it is that we Christians are to draw near to God. But observe, again, while he was on the mount, what was going on in the plain. *There* was the turbulence, the ungodliness, the sin of the world. His servant Joshua said, as they heard the noise of the shouting, "There is a noise of war in the camp:" but Moses said, "It is not the voice of them that shout for mastery, neither is it the voice of them that cry for being overcome: but the noise of them that sing do I hear."[1]

Our Saviour's own history gives us another striking instance of this Divine communion, and the troublesome world in contrast. When He ascended the Mount of Transfiguration with His three Apostles, on the summit all was still and calm as heaven. He appeared in glory; Moses and Elias with Him; the Father's voice was heard: St. Peter said, "Master, it is good for us to be here." Then he and his brother Apostles felt that their life was hid with Christ in God. But when they came down the mountain, how the scene was changed! It was descending from heaven to the world. "When He came to His disciples," says the Evangelist, "He saw a great multitude about them, and the scribes questioning with them. And straightway all the people, when they beheld Him, were greatly amazed, and running to Him, saluted Him." And He found that the Apostles were trying to cast out a devil, and could not. And then He spoke the word, conformable with Moses' deed, "This kind can come forth by nothing but by prayer and fasting."[2]

And again; we may even say that, when our Lord was lifted up on the Cross, then, too, He presented to us the same example of a soul raised heavenwards and hid in God, with the tumultuous world at its feet. The unbelieving multitude swarmed about the Cross, they that passed by reviled Him, and the scribes mocked Him. Meanwhile, He Himself was, amid His agony, in Divine contemplations. He said, "Father, forgive them;" "Why hast Thou forsaken Me?" "It is finished;" "Into Thy hands I commend My Spirit." And as He was hid in God, so too, even at that awful moment, one was at His side gazing on Him, and hid in God with Him. The penitent thief said, "Lord, remember me when Thou comest into Thy kingdom; and

[1] Exod. xxxii. 17, 18.　　　[2] Mark ix. 5, 14, 15. 29.

Jesus said unto Him, Verily, I say unto thee, To-day shalt thou be with Me in paradise." [1]

And much more on His resurrection was He withdrawn from this troublesome world, and at peace, as the Psalmist foretold it. "I have set My King upon My holy *hill* of Sion." "Ever since the world began hath Thy seat been prepared; Thou art from everlasting. The floods are risen, O Lord, the floods have lift up their voice; the floods lift up their waves. The waves of the sea are mighty and rage horribly; but yet the Lord, who dwelleth on high, is mightier." [2]

These passages may be taken as types, if not as instances, of the doctrine and precept which the text contains. Christ is risen on high, we must rise with Him. He is gone away out of sight, and we must follow Him. He is gone to the Father, we, too, must take care that our new life is hid with Christ in God. This was the gracious promise, which is signified in the prayer He offered before His Passion for all His disciples, even to the end of the world. "Holy Father," He said, "keep through Thine own Name those whom Thou hast given Me, that they may be one, as We are. . . . I pray not that Thou shouldest take them out of the world, but that Thou shouldest keep them from the evil. They are not of the world, even as I am not of the world. . . . Neither pray I for these alone, but for them also which shall believe on Me through their word; that they all may be one, as Thou, Father, art in Me, and I in Thee; that they may be one in Us. . . . I in them, and Thou in Me, that they may be made perfect in one . . . that the love wherewith Thou hast loved Me, may be in them, and I in them." [3] Agreeably to this sacred and awful announcement, St. Paul speaks in the text and following verses : "If ye then be risen with Christ," he says, "seek those things which are above, where Christ sitteth on the right hand of God. Set your affection on things above, not on things on the earth. For ye are dead, and your life is hid with Christ in God. Mortify therefore your members which are upon the earth."

It is then the duty and the privilege of all disciples of our glorified Saviour to be exalted and transfigured with Him ; to live in heaven in their thoughts, motives, aims, desires, likings, prayers, praises, intercessions, even while they are in the flesh ; to look like other men, to be busy like other men, to be passed over in the crowd of men, or even to be scorned or oppressed,

[1] Luke xxiii. 42, 43. [2] Ps. ii. 6; xciii. 3-5.
[3] John xvii. 11, 15, 16, 20, 21, 23, 26.

as other men may be, but the while to have a secret channel of communication with the Most High, a gift the world knows not of; to have their life *hid* with Christ in God. Men of this world live in this world, and depend upon it; they place their happiness in this world; they look out for its honours or comforts. *Their* life is not hid. And every one they meet they suppose to be like-minded. They think they can be *as* sure that every other man looks out for the things which they covet, as they can be sure he has the same outward appearance, the same make, a soul and body, eyes and tongue, hands and feet. They look up and down the world, and, as far as they see, one man is just like another. They know that a great many, nay, far the greater part, are like themselves, lovers of this world, and they infer, in consequence, that all are such. They discredit the possibility of any other motives and views being paramount in a man but those of this world. They admit, indeed, that a man may be *influenced* by religious motives, but to be *governed* by them, to *live* by them, to own them as turning-points, and primary and ultimate laws of his conduct, this is what they do not credit. They have devised proverbs and sayings to the effect that every man has his price; that all of us have our weak side; that religion is a beautiful theory; and that the most religious man is only he who hides most skilfully from himself, as well as from others, his own love of the world; and that men would not be men if they did not love and desire wealth and honour. And, in accordance with these views, they imputed all base and evil things to our Lord Himself, rather than believe Him to be what He said He was. They said He was a deceiver; that He wished to make Himself a king; that His miracles were wrought through Beelzebub. But He all the while, the Son of Man, was but in outward act sojourning here, and was in spirit in heaven. Follow Him into the wilderness during His forty days' fast, when He did neither eat nor drink; or after the devil's temptation, when Angels came and ministered unto Him; or go with Him up that mountain to pray, where, as I have already said, He was transfigured, and talked with Moses and Elias; and you will see where He really was, and with whom, while He sojourned upon earth,—with Saints and Angels, with His Father, who announced Him as His beloved Son, and with the Holy Ghost, who descended upon Him. He was "the Son of Man which is in heaven," and "had meat to eat" which others "knew not of."

And such in our measure shall we be, both in the appearance and in the reality, if we be His. "Truly our fellowship is with the Father, and with His Son Jesus Christ;" but, as far as this world goes, we shall be of little account. "The world knoweth us not, because it knew Him not." [1] Or, more than this, we may be perhaps ridiculed for our religion, despised, or punished : "If they have called the Master of the house Beelzebub, how much more them of His household?" [2] Such is the condition of those who rise with Christ. He rose in the night, when no one saw Him; and we, too, rise we know not when nor how. Nor does any one know anything of our religious history, of our turnings to God, of our growings in grace, of our successes, but God Himself, who secretly is the cause of them.

In this way let us enjoy and profit by this holy season ; Christ hath "died, yea, rather hath risen again, who is even at the right hand of God, who also maketh intercession for us." Wonderful things had taken place, while the world seemed to go on as usual. Pontius Pilate thought himself like other governors. The Jewish rulers went on with the aims and the prejudices which had heretofore governed them. Herod went on in his career of sin, and having seen and put to death one prophet, hoped to see miracles from a second. They all viewed all things as of this world ; they said, "To-morrow shall be as to-day, and much more abundant." They heard the news and saw the sights and provided for the needs of the moment, and forgot the thought of God. Thus men went on at the foot of the mount, and they cared not for what was on the summit. They did not understand that another and marvellous system, contrary to this world, was proceeding forward under the veil of this world. So it was then : so it is now. The world witnesses not the secret communion of the Saints of God, their prayers, praises, and intercessions. But *they* have the present privileges of saints notwithstanding,—a knowledge, and a joy, and a strength, which they cannot compass or describe, and would not if they could. " O how plentiful is Thy goodness, which Thou hast laid up for them that fear Thee ; and that Thou hast prepared for them that put their trust in Thee, even before the sons of men." Are they in anxiety? "Thou shalt hide them privily by Thine own presence from the provoking of all men ; Thou shalt keep them secretly in Thy tabernacle from the strife of tongues." Are they in disappointment? "Thou hast put gladness in their heart, since the time that their enemies' corn, and wine, and oil increased." Are they despised by the prosperous? "*They* have children at their desire," says another Psalm, "and leave the rest of their substance for their

[1] 1 John i. 3; iii. 1.   [2] Matt. x. 25.

R

babes ; but as for me, I will behold Thy presence in righteousness,
and when I awake up after Thy likeness, I shall be satisfied with
it." Are they in despondency ? The Psalmist has provided
them with a consolation : "Nevertheless, 1 am alway by Thee,
for Thou hast holden me by my right hand ; Thou shalt guide
me with Thy counsel, and after that receive me with glory. Whom
have I in heaven but Thee ? and there is none upon earth that I
desire in comparison of Thee. My flesh and my heart faileth,
but God is the strength of my heart, and my portion for ever.'
Are they in peril ? "Whoso dwelleth under the defence of the
Most High, shall abide under the shadow of the Almighty . . . a
thousand shall fall beside thee, and ten thousand at thy right
hand, but it shall not come nigh thee." Thus there is fulness
without measure for every need, to be found in Him with whom
our life is lodged ; there is what will "satisfy us with the
plenteousness of His house, who gives us to drink of His pleasures,
as out of the river. For with Him is the well of life, and in His
light shall we see light." So that they may fittingly cry out,
"Praise the Lord, O my soul, and all that is within me praise His
holy name . . . who forgiveth all thy sin, and healeth all thine
infirmities ; who saveth thy life from destruction, and crowneth
thee with mercy and loving-kindness ; who satisfieth thy mouth
with good things, making thee young and lusty as an eagle."[1]

All this, my brethren, I say is our portion, if we choose but to
accept it. "Who shall ascend into the hill of the Lord, or who
shall rise up in His holy place ? Who shall dwell in Thy tabernacle, or who shall rest upon Thy holy hill ? Even he that leadeth
an uncorrupt life, and doeth the thing that is right, and speaketh
the truth from his heart. He shall receive the blessing from the
Lord, and righteousness from the God of his salvation. This is
the generation of them that seek Him, even of them that seek
thy face, O Jacob." Aspire, then, to be "fellow-citizens of the
Saints and of the household of God." Follow their steps as they
have followed Christ. Though the hill be steep, yet faint not,
for the reward is great ; and till you have made the trial, you can
form no idea how great that reward is, or how high its nature.
The invitation runs, "O taste, and see how gracious the Lord is."
If you have hitherto thought too little of these things, if you have
thought religion lies *merely* in what it certainly does consist in
also, in filling your worldly station well, in being amiable, and
well-behaved, and considerate, and orderly,—but if you have

[1] Ps. xxxi. 21, 22 ; iv. 8 ; xvii. 15, 16 ; lxxiii. 22-25 ; xci. 1-7 ;
xxxvi. 8, 9 ; ciii. 1, 3-5.

thought it was nothing more than this, if you have neglected to stir up the great gift of God which is lodged deep within you, the gift of election and regeneration, if you have been scanty in your devotions, in intercession, prayer, and praise, and if, in consequence, you have little or nothing of the sweetness, the winning grace, the innocence, the freshness, the tenderness, the cheerfulness, the composure of the elect of God, if you are at present really deficient in praying, and other divine exercises, make a new beginning henceforth. Start, now, with this holy season, and rise with Christ. See, He offers you His hand; He is rising; rise with Him. Mount up from the grave of the old Adam; from grovelling cares, and jealousies, and fretfulness, and worldly aims; from the thraldom of habit, from the tumult of passion, from the fascinations of the flesh, from a cold, worldly, calculating spirit, from frivolity, from selfishness, from effeminacy, from self-conceit and high-mindedness. Henceforth set about doing what it is so difficult to do, but what should not, must not be left undone; watch, and pray, and meditate, that is, according to the leisure which God has given you. Give freely of your time to your Lord and Saviour, if you have it. If you have little, show your sense of the privilege by giving that little. But anyhow, show that your heart and your desires, show that your life is with your God. Set aside every day times for seeking Him. Humble yourself that you have been hitherto so languid and uncertain. Live more strictly to Him; take His yoke upon your shoulder; live by rule. I am not calling on you to go out of the world, or to abandon your duties in the world, but to redeem the time; not to give hours to mere amusement or society, while you give minutes to Christ; not to pray to Him only when you are tired, and fit for nothing but sleep; not altogether to omit to praise Him, or to intercede for the world and the Church; but in good measure to realize honestly the words of the text, to "set your affection on things above;" and to prove that you are His, in that your heart is risen with Him, and your life hid in Him.

SERMON XXXI.

(WHIT SUNDAY.)

The Weapons of Saints.

" Many that are first shall be last, and the last shall be first."—
MATT. xix. 30.

THESE words are fulfilled under the Gospel in many ways.
Our Saviour in one place applies them to the rejection of
the Jews and the calling of the Gentiles; but in the context, in
which they stand as I have cited them, they seem to have a
further meaning, and to embody a great principle, which we all
indeed acknowledge, but are deficient in mastering. Under the
dispensation of the Spirit all things were to become new and to
be reversed. Strength, numbers, wealth, philosophy, eloquence,
craft, experience of life, knowledge of human nature, these are
the means by which worldly men have ever gained the world.
But in that kingdom which Christ has set up, all is contrariwise.
" The weapons of our warfare are not carnal, but mighty through
God to the pulling down of strongholds." What was before in
honour, has been dishonoured; what before was in dishonour,
has come to honour; what before was successful, fails; what
before failed, succeeds. What before was great, has become
little; what before was little, has become great. Weakness has
conquered strength, for the hidden strength of God "is made
perfect in weakness." Death has conquered life, for in that
death is a more glorious resurrection. Spirit has conquered
flesh; for that spirit is an inspiration from above. A new
kingdom has been established, not merely different from all
kingdoms before it, but contrary to them; a paradox in the eyes
of man,—the visible rule of the invisible Saviour.

This great change in the history of the world is foretold or
described in very many passages of Scripture. Take, for in-

stance, St. Mary's Hymn, which we read every evening; she was no woman of high estate, the nursling of palaces and the pride of a people, yet she was chosen to an illustrious place in the kingdom of heaven. What God began in her was a sort of type of His dealings with His Church. So she spoke of His "scattering the proud," "putting down the mighty," "exalting the humble and meek," "filling the hungry with good things," and "sending the rich empty away." This was a shadow or outline of that kingdom of the Spirit which was then coming on the earth.

Again; when our Lord, in the beginning of His ministry, would declare the great principles and laws of His kingdom, after what manner did He express Himself? Turn to the Sermon on the Mount. "He opened His mouth and said, Blessed are the poor in spirit, blessed are they that mourn, blessed are the meek, blessed are they which are persecuted for righteousness' sake."[1] Poverty was to bring into the Church the riches of the Gentiles; meekness was to conquer the earth; suffering was "to bind their kings in chains, and their nobles with links of iron."

On another occasion He added the counterpart: "Woe unto you that are rich! for ye have received your consolation; woe unto you that are full! for ye shall hunger; woe unto you that laugh now! for ye shall mourn and weep; woe unto you when all men shall speak well of you! for so did their fathers to the false prophets."[2]

St. Paul addresses the Corinthians in the same tone: "Ye see your calling, brethren, how that not many wise men after the flesh, not many mighty, not many noble, are called: but God hath chosen the foolish things of the world to confound the wise; and God hath chosen the weak things of the world to confound the things which are mighty; and base things of the world, and things which are despised, hath God chosen, yea, and things which are not, to bring to nought things that are: that no flesh should glory in His presence."[3]

Once more; consider the Book of Psalms, which, if any part of the Old Testament, belongs immediately to Gospel times, and is the voice of the Christian Church; what is the one idea in that sacred book of devotion from beginning to end? This: that the weak, the oppressed, the defenceless, shall be raised to rule the world in spite of its array of might, its threats, and its terrors; that "the first shall be last, and the last first."

[1] Matt. v. 2-10.   [2] Luke vi. 24-26.   [3] 1 Cor. i. 26-29.

Such is the kingdom of the sons of God; and while it endures, there is ever a supernatural work going on by which all that man thinks great is overcome, and what he despises prevails.

Yes, so it is; since Christ sent down gifts from on high, the Saints are ever taking possession of the kingdom, and with the weapons of Saints. The invisible powers of the heavens, truth, meekness, and righteousness, are ever coming in upon the earth, ever pouring in, gathering, thronging, warring, triumphing, under the guidance of Him who "is alive and was dead, and is alive for evermore." The beloved disciple saw Him mounted on a white horse, and going forth "conquering and to conquer." "And the armies which were in heaven followed Him upon white horses, clothed in fine linen, white and clean. And out of His mouth goeth a sharp sword, that with it He should smite the nations, and He shall rule them with a rod of iron."[1]

Now let us apply this great truth to ourselves; for be it ever recollected, *we* are the sons of God, *we* are the soldiers of Christ. The kingdom is within us, and among us, and around us. We are apt to speak of it as a matter of history; we speak of it as at a distance; but really we are a part of it, or ought to be; and, as we wish to be a living portion of it, which is our only hope of salvation, we must learn what its characters are in order to imitate them. It is the characteristic of Christ's Church, that the first should be last, and the last first; are we realizing in ourselves and taking part in this wonderful appointment of God?

Let me explain what I mean :—We have most of us by nature longings more or less, and aspirations, after something greater than this world can give. Youth, especially, has a natural love of what is noble and heroic. We like to hear marvellous tales, which throw us out of things as they are, and introduce us to things that are not. We so love the idea of the invisible, that we even build fabrics in the air for ourselves, if heavenly truth be not vouchsafed us. We love to fancy ourselves involved in circumstances of danger or trial, and acquitting ourselves well under them. Or we imagine some perfection, such as earth has not, which we follow, and render it our homage and our heart. Such is the state more or less of young persons before the world alters them, before the world comes upon them, as it often does very soon, with its polluting, withering, debasing, deadening influence, before it breathes on them, and blights and parches, and strips off their green foliage, and leaves them, as dry and wintry trees without sap or sweetness. But in early youth we stand

[1] Rev. xix. 14, 15.

with our leaves and blossoms on, which promise fruit ; we stand by the side of the still waters, with our hearts beating high, with longings after our unknown good, and with a sort of contempt for the fashions of the world ; with a contempt for the world, even though we engage in it. Even though we allow ourselves in our degree to listen to it, and to take part in its mere gaieties and amusements, yet we feel the while that our happiness is not there ; and we have not yet come to think, though we are in the way to think, that all that is beyond this world is after all an idle dream. We are on our way to think it, for no one stands where he was ; his desires after what he has not, his earnest thoughts after things unseen, if not fixed on their true objects, catch at something which he does see, something earthly and perishable, and seduce him from God. But I am speaking of men *before* that time, before they have given their hearts to the world, which promises them true good, then cheats them, and then makes them believe that there is no truth anywhere, and that they were fools for thinking it. But before that time, they have desires after things above this world, which they embody in some form of this world, because they have no other way at all of realizing them. If they are in humble life, they dream of becoming their own masters, rising in the world, and securing an independence ; if in a higher rank, they have ambitious thoughts of gaining a name and exercising power. While their hearts are thus unsettled, Christ comes to them, if they will receive Him, and promises to satisfy their great need, this hunger and thirst which wearies them. He does not wait till they have learned to ridicule high feelings as mere romantic dreams : He comes to the young ; He has them baptized betimes, and then promises them, and in a higher way, those unknown blessings which they yearn after. He seems to say, in the words of the Apostle, "What ye ignorantly worship, that declare I unto you." You are seeking what you see not, I give it you ; you desire to be great, I will make you so ; but observe how,—just in the reverse way to what you expect ; the way to real glory is to become unknown and despised.

He says, for instance, to the aspiring, as to His two Apostles, "Whosoever will be great among you, let him be your minister ; and whosoever will be chief among you, let him be your servant ; even as the Son of Man came not to be ministered unto, but to minister." [1] Here is our rule. The way to mount up is to go down. Every step we take downward makes us higher in the

[1] Matt. xx. 26-28.

kingdom of heaven.   Do you desire to be great? make yourselves
little.   There is a mysterious connection between real advancement and self-abasement.   If you minister to the humble and
despised, if you feed the hungry, tend the sick, succour the distressed; if you bear with the froward, submit to insult, endure
ingratitude, render good for evil, you are, as by a divine charm,
getting power over the world and rising among the creatures.
God has established this law.   Thus He does His wonderful
works.   His instruments are poor and despised; the world hardly
knows their names, or not at all.   They are busied about what
the world thinks petty actions, and no one minds them.   They
are apparently set on no great works; nothing is seen to come of
what they do: they seem to fail.   Nay, even as regards religious
objects which they themselves profess to desire, there is no
natural and visible connection between their doings and sufferings
and these desirable ends; but there is an unseen connection in
the kingdom of God.   They rise by falling.   Plainly so, for no
condescension *can* be so great as that of our Lord *Himself.*
Now the more they abase themselves the more *like* they are to
Him; and the more like they are to Him, the greater must be
their power with Him.

When we once recognise this law of God's providence we shall
understand better, and be more desirous to imitate, our Lord's
precepts, such as the following:—

"Ye call Me Master and Lord: and ye say well; for so I am.
If I then, your Lord and Master, have washed your feet; ye also
ought to wash one another's feet.   For I have given you an
example, that ye should do as I have done to you.   Verily,
verily, I say unto you, The servant is not greater than his lord;
neither he that is sent greater than he that sent him."   And
then our Lord adds, "If ye know these things, happy are ye if
ye do them."[1]   As if He should say to us of this day, You know
well that the Gospel was at the first preached and propagated by
the poor and lowly against the world's power; you know that
fishermen and publicans overcame the world.   You know it;
you are fond of bringing it forward as an evidence of the truth
of the Gospel, and of enlarging on it as something striking, and
a topic for many words; happy are ye if ye yourselves fulfil it;
happy are ye if *ye* carry on the work of those fishermen; if ye in
your generation follow them as they followed Me, and triumph
over the world and ascend above it by a like self-abasement.

Again, "When thou art bidden of any man to a wedding, sit not

[1] John xiii. 13-17.

down in the highest room . . . but when thou art bidden, go and sit down in the lowest room, that when he that bade thee cometh, he may say unto thee, Friend, go up higher: then shalt thou have worship in the presence of them that sit at meat with thee ; for whosoever exalteth himself shall be abased, and he that humbleth himself shall be exalted." [1] Here is a rule which extends to whatever we do. It is plain that the spirit of this command leads us, as a condition of being exalted hereafter, to cultivate here all kinds of little humiliations ; instead of loving display, putting ourselves forward, seeking to be noticed, being loud or eager in speech, and bent on having our own way, to be content, nay, to rejoice in being made little of, to perform what to the flesh are servile offices, to think it enough to be barely suffered among men, to be patient under calumny ; not to argue, not to judge, not to pronounce censures, unless a plain duty comes in ; and all this because our Lord has said that such conduct is the very way to be exalted in His presence.

Again, "I say unto you, That ye resist not evil ; but whosoever shall smite thee on thy right cheek, turn to him the other also." [2] What a precept is this ? why is this voluntary degradation ? what good can come to it ? is it not an extravagance ? Not to *resist* evil is going far ; but to court it, to turn the left cheek to the aggressor and to offer to be insulted ! what a wonderful command ! What ! must we take pleasure in indignities ? Surely we must ; however difficult it be to understand it, however arduous and trying to practise it. Hear St. Paul's words, which are a comment on Christ's : "Therefore I *take pleasure* in infirmities, in reproaches, in necessities, in persecutions, in distresses for Christ's sake ;" he adds the reason ; "*for when I am weak, then* am I strong." [3] As health and exercise and regular diet are necessary to strength of the body, so an enfeebling and afflicting of the natural man, a chastising and afflicting of soul and body, are necessary to the exaltation of the soul.

Again, St. Paul says, "Avenge not yourselves, but rather give place unto wrath : for it is written, Vengeance is Mine ; I will repay, saith the Lord. Therefore if thine enemy hunger, feed him ; if he thirst, give him drink : for in so doing thou shalt heap coals of fire on his head." [4] As if he said, *This* is a *Christian's* revenge ; *this* is how a *Christian* heaps punishment and suffering on the head of his enemy ; viz. by returning good for evil. Is there pleasure in seeing an injurer and oppressor at your feet ? has

---

[1] Luke xiv. 8, 10, 11.
[2] Matt. v. 39.
[3] 2 Cor. xii. 10.
[4] Rom. xii. 19, 20.

a man wronged you, slandered you, tyrannized over you, abused
your confidence, been ungrateful to you? or to take what is more
common, has a man been insolent to you, shown contempt of
you, thwarted you, outwitted you, been cruel to you, and you feel
resentment,—and your feeling is this, "I wish him no ill, but I
should like him just to be brought down for this, and to make
amends to me;" rather say, hard though it be, "I will overcome
him with love; except severity be a duty, I will say nothing, do
nothing; I will keep quiet, I will seek to do him a service; I
owe him a service, not a grudge; and I will be kind, and sweet,
and gentle, and composed; and while I cannot disguise from
him that I know well where he stands, and where I, still this shall
be with all peaceableness and purity of affection." O hard duty,
but most blessed! for even to take into account the *pleasure* of
revenge, such as it is, is there not greater gratification in thus
melting the proud and injurious heart, than in triumphing over
it outwardly, without subduing it within? Is there not more of
true enjoyment, in looking up to God, and calling Him (so to
speak) as a witness of what is done, and having His Angels as
conscious spectators of your triumph, though not a soul on earth
knows anything of it, than to have your mere carnal retaliation of
evil for evil known and talked of, in the presence of all, and more
than all, who saw the insult or heard of the wrong?

The case is the same as regards poverty, which it is the fashion
of the world to regard not only as the greatest of evils, but as the
greatest *disgrace*. Men count it a disgrace, because it certainly
does often arise from carelessness, sloth, imprudence, and other
faults. But, in many cases, it is nothing else but the very state
of life in which God has placed a man; but still, even then, it is
equally despised by the world. Now if there is one thing clearly
set forth in the Bible it is this, that "blessed are the poor."
Our Saviour was the great example of poverty; He was a poor
man. St. Paul says, "Ye know the grace of our Lord Jesus
Christ, that, though He was rich, yet for your sakes He became
poor, that ye through His poverty might be rich."[1] Or consider
St. Paul's very solemn language about the danger of wealth:
"The love of money is the root of all evil, which while some
coveted after, they have erred from the faith, and pierced themselves through with many sorrows."[2] Can we doubt that poverty
is under the Gospel *better* than riches? I say *under* the Gospel,
and *in* the regenerate, and *in* the true servants of God. Of
course out of the Gospel, among the unregenerate, among the

[1] 2 Cor. viii. 9.   [2] 1 Tim. vi. 10.

lovers of this world, it matters not whether one is rich or poor; a man is any how unjustified, and there is no better or worse in his outward circumstances. But, I say, *in Christ* the poor is in a more blessed lot than the wealthy. Ever since the Eternal Son of God was born in a stable, and had not a place to lay His head, and died an outcast and as a malefactor, heaven has been won by poverty, by disgrace, and by suffering. Not by these things in themselves, but by faith working in and through them.

These are a few out of many things which might be said on this most deep and serious subject. It is strange to say, but it is a truth which our own observation and experience will confirm, that when a man discerns in himself most sin and humbles himself most, when his comeliness seems to him to vanish away and all his graces to wither, when he feels disgust at himself, and revolts at the thought of himself,—seems to himself all dust and ashes, all foulness and odiousness, then it is that he is really rising in the kingdom of God : as it is said of Daniel, "From the first day that thou didst set thine heart to understand and to chasten thyself before thy God, thy words were heard, and I am come for thy words."[1]

Let us then, my brethren, understand our place, as the redeemed children of God. Some *must* be great in this world, but woe to those who make themselves great; woe to any who take one step out of their way with this object before them. Of course no one is safe from the intrusion of corrupt motives ; but I speak of persons *allowing* themselves in such a motive, and acting mainly from such a motive. Let this be the settled view of all who would promote Christ's cause upon earth. If we are true to ourselves, nothing can really thwart us. Our warfare is not with carnal weapons, but with heavenly. The world does not understand what our real power is, and where it lies. And until we put ourselves into its hands of our own act, it can do nothing against us. Till we leave off patience, meekness, purity, resignation, and peace, it can do nothing against that Truth which is our birthright, that Cause which is ours, as it has been the cause of all Saints before us. But let all who would labour for God in a dark time beware of anything which ruffles, excites, and in any way withdraws them from the love of God and Christ, and simple obedience to Him.

This be our duty in the dark night, while we wait for the day ; while we wait for Him who is our Day, while we wait for His coming, who is gone, who will return, and before whom all the

[1] Dan. x. 12.

tribes of the earth will mourn, but the sons of God will rejoice
"It doth not yet appear what we shall be : but we know that,
when He shall appear, we shall be like Him ; for we shall see
Him as He is. And every man that hath this hope in Him
purifieth himself, even as He is pure."[1]   It is our blessedness to
be made like the all-holy, all-gracious, long-suffering, and merciful God ; who made and who redeemed us ; in whose presence
is perfect rest and perfect peace ; whom the Seraphim are
harmoniously praising, and the Cherubim tranquilly contemplating, and Angels silently serving, and the Church thankfully
worshipping.   All is order, repose, love, and holiness in heaven.
There is no anxiety, no ambition, no resentment, no discontent,
no bitterness, no remorse, no tumult.   "Thou wilt keep him in
perfect peace whose mind is stayed on Thee : because he trusteth
in Thee.   Trust ye in the Lord for ever : for in the Lord Jehovah
is everlasting strength."[2]

[1] 1 John iii. 2, 3.   [2] Isa xxvi. 3, 4.

SERMON XXXII.

(TRINITY SUNDAY.)

𝕿𝔥𝔢 𝔐𝔶𝔰𝔱𝔢𝔯𝔦𝔬𝔲𝔰𝔫𝔢𝔰𝔰 𝔬𝔣 𝔬𝔲𝔯 𝔓𝔯𝔢𝔰𝔢𝔫𝔱 𝔅𝔢𝔦𝔫𝔤.

" I will praise Thee, for I am fearfully and wonderfully made ; marvellous are Thy works, and that my soul knoweth right well."—Psalm cxxxix. 14.

IN the very impressive Psalm from which these words are taken, this is worth noticing among other things,—that the inspired writer finds in the mysteries without and within him a source of admiration and praise. "I will *praise* Thee, *for* I am fearfully and wonderfully made ; *marvellous* are Thy works." When Nicodemus heard of God's wonderful working, he said, "How can these things be ?" But holy David glories in what the natural man stumbles at. It awes his heart and imagination, to think that God sees him, wherever he is, yet without provoking or irritating his reason. He has no proud thoughts rising against what he cannot understand, and calling for his vigilant control. He does not submit his reason by an effort, but he bursts forth in exultation, to think that God is so mysterious. "Such knowledge," he says, "is too wonderful for me; it is high, I cannot attain unto it." Again, "How precious are Thy thoughts unto me, O God !"

This reflection is suitable on the festival which we are at present engaged in celebrating, on which our thoughts are especially turned to the great doctrine of the Trinity in Unity. It is my intention now to make some remarks upon it ; not however explanatory of the doctrine itself, which we have to-day confessed in the Athanasian Creed as fully and explicitly as it can be set forth in human words ; but I will endeavour from the text to show, that the difficulty which human words have in expressing it, is no greater than we meet with when we would express in human words even those earthly things of which we actually have experience, and which we cannot deny to exist, because we witness them : so that our part evidently lies in using the mysteries of religion, as David did, simply as a means of impressing on our minds the inscrutableness of Almighty God. Mysteries in religion are measured by the proud according to their own comprehension, by the humble according to the power of God ; the humble glorify God for them, the proud exalt themselves against them.

The text speaks of earthly things, "I am fearfully and wonderfully made." Now, let us observe some of the mysteries which are involved in our own nature.

1. First, we are made up of soul and body. Now, if we did not know this, so that we cannot deny it, what notion could our minds ever form of such a mixture of natures, and how should we ever succeed in making those who go only by abstract reason take in what we meant ? The body is made of matter ; this we see ; it has a certain extension, make, form, and solidity : by the soul we mean that invisible principle which thinks. We are conscious we are alive, and are rational ; each man has his own thoughts, feelings, and desires ; each man is one to himself, and he knows himself to be one and indivisible,—one in such sense, that while he exists, it were an absurdity to suppose he can be any other than himself ; one in a sense in which no material body which consists of parts can be one. He is sure that he is distinct from the body, though joined to it, because he is one, and the body is not one, but a collection of many things. He feels moreover that he is distinct from it, because he uses it ; for what a man can use, to that he is superior. No one can by any possibility mistake his body for himself. It is *his ;* it is not he. This principle, then, which thinks and acts in the body, and which each person feels to be himself, we call the soul. We do not know what it is ; it cannot be reached by any of the senses ; we cannot see it or touch it. It has nothing in common with extension or form ; to ask what shape the soul is, would be as absurd as to ask what is the shape of a thought, or a wish, or a regret, or a hope. And hence we call the soul spiritual and immaterial, and say that it has no parts, and is of no size at all. All this seems undeniable. Yet observe, if all this be true, what is meant by saying that it is *in* the body, any more than saying that a thought or a hope is in a stone or a tree ? *How* is it joined to the body ? what keeps it one with the body ? what

keeps it in the body? what prevents it any moment from separating from the body? when two things which we see are united, they are united by some connection which we can understand. A chain or cable keeps a ship in its place; we lay the foundation of a building in the earth, and the building endures. But what is it which unites soul and body? how do they touch? how do they keep together? how is it we do not wander to the stars or the depths of the sea, or to and fro as chance may carry us, while our body remains where it was on earth? So far from its being wonderful that the body one day dies, how is it that it is made to live and move at all? how is it that it keeps from dying a single hour? Certainly it is as incomprehensible as anything can be, how soul and body can make up one man; and, unless we had the instance before our eyes, we should seem in saying so to be using words without meaning. For instance, would it not be extravagant and idle to speak of time as deep or high, or of space as quick or slow? Not less idle, surely, it perhaps seems to some races of spirits to say that thought and mind have a body, which in the case of man they have, according to God's marvellous will. It is certain, then, that experience outstrips reason in its capacity of knowledge; why then should reason circumscribe faith, when it cannot compass sight?

2. Again: the soul is not only one, and without parts, but moreover, as if by a great contradiction even in terms, it is in every part of the body. It is nowhere, yet everywhere. It may be said, indeed, that it is especially in the brain; but, granting this for argument's sake, yet it is quite certain, since every part of his body belongs to him, that a man's self is in every part of his body. No part of a man's body is like a mere instrument, as a knife, or a crutch might be, which he takes up and may lay down. Every part of it is part of himself; it is connected into one by his soul, which is one. Supposing we take stones and raise a house, the building is not *really* one; it is composed of a number of separate parts, which viewed as collected together, we call one, but which are not one except in our notion of them. But the hands and feet, the head and trunk, form one body under the presence of the soul within them. Unless the soul were in every part, they would not form one body; so that the soul is in every part, uniting it with every other, though it consists of no parts at all. I do not of course mean that there is any real contradiction in these opposite truths; indeed, we know there is not, and cannot be, because they *are* true, because human nature is a

fact before us. But the state of the case is a contradiction *when put into words;* we cannot so express it as not to involve an apparent contradiction; and then, if we discriminate our terms, and make distinctions, and balance phrases, and so on, we shall seem to be technical, artificial, and speculative, and to use words without meaning.

Now, this is precisely our difficulty, as regards the doctrine of the Ever-blessed Trinity. We have never been in heaven; God, as He is in Himself, is hid from us. We are informed concerning Him by those who were inspired by Him for the purpose, nay, by One who "knoweth the Father," His Co-eternal Son Himself, when He came on earth. And, in the message which they brought to us from above, are declarations concerning His nature, which seem to run counter the one to the other. He is revealed to us as One God, the Father, One indivisible Spirit; yet there is said to exist in Him from everlasting His Only-begotten Son, the same as He is, and yet distinct, and from and in Them both, from everlasting and indivisibly, exists the Co-equal Spirit. All this, put into words, seems a contradiction in terms; men have urged it as such; then Christians, lest they should seem to be unduly and harshly insisting upon words which clash with each other, and so should dishonour the truth of God, and cause hearers to stumble, have guarded their words, and explained them; and then for doing this they have been accused of specu lating and theorizing. The same result, doubtless, would take place in the parallel case already mentioned. Had we no bodies, and were a revelation made us that there was a race who had bodies as well as souls, what a number of powerful objections should we seem to possess against that revelation! We might plausibly say, that the words used in conveying it were arbitrary and unmeaning. What (we should ask) was the meaning of saying that the soul had no parts, yet was in every part of the body? what was meant by saying it was everywhere and no- where? how could it be one, and yet repeated, as it were, ten thousand times over in every atom and pore of the body, which it was said to exist in? how could it be confined to the body at all? how did it act upon the body? how happened it, as was pretended, that, when the soul did but will, the arm moved or the feet walked? how can a spirit which cannot touch anything, yet avail to move so large a mass of matter, and so easily, as the human body? These are some of the questions which might be asked, partly on the ground that the alleged fact was impossible, partly that the idea was self-contradictory. And these are just the kind of questions with which arrogant and profane minds do assail the revealed doctrine of the Holy Trinity.

3. Further consider what a strange state we are in when we dream, and how difficult it would be to convey to a person who had never dreamed what was meant by dreaming. *His* vocabulary would contain no words to express any middle idea between perfect possession and entire suspension of the mind's powers. He would understand what it was to be awake, what it was to be insensible ; but a state between the two he would neither have words to describe, nor, if he were self-confident and arrogant, inclination to believe, however well it was attested by those who ought to know. I do not say there is no conceivable accumulation of evidence that would subdue such a man's reason, since we see sometimes men's reason subdued by the evidences of the Gospel, whose hearts are imperfectly affected : but I mean, that this earthly mystery *might* be brought before a man with about that degree of evidence in its favour which the Gospel actually has, not ordinarily overpowering, but constituting a *trial* of his heart, a trial, that is, whether the mysteries contained in it do or do not rouse his pride. Dreaming is not a fiction, but a real state of the mind, though only one or two in the whole world ever dreamed ; and if these one or two or a dozen men spoke to the rest of the world, and unanimously witnessed to the existence of that mysterious state, many doubtless would resist their report, as they do the mysteries of the Gospel, on the ground of its being unintelligible : yet in that case they would be resisting a truth, and would be wrong (not indeed blameably so, compared with those who on a like account reject the Gospel, which comes to us as a practical, not a mere abstract matter), yet they would undeniably be considering a thing false which was true.

It is no great harm to be wrong in a matter of opinion ; but in matters which influence conduct, which bear upon our eternal interests, such as revealed religion, surely it is most hazardous, most unwise, though it is so common, to stumble at its mysteries, instead of believing and acting upon its threats and promises. Instead of embracing what they can understand, together with what they cannot, men criticise the wording in which truths are conveyed, which came from heaven. The inspired Apostles taught them to the first Christian converts, and they, according to the capacities of human language, whether their own or the Apostles', partly one and partly the other, preserved them ; and we, instead of thanking them for the benefit, instead of rejoicing that they should have handed on to us those secrets concerning God, instead

s

of thanking Him for His condescension in allowing us to hear them, have hearts cold enough to complain of their mysteriousness. Profane minds ask, "Is God one, or three?" They are answered, "He is One and He is also Three." They reply, "He cannot be One in the same sense in which He is Three." It is in reply allowed to them, "He is Three in one sense, One in another." They ask, "In what sense? what is that sense in which He is Three Persons,—what is that sense of the word Person, such that it neither stands for one separate Being, as it does with men, nor yet comes short of such a real and sufficient sense as the word requires?" We reply that we do *not know* that intermediate sense; we cannot reconcile, we confess, the distinct portions of the doctrine; we can but take what is given us, and be content. They rejoin, that, if this be so, we are using words without meaning. We answer, No, not without meaning in themselves, but without meaning which *we* fully apprehend. God understands His own words, though human. God, when He gave the doctrine, put it into words, and the doctrine, as we word it, is the doctrine as the Apostles worded it; it is conveyed to us with the same degree of meaning in it, intelligible to us, with which the Apostles received it; so that it is no reason for giving it up that in part it is not intelligible. This we say; and they insist in reply, as if it were a sufficient answer, that the doctrine, as a whole, *is* unintelligible to us (which we grant); that the words which we use have very little meaning (which is not true, though *we* may not see the full meaning); and so they think to excuse their rejection of them.

But surely all this, I say, is much the same as what might take place in any discussion about dreaming, in a company where one or two persons had experienced it, and the multitude not. It might be said to those who told us of it, Do you mean that it is a state of waking or insensibility? is it one or the other? what is that sense in which we are not insensible in dreaming, and yet are not awake and ourselves? Now if we have mysteries even about ourselves, which we cannot even put into words accurately, much more may we suppose, even were we not told it, that there are mysteries in the nature of Almighty God; and so far from its being improbable that there should be mysteries, the declaration that there are even adds some probability to the revelation which declares them. On the other hand, still more unreasonable is disbelief, if it be grounded on the mysteriousness of the revelation; because, if we cannot put into consistent human language human things, if the state of dreaming, which we experience commonly, must be described in words either vague or contradictory, much less is there to surprise us if human words are insufficient to describe heavenly things.

These are a few, out of the many remarks which might be made concerning our own mysterious state,—that is, concerning things in us which we know to *be* really and truly, yet which we cannot accurately reflect upon and contemplate, cannot describe, cannot put into words, and cannot convey to another's comprehension who does not experience them. But this is a very large subject. Let a man consider how hardly he is able and how circuitously he is forced to describe the commonest objects of nature, when he attempts to substitute reason for sight, how difficult it is to define things, how impracticable it is to convey to another any complicated, or any deep or refined feeling, how inconsistent and self-contradictory his own feelings seem, when put into words, how he subjects himself in consequence to misunderstanding, or ridicule, or triumphant criticism ; and he will not wonder at the impossibility of duly delineating in earthly words the first Cause of all thought, the Father of spirits, the One Eternal Mind, the King of kings and Lord of lords, who only hath immortality, dwelling in light unapproachable, whom no man hath seen nor can see, the incomprehensible infinite God.

To conclude. One objection only, as it seems to me, can be made to these reflections, and that is soon answered. It may be said that, though there be, as there well may be, ten thousand mysteries about the Divine Nature, yet why should they be disclosed in the Gospel ? because the very circumstance that they *cannot* be put into words is a reason why this should not be attempted. But this surely is a very bold and presumptuous way of speaking, not to say more about it ; as if we had any means of knowing, as if we had any right to ask, why God does what He does in the very way He does it ; as if sinners, receiving a great and unmerited favour, were not very unthankful and acting almost madly, in saying, Why was it given us in this way, not in that ? Is God obliged to take us into counsel, and explain to us the reason for everything He does ; or is it our plain duty to take what is given us, and feed upon it in faith ? And to those who do thus receive the blessed doctrine under consideration, it will be found to produce special and singular practical effects on them, on the very ground of its mysteriousness. There is nothing, according as we are given to see and judge of things, which will make a greater difference in the temper, character, and habits of an individual, than the circumstance of his holding or not holding the Gospel to be mysterious. Even then, if we go by its influence on our minds, we might safely pronounce that the doctrine of the Holy Trinity, and of other like mysteries, cannot be unimportant. If it be true (as we hold it to be), it must be of consequence; for it tends to draw the mind in one particular direction, and to form it on a different mould from theirs who do not believe in it. And thus what we actually are given to see, does go a certain way in confirming to us what Scripture and the Church declare to us, that belief in this doctrine is actually necessary to salvation, by showing us that such belief has a moral effect on us. The temper of true faith is described in the text: "Marvellous are Thy works; and that my soul knoweth right well." A religious mind is ever marvelling, and irreligious men laugh and scoff at it because it marvels. A religious mind is ever looking out of itself, is ever pondering God's words, is ever "looking into" them with the angels, is ever realizing to itself Him on whom it depends, and who is the centre of all truth and good. Carnal and proud minds are contented with self; they like to remain at home; when they hear of mysteries, they have no devout curiosity to go and see the great sight, though it be ever so little out of their way; and when it actually falls in their path, they stumble at it. As great then as is the difference between hanging upon the thought of God and resting in ourselves, lifting up the heart to God and bringing all things in heaven and earth down to ourselves, exalting God and exalting reason, measuring things by God's power and measuring them by our own ignorance, so great is the difference between him who believes in the Christian mysteries and him who does not. And were there no other reason for the revelation of them but this gracious one, of raising us, refining us, making us reverent, making us expectant and devout, surely this would be more than a sufficient one.

Let us then all, learned and unlearned, gain this great benefit from the mystery of the Ever-blessed Trinity. It is calculated to humble the wise in this world with the thought of what is above them, and to encourage and elevate the lowly with the thought of Almighty God, and the glories and marvels which shall one day be revealed to them. In the Beatific Vision of God, should we through His grace be found worthy of it, we shall comprehend clearly what we now dutifully repeat and desire to know, how the Father Almighty is truly and by Himself God, the Eternal Son truly and by Himself God, and the Holy Ghost truly and by Himself God, and yet not three Gods but one God.

SERMON XXXIII.

(SUNDAYS AFTER TRINITY.)

Holiness necessary for Future Blessedness.

" Holiness, without which no man shall see the Lord."—HEB. xii. 14.

IN this text it has seemed good to the Holy Spirit to convey a chief truth of religion in a few words. It is this circumstance which makes it especially impressive; for the truth itself is declared in one form or other in every part of Scripture. It is told us again and again, that to make sinful creatures holy was the great end which our Lord had in view in taking upon Him our nature, and thus none but the holy will be accepted for His sake at the last day. The whole history of redemption, the covenant of mercy in all its parts and provisions, attests the necessity of holiness in order to salvation; as indeed even our natural conscience bears witness also. But in the text what is elsewhere implied in history, and enjoined by precept, is stated doctrinally, as a momentous and necessary fact, the result of some awful irreversible law in the nature of things, and the inscrutable determination of the Divine Will.

Now some one may ask, " Why is it that holiness is a necessary qualification for our being received into heaven? why is it that the Bible enjoins upon us so strictly to love, fear, and obey God, to be just, honest, meek, pure in heart, forgiving, heavenly-minded, self-denying, humble, and resigned? Man is confessedly weak and corrupt; *why* then is he enjoined to be so religious, so unearthly? *why* is he required (in the strong language of Scripture) to become 'a new creature'? Since he is by nature what he is, would it not be an act of greater mercy in God to save him altogether without this holiness, which it is so difficult, yet (as it appears) so necessary for him to possess?"

Now we have no right to ask this question. Surely it is quite enough for a sinner to know, that a way has been opened through God's grace for his salvation, without being informed why that way, and not another way, was chosen by Divine Wisdom. Eternal life is "the *gift* of God." Undoubtedly He may pre-scribe the terms on which He will give it; and if He has deter-mined holiness to be the way of life, it is enough; it is not for us to inquire why He has so determined.

Yet the question may be asked reverently, and with a view to enlarge our insight into our own condition and prospects; and in that case the attempt to answer it will be profitable, if it be made soberly. I proceed, therefore, to state one of the reasons, assigned in Scripture, why present holiness is necessary, as the text declares to us, for future happiness.

To be holy is, in our Church's words, to have "the true cir-cumcision of the Spirit;" that is, to be separate from sin, to hate the works of the world, the flesh, and the devil; to take pleasure in keeping God's commandments; to do things as He would have us do them; to live habitually as in the sight of the world to come, as if we had broken the ties of this life, and were dead already. Why cannot we be saved without possessing such a frame and temper of mind?

I answer as follows: That, even supposing a man of unholy life were suffered to enter heaven, *he would not be happy there;* so that it would be no mercy to permit him to enter.

We are apt to deceive ourselves, and to consider heaven a place like this earth; I mean, a place where every one may choose and take his *own* pleasure. We see that in this world, active men have their own enjoyments, and domestic men have theirs; men of literature, of science, of political talent, have their respective pursuits and pleasures. Hence we are led to act as if it will be the same in another world. The only difference we put between this world and the next, is that *here* (as we know well) men are *not always sure*, but *there*, we suppose they *will be always sure*, of obtaining what they seek after. And accordingly we conclude, that *any man*, whatever his habits, tastes, or manner of life, if *once admitted* into heaven, would be happy there. Not that we altogether deny that some preparation is necessary for the next world; but we do not estimate its real extent and importance. We think we can reconcile ourselves to God when we will; as if nothing were required in the case of men in general, but some temporary attention, more than ordinary, to our religious duties, —some strictness, during our last sickness, in the services of the

Church, as men of business arrange their letters and papers on taking a journey or balancing an account. But an opinion like this, though commonly acted on, is refuted as soon as put into words. For heaven, it is plain from Scripture, is not a place where many different and discordant pursuits can be carried on at once, as is the case in this world. Here every man can do his *own* pleasure, but there he must do *God's* pleasure. It would be presumption to attempt to determine the employments of that eternal life which good men are to pass in God's presence, or to deny that that state which eye hath not seen, nor ear heard, nor mind conceived, may comprise an infinite variety of pursuits and occupations. Still so far we are distinctly told, that that future life will be spent in God's *presence*, in a sense which does not apply to our present life; so that it may be best described as an endless and uninterrupted worship of the Eternal Father, Son, and Spirit. "They serve Him day and night in His temple, and He that sitteth on the throne shall dwell among them. . . . The Lamb which is in the midst of the throne shall feed them, and shall lead them unto living fountains of waters." Again, "The city had no need of the sun, neither of the moon to shine in it, for the glory of God did lighten it, and the Lamb is the light thereof. And the nations of them which are saved shall walk in the light of it, and the kings of the earth do bring their glory and honour into it."[1] These passages from St. John are sufficient to remind us of many others.

Heaven then is not like this world; I will say what it is much more like—*a church*. For in a place of public worship no language of this world is heard; there are no schemes brought forward for temporal objects, great or small; no information how to strengthen our worldly interests, extend our influence, or establish our credit. These things indeed may be right in their way, so that we do not set our hearts upon them; still (I repeat), it is certain that we hear nothing of them in a church. Here we hear solely and entirely of *God*. We praise Him, worship Him, sing to Him, thank Him, confess to Him, give ourselves up to Him, and ask His blessing. And *therefore*, a church is like heaven; viz. because, both in the one and the other, there is one single sovereign subject—religion—brought before us.

Supposing, then, instead of it being said that no irreligious man could serve and attend on God in heaven (or see Him, as the text expresses it), we were told that no irreligious man could worship, or spiritually see Him in church; should we not at once

[1] Rev. vii. 15, 17; xxi. 23, 24.

perceive the meaning of the doctrine? viz. that, were a man to come hither, who had suffered his mind to grow up in its own way, as nature or chance determined, without any deliberate habitual effort after truth and purity, he would find no real pleasure here, but would soon get weary of the place; because, in this house of God, he would hear only of that one subject which he cared little or nothing about, and nothing at all of those things which excited his hopes and fears, his sympathies and energies. If then a man without religion (supposing it possible) were admitted into heaven, doubtless he would sustain a great disappointment. Before, indeed, he fancied that he could be happy there; but when he arrived there, he would find no discourse but that which he had shunned on earth, no pursuits but those he had disliked or despised, nothing which bound him to aught *else* in the universe, and made him feel at home, nothing which he could enter into and rest upon. He would perceive himself to be an isolated being, cut away by Supreme Power from those objects which were still entwined around his heart. Nay, he would be in the presence of that Supreme Power, whom he never on earth could bring himself steadily to think upon, and whom now he regarded only as the destroyer of all that was precious and dear to him. Ah! he could not *bear* the face of the Living God; the Holy God would be no object of joy to him. "Let us alone! What have we to do with thee?" is the sole thought and desire of unclean souls, even while they acknowledge His majesty. None but the holy can look upon the Holy One; without holiness no man can endure to see the Lord.

When, then, we think to take part in the joys of heaven without holiness, we are as inconsiderate as if we supposed we could take an interest in the worship of Christians here below without possessing it in our measure. A careless, a sensual, an unbelieving mind, a mind destitute of the love and fear of God, with narrow views and earthly aims, a low standard of duty, and a benighted conscience, a mind contented with itself, and unresigned to God's will, would feel as little pleasure, at the last day, at the words, "Enter into the joy of thy Lord," as it does now at the words, "Let us pray." Nay, much less, because, while we are in a church, we may turn our thoughts to other subjects, and contrive to forget that God is looking on us; but that will not be possible in heaven.

We see, then, that holiness, or inward separation from the world, is necessary to our admission into heaven, because heaven is *not* heaven, is not a place of happiness, *except* to the holy.

There are bodily indispositions which affect the taste, so that the sweetest flavours become ungrateful to the palate; and indispositions which impair the sight, tinging the fair face of nature with some sickly hue. In like manner, there is a moral malady which disorders the inward sight and taste; and no man labouring under it is in a condition to enjoy what Scripture calls "the fulness of joy in God's presence, and pleasures at His right hand for evermore."

Nay, I will venture to say more than this;—it is fearful, but it is right to say it;—that if we wished to imagine a punishment for an unholy, reprobate soul, we perhaps could not fancy a greater than to *summon it to heaven.* Heaven would be hell to an irreligious man. We know how unhappy we are apt to feel at present, when alone in the midst of strangers, or of men of different tastes and habits from ourselves. How miserable, for example, would it be to have to live in a foreign land, among a people whose faces we never saw before, and whose language we could not learn. And this is but a faint illustration of the loneliness of a man of earthly dispositions and tastes, thrust into the society of Saints and Angels. How forlorn would he wander through the courts of heaven! He would find no one like himself; he would see in every direction the marks of God's holiness, and these would make him shudder. He would feel himself always in His presence. He could no longer turn his thoughts another way, as he does now, when conscience reproaches him. He would know that the Eternal Eye was ever upon him; and that Eye of holiness, which is joy and life to holy creatures, would seem to him an Eye of wrath and punishment. God cannot change His nature. Holy He must ever be. But while He is holy, no unholy soul can be happy in heaven. Fire does not inflame iron, but it inflames straw. It would cease to be fire if it did not. And so heaven itself would be fire to those who would fain escape across the great gulf from the torments of hell. The finger of Lazarus would but increase their thirst. The very "heaven that is over their head" will be "brass" to them.

And now I have partly explained why it is that holiness is prescribed to us as the condition on our part for our admission into heaven. It seems to be necessary from the very nature of things. We do not see how it could be otherwise. Now, then, I will mention two important truths which seem to follow from what has been said.

1. If a certain character of mind, a certain state of the heart

and affections, be necessary for entering heaven, our *actions* will avail for our salvation, chiefly as they tend to produce or evidence this frame of mind. Good works (as they are called) are required, not as if they had anything of merit in them, not as if they could of themselves turn away God's anger for our sins, or purchase heaven for us, but because they are the means, under God's grace, of strengthening and showing forth that holy principle which God implants in the heart, and without which (as the text tells us) we cannot see Him. The more numerous are our acts of charity, self-denial, and forbearance, of course the more will our minds be schooled into a charitable, self-denying, and for-bearing temper. The more frequent are our prayers, the more humble, patient, and religious are our daily deeds, this communion with God, these holy works, will be the means of making our hearts holy, and of preparing us for the future presence of God. Outward acts, done on principle, create inward habits. I repeat, the separate acts of obedience to the will of God, good works as they are called, are of service to us, as gradually severing us from this world of sense, and impressing our hearts with a heavenly character.

It is plain, then, what works are *not* of service to our salvation; —all those which either have no effect upon the heart to change it, or which have a bad effect. What then must be said of those who think it an easy thing to please God, and to recommend themselves to Him; who do a few scanty services, call these the walk of faith, and are satisfied with them? Such men, it is too evident, instead of being themselves profited by their acts, such as they are, of benevolence, honesty, or justice, may be (I might even say) injured by them. For these very acts, even though good in themselves, are made to foster in these persons a bad spirit, a corrupt state of heart; viz. self-love, self-conceit, self-reliance, instead of tending to turn them from this world to the Father of spirits. In like manner, the mere outward acts of coming to church, and saying prayers, which are, of course, duties imperative upon all of us, are really serviceable to those only who do them in a heavenward spirit. Because such men only use these good deeds to the improvement of the heart; whereas even the most exact outward devotion avails not a man, if it does not improve it.

2. But observe what follows from this. If holiness be not merely the doing a certain number of good actions, but is an inward character which follows, under God's grace, from doing them how far distant from that holiness are the multitude of

men. They are not yet even obedient in outward deeds, which is the first step towards possessing it. They have even to learn to practise good works, as the means of changing their hearts, which is the end. It follows at once, even though Scripture did not plainly tell us so, that no one is able to prepare himself for heaven, that is, make himself holy, in a short time ;—at least we do not see how it is possible; and this, viewed merely as a deduction of the reason, is a serious thought. Yet, alas! as there are persons who think to be saved by a few scanty performances, so there are others who suppose they may be saved all at once by a sudden and easily acquired faith. Most men who are living in neglect of God silence their consciences, when troublesome, with the promise of repenting some future day. How often are they thus led on till death surprises them! But we will suppose they *do* begin to repent when that future day comes. Nay, we will even suppose that Almighty God were to forgive them, and to admit them into His holy heaven. Well, but is nothing more requisite? are they in a fit state to *do Him service in heaven?* is not this the very point I have been so insisting on, that they are *not* in a fit state? has it not been shown that, even if admitted thero without a change of heart, they would find no pleasure in heaven? and is a change of heart wrought in a day? Which of our tastes or likings can we change at our will in a moment? Not the most superficial. Can we then at a word change the whole frame and character of our minds? Is not holiness the result of many patient, repeated efforts aiter obedience, gradually working on us, and first modifying and then changing our hearts? We dare not, of course, set bounds to God's mercy and power in cases of repentance late in life, even where He has revealed to us the general rule of His moral governance; yet, surely, it is our duty ever to keep steadily before us, and act upon, those general truths which His Holy Word has declared. His Holy Word in various ways warns us, that, as no one will find happiness in heaven who is not holy, so no one can learn to be so in a short time, and when he will. It implies it in the text, which names a qualification, which we know in matter of fact does ordinarily take time to gain. It propounds it clearly, though in figure, in the parable of the wedding garment, in which inward sanctification is made a condition distinct from our acceptance of the proffer of mercy, and not negligently to be passed over in our thoughts as if a necessary consequence of it; and in that of the ten virgins, which shows us that we must meet the bridegroom with the oil of holiness, and that it takes time to procure it.

And it solemnly assures us in St. Paul's Epistles, that it is possible so to presume on Divine grace, as to let slip the accepted time, and be sealed even before the end of life to a reprobate mind.[1]

I wish to speak to you, my brethren, not as if aliens from God's mercies, but as partakers of His gracious covenant in Christ; and for this reason in especial peril, since those only can incur the sin of making void His covenant who have the privilege of it. Yet neither on the other hand do I speak to you as wilful and obstinate sinners, exposed to the imminent risk of forfeiting, or the chance of having forfeited, your hope of heaven. But I fear there are those who, if they dealt faithfully with their consciences, would be obliged to own that they had not made the service of God their first and great concern; that their obedience, so to call it, has been a matter of course, in which the heart has had no part; that they have acted uprightly in worldly matters chiefly for the sake of their worldly interest. I fear there are those who, whatever be their sense of religion, still have such misgivings about themselves, as lead them to make resolve to obey God more exactly some future day, such misgivings as convict them of sin, though not enough to bring home to them its heinousness or its peril. Such men are trifling with the appointed season of mercy. To obtain the gift of holiness is the work of *a life*. No man will ever be perfect here, so sinful is our nature. Thus, in putting off the day of repentance, these men are reserving for a few chance years, when strength and vigour are gone, that WORK for which a *whole* life would not be enough. That work is great and arduous beyond expression. There is much of sin remaining even in the best of men, and "if the righteous scarcely be saved, where shall the ungodly and the sinner appear?"[2] Their doom may be fixed any moment; and though this thought should not make a man despair to-day, yet it should ever make him tremble for to-morrow.

Perhaps, however, others may say: "We know something of the power of religion—we love it in a measure—we have many right thoughts—we come to church to pray; this is a proof that we are prepared for heaven:—we are safe, and what has been said does not apply to us." But be not you, my brethren, in the number of these. One principal test of our being true servants of God is our wishing to serve Him better; and be quite sure that a man who is contented with his own proficiency in Christian

[1] Heb. vi. 4-6; x. 26-29.   Vide also 2 Pet. ii. 20, 22.
[2] 1 Pet. iv. 18.

holiness is at best in a dark state, or rather in great peril. If we are really imbued with the grace of holiness, we shall abhor sin as something base, irrational, and polluting. Many men, it is true, are contented with partial and indistinct views of religion and mixed motives. Be you content with nothing short of perfection; exert yourselves day by day to grow in knowledge and grace ; that, if so be, you may at length attain to the presence of Almighty God.

Lastly ; while we thus labour to mould our hearts after the pattern of the holiness of our Heavenly Father, it is our comfort to know, what I have already implied, that we are not left to ourselves, but that the Holy Ghost is graciously present with us, and enables us to triumph over, and to change our own minds. It is a comfort and encouragement, while it is an anxious and awful thing, to know that God works in and through us.[1] We are the instruments, but we are only the instruments, of our own salvation. Let no one say that I discourage him, and propose to him a task beyond his strength. All of us have the gifts of grace pledged to us from our youth up. We know this well ; but we do not use our privilege. We form mean ideas of the diffi- culty, and in consequence never enter into the greatness of the gifts given us to meet it. Then afterwards, if perchance we gain a deeper insight into the work we have to do, we think God a hard master, who commands much from a sinful race. Narrow, indeed, is the way of life, but infinite is His love and power who is with the Church, in Christ's place, to guide us along it.

[1] Phil. ii. 12. 13.

SERMON XXXIV.

(SUNDAYS AFTER TRINITY.)

𝕿𝖍𝖊 𝕽𝖊𝖑𝖎𝖌𝖎𝖔𝖚𝖘 𝖀𝖘𝖊 𝖔𝖋 𝕰𝖝𝖈𝖎𝖙𝖊𝖉 𝕱𝖊𝖊𝖑𝖎𝖓𝖌𝖘.

" *The man out of whom the devils were departed besought Him that he might be with Him ; but Jesus sent him away, saying, Return to thine own house, and show how great things God hath done unto thee.*"— LUKE viii. 38, 39.

IT was very natural in the man whom our Lord had set free from this dreadful visitation to wish to continue with Him. Doubtless his mind was transported with joy and gratitude ; whatever consciousness he might possess of his real wretchedness while the devils tormented him, now at least, on recovering his reason, he would understand that he had been in a very miserable state, and he would feel all the lightness of spirits and activity of mind which attend any release from suffering or constraint. Under these circumstances he would imagine himself to be in a new world ; he had found deliverance ; and what was more, a Deliverer too, who stood before him. And whether from a wish to be ever in His Divine presence, ministering to Him, or from a fear lest Satan would return, nay, with sevenfold power, did he lose sight of Christ, or from an undefined notion that all his duties and hopes were now changed, that his former pursuits were unworthy of him, and that he must follow up some great undertakings with the new ardour he felt glowing within him ;—from one or other, or all of these feelings combined, he besought our Lord that he might be with Him. Christ imposed this attendance as a command on others ; He bade, for instance, the young ruler follow Him ; but He gives opposite commands, according to our tempers and likings ; He thwarts us that He may try our faith. In the case before us He suffered not what at other times He had bidden. "Return to thine own house," He said or as it is in St. Mark's Gospel, "Go home to thy friends, and tell them how great things the Lord hath done for thee, and hath had compassion on thee." [1] He directed the current of his newly awakened feelings into another channel; as if He said, "Lovest thou Me? this do; return home to your old occupations and pursuits. You did them ill before, you lived to the world; do them well now, live to Me. Do your duties, little as well as great, heartily for My sake; go among your friends; show them what God hath done for thee; be an example to them, and teach them." [2] And further, as He said on another occasion, "Show thyself to the priest, and offer the gift that Moses commanded, for a testimony unto them," [3]—show forth that greater light and truer love which you now possess in a conscientious, consistent obedience to all the ordinances and rites of your religion.

Now from this account of the restored demoniac, his request, and our Lord's denial of it, a lesson may be drawn for the use of those who, having neglected religion in early youth, at length begin to have serious thoughts, try to repent, and wish to serve God better than hitherto, though they do not know how to set about it. We know that God's commandments are pleasant, and "rejoice the heart," if we accept them in the order and manner in which He puts them upon us; that Christ's yoke, as He has promised, is (on the whole) very easy, if we submit to it betimes; that the practice of religion is full of comfort to those who, being first baptized with the Spirit of grace, receive thankfully His influences as their minds open, inasmuch as they are gradually, and almost without sensible effort on their part, imbued in all their heart, soul, and strength, with that true heavenly life which will last for ever.

But here the question meets us, "But what are those to do who *have* neglected to remember their Creator in the days of their youth, and so have lost all claim on Christ's promise, that His yoke shall be easy, and His commandments not grievous?" I answer, that of course they must not be surprised if obedience is with them a laborious uphill work all their days; nay, as having been "once enlightened, and partaken of the Holy Ghost" in baptism, they would have no right to complain even though "it were impossible for them to renew themselves again unto repentance." But God is more merciful than this just severity; merciful not only above our deservings, but even above His own promises. Even for those who have neglected Him when young, He has found (if they will avail themselves of it) some sort of

[1] Mark v. 19.   [2] Col. iii. 17.   [3] Matt. viii. 4.

remedy of the difficulties in the way of obedience which they have brought upon themselves by sinning; and what this remedy is, and how it is to be used, I proceed to describe in connection with the account in the text.

The help I speak of is the excited feeling with which repentance is at first attended. True it is, that all the passionate emotion, or fine sensibility, which ever man displayed, will never by itself make us change our ways and do our duty. Impassioned thoughts, high aspirations, sublime imaginings, have no strength in them. They can no more make a man obey consistently than they can move mountains. If any man truly repent, it must be in consequence, not of these, but of a settled conviction of his guilt, and a deliberate resolution to leave his sins and serve God. Conscience, and Reason in subjection to Conscience, *these* are those powerful instruments (under grace) which change a man. But you will observe, that though Conscience and Reason lead us to resolve on and to attempt a new life, they cannot at once make us *love* it. It is long practice and habit which make us love religion; and in the beginning, obedience, doubtless, is very grievous to habitual sinners. Here, then, is the use of those earnest, ardent feelings of which I just now spoke, and which attend on the first exercise of Conscience and Reason,—to take away from the *beginnings* of obedience its *grievousness*, to give us an impulse which may carry us over the first obstacles, and send us on our way rejoicing. Not as if all this excitement of mind were to last (which cannot be), but it will do its office in thus setting us off; and then will leave us to the more sober and higher comfort resulting from that real *love* for religion, which obedience itself will have by that time begun to form in us, and will gradually go on to perfect.

Now it is well to understand this fully, for it is often mistaken. When sinners at length are led to think seriously, strong feelings generally precede or attend their reflections about themselves. Some book they have read, some conversation of a friend, some remarks they have heard made in church, or some occurrence or misfortune, rouses them. Or, on the other hand, if in any more calm and deliberate manner they have commenced their self-examination, yet in a little time the very view of their manifold sins, of their guilt, and of their heinous ingratitude to their God and Saviour, breaking upon them, and being new to them, strikes, and astonishes, and then agitates them. Here, then, let them know the *intention* of all this excitement of mind in the order of Divine Providence. It will not continue; it arises from the novelty of the view presented to them. As they become accustomed to religious contemplations it will wear away. It is not religion itself, though it is accidentally connected with it, and may be made a means of leading them into a sound religious course of life. It is graciously intended to be a set-off in their case against the first distastefulness and pain of doing their duty ; it must be used as such, or it will be of no use at all, or worse than useless. My brethren, bear this in mind (and I may say this generally,—not confining myself to the excitement which attends repentance,—of all that natural emotion prompting us to do good, which we involuntarily feel on various occasions), it is given you in order that you may find it easy to obey at starting. Therefore obey *promptly ;* make use of it whilst it lasts ; it waits for no man. Do you feel natural pity towards some case which reasonably demands your charity ? or the impulse of generosity in a case where you are called to act a manly self-denying part ? Whatever the emotion may be, whether these or any other, do not imagine you will always feel it. Whether you avail yourselves of it or not, still anyhow you will feel it less and less, and, as life goes on, at last you will not feel such sudden vehement excitement at all. But this is the difference between seizing or letting slip these opportunities ;—if you avail yourselves of them for acting, and yield to the impulse so far as conscience tells you to do, you have made a leap (so to say) across a gulf, to which your ordinary strength is not equal ; you will have secured the beginning of obedience, and the further steps in the course are (generally speaking) far easier than those which first determine its direction. And so, to return to the case of those who feel any accidental remorse for their sins violently exerting itself in their hearts, I say to them, Do not loiter ; go home to your friends, and repent in *deeds* of righteousness and love ; hasten to commit yourselves to certain definite *acts* of obedience. Doing is at a far greater distance from intending to do than you at first sight imagine. Join them together while you can ; you will be depositing your good feelings into your heart itself by thus making them influence your conduct ; and they will "spring up into fruit." This was the conduct of the conscience-stricken Corinthians, as described by St. Paul ; who rejoiced " not that they were made *sorry*" (not that their feelings merely were moved), "but that they sorrowed *to change of mind.* . . . For godly sorrow," he continues, "worketh repentance to salvation not to be repented of ; but the sorrow of the world worketh death." [1]

[1] 2 Cor. vii. 9, 10.

T

But now let us ask, How do men usually conduct themselves in matter of fact, when under visitings of conscience for their past sinful lives? They are far from thus acting. They look upon the turbid zeal and feverish devotion which attend their repentance, not as in part the corrupt offspring of their own previously corrupt state of mind, and partly a gracious natural provision, only temporary, to encourage them to set about their reformation, but as the substance and real excellence of religion. They think that to be thus agitated is to be religious; they indulge themselves in these warm feelings for their own sake, resting in them as if they were then engaged in a religious exercise, and boasting of them as if they were an evidence of their own exalted spiritual state; not *using them* (the one only thing they ought to do), using them as an incitement to *deeds* of love, mercy, truth, meekness, holiness. After they have indulged this luxury of feeling for some time, the excitement of course ceases; they do not feel as they did before. This (I have said) might have been anticipated, but they do not understand it so. See then their unsatisfactory state. They have lost an opportunity of overcoming the first difficulties of active obedience, and so of fixing their conduct and character, which may never occur again. This is one great misfortune; but more than this, what a perplexity they have involved themselves in! Their warmth of feeling is gradually dying away. Now they think that *in it* true religion consists; therefore they believe that they are losing their faith, and falling into sin again.

And this, alas! *is* too often the case; they *do* fall away, for they have no root in themselves. Having neglected to turn their feelings into principles by acting upon them, they have no inward strength to overcome the temptation to live as the world, which continually assails them. Their minds have been acted upon as water by the wind, which raises waves for a time, then ceasing, leaves the water to subside into its former stagnant state. The precious opportunity of improvement has been lost; "and the latter end is worse with them than the beginning."[1]

But let us suppose, that when they first detect this declension (as they consider it), they are alarmed, and look around for a means of recovering themselves. What do they do? Do they at once begin those practices of lowly obedience which alone can prove them to be Christ's at the last day? such as the government of their tempers, the regulation of their time, self-denying charity, truth-telling sobriety. Far from it; they despise this plain obedience to God as a mere unenlightened morality, as they

[1] 2 Pet. ii. 20.

call it, and they seek for potent stimulants to sustain their minds in that state of excitement which they have been taught to consider the essence of a religious life, and which they cannot produce by the means which before excited them. They have recourse to new doctrines, or follow strange teachers, in order that they may dream on in this their artificial devotion, and may avoid that conviction which is likely sooner or later to burst upon them, that emotion and passion are in our power indeed to repress, but not to *excite;* that there is a limit to the tumults and swellings of the heart, foster them as we will; and, when that time comes, the poor, misused soul is left exhausted and resourceless. Instances are not rare in the world of that fearful, ultimate state of hard-heartedness which then succeeds; when the miserable sinner believes indeed as the devils may, yet not even with the devils' trembling, but sins on without fear.

Others, again, there are, who, when their feelings fall off in strength and fervency, are led to despond; and so are brought down to fear and bondage, when they might have been rejoicing in cheerful obedience. These are the better sort, who, having something of true religious principle in their hearts, still are misled in part,—so far, that is, as to rest in their feelings as tests of holiness; therefore they are distressed and alarmed at their own tranquillity, which they think a bad sign, and, being dispirited, lose time, others outstripping them in the race.

And others might be mentioned who are led by this same first eagerness and zeal into a different error. The restored sufferer in the text wished to be with Christ. Now it is plain, all those who indulge themselves in the false devotion I have been describing, may be said to be desirous of thus keeping themselves in Christ's immediate sight, instead of returning to their own home, as He would have them, that is, to the common duties of life: and they do this, some from weakness of faith, as if He could not bless them, and keep them in the way of grace, though they pursued their worldly callings; others from an ill-directed love of Him. But there are others, I say, who, when they are awakened to a sense of religion, forthwith despise their former condition altogether, as beneath them; and think that they are now called to some high and singular office in the Church. These mistake their duty as those already described neglect it; they do not waste their time in mere good thoughts and good words, as the others, but they are impetuously led on to *wrong acts*, and that from the influence of those same strong emotions which they have not learned to use aright or direct to their proper end. But to speak of these now at any length would be beside my subject.

To conclude ;—let me repeat and urge upon you, my brethren, the lesson which I have deduced from the narrative of which the text forms part. Your Saviour calls you from infancy to serve Him, and has arranged all things well, so that His service shall be perfect freedom. Blessed above all men are they who heard His call then, and served Him day by day, as their strength to obey increased. But further, are you conscious that you have more or less neglected this gracious opportunity, and suffered yourselves to be tormented by Satan? See, He calls you a second time; He calls you by your roused affections once and again, ere He leave you finally. He brings you back for the time (as it were) to a second youth by the urgent persuasions of excited fear, gratitude, love, and hope. He again places you for an instant in that early, unformed state of nature when habit and character were not. He takes you out of yourselves, robbing sin for a season of its indwelling hold upon you. Let not those visitings pass away "as the morning cloud and the early dew."[1] Surely, you must still have occasional compunctions of conscience for your neglect of Him. Your sin stares you in the face; your ingratitude to God affects you. Follow on to know the Lord, and to secure His favour by *acting* upon these impulses; by them He pleads with you, as well as by your conscience; they are the instruments of His Spirit, stirring you up to seek your true peace. Nor be surprised, though you obey them, that they die away; they have done their office, and if they die, it is but as blossom changes into the fruit, which is far better. They *must* die. Perhaps you will have to labour in darkness afterwards, out of your Saviour's sight, in the home of your own thoughts, surrounded by sights of this world, and showing forth His praise among those who are cold-hearted. Still be quite sure that resolute, consistent obedience, though unattended with high transport and warm emotion, is far more acceptable to Him than all those passionate longings to live in His sight, which look more like religion to the uninstructed. At the very best these latter are but the graceful beginnings of obedience, graceful and becoming in children, but in grown spiritual men indecorous, as the sports of boyhood would seem in advanced years. Learn to live by faith, which is a calm, deliberate, rational principle, full of peace and comfort, and sees Christ, and rejoices in Him, though sent away from His presence to labour in the world. You will have your reward. He will "see you again, and your heart shall rejoice, and your joy no man taketh from you."

[1] Hosea vi. 4.

SERMON XXXV.

(SUNDAYS AFTER TRINITY.)

The Self-wise Inquirer.

" Let no man deceive himself. If any man among you seemeth to be wise in this world, let him become a fool, that he may be wise. For the wisdom of this world is foolishness with God. For it is written, He taketh the wise in their own craftiness."—1 COR. iii. 18, 19.

AMONG the various deceptions against which St. Paul warns us, a principal one is that of a *false wisdom ;* as in the text. The Corinthians prided themselves on their intellectual acuteness and knowledge ; as if anything could equal the excellence of Christian love. Accordingly, St. Paul writing to them says, "Let no man deceive himself. If any man among you seemeth to be wise in this world" (*i.e.* has the reputation of wisdom in the world), "let him become a fool" (what the world calls a fool), "that he may [really] be wise." "For," he proceeds (just as real wisdom is foolishness in the eyes of the world, so in turn), "the wisdom of this world is foolishness with God."

This warning of the Apostle against *our trusting our own wisdom*, may lead us, through God's blessing, to some profitable reflections to-day.

The world's wisdom is said to be *foolishness* in God's sight ; and the end of it error, perplexity, and then ruin. "He taketh the wise in their own craftiness." Here is one especial reason why professed inquirers after truth do not find it. They seek it in a wrong way, by a vain wisdom, which leads them away from the truth, however it may seem to promise success.

Let us then inquire what is this *vain wisdom*, and then we shall the better see how it leads men astray.

Now, when it is said that to trust our own notions is a wrong thing and a vain wisdom, of course this is not meant of all our own notions whatever; for we must trust our own notions in one shape or other, and some notions which we form are right and true. The question, therefore, is, What is that *evil* trusting to ourselves, that sinful self-confidence, or self-conceit, which is called in the text the "wisdom of the world," and is a chief cause of our going wrong in our religious inquiries?

These are the notions which we may trust *without* blame; viz. such as come to us by way of our conscience, for such come from God. I mean our certainty that there is a right and a wrong, that some things ought to be done, and other things not done; that we have duties, the neglect of which brings remorse; and further, that God is good, wise, powerful, and righteous, and that we should try to obey Him. All these notions, and a multitude of others like these, come by natural conscience, *i.e.* they are impressed on all our minds from our earliest years without our trouble. They do not proceed from the mere exercise of our minds, though it is true they are strengthened and formed thereby. They proceed from God, whether within us or without us; and though we cannot trust them so implicitly as we can trust the Bible, because the truths of the Bible are actually preserved in writing, and so cannot be lost or altered, still, as far as we have reason to think them true, we may rely in them, and make much of them, without incurring the sin of self-confidence. These notions which we obtain without our exertion will never make us proud or conceited, because they are ever attended with a sense of sin and guilt, from the remembrance that we have at times transgressed and injured them. To trust them is not the false wisdom of the world, or foolishness, because they come from the All-wise God. And far from leading a man into error, they will, if obeyed, of a certainty lead him to a firm belief in Scripture; in which he will find all those vague conjectures and imperfect notions about truth, which his own heart taught him, abundantly sanctioned, completed, and illustrated.

Such then are the opinions and feelings of which a man is *not* proud. What are those of which he is likely to be proud? those which he obtains, *not* by nature, but by his own industry, ability, and research; those which he possesses and others not. Every one is in danger of valuing himself for what he does; and hence truths (or fancied truths) which a man has obtained for himself after much thought and labour, such he is apt to make much of, and to rely upon; and this is the source of that vain wisdom of which the Apostle speaks in the text.

Now (I say) this confidence in our own reasoning powers not only leads to pride, but to "*foolishness*" also, and destructive error, because it will oppose itself to Scripture. A man who fancies he can find out truth by himself, disdains revelation. He who thinks he *has* found it out is *impatient* of revelation. He fears it will interfere with his own imaginary discoveries, he is unwilling to consult it; and when it does interfere, then he is angry. We hear much of this proud rejection of the truth in the Epistle from which the text is taken. The Jews felt anger, and the Greeks disdain, at the Christian doctrine. "The Jews required a sign" (according to their preconceived notions concerning the Messiah's coming), "and the Greeks seek after wisdom" (some subtle train of reasoning), "but we preach Christ crucified, unto the Jews a stumblingblock, and to the Greeks foolishness."[1] In another place the Apostle says of the misled Christians of Corinth, "Now ye are full" of your own notions, "now ye are rich, ye have reigned as kings *without us;*"[2] *i.e.* you have prided yourselves on a wisdom, "without," separate from, the truth of Apostolic doctrine. Confidence, then, in our own reasoning powers leads to (what St. Paul calls) foolishness, by causing in our hearts an indifference towards, or a distaste for Scripture information.

But, besides thus keeping us from the best of guides, it also makes us fools, because it is a confidence in a *bad* guide. Our reasoning powers are very weak in all inquiries into moral and religious truth. Clear-sighted as reason is on other subjects, and trustworthy as a guide, still in questions connected with our duty to God and man it is very unskilful and equivocating. After all, it barely reaches the same great truths which are authoritatively set forth by conscience and by Scripture; and if it be used in religious inquiries, without reference to these divinely-sanctioned informants, the probability is, it will miss the truth altogether. Thus the (so-called) wise will be taken in their own craftiness. All of us, doubtless, recollect our Lord's words, which are quite to the purpose: "I thank Thee, O Father, Lord of heaven and earth, because Thou hast hid these things from the *wise and prudent*" (those who trust in their own intellectual powers), "and hast revealed them unto *babes*,"[3] those, *i.e.* that act by faith and for conscience' sake.

The false wisdom, then, of which St. Paul speaks in the text, is a trusting our own powers for arriving at religious truth, instead of taking what is divinely provided for us, whether in

[1] 1 Cor. i. 22, 23.   [2] 1 Cor. iv. 8.   [3] Matt. xi. 25.

nature or revelation. This is the way of the world. In the world, reason is set against conscience, and usurps its power; and hence men become " wise in their own conceits," and " leaning to their own understandings," " err from the truth." Let us now review some particulars of this contest between our instinctive sense of right and wrong and our weak and conceited reason.

It begins within us, when childhood and boyhood are past, and the time comes for our entrance into life. Before that time we trusted our divinely-enlightened sense of duty and our right feeling implicitly; and though (alas!) we continually transgressed, and thereby impaired this inward guide, at least we did not question its authority. *Then* we had that original temper of faith, wrought in us by baptism, the spirit of little children, without which our Lord assures us, none of us, young or old, can enter the kingdom of heaven.[1]

But when our minds became more manly, and the world opened upon us, then, in proportion to the intellectual gifts with which God had honoured us, came the temptation of unbelief and dis-obedience. Then came reason, led on by passion, to war against our better knowledge. We were driven into the wilderness, after our Lord's manner, by the very Spirit given us, which exposed us to the devil's devices, before the time or power came of using the gift in God's service. And how many of the most highly endowed then fall away under trials which the sinless Son of God withstood! He feels for all who are tempted, having Himself suffered temptation; yet what a sight must He see, and by what great exercise of mercy must the holy Jesus endure, the bold and wicked thoughts which often reign the most triumphantly in the breasts of those (at least for a time) whom He has commissioned by the abundance of their talents to be the especial ministers of His will!

A murmuring against that religious service which is perfect freedom, complaints that Christ's yoke is heavy, a rebellious rising against the authority of conscience, and a proud arguing against the truth, or at least an endurance of doubt and scoffing, and a light, unmeaning use of sceptical arguments and assertions, these are the beginnings of apostasy. Then come the affectation of originality, the desire to appear manly and independent, and the fear of the ridicule of our acquaintance, all combining to make us first speak, and then really think evil of the supreme authority of religion. This gradual transgression of the first commandment of the Law is generally attended by a transgres-

[1] Matt. xviii. 3.

sion of the fifth. In our childhood we loved both religion and our home; but as we learn to despise the voice of God, so do we first affect, and then feel, an indifference towards the opinions of our superiors and elders. Thus our minds become gradually hardened against the purest pleasures, both divine and human.

As this progress in sin continues, our disobedience becomes its own punishment. In proportion as we lean to our own understanding, we are driven to do so for want of a better guide. Our first true guide, the light of innocence, is gradually withdrawn from us; and nothing is left for us but to "grope and stumble in the desolate places," by the dim, uncertain light of reason. Thus we are taken in our own craftiness. This is what is sometimes called *judicial blindness;* such as Pharaoh's, who, from resisting God's will, at length did not know the difference between light and darkness.

How far each individual proceeds in this bad course depends on a variety of causes, into the consideration of which I need not enter. Some are frightened at themselves, and turn back into the right way before it is too late. Others are checked; and though they do not seek God with all their heart, yet are preserved from any strong and full manifestation of the evil principles which lurk within them; and others are kept in a correct outward form of religion by the circumstances in which they are placed. But there are others, and these many in number, perhaps in all ranks of life, who proceed onwards in evil; and I will go on to describe in part their condition,—the condition, that is, of those in whom intellectual power is fearfully unfolded amid the neglect of moral truth.

The most common case, of course, is that of those who, with their principles thus unformed, or rather unsettled, become engaged, in the ordinary way, in the business of life. Their first simplicity of character went early. The violence of passion followed, and was indulged; and it is gone too, leaving (without their suspecting it) most baneful effects on their mind; just as some diseases silently change the constitution of the body. Lastly, a vain reason has put into disorder their notions about moral propriety and duty, both as to religion and the conduct of life. It is quite plain that, having nothing of that faith which "overcomes the world," they must be overcome by it. Let it not be supposed I am speaking of some strange case which does not concern us; for what we know, it concerns some of us most nearly. The issue of our youthful trial in good and evil probably has had somewhat of a decided character one way or the other; and we may be quite sure that, if it has issued in evil, we shall not know it.   Deadness to the voice of God, hardness of heart, is one of the very symptoms of unbelief.   God's judgments, whether to the world or the individual, are not loudly spoken. The decree goes forth to build or destroy; Angels hear it; but we go on in the way of the world as usual, though our souls may have been, at least for a season, abandoned by God.   I mean, that it is not at all unlikely that, in the case of some of those who now hear me, a great part of their professed faith is a mere matter of *words*, not *ideas and principles;* that what opinions they really hold by any exertion of their own minds, have been reached by the mere exercise of their intellect, the random and accidental use of their mere reasoning powers, whether they be strong or not, and are not the result of habitual, firm, and progressive obedience to God, not the knowledge which an honest and good heart imparts.   Our religious notions may lie on the mere surface of our minds, and have no root within them; and (I say) from this circumstance,—that the indulgence of early passions, though forgotten now, and the misapplication of reason in our youth, have left an indelibly evil character upon our heart, a judicial hardness and blindness.   Let us think of this; it may be the state of those who have had to endure only ordinary temptations, from the growth of that reasoning faculty with which we are all gifted.

But when that gift of reason is something especial,—clear, brilliant, or powerful,—then our danger is increased.   The first sin of men of superior understanding is to *value* themselves upon it, and look down upon others.   They make intellect the measure of praise and blame; and instead of considering a common *faith* to be the bond of union between Christian and Christian, they dream of some other fellowship of civilization, refinement, literature, science, or general mental illumination, to unite gifted minds one with another.   Having thus cast down moral excellence from its true station, and set up the usurping empire of mere reason, next they place a value upon all truths exactly in proportion to the possibility of proving them by means of that mere reason.   Hence, moral and religious truths are thought little of by them, because they fall under the province of *conscience* far more than of the intellect.   Religion sinks in their estimation, or becomes of no account; they begin to think all religions alike; and no wonder, for they are like men who have lost the faculty of discerning colours, and who never, by any exercise of reason, can make out the difference between white and black.   As to the code of morals, they acknowledge it in a measure, that is, so far as its dicta can be *proved* by reasoning, by an appeal to sight, and to expedience, and without reference to a natural sense of right and wrong as the sanction of these informants. Thinking much of intellectual advancement, they are much bent on improving the world by making *all men* intellectual; and they labour to convince themselves, that as men grow in knowledge they will grow in virtue.

As they proceed in their course of judicial blindness, from *undervaluing* they learn to *despise* or to *hate* the authority of conscience. They treat it as a weakness, to which all men indeed are subject,—they themselves in the number,—especially in seasons of sickness, but of which they have cause to be ashamed. The notions of better men about an overruling Providence, and the Divine will, designs, appointments, works, judgments, they treat with scorn, as irrational; especially if (as will often be the case) these notions are conveyed in incorrect language, with some accidental confusion or intellectual weakness of expression.

And all these inducements to live by sight and not by faith are greatly increased, when men are engaged in any pursuit which properly *belongs* to the intellect. Hence sciences conversant with experiments on the material creation tend to make men forget the existence of spirit and the Lord of spirits.

I will not pursue the course of infidelity into its worst and grossest forms; but it may be instructive, before I conclude, to take the case of such a man as I have been describing, when under the influence of some relentings of conscience towards the close of his life.

This is a case of no unfrequent occurrence; that is, it must frequently happen that the most hardened conscience is at times visited by sudden compunctions, though generally they are but momentary. But it sometimes happens, further than this, that a man, from one cause or other, feels he is not in a safe state, and struggles with himself, and the struggle terminates in a manner which affords a fresh illustration of the working of that wisdom of the world which in God's sight is foolishness.

How shall a sinner, who has formed his character upon unbelief, trusting sight and reason rather than conscience and Scripture, how shall he begin to repent? What must he do? Is it possible he can overcome himself, and new make his heart in the end of his days? it *is* possible,—not with man, but with God, who gives grace to all who ask for it; but in only one way, *in the way of*

His commandments, by a slow, tedious, toilsome self-discipline; slow, tedious, and toilsome, that is, to one who has been long hardening himself in a dislike of it, and indulging himself in the rapid flights and easy victories of his reason. There is but one way to heaven; the narrow way; and he who sets about to seek God, though in old age, must enter it at the same door as others. He must retrace his way, and begin again with the very beginning as if he were a boy. And so proceeding,—labouring, watching, and praying,—he seems likely, after all, to make but little progress during the brief remnant of his life; both because the time left to him is short, and because he has to undo while he does a work;—he has to overcome that resistance from his old stout will and hardened heart which in youth he would not have experienced.

Now it is plain how humbling this is to his pride: he wishes to be saved; but he cannot stoop to be a penitent all his days: to beg he is ashamed. Therefore he looks about for other means of finding a safe hope. And one way among others by which he deceives himself, is this same idea that he may gain religious knowledge merely by his reason.

Thus it happens, that men who have led profligate lives in their youth, or who have passed their days in the pursuit of wealth, or in some other excitement of the world, not unfrequently settle down into *heresies* in their latter years. Before, perhaps, they professed nothing, and suffered themselves to be called Christians and members of the Church; but at length, roused to inquire after truth, and forgetting that the pure in heart alone can see God, and therefore that they must begin by a *moral* reformation, by self-denial, they inquire merely by the way of reasoning. No wonder they err; they cannot understand any part of the Church's system whether of doctrine or discipline; yet they *think* themselves judges; and they treat the most sacred ordinances and the most solemn doctrines with scorn and irreverence. Thus "the last state of such men is worse than the first." In the words of the text, they ought to have become fools, that they might have been in the end really wise; but they prefer another way, and are taken in their own craftiness.

May we ever bear in mind that the "fear of the Lord is the beginning of wisdom;"[1] that obedience to our conscience, in all things, great and small, is the way to know the truth; that pride hardens the heart, and sensuality debases it; and that all those who live in pride and sensual indulgence, can no more comprehend

[1] Prov. i. 7.

the way of the Holy Spirit, or know the voice of Christ, than the devils who believe with a dead faith and tremble !

"Blessed are they that do His commandments, that they may have right to the tree of life, and may enter in through the gates into the city " . . . where there is "no need of the sun, neither of the moon to shine in it; for the glory of God doth lighten it, and the Lamb is the light thereof." [1]

[1] Rev. xxi. 23; xxii. 14.

SERMON XXXVI.

(SUNDAYS AFTER TRINITY.)

Scripture a Record of Human Sorrow.

*" There is at Jerusalem by the sheepmarket a pool, which is called in the
Hebrew tongue Bethesda, having five porches. In these lay a great multitude of impotent folk, of blind, halt, withered, waiting for the moving
of the water."*—JOHN v. 2, 3.

WHAT a scene of misery this pool of Bethesda must have
presented! of pain and sickness triumphing unto death!
the "blind, halt, withered, and impotent," persuaded by the hope
of cure to disclose their sufferings in the eye of day in one large
company. This pool was endued, at certain times, with a
wonderful virtue by the descent of an Angel into it, so that its
waters effected the cure of the first who stepped into it, whatever was his disease. However, I shall not speak of this wonderful pool; nor of our Saviour's miracle, wrought there upon the
man who had no one to put him in before the rest, when the water
was troubled, and who had been for thirty-eight years afflicted
with his infirmity. Without entering into these subjects, let us
take the text as it stands in the opening of the chapter which
contains it, and deduce a lesson from it.

There lay about the pool "a great multitude of impotent folk,
of blind, halt, and withered." This is a painful picture, such as
we do not like to dwell upon,—a picture of a chief kind of human
suffering, bodily disease; one which suggests to us and typifies
all other suffering,—the most obvious fulfilment of that curse
which Adam's fall brought upon his descendants. Now it must
strike every one who thinks at all about it, that the Bible is full
of such descriptions of human misery. We know it also abounds
in accounts of human sin; but not to speak of these, it abounds

in accounts of human distress and sufferings, of our miserable condition, of the vanity, unprofitableness, and trials of life. The Bible begins with the history of the curse pronounced on the earth and man; it ends with the Book of Revelation, a portion of Scripture fearful for its threats, and its prediction of judgments; and whether the original curse on Adam be now removed from the world or not, it is certain that God's awful curses, foretold by St. John, are on all sides of us. Surely, in spite of the peculiar promises made to the Church in Christ our Saviour, yet as regards the world, the volume of inspiration is still a dreary record, "written within and without with lamentations, and mourning, and woe." And further, you will observe that it seems to drop what might be said in favour of this life, and enlarges on the unpleasant side of it. The history passes quickly from the Garden of Eden, to dwell on the sufferings which followed, when our first parents were expelled thence; and though, in matter of fact, there are traces of paradise still left among us, yet it is evident, Scripture says little of them in comparison of its accounts of human misery. Little does it say concerning the innocent pleasures of life; of those temporal blessings which rest upon our worldly occupations, and make them easy; of the blessings which we derive from "the sun and moon, and the everlasting hills," from the succession of the seasons, and the produce of the earth;—little about our recreations and our daily domestic comforts;—little about the ordinary occasions of festivity and mirth which occur in life, and nothing at all about those various other enjoyments which it would be going too much into detail to mention. Human tales and poems are full of pleasant sights and prospects; they make things better than they are, and portray a sort of imaginary perfection; but Scripture (I repeat) seems to abstain even from what might be said in praise of human life as it is. We read, indeed, of the feast made when Isaac was weaned, of Jacob's marriage, of the domestic and religious festivities of Job's family; but these are exceptions in the tenor of the Scripture history. "Vanity of vanities, all is vanity;" "man is born to trouble:" these are its customary lessons. The text is but a specimen of the descriptions repeated again and again throughout Scripture of human infirmity and misery.

So much is this the case, that thoughtless persons are averse to the Scripture narrative for this very reason. I do not mean bad men, who speak hard, presumptuous words against the Bible, and in consequence expose themselves to the wrath of God; but I speak of *thoughtless* persons; and of these there are many, who consider the Bible a gloomy book, and on that account seldom look into it, saying that it makes them melancholy. Accordingly, there have been attempts made on the other hand to hide this austere character of Scripture, and make it a bright interesting picture of human life. Its stories have before now been profanely embellished in human language, to suit the taste of weak and cowardly minds. All this shows, that in the common opinion of mankind, the Bible does not take a pleasant sunshine view of the world.

Now why have I thus spoken of this general character of the sacred history?—in order to countenance those who complain of it?—let it not be imagined;—far from it. God does nothing without some wise and good reason, which it becomes us devoutly to accept and use. He has not given us this dark view of the world without a cause. In truth, this view is the ultimate *true* view of human life. But this is not all; it is a view which it concerns us much to know. It concerns us (I say) much to be told that this world is, after all, in spite of first appearances and partial exceptions, a dark world; else we shall be obliged to learn it (and, sooner or later, we must learn it) by sad *experience;* whereas, if we are forewarned, we shall unlearn false notions of its excellence, and be saved the disappointment which follows them. And therefore it is that Scripture omits even what might be said in praise of this world's pleasures;—not denying their value, such as it is, or forbidding us to use them religiously, but knowing that we are sure to find them out for ourselves without being told of them, and that our danger is on the side, not of undervaluing, but of overvaluing them; whereas, by being told of the world's vanity, *at first*, we shall learn (what else we should only attain *at last*), not indeed to be gloomy and discontented, but to bear a sober and calm heart under a smiling cheerful countenance. This is one chief reason of the solemn character of the Scripture history; and if we keep it in view, so far from being offended and frightened away by its notes of sorrow, because they grate on the ear at first, we shall stedfastly listen to them, and get them by heart, as a gracious gift from God sent to us, as a remedy for all dangerous overflowing joy in present blessings, in order to save us far greater pain (if we use the lesson well), the pain of actual disappointment, such as the overthrow of vainly cherished hopes of lasting good upon earth will certainly occasion.

Do but consider what is the consequence of ignorance or distrust of God's warning voice, and you will see clearly how merciful He is, and how wise it is to listen to Him. I will not suppose a case of gross sin, or of open contempt for religion; but let a man have a general becoming reverence for the law and Church of God, and an unhesitating faith in his Saviour Christ, yet suppose him so to be taken with the goods of this world, as (without his being aware of it) to give his heart to them. Let him have many good feelings and dispositions; but let him love his earthly pursuits, amusements, friends, too well;—by which I mean, so well as to forget that he is bound to live in the spirit of Abraham's faith, who gave up home, kindred, possessions, all his eye ever loved, at God's word,—in the spirit of St. Paul's faith, who "counted all things but loss for the excellency of the knowledge of Christ Jesus his Lord," and to win His favour "suffered the loss of all things." How will the world go with a man thus forgetful of his true interests? For a while all will be enjoyment;—if at any time weariness comes, he will be able to change his pleasure, and the variety will relieve him. His health is good and his spirits high, and easily master and bear down all the accidental troubles of life. So far is well; but, as years roll on, by little and little he will discover that, after all, he is not, as he imagined, possessed of any real substantial good. He will begin to find, and be startled at finding, that the things which once pleased, please less and less, or not at all. He will be unable to recall those lively emotions in which he once indulged; and he will wonder why. Thus, by degrees, the delightful visions which surrounded him will fade away, and in their stead, melancholy forms will haunt him, such as crowded round the pool of Bethesda. Then will be fulfilled the words of the wise man. The days will have come, "when thou shalt say, I have no pleasure in them; the sun and the light and the moon and the stars shall be darkened, and the clouds return after the rain; then they who look out of the window shall be darkened, the doors shall be shut in the streets, all the daughters of music shall be brought low, fears shall be in the way, and desire shall fail." [1] Then a man will begin to be restless and discontented, for he does not know how to amuse himself. Before, he was cheerful only from the natural flow of his spirits, and when such cheerfulness is lost with increasing years, he becomes evil-natured. He has made no effort to change his heart,—to raise, strengthen, and purify his faith,—to subdue his bad passions and tempers. Now their day is come; they have sprung up and begin to domineer. When he was in health, he thought about his farm, or his merchandise, and lived to himself; he laid out his strength

---

[1] Eccles. xii. 1-5.

U

on the world, and the world is nothing to him, as a worthless bargain (so to say), seeing it is nothing worth to one who cannot take pleasure in it. He had no habitual thought of God in the former time, however he might have a general reverence for His Name; and now he dreads Him, or (if the truth must be said) even begins to hate the thought of Him. Where shall he look for succour? Perhaps, moreover, he is a burden to those around him; they care not for him,—he is in their way. And so he will lie year after year, by the pool of Bethesda, by the waters of health, with no one helping him;—unable to advance himself towards a cure, in consequence of his long habits of sin, and others passing him by, perhaps unable to help one who obstinately refuses to be comforted. Thus he has at length full personal, painful experience, that this world is really vanity or worse, and all this because he would not believe it from Scripture.

Now, should the above description appear overcharged, should it be said that it supposes a man to be possessed of more of the pleasures of life than most men have, and of keener feelings,— should it be said that most men have little to enjoy, and that most of those who have much go on in an ordinary tranquil way, and take and lose things without much thought, not pleased much in their vigorous days, and not caring much about the change when the world deserts them,—then I must proceed to a more solemn consideration still, on which I do not like to dwell, but would rather leave it for your own private reflection upon it. There is a story in the Gospels of a man who was taken out of this life before he had turned his thoughts heavenward, and in another world he lift up his eyes being in torments. Be quite sure that every one of us, even the poorest and the most dull and insensible, is far more attached to this world than he can possibly imagine. We get used to the things about us, and forget they are necessary for our comfort. Every one, when taken out of this world, would miss a great deal that he was used to depend on, and would in consequence be in great discomfort and sorrow in his new abode, as a stranger in an unknown place; every one, that is, who had not, while on earth, made God his Father and Protector,—that Great God who alone will there be found. We do not, then, mend the matter at all in supposing a man not to find out the world's vanity here; for, even should the world remain his faithful friend, and please him with its goods, to his dying day, still that world will be burnt up at the day of his resurrection; and even had he little of its comforts here, that little he will then miss. Then all men, small and great, will know it to be vanity, and feel their infinite loss if they have trusted it, when all the dead stand before God.

Let this suffice on the use we must make of the solemn view which the Scripture takes of this life. Those disclosures are intended to save us pain, by preventing us from enjoying the world unreservedly ; that we may use, not abusing it.

Nor let it seem as if this view of life must make a man melancholy and gloomy. There are, it is true, men of ill-constituted minds, whom it has driven out of the world; but, rightly understood, it has no such tendency. The great rule of our conduct is to take things as they come. He who goes out of his way as shrinking from the varieties of human life which meet him, has weak faith, or a strangely perverted conscience,— he wants elevation of mind. The true Christian rejoices in those earthly things which give joy, but in such a way as not to care for them when they go. For no blessings does he care much, except those which are immortal, knowing that he shall receive all such again in the world to come. But the least and the most fleeting, he is too religious to contemn, considering them God's gift; and the least and most fleeting, thus received, yield a purer and deeper, though a less tumultuous joy. And if he at times refrains, it is lest he should encroach upon God's bounty, or lest by a constant use of it he should forget how to do without it.

Our Saviour gives us a pattern which we are bound to follow. He was a far greater than John the Baptist, yet He came, not with St. John's outward austerity,—condemning the *display* of strictness or gloominess, that we, His followers, might fast the more in private, and be the more austere in our secret hearts. True it is, that such self-command, composure, and inward faith, are not learned in a day; but if they were, why should this life be given us? It is given us as a very preparation-time for obtaining them. Only look upon the world in this light ;—its sights of sorrows are to calm you, and its pleasant sights to try you. There is a bravery in thus going straightforward, shrinking from no duty little or great, passing from high to low, from pleasure to pain, and making your principles strong without their becoming formal. Learn to be as the Angel, who could descend among the miseries of Bethesda, without losing his heavenly purity or his perfect happiness. Gain healing from troubled waters. Make up your mind to the prospect of sustaining a certain measure of pain and trouble in your passage through life ; by the blessing of God this will prepare you for it,—it will make you thoughtful and resigned without interfering with your cheerfulness. It will connect you in your own thoughts with the Saints of Scripture, whose lot it was to be patterns of patient endurance; and this association brings to the mind a peculiar consolation. View yourselves and all Christians as humbly following the steps of Jacob, whose days were few and evil; of David, who in his best estate was as a shadow that declineth, and was withered like grass; of Elijah, who despised soft raiment and sumptuous fare; of forlorn Daniel, who led an Angel's life; and be light-hearted and contented, *because* you are thus called to be a member of Christ's pilgrim Church. Realize the paradox of making merry and rejoicing in the world because it is *not* yours. And if you are hard to be affected (as many men are), and think too little about the changes of life, going on in a dull way without hope or fear, feeling neither your need nor the excellence of religion; then, again, meditate on the mournful histories recorded in Scripture, in order that your hearts may be opened thereby and roused. Read the Gospels in particular; you there find accounts of sick and afflicted persons in every page as mementoes. Above all, you there read of Christ's sufferings, which I am not now called upon to speak of; but the thought of which is far more than enough to make the world, bright as it may be, look dark and miserable in itself to all true believers, even if the record of *them* were the only sorrowful part of the whole Bible.

And now I conclude, bidding you think much of the Scripture history in the light in which I have put it,—that you may not hereafter find that you have missed one great benefit which it was graciously intended to convey.

SERMON XXXVII.

(SUNDAYS AFTER TRINITY.)

The Danger of Riches.

" Woe unto you that are rich! for ye have received your consolation."—
LUKE vi. 24.

UNLESS we were accustomed to read the New Testament
from our childhood, I think we should be very much
struck with the warnings which it contains, not only against the
love of riches, but the very possession of them; we should
wonder with a portion of that astonishment which the Apostles
at first felt, who had been brought up in the notion that they
were a chief reward which God bestowed on those He loved.
As it is, we have heard the most solemn declarations so continually, that we have ceased to attach any distinct meaning to
them; or, if our attention is at any time drawn more closely to
them, we soon dismiss the subject on some vague imagination,
that what is said in Scripture had a reference to the particular
times when Christ came, without attempting to settle its exact
application to us, or whether it has any such application at all,—
as if the circumstance, that the interpretation requires care and
thought, were an excuse for giving no thought or care whatever
to the settling of it.

But, even if we had ever so little concern in the Scripture
denunciations against riches and the love of riches, the very
awfulness of them might have seemed enough to save them from
neglect; just as the Flood, and the judgment upon Sodom and
Gomorrah, are still dwelt upon by Christians with solemn attention, though we have a promise against the recurrence of the one,
and trust we shall never be so deserted by God's grace as to call
down upon us the other. And this consideration may lead a man

to suspect that the neglect in question does not entirely arise from unconcern, but from a sort of misgiving that the subject of riches is one which cannot be safely or comfortably discussed by the Christian world at this day; that is, which cannot be discussed without placing the claims of God's Law and the pride of life into visible and perplexing opposition.

Let us then see what the letter of Scripture says on the subject. For instance, consider the text : "Woe unto you that are rich! for ye have received your consolation." The words are sufficiently clear (it will not be denied), as spoken of rich persons in our Saviour's day. Let the full force of the word "consolation" be observed. It is used by way of contrast to the comfort which is promised to the Christian in the list of Beatitudes.[1] Comfort, in the fulness of that word, as including help, guidance, encouragement, and support, is the peculiar promise of the Gospel. The Promised Spirit, who has taken Christ's place, was called by Him "the Comforter." There is then something very fearful in the intimation of the text, that those who have riches thereby receive their portion, such as it is, in full, instead of the Heavenly Gift of the Gospel. The same doctrine is implied in our Lord's words in the parable of Dives and Lazarus : "Son, remember thou in thy lifetime receivedst *thy* good things, and likewise Lazarus evil things; but *now* he is *comforted*, and thou art tormented." At another time He said to His disciples, "How hardly shall they that have riches enter into the kingdom of God! for it is easier for a camel to go through a needle's eye, than for a rich man to enter into the kingdom of God."[2]

Now, it is usual to dismiss such passages with the remark, that they are directed, not against those who have, but against those who trust in, riches ; as if forsooth they implied no *connection* between the having and the trusting, no warning *lest* the possession led to the idolatrous reliance on them, no necessity of fear and anxiety in the possessors, lest they should become castaways. And this irrelevant distinction is supposed to find countenance in our Lord's own language on one of the occasions above referred to, in which He first says, "How hardly shall they that *have* riches," then, "How hard is it for them that *trust* in riches, to enter into the kingdom of God ;" whereas surely, He only removes His disciples' false impression, that the bare circumstance of possessing wealth was inconsistent with a state of salvation, and no more interprets *having* by *trusting* than makes *trusting* essential to *having*. He connects the two, without identifying,

[1] Matt. v. 4.   [2] Luke xvi. 25 ; xviii. 24, 25.

without explaining away; and the simple question which lies for our determination is this:—whether, considering that they who had riches when Christ came, were likely in His judgment idolatrously to trust in them, there is, or is not, reason for thinking that this likelihood varies materially in different ages; and, according to the solution of this question, must we determine the application of the woe pronounced in the text to these times. And, at all events, let it be observed, it is for those who would make out that these passages do *not* apply now, to give their reasons for their opinion; the burden of proof is with them. Till they draw their clear and reasonable distinctions between the first and the nineteenth century, the denunciation hangs over the world,—that is, as much as over the Pharisees and Sadducees at our Lord's coming.

But, in truth, that our Lord meant to speak of riches as being in some sense a calamity to the Christian, is plain, not only from such texts as the foregoing, but from His praises and recommendation on the other hand of poverty. For instance, " Sell that ye have and give alms; provide yourselves bags which wax not old." "If thou wilt be perfect, go sell that thou hast and give to the poor, and thou shalt have treasure in heaven." "Blessed be ye poor : for yours is the kingdom of God." "When thou makest a dinner or a supper, call not thy friends, nor thy brethren, neither thy kinsmen, nor thy rich neighbours . . . . but . . . . call the poor, the maimed, the lame, the blind." And in like manner, St. James : "Hath not God chosen the poor of this world rich in faith, and heirs of that kingdom which He hath promised to them that love Him ? " [1] Now, I cite these texts in the way of doctrine, not of precept. Whatever be the line of conduct they prescribe to this or that individual (with which I have nothing to do at present), so far seems clear, that according to the rule of the Gospel, the absence of wealth is, as such, a more blessed and a more Christian state than the possession of it.

The most obvious danger which worldly possessions present to our spiritual welfare is, that they become practically a substitute in our hearts for that One Object to which our supreme devotion is due. They are present; God is unseen. They are means at hand of effecting what we want : whether God will hear our petitions for those wants is uncertain; or rather I may say, certain in the negative. Thus they minister to the corrupt inclinations of our nature; they promise and are able to be gods

[1] Luke xii. 33.   Matt. xix. 21.   Luke vi. 20 ; xiv. 12, 13.   James ii. 5.

to us, and such gods too as require no service, but, like dumb idols, exalt the worshipper, impressing him with a notion of his own power and security. And in this consist their chief and most subtle mischief. Religious men are able to repress, nay extirpate sinful desires, the lust of the flesh and of the eyes, gluttony, drunkenness, and the like, love of amusements and frivolous pleasures and display, indulgence in luxuries of whatever kind ; but as to wealth, they cannot easily rid themselves of a secret feeling that it gives them a footing to stand upon, an importance, a superiority, and in consequence they get attached to this world, lose sight of the duty of bearing the Cross, become dull and dim-sighted, and lose their delicacy and precision of touch, are numbed (so to say) in their fingers' ends, as regards religious interests and prospects. To risk all upon Christ's word seems somehow unnatural to them, extravagant, and evidences a morbid excitement ; and death, instead of being a gracious, however awful release, is not a welcome subject of thought. They are content to remain as they are, and do not contemplate a change. They desire and mean to serve God, nay actually do serve Him in their measure ; but not with the keen sensibilities, the noble enthusiasm, the grandeur and elevation of soul, the dutifulness and affectionateness towards Christ which become a Christian, but as Jews might obey, who had no Image of God given them except this created world, " eating their bread with joy, and drinking their wine with a merry heart," caring that " their garments be always white, and their head lacking no ointment, living joyfully with the wife whom they love all the days of the life of their vanity," and " enjoying the good of their labour." [1] Not, of course, that the due use of God's temporal blessings is wrong, but to make them the object of our affections, to allow them to beguile us from the " One Husband " to whom we are espoused, is to mistake the Gospel for Judaism.

This, then, if we may venture to say so, was some part of our Saviour's meaning, when He connects together the having with the trusting in riches ; and it is especially suitable to consider it upon this day, [2] when we commemorate an Apostle and an Evangelist, whose history is an example and encouragement for all those who have, and fear lest they should trust. But St. Matthew was exposed to an additional temptation, which I shall proceed to consider ; for he not only possessed, but he was engaged also in the pursuit of wealth. Our Saviour seems to warn us against this further danger in His description of the thorns in the parable

[1] Eccles. ix. 7-9 ; v. 18.   [2] Preached on St. Matthew's Day.

of the Sower, as being "the care of this world and the deceitfulness of riches;" and more clearly in the parable of the Great Supper, where the guests excuse themselves, one as having "bought a piece of ground," another "five yoke of oxen." Still more openly does St. Paul speak in his First Epistle to Timothy: "They that desire to be rich, fall into temptation and a snare, and into many foolish and hurtful lusts, which drown men in destruction and perdition. For the love of money is the root of all evil; which, while some coveted after, they have erred from the Faith, and pierced themselves through with many sorrows."[1]

The danger of *possessing* riches is the carnal security to which they lead; that of "*desiring*" and *pursuing* them, is, that an object of this world is thus set before us as the aim and end of life. It seems to be the will of Christ that His followers should have no aim or end, pursuit or business, merely of this world. Here, again, I speak as before, not in the way of precept, but of doctrine. I am looking at His holy religion as at a distance, and determining what is its general character and spirit, not what may happen to be the duty of this or that individual who has embraced it. It is His will that all we do should be done, not unto men, or to the world, or to self, but to His glory; and the more we are enabled to do this simply, the more favoured we are. Whenever we act with reference to an object of this world, even though it be ever so pure, we are exposed to the temptation— (not irresistible, God forbid!) still to the temptation—of setting our hearts upon obtaining it. And therefore, we call all such objects *excitements*, as stimulating us incongruously, casting us out of the serenity and stability of heavenly faith, attracting us aside by their proximity from our harmonious round of duties, and making our thoughts converge to something short of that which is infinitely high and eternal. Such excitements are of perpetual occurrence, and the mere undergoing them, so far from involving guilt in the act itself or its results, is the great business of life and the discipline of our hearts. It is often a sin to withdraw from them, as has been the case of some perhaps who have gone into monasteries to serve God more entirely. On the other hand, it is the very duty of the Spiritual Ruler to labour for the flock committed to him, to suffer and to dare; St. Paul was encompassed with excitements hence arising, and his writings show the agitating effect of them on his mind. He was like David, a man of war and blood; and that for our sakes. Still

[1] Matt. xiii. 22. Luke xiv. 18, 19. 1 Tim. vi. 9, 10.

it holds good that the essential spirit of the Gospel is "quietness and confidence ;" that the possession of these is the highest gift, and to gain them perfectly our main aim.

Consequently, however much a duty it is to undergo excitements when they are sent upon us, it is plainly unchristian, a manifest foolishness and sin, to seek out any such, whether secular or religious. Hence gaming is so great an offence ; as being a presumptuous creation on our part of a serious, if not an overpowering temptation to fix the heart upon an object of this world. Hence, the mischief of many amusements, of (what is called) the fashion of the day ; which are devised for the very purpose of taking up the thoughts, and making time pass easy. Quite contrary is the Christian temper, which is in its perfect and peculiar enjoyment when engaged in that ordinary, unvaried course of duties which God assigns, and which the world calls dull and tiresome. To get up day after day to the same employments, and to feel happy in them, is the great lesson of the Gospel ; and, when exemplified in those who are alive to the temptation of being busy, it implies a heart weaned from the love of this world. True it is that illness of body, as well as restlessness of mind, may occasionally render such a life a burden ; it is true also that indolence, self-indulgence, timidity, and other similar bad habits, may adopt it by preference, as a pretext for neglecting more active duties. Men of energetic minds and talents for action are called to a life of trouble ; they are the compensations and antagonists of the world's evils : still let them never forget their place ; they are men of war, and we war that we may obtain peace. They are but men of war, honoured indeed by God's choice, and, in spite of all momentary excitements, resting in the depth of their hearts upon the One true Vision of Christian faith ; still, after all, they are but soldiers in the open field, not builders of the Temple, nor inhabitants of those "amiable" and specially blessed "Tabernacles" where the worshipper lives in praise and intercession, and is militant amid the unostentatious duties of ordinary life. "Martha, Martha, thou art anxious and troubled about many things ; but one thing is needful, and Mary has chosen that good part which shall not be taken away from her." [1] Such is our Lord's judgment, showing that our true happiness consists in being at leisure to serve God without excitements. For this gift we especially pray in one of our Collects : "Grant, O Lord, that the course of this world may be so peaceably ordered by Thy governance, that Thy Church may joyfully serve Thee in all godly

[1] Luke x. 41, 42.

quietness." [1] Persecution, civil changes, and the like break in upon the Church's calm. The greatest privilege of a Christian is to have nothing to do with worldly politics,—to be governed and to submit obediently; and though here again selfishness may creep in, and lead a man to neglect public concerns in which he is called to take his share, yet, after all, such participation must be regarded as a duty, scarcely as a privilege, as the fulfilment of trusts committed to him for the good of others, not as the enjoyment of rights (as men talk in these days of delusion), not as if political power were in itself a good.

To return to the subject immediately before us; I say then, that it is a part of Christian caution to see that our engagements do not become pursuits. Engagements are our portion, but pursuits are for the most part of our own choosing. We may be engaged in worldly business, without pursuing worldly objects; "not slothful in business," yet "serving the Lord." In this then consists the danger of the pursuit of gain, as by trade and the like. It is the most common and widely extended of all excitements. It is one in which every one almost may indulge, nay, and will be praised by the world for indulging. And it lasts through life; in that differing from the amusements and pleasures of the world, which are short-lived, and succeed one after another. Dissipation of mind, which these amusements create, is itself indeed miserable enough : but far worse than this dissipation is the concentration of mind upon some worldly object, which admits of being constantly pursued,—and such is the pursuit of gain. Nor is it a slight aggravation of the evil, that anxiety is almost sure to attend it. A life of money-getting is a life of care; from the first there is a fearful anticipation of loss in various ways to depress and unsettle the mind, nay to haunt it, till a man finds he can think about nothing else, and is unable to give his mind to religion, from the constant whirl of business in which he is involved. It is well this should be understood. You may hear men talk as if the pursuit of wealth was the business of life. They will argue, that by the law of nature a man is bound to gain a livelihood for his family, and that he finds a reward in doing so, an innocent and honourable satisfaction, as he adds one sum to another, and counts up his gains. And perhaps they go on to argue, that it is the very duty of man since Adam's fall, "in the sweat of his face," by effort and anxiety, "to eat bread." How strange it is that they do not remember Christ's gracious promise, repealing that original curse, and

[1] *Vide* 1 Tim. ii. 2.

obviating the necessity of any real pursuit after "the meat that perisheth"! In order that we might be delivered from the bondage of corruption, He has expressly told us that the necessaries of life shall never fail His faithful follower, any more than the meal and oil the widow woman of Sarepta; that, while he is bound to labour for his family, he need not be engrossed by his toil,—that while he is busy, his heart may be at leisure for his Lord. "Be not anxious, saying, What shall we eat? or, What shall we drink? or, Wherewithal shall we be clothed? For after all these things do the Gentiles seek; for your heavenly Father knoweth that ye have need of all these things. But seek ye first the kingdom of God and His righteousness; and all these things shall be added unto you." Here is revealed to us at once our privilege and our duty, the Christian portion of having engagements of this world without pursuing objects. And in accordance with our Divine Teacher are the words of the Apostle, introductory of a passage already cited : "We brought nothing into this world, and it is certain we can carry nothing out. And having food and raiment, let us therewith be content." [1] There is no excuse then for that absorbing pursuit of wealth, which many men indulge in as if a virtue, and expatiate upon as if a science. "After all these things do the Gentiles seek!" Consider how different is the rule of life left us by the Apostles. "I speak this for your own profit," says St. Paul, "that ye may attend upon the Lord, without distraction." "This I say, brethren, the time is short; it remaineth, that both they that have wives be as though they had none, and they that weep as though they wept not, and they that rejoice as though they rejoiced not, and they that buy as though they possessed not, and they that use this world as not abusing it, for the fashion of this world passeth away." "Be anxious for nothing; but in every thing, by prayer and supplication with thanksgiving, let your requests be made known unto God." And St. Peter, "Casting all your anxiety upon Him, for He careth for you." [2]

I have now given the main reason why the pursuit of gain, whether in a large or small way, is prejudicial to our spiritual interests, that it fixes the mind upon an object of this world; yet others remain behind. Money is a sort of creation, and gives the acquirer, even more than the possessor, an imagination of his own power; and tends to make him idolize self. Again, what we have hardly won we are unwilling to part with; so that a man

---

[1] Matt. vi. 1 Tim. vi. 7, 8.
[2] 1 Cor. vii. 29-31, 35. Phil. iv. 6. 1 Pet. v. 7.

who has himself made his wealth will commonly be penurious, or at least will not part with it except in exchange for what will reflect credit upon himself, or increase his importance. Even when his conduct is most disinterested and amiable (as in spending for the comfort of those who depend upon him), still this indulgence of self, of pride and worldliness, insinuates itself. Very unlikely therefore is it that he should be liberal towards God; for religious offerings are an expenditure without sensible return, and that upon objects for which the very pursuit of wealth has indisposed his mind. Moreover, if it may be added, there is a considerable tendency in occupations connected with gain to make a man unfair in his dealings,—that is, in a subtle way. There are so many conventional deceits and prevarications in the details of the world's business, so much intricacy in the management of accounts, so many perplexed questions about justice and equity, so many plausible subterfuges and fictions of law, so much confusion between the distinct yet approximating outlines of honesty and civil enactment, that it requires a very straightforward mind to keep firm hold of strict conscientiousness, honour, and truth, and to look at matters in which he is engaged, as he would have looked on them, supposing he now came upon them all at once as a stranger.

And if such be the effect of the pursuit of gain on an individual, doubtless it will be the same on a nation; and if the peril be so great in the one case, why should it be less in the other? Rather, considering that the tendencies of things are sure to be brought out, where time and numbers allow them fair course, is it not certain that any multitude, any society of men, whose object is gain, will on the whole be actuated by those feelings, and moulded into that character, which has been above described? With this thought before us, it is a very fearful consideration that we belong to a nation which in good measure subsists by making money. I will not pursue it; nor inquire whether the especial political evils of the day have not their root in that principle, which St. Paul calls the root of all evil, the love of money. Only let us consider the fact, that we *are* money-making people, with our Saviour's declarations before us against wealth, and trust in wealth: and we shall have abundant matter for serious thought.

Lastly, with this dreary view before us of our condition and prospects as a nation, the pattern of St. Matthew is our consolation; for it suggests that we, Christ's ministers, may use great freedom of speech, and state unreservedly the peril of wealth and

gain, without aught of harshness or uncharitableness towards
individuals who are exposed to it.   They may be brethren of the
Evangelist, who left all for Christ's sake.   Nay, such there have
been (blessed be God!) in every age; and in proportion to the
strength of the temptation which surrounds them, is their blessedness and their praise, if they are enabled amid the "wares of the
seas" and the "great wisdom of their traffic" to hear Christ's
voice, to take up their cross, and follow Him.

SERMON XXXVIII.

Obedience without Love, as instanced in the Character of Balaam.

" The word that God putteth in my mouth, that shall I speak."—
NUMB. xxii. 38.

WHEN we consider the Old Testament as written by divine
inspiration, and preserved, beyond the time of its own
Dispensation, for us Christians,—as acknowledged and delivered
over to us by Christ Himself, and pronounced by St. Paul to be
"profitable for doctrine, reproof, correction, and instruction in
righteousness," [1]—we ought not surely to read any portion of
it with indifference, nay, without great and anxious interest.
"Lord, what wilt Thou have me to do ?" is the sort of inquiry
which spontaneously arises in the serious mind. Christ and His
Apostle cannot have put the Law and the Prophets into our
hands for nothing. I would this thought were more carefully
weighed than it commonly is. We profess indeed to revere the
Old Testament ; yet, for some reason or other, at least one considerable part of it, the historical, is regarded by the mass, even
of men who think about religion, as merely historical, as a relation of facts, as antiquities ; not in its divine characters, not in
its practical bearings, not in reference to themselves. The notion
that God speaks in it to them personally, the question, " What
does He say ?" " What must I *do ?*" does not occur to them.
They consider that the Old Testament concerns them only as far
as it can be made typical of one or two of the great Christian
doctrines ; they do not consider it in its fulness, and in its literal
sense, as a collection of deep moral lessons, such as are not

[1] 2 Tim. iii. 16.

vouchsafed in the New, though St. Paul expressly says that it is "profitable for instruction in righteousness."

If the Old Testament history generally be intended as a permanent instruction to the Church, much more, one would think, must such prominent and remarkable passages in it as the history of Balaam. Yet I suspect a very great number of readers carry off little more from it than the impression of the miracle which occurs in it, the speaking of his ass. And not unfrequently they talk more lightly on the subject than is expedient. Yet I think some very solemn and startling lessons may be drawn from the history, some of which I shall now attempt to set before you.

What is it which the chapters in question present to us? The first and most general account of Balaam would be this;—that he was a very eminent person in his age and country, that he was courted and gained by the enemies of Israel, and that he promoted a wicked cause in a very wicked way; that, when he could do nothing else for it, he counselled the Moabites to employ their women as means of seducing the chosen people into idolatry; and that he fell in battle in the war which ensued. These are the chief points, the prominent features of his history as viewed at a distance;—and repulsive indeed they are. He took on him the office of a tempter, which is especially the Devil's office. But Satan himself does not seem so hateful near as at a distance; and when we look into Balaam's history closely we shall find points of character which may well interest those who do not consider his beginning and his end. Let us then approach him more nearly, and forget for a moment the summary account of him which I have just been giving.

Now, first he was blessed with God's especial favour. You will ask at once, How could so bad a man be in God's favour? but I wish you to put aside reasonings and contemplate facts. I say he was especially favoured by God; God has a store of favours in His treasure-house, and of various kinds,—some for a time, some for ever,—some implying His approbation, others not. He showers favours even on the bad. He makes His sun to rise on the unjust as well as on the just. He willeth not the death of a sinner. He is said to have loved the young ruler, whose heart, notwithstanding, was upon the world. His loving-mercy extends over all His works. How He separates in His own divine thought, kindness from approbation, time from eternity, what He does from what He foresees, we know not and need not inquire. At present He is loving to all men, as if He did not foresee that some are to be saints, others reprobates to all eternity. He dispenses His favours variously,—gifts, graces, rewards, faculties, circumstances being indefinitely diversified, nor admitting of discrimination or numbering on our part. Balaam, I say, was in His favour; not indeed for his holiness' sake, not for ever; but in a certain sense, according to His inscrutable purpose,—who chooses whom He will choose, and exalts whom He will exalt, without destroying man's secret responsibilities or His own governance, and the triumph of truth and holiness, and His own strict impartiality in the end. Balaam was favoured in an especial way above the mere heathen. Not only had he the grant of inspiration, and the knowledge of God's will, an insight into the truths of morality, clear and enlarged, such as even we Christians cannot surpass; but he was even admitted to conscious intercourse with God, such as we Christians have not. In our Sunday services, you may recollect, we read the chapters which relate to this intercourse; and we do not read those which record the darker passages of his history. Now, do you not think that most persons, who know only so much of him as our Sunday lessons contain, form a very mild judgment about him? They see him indeed to be on the wrong side, but still view him as a prophet of God. Such a judgment is not incorrect as far as it goes; and I appeal to it, if it be what I think it is, as a testimony how highly Balaam was in God's favour.

But again, Balaam was, in the ordinary and commonly received sense of the word, without straining its meaning at all, a very *conscientious* man. That this is so, will be plain from some parts of his conduct and some speeches of his, of which I proceed to remind you; and which will show also his enlightened and admirable view of moral and religious obligation. When Balak sent to him to call him to curse Israel, he did not make up his mind for himself, as many a man might do, or according to the suggestions of avarice and ambition. No, he brought the matter before God in prayer. He *prayed* before he did what he did, as a religious man ought to do. Next, when God forbade his going, he at once, as he ought, positively refused to go. "Get you into your land," he said, "for the Lord refuseth to give me leave to go with you." Balak sent again a more pressing message and more lucrative offers, and Balaam was even more decided than before. "If Balak," he said, "would give me his house full of silver and gold, I cannot go beyond the word of the Lord my God, to do less or more." Afterwards God gave him

x

leave to go. "If the men come to call thee, rise up, and go with them."[1] Then, and not till then, he went.

Almighty God added, "Yet the word which I shall say unto thee, that shalt thou do." Now, in the next place, observe how strictly he obeyed this command. When he first met Balak, he said, in the words of the text, "Lo, I am come unto thee; have I now any power at all to say any thing? the word that God putteth in my mouth, that shall I speak." Again, when he was about to prophesy, he said, "Whatsoever He showeth me I will tell thee;"[2] and he did so, in spite of Balak's disappointment and mortification to hear him bless Israel. When Balak showed his impatience, he only replied calmly, "Must I not take heed to speak that which the Lord hath put in my mouth?" Again he prophesied, and again it was a blessing; again Balak was angered, and again the prophet firmly and serenely answered, "Told not I thee, saying, All that the Lord speaketh, that I must do?" A third time he prophesied blessing; and now Balak's anger was kindled, and he smote his hands together, and bade him depart to his place. But Balaam was not thereby moved from his duty. "The wrath of a king is as messengers of death."[3] Balak might have instantly revenged himself upon the prophet; but Balaam, not satisfied with blessing Israel, proceeded, as a prophet should, to deliver himself of what remained of the prophetic burden, by foretelling more pointedly than before, destruction to Moab and the other enemies of the chosen people. He prefaced his prophecy with these unacceptable words: "Spake I not also unto thy messengers which thou sentest unto me, saying, If Balak would give me his house full of silver and gold, I cannot go beyond the commandment of the Lord, to do either good or bad of mine own mind? but what the Lord saith, that will I speak. And now behold, I go unto my people; come, therefore, and I will advertise thee what this people shall do to thy people in the latter days." After delivering his conscience, he "rose up, and went and returned to his place."

All this surely expresses the conduct and the feelings of a high-principled, honourable, conscientious man. Balaam, I say, was certainly such, in that very sense in which we commonly use those words. He said, and he did; he professed, and he acted according to his professions. There is no inconsistency in word and deed. He obeys as well as talks about religion; and this being the case, we shall feel more intimately the value of the following noble sentiments which he lets drop from time to

[1] Numb. xxii.   [2] Numb. xxiii.   [3] Prov. xvi. 14.

time, and which, if he had shown less firmness in his conduct, might have passed for mere words, the words of a maker of speeches, a sophist, moralist, or orator. "Let me die the death of the righteous, and let my last end be like his." God is not a man that He should lie; neither the son of man, that He should repent. . . . Behold, I have received commandment to bless; and He hath blessed, and I cannot reverse it." "I shall see Him, but not now; I shall behold Him, but not nigh." It is remarkable that these declarations are great and lofty in their mode of expression; and the saying of his recorded by the prophet Micah is of the same kind. Balak asked what sacrifices were acceptable to God. Balaam answered, "He hath showed thee, O man, what is good; and what doth the Lord require of thee, but to do justly, and to love mercy, and to walk humbly with thy God?"[1]

Viewing, then, the inspired notices concerning Balaam in all their parts, we cannot deny to him the praise which, if those notices have a plain meaning, they certainly do convey, that he was an honourable and religious man, with a great deal of what was great and noble about him; a man whom any one of us at first sight would have trusted, sought out in our difficulties, perhaps made the head of a party, and anyhow spoken of with great respect. We may indeed, if we please, say that he fell away afterwards from all this excellence : though, after all, there is something shocking in such a notion. Nay, it is not natural even that ordinarily honourable men should suddenly change; but however this *may* be said,—it may be said he fell away; but, I presume, it *cannot* be said that he was other than a high-principled man (in the language of the world) *when* he so spoke and acted.

But now the strange thing is, that at this very time, *while* he so spoke and acted, he seems, as in one sense to be in God's favour, so in another and higher to be under His displeasure. If this be so, the supposition that he fell away will not be in point; the difficulty it proposes to solve will remain; for it will turn out that he was displeasing to God *amid* his many excellences. The passage I have in mind is this, as you will easily suppose : "God's anger was kindled, because he went" with the princes of Moab, "and the Angel of the Lord stood in the way for an adversary against him." Afterwards, when God opened his eyes, "he saw the Angel of the Lord standing in the way, and his sword drawn in his hand. . . . And Balaam said, I have *sinned*, for I knew

[1] Micah vi. 8.

not that thou stoodest in the way against me; now, therefore, if it displease thee, I will get me back again." You observe Balaam said, "I have sinned," *though* he avers he did not *know* that God was his adversary. What makes the whole transaction the more strange is this,—that Almighty God had said before, "If the men come to call thee, rise up, and go with them;" and that when Balaam offered to go back again, the Angel repeated, "Go with the men." And afterwards we find in the midst of his heathen enchantments "God met Balaam," and "put a word in his mouth;" and afterwards "the Spirit of God came unto him."

Summing up, then, what has been said, we seem, in Balaam's history, to have the following remarkable case, that is, remarkable according to our customary judgment of things : a man divinely favoured, visited, influenced, guided, protected, eminently honoured, illuminated,—a man possessed of an enlightened sense of duty, and of moral and religious acquirements, educated, high-minded, conscientious, honourable, firm ; and yet on the side of God's enemies, personally under God's displeasure, and in the end (if we go on to that) the direct instrument of Satan, and having his portion with the unbelievers. I do not think I have materially overstated any part of this description ; but if it be correct only in substance, it certainly is most fearful, after allowing for incidental exaggeration,—most fearful to every one of us, the more fearful the more we are conscious to ourselves in the main of purity of intention in what we do, and conscientious adherence to our sense of duty.

And now it is natural to ask, What is the *meaning* of this startling exhibition of God's ways? Is it really possible that a conscientious and religious man should be found among the enemies of God, nay, should be personally displeasing to Him, and that at the very time God was visiting him with extraordinary favour? What a mystery is this ! Surely, if this be so, Revelation has added to our perplexities, not relieved them ! What instruction, what profit, what correction, what doctrine is there in such portions of inspired Scripture ?

In answering this difficulty, I observe, in the first place, that it certainly is impossible, quite impossible, that a really conscientious man should be displeasing to God; at the same time it is possible to be *generally* conscientious, or what the world calls honourable and high-principled, yet to be destitute of that religious fear and strictness which God calls conscientiousness, but which the world calls superstition or narrowness of mind

And bearing this in mind, we shall, perhaps, have a solution of our perplexities concerning Balaam.

And here I would make a remark : that when a passage of Scripture, descriptive of God's dealings with man, is obscure or perplexing, it is as well to ask ourselves whether this may not be owing to some insensibility, in ourselves or in our age, to certain peculiarities of the Divine law or government therein involved. Thus, to those who do not understand the nature and history of religious truth, our Lord's assertion about sending a sword on earth is an obscurity. To those who consider sin a light evil, the doctrine of eternal punishment is a difficulty. In like manner the history of the Flood, of the call of Abraham, of the plagues of Egypt, of the wandering in the desert, of the judgment on Korah, Dathan, and Abiram, and a multitude of other occurrences, may be insuperable difficulties, except to certain states and tempers of mind, to which, on the contrary, they will seem quite natural and obvious. I consider that the history of Balaam is a striking illustration of this remark. Those whose hearts, like Josiah's, are " tender," scrupulous, sensitive in religious matters, will see with clearness and certainty what the real state of the case was as regards him; on the other hand, our difficulties about it, if we have them, are a presumption that the age we live in has not the key to a certain class of Divine providences, is deficient in a certain class of religious principles, ideas, and sensibilities. Let it be considered, then, whether the following remarks may not tend to lessen our perplexity.

Balaam obeyed God from a sense of its being right to do so, but not from a *desire to please Him,* not from *fear and love.* He had other ends, aims, wishes of his own, distinct from God's will and purpose, and he would have effected these if he could. His endeavour was, not to please God, but to please self without displeasing God ; to pursue his own ends *as far* as was consistent with his duty. In a word, he did not give his heart to God, but obeyed Him, as a man may obey human law, or observe the usages of society or his country, as something external to himself, because he knows he ought to do so, from a sort of rational good sense, a conviction of its propriety, expediency, or comfort, as the case may be.

You will observe he *wished* to go with Balak's messengers, only he felt he *ought not* to go ; and the problem which he attempted to solve was *how* to go and yet not offend God. He was quite resolved he *would* anyhow act religiously and conscientiously ; he was too honourable a man to break any of his engagements; if he had given his word, it was sacred; if he had duties, they were imperative : he had a character to maintain, and an inward sense of propriety to satisfy ; but he would have given the world to have got rid of his duties; and the question was, *how* to do so without violence; and he did not care about walking on the very brink of transgression, so that he could keep from falling over. Accordingly he was not content with *ascertaining* God's will, but he attempted to *change* it. He inquired of Him a *second time*, and this was to tempt Him. Hence, while God bade him go, His anger was kindled against him because he went.

This surely is no uncommon character; rather, it is the common case even with the more respectable and praiseworthy portion of the community. I say plainly, and without fear of contradiction, though it is a serious thing to say, that the aim of most men esteemed conscientious and religious, or who are what is called honourable, upright, men, is, to all appearance, not how to please God, but how to please themselves without displeasing Him. I say confidently,—that is, if we may judge of men in general by what we see,—that they make this world the first object in their minds, and use religion as a corrective, a restraint, upon *too much* attachment to the world. They think that religion is a negative thing, a sort of moderate love of the world, a moderate luxury, a moderate avarice, a moderate ambition, and a moderate selfishness. You see this in numberless ways. You see it in the course of trade, of public life, of literature, in all matters where men have objects to pursue. Nay, you see it in religious exertions; of which it too commonly happens that the chief aim is, to attain *anyhow* a certain definite end, religious indeed, but of man's own choosing ; not, to please God, and *next*, if possible, to attain it; not, to attain it religiously, or not at all.

This surely is so plain that it is scarcely necessary to enlarge upon it. Men do not take for the object towards which they **act,** God's will, but certain maxims, rules, or measures, right perhaps as far as they go, but defective because they admit of being subjected to certain other ultimate ends, which are not religious. Men are just, honest, upright, trustworthy; but all this not from the love and fear of God, but from a mere feeling of obligation to be so, and in subjection to certain worldly objects. And thus they are what is popularly called moral, without being religious. Such was Balaam. He was in a popular sense a strictly moral, honourable, conscientious man ; that he was not so in a heavenly and true sense is plain, if not from the considerations here insisted on, at least from his after-history, which (we may presume) brought to light his secret defect, in whatever it consisted.

And here we see why he spoke so much and so vauntingly of his determination to follow God's direction. He made a great *point* of following it; his end was not to please God, but to keep straight with Him. He who loves does not act from calculation or reasoning; he does not in his cool moments reflect upon or talk of what he is doing, as if it were a great sacrifice. Much less does he pride himself on it; but this is what Balaam seems to have done.

I have been observing that his defect lay in this, that he had not a single eye towards God's will, but was ruled by other objects. But, moreover, this evil heart of unbelief showed itself in a peculiar way, to which it is necessary to draw your attention, and to which I alluded just now in saying that the difficulties of Scripture often arose from the defective moral condition of our hearts.

Why did Almighty God give Balaam leave to go to Balak, and then was angry with him for going? I suppose for this reason, because his asking twice was tempting God. God is a jealous God. Sinners as we are, nay as creatures of His hands, we may not safely intrude upon Him, and make free with Him. We may not dare to do that which we should not dare to do with an earthly superior, which we should be punished, for instance, for attempting in the case of a king or noble of this world. To rush into His presence, to address Him familiarly, to urge Him, to strive to make our duty lie in one direction when it lies in another, to handle rudely and practise upon His holy Word, to trifle with truth, to treat conscience lightly, to take liberties (as it may be called) with anything that is God's, all irreverence, profaneness, unscrupulousness, wantonness, is represented in Scripture not only as a sin, but as felt, noticed, quickly returned on God's part (if I may dare use such human words of the Almighty and All-holy God, without transgressing the rule I am myself laying down,—but He vouchsafes in Scripture to represent Himself to us in that only way in which we can attain to the knowledge of Him), I say all irreverence towards God is represented as being jealously and instantly and fearfully noticed and visited, as friend or stranger among men might resent an insult shown him. This should be carefully considered; we are apt to act towards God and the things of God as towards a mere system, a law, a name, a religion, a principle, not as against a Person, a living, watchful, present, prompt, and powerful Eye and Arm.

That all this is a great error, is plain to all who study Scripture; as is sufficiently shown by the death of that multitude of persons for looking into the ark—the death of the prophet by the lion, who was sent to Jeroboam from Judah, and did not minutely obey the instructions given him—the slaughter of the children at Bethel by the bears, for mocking Elisha—the exclusion of Moses from the promised land, for smiting the rock twice—and the judgment on Ananias and Sapphira. Now Balaam's fault seems to have been of this nature. God told him distinctly not to go to Balak. He was rash enough to ask a second time, and God as a punishment gave him leave to ally himself with His enemies, and to take part against His people. With this presumptuousness and love of self in his innermost heart, his prudence, firmness, wisdom, illumination, and general conscientiousness, availed him nothing.

A number of reflections crowd upon the mind on the review of this awful history, as I may well call it; and with a brief notice of some of these I shall conclude.

1. First, we see how little we can depend, in judging of right and wrong, on the apparent excellence and high character of individuals. There *is* a right and a wrong in matters of conduct, in spite of the world; but it is the world's aim and Satan's aim to take our minds off from the indelible distinctions of things, and to fix our thoughts upon man, to make us the slaves of man, to make us dependent on his opinion, his patronage, his honour, his smiles, and his frowns. But if Scripture is to be our guide, it is quite plain that the most conscientious, religious, high-principled, honourable men (I use the words in their ordinary, not in their Scripture sense), may be on the side of evil, may be Satan's instruments in cursing, if that were possible, and at least in seducing and enfeebling the people of God. For in the world's judgment, even when most refined, a person is conscientious and consistent who acts up to his standard, *whatever that is*, not he only who aims at taking the highest standard. This is the world's highest flight; but in its ordinary judgment, a man is conscientious and consistent who is only inconsistent and goes against conscience in any extremity, when hardly beset, and when he must cut the knot or remain in present difficulties. That is, *he* is thought to obey conscience who only disobeys it when it is a praise and merit to obey it. This, alas! is the way with some of the most honourable of mere men of the world, nay of the mass of (so-called) respectable men. They never tell untruths, or break their word, or profane the Lord's day, or are dishonest in trade, or falsify their principles, or insult religion, except in very great

straits or great emergencies, when driven into a corner; and then perhaps they force themselves, as Saul did when he offered sacrifice instead of Samuel;—they force themselves, and (as it were) undergo their sin as a sort of unpleasant self-denial or penance, being ashamed of it all the while, getting it over as quickly as they can, shutting their eyes and leaping blindfold, and then forgetting it, as something which is bitter to think about. And if memory is ever roused and annoys them, they console themselves that after all they have only gone against their conscience now and then. This is their view of themselves and of each other, taken at advantage; and if any one come across them who has lived more out of the world than themselves, and has a truer sense of right and wrong, and who fastens on some one point in them which to his mind is a token and warning to himself against them, such a one seems of course narrow-minded and overstrict in his notions. For instance; supposing some such man had fallen in with Balaam, and had been privy to the history of his tempting God, it is clear that Balaam's general correctness, his nobleness of demeanour, and his enlightened view of duty, would not have availed one jot or tittle to overcome such a man's repugnance to him. He would have been startled and alarmed, and would have kept at a distance, and in consequence he would have been called by the world uncharitable and bigoted.

2. A second reflection which rises in the mind has relation to the wonderful secret providence of God, while all things seem to go on according to the course of this world. Balaam did not see the Angel, yet the Angel went out against him as an adversary. He had no open denunciation of God's wrath directed against him. He had sinned, and nothing happened outwardly, but wrath was abroad and in his path. *This*, again, is a very serious and awful thought. God's arm is not shortened. What happened to Balaam is as if it took place yesterday. God is what He ever was; we sin as man has ever sinned. We sin without being aware of it. God is our enemy without our being aware of it; and when the blow falls, we turn our thoughts to the creature, we ill-treat our ass, we lay the blame on circumstances of this world, instead of turning to Him. "Lord, when Thy hand is lifted up, they will not see: but they shall see," in the next world if not here, "and be ashamed for their envy at the people; yea, the fire of Thine enemies shall devour them."[1]

3. Here too is a serious reflection, if we had time to pursue it, that when we have begun an evil course, we cannot retrace our

[1] Isa. xxvi. 11.

steps.   Balaam was forced to go with the men; he offered to draw back—he was not allowed—yet God's wrath followed him. This is what comes of committing ourselves to an evil line of conduct; and we see daily instances of it in our experience of life. Men get entangled, and are bound hand and foot in unadvisable courses.   They make imprudent marriages or connections; they place themselves in dangerous situations; they engage in unprofitable or harmful undertakings.   Too often, indeed, they do not discern their evil plight; but when they do, they cannot draw back.   God seems to say, "Go with the men."   They are in bondage, and they must make the best of it; being the slave of the creature, without ceasing to be the responsible servants of God; under His displeasure, yet bound to act as if they could please Him.   All this is very fearful.

4. Lastly, I will but say this in addition,—God gives us warnings now and then, but does not repeat them.   Balaam's sin consisted in not acting upon what was told him *once for all*.   In like manner, you, my brethren, now hear what you may never hear again, and what perchance in its substance is the word of God.   You may never hear it again, though with your outward ears you hear it a hundred times, because you may be impressed with it now, but never may again.   You may be impressed with it now, and the impression may die away; and some time hence, if you ever think about it, you may then speak of it thus,—that the view struck you at the time, but somehow the more you thought about it, the less you liked or valued it.   True; this *may* be so, and it *may* arise, as you think, from the doctrine I have been setting before you not being true and scriptural; but it *may* also arise from your having heard God's voice and not obeyed it.   It may be that you have become blind, not the doctrine been disproved.   Beware of trifling with your conscience. It is often said that second thoughts are best; so they are in matters of judgment, but not in matters of conscience.   In matters of duty first thoughts are commonly best—they have more in them of the voice of God.   May He give you grace so to hear what has been said, as you will wish to have heard when life is over; to hear in a practical way, with a desire to profit by it, to learn God's will, and to do it !

SERMON XXXIX

(SUNDAYS AFTER TRINITY.)

Moral Consequences of Single Sins.

" Be sure your sin will find you out."—NUMB. xxxii. 23.

THIS is one of those passages in the inspired writings which, though introduced on a particular occasion and with a limited meaning, express a general truth, such as we seem at once to feel as being far greater than the context requires, and which we use apart from it. Moses warned the Reubenites and Gadites, that, if they, who had already been allotted their inheritance, did not assist their brethren in gaining theirs, their sin would find them out, or be visited on them. And, while he so spoke, He who spoke through him, God, the Holy Spirit, conveyed, as we believe, a deeper meaning under his words, for the edification of His Church to the end; viz. He intimated that great law of God's governance, to which all who study that governance will bear witness, that sin is ever followed by punishment. Day and night follow each other not more surely than punishment comes upon sin. Whether the sin be great or little, momentary or habitual, wilful or through infirmity, its own peculiar punishment seems, according to the law of nature, to follow, as far as our experience of that law carries us,—sooner or later, lighter or heavier, as the case may be.

We Christians, indeed, are under a Dispensation of grace, and are blessed with a certain suspension of this awful law of natural religion. The blood of Christ, as St. John says, is of such wonderful efficacy as to "cleanse us from all sin;" to interpose between our sin and its punishment, and to wipe out the former before the latter has overtaken us. This inestimable benefit is applied to our souls in various ways, according to God's inscrutable pleasure; and so far as this is the case, it supersedes or reverses the law of nature which has annexed suffering to disobedience. But, however effectually and extensively it is applied, still experience assures us that it is not yet vouchsafed to us in full measure and under all circumstances. It is an undeniable fact still, that penitents, however truly such, are not secured from the present consequences of their past offences, whether outward or inward, in mind, body, or estate. And we know that there are cases in which Christians fall away and do not repent again. Nay, we have reason for saying that those who sin after grace given, are, as such, in a worse state than if they had not received it. Great, then, as are our privileges under the Gospel, they in no degree supersede the force and the serious warning of the words in the text. Still it is true, and in many frightful ways, nay more so even than before Christ died, that our sin finds us out, and brings punishment after it, in due course; just as a stone falls to the earth, or as fire burns, or as poison kills, as if by the necessary bond of cause and effect.

The text leads us to consider the consequences of a single sin, such as a breach of their engagement would have been in the Reubenites and Gadites; and to narrow the subject, I shall speak only of the moral consequences. Let us then consider the influence which single sins, past or present, may have on our present moral character in God's sight; how great it may be, will be plain from such reflections as the following :—

And first of all, it is natural to reflect on the probable influence upon us of sins committed in our childhood, and even infancy, which we never realized or have altogether forgotten. Ignorant as we may be when children begin to be responsible beings, yet we are ignorant also when they are not so; nor can we assign a date ever so early at which they certainly are not. And even the latest assignable date is very early; and thenceforward, whatever they do exerts, we cannot doubt, a most momentous influence on their character. We know that two lines starting at a small angle diverge to greater and greater distances the further they are produced; and surely in like manner a soul living on into eternity may be infinitely changed for the better or the worse by very slight influences exerted on it in the beginning of its course. A very slight deviation at setting out may be the measure of the difference between tending to hell and tending to heaven.

To give due weight to this thought, we should recollect that children's minds are impressible in a very singular way, such as is not common afterwards. The passing occurrences which meet them, these, whether from their novelty or other cause, rest upon their imagination, as if they had duration; and days or hours, having to them the semblance, may do the work of years. Any one, on casting his thoughts back on his first years, may convince himself of this; the character which his childhood bears in his memory as a whole being traceable to a few external circumstances, which lasted through a very small portion of it, a certain abode, or a visit to some particular place, or the presence of certain persons, or some one spring or summer,—circumstances which he at first cannot believe to have been so transitory as on examination he finds they certainly were.

On the other hand, let it be observed, that we are certainly ignorant of a great deal that goes on in us in infancy and childhood; I mean our illnesses and sufferings as children, which we are either not conscious of at the time, or at any rate forget soon afterwards;—which yet are of a very serious nature, and while they must have a moral cause, known or unknown, must, one would think, have a moral effect also; and while they suggest by their occurrence the possibility of other serious things going on in us also, have moreover a natural tendency to affect us in some way or other. Mysterious as it is that infants and children should suffer pain, surely it is not less so that, when they come to years of reason, they should so forget it as hardly to be able to believe, when told of it, that they themselves were the very sufferers; yet as sicknesses and accidents then happening permanently affect their body, though they recollect nothing of them, there is no extravagance in the idea that passing sins then contracted and forgotten for ever afterwards, should so affect the soul as to cause those moral differences between man and man which, however originating, are too clear to be denied. And with this fearful thought before us of the responsibility attaching to the first years of our life, how miserable is it to reflect on the other hand that children are commonly treated as if they were not responsible, as if it did not matter what they did or were! They are indulged, humoured, spoiled, or at best neglected. Bad examples are set them; things are done or said before them which they understand and catch up, when others least think it, and store in their minds, or act upon; and thus the indelible hues of sin and error are imprinted on their souls, and become as really part of their nature as that original sin in which they were born.

And what is true in infancy and childhood is in its degree true in after-life. Though our earliest years have especially the characteristic of being impressible by outward things, and of being unconscious or forgetful of them, yet at particular seasons afterwards, when the mind is excited, thrown out of its ordinary state, thrown for a while out of its subjection to habit, as if into that original unformed state when it was more free to choose good and evil, then in like manner it takes impressions, and those indelible ones, and withal almost unconsciously, after the manner of childhood. This is one reason why a time of trial is often such a crisis in a man's spiritual history. It is a season when the iron is heated and malleable; one or two strokes serve to fashion it as a weapon for God or for Satan. Or in other words, if a man is then taken at unawares, an apparently small sin leads to consequences in years and ages to come so fearful, that one can hardly dare contemplate them. This may serve to make us understand the shortness and apparent simplicity of the trial which is sometimes represented in Scripture as sealing the fate of those who succumb to it; Saul's trial, for instance, or Esau's; as on the other hand, indefinitely great results may follow from one act of obedience, as Joseph's in resisting his master's wife, or David's in sparing the life of Saul. Such great occasions, good or evil, occur all through life, but especially in youth; and it were well if young persons would realize that they do occur and are momentous. Alas! what would they give afterwards, when they come to repent (not to speak of that most awful season, the future judgment, when they stand before God, and are shortly to enter heaven or hell), not to have done what in a moment of excitement they did—to recall the blasphemous avowal, or the guilty deed— to be what they then were and now are not, free to serve God, free from the brand and the yoke of Satan! How will they bitterly bewail that fascination, or delirium, or sophistry, which made them what they need not have been, had they used against it the arms which Christ gave them!

But to return:—to these single or forgotten sins, such as I have described them, are not improbably to be traced the strange inconsistencies of character which we often witness in our experience of life. I mean, you meet continually with men possessed of a number of good points, amiable and excellent men, yet in one respect perhaps strangely perverted. And you cannot move them, or succeed at all with them, but must leave them as you find them. Perhaps they are weak and over-indulgent towards others, perhaps they are harsh, perhaps they are obstinate, perhaps they are perversely wedded to some wrong opinion, perhaps they are irresolute and undecided,—some fault or other they have, and you lament it, but cannot mend it, and are obliged to take them for what they are, and be resigned, however you may regret. Men are sometimes so good and so great, that one is led to exclaim, Oh that they were only a little better, and a little greater!

This indeed is all the difference between being a true saint of God and a second-rate or third-rate Christian. Few men are great saints. There is always a something; I am not speaking of wilful or admitted sins—sins against the conscience (they of course exclude a man altogether from any hope), but of a defect of view and principle, a perversion of character. This is the common case even with the better sort of Christians; they are deformed in stature, they are not upright, they do not walk perfectly with God. And you cannot tell why it is;—they have ever lived religiously,—they have been removed from temptation, had good training and instruction, and they fulfil their calling, are good husbands or wives, good parents, good neighbours,—still when you come to know them well, there is in them this or that great inconsistency.

This consideration, moreover, tends to account for the strange way in which defects of character are buried in a man. He goes on, for years perhaps, and no one ever discovers his particular failings, nor does he know them himself; till at length he is brought into certain circumstances, which bring them out. Hence men turn out so very differently from what was expected; and we are seldom able to tell beforehand of another, and scarcely ever dare we promise for ourselves, as regards the future. The proverb, for instance, says, power tries a man; so do riches, so do various changes of life. We find that, after all, we do not know him, though we have been acquainted with him for years. We are disappointed, nay sometimes startled, as if he had almost lost his identity; whereas perchance it is but the coming to light of sins committed long before we knew him.

Again: single sins indulged or neglected are often the cause of other defects of character, which seem to have no connection with them, but which after all are rather symptomatic of the former, than themselves at the bottom of the mischief. This is generally acknowledged as regards a sceptical temper of mind, which commonly is assailed by argument in vain, the root of the evil lying deeper, viz. in habits of vice, which however the guilty parties strenuously maintain to be quite a distinct matter, to relate to their conduct, and to have no influence whatever upon their reason or their opinions. And the same thing perhaps holds true

in other cases ; softness of mind and manner and false refinement
may sometimes be the result of allowing ourselves in impure
thoughts ; or wanderings in prayer may have some subtle connection with self-conceit ; or passionateness may owe its power
over us to indulgence, though without excess, in eating and drinking.   I am not connecting these several sins together as if in the
way of cause and effect, but stating a connection which sometimes
holds in matter of fact, however we account for it.

Now I will proceed to consider the existence of single sins, and
the state of persons labouring under them, in another point of
view.   I suppose there are few persons indeed, if any, but have
some besetting sin or other, some infirmity, some temptation ; and
in resisting this lies their trial.   Now a man may be very
religious *all but* this one infirmity, and this one indulged infirmity
may in consequence be producing most distressing effects on his
spiritual state considered both in itself and in God's sight,
without his being aware of it.   Suppose, for instance, that a man
is naturally resentful and unforgiving.   He may, in spite of this,
have a great number of excellences, very high views, very deeply-
seated principles, very great points, great self-devotion to God's
service, great faith, great sanctity.   I can fancy such a person
almost arguing himself out of his own conviction, that he is
fostering the secret sin in question, from his consciousness of his
own integrity, and his devotional spirit in the general round of
his duties.   There are sins which, when committed, so acutely
distress the mind, that they are far less dangerous to it than
their intrinsic heinousness would otherwise make them.   Never
must we undervalue of course the extreme misery and guilt of
evil thoughts which are often indulged by the young ; still
afterwards they fill a person with remorse, and are clamorous for
his repentance, and before he repents they so burden him, that he
has no ease, no satisfaction.   He cannot go about his ordinary
duties as before : and, while all this is felt, great as is their
sinfulness, they strike no secret blow, but in a certain sense
counteract their own effects.   But far different is it with covetousness, conceit, ambition, or resentment, which is the particular
sin I am speaking of.   It may have ten thousand palliations ; it
may be disguised by fair names ; it affects the conscience only
now and then, for a moment, and that is all ; the pang is soon
over.   The pang is momentary, but the ease and satisfaction and
harmony of mind arising from the person's exact performance of
his general duties are abiding guests within him.   Whatever his
duties are, this consciousness is with him : he is honest, just,

temperate, self-denying; he mixes with others, and is perhaps meek and lowly, unassuming and affectionate, or, if need be, firm, clear-sighted in matters of principle, zealous in conduct, pure in his motives. He enters God's house, and his heart responds to what he sees and hears there. He seems to himself to be able to say, "Thou God seest me !" as if he had no secret fault at all in his heart. He prays as calmly and seriously as before; he feels, as before, his heart drawn upwards by his Lord's history, or the Psalms of David. He is conscious to himself that he is not of this world. He humbly trusts that there is nothing in this world (through God's grace) that can tempt his heart from his God and Saviour. Do you not see how his imagination is affected by all this ? he is in the main what he thinks he is ; he thinks himself devoted to God in all active services, in all inward thoughts ; and so he is. He is not wrong in thinking so ; but in spite of all this, he has just one fault in a different direction,—there is a fault out of sight. He forgets, that in spite of this harmony between all within and all without for twenty-three hours of the day, there is one subject, now and then recurring, which jars with his mind,—there is just one string out of tune Some particular person has injured him or dishonoured him, and a few minutes of each day or of each week are given to the indulgence of harsh, unforgiving thoughts, which at first he suspected were what they really are, sinful, but which he has gradually learned to palliate, or rather account for, on other principles, to refer to other motives, to justify on religious or other grounds. Solomon says, " Dead flies cause the ointment of the apothecary to send forth a stinking savour ; so doth a little folly him that is in reputation for wisdom and honour." [1] Alas ! who can pretend to estimate the effect of this apparently slight transgression upon the spiritual state of any one of us ? Who can pretend to say what the effect of it is in God's sight ? What do the Angels think of it ? What does our own guardian Angel, if one be vouchsafed us, who has watched over us, and been intimate with us from our youth up ; who joyed to see how we once grew together with God's grace, but who now is in fear for us ? Alas ! what is the real condition of our heart itself ? Dead bodies keep their warmth a short time ; and who can tell but a soul so circumstanced may be severed from the grace of the Ordinances, though he partakes them outwardly, and is but existing upon and exhausting the small treasure of strength and life which is laid up within him ? Nay, we know that so it

[1] Eccles. x. 1.

Y

really is, if the sin be deliberate and wilful; for the word of Scripture assures us that such sin shuts us out from God's presence, and obstructs the channels by which He gives us grace.

Consider, again, how miserable a calamity may from such a cause be inflicted on a whole Church. The intercessions of the saints are the life of the Church. The alms and good works, the prayers and fastings, the purity, the strict conscientiousness, the devotion of all true believers, high and low, are our safety and protection. When Satan, then, would afflict her in any of her branches, he begins doubtless by attempting to rob her of that in which her strength lies. He has gained a point whenever he can entangle religious persons in some deliberate sin, when he can rouse their pride, inflame their resentment, allure their covetousness, or feed their ambitious hopes. One sin is enough: his work is done, when he can put one single obstacle in their road; and there he leaves it, satisfied. And let it be observed, this applies both to the case of individuals and of the Church itself at a given time. For what we know, at this very time Satan may have succeeded in attaching some sin upon us as a people, which is working our destruction, in spite of whatever good points we may really have besides. Love of the world's good things, for instance, may be sufficient to ruin many graces. As to individuals, the case of Achan is quite in point, as you must well recollect. His one sin, secreting from among the spoils of Jericho a goodly Babylonish garment and some gold and silver, brought defeat upon the forces of Israel, and next death upon himself, and death upon his sons and his daughters. Let us not think that God's providence is materially different now, because we do not happen to see it. The chief difference between His dealings with Jews and with Christians is surely but this: they were visible to the one, to the other invisible. We do not *see* the effects of His wrath now as then, but they are as real, and more terrible as being proportioned to the greatness of the privileges abused.

And here I will notice another instance, as it may be considered, of a disobedience in one particular only, which sometimes consists with much excellence in other respects; that of separation or alienation from the Church. When we come across persons who have seceded from the Church, or who actively oppose her, or who disbelieve some of her doctrines, it may sometimes happen that we see so much of good principle and right conduct in them, as to be perplexed, and to begin to ask ourselves whether they can be very wrong in their opinions, or whether they themselves gain any harm from them. Now here let it be observed, I am

speaking of those who go counter to the truth, when they might
have known better. Again, I would not have you forget that the
higher gifts of grace are altogether unseen, as well as the inflictions
of God's wrath ; but still let us speak of what *is* seen in those
who deliberately oppose the Church. I say our imagination is
likely to be affected by what appears in them of faith and holiness ; and much more the imagination of the persons themselves,
who often have no doubt whatever that they are in God's favour.
I repeat, I am speaking of those whom God sees to be wilful in
their separation ; and though we cannot know who are such, and
therefore can pronounce judgment absolutely on no one, yet I would
have all those who are thrown with persons who, being separatists,
may be such, to bear in mind that their seeming to be holy and
religious ever so much, does not prove they are really so, supposing they have this one secret sin chargeable upon them in God's
books. Just as a man may be in good health, may have his arms
and hands his own, his head clear, his mind active, and yet may
just have one organ diseased, and the disease not at once appear,
but be latent, and yet be mortal, bringing certain death in the
event, so may it be with them. As in the instance just now
taken, a man may be upright and noble-minded, with a single
purpose and a high resoluteness, kind and gentle, self-denying
and charitable, and yet towards one certain individual may cherish
feelings of revenge, and thereby show that some principle short
of the love of God rules his heart,—so may it be with those who
seem to be good men, and wilfully leave the Church. Their
religious excellences, whatever these may be, are of no avail really
against this or any other wilful sin.

To conclude. I have suggested but one or two thoughts on a
very large subject, yet through God's mercy they may be useful.
They must be useful, if they lead us to be frightened at ourselves.
"Who can understand his errors ? " says holy David. "Cleanse
Thou me from secret faults." And how awful is the text,
"Your sin will find you out ! " Who can undertake to say for
himself what and when have been his wilful sins, how frequently
they recur, and how continually in consequence he is falling from
grace ! What need have we of a cleansing and a restoration day
by day ! What need have we of drawing near to God in faith
and penitence, to seek from Him such pardon, such assurance,
such strength, as He will vouchsafe to bestow ! What need have
we to continue in His presence, to remain under the shadow of
His throne, to make use of all the means and expedients He

allows us, to be steadfast in His Ordinances, and zealous in His precepts, lest we be found shelterless and helpless when He visits the earth !

Moreover, what constant prayers should we offer up to Him that He would be merciful to us in the dreadful day of judgment ! It will indeed be a fearful moment when we stand before Him in the sight of men and Angels, to be judged according to our works ! It will be fearful for ourselves and for all our friends. Then the day of grace will be over; prayers will not avail then, when the books are opened. Let us then plead for ourselves and for each other while it is called to-day. Let us pray Him, by the merits of His cross and passion, to have mercy on us, to have mercy on all we love, on all the Church; to pardon us, to reveal to us our sins, to give us repentance and amendment of life, to give us present grace, and to bestow on us, according to the riches of His love, future blessedness in His eternal kingdom.

SERMON XL.

(SUNDAYS AFTER TRINITY.)

The Greatness and Littleness of Human Life.

" The days of the years of my pilgrimage are an hundred and thirty years: few and evil have the days of the years of my life been ; and have not attained unto the days of the years of the life of my fathers, in the days of their pilgrimage."—GEN. xlvii. 9.

WHY did the aged Patriarch call his days few, who had lived twice as long as men now live, when he spoke? why did he call them evil, seeing he had on the whole lived in riches and honour, and, what is more, in God's favour? yet he described his time as short, his days as evil, and his life as but a pilgrimage. Or if we allow that his afflictions were such as to make him reasonably think cheaply of his life, in spite of the blessings which attended it, yet that he should call it short, considering he had so much more time for the highest purposes of his being than we have, is at first sight surprising. He alludes indeed to the longer life which had been granted to his fathers, and perhaps felt a decrepitude greater than theirs had been; yet this difference between him and them could hardly be the real ground of his complaint in the text, or more than a confirmation or occasion of it. It was not because Abraham had lived one hundred and seventy-five years, and Isaac one hundred and eighty, and he himself, whose life was not yet finished, but one hundred and thirty, that he made this mournful speech. For it matters not, when time is gone, what length it has been; and this doubtless was the real cause why the Patriarch spoke as he did, not because his life was shorter than his fathers', but because it was wellnigh over. When life is past, it is all one whether it has lasted two hundred years or fifty. And it is this characteristic, stamped on human life in the day of its birth, viz. that it is mortal, which makes it under all circumstances and in every form equally feeble and despicable. All the points in which men differ, health and strength, high or low estate, happiness or misery, vanish before this common lot, mortality. Pass a few years, and the longest-lived will be gone; nor will what is past profit him then, except in its consequences.

And this sense of the nothingness of life, impressed on us by the very fact that it comes to an end, is much deepened, when we contrast it with the capabilities of us who live it. Had Jacob lived Methuselah's age, he would have called it short. This is what we all feel, though at first sight it seems a contradiction, that even though the days as they go be slow, and be laden with many events, or with sorrows or dreariness, lengthening them out and making them tedious, yet the year passes quick though the hours tarry, and time bygone is as a dream, though we thought it would never go while it was going. And the reason seems to be this; that, when we contemplate human life in itself, in how-ever small a portion of it, we see implied in it the presence of a soul, the energy of a spiritual existence, of an accountable being; consciousness tells us this concerning it every moment. But when we look back on it in memory, we view it but externally, as a mere lapse of time, as a mere earthly history. And the longest duration of this external world is as dust, and weighs nothing against one moment's life of the world within. Thus we are ever expecting great things from life, from our internal consciousness every moment of our having souls; and we are ever being disappointed, on considering what we have gained from time past, or can hope from time to come. And life is ever promising and never fulfilling; and hence, however long it be, our days are few and evil. This is the particular view of the subject on which I shall now dwell.

Our earthly life, then, gives promise of what it does not accom-plish. It promises immortality, yet it is mortal; it contains life in death and eternity in time; and it attracts us by begin-nings which faith alone brings to an end. I mean, when we take into account the powers with which our souls are gifted as Chris-tians, the very consciousness of these fills us with a certainty that they must last beyond this life; that is, in the case of good and holy men, whose present state, I say, is to them who know them well, an earnest of immortality. The greatness of their gifts, contrasted with their scanty time for exercising them, forces the mind forward to the thought of another life, as almost the necessary counterpart and consequence of this life, and certainly implied in this life, provided there be a righteous Governor of the world who does not make man for nought.

This is a thought which will come upon us not always, but under circumstances. And many perhaps of those who at first hearing may think they never felt it, may recognise what I mean while I describe it.

I mean, when one sees some excellent person, whose graces we know, whose kindliness, affectionateness, tenderness, and generosity, —when we see him dying (let him have lived ever so long ; I am not supposing a premature death ; let him live out his days), the thought is forced upon us with a sort of surprise: "Surely, he is not to die yet ; he has not yet had any opportunity of exercising duly those excellent gifts with which God has endowed him." Let him have lived seventy or eighty years, yet it seems as if he had done nothing at all, and his life were scarcely begun. He has lived all his days perhaps in a private sphere ; he has been engaged on a number of petty matters which died with the day, and yielded no apparent fruit. He has had just enough of trial under various circumstances, to evidence, but not adequately to employ, what was in him. He has, we perhaps perceive, a noble benevolence of mind, a warmth of heart, and a beneficent temper, which, had it the means, would scatter blessings on every side ; yet he has never been rich,—he dies poor. We have been accustomed to say to ourselves, "What would such a one be were he wealthy?" not as fancying he ever *will* have riches, but from feeling how he would become them ; yet, when he actually does die as he lived, without them, we feel somehow disappointed,— there has been a failure,—his mind, we think, has never reached its scope,—he has had a treasure within him which has never been used. His days have been but few and evil, and have become old unseasonably, compared with his capabilities ; and we are driven by a sense of these, to look on to a future state as a time when they will be brought out and come into effect. I am not attempting by such reflections to prove that there is a future state ; let us take that for granted. I mean, over and above our positive belief in this great truth, we are actually driven to a belief, we attain a sort of sensible conviction of that life to come, a certainty striking home to our hearts and piercing them, by this imperfection in what is present. The very greatness of our powers makes this life look pitiful ; the very pitifulness of this life forces on our thoughts to another ; and the prospect of another gives a dignity and value to this life which promises it ;

and thus this life is at once great and little, and we rightly contemn it while we exalt its importance.

And, if this life is short, even when longest, from the great
disproportion between it and the powers of regenerate man, still
more is this the case, of course, where it is cut short, and death
comes prematurely. Men there are, who, in a single moment of
their lives, have shown a superhuman height and majesty of mind
which it would take ages for them to employ on its proper objects,
and, as it were, to exhaust; and who by such passing flashes, like
rays of the sun, and the darting of lightning, give token of their
immortality, give token to us that they are but Angels in disguise,
the elect of God sealed for eternal life, and destined to judge the
world and to reign with Christ for ever. Yet they are suddenly
taken away, and we have hardly recognised them when we lose
them. Can we believe that they are not removed for higher
things elsewhere? This is sometimes said with reference to our
intellectual powers; but it is still more true of our moral nature.
There is something in moral truth and goodness, in faith, in firmness, in heavenly-mindedness, in meekness, in courage, in loving-
kindness, to which this world's circumstances are quite unequal,
for which the longest life is insufficient, which makes the highest
opportunities of this world disappointing, which must burst the
prison of this world to have its appropriate range. So that when
a good man dies, one is led to say, " He has not half showed himself, he has had nothing to exercise him; his days are gone like
a shadow, and he is withered like grass."

I say the word "disappointing" is the only word to express
our feelings on the death of God's Saints. Unless our faith
be very active, so as to pierce beyond the grave, and realize the
future, we feel depressed at what seems like a failure of great
things. And from this very feeling surely, by a sort of contradiction, we may fairly take hope; for if this life be so disappointing, so unfinished, surely it is not the whole. This feeling of
disappointment will often come upon us in an especial way, on
happening to hear of or to witness the deathbeds of holy men.
The hour of death seems to be a season, of which, in the hands
of Providence, much might be *made*, if I may use the term; much
might be done for the glory of God, the good of man, and the
manifestation of the person dying. And beforehand friends will
perhaps look forward, and expect that great things are then to
take place, which they shall never forget. Yet, "how dieth the
wise man? as the fool."[1] Such is the Preacher's experience, and

[1] Eccles. ii. 16.

our own bears witness to it. King Josiah, the zealous servant of the Living God, died the death of wicked Ahab, the worshipper of Baal. True Christians die as other men. One dies by a sudden accident, another in battle, another without friends to see how he dies, a fourth is insensible or not himself. Thus the opportunity seems thrown away, and we are forcibly reminded that "the manifestation of the sons of God"[1] is hereafter; that "the earnest expectation of the creature" is but waiting for it; that this life is unequal to the burden of so great an office as the due exhibition of those secret ones who shall one day "shine forth as the sun in the kingdom of their Father."[2]

But further (if it be allowable to speculate), one can even conceive the same kind of feeling, and a most transporting one, to come over the soul of the faithful Christian, when just separated from the body, and conscious that his trial is once for all over. Though his life has been a long and painful discipline, yet when it is over, we may suppose him to feel at the moment the same sort of surprise at its being ended as generally follows any exertion in this life, when the object is gained and the anticipation over. When we have wound up our minds for any point of time, any great event, an interview with strangers, or the sight of some wonder, or the occasion of some unusual trial, when it comes, and is gone, we have a strange reverse of feeling from our changed circumstances. Such, but without any mixture of pain, without any lassitude, dulness, or disappointment, may be the happy contemplation of the disembodied spirit; as if it said to itself, "So all is now over; this is what I have so long waited for; for which I have nerved myself; against which I have prepared, fasted, prayed, and wrought righteousness. Death is come and gone,—it is over. Ah! is it possible? What an easy trial, what a cheap price for eternal glory! A few sharp sicknesses, or some acute pain awhile, or some few and evil years, or some struggles of mind, dreary desolateness for a season, fightings and fears, afflicting bereavements, or the scorn and ill-usage of the world,—how they fretted me, how much I thought of them, yet how little really they are! How contemptible a thing is human life,—contemptible in itself, yet in its effects invaluable! for it has been to me like a small seed of easy purchase, germinating and ripening into bliss everlasting."

Such being the unprofitableness of this life, viewed in itself, it is plain how we should regard it while we go through it. We should remember that it is scarcely more than an accident of our

[1] Rom. viii. 19. [2] Matt. xiii. 43.

being—that it is no part of ourselves, who are immortal; that we are immortal spirits, independent of time and space, and that this life is but a sort of outward stage, on which we act for a time, and which is only sufficient and only intended to answer the purpose of trying whether we will serve God or no.   We should consider ourselves to be in this world in no fuller sense than players in any game are in the game; and life to be a sort of dream, as detached· and as different from our real eternal existence, as a dream differs from waking; a serious dream, indeed, as affording a means of judging us, yet in itself a kind of shadow without substance, a scene set before us, in which we seem to be, and in which it is our duty to act just as if all we saw had a truth and reality, because all that meets us influences us and our destiny. The regenerate soul is taken into communion with Saints and Angels, and its "life is hid with Christ in God;"[1] it has a place in God's court, and is not of this world,—looking into this world as a spectator might look at some show or pageant, except when called from time to time to take a part.   And while it obeys the instinct of the senses, it does so for God's sake, and it submits itself to things of time so far as to be brought to perfection by them, that, when the veil is withdrawn and it sees itself to be, where it ever has been, in God's kingdom, it may be found worthy to enjoy it.   It is this view of life, which removes from us all surprise and disappointment that it is so incomplete: as well might we expect any chance event which happens in the course of it to be complete, any casual conversation with a stranger, or the toil or amusement of an hour.

Let us, then, thus account of our present state: it is precious as revealing to us, amid shadows and figures, the existence and attributes of Almighty God and His elect people: it is precious, because it enables us to hold intercourse with immortal souls who are on their trial as we are.   It is momentous, as being the scene and means of our trial; but beyond this it has no claims upon us. "Vanity of vanities, says the Preacher, all is vanity."   We may be poor or rich, young or old, honoured or slighted, and it ought to affect us no more, neither to elate us nor depress us, than if we were actors in a play, who know that the characters they represent are not their own, and that though they may appear to be superior one to another, to be kings or to be peasants, they are in reality all on a level.   The one desire which should move us should be, first of all, that of seeing Him face to face who is now hid from us; and next of enjoying eternal and direct communion,

[1] Col. iii. 3.

in and through Him, with our friends around us, whom at present we know only through the medium of sense, by precarious and partial channels, which give us little insight into their hearts.

These are suitable feelings towards this attractive but deceitful world. What have we to do with its gifts and honours, who, having been already baptized into the world to come, are no longer citizens of this? Why should we be anxious for a long life, or wealth, or credit, or comfort, who know that the next world will be everything which our hearts can wish, and that not in appearance only, but truly and everlastingly? Why should we rest in this world, when it is the token and promise of another? Why should we be content with its surface, instead of appropriating what is stored beneath it? To those who live by faith, everything they see speaks of that future world; the very glories of nature, the sun, moon, and stars, and the richness and the beauty of the earth, are as types and figures witnessing and teaching the invisible things of God. All that we see is destined one day to burst forth into a heavenly bloom, and to be transfigured into immortal glory. Heaven at present is out of sight, but in due time, as snow melts and discovers what it lay upon, so will this visible creation fade away before those greater splendours which are behind it, and on which at present it depends. In that day shadows will retire, and the substance show itself. The sun will grow pale and be lost in the sky, but it will be before the radiance of Him whom it does but image, the Sun of Righteousness, with healing on His wings, who will come forth in visible form, as a bridegroom out of his chamber, while His perishable type decays. The stars which surround it will be replaced by Saints and Angels circling His throne. Above and below, the clouds of the air, the trees of the field, the waters of the great deep will be found impregnated with the forms of everlasting spirits, the servants of God which do His pleasure. And our own mortal bodies will then be found in like manner to contain within them an inner man, which will then receive its due proportions, as the soul's harmonious organ, instead of that gross mass of flesh and blood which sight and touch are sensible of. For this glorious manifestation the whole creation is at present in travail, earnestly desiring that it may be accomplished in its season.

These are thoughts to make us eagerly and devoutly say, "Come, Lord Jesus, to end the time of waiting, of darkness, of turbulence, of disputing, of sorrow, of care." These are thoughts to lead us to rejoice in every day and hour that passes, as bringing us nearer the time of His appearing, and the termination of sin and misery. They are thoughts which ought thus to affect us; and so they would, were it not for the load of guilt which weighs upon us, for sins committed against light and grace. O that it were otherwise with us! O that we were fitted duly to receive this lesson which the world gives us, and had so improved the gifts of life, that while we felt it to be perishing, we might rejoice in it as precious! O that we were not conscious of deep stains upon our souls, the accumulations of past years, and of infirmities continually besetting us! Were it not for all this,—were it not for our unprepared state, as in one sense it may truly be called, how gladly should we hail each new month and year as a token that our Saviour is so much nearer to us than He ever has been yet! May He grant His grace abundantly to us, to make us meet for His presence, that we may not be ashamed before Him at His coming! May He vouchsafe to us the full grace of His ordinances: may He feed us with His choicest gifts: may He expel the poison from our souls: may He wash us clean in His precious blood, and give us the fulness of faith, love, and hope, as foretastes of the heavenly portion which He destines for us!

SERMON XLI.

(SUNDAYS AFTER TRINITY.)

Moral Effects of Communion with God.

" One thing have I desired of the Lord, which I will require; even that I may dwell in the house of the Lord all the days of my life, to behold the fair beauty of the Lord, and to visit His Temple."—PSALM xxvii. 4.

WHAT the Psalmist desired, we Christians enjoy to the full—the liberty of holding communion with God in His Temple all through our life. Under the Law, the presence of God was but in one place; and therefore could be approached and enjoyed only at set times. For far the greater part of their lives, the chosen people were in one sense "cast out of the sight of His eyes;" [1] and the periodical return to it which they were allowed was a privilege highly coveted and earnestly expected. Much more precious was the privilege of continually dwelling in His sight, which is spoken of in the text. "One thing," says the Psalmist, "have I desired of the Lord . . . . that I may dwell in the house of the Lord all the days of my life, to behold the fair beauty of the Lord, and to visit His Temple." He desired to have continually that communion with God in prayer, praise, and meditation, to which His presence admits the soul; and this, I say, is the portion of Christians. Faith opens upon us Christians the Temple of God wherever we are; for that Temple is a spiritual one, and so is everywhere present. "We have access," says the Apostle—that is, we have admission or introduction—"by faith into this grace wherein we stand, and rejoice in hope of the glory of God." And hence he says elsewhere, "Rejoice in the Lord alway, and again I say, Rejoice." "Rejoice evermore, pray without ceasing; in every thing give

[1] Psalm xxxi. 24.

thanks." And St. James, "Is any afflicted? let him pray: is any merry? let him sing psalms."[1] Prayer, praise, thanksgiving, contemplation, are the peculiar privilege and duty of a Christian, and that for their own sakes, from the exceeding comfort and satisfaction they afford him, and without reference to any definite results to which prayer tends, without reference to the answers which are promised to it, from a general sense of the blessedness of being under the shadow of God's throne.

I propose, then, in what follows, to make some remarks on communion with God, or prayer in a large sense of the word; not as regards its external consequences, but as it may be considered to affect our own minds and hearts.

What, then, is prayer? It is (if it may be said reverently) *conversing* with God. We converse with our fellow-men, and then we use familiar language, because they *are* our fellows. We converse with God, and then we use the lowliest, awfullest, calmest, concisest language we can, because He *is* God. Prayer, then, is *divine* converse, differing from human as God differs from man. Thus St. Paul says, "Our conversation is in heaven,"[2]— not indeed thereby meaning converse of words only, but intercourse and manner of living generally; yet still in an especial way converse of words or prayer, because language is the special means of all intercourse. Our intercourse with our fellow-men goes on, not by sight, but by sound, not by eyes, but by ears. Hearing is the social sense, and language is the social bond. In like manner, as the Christian's conversation is in heaven, as it is his duty, with Enoch and other saints, *to walk with God*, so his voice is in heaven, his heart "inditing of a good matter," of prayers and praises. Prayers and praises are the mode of his intercourse with the next world, as the converse of business or recreation is the mode in which this world is carried on in all its separate courses. He who does not pray does not claim his citizenship with heaven, but lives, though an heir of the kingdom, as if he were a child of earth.

Now, it is not surprising if that duty or privilege, which is the characteristic token of our heavenly inheritance, should also have an especial influence upon our fitness for claiming it. He who does not use a gift, loses it; the man who does not use his voice or limbs, loses power over them, and becomes disqualified for the state of life to which he is called. In like manner, he who neglects to pray, not only suspends the enjoyment, but is in a

---

[1] Rom. v. 2. Phil. iv. 4. 1 Thess. v. 16-18. James v. 13.
[2] Phil. iii. 20.

way to lose the possession, of his divine citizenship. We are members of another world; we have been severed from the companionship of devils, and brought into that invisible kingdom of Christ which faith alone discerns,—that mysterious Presence of God which encompasses us, which is in us, and around us, which is in our heart, which enfolds us as though with a robe of light, hiding our scarred and discoloured souls from the sight of Divine Purity, and making them shining as the Angels; and which flows in upon us too by means of all forms of beauty and grace which this visible world contains, in a starry host or (if I may so say) a milky way of divine companions, the inhabitants of Mount Zion, where we dwell. Faith, I say, alone apprehends all this; but yet there *is* something which is not left to faith,— our own tastes, likings, motives, and habits. Of these we are conscious in our degree, and we can make ourselves more and more conscious; and as consciousness tells us what they are, reason tells us whether they are such as become, as correspond with, that heavenly world into which we have been translated.

I say, then, it is plain to common sense that the man who has not accustomed himself to the language of heaven will be no fit inhabitant of it when, in the Last Day, it is perceptibly revealed. The case is like that of a language or style of speaking of this world; we know well a foreigner from a native. Again, we know those who have been used to kings' courts or educated society from others. By their voice, accent, and language, and not only so, by their gestures and gait, by their usages, by their mode of conducting themselves and their principles of conduct, we know well what a vast difference there is between those who have lived in good society and those who have not. What indeed is called "*good* society" is often very worthless society. I am not speaking of it to praise it; I only mean, that, as the manners which men call refined or courtly are gained only by in-tercourse with courts and polished circles, and as the influence of the words there used (that is, of the ideas which those words, striking again and again on the ear, convey to the mind) extends in a most subtle way over all that men do, over the turn of their sentences, and the tone of their questions and replies, and their general bearing, and the spontaneous flow of their thoughts, and their mode of viewing things, and the general maxims or heads to which they refer them, and the motives which determine them, and their likings and dislikings, hopes and fears, and their relative estimate of persons, and the intensity of their perceptions towards particular objects; so a habit of prayer, the practice of turning to God and the unseen world, in every season, in every place, in every emergency (let alone its supernatural effect of prevailing with God),—prayer, I say, has what may be called a *natural* effect, in spiritualizing and elevating the soul. A man is no longer what he was before ; gradually, imperceptibly to himself, he has imbibed a new set of ideas, and become imbued with fresh principles. He is as one coming from kings' courts, with a grace, a delicacy, a dignity, a propriety, a justness of thought and taste, a clearness and firmness of principle, all his own. Such is the power of God's secret grace acting through those ordinances which He has enjoined us ; such the evident fitness of those ordinances to produce the results which they set before us. As speech is the organ of human society, and the means of human civilization, so is prayer the instrument of divine fellowship and divine training.

I will give, for the sake of illustration, some instances in detail of one particular fault of mind which among others a habit of prayer is calculated to cure.

For instance ; many a man seems to have no grasp at all of doctrinal truth. He cannot get himself to think it of importance what a man believes, and what not. He tries to do so ; for a time he does ; he does for a time think that a certain faith is necessary for salvation, that certain doctrines are to be put forth and maintained in charity to the souls of men. Yet though he thinks so one day, he changes the next ; he holds the truth, and then lets it go again. He is filled with doubts ; suddenly the question crosses him, "Is it possible that such and such a doctrine *is* necessary?" and he relapses into an uncomfortable sceptical state, out of which there is no outlet. Reasonings do not convince him ; he *cannot* be convinced ; he has no grasp of truth. Why? Because the next world is not a reality to him ; it only exists in his mind in the form of certain conclusions from certain reasonings. It is but an inference ; and never can be more, never can be present to his mind, until he acts, instead of arguing. Let him but act as if the next world were before him ; let him but give himself to such devotional exercises as we ought to observe in the presence of an Almighty, All-holy, and All-merciful God, and it will be a rare case indeed if his difficulties do not vanish.

Or again : a man may have a natural disposition towards caprice and change ; he may be apt to take up first one fancy, then another, from novelty or other reason ; he may take sudden likings or dislikings, or be tempted to form a scheme of religion for himself, of what he thinks best or most beautiful out of all the systems which divide the world.

Again : he is troubled perhaps with a variety of unbecoming thoughts, which he would fain keep out of his mind if he could. He finds himself unsettled and uneasy, dissatisfied with his condition, easily excited, sorry at sin one moment, forgetting it the next, feeble-minded, unable to rule himself, tempted to dote upon trifles, apt to be caught and influenced by vanities, and to abandon himself to languor or indolence.

Once more : he has not a clear perception of the path of truth and duty. This is an especial fault among us nowadays : men are actuated perhaps by the best feelings and the most amiable motives, and are not fairly chargeable with insincerity ; and yet there is a want of straightforwardness in their conduct. They allow themselves to be guided by expediency, and defend themselves, and perhaps so plausibly, that though you are not convinced, you are silenced. They attend to what others think more than to what God says ; they look at Scripture more as a gift to man than as a gift from God ; they consider themselves at liberty to modify its plain precepts by a certain discretionary rule ; they listen to the voice of great men, and allow themselves to be swayed by them ; they make comparisons and strike the balance between the impracticability of the whole that God commands, and the practicability of effecting a part, and think they may consent to give up something, if they can secure the rest. They shift about in opinion, going first a little this way, then a little that, according to the loudness and positiveness with which others speak ; they are at the mercy of the last speaker, and they think they observe a safe, judicious, and middle course, by always keeping a certain distance behind those who go furthest. Or they are rash in their religious projects and undertakings, and forget that they may be violating the lines and fences of God's law, while they move about freely at their pleasure. Now, I will not judge another ; I will not say that in this or that given case the fault of mind in question (for anyhow it is a fault), does certainly arise from some certain cause which I choose to guess at : but at least there *are* cases where this wavering of mind *does* arise from scantiness of prayer ; and if so, it is worth a man's considering, who is thus unsteady, timid, and dimsighted, whether this scantiness be not perchance the true reason of such infirmities in his own case, and whether a " continuing instant in prayer,' —by which I mean, not merely prayer morning and evening, but something suitable to his disease, something extraordinary, as

z

medicine is extraordinary, a "redeeming of time" from society and recreation in order to pray more,—whether such a change in his habits would not remove them?

For what is the very promise of the New Covenant but stability? what is it, but a clear insight into the truth, such as will enable us to know how to walk, how to profess, how to meet the circumstances of life, how to withstand gainsayers? Are we built upon a rock or upon the sand? are we after all tossed about on the sea of opinion, when Christ has stretched out His hand to us, to help and encourage us? "Thou wilt keep him in perfect peace whose mind is stayed on Thee, because he trusteth in Thee."[1] Such is the word of promise. Can we possibly have apprehensions about what man will do to us or say of us, can we flatter the great ones of earth, or timidly yield to the many, or be dazzled by talent, or drawn aside by interest, who are in the habit of divine conversations? "Ye have an unction from the Holy One," says St. John, "and ye know all things. I have not written unto you because ye know not the truth, but because ye know it, and that no lie is of the truth. . . . The anointing which ye have received of Him abideth in you, and ye need not that any man teach you. . . . Whosoever is born of God doth not commit sin, for his seed remaineth in him; and he cannot sin, because he is born of God."[2] This is that birth by which the baptized soul not only enters, but actually embraces and realizes the kingdom of God. This is the true and effectual regeneration, when the seed of life takes root in man and thrives. Such men have accustomed themselves to speak to God, and God has ever spoken to them; and they feel "the powers of the world to come" as truly as they feel the presence of this world, because they have been accustomed to speak and act as if it were real. All of us must rely on something; all must look up to, admire, court, make themselves one with something. Most men cast in their lot with the visible world; but true Christians with Saints and Angels.

Such men are little understood by the world because they are not of the world; and hence it sometimes happens that even the better sort of men are often disconcerted and vexed by them. It cannot be otherwise; they move forward on principles, so different from what are commonly assumed as true. They take for granted, as first principles, what the world wishes to have proved in detail. They have become familiar with the sights of the next world, till they talk of them as if all men admitted them.

---

[1] Isa. xxvi. 3. [2] 1 John ii. 20, 21, 27 ; iii. 9.

The immortality of truth, its oneness, the impossibility of false-hood coalescing with it, what truth is, what it should lead one to do in particular cases, how it lies in the details of life,—all these points are mere matters of debate in the world, and men go through long processes of argument, and pride themselves on their subtleness in defending or attacking, in making probable or improbable, ideas which are assumed without a word by those who have lived in heaven, as the very ground to start from. In consequence, such men are called bad disputants, inconsecutive reasoners, strange, eccentric, or perverse thinkers, merely because they do not take for granted, nor go to prove, what others do,—because they do not go about to define and determine the sights (as it were), the mountains and rivers and plains, and sun, moon, and stars, of the next world. And hence in turn they are commonly unable to enter into the ways of thought or feelings of other men, having been engrossed with God's thoughts and God's ways. Hence, perhaps, they seem abrupt in what they say and do ; nay, even make others feel constrained and uneasy in their presence. Perhaps they appear reserved too, because they take so much for granted which might be drawn out, and because they cannot bring themselves to tell all their thoughts from their sacredness, and because they are drawn off from free conversation to the thought of heaven, on which their minds rest. Nay, per-chance, they appear severe, because their motives are not under-stood, nor their sensitive jealousy for the honour of God and their charitable concern for the good of their fellow-Christians duly appreciated. In short, to the world they seem like *foreigners.* We know how foreigners strike us ; they are often to *our* notions strange and unpleasing in their manners ; why is this ? merely *because* they are of a different country. Each country has its own manners,—one may not be better than other ; but we naturally like our own ways, and we do not understand other. We do not see their meaning. We misconstrue them ; we think they mean something unpleasant, something rude, or over-free, or haughty, or unrefined, when they do not. And in like manner, the world at large, not only is not Christian, but cannot discern or understand the Christian. Thus our Blessed Lord Himself was not recognised or honoured by His relatives, and (as is plain to every reader of Scripture) He often seems to speak abruptly and severely. So too St. Paul was considered by the Corinthians as contemptible in speech. And hence St. John, speaking of "what manner of love the Father hath bestowed upon us that we should be called the sons of God," adds, "there-

fore the world *knoweth* us not, because it knew Him not."[1]
Such is the effect of divine meditations: admitting us into the
next world, and withdrawing us from this ; making us children
of God, but withal "strangers unto our brethren, even aliens unto
our mother's children."[2] Yea, though the true servants of God
increase in meekness and love day by day, and to those who know
them will seem what they really are ; and though their good
works are evident to all men, and cannot be denied, yet such is
the eternal law which goes between the Church and the world—
we cannot be friends of both ; and they who take their portion
with the Church, will seem, except in some remarkable cases,
unamiable to the world, for the "world knoweth them not," and
does not like them though it can hardly tell why ; yet (as St.
John proceeds) they have this blessing, that "when He shall
appear, they shall be like Him, for they shall see Him as He
is."[3]

And if, as it would seem, we must choose between the two,
surely the world's friendship may be better parted with than our
fellowship with our Lord and Saviour. What indeed have we to
do with courting men whose faces are turned towards God ? We
know how men feel and act when they come to die ; they discharge
their worldly affairs from their minds, and try to realize the unseen
state. Then this world is nothing to them. It may praise, it
may blame ; but they feel it not. They are leaving their goods,
their deeds, their sayings, their writings, their names, behind
them ; and they care not for it, for they wait for Christ. To one
thing alone they are alive, His coming ; they watch against it,
if so be they may then be found without shame. Such is the
conduct of dying men ; and what all but the very hardened do at
the last, if their senses fail not and their powers hold, that does
the true Christian all life long. He is ever dying while he lives ;
he is on his bier, and the prayers for the sick are saying over
him. He has no work but that of making his peace with God,
and preparing for the judgment. He has no aim but that of
being found worthy to escape the things that shall come to pass
and to stand before the Son of Man. And therefore day by day
he unlearns the love of this world, and the desire of its praise ;
he can bear to belong to the nameless family of God, and to seem
to the world strange in it and out of place, for so he is.

And when Christ comes at last, blessed indeed will be his lot.
He has joined himself from the first to the conquering side ; he
has risked the present against the future, preferring the chance of

----

[1] 1 John iii. 1.   [2] Ps. lxix. 8.   [3] 1 John iii. 2.

eternity to the certainty of time; and then his reward will be but beginning, when that of the children of this world is come to an end. In the words of the wise man, "Then shall the righteous man stand in great boldness before the face of such as have afflicted him, and made no account of his labours. When they see it they shall be troubled with terrible fear, and shall be amazed at the strangeness of His salvation, so far beyond all that they looked for. And they, repenting and groaning for anguish of spirit, shall say within themselves, This is he whom we had sometimes in derision and a proverb of reproach; we fools counted his life madness, and his end to be without honour. How is he numbered among the children of God, and his lot is among the Saints !" [1]

[1] Wisd. v. 1-5.

SERMON XLII.

(SUNDAYS AFTER TRINITY.)

The Thought of God the Stay of the Soul.

" Ye have not received the spirit of bondage again to fear, but ye have received the Spirit of adoption, whereby we cry, Abba, Father."—ROM. viii. 15.

WHEN Adam fell, his soul lost its true strength; he forfeited the inward light of God's presence, and became the wayward, fretful, excitable, and miserable being which his history has shown him to be ever since; with alternate strength and feebleness, nobleness and meanness, energy in the beginning and failure in the end. Such was the state of his soul in itself, not to speak of the Divine wrath upon it, which followed, or was involved in the Divine withdrawal. It lost its spiritual life and health, which was necessary to complete its nature, and to enable it to fulfil the ends for which it was created,—which was necessary both for its moral integrity and its happiness; and as if faint, hungry, or sick, it could no longer stand upright, but sank on the ground. Such is the state in which every one of us lies as born into the world; and Christ has come to reverse this state, and restore us the great gift which Adam lost in the beginning. Adam fell from his Creator's favour to be a bond-servant; and Christ has come to set us free again, to impart to us the Spirit of adoption, whereby we become God's children, and again approach Him as our Father.

I say, by birth we are in a state of defect and want; we have not all that is necessary for the perfection of our nature. As the body is not complete in itself, but requires the soul to give it a meaning, so again the soul till God is present with it, and manifested in it, has faculties and affections without a ruling principle, object, or purpose. Such it is by birth, and this Scripture signifies to us by many figures; sometimes calling human nature blind, sometimes hungry, sometimes unclothed, and calling the gift of the Spirit light, health, food, warmth, and raiment; all by way of teaching us what our first state is, and what our gratitude should be to Him who has brought us into a new state. For instance, "Because thou sayest, I am rich, and increased in goods, and have need of nothing; and knowest not that thou art wretched, and miserable, and poor, and blind, and naked: I counsel thee to buy of Me gold tried in the fire, that thou mayest be rich; and white raiment, that thou mayest be clothed, . . . and anoint thine eyes with eye-salve, that thou mayest see." Again, "God, who commanded the light to shine out of darkness, hath shined in our hearts, to give the light of the knowledge of the glory of God, in the face of Jesus Christ." Again, "Awake, thou that sleepest, and arise from the dead, and Christ shall give thee light." Again, "Whosoever drinketh of the water that I shall give him, shall never thirst; but the water that I shall give him shall be in him a well of water springing up into everlasting life." And in the Book of Psalms, "They shall be satisfied with the plenteousness of Thy house; and Thou shalt give them drink of Thy pleasures as out of the river. For with Thee is the well of life, and in Thy Light shall we see light." And in another Psalm, "My soul shall be satisfied, even as it were with marrow and fatness, when my mouth praiseth Thee with joyful lips." And so again, in the Prophet Jeremiah, "I will satiate the souls of the priests with fatness; and My people shall be satisfied with My goodness. . . . I have satiated the weary soul, and I have replenished every sorrowful soul." [1]

Now the doctrine which these passages contain is often truly expressed thus : that the soul of man is made for the contemplation of its Maker; and that nothing short of that high contemplation is its happiness; that, whatever it may possess besides, it is unsatisfied till it is vouchsafed God's presence, and lives in the light of it. There are many aspects in which the same solemn truth may be viewed; there are many ways in which it may be signified. I will now dwell upon it as I have been stating it.

I say, then, that the happiness of the soul consists in the exercise of the affections; not in sensual pleasures, not in activity,

[1] Rev. iii. 17, 18. 2 Cor. iv. 6. Ephes. v. 14. John iv. 14. Ps. xxxvi. 8, 9; lxiii. 5. Jer. xxxi. 14, 25.

not in excitement, not in self-esteem, not in the consciousness of power, not in knowledge; in none of these things lies our happiness, but in our affections being elicited, employed, supplied. As hunger and thirst, as taste, sound, and smell, are the channels through which this bodily frame receives pleasure, so the affections are the instruments by which the soul has pleasure. When they are exercised duly, it is happy; when they are undeveloped, restrained, or thwarted, it is not happy. This is our real and true bliss, not to know, or to affect, or to pursue; but to love, to hope, to joy, to admire, to revere, to adore. Our real and true bliss lies in the possession of those objects on which our hearts may rest and be satisfied.

Now, if this be so, here is at once a reason for saying that the thought of God, and nothing short of it, is the happiness of man; for though there is much besides to serve as subject of knowledge, or motive for action, or means of excitement, yet the affections require a something more vast and more enduring than anything created. What is novel and sudden excites, but does not influence; what is pleasurable or useful raises no awe; self moves no reverence, and mere knowledge kindles no love. He alone is sufficient for the heart who made it. I do not say, of course, that nothing short of the Almighty Creator can awaken and answer to our love, reverence, and trust; man can do this for man. Man doubtless is an object to rouse his brother's love, and repays it in his measure. Nay, it is a great duty, one of the two chief duties of religion, thus to be minded towards our neighbour. But I am not speaking here of what we can do, or ought to do, but what it is our happiness to do; and surely it may be said that though the love of the brethren, the love of all men, be one half of our obedience, yet exercised by itself, were that possible, which it is not, it would be no part of our reward. And for this reason, if for no other, that our hearts require something more permanent and uniform than man can be. We gain much for a time from fellowship with each other. It is a relief to us, as fresh air to the fainting, or meat and drink to the hungry, or a flood of tears to the heavy in mind. It is a soothing comfort to have those whom we may make our confidants; a comfort to have those to whom we may confess our faults; a comfort to have those to whom we may look for sympathy. Love of home and family in these and other ways is sufficient to make this life tolerable to the multitude of men, which otherwise it would not be; but still, after all, our affections exceed such exercise of them, and demand what is more stable. Do not all men die? are they not taken from us? are they not as uncertain as the grass of the field? We do not give our hearts to things irrational, because these have no permanence in them. We do not place our affections in sun, moon, and stars, or this rich and fair earth, because all things material come to nought, and vanish like day and night. Man, too, though he has an intelligence within him, yet in his best estate he is altogether vanity. If our happiness consists in our affections being employed and recompensed, "man that is born of a woman" cannot be our happiness; for how can he stay another who "continueth not in one stay" himself?

But there is another reason why God alone is the happiness of our souls, to which I wish rather to direct attention :—the contemplation of Him, and nothing but it, is able fully to open and relieve the mind, to unlock, occupy, and fix our affections. We may indeed love things created with great intenseness, but such affection, when disjoined from the love of the Creator, is like a stream running in a narrow channel, impetuous, vehement, turbid. The heart runs out, as it were, only at one door; it is not an expanding of the whole man. Created natures cannot open us, or elicit the ten thousand mental senses which belong to us, and through which we really live. None but the presence of our Maker can enter us; for to none besides can the whole heart in all its thoughts and feelings be unlocked and subjected. "Behold," He says, "I stand at the door and knock; if any man hear My voice and open the door, I will come in to him, and will sup with him, and he with Me." "My Father will love him, and We will come unto him, and make Our abode with him." "God hath sent forth the Spirit of His Son into your hearts." "God is greater than our heart, and knoweth all things."[1] It is this feeling of simple and absolute confidence and communion which soothes and satisfies those to whom it is vouchsafed. We know that even our nearest friends enter into us but partially, and hold intercourse with us only at times; whereas the consciousness of a perfect and enduring Presence, and it alone, keeps the heart open. Withdraw the Object on which it rests, and it will relapse again into its state of confinement and constraint; and in proportion as it is limited, either to certain seasons or to certain affections, the heart is straitened and distressed. If it be not overbold to say it, He who is infinite can alone be its measure; He alone can answer to the mysterious assemblage of feelings and thoughts which it has within it. "There is no creature that is not mani-

[1] Rev. iii. 20.   John xiv. 23.   Gal. iv. 6.   1 John iii. 20.

fest in His sight, but all things are naked and opened unto the eyes of Him with whom we have to do." [1]

This is what is meant by the peace of a good conscience; it is the habitual consciousness that our hearts are open to God, with a desire that they should be open.   It is a confidence in God, from a feeling that there is nothing in us which we need be ashamed or afraid of.   You will say that no man on earth is in such a state; for we are all sinners, and that daily.   It is so; certainly we are quite unfitted to endure God's all-searching Eye, to come into direct contact (if I may so speak) with His glorious Presence, without any medium of intercourse between Him and us.   But, first, there may be degrees of this confidence in different men, though the perfection of it be in none.   And again, God in His great mercy, as we all well know, has revealed to us that there is a Mediator between the sinful soul and Himself. And as His merits most wonderfully intervene between our sins and God's judgment, so the thought of those merits, when present with the Christian, enables him, in spite of his sins, to lift up his heart to God; and believing, as he does, that he is (to use Scripture language) in Christ, or, in other words, that he addresses Almighty God, not simply face to face, but in and through Christ, he can bear to submit and open his heart to God, and to wish it open.   For while he is very conscious both of original and actual sin, yet still a feeling of his own sincerity and earnestness is possible; and in proportion as he gains as much as this, he will be able to walk unreservedly with Christ his God and Saviour, and desire His continual presence with him, though he be a sinner, and will wish to be allowed to make Him the one Object of his heart.   Perhaps, under somewhat of this feeling, Hagar said, "Thou God seest me."   It is under this feeling that holy David may be supposed to say, "Examine me, O Lord, and prove me; try out my reins and my heart."   "Try me, O God, and seek the ground of my heart; prove me, and examine my thoughts.   Look well, if there be any way of wickedness in me; and lead me in the way everlasting." [2]   And especially is it instanced in St. Paul, who seems to delight in the continual laying open of his heart to God, and submitting it to His scrutiny, and waiting for His Presence upon it; or, in other words, in the joy of a good conscience.   For instance, "I have lived in all good conscience before God until this day."   "Herein do I exercise myself, to have always a conscience void of offence toward God, and toward men."   "I say the truth in Christ, I lie

[1] Heb. iv. 13.   [2] Ps. xxvi. 2; cxxxix. 23, 24.

not; my conscience also bearing me witness in the Holy Ghost." "Our rejoicing is this, the testimony of our conscience, that in simplicity and godly sincerity, not with fleshly wisdom, but by the grace of God, we have had our conversation in the world, and more abundantly to you-ward."[1] It is, I say, the characteristic of St. Paul, as manifested to us in his Epistles, to live in the sight of Him who "searcheth the reins and the heart," to love to place himself before Him, and, while contemplating God, to dwell on the thought of God's contemplating him.

And, it may be, this is something of the Apostle's meaning, when he speaks of the witness of the Spirit. Perhaps he is speaking of that satisfaction and rest which the soul experiences in proportion as it is able to surrender itself wholly to God, and to have no desire, no aim, but to please Him. When we are awake, we are conscious we are awake, in a sense in which we cannot fancy we are when we are asleep. When we have discovered the solution of some difficult problem in science, we have a conviction about it which is distinct from that which accompanies fancied discoveries or guesses. When we realize a truth we have a feeling which they have not, who take words for things. And so, in like manner, if we are allowed to find that real and most sacred Object on which our heart may fix itself, a fulness of peace will follow, which nothing but it can give. In proportion as we have given up the love of the world, and are dead to the creature, and, on the other hand, are born of the Spirit unto love of our Maker and Lord, this love carries with it its own evidence whence it comes. Hence the Apostle says, "The Spirit itself beareth witness with our spirit, that we are the children of God." Again, he speaks of Him "who hath sealed us, and given the earnest of the Spirit in our hearts."[2]

I have been saying that our happiness consists in the contemplation of God (such a contemplation is alone capable of accompanying the mind always and everywhere, for God alone can be always and everywhere present);—and that what is commonly said about the happiness of a good conscience confirms this; for what is it to have a good conscience, when we examine the force of our words, but to be ever reminded of God by our own hearts, to have our hearts in such a state as to be led thereby to look up to Him, and to desire His Eye to be upon us through the day? It is in the case of holy men the feeling attendant on the contemplation of Almighty God.

[1] Acts xxiii. 1; xxiv. 16. Rom. ix. 1. 2 Cor. i. 12.
[2] Rom. viii. 16. 2 Cor. i. 22.

But, again, this sense of God's presence is not only the ground of the peace of a good conscience, but of the peace of repentance also.   At first sight it might seem strange how repentance can have in it anything of comfort and peace.   The Gospel, indeed, promises to turn all sorrow into joy.   It makes us take pleasure in desolateness, weakness, and contempt.   " We glory in tribulations also," says the Apostle, " because the love of God is shed abroad in our hearts by the Holy Ghost which is given unto us." It destroys anxiety : " Take no thought for the morrow, for the morrow shall take thought for the things of itself."   It bids us take comfort under bereavement : " I would not have you ignorant, brethren, concerning them which are asleep, that ye sorrow not, even as others which have no hope."[1]   But if there be one sorrow which might seem to be unmixed misery, if there be one misery left under the Gospel, the awakened sense of having abused the Gospel might have been considered that one.   And, again, if there be a time when the presence of the Most High would at first sight seem to be intolerable, it would be then, when first the consciousness vividly bursts upon us that we have ungratefully rebelled against Him.   Yet so it is that true repentance cannot be without the thought of God ; it has the thought of God, for it seeks Him ; and it seeks Him, because it is quickened with love ; and even sorrow must have a sweetness, if love be in it.   For what is to repent but to surrender ourselves to God for pardon or punishment ; as loving His presence for its own sake, and accounting chastisement from Him better than rest and peace from the world ?   While the prodigal son remained among the swine he had sorrow enough, but no repentance ; remorse only ; but repentance led him to rise and go to his father, and to confess his sins.   Thus he relieved his heart of its misery, which before was like some hard and fretful tumour weighing upon it.   Or, again, consider St. Paul's account of the repentance of the Corinthians ; there is sorrow in abundance, nay, anguish, but no gloom, no dryness of spirit, no sternness. The penitents afflict themselves, but it is from the fulness of their hearts, from love, gratitude, devotion, horror of the past, desire to escape from their present selves into some state holier and more heavenly.   St. Paul speaks of their " earnest desire, their mourning, their fervent mind towards him."   He rejoices, " not that they were made sorry, but that they sorrowed to repentance."   " For ye were made sorry," he proceeds, " after a godly manner, that ye might receive damage by us in nothing."   And he

[1] Rom. v. 3. 5.   Matt. vi. 34.   1 Thess. iv. 13.

describes this "sorrowing after a godly sort" to consist in "carefulness, which it wrought in them," "clearing of themselves,"— "indignation,"—"fear,"—"vehement desire,"—"zeal,"—"revenge,"[1]—feelings, all of them, which open the heart, yet without relaxing it, in that they terminate in acts or works.

On the other hand, remorse, or what the Apostle calls "the sorrow of the world," worketh death. Instead of coming to the Fount of Life, to the God of all consolation, remorseful men feed on their own thoughts, without any confidant of their sorrow. They disburden themselves to no one : to God they will not, to the world they cannot confess. The world will not attend to their confession; it is a good associate, but it cannot be an intimate. It cannot approach us or stand by us in trouble; it is no Paraclete; it leaves all our feelings buried within us, either tumultuous, or, at best, dead : it leaves us gloomy or obdurate. Such is our state, while we live to the world, whether we be in sorrow or in joy. We are pent up within ourselves, and are therefore miserable. Perhaps we may not be able to analyse our misery, or even to realize it, as persons oftentimes who are in bodily sicknesses. We do not know, perhaps, what or where our pain is ; we are so used to it that we do not call it pain. Still so it is ; we need a relief to our hearts, that they may be dark and sullen no longer, or that they may not go on feeding upon themselves ; we need to escape from ourselves to something beyond ; and much as we may wish it otherwise, and may try to make idols to ourselves, nothing short of God's presence is our true refuge ; everything else is either a mockery, or but an expedient useful for its season or in its measure.

How miserable then is he who does not practically know this great truth ! Year after year he will be a more unhappy man, or, at least, he will emerge into a maturity of misery at once, when he passes out of this world of shadows into that kingdom where all is real. He is at present attempting to satisfy his soul with that which is not bread ; or he thinks the soul can thrive without nourishment. He fancies he can live without an object. He fancies that he is sufficient for himself ; or he supposes that knowledge is sufficient for his happiness ; or that exertion, or that the good opinion of others, or (what is called) fame, or that the comforts and luxuries of wealth, are sufficient for him. What a truly wretched state is that coldness and dryness of soul, in which so many live and die, high and low, learned and unlearned ! Many a great man, many a peasant,

[1] 2 Cor. vii. 7. 9. 11.

many a busy man, lives and dies with closed heart, with affections undeveloped, unexercised. You see the poor man, passing day after day, Sunday after Sunday, year after year, without a thought in his mind, to appearance almost like a stone. You see the educated man, full of thought, full of intelligence, full of action, but still with a stone heart, as cold and dead as regards his affections, as if he were the poor ignorant countryman. You see others, with warm affections, perhaps, for their families, with benevolent feelings towards their fellow-men, yet stopping there; centring their hearts on what is sure to fail them, as being perishable. Life passes, riches fly away, popularity is fickle, the senses decay, the world changes, friends die. One alone is constant; One alone is true to us; One alone can be true; One alone can be all things to us; One alone can supply our needs; One alone can train us up to our full perfection; One alone can give a meaning to our complex and intricate nature; One alone can give us tune and harmony; One alone can form and possess us. Are we allowed to put ourselves under His guidance? this surely is the only question. Has He really made us His children, and taken possession of us by His Holy Spirit? Are we still in His kingdom of grace, in spite of our sins? The question is not whether we should go, but whether He will receive. And we trust that, in spite of our sins, He will receive us still, every one of us, if we seek His face in love unfeigned and holy fear. Let us then do our part, as He has done His, and much more. Let us say with the Psalmist, "Whom have I in heaven but Thee? and there is none upon earth I desire in comparison of Thee. My flesh and my heart faileth; but God is the strength of my heart, and my portion for ever."[1]

[1] Ps. lxxiii. 25, 26.

SERMON XLIII.

(SUNDAYS AFTER TRINITY.)

The Power of the Will.

" Finally, my brethren, be strong in the Lord, and in the power of His might."—EPHES. vi. 10.

WE know that there are great multitudes of professed Christians, who, alas! have actually turned from God with a deliberate will and purpose, and, in consequence, are at present strangers to the grace of God; though they do not know, or do not care about this. But a vast number of Christians, half of the whole number at least, are in other circumstances. They have not thrown themselves out of a state of grace, nor have they to repent and turn to God, in the sense in which those must, who have allowed themselves in wilful transgression, after the knowledge of the truth has been imparted to them. Numbers there are in all ranks of life, who, having good parents and advisers, or safe homes, or religious pursuits, or being without strong feelings and passions, or for whatever reason, cannot be supposed to have put off from them the garment of divine grace, and deserted to the ranks of the enemy. Yet are they not safe, nevertheless. It is plain,—for surely it is not enough to avoid evil in order to attain to heaven,—we must follow after good. What, then, is their danger?—That of the unprofitable servant who hid his Lord's money. As far removed as that slothful servant was from those who traded with their talents, in his state and in his destiny, so far separate from one another are two classes of Christians who live together here as brethren,—the one class is using grace, the other neglecting it; one is making progress, the other sitting still; one is working for a reward, the other is idle and worthless.

This view of things should ever be borne in mind when we speak of the state of grace. There are different degrees in which we may stand in God's favour; we may be rising or sinking in His favour; we may not have forfeited it, yet we may not be securing it; we may be safe for the present, but have a dangerous prospect before us. We may be more or less "hypocrites," "slothful," "unprofitable," and yet our day of grace not be passed. We may still have the remains of our new nature lingering on us, the influences of grace present with us, and the power of amendment and conversion within us. We may still have talents which we may put to account, and gifts which we may stir up. We may not be cast out of our state of justification, and yet may be destitute of that love of God, love of God's truth, love of holiness, love of active and generous obedience, that honest surrender of self, which alone will secure to us hereafter the blessed words, "Well done, good and faithful servant; enter thou into the joy of thy Lord." [1]

The only qualification which will avail us for heaven is the love of God. We may keep from gross sinning, and yet not have this divine gift, "without which we are dead" in God's sight. This changes our whole being; this makes us live; this makes us grow in grace and abound in good works; this makes us fit for God's presence hereafter.

Now, here I have said a number of things, each of which will bear drawing out by itself, and insisting on.

No one can doubt that we are again and again exhorted in Scripture to be holy and perfect, to be holy and blameless in the sight of God, to be holy as He is holy, to keep the commandments, to fulfil the Law, to be filled with the fruit of righteousness. Why do we not obey as we ought? Many people will answer that we have a fallen nature, which hinders us; that we cannot help it, though we ought to be very sorry for it; that this is the reason of our shortcomings. Not so : we can help it; we are not hindered; what we want is the will; and it is our own fault that we have it not. We have all things granted to us; God has abounded in His mercies to us; we have a depth of power and strength lodged in us; but we have not the heart, we have not the will, we have not the love to use it. We lack this one thing, a desire to be new made; and I think any one who examines himself carefully, will own that he does, and that this is the reason why he cannot and does not obey or make progress in holiness.

[1] Matt. xxv. 21.

That we have this great gift within us, or are in a state of grace, for the two statements mean nearly the same thing, is very plain of course from Scripture. We all know what Scripture says on the subject, and yet even here it may be as well to dwell on one or two passages by way of reminding and impressing ourselves.

Consider then our Saviour's words : "The water that I shall give him, shall be in him a *well of water* springing up into everlasting life."[1] Exhaust the sea, it will not fill the infinite spaces of the heavens, but the gift within us may be drawn out till it fills eternity.

Again, consider St. Paul's most wonderful words in the Epistle from which the text is taken, when he gives glory to "Him who is able to do exceeding abundantly above all that we ask or think, according to the power that worketh in us."[2] You observe here, that there is a power given to us Christians, which "worketh in us," a special hidden mysterious power, which makes us its instruments. Even that we have souls, is strange and mysterious. We do not see our souls; but we see in others and we are conscious in ourselves of a principle which rules our bodies, and makes them what the brutes are not. We have that in us which informs our bodies, and changes them from mere animal bodies into human. Brutes cannot talk; brutes have little expression of countenance; they cannot form into societies; they cannot progress. Why? Because they have not that hidden gift which we have?—reason. Well, in like manner St. Paul speaks of Christians too as having a special power within them, which they gain because they are, and when they become Christians ; and he calls it, in the text to which I am referring, "the power that worketh in us." In a former chapter of the Epistle, he speaks of "the exceeding greatness of His power to us-ward who believe, according to the working of His mighty power;"[3] and he says that our eyes must be enlightened in order to recognise it ; and he compares it to that divine power in Christ our Saviour, by which, working in due season, He was raised from the dead, so that the bonds of death had no dominion over Him. As seeds have life in them, which seem lifeless, so the Body of Christ had life in itself, when it was dead ; and so also, though not in a similar way, we too, sinners as we are, have a spiritual principle in us, if we did but exert it, so great, so wondrous, that all the powers in the visible world, all the conceivable forces and appetites of matter, all the physical miracles which are at this day in process of discovery, almost superseding time and space,

[1] John iv. 14. [2] Ephes. iii. 20. [3] Ephes. i. 19.

2 A

dispensing with numbers, and rivalling mind, all these powers of nature are nothing to this gift within us. Why do I say this? because the Apostle tells us that God is able thereby "to do *exceeding abundantly above all* that we ask or think." You see he labours for words to express the exuberant, overflowing fulness, the vast and unfathomable depth, or what he has just called "the breadth, and length, and depth, and height" of the gift given us. And hence he elsewhere says, "I can do *all things* through Christ, which *strengtheneth* me;"[1] where he uses the same word which occurs also in the text, "My brethren, be *strong* in the Lord, and in the power of His might." See, what an accumulation of words! First, be *strong*, or be ye made strong. Strong in what? strong in power. In the power of what? in the power of His might, the might of God. Three words are used one on another, to express the manifold gift which God has given us. He to might has added power, and power He has made grow into strength. We have the power of His might; nor only so, but the strength of the power of His might who is Almighty.

And this is the very account which St. Luke gives us of St. Paul's own state in the Acts, after his conversion. The Jews wondered, but "Saul increased the more in *strength*, and confounded the Jews who dwelt at Damascus."[2] He became more and more strong. And at the end of his course, when brought before the Romans, "the Lord," as he says, "stood with him, and *strengthened* him;" and in turn he too exhorts Timothy, "Thou, therefore, my son, be *strong* in the grace that is in Christ Jesus; and the things that thou hast heard of me among many witnesses, the same commit thou to faithful men, who shall be able to teach others also. Thou therefore endure hardness, as a good soldier of Jesus Christ."[3]

I said just now that we did not need Scripture to tell us of our divinely-imparted power; that our own consciousness was sufficient. I do not mean to say that our consciousness will enable us to rise to the fulness of the Apostle's expressions; for trial, of course, cannot ascertain an inexhaustible gift. All we can know of it by experience is, that it goes beyond *us*, that *we* have never fathomed it, that we have drawn from it, and never emptied it; that we have evidence that there is *a* power with us, how great we know not, which does for us what we cannot do for ourselves, and is always equal to all our needs. And of as much as this, I think, we have abundant evidence.

[1] Phil. iv. 13.   [2] Acts ix. 22.   [3] 2 Tim. ii. 1-3; iv. 17.

Let us ask ourselves, why is it that we so often wish to do right and cannot? why is it that we are so frail, feeble, languid, wayward, dim-sighted, fluctuating, perverse? why is it that we cannot "do the things that we would?" why is it that, day after day, we remain irresolute, that we serve God so poorly, that we govern ourselves so weakly and so variably, that we cannot command our thoughts, that we are so slothful, so cowardly, so discontented, so sensual, so ignorant? Why is it that we, who trust that we are not by wilful sin thrown out of grace (for of such I am all along speaking), why is it that we, who are ruled by no evil masters and bent upon no earthly ends, who are not covetous, or profligate livers, or worldly-minded, or ambitious, or envious, or proud, or unforgiving, or desirous of name,—why is it that we, in the very kingdom of grace, surrounded by Angels, and preceded by Saints, nevertheless can do so little, and instead of mounting with wings like eagles, grovel in the dust, and do but sin, and confess sin, alternately? Is it that the *power* of God is not within us? Is it literally that we are *not able* to perform God's commandments? God forbid! We are able. We have that given us which makes us able. We are not in a state of nature. We have had the gift of grace implanted in us. We have a power within us to do what we are commanded to do. What is it we lack? The power? No; the will. What we lack is the real, simple, earnest, sincere inclination and aim to use what God has given us, and what we have in us. I say, our experience tells us this. It is no matter of mere doctrine, much less a matter of words, but of things; a very practical plain matter.

To take an instance of the simple kind. Is not the power to use our limbs our own, nay, even by nature? What then is sloth but a want of will? When we are not set on an object so greatly as to overcome the inconvenience of an effort, we remain as we are;—when we ought to exert ourselves we are slothful. But is the effort any effort at all, when we desire that which needs the effort?

In like manner, to take a greater thing. Are not the feelings as distinct as well can be, between remorse and repentance? In both a man is very sorry and ashamed of what he has done; in both he has a painful foreboding that he may perchance sin again in spite of his present grief. You will hear a man perhaps lament that he is so weak, so that he quite dreads what is to come another time, after all his good resolutions. There are cases, doubtless, in which a man *is* thus weak in power, though earnest in will ; and, of course, it continually happens that he has ungovernable feelings and passions in spite of his better nature. But in a very great multitude of cases this pretence of want of power is really but a want of will. When a man complains that he is under the dominion of any bad habit, let him seriously ask himself whether he has ever *willed* to get rid of it. Can he, with a simple mind, say in God's sight, " I wish it removed " ?

A man, for instance, cannot attend to his prayers ; his mind wanders ; other thoughts intrude ; time after time passes, and it is the same. Shall we say this arises from want of power ? Of course it may be so ; but before he says so, let him consider whether he has ever roused himself, shaken himself, awakened himself, got himself to will, if I may so say, attention. We know the feeling in unpleasant dreams, when we say to ourselves, " This is a dream," and yet cannot exert ourselves to will to be free from it ; and how at length by an effort we will to move, and the spell at once is broken ; we wake. So it is with sloth and indolence ; the Evil One lies heavy on us, but he has no power over us except in our unwillingness to get rid of him. He cannot battle with us ; he flies ; he can do no more, as soon as we propose to fight with him.

There is a famous instance of a holy man of old time, who before his conversion felt indeed the excellence of purity, but could not get himself to say more in prayer than " Give me chastity, but not yet." I will not be inconsiderate enough to make light of the power of temptation of any kind, nor will I presume to say that Almighty God will certainly shield a man from temptation for his wishing it ; but whenever men complain, as they often do, of the arduousness of a high virtue, at least it were well that they should first ask themselves the question, whether they desire to have it. We hear much in this day of the impossibility of heavenly purity ;—far be it from me to say that every one has not his proper gift from God, one after this manner, another after that ;—but, O ye men of the world, when ye talk, as ye do, so much of the impossibility of this or that supernatural grace, when you disbelieve in the existence of severe self-rule, when you scoff at holy resolutions, and affix a slur on those who make them, are you sure that the impossibility which you insist upon does not lie, not in nature, but in the will ? Let us but will, and our nature is changed, " according to the power that worketh in us." Say not, in excuse for others or for yourselves, that you cannot be other than Adam made you ; you have never brought yourselves to will it,—you cannot bear to will it. You cannot bear to be other than you are. Life would seem a blank to you, were you other; yet what you are from not desiring a gift, this you make an excuse for not possessing it.

Let us take what trial we please,—the world's ridicule or censure, loss of prospects, loss of admirers or friends, loss of ease, endurance of bodily pain,—and recollect how easy our course has been, directly we had once made up our mind to submit to it; how simple all that remained became, how wonderfully difficulties were removed from without, and how the soul was strengthened inwardly to do what was to be done. But it is seldom we have heart to throw ourselves, if I may so speak, on the Divine Arm; we dare not trust ourselves on the waters, though Christ bids us. We have not St. Peter's love to ask leave to come to Him upon the sea. When we once are filled with that heavenly charity, we can do all things, because we attempt all things,— for to attempt is to do.

I would have every one carefully consider whether he has ever found God fail him in trial, when his own heart had not failed him; and whether he has not found strength greater and greater given him according to his day; whether he has not gained clear proof on trial that he *has* a divine power lodged within him, and a certain conviction withal that he has not made the extreme trial of it, or reached its limits. Grace ever outstrips prayer. Abraham ceased interceding ere God stayed from granting. Joash smote upon the ground but thrice, when he might have gained five victories or six. All have the gift, many do not use it at all, none expend it. One wraps it in a napkin, another gains five pounds, another ten. It will bear thirty-fold, or sixty, or a hundred. We know not what we are, or might be. As the seed has a tree within it, so men have within them Angels.

Hence the great stress laid in Scripture on growing in grace. Seeds are intended to grow into trees. We are regenerated in order that we may be renewed daily after the Image of Him who has regenerated us. In the text and verses following, we have our calling set forth, in order to "stir up our pure minds, by way of remembrance,"[1] to the pursuit of it. "Be strong in the Lord," says the Apostle, "and in the power of His might. Put on the whole armour of God," with your loins girt about with truth, the breastplate of righteousness, your feet shod with the preparation of the gospel of peace, the shield of faith, the helmet of salvation, the sword of the Spirit. One grace and then another is to be perfected in us. Each day is to bring forth its

[1] 2 Pet. iii. 1.

own treasure, till we stand, like blessed spirits, able and waiting
to do the will of God.

Still more apposite are St. Peter's words, which go through the
whole doctrine which I have been insisting on, point by point.
First, he tells us that "divine power hath given unto us all
things that pertain unto life and godliness;"[1] that is, we have the
gift. Then he speaks of the *object* which the gift is to effect,—
"exceeding great and precious promises are given unto us, that
by these we may be *partakers of the divine nature;*" that we who,
by birth, are children of wrath, should become inwardly and really
sons of God; putting off our former selves, or, as he says,
"having escaped the corruption that is in the world through lust;"
that is, cleansing ourselves from all that remains in us of original
sin, the infection of concupiscence. With which closely agree
St. Paul's words to the Corinthians, "Having these promises," he
says, "dearly beloved, let us cleanse ourselves from all defilement
of the flesh and spirit, perfecting holiness in the fear of God."[2]
But to continue with St. Peter,—"Giving all diligence," he says,
"add to your faith virtue, and to virtue knowledge, and to knowledge temperance, and to temperance patience, and to patience
godliness, and to godliness brotherly kindness, and to brotherly
kindness charity." Next he speaks of those who, though they
cannot be said to have forfeited God's grace, yet by a sluggish
will and a lukewarm have become but unprofitable, and
"cumber the ground" in the Lord's vineyard. "He that lacketh
these things is blind, and cannot see afar off, and hath forgotten
that he was purged from his old sins,"—has forgotten that
cleansing which he once received, when he was brought into the
kingdom of grace. "Wherefore the rather, brethren, give diligence to make your calling and election sure; for if ye do these
things, ye shall never fall; for so an entrance shall be ministered
unto you abundantly, into the everlasting kingdom of our Lord
and Saviour Jesus Christ." Day by day shall ye enter deeper
and deeper into the fulness of the riches of that kingdom, of
which ye are made members.

Or, lastly, consider St. Paul's account of the same growth, and
of the course of it, in his Epistle to the Romans. "Tribulation
worketh patience, and patience experience, and experience hope,
and hope maketh not ashamed." Such is the series of gifts,
patience, experience, hope, a soul without shame,—and whence
all this? He continues, "Because the *love* of God is shed abroad
in our hearts, by the Holy Ghost which is given unto us."[3]

[1] 2 Pet. i. 3.   [2] 2 Cor. vii. 1.   [3] Rom. v. 3-5.

Love can do all things; "charity never faileth;" he that has the will, has the power. You will say, "But is not the will itself from God? and, therefore, is it not after all *His* doing, not ours, if we have *not* the will?" Doubtless, by nature, our will is in bondage; we cannot will good; but by the grace of God our will has been set free; we obtain again, to a certain extent, the gift of free-will; henceforth, we can will, or not will. If we will, it is doubtless from God's grace, who gave us the power to will, and to Him be the praise; but it is from ourselves too, because we have used that power which God gave. God enables us to will and to do; by nature we cannot will, but by grace we can; and now if we do not will, we are the cause of the defect. What can Almighty Mercy do for us which He hath not done? "He has given *all* things which pertain to life and godliness;" and we, in consequence, can "make our calling and election sure," as the holy men of God did of old time. Ah, how do those ancient Saints put us to shame! how were they "out of weakness made strong," how "waxed" they "valiant in fight," and became as Angels upon earth instead of men! And why?—because they had a heart to contemplate, to design, to *will* great things. Doubtless, in many respects, we all are but men to the end; we hunger, we thirst, we need sustenance, we need sleep, we need society, we need instruction, we need encouragement, we need example; yet who can say the heights to which in time men can proceed in all things, who beginning by little and little, yet in the distance shadow forth great things? "Enlarge the place of thy tent, and let them stretch forth the curtains of thine habitations; spare not, lengthen thy cords, and strengthen thy stakes; for thou shalt break forth on the right hand and on the left. . . . Fear not; for thou shalt not be ashamed; neither shalt thou be confounded, for thou shalt not be put to shame. . . . In righteousness shalt thou be established; thou shalt be far from oppression, for thou shalt not fear; and from terror, for it shall not come near thee. . . . This is the heritage of the servants of the Lord, and their righteousness is of Me, saith the Lord."[1]

High words like these relate in the first place to the Church, but doubtless they are also fulfilled in their measure in each of her true children. But we sit coldly and sluggishly at home; we fold our hands and cry, "A little more slumber;" we shut our eyes, we cannot see things afar off, we cannot "see the land which is very far off;" we do not understand that Christ calls us after

[1] Isa. liv. 2-4, 14, 17.

Him; we do not hear the voice of His heralds in the wilderness; we have not the heart to go forth to Him who multiplies the loaves, and feeds us by every word of His mouth. Other children of Adam have before now done in His strength what we put aside. We fear to be too holy. Others put us to shame; all around us, others are doing what we will not. Others are entering deeper into the kingdom of heaven than we. Others are fighting against their enemies more truly and bravely. The unlettered, the ungifted, the young, the weak and simple, with sling and stones from the brook, are encountering Goliath, as having on divine armour. The Church is rising up around us day by day towards heaven, and we do nothing but object, or explain away, or criticise, or make excuses, or wonder. We fear to cast in our lot with the Saints, lest we become a party; we fear to seek the strait gate, lest we be of the few, not the many. O may we be loyal and affectionate before our race is run! Before our sun goes down in the grave, O may we learn somewhat more of what the Apostle calls the love of Christ which passeth knowledge, and catch some of the rays of love which come from Him! Especially at the season of the year now approaching, when Christ calls us into the wilderness, let us gird up our loins and fearlessly obey the summons.[1] Let us take up our cross and follow Him. Let us take to us "the whole armour of God, that we may be able to stand against the wiles of the devil; for we wrestle not against flesh and blood, but against principalities, against powers, against the rulers of the darkness of this world, against spiritual wickedness in high places; wherefore, take unto you the whole armour of God, that ye may be able to withstand in the evil day, and, having done all, to stand."

Preached on Quinquagesima.

SERMON XLIV.

(SUNDAYS AFTER TRINITY.)

The Gospel Palaces.

" *He built His sanctuary like high palaces, like the earth which He hath established for ever.*"—PSALM lxxviii. 69.

THERE was one occasion when our Saviour said, " The hour cometh, when ye shall neither in this mountain, nor yet at Jerusalem, worship the Father. The hour cometh, when the true worshippers shall worship the Father in spirit and in truth."[1] Did we take these words by themselves, we might consider they implied that, under the Gospel, there would be no outward tokens of religion, no rites and ordinances at all, no public services, no assemblings of ourselves together, and especially no sacred buildings. Such an inference, however, would be a great error, if it were only for this reason, that it has never been received, never acted on in any age of the Church; so far from it, that I suppose there are few indeed but would shrink from the very mention of it, and none at all who could be found to testify that they had adopted it in their own case, yet had not suffered from it in point of inward devotion to God's service. That cannot be the true sense of Scripture, which never has been fulfilled, which ever has been contradicted and disobeyed; for God's word shall not return unto Him void, but shall accomplish His pleasure and prosper in His purpose. Our Saviour did *not* say to the Samaritan woman that there should be no places and buildings for worship under the Gospel, *because* He has *not* brought it to pass, *because* such ever have been, at all times and in all countries, and amid all differences of faith. And the same reasons which lead us to

[1] John iv. 21, 23.

believe that religious edifices are a Christian ordinance, though so very little is said about them in Scripture, will also show that it is right and pious to make them enduring, and stately, and magnificent, and ornamental ; so that our Saviour's declaration, when He foretold the destruction of the Temple at Jerusalem, was not that there should never be any other house built to His honour, but rather that there should be many houses ; that they should be built, not merely at Jerusalem, or at Gerizim, but everywhere ; what was under the Law a local ordinance, being henceforth a Catholic privilege, allowed not here and there, but wherever was the Spirit and the Truth. The glory of the Gospel is not the *abolition* of rites, but their *dissemination ;* not their absence, but their living and efficacious presence through the grace of Christ. Accordingly, such passages as the text, though spoken in the times of the Law, are fulfilled even at this day, and, as we trust, among ourselves. The Jewish Temple, indeed, of which the Psalmist spoke in the first instance, has come to nought; but he has a meaning still, and a noble one, as signifying the Christian institution of churches.

" He built His sanctuary like high palaces, like the earth which He hath established for ever." How much more strikingly and fully is this accomplished in our times than in those of the Law ! Rich and " exceeding magnifical " as was Solomon's Temple, and built at the immediate command of God, it is not presumptuous surely to say that Christian temples have as far surpassed it in size, beauty, and costliness, as in divine gifts and privileges, as in spirit and in truth. " He built His sanctuary like high palaces ; " look through this very country,—compare its palaces with its cathedrals and churches, even in their present state of disadvantage, and say whether these words are not more than accomplished ; so that the palaces of England should rather, by way of honour, be compared to the cathedrals, than the cathedrals to the palaces. And rightly so ; for our first duty is towards our Lord and His Church, and our second towards our earthly sovereign. And still more strikingly has the promise of permanence been fulfilled to us. For what were the years of Solomon's Temple ? Four hundred. What of the second Temple? Six hundred. These were long periods, certainly ; yet is it plain that the Church of Christ can more than equal them, and that in a great number of cases. Nay, there are Christian temples in some parts of the world which have lasted as much as fourteen hundred years. Surely, then, when Christ multiplied His sacred palaces, He also gave them an extended age, bringing back under the Gospel the days of the Antediluvian patriarchs. The times are reversed, and a more vigorous life has been infused among us than at the first, and the reign of Christ and His Saints has begun long since, and the Apostles fill their thrones in His temples. "He hath built His sanctuary like high palaces, like the earth which He hath established for ever."

Stability and permanence are, perhaps, the especial ideas which a church brings before the mind. It represents, indeed, the beauty, the loftiness, the calmness, the mystery, and the sanctity of religion also, and that in many ways; still, I will say, more than all these, it represents to us its eternity. It is the witness of Him who is the beginning and the ending, the first and the last; it is the token and emblem of "Jesus Christ, the same yesterday, to-day, and for ever;" it is the pledge of One who has said, "I will never leave thee nor forsake thee," but "even to your old age I am He, and even to hoar hairs I will carry you." All ye who take part in the building of a church, know that you have been admitted to the truest symbol of God's eternity. You have built what may be destined to have no end but in Christ's coming. Cast your thoughts back on the time when our ancient buildings were first reared. Consider the churches all around us; how many generations have passed since stone was put upon stone till the whole edifice was finished! The first movers and instruments of its erection, the minds that planned it, and the limbs that wrought at it, the pious hands that contributed to it, and the holy lips that consecrated it, have long, long ago, been taken away; yet we benefit by their good deed. Does it not seem a very strange thing that *we* should be fed, and lodged, and clothed in spiritual things, by persons we never saw or heard of, and who never saw us, or could think of us, hundreds of years ago? Does it not seem strange that men should be able, not merely by acting on others, not by a continued influence carried on through many minds in a long succession, but by one simple and direct act, to come into contact with us, and as if with their own hand to benefit us, who live centuries later? What a visible, palpable specimen this of the communion of saints! What a privilege thus to be immediately interested in the deeds of our forefathers! and what a call on us, in like manner, to reach out our own hands towards our posterity! Freely we have received; let us freely give. Let us not be slack to do what our fathers have done; to do a work, the fruits of which we cannot see, because they are too vast to be seen. If it were told us, that a word of ours, uttered by the mouth, should take, as it were, consistence, and float and continue in the air, and impart advice or comfort to men who were to live five hundred years to come, it would be an inspiring thought; and what but this is our very privilege, in the leave granted us to multiply the One Temple of God all over the earth, unto all time? It is to make our deeds live; it is to hold fellowship with the future.

See what a noble principle faith is. Faith alone lengthens a man's existence, and makes him, in his own feelings, live in the future and in the past. Men of this world are full of plans of the day. Even in religion they are ever coveting immediate results, and will do nothing at all, unless they can do everything, —can have their own way, choose their methods, and see the end. But the Christian throws himself fearlessly upon the future, because he believes in Him which is, and which was, and which is to come. He can endure to be one of an everlasting company while in this world, as well as in the next. He is content to begin, and break off; to do his part, and no more; to set about what others must accomplish; to sow where others must reap. None has finished his work and cut it short in righteousness but He who is One. We, His members, who have but a portion of His fulness, execute but a part of His purpose. One lays the foundation, and another builds thereupon; one levels the mountain, and another "brings forth the headstone with shoutings." Thus were our churches raised. One age would build a chancel, and another a nave, and a third would add a chapel, and a fourth a shrine, and a fifth a spire. By little and little the work of grace went forward; and they could afford to take time about it, and be at pains to do it best, who had a promise that the gates of hell should not prevail against it. Powers of the earth rise and fall; revolutions come in course; great families appear, and are swept away; wise men are in high places, and walk amid the sparks which they have kindled. They *feel* that they are short-lived, and they determine to make the most of their time. They grasp and push forwards, they are busy and feverish, not only from the feebleness and waywardness of their nature, but from the conviction of their reason, that they have but a short time. "Our time is short," say they; "let us buy and sell, and plant and build, and marry wives, and give in marriage, and eat and drink, for to-morrow we die." Poor worms of the earth, it is too true of them! Their aims and desires, their instruments, their goods, their bodies, their souls, are all perishable. In the words of the wise man, "as soon as they are born, they *begin* to draw to an end,"[1] they begin to die. Their growth and progress, their successes, are but the first stages of corruption and dissolution. Poor children of time, what are they? They triumph over religion in their day; they insult its ordinances and its ministers; they tyrannize in its temples, showing themselves that they are gods. They carry away its massive stones to their own houses, and trick themselves out with its jewels. They build up their families by rapine and sacrilege; they are wanton when they are not covetous; and, when satiated with pillage, they mutilate and defile what they do not destroy. But, after all, how speaks the Psalmist? "I have said, Ye are gods, and ye are all the children of the Most Highest. But ye shall die like men, and fall like one of the princes." "The proud have robbed, they have slept their sleep, and all the men whose hands were mighty have found nothing." "Fret not thyself because of the ungodly; neither be thou envious against the evil-doers; for they shall soon be cut down like the grass, and be withered even as the green herb. I myself have seen the ungodly in great power, and flourishing like a green bay tree; I went by, and lo, he was gone; I sought him, but his place could nowhere be found."[2] We rise in the morning, and, behold, they are all dead corpses. The storm has passed, the morning has broken, the Egyptians are cast on the sea-shore, God's Tabernacle is still standing. As though no violence had been in the night, no assaults of Satan and Antichrist, no arm of force, no envious or covetous eye, they remain, those holy places, where they were; for the Church abides for evermore, and her temples, in their deep foundations and their arching heights, are her image and manifestation.

I have said that the sacred edifices which we see around us, and in which we worship, remind us of their builders, though they lived so long ago; but in truth they remind us of a time far earlier even than theirs. Do we suppose that the very builders of these shrines were all in all in their building? Could any men whatever, did they but will it, at any time, build what they have built? is a cathedral the offspring of a random thought, a thing to will and to accomplish at our pleasure? or rather, were not those builders merely the successors and the children of others long before them, who made them what they were, and enabled them, under God, to do works, which it was not given to every one to do, but only to the sons of such fathers? Surely the churches which we inherit are not the purchase of wealth nor the creation of genius, they are the fruits of martyrdom. They come

[1] Wisd. v. 13.   [2] Ps. lxxxii. 6, 7; lxxvi. 5; xxxvii. 1, 2, 36, 37.

of high deeds and sufferings, as long before their very building as we are after it. Their foundations are laid very deep, even in the preaching of Apostles, and the confession of Saints, and the first victories of the Gospel in our land. All that is so noble in their architecture, all that captivates the eye and makes its way to the heart, is not a human imagination, but a divine gift, a moral result, a spiritual work. The Cross is ever planted in hazard and suffering, and is watered with tears and blood. Nowhere does it take root and bear fruit, except its preaching be with self-denial. It is easy, indeed, for the ruling powers to make a decree, and set religion on high, and extend its range, and herald its name ; but they cannot plant it, they can but impose it. The Church alone can plant the Church. The Church alone can found her sees, and enclose herself within walls. None but saintly men, mortified men, preachers of righteousness, and confessors for the truth, can create a home for the truth in any land. Thus the temples of God are withal the monuments of His Saints, and we call them by their names while we consecrate them to His glory. Their simplicity, grandeur, solidity, elevation, grace, and exuberance of ornament, do but bring to remembrance the patience and purity, the courage, meekness, and great charity, the heavenly affections, the activity in well-doing, the faith and resignation, of men who themselves did but worship in mountains, and in deserts, and in caves and dens of the earth. They laboured, but not in vain, for other men entered into their labours ; and, as if by natural consequence, at length their word prospered after them, and made itself a home, even these sacred palaces in which it has so long dwelt, and which are still vouchsafed to us, in token, as we trust, that they too are still with us who spoke that word, and, with them, His Presence, who gave them grace to speak it.

O happy they who, in a sorrowful time, avail themselves of this bond of communion with the Saints of old and with the Universal Church ! O wise and dutiful who, when the world has robbed them of so much, set the more account upon what remains ! We have not lost all, while we have the dwelling-places of our forefathers ; while we can repair those which are broken down, and build upon the old foundations, and propagate them upon new sites ! Happy they who, when they enter within their holy limits, enter in heart into the court of heaven ! And most unhappy who, while they have eyes to admire, admire them only for their beauty's sake and the skill they exhibit ; who regard them as works of art, not fruits of grace ; bow down before their

material forms, instead of worshipping " in spirit and in truth ; "
count their stones, and measure their spaces, but discern in them
no tokens of the invisible, no canons of truth, no lessons of
wisdom, to guide them forward in the way heavenward !

In heaven is the substance, of which here below we are vouchsafed the image ; and thither, if we be worthy, we shall at length
attain.   There is the holy Jerusalem, whose light is like unto a
stone most precious, even like a jasper stone, clear as crystal ;
and whose wall is great and high, with twelve gates, and an
Angel at each ;—whose glory is the Lord God Almighty, and the
Lamb is the light thereof.

SERMON XLV.

Religion a Weariness to the Natural Man.

" He hath no form nor comeliness; and when we shall see Him, there is no beauty that we should desire Him."—ISAIAH liii. 2.

"RELIGION is a weariness;" such is the judgment commonly passed, often avowed, concerning the greatest of blessings which Almighty God has bestowed upon us. And when God gave the blessing, He at the same time foretold that such would be the judgment of the world upon it, even as manifested in the gracious Person of Him whom He sent to give it to us. "He hath no form nor comeliness," says the prophet, speaking of our Lord and Saviour, "and when we shall see Him, there is no beauty that we should desire Him." He declared beforehand, that to man His religion would be uninteresting and distasteful. Not that this prediction excuses our deadness to it ; this dislike of the religion given us by God Himself, seen as it is on all sides of us,—of religion in all its parts, whether its doctrines, its precepts, its polity, its worship, its social influence,—this distaste for its very name must obviously be an insult to the Giver. But the text speaks of it as a fact, without commenting on the guilt involved in it ; and as such I wish you to consider it, as far as this may be done in reverence and seriousness. Putting aside for an instant the thought of the ingratitude and the sin which indifference to Christianity implies, let us, as far as we dare, view it merely as a matter of fact, after the manner of the text, and form a judgment on the probable consequences of it. Let us take the state of the case as it is found, and survey it dispassionately, as even an unbeliever might survey it, without at the moment considering whether it is sinful or not; as a misfortune, if we will, or a strange accident, or a necessary condition of our nature,—one of the phenomena, as it may be called, of the present world.

Let me then review human life in some of its stages and conditions, in order to impress upon you the fact of this contrariety between ourselves and our Maker : He having one will, we another ; He declaring one thing to be good for us, and we fancying other objects to be our good.

1. "Religion is a weariness ;" alas! so feel even children before they can well express their meaning. Exceptions of course now and then occur; and of course children are always more open to religious impressions and visitations than grown persons. They have many good thoughts and good desires, of which, in after-life, the multitude of men seem incapable. Yet who, after all, can have a doubt that, in spite of the more intimate presence of God's grace with those who have not yet learned to resist it, still, on the whole, religion is a weariness to children ? Consider their amusements, their enjoyments,—what they hope, what they devise, what they scheme, and what they dream about themselves in time future, when they grow up ; and say what place religion holds in their hearts. Watch the reluctance with which they turn to religious duties, to saying their prayers, or reading the Bible ; and then judge. Observe, as they get older, the influence which the fear of the ridicule of their companions has in deterring them even from speaking of religion, or seeming to be religious. Now the dread of ridicule, indeed, is natural enough ; but why should religion inspire ridicule ? What is there absurd in thinking of God ? Why should we be ashamed of worshipping Him ? It is unaccountable, but it is natural. We may call it an accident, or what we will ; still it is an undeniable fact, and that is what I insist upon. I am not forgetful of the peculiar character of children's minds : sensible objects first meet their observation ; it is not wonderful that they should at first be inclined to limit their thoughts to things of sense. A distinct profession of faith, and a conscious maintenance of principle, may imply a strength and consistency of thought to which they are as yet unequal. Again, childhood is capricious, ardent, light-hearted ; it cannot think deeply or long on any subject. Yet all this is not enough to account for the fact in question—why they should feel this distaste for the very subject of religion. Why should they be ashamed of paying reverence to an unseen, all-powerful God, whose existence they do not disbelieve ? Yet they do feel

2 B

ashamed of it. Is it that they are ashamed of themselves, not of their religion; feeling the inconsistency of professing what they cannot fully practise? This refinement does not materially alter the view. of the case; for it is merely their own acknowledgment that they do not love religion as much as they ought. No; we seem compelled to the conclusion, that there is by nature some strange discordance between what we love and what God loves. So much, then, on the state of boyhood.

2. "Religion is a weariness." I will next take the case of young persons when they first enter into life. Here I may appeal to some perhaps who now hear me. Alas! my brethren, is it not so? Is not religion associated in your minds with gloom, melancholy, and weariness? I am not at present going so far as to reprove you for it, though I might well do so; if I did, perhaps you might at once turn away, and I wish you calmly to think the matter over, and bear me witness that I state the fact correctly. It is so; you cannot deny it. The very terms "religion," "devotion," "piety," "conscientiousness," "mortification," and the like, you find to be inexpressibly dull and cheerless : you cannot find fault with them, indeed, you would if you could; and whenever the words are explained in particulars and realized, then you do find occasion for exception and objection. But though you cannot deny the claims of religion used as a vague and general term, yet how irksome, cold, uninteresting, uninviting, does it at best appear to you! how severe its voice! how forbidding its aspect! With what animation, on the contrary, do you enter into the mere pursuits of time and the world! What bright anticipations of joy and happiness flit before your eyes! How you are struck and dazzled at the view of the prizes of this life, as they are called! How you admire the elegancies of art, the brilliance of wealth, or the force of intellect! According to your opportunities you mix in the world, you meet and converse with persons of various conditions and pursuits, and are engaged in the numberless occurrences of daily life. You are full of news; you know what this or that person is doing, and what has befallen him; what has not happened, which was near happening, what may happen. You are full of ideas and feelings upon all that goes on around you. But, from some cause or other, religion has no part, no sensible influence, in your judgment of men and things. It is out of your way. Perhaps you have your pleasure parties; you readily take your share in them time after time; you pass continuous hours in society where you know that it is quite impos-

sible even to mention the name of religion. Your heart is in
scenes and places where conversation on serious subjects is
strictly forbidden by the rules of the world's propriety. I do
not say we should discourse on religious subjects wherever we
go; I do not say we should make an effort to discourse on them
at any time, nor that we are to refrain from social meetings in
which religion does not lie on the surface of the conversation :
but I do say, that when men find their pleasure and satisfaction
to lie in society which proscribes religion, and when they
deliberately and habitually prefer those amusements which have
necessarily nothing to do with religion, such persons cannot
view religion as God views it. And this is the point : that
the feelings of our hearts on the subject of religion are
different from the declared judgment of God ; that we have
a natural distaste for that which He has said is our chief
good.

3. Now let us pass to the more active occupations of life.
Here, too, religion is confessedly felt to be wearisome, it is out
of place. The transactions of worldly business, speculations in
trade, ambitious hopes, the pursuit of knowledge, the public
occurrences of the day, these find a way directly to the heart ;
they rouse, they influence. It is superfluous to go about to prove
this innate power over us of things of time and sense, to make
us think and act. The name of religion, on the other hand, is
weak and impotent ; it contains no spell to kindle the feelings
of man, to make the heart beat with anxiety, and to produce
activity and perseverance. The reason is not merely that men
are in want of leisure, and are sustained in a distressing continuance of exertion, by their duties towards those dependent on
them. They have their seasons of relaxation, they turn for a
time from their ordinary pursuits ; still religion does not attract
them, they find nothing of comfort or satisfaction in it. For a
time they allow themselves to be idle. They want an object to
employ their minds upon ; they pace to and fro in very want of
an object ; yet their duties to God, their future hopes in another
state of being, the revelation of God's mercy and will, as contained in Scripture, the news of redemption, the gift of regeneration, the sanctities, the devotional heights, the nobleness and
perfection which Christ works in His elect, do not suggest
themselves as fit subjects to dispel their weariness. Why?
Because religion makes them melancholy, say they, and they
wish to relax. Religion is a labour, it is a weariness, a greater
weariness than the doing nothing at all. "Wherefore," says

Solomon, " is there a price in the hand of a fool to get wisdom, seeing he hath no heart to it?"[1]

4. But this natural contrariety between man and his Maker is still more strikingly shown by the confessions of men of the world who have given some thought to the subject, and have viewed society with somewhat of a philosophical spirit. Such men treat the demands of religion with disrespect and negligence, on the ground of their being unnatural. They say, "It is natural for men to love the world for its own sake; to be engrossed in its pursuits, and to set their hearts on the rewards of industry, on the comforts, luxuries, and pleasures of this life. Man would not be man if he could be made otherwise; he would not be what he was evidently intended for by his Maker." Let us pass by the obvious *answer* that might be given to this objection; it is enough for my purpose that it is *commonly urged*, recognising as it does the fact of the disagreement existing between the claims of God's Word, and the inclinations and natural capacities of man. Many, indeed, of those unhappy men who have denied the Christian faith, treat the religious principle altogether as a mere unnatural, eccentric state of mind, a peculiar untoward condition of the affections to which weakness will reduce a man, whether it has been brought on by anxiety, oppressive sorrow, bodily disease, excess of imagination or the like, and temporary or permanent, according to the circumstances of the disposing cause; a state to which we all are liable, as we are liable to any other mental injury, but unmanly and unworthy of our dignity as rational beings. Here again it is enough for our purpose, that it is allowed by these persons that the love of religion is unnatural and inconsistent with the original condition of our minds.

The same remark may be made upon the notions which secretly prevail in certain quarters at the present day, concerning the unsuitableness of Christianity to an enlightened age. Men there are who look upon the inspired Word of God with a sort of indulgence, as if it had its use, and had done service in its day; that in times of ignorance it awed and controlled fierce barbarians, whom nothing else could have subdued; but that from its very claim to be divine and infallible, and its consequent unalterableness, it is an obstacle to the improvement of the human race beyond a certain point, and must ultimately fall before the gradual advancement of mankind in knowledge and virtue. In other words, the literature of the day is weary of Revealed Religion.

[1] Prov. xvii. 16.

5. Once more; that religion is in itself a weariness is seen even in the conduct of the better sort of persons, who really on the whole are under the influence of its spirit. So dull and uninviting is calm and practical religion, that religious persons are ever exposed to the temptation of looking out for excitements of one sort or other, to make it pleasurable to them. The spirit of the Gospel is a meek, humble, gentle, unobtrusive spirit. It doth not cry nor lift up its voice in the streets, unless called upon by duty so to do, and then it does it with pain. Display, pretension, conflict, are unpleasant to it. What then is to be thought of persons who are ever on the search after novelties to make religion interesting to them; who seem to find that Christian activity cannot be kept up without unchristian party-spirit, or Christian conversation without unchristian censoriousness? Why, this; that religion is to them as to others, taken by itself, a weariness, and requires something foreign to its own nature to make it palatable. Truly it is a weariness to the natural man to serve God humbly and in obscurity; it is very wearisome, and very monotonous, to go on day after day watching all we do and think, detecting our secret failings, denying ourselves, creating within us, under God's grace, those parts of the Christian character in which we are deficient; wearisome to learn modesty, love of insignificance, willingness to be thought little of, backwardness to clear ourselves when slandered, and readiness to confess when we are wrong; to learn to have no cares for this world, neither to hope nor to fear, but to be resigned and contented !

I may close these remarks, by appealing to the consciences of all who have ever set about the work of religion in good earnest, whoever they may be, whether they have made less, or greater progress in their noble toil, whether they are matured saints, or feeble strugglers against the world and the flesh. They have ever confessed how great efforts were necessary to keep close to the commandments of God; in spite of their knowledge of the truth, and their faith, in spite of the aids and consolations they receive from above, still how often do their corrupt hearts betray them ! Even their privileges are often burdensome to them, even to pray for the grace which in Christ is pledged to them is an irksome task. They know that God's service is perfect freedom, and they are convinced, both in their reason and from their own experience of it, that it is true happiness ; still they confess withal the strange reluctance of their nature to love their Maker and His Service. And this is the point in question ; not only the mass of mankind, but even the confirmed servants of Christ, witness to the opposition which exists between their own nature and the demands of religion.

This, then, is the remarkable fact which I proposed to show. Can we doubt that man's will runs contrary to God's will—that the view which the inspired Word takes of our present life, and of our destiny, does not satisfy us, as it rightly ought to do? that Christ hath no form nor comeliness in our eyes; and though we see Him, we see no desirable beauty in Him? That holy, merciful, and meek Saviour, the Eternal, the Only-begotten Son of God, our friend and infinite benefactor—He who left the glory of His Father and died for us, who has promised us the overflowing riches of His grace both here and hereafter, He is a light shining in a dark place, and "the darkness comprehendeth it not." "Light is come into the world, and men love darkness rather than light." The nature of man is flesh, and that which is born of the flesh is flesh, and ever must so remain; it never can discern, love, accept, the holy doctrines of the Gospel. It will occupy itself in various ways, it will take interest in things of sense and time, but it can never be religious. It is at enmity with God.

And now we see what must at once follow from what has been said. If our hearts are by nature set on the world for its own sake, and the world is one day to pass away, what are they to be set on, what to delight in, then? Say, how will the soul feel when, stripped of its present attire, which the world bestows, it stands naked and shuddering before the pure, tranquil, and severe majesty of the Lord its God, its most merciful yet dishonoured Maker and Saviour? What are to be the pleasures of the soul in another life? Can they be the same as they are here? They cannot; Scripture tells us they cannot; the world passeth away —now what is there left to love and enjoy through a long eternity? What a dark, forlorn, miserable eternity that will be!

It is then plain enough, though Scripture said not a word on the subject, that if we would be happy in the world to come, we must make us new hearts, and begin to love the things we naturally do not love. Viewing it as a practical point, the end of the whole matter is this, we must be changed; for we cannot, we cannot expect the system of the universe to come over to us; the inhabitants of heaven, the numberless creations of Angels, the glorious company of the Apostles, the goodly fellowship of the Prophets, the noble army of Martyrs, the holy Church universal, the Will and Attributes of God, these are fixed. We must go over to them. In our Saviour's own authoritative words : "Verily, verily, except a man be born again, he cannot see the kingdom of God." [1] It is a plain matter of self-interest to turn our thoughts to the means of changing our hearts, putting out of the question our duty towards God and Christ, our Saviour and Redeemer.

"He hath no form nor comeliness, and when we see Him, there is no beauty that we should desire Him." It is not His loss that we love Him not, it is our loss. He is All-blessed, whatever becomes of us. He is not less blessed because we are far from Him. It is we who are not blessed, except as we approach Him, except as we are like Him, except as we love Him. Woe unto us, if in the day in which He comes from heaven we see nothing desirable or gracious in His wounds ; but instead, have made for ourselves an ideal blessedness, different from that which will be manifested to us in Him. Woe unto us, if we have made pride, or selfishness, or the carnal mind, our standard of perfection and truth ; if our eyes have grown dim, and our hearts gross, as regards the true light of men, and the glory of the Eternal Father. May He Himself save us from our self-delusions, whatever they are, and enable us to give up this world, that we may gain the next ;—and to rejoice in Him, who had no home of His own, no place to lay His head, who was poor and lowly, and despised and rejected, and tormented and slain !

[1] John iii. 3.

SERMON XLVI.

(SUNDAYS AFTER TRINITY.)

The World our Enemy.

" We know that we are of God, and the whole world lieth in wickedness."
—I JOHN v. 19.

FEW words are of more frequent occurrence in the language
of religion than "the world;" Holy Scripture makes continual mention of it, in the way of censure and caution; in the
Service for Baptism it is described as one of three great enemies
of our souls; and in the ordinary writings and conversation of
Christians, I need hardly say, mention is made of it continually.
Yet most of us, it would appear, have very indistinct notions
what the world means. We know that the world is a something
dangerous to our spiritual interests, and that it is in some way
connected with human society—with men as a mixed multitude,
contrasted with men one by one, in private and domestic life;
but what it is, how it is our enemy, how it attacks, and how it
is to be avoided, is not so clear. Or if we conceive some distinct
notion concerning it, still probably it is a wrong notion,—which
leads us, in consequence, to misapply the Scripture precepts relat-
ing to the world; and this is even worse than overlooking them.
I shall now, then, attempt to show what is meant by the world,
and how, in consequence, we are to understand the information
and warnings of the sacred writers concerning it.

1. Now, first, by the world is very commonly meant the present visible system of things, without taking into consideration
whether it is good or bad. Thus St. John contrasts the world
with the things that are in it, which are evil, "Love not the
world, *neither* the things that are in the world."[1] Again, he

[1] 1 John ii. 15.

presently says, "The world passeth away, *and* the lust thereof."
Here, as in many other parts of Scripture, the world is not spoken
of as actually sinful in itself (though its lusts are so, of course),
but merely as some present visible system which is likely to
attract us, and is not to be trusted, because it cannot last. Let
us first consider it in this point of view.

There is, as a matter of necessity, a great variety of stations
and fortunes among mankind; hardly two persons are in the
same outward circumstances, and possessed of the same mental
resources. Men differ from each other, and are bound together
into one body or system by the very points in which they differ;
they depend on each other; such is the will of God. This system
is the world, to which it is plain belong our various modes of
supporting ourselves and families by exertion of mind and body,
our intercourse with others, our duty towards others, the social
virtues,—industry, honesty, prudence, justice, benevolence, and
the like. These spring all from our present lot in life, and tend
to our present happiness. This life holds out prizes to merit
and exertion. Men rise above their fellows; they gain fame
and honours, wealth and power, which we therefore call worldly
goods. The affairs of nations, the dealings of people with people,
the interchange of productions between country and country, are
of this world. We are educated in boyhood for this world; we
play our part on a stage more or less conspicuous, as the case may
be; we die, we are no more, we are forgotten, as far as the present state of things is concerned; all this is of the world.

By the world, then, is meant this course of things which we
see carried on by means of human agency, with all its duties and
pursuits. It is not necessarily a sinful system; rather it is
framed, as I have said, by God Himself, and therefore cannot be
otherwise than good. And yet even thus considering it, we are
bid not to love the world : even in this sense the world is an
enemy of our souls; and for this reason, because the love of it
is dangerous to beings circumstanced as we are,—things in themselves good being not good to us sinners. And this state of
things which we see, fair and excellent in itself, is very likely
(for the very reason that it is seen, and because the spiritual and
future world is not seen) to seduce our wayward hearts from our
true and eternal good. As the traveller on serious business may
be tempted to linger, while he gazes on the beauty of the prospect which opens on his way, so this well-ordered and divinely-
governed world, with all its blessings of sense and knowledge,
may lead us to neglect those interests which will endure when

itself has passed away. In truth, it promises more than it can fulfil. The goods of life and the applause of men have their excellence, and, as far as they go, are really good ; but they are short-lived. And hence it is that many pursuits in themselves honest and right are nevertheless to be engaged in with caution, lest they seduce us ; and those perhaps with especial caution which tend to the wellbeing of men in this life. The sciences, for instance, of good government, of acquiring wealth, of preventing and relieving want, and the like, are for this reason especially dangerous ; for fixing, as they do, our exertions on this world as an end, they go far to persuade us that they have no other end ; they accustom us to think too much of success in life and temporal prosperity ; nay, they may even teach us to be jealous of religion and its institutions, as if these stood in our way, preventing us from doing so much for the worldly interests of mankind as we might wish.

In this sense it is that St. Paul contrasts sight and faith. We see this world ; we only believe that there is a world of spirits, we do not see it : and inasmuch as sight has more power over us than belief, and the present than the future, so are the occupations and pleasures of this life injurious to our faith. Yet not, I say, in themselves sinful ; as the Jewish system was a temporal system, yet divine, so is the system of nature—this world— divine, though temporal. And as the Jews became carnal-minded even by the influence of their divinely-appointed system, and thereby rejected the Saviour of their souls ; in like manner, men of the world are hardened by God's own good world into a rejection of Christ. In neither case through the fault of the things which are seen, whether miraculous or providential, but accidentally, through the fault of the human heart.

2. But now, secondly, let us proceed to consider the world, not only as dangerous, but as positively sinful, according to the text—"the whole world lieth in wickedness." It was created well in all respects, but even before it as yet had fully grown out into its parts, while as yet the elements of human society did but lie hid in the nature and condition of the first man, Adam fell ; and thus the world, with all its social ranks, and aims, and pursuits, and pleasures, and prizes, has ever from its birth been sinful. The infection of sin spread through the whole system, so that although the framework is good and divine, the spirit and life within it are evil. Thus, for instance, to be in a high station is the gift of God ; but the pride and injustice to which it has given scope is from the Devil. To be poor and obscure is

also the ordinance of God; but the dishonesty and discontent which are often seen in the poor is from Satan. To cherish and protect wife and family is God's appointment; but the love of gain, and the low ambition, which lead many a man to exert himself, are sinful. Accordingly, it is said in the text, "The world lieth in wickedness,"—it is plunged and steeped, as it were, in a flood of sin, not a part of it remaining as God originally created it, not a part pure from the corruptions with which Satan has disfigured it.

Look into the history of the world, and what do you read there? Revolutions and changes without number, kingdoms rising and falling; and when without crime? States are established by God's ordinance, they have their existence in the necessity or man's nature; but when was one ever established, nay, or maintained, without war and bloodshed? Of all natural instincts, what is more powerful than that which forbids us to shed our fellows' blood? We shrink with natural horror from the thought of a murderer; yet not a government has ever been settled, or a state acknowledged by its neighbours, without war and the loss of life; nay, more than this, not content with unjustifiable bloodshed, the guilt of which must lie somewhere, instead of lamenting it as a grievous and humiliating evil, the world has chosen to honour the conqueror with its amplest share of admiration. To become a hero, in the eyes of the world, it is almost necessary to break the laws of God and man. Thus the deeds of the world are matched by the opinions and principles of the world: it adopts bad doctrine to defend bad practice; it loves darkness because its deeds are evil.

And as the affairs of nations are thus depraved by our corrupt nature, so are all the appointments and gifts of Providence perverted in like manner. What can be more excellent than the vigorous and patient employment of the intellect; yet in the hands of Satan it gives birth to a proud philosophy. When St. Paul preached, the wise men of the world, in God's eyes, were but fools, for they had used their powers of mind in the cause of error; their reasonings even led them to be irreligious and immoral; and they despised the doctrine of a resurrection which they neither loved nor believed. And again, all the more refined arts of life have been disgraced by the vicious tastes of those who excelled in them; often they have been consecrated to the service of idolatry; often they have been made the instruments of sensuality and riot. But it would be endless to recount the manifold and complex corruption which man has introduced into the world which God made good; evil has preoccupied the whole of it, and holds fast its conquest. We know, indeed, that the gracious God revealed Himself to His sinful creatures very soon after Adam's fall. He showed His will to mankind again and again, and pleaded with them through many ages; till at length His Son was born into this sinful world in the form of man, and taught us how to please Him. Still, hitherto the good work has proceeded slowly: such is His pleasure. Evil had the start of good by many days; it filled the world, it holds it: it has the strength of possession, and it has its strength in the human heart; for though we cannot keep from approving what is right in our conscience, yet we love and encourage what is wrong; so that when evil was once set up in the world, it was secured in its seat by the unwillingness with which our hearts relinquish it.

And now I have described what is meant by the sinful world; that is, the world as corrupted by man, the course of human affairs viewed in its connection with the principles, opinions, and practices which actually direct it. There is no mistaking these; they are evil; and of these it is that St. John says, "If any man love the world, the love of the Father is not in him. For all that is in the world, the lust of the flesh, and the lust of the eyes, and the pride of life, is not of the Father, but is of the world." [1]

The world, then, is the enemy of our souls; first, because, however innocent its pleasures, and praiseworthy its pursuits may be, they are likely to engross us unless we are on our guard : and secondly, because in all its best pleasures, and noblest pursuits, the seeds of sin have been sown; an enemy hath done this; so that it is most difficult to enjoy the good without partaking of the evil also. As an orderly system of various ranks, with various pursuits and their several rewards, it is to be considered not sinful indeed, but dangerous to us. On the other hand, considered in reference to its principles and actual practices, it is really a sinful world. Accordingly, when we are bid in Scripture to shun the world, it is meant that we must be cautious, lest we love what is good in it too well, and lest we love the bad at all.— However, there is a mistaken notion sometimes entertained, that the world is some particular set of persons, and that to shun the world is to shun them; as if we could point out, as it were, with the finger, what is the world, and thus could easily rid ourselves of one of our three great enemies. Men who are beset with this notion are often great lovers of the world notwithstanding, while

[1] 1 John ii. 15, 16.

they think themselves at a distance from it altogether. They love its pleasures, and they yield to its principles, yet they speak strongly against men of the world, and avoid them. They act the part of superstitious people, who are afraid of seeing evil spirits in what are considered haunted places, while these spirits are busy at their hearts instead, and they do not suspect it.

3. Here, then, is a question which it will be well to consider, viz. how far the world is a separate body from the Church of God. The two are certainly contrasted in the text, as elsewhere in Scripture. "We know that *we* are of God, and *the whole world* lieth in wickedness." Now the true account of this is, that the Church, so far from being literally, and in fact, separate from the wicked world, is within it. The Church is a body, gathered together in the world, and in a process of separation from it. The world's power, alas ! is over the Church, because the Church has gone forth into the world to save the world. All Christians are in the world, and of the world, so far as sin still has dominion over them ; and not even the best of us is clean every whit from sin. Though then, in our idea of the two, and in their principles, and in their future prospects, the Church is one thing, and the world is another, yet in present matter of fact, the Church is of the world, not separate from it ; for the grace of God has but partial possession even of religious men, and the best that can be said of us is, that we have two sides, a light side and a dark, and that the dark happens to be the outermost. Thus we form part of the world to each other, though we be not of the world. Even supposing there were a society of men influenced individually by Christian motives, still this society, viewed as a whole, would be a worldly one ; I mean a society holding and maintaining many errors, and countenancing many bad practices. Evil ever floats at the top. And if we inquire why it is that the good in Christians is seen less than the bad ? I answer, first, because there is less of it ; and secondly because evil forces itself upon general notice, and good does not. So that in a large body of men, each contributing his portion, evil displays itself on the whole conspicuously, and in all its diversified shapes. And thirdly, from the nature of things, the soul cannot be understood by any but God, and a religious spirit is, in St. Peter's words, "the hidden man of the heart." It is only the actions of others which we see for the most part, and since there are numberless ways of doing wrong, and but one of doing right, and numberless ways too of regarding and judging the conduct of others, no wonder that even the better sort of

men, much more the generality, are, and seem to be, so sinful. God only sees the circumstances under which a man acts, and why he acts in this way and not in that. God only sees perfectly the train of thought which preceded his action, the motive, and the reasons. And God alone (if aught is ill done, or sinfully) sees the deep contrition afterwards,—the habitual lowliness, then bursting forth into special self-reproach,—and the meek faith casting itself wholly upon God's mercy. Think for a moment how many hours in the day every man is left wholly to himself and his God, or rather how few minutes he is in intercourse with others—consider this, and you will perceive how it is that the life of the Church is hid with God, and how it is that the outward conduct of the Church must necessarily look like the world, even far more than it really is like it, and how vain, in consequence, the attempt is (which some make) of separating the world distinctly from the Church. Consider, moreover, how much there is, while we are in the body, to stand in the way of one mind communicating with another. We are imprisoned in the body, and our intercourse is by means of words, which feebly represent our real feelings. Hence the best motives and truest opinions are misunderstood, and the most sound rules of conduct misapplied by others. And Christians are necessarily more or less strange to each other ; nay, and as far as the appearance of things is concerned, almost mislead each other, and are, as I have said, the world one to another. It is long, indeed, before we become at all acquainted with each other, and we appear the one to the other cold, or harsh, or capricious, or self-willed, when we are not so. So that it unhappily comes to pass, that even good men retire from each other into themselves, and to their God, as if retreating from the rude world.

And if all this takes place in the case of the better sort of men, how much more will it happen in the case of those multitudes who are still unstable in faith and obedience, half Christians, not having yet wrought themselves into any consistent shape of opinion and practice ! These, so far from showing the better part of themselves, often affect to be worse even than they are. Though they have secret fears and misgivings, and God's grace pleads with their conscience, and seasons of seriousness follow, yet they are ashamed to confess to each other their own seriousness, and they ridicule religious men lest they should be themselves ridiculed.

And thus, on the whole, the state of the case is as follows : that if we look through mankind in order to find out who make up the world, and who do not, we shall find none who are not of the world ; inasmuch as there are none who are not exposed to infirmity. So that if to shun the world is to shun some body of men so called, we must shun all men, nay, ourselves too—which is a conclusion which means nothing at all.

But let us, avoiding all refinements which lead to a display of words only, not to the improvement of our hearts and conduct, let us set to work practically ; and instead of attempting to judge of mankind on a large scale, and to settle deep questions, let us take what is close at hand and concerns ourselves, and make use of such knowledge as we can obtain. Are we tempted to neglect the worship of God for some temporal object ? this is of the world, and not to be admitted. Are we ridiculed for our conscientious conduct ? this again is a trial of the world, and to be withstood. Are we tempted to give too much time to our recreations ; to be idling when we should be working ; reading or talking when we should be busy in our temporal calling ; hoping for impossibilities, or fancying ourselves in some different state of life from our own ; over-anxious of the good opinion of others ; bent upon getting the credit of industry, honesty, and prudence ? all these are temptations of this world. Are we discontented with our lot, or are we over-attached to it, and fretful and desponding when God recalls the good He has given ? this is to be worldly-minded.

Look not about for the world as some vast and gigantic evil far off—its temptations are close to you, apt and ready, suddenly offered and subtle in their address. Try to bring down the words of Scripture to common life, and to recognise the evil in which this world lies in your own hearts.

When our Saviour comes He will destroy this world, even His own work, and much more the lusts of the world, which are of the Evil One ; then at length we must lose the world, even if we cannot bring ourselves to part with it now. And we shall perish with the world, if on that day its lusts are found within us. "The world passeth away, and the lust thereof, but he that doeth the will of God abideth for ever."

SERMON XLVII.

(SUNDAYS AFTER TRINITY.)

The Praise of Men.

" *They loved the praise of men more than the praise of God.*"
—JOHN xii. 43.

THIS is spoken of the chief rulers of the Jews, who, though they believed in Christ's Divine mission, were afraid to confess Him, lest they should incur temporal loss and shame from the Pharisees. The censure passed by St. John on these persons is too often applicable to Christians at the present day; perhaps, indeed, there is no one among us who has not at some time or other fallen under it. We love the good opinion of the world more than the approbation of Him who created us, redeemed us, has regenerated us, and who still preserves to us the opportunity of preparing ourselves for His future presence. Such is too often the case with us. It is well we should be aware that it is so; it is well we should dwell upon it, and that we should understand and feel that it is wrong, which many men do not.

Now it is an obvious question, Why is it wrong to love the praise of men? For it may be objected, that we are accustomed to educate the young by means of praise and blame; that we encourage them by kind words *from us*, that is, from man; and punish them for disobedience. If, then, it may be argued, it is right to regard the opinions of others concerning us in our youth, it cannot be in itself wrong to pay attention to it at any other period of life. This is true; but I do not say that the mere love of praise and fear of shame are evil: regard to the corrupt world's praise or blame, this is what is sinful and dangerous. St. John, in the text, implies that the praise of men was, at the time spoken of, in opposition to the praise of God. It *must* be wrong to prefer anything to the will of God. To seek praise is in itself as little wrong as it is wrong to hope, and to fear, and to love, and to trust; all depends upon the object hoped, or feared, or loved, or trusted; to seek the praise of good men is not wrong, any more than to love or to reverence good men; only wrong when it is in excess, when it interferes with the exercise of love and reverence towards God. Not wrong while we look on good men singly as instruments and servants of God; or, in the words of Scripture, while "we glorify God in them."[1] But to seek the praise of bad men is in itself as wrong as to love the company of bad men, or to admire them. It is not, I say, merely the love of praise that is a sin, but love of the corrupt world's praise. This is the case with all our natural feelings and affections; they are all in themselves good, and implanted by God; they are sinful, because we have in us by nature a something more than them, viz. an evil principle which perverts them to a bad end. Adam, before his fall, felt, we may suppose, love, fear, hope, joy, dislike, as we do now; but then he felt them only when he ought, and as he ought; all was harmoniously attempered and rightly adjusted in his soul, which was at unity with itself. But, at the fall, this beautiful order and peace was broken up; the same passions remained, but their use and action were changed; they rushed into extremes, sometimes excessive, sometimes the reverse. Indignation was corrupted into wrath, self love became selfishness, self-respect became pride, and emulation envy and jealousy. They were at variance with each other; pride struggled with self-interest, fear with desire. Thus his soul became a chaos, and needed a new creation. Moreover, as I have said, his affections were set upon unsuitable objects. The natural man looks to this world, the world is his god; faith, love, hope, joy, are not excited in his mind by things spiritual and divine, but by things seen and temporal.

Considering, then, that love of praise is not a bad principle in itself, it is plain that a parent may very properly teach his child to love his praise, and fear his blame, when that praise and blame are given in accordance with God's praise and blame, and made subservient to them. And, in like manner, if the world at large took a correct and religious view of things, then its praise and blame would in its place be valuable too. Did the world admire what God admires; did it account humility, for instance, a great

Gal. i. 24.

2 c

virtue, and pride a great sin; did it condemn that spirit of self-importance and sensitiveness of disgrace which calls itself a love of honour; did it think little of temporal prosperity, wealth, rank, grandeur, and power; did it condemn arrogant and irreverent disputing, the noisy, turbulent spirit of ambition, the love of war and conquest, and the perverse temper which leads to jealousy and hatred; did it prefer goodness and truth to gifts of the intellect; did it think little of quickness, wit, shrewdness, power of speech and general acquirements, and much of patience, meekness, gentleness, firmness, faith, conscientiousness, purity, forgiveness of injuries,—then there would be no sin in our seeking the world's praise; and though we still ought to love God's praise above all, yet we might love the praise of the world in its degree, for it would be nothing more nor less than the praise of good men. But since, alas! the contrary is the case, since the world (as Scripture tells us) "lieth in wickedness," and the principles and practices which prevail on all sides of us are not those which the All-holy God sanctions, we cannot lawfully seek the world's praise. We cannot serve two masters who are enemies the one to the other. We are forbidden to love the world or anything that is of the world, for it is not of the Father, but passeth away.

This is the reason why it is wrong to pursue the world's praise; viz. because we cannot have it and God's praise too. And yet, as the pursuit of it is wrong, so is it common,—for this reason: because God is unseen, and the world is seen; because God's praise and blame are future, the world's are present; because God's praise and blame are inward, and come quietly and without keenness, whereas the world's are very plain and intelligible, and make themselves felt.

Take, for instance, the case of the young, on (what is called) entering into life. Very many, indeed, there are, whether in a higher or lower station, who enter into the mixed society of others early; so early, that it might be thought they had hardly had time to acquire any previous knowledge of right and wrong, any standard of right and wrong, other than the world gives, any principles by which to fight against the world. And yet it cannot quite be so. Whatever is the first time persons hear evil, it is quite certain that good has been beforehand with them, and they have a something within them which tells them it is evil. And much more, if they have been blessed, as most men are, with the protection of parents, or the kind offices of teachers or of God's ministers, they generally have principles of duty more or less strongly imprinted on their minds; and on their first intercourse with strangers they are shocked or frighted at seeing the improprieties and sins which are openly countenanced. Alas! there are persons, doubtless (though God forbid it should be the case with any here present!), whose consciences have been so early trained into forgetfulness of religious duties, that they can hardly, or cannot at all, recollect the time I speak of; the time when they acted with the secret feeling that God saw them, saw all they did and thought. I will not fancy this to be the case with any who hear me. Rather, there are many of you, in different ranks and circumstances, who have, and ever have had, general impressions on your minds of the claims which religion has on you, but, at the same time, have been afraid of acting upon them, afraid of the opinion of the world, of what others would say if you set about obeying your conscience. Ridicule is a most powerful instrument in the hands of Satan, and it is most vividly felt by the young. If any one wishes to do his duty, it is most easy for the cold, the heartless, and the thoughtless, to find out harsh, or provoking, or ridiculous names to fix upon him. My brethren, so many of you as are sensitive of the laughter or contempt of the world, this is your cross; you must wear it, you must endure it patiently; it is the mark of your conformity to Christ; He despised the shame: you must learn to endure it, from the example and by the aid of your Saviour. You must love the praise of God more than the praise of men. It is the very trial suited to you, appointed for you, to establish you in the faith. You are not tempted with gain or ambition, but with ridicule. And be sure, that unless you withstand it, you cannot endure hardships as good soldiers of Jesus Christ, you will not endure other temptations which are to follow. How can you advance a step in your after and more extended course till the first difficulty is overcome? You need faith, and "a double-minded man," says St. James, "is unstable in all his ways." Moreover, be not too sure that all who show an inclination to ridicule you feel exactly as they say. They speak with the loudest speaker; speak you boldly, and they will speak with you. They have very little of definite opinion themselves, or probably they even feel with you, though they speak against you. Very likely they have uneasy, unsatisfied consciences, though they seem to sin so boldly; and are as afraid of the world as you can be, nay, more so; they join in ridiculing you, lest others should ridicule them; or they do so in a sort of self-defence against the reproaches of their own consciences. Numbers in this bad world talk loudly against

religion in order to encourage each other in sin, because they
need encouragement. They are cowards, and rely on each other
for support against their fears. They know they ought to be
other than they are, but are glad to avail themselves of anything that looks like argument to overcome their consciences
withal. And ridicule is a kind of argument—such as it is; and
numbers ridiculing together are a still stronger one—of the same
kind. Anyhow, there are few indeed who will not feel afterwards, in times of depression or alarm, that you are right, and
they themselves are wrong. Those who serve God faithfully
have a friend of their own, in each man's bosom, witnessing for
them; even in those who treat them ill. And I suppose no
young person has been able, through God's mercy, to withstand
the world's displeasure, but has felt at this time or that, that
this is so, and in a little time will, with all humility, have the
comfort of feeling it while he is withstanding the world.

But now supposing he has not had strength of mind to withstand the world, but has gone the way of the world. Suppose
he has joined the multitude in saying and doing what he should
not. We know the careless, thoughtless, profane habits which
most men live in, making light of serious subjects, and being
ashamed of godliness and virtue; ashamed of going to church
regularly, ashamed of faith, ashamed of chastity, ashamed of
innocence, ashamed of obedience to persons in authority. Supposing a person has been one of these, and then through God's
grace repents. It often pleases God, in the course of His
Providence, to rouse men to reflection by the occurrences of life.
In such circumstances they certainly will have a severe trial to
stand against the world. Nothing is more painful in the case
of such persons than the necessity often imposed upon them
of acting contrary to the opinion and wishes of those with
whom they have till now been intimate,—whom they have
admired and followed. Intimacies have already been formed,
and ties drawn tight, which it is difficult to sever. What is the
person in question to do? rudely to break them at once? no.
But is he to share in sins in which he formerly took part? no;
whatever censure, contempt, or ridicule attaches to him in consequence. But what, then, is he to do? His task, I say, is painful and difficult, but he must not complain, for it is his own
making; it is the natural consequence of his past neglect of God.
So much is plain,—he must abstain from all sinful actions; not
converse lightly or irreverently where formerly he was not unwilling so to do; not spend his time, as heretofore, in idleness or

riot; avoid places whither he is not called by actual duty, which offer temptation to sin; observe diligently attendance on church; not idle away the Lord's Day in vanity, or worse; not add to the number of his acquaintance any thoughtless persons. All this is quite plain, and in doing this I know he will incur the ridicule of his companions. He will have much to bear. He must bear to be called names, to be thought a hypocrite, to be thought to be affecting something out of the way, to be thought desirous of recommending himself to this or that person. He must be prepared for malicious and untrue reports about himself; many other trials must he look for. They are his portion. He must pray God to enable him to bear them meekly. He must pray for himself, he must pray for those who ridicule him. He has deserved ridicule. He has nothing to boast of, if he bears it well. He has nothing to boast of that he incurs it. He has nothing to boast of, as if he were so much better than those who ridicule him; he was once as they are now. He is now just a little better than they are. He has just begun a new life. He has got a very little way in it, or rather no way, nothing beyond professing it; and he has the reproach of the world in consequence of his profession. Well, let him see to it that this reproach is not in vain, that he has a right to the reproach. Let him see to it that he acts as well as professes. It will be miserable indeed if he incurs the reproach, and yet does not gain the reward. Let him pray God to perfect in him what He has begun in him, and to begin and perfect it also in all those that reproach him. Let him pray for Christ's grace to bear hardships in Christ's spirit; to be able to look calmly in the world's face, and bear its frown; to trust in the Lord, and be doing good; to obey God, and so to be reproached, not for professing only, but for performing, not for doing nothing, but for doing something, and in God's cause. If we *are* under reproach, let us have something to show for it. At present, such a one is but a child in the Gospel; but in time, St. Peter's words will belong to him, and he may appropriate them. "This is thankworthy, if a man for conscience towards God endure grief, suffering wrongfully. For what glory is it, if when ye be buffeted for your faults ye shall take it patiently? but if, when ye do well and suffer for it, ye take it patiently, this is acceptable with God."

What happens to the young in one way, and to penitent sinners in another, happens in one way or other to all of us. In the case of all of us occasions arise, when practices countenanced by others do not approve themselves to our consciences. If after serious thought we find we cannot acquiesce in them, we must follow our consciences, and stand prepared for the censure of others. We must submit (should it be unavoidable) to appear to those who have no means of understanding us, self-willed, or self-conceited, or obstinate, or eccentric, or headstrong, praying the while that God's mercy may vouchsafe to us that we be not really what we seem to the world.

Some are exposed to a temptation of a different kind, that of making themselves seem more religious than they really are. It may happen, that to advocate right opinions may be profitable to our worldly interests, and be attended by the praise of men. You may ask, since in such cases God and man approve the same thing, why should the applause of the world be accounted dangerous then? I answer, it is dangerous because God requires of us a modest silence in our religion; but we cannot be religious in the eyes of men without displaying religion. I am now speaking of display. God sees our thoughts without our help, and praises *them;* but we cannot be praised by men without being seen by men: whereas often the very excellence of a religious action, according to our Saviour's precept, consists in the not being seen by others. This is a frequent cause of hypocrisy in religion. Men begin by feeling as they should feel, then they think it a very hard thing that men should not know how well they feel, and in course of time they learn to speak without feeling. Thus they have learned to "love the praise of men more than the praise of God."—We have to guard against another danger, against the mistake of supposing that the world's despising us is a proof that we are particularly religious; for this, too, is often supposed. Frequently it happens that we encumber our religion with extravagances, perversions, or mistakes, with which religion itself has no necessary connection, and these, and not religion, excite the contempt of the world. So much is this the case, that the censure of numbers, or of the sober-minded, or of various and distinct classes of men, or censure consistently urged, or continued consistently, ought always to lead a man to be very watchful as to what he considers right to say or do in the line of duty, to lead him to examine his principles; to lead him, however thoroughly he adheres to these after all, to be unaffectedly humble about himself, and to convince him in matter of fact (what he might be quite sure of beforehand, from the nature of the case), that, however good his principles are in themselves, he is mixing up with them the alloy of his own frail and corrupt nature.

In conclusion, I would say to those who fear the world's cen
sure, this :—

1. Recollect you cannot please all parties, you must disagree
with some or other : you have only to choose (if you are determined to look to man) with which you will disagree. And,
further, you may be sure that those who attempt to please all
parties, please fewest; and that the best way to gain the world's
good opinion (even if you were set upon this, which you must
not be) is to show that you prefer the praise of God. Make up
your mind to be occasionally misunderstood, and undeservedly
condemned. You must, in the Apostle's words, go through evil
report, and good report, whether on a contracted or a wider field
of action. And you must not be anxious even for the praise of
good men. To have, indeed, the approbation of those whose
hearts are guided by God's Holy Spirit, is indeed much to be
coveted. Still this is a world of discipline, not of enjoyment;
and just as we are sometimes bound in duty to abstain from
indulgences of sense in themselves innocent, so are we sometimes
bound to deny ourselves the satisfaction derived from the praise
even of the religious and conscientious. Only let us beware in
all this lest we act from pride and self-conceit.

2. In the next place, think of the multitude of beings who,
unseen themselves, may yet be surveying our conduct. St. Paul
charges Timothy by the elect Angels ; [1] and elsewhere he declares
that the Apostles were made "a spectacle unto the world, and to
Angels, and to men." [2] Are we then afraid to follow what is
right, lest the world should scoff? rather let us be afraid not to
follow it, because God sees us, and Christ, and the holy Angels.
They rejoice over one sinner that repenteth ; how must they
mourn over those who fall away ! What interest, surely, is
excited among them by the sight of the Christian's trial, when
faith and the desire of the world's esteem are struggling in his
heart for victory ! what rejoicing if, through the grace of God,
he overcomes ! what sorrow and pity if he is overcome by the
world ! Accustom yourselves, then, to feel that you are on a
public stage, whatever your station of life may be ; that there are
other witnesses to your conduct besides the world around you ;
and, if you feel shame of men, you should much more feel shame
in the presence of God, and those servants of His that do His
pleasure.

3. Still further : you fear the judgment of men upon you.
What will you think of it on your deathbed? The hour must

[1] 1 Tim. v. 21. [2] 1 Cor. iv. 9.

come, sooner or later, when your soul is to return to Him who
gave it.   Perhaps you will be sensible of your awful state.
What will you then think of the esteem of the world?   will not
all below seem to pass away, and be rolled up as a scroll, and the
extended regions of the future solemnly set themselves before
you?   Then how vain will appear the applause or blame of
creatures, such as we are, all sinners and blind judges, and feeble
aids, and themselves destined to be judged for their deeds.
When, then, you are tempted to dread the ridicule of man, throw
your mind forward to the hour of death.   You know what you
will then think of it, if you are then able to think at all.

4. The subject is not exhausted.   You fear shame ; well, and
will you not shrink from shame at the judgment-seat of Christ?
There will be assembled all the myriads of men who ever lived,
a vast multitude !   There will be Apostles, Prophets, Martyrs,
and all Saints from the beginning of time.   There will be all the
good men you ever heard of or knew.   There will be your own
kindest and best friends, your pious parents, or brothers, or
children.   Now what think you of being put to shame before all
these?   You fear the contempt of one small circle of men; what
think you of the Saints of God, of St. Mary, of St. Peter and St.
Paul, of the ten thousand generations of mankind, being witnesses of your disgrace ?   You dread the opinion of those whom
you do not love ; but what if a father then shrink from a dear
son, or the wife, or husband, your earthly companion, then
tremble at the sight of you, and feel ashamed of you ?   Nay,
there is One greater than parents, husbands, or brothers ; One of
whom you have been ashamed on earth ; and what will He, that
merciful but neglected Saviour, think of you then ?   Hear His
own words : "Whosoever shall be ashamed of Me and of My
words, of him shall the Son of Man be ashamed, when He shall
come in His own glory, and in His Father's, and of the holy
Angels."   Then such unhappy men, how will they feel shame at
themselves !   they will despise and loathe themselves ; they will
hate and abominate their own folly ; they will account themselves brutish and mad, so to have been beguiled by the devil,
and to have trifled with the season of mercy.   "Many of them
that sleep in the dust of the earth," says Daniel, "shall awake,
some to everlasting life, and some to shame and everlasting
contempt."

Let us, then, rouse ourselves, and turn from man to God ;
what have we to do with the world, who from our infancy have
been put on our journey heavenward ?   Take up your cross and

follow Christ. He went through shame far greater than can be yours. Do you think He felt nothing when He was lifted up on the Cross to public gaze, amid the contempt and barbarous triumphings of His enemies, the Pharisees, Pilate and his Roman guard, Herod and his men of war, and the vast multitude collected from all parts of the world? They all looked on Him with hatred and insult; yet He endured (we are told), "despising the shame."[1] It is a high privilege to be allowed to be conformed to Christ; St. Paul thought it so, so have all good men. The whole Church of God, from the days of Christ to the present, has been ever held in shame and contempt by men of this world. Proud men have reasoned against its divine origin; crafty men have attempted to degrade it to political purposes: still it has lasted for many centuries; it will last still, through the promised help of God the Holy Ghost; and that same promise which is made to it first as a body is assuredly made also to every one of us who seeks grace from God through it. The grace of our Lord and Saviour is pledged to every one of us without measure, to give us all necessary strength and holiness when we pray for it; and Almighty God tells us Himself, "Fear ye not the reproach of men, neither be ye afraid of their revilings. For the moth shall eat them up like a garment, and the worm shall eat them like wool; but My righteousness shall be for ever, and My salvation from generation to generation."

[1] Heb. xii. 2.

SERMON XLVIII.

(SUNDAYS AFTER TRINITY.)

Religion pleasant to the Religious.

" O taste and see how gracious the Lord is: blessed is the man that trusteth in Him."—PSALM xxxiv. 8.

YOU see by these words what love Almighty God has towards us, and what claims He has upon our love. He is the Most High, and All-Holy. He inhabiteth eternity: we are but worms compared with Him. He would not be less happy though He had never created us; He would not be less happy though we were all blotted out again from creation. But He is the God of love; He brought us all into existence, because He found satis-faction in surrounding Himself with happy creatures: He made us innocent, holy, upright, and happy. And when Adam fell into sin, and his descendants after him, then ever since He has been imploring us to return to Him, the Source of all good, by true repentance. "Turn ye, turn ye," He says, "why will ye die? As I live I have no pleasure in the death of the wicked." "What could have been done more to My vineyard that I have not done to it?"[1] And in the text He condescends to invite us to Him: "O taste and see how gracious the Lord is: blessed is the man that trusteth in Him." As if He said, "If you would but make trial, one trial, if you would but be persuaded to taste and judge for yourself, so excellent is His graciousness, that you would never cease to desire, never cease to approach Him:" ac-cording to the saying of the wise man, "They that eat Me shall yet be hungry, and they that drink Me shall yet be thirsty."[2]

This excellence and desirableness of God's gifts is a subject again and again set before us in Holy Scripture. Thus the

[1] Ezek. xxxiii. 11. Isa. v. 4.   [2] Ecclus. xxiv. 21.

Prophet Isaiah speaks of the "feast of fat things, a feast of wines on the lees; of fat things full of marrow, of wines on the lees well refined."[1] And again, under images of another kind: "He hath sent Me . . . . to give . . . . beauty for ashes, the oil of joy for mourning, the garment of praise for the spirit of heaviness, that they may be called Trees of Righteousness."[2] Or again, the Prophet Hosea: "I will be as the dew unto Israel: he shall grow as the lily, and cast forth his roots as Lebanon. His branches shall spread, and his beauty shall be as the olive-tree, and his smell as Lebanon. They that dwell under his shadow shall return; they shall revive as the corn, and grow as the vine: the scent thereof shall be as the wine of Lebanon."[3] And the Psalmist: "O that My people would have hearkened unto Me . . . . the haters of the Lord should have been found liars, but their time should have endured for ever. He should have fed them also with the finest wheat flour, and with honey out of the stony rock should I have satisfied thee."[4] You see all images of what is pleasant and sweet in nature are brought together to describe the pleasantness and sweetness of the gifts which God gives us in grace. As wine enlivens, and bread strengthens, and oil is rich, and honey is sweet, and flowers are fragrant, and dew is refreshing, and foliage is beautiful; so, and much more, are God's gifts in the Gospel enlivening, and strengthening, and rich, and sweet, and fragrant, and refreshing, and excellent. And as it is natural to feel satisfaction and comfort in these gifts of the visible world, so it is but natural and necessary to be delighted and transported with the gifts of the world invisible; and as the visible gifts are objects of desire and search, so much more is it, I do not merely say a duty, but a privilege and blessedness, to "taste and see how gracious the Lord is."

Other passages in the Psalms speak of this blessedness besides the text. "Thou hast put gladness in my heart," says the Psalmist, "since the time that their corn and wine and oil increased."[5] "The lot is fallen unto me in a fair ground, yea, I have a goodly heritage."[6] Again, "The statutes of the Lord are right, and rejoice the heart . . . . more to be desired are they than gold, yea, than much fine gold, sweeter also than honey and the honeycomb."[7] "My heart trusted in Him, and I am helped; therefore my heart danceth for joy, and in my song will I praise Him."[8] Once more: "Blessed is the man whom Thou choosest

---

[1] Isa. xxv. 6.
[2] Isa. lxi. 1-3.
[3] Hos. xiv. 5-7.
[4] Ps. lxxxi. 13-16.
[5] Ps. iv. 7.
[6] Ps. xvi. 6.
[7] Ps. xix. 10.
[8] Ps. xxviii. 7.

and receivest unto Thee : he shall dwell in Thy courts, and shall be satisfied with the pleasures of Thy house, even of Thy holy temple."[1]

I wish it were possible, my brethren, to lead men to greater holiness and more faithful obedience by setting before them the high and abundant joys which they have who serve God : "In His presence is fulness of joy," "the well of life ; " and they are satisfied with "the plenteousness of His house," and "drink of His pleasures as out of a river ; " but this is, I know, just what most persons will not believe. They think that it is very right and proper to be religious ; they think that it would be better for themselves in the world to come if they were religious now. They do not at all deny either the duty or the expedience of leading a new and holy life ; but they cannot understand how it can be pleasant : they cannot believe or admit that it is more pleasant than a life of liberty, laxity, and enjoyment. They, as it were, say, "Keep within bounds, speak within probability, and we will believe you ; but do not shock our reason. We will admit that we *ought* to be religious, and that, when we come to die, we shall be very glad to have led religious lives : but to tell us that it is a *pleasant* thing to be religious, this is too much : it is not true ; we feel that it is not true ; all the world knows and feels it is not true ; religion is something unpleasant, gloomy, sad, and troublesome. It imposes a number of restraints on us ; it keeps us from doing what we would ; it will not let us have our own way ; it abridges our liberty ; it interferes with our enjoyments ; it has fewer, far fewer, joys at present than a worldly life, though it gains for us more joys hereafter." This is what men say, or would say, if they understood what they feel, and spoke their minds freely.

Alas ! I cannot deny that this *is* true in the case of most men. Most men do not like the service of God, though it be perfect freedom ; they like to follow their own ways, and they are only religious so far as their conscience obliges them ; they are like Balaam, desirous of "the death of the righteous," not of his life. Indeed, this is the very thing I am lamenting and deploring. I lament, my brethren, that so many men, nay, I may say, that so many of you, do *not* like religious service. I do not deny it ; but I lament it. I do not deny it : far from it. I know quite well how many there are who do not like coming to church, and who make excuses for keeping away at times when they might come. I know how many there are who do not come to the Most Holy

[1] Ps. lxv. 4.

Sacrament, I know that there are numbers who do not say their prayers in private morning and evening. I know how many there are who are ashamed to be thought religious, who take God's Name in vain, and live like the world. Alas! this is the very thing I lament,—that God's service is not pleasant to you. It is not pleasant to those who do not like it : true; but it *is* pleasant to those who *do*. Observe, this is what I say; not that it is pleasant to those who like it not, but that it is pleasant to those who like it. Nay, what I say is, that it is much *more* pleasant to those who like it than anything of this world is pleasant to those who do not like it. This is the point. I do not say that it is pleasant to most men ; but I say that it is in itself the most pleasant thing in the world. Nothing is so pleasant as God's service to those *to whom* it is pleasant. The pleasures of sin are not to be compared in fulness and intensity to the pleasures of holy living. The pleasures of holiness are far more pleasant to the holy than the pleasures of sin to the sinner. O that I could get you to believe this ! O that you had a heart to feel it and know it ! O that you had a heart to taste God's pleasures and to make proof of them ; to taste and see how gracious the Lord is !

None can know, however, the joys of being holy and pure but the holy. If an Angel were to come down from heaven, even he could not explain them to you ; nor could he in turn understand what the pleasures of sin are. Do you think that an Angel could be made to understand what are the pleasures of sin? I trow not. You might as well attempt to persuade him that there was pleasure in feasting on dust and ashes. There are brute animals who wallow in the mire and eat corruption. This seems strange to us : much stranger to an Angel is it how any one can take pleasure in anything so filthy, so odious, so loathsome as sin. Many men, as I have been saying, wonder what possible pleasure there can be in anything so melancholy as religion. Well : be sure of this,—it is *more* wonderful to an Angel what possible pleasure there can be in sinning. It is *more* wonderful, I say. He would turn away with horror and disgust, both because sin is so base a thing in itself and because it is so hateful in God's sight.

Let no persons, then, be surprised that religious obedience should really be so pleasant in itself when it seems to them so distasteful. Let them not be surprised that *what* the pleasure is cannot be explained to *them*. It is a secret till they try to be religious. Men know what sin is by experience. They do not know what holiness is; and they cannot obtain the knowledge of its secret pleasure, till they join themselves truly and heartily to Christ, and devote themselves to His service,—till they "taste," and thereby try.   This pleasure is as hidden from them as the pleasures of sin are hidden from the Angels.   The Angels have never eaten the forbidden fruit, and their eyes are not open to know good and evil.   And we *have* eaten the forbidden fruit, —at least Adam did, and we are his descendants,—and our eyes *are* open to know evil.   And, alas! on the other hand, they have become blinded to good; they require opening to see, to know, to understand good.   And till our eyes *are* opened spiritually, we *shall* ever think religion distasteful and unpleasant, and shall wonder how any one can like it.   Such is our miserable state,— we are blind to the highest and truest glories, and dead to the most lively and wonderful of all pleasures;—and no one can describe them to us.   None other than God the Holy Spirit can help us in this matter, by enlightening and changing our hearts. So it is; and yet I will say one thing, by way of suggesting to you how great and piercing the joys of religion are.   Think of this.   Is there any one who does not know how very painful the feeling of a bad conscience is?   Do not you recollect, my brethren, some time or other, having done something you knew to be wrong? and do you not remember afterwards what a piercing bitter feeling came on you?   Is not the feeling of a bad conscience different from any other feeling, and more distressing than any other, till we have accustomed ourselves to it? Persons do accustom themselves and lose this feeling; but till we blunt our conscience, it is very painful.   And why?   It is the feeling of God's displeasure, and therefore it is so painful. Consider then: if God's displeasure is so distressing to us, must not God's approval and favour be just the reverse; like life from the dead, most exceedingly joyful and transporting?   And this is what it is to be holy and religious.   It is to have God's favour. And, as it is a great misery to be under God's wrath, so it is a great and wonderful joy to be in God's favour; and those who know what a misery the former is, may fancy, though they do not know, how high a blessing the latter is.   From what you know, then, judge of what you do not know.   From the miseries of guilt, which, alas! you have experienced, conjecture the blessedness of holiness and purity which you have not experienced.   From the pain of a bad conscience, believe in the unspeakable joy and gladness of a good conscience.

I have been addressing those who do not know what religious

peace and divine pleasures are; but there are those present, I hope, who in a measure are not strangers to them. I know that none of us gain all the pleasure from God's service which it might afford us; still some of us, I hope, gain some pleasure. I hope there are some of those who hear me, who take a pleasure in coming to church, in saying their prayers, in thinking of God, in singing Psalms, in blessing Him for the mercies of the Gospel, and in celebrating Christ's death and resurrection, as at this season of the year.[1] These persons have "tasted" and tried. I trust they find the taste so heavenly, that *they* will not need any proof that religion is a pleasant thing; nay, more pleasant than anything else, worth the following above all other things, and unpleasant only to those who are not religious.

Let such persons then think of this, that if a religious life is pleasant here, in spite of the old Adam interrupting the pleasure and defiling them, what a glorious day it will be, if it is granted to us hereafter to enter into the Kingdom of Heaven! None of us, even the holiest, can guess *how* happy we shall be; for St. John says, "We know not what we shall be;"[2] and St. Paul, "Now we see in a glass darkly, but then face to face." Yet in proportion to our present holiness and virtue, we have some faint ideas of what will then be our blessedness. And in Scripture various descriptions of heaven are given us, in order to arrest, encourage, and humble us. We are told that the Angels of God are very bright, and clad in white robes. The Saints and Martyrs too are clad in white robes, with palms in their hands; and they sing praises unto Him that sitteth upon the Throne, and to the Lamb. When our Lord was transfigured, He showed us what Heaven is. His raiment became white as snow, white and glistening. Again, at one time He appeared to St. John, and then, "His head and His hairs were white like wool, as white as snow; and His eyes were as a flame of fire; and His feet like unto fine brass, as if they burned in a furnace; and His countenance was as the sun shineth in his strength."[3] And what Christ is, such do His Saints become hereafter. Here below they are clad in a garment of sinful flesh; but when the end comes, and they rise from the grave, they shall inherit glory, and shall be ever young and ever shining. In that day, all men will see and be convinced, even bad men, that God's servants are really happy, and only they. In that day, even lost souls, though they will not be able to understand the blessedness of religion, will have no doubt at all of what they now doubt, or pretend to doubt,

[1] Easter.   [2] 1 John iii. 2.   [3] Rev. i. 14-16.

that religion *is* blessed.   They laugh at religion, think strictness to be narrowness of mind, and regularity to be dulness; and give bad names to religious men.   They will not be able to do so then. They think themselves the great men of the earth now, and look down upon the religious; but then, who would not have been a religious man to have so great a reward? who will then have any heart to speak against religion, even though he has not " a heart to fear God and keep all His commandments always"?   In that day, they will look upon the righteous man, and "be amazed at the strangeness of his salvation, so far beyond all that they looked for.   And they, repenting and groaning for anguish of spirit, shall say within themselves, This was he whom we had sometimes in derision, and a proverb of reproach.   We fools accounted his life madness, and his end to be without honour; how is he numbered among the children of God, and his lot is among the saints !"[1]

Think of all this, my brethren, and rouse yourselves, and run forward with a good courage on your way towards heaven.   Be not weary in welldoing, for in due season we shall reap, if we faint not.   Strive to enter in at the strait gate.   Strive to get holier and holier every day, that you may be worthy to stand before the Son of Man.   Pray God to teach you His will, and to lead you forth in the right way, because of your enemies.   Submit yourselves to His guidance, and you will have comfort given you, according to your day, and peace at the last.

[1] Wisd. v. 2-5.

SERMON XLIX.

(SUNDAYS AFTER TRINITY.)

Mental Prayer.

"Pray without ceasing."—I THESS. v. 17.

THERE are two modes of praying mentioned in Scripture; the one is prayer at set times and places, and in set forms; the other is what the text speaks of,—continual or habitual prayer. The former of those is what is commonly called prayer, whether it be public or private. The other kind of praying may also be called holding communion with God, or living in God's sight, and this may be done all through the day, wherever we are, and is commanded us as the duty, or rather the characteristic, of those who are really servants and friends of Jesus Christ.

These two kinds of praying are also natural duties. I mean, we should in a way be bound to attend to them, even if we were born in a heathen country, and had never heard of the Bible. For our conscience and reason would lead us to practise them, if we did but attend to these divinely-given informants. I shall here confine myself to the consideration of the latter of the two, habitual or inward prayer, which is enjoined in the text, with the view of showing what it is, and how we are to practise it; and I shall speak of it, first, as a natural duty, and then as the characteristic of a Christian.

1. At first sight, it may be difficult to some persons to understand what is meant by praying always. Now consider it as a natural duty, that is, a duty taught us by natural reason and religious feeling, and you will soon see what it consists in.

What does nature teach us about ourselves, even before opening the Bible?—that we are creatures of the Great God, the Maker of heaven and earth; and that, as His creatures, we are

2 D

bound to serve Him and give Him our hearts; in a word, to be religious beings. And next, what is religion but a habit? and what is a habit but a state of mind which is always upon us, as a sort of ordinary dress or inseparable garment of the soul? A man cannot really be religious one hour, and not religious the next. We might as well say he could be in a state of good health one hour, and in bad health the next. A man who is religious, is religious morning, noon, and night; his religion is a certain character, a mould in which his thoughts, words, and actions are cast, all forming parts of one and the same whole. He sees God in all things; every course of action he directs towards those spiritual objects which God has revealed to him; every occurrence of the day, every event, every person met with, all news which he hears, he measures by the standard of God's will. And a person who does this may be said almost literally to pray without ceasing; for, knowing himself to be in God's presence, he is continually led to address Him reverently, whom he sets always before him, in the inward language of prayer and praise, of humble confession and joyful trust.

All this, I say, any thoughtful man acknowledges from mere natural reason. To be religious is, in other words, to have the habit of prayer, or to pray always. This is what Scripture means by doing all things to God's glory; that is, so placing God's presence and will before us, and so consistently acting with a reference to Him, that all we do becomes one body and course of obedience, witnessing without ceasing to Him who made us, and whose servants we are; and in its separate parts promoting more or less directly His glory, according as each particular thing we happen to be doing admits more or less of a religious character. Thus religious obedience is, as it were, a spirit dwelling in us, extending its influence to every motion of the soul; and just as healthy men and strong men show their health and strength in all they do (not indeed equally in all things, but in some things more than in others, because all actions do not require or betoken the presence of that health and strength, and yet even in their step, and their voice, and their gestures, and their countenance, showing in due measure their vigour of body), so they who have the true health and strength of the soul, a clear, sober, and deep faith in Him in whom they have their being, will in all they do, nay (as St. Paul says), even whether they "eat or drink,"[1] be living in God's sight, or, in the words of the same Apostle in the text, live in ceaseless prayer.

[1] 1 Cor. x. 31.

If it be said that no man on earth does thus continually and perfectly glorify and worship God, this we all know too well; this is only saying that none of us has reached perfection. We know, alas! that in many things all of us offend. But I am speaking not of what we *do,* but of what we *ought to do,* and must aim at doing,—of *our duty;* and, for the sake of impressing our duty on our hearts, it is of use to draw the picture of a man perfectly obedient, as a pattern for us to aim at. In proportion as we grow in grace and in the knowledge of our Saviour, so shall we approximate to Him in obedience, who is our great example, and who alone of all the sons of Adam lived in the perfection of unceasing prayer.

Thus the meaning and reasonableness of the command in the text is shown by considering it as a natural duty, religion being no accident which comes and goes by fits and starts, but a certain spirit or life.

2. Now, secondly, I will state all this in the language of Scripture ; that is, I will confirm this view of our duty, which natural reason might suggest, by that other and far clearer voice of God, His inspired Word.

How is religious obedience described in Scripture? Surely as a certain kind of life. We know what life of the body is; it is a state of the body : the pulse beats ; all things are in motion. The hidden principle of life, though we know not how or what it is, is seen in these outward signs of it. And so of the life of the soul. The soul, indeed, was not possessed of this life of God when first born into the world. We are born with dead souls; that is, dead as regards religious obedience. If left to ourselves we should grow up haters of God, and tend nearer and nearer, the longer we had existence, to utter spiritual death, that inward fire of hell torments, maturing in evil through a long eternity. Such is the course we are beginning to run when born into the world ; and were it not for the Gospel promise, what a miserable event would the birth of children be! Who could take pleasure at the sight of such poor beings, unconscious as yet of their wretchedness, but containing in their hearts that fearful root of sin which is sure in the event of reigning and triumphing unto everlasting woe? But God has given us all, even the little children, a good promise through Christ; and our prospects are changed. And He has given not only a promise of future happiness, but through His Holy Spirit He implants here and at once a new principle within us, a new spiritual life, a life of the soul, as it is called. St. Paul tells us that " God hath quickened us," made us *live*, "together with Christ, . . . and hath raised us up together" from the death of sin, "and made us sit together in heavenly places in Christ Jesus."[1] Now how God quickens our souls we do not know; as little as how He quickens our bodies. Our spiritual "life" (as St. Paul says) "is *hid* with Christ in God."[2] But as our bodily life discovers itself by its activity, so is the presence of the Holy Spirit in us discovered by a spiritual activity; and this activity is the spirit of continual prayer. Prayer is to spiritual life what the beating of the pulse and the drawing of the breath are to the life of the body. It would be as absurd to suppose that life could last when the body was cold and motionless and senseless, as to call a soul alive which does not pray. The state or habit of spiritual life exerts itself, consists, in the continual activity of prayer.

Do you ask, where does Scripture say this? Where? In all it tells us of the connection between the new birth and faith; for what is prayer but the expression, the voice, of faith? For instance, St. Paul says to the Galatians, "The *life* which I now live in the flesh" (*i.e.* the new and spiritual life), "I live by the *faith* of the Son of God, who loved me."[3] For what, I say, is faith, but the looking to God and thinking of Him continually, holding habitual fellowship with Him, that is, speaking to Him in our hearts all through the day, praying without ceasing? Afterwards, in the same Epistle, he tells us first that nothing avails but faith working by love; but soon after, he calls this same availing principle a new creature: so that the new birth and a living faith are inseparable. Never, indeed, must it be supposed, as we are indolently apt to suppose, that the gift of grace which we receive at baptism is a mere outward privilege, a mere outward pardon, in which the heart is not concerned; or as if it were some mere mark put on the soul, distinguishing it indeed from souls unregenerate, as if by a colour or seal, but not connected with the thoughts, mind, and heart of a Christian. This would be a gross and false view of the nature of God's mercy given us in Christ. For the new birth of the Holy Spirit sets the soul in motion in a heavenly way: it gives us good thoughts and desires, enlightens and purifies us, and prompts us to seek God. In a word (as I have said), it gives a spiritual *life;* it opens the eyes of our mind, so that we begin to see God in all things by faith, and hold continual intercourse with Him by prayer; and if we cherish these gracious influences, we shall become holier and wiser and more heavenly, year by year, our

[1] Eph. ii. 5, 6.   [2] Col. iii. 3.   [3] Gal. ii. 20.

hearts being ever in a course of change from darkness to light, from the ways and works of Satan to the perfection of Divine obedience.

These considerations may serve to impress upon our minds the meaning of the precept in the text, and others like it which are found in St. Paul's Epistles. For instance, he enjoins the Ephesians to "pray always with all prayer and supplication in the Spirit." To the Philippians he says, "Be careful for nothing; but in every thing by prayer and supplication let your requests be made known unto God." [1] To the Colossians, "Continue in prayer, and watch in the same with thanksgiving." To the Romans, "Continue instant in prayer." [2]

Thus the true Christian pierces through the veil of this world and sees the next. He holds intercourse with it; he addresses God, as a child might address his parent, with as clear a view of Him, and with as unmixed a confidence in Him; with deep reverence indeed, and godly fear and awe, but still with certainty and exactness: as St. Paul says, "I know whom I have believed," [3] with the prospect of judgment to come to sober him, and the assurance of present grace to cheer him.

If what I have said is true, surely it is well worth thinking about. Most men indeed, I fear, neither pray at fixed times, nor do they cultivate an habitual communion with Almighty God. Indeed, it is too plain how most men pray. They pray now and then, when they feel particular need of God's assistance; when they are in trouble or in apprehension of danger; or when their feelings are unusually excited. They do not know what it is either to be habitually religious, or to devote a certain number of minutes at fixed times to the thought of God. Nay, the very best Christian, how lamentably deficient is he in the spirit of prayer! Let any man compare in his mind how many times he has prayed when in trouble, with how seldom he has returned thanks when his prayers have been granted; or the earnestness with which he prays against expected suffering, with the languor and unconcern of his thanksgivings afterwards, and he will soon see how little he has of the real habit of prayer, and how much his religion depends on accidental excitement, which is no test of a religious heart. Or supposing he has to repeat the same prayer for a month or two, the cause of using it continuing, let him compare the earnestness with which he first said it, and tried to enter into it, with the coldness with which he at length uses

[1] Eph. vi. 18. Phil. iv. 6. [2] Col. iv. 2. Rom. xii. 12.
[3] 2 Tim. i. 12.

it. Why is this, except that his perception of the unseen world
is not the true view which faith gives (else it would last as that
world itself lasts), but a mere dream, which endures for a night,
and is succeeded by a hard worldly joy in the morning? Is
God habitually in our thoughts? Do we think of Him, and of
His Son our Saviour, through the day? When we eat and
drink, do we thank Him, not as a mere matter of form, but in
spirit? When we do things in themselves right, do we lift up
our minds to Him, and desire to promote His glory? When we
are in the exercise of our callings, do we still think of Him,
acting ever conscientiously, desiring to know His will more
exactly than we do at present, and aiming at fulfilling it more
completely and abundantly? Do we wait on His grace to
enlighten, renew, strengthen us?

I do not ask whether we use many words about religion.
There is no need to do this: nay, we should avoid a boastful
display of our better feelings and practices, silently serving God
without human praise, and hiding our conscientiousness except
when it would dishonour God to do so. There are times,
indeed, when, in the presence of a holy man, to confess is a
benefit, and there are times when, in the presence of worldly
men, to confess becomes a duty; but these seasons, whether of
privilege or of duty, are comparatively rare. But we are always
with ourselves and our God; and that silent inward confession
in His presence may be sustained and continual, and will end in
durable fruit.

But if those persons come short of their duty who make
religion a matter of impulse and mere feeling, what shall be said
to those who have no feeling or thought of religion at all?
What shall be said of the multitude of young people who ridicule seriousness, and deliberately give themselves up to vain
thoughts? Alas! my brethren, you do not even observe or
recognise the foolish empty thoughts which pass through your
minds; you are not distressed even at those of them you
recollect; but what will you say at the last day, when, instead
of the true and holy visions in which consists divine communion,
you find recorded against you in God's book an innumerable
multitude of the idlest, silliest imaginings, nay, of the wickedest,
which ever disgraced an immortal being? What will you say,
when heaven and hell are before you, and the books are opened,
and therein you find the sum total of your youthful desires and
dreams, your passionate wishes for things of this world, your
low-minded, grovelling tastes, your secret contempt and aversion

for serious subjects and persons, your efforts to attract the looks
of sinners and to please those who displease God ; your hanker-
ings after worldly gaieties and luxuries, your admiration of the
rich or titled, your indulgence of impure thoughts, your self-
conceit and pitiful vanity ? Ah, I may seem to you to use harsh
words ; but be sure I do not use terms near so severe as you will
use against yourselves in that day. Then those men, whom you
now think gloomy and over-strict, will seem to you truly wise ;
and the advice to pray without ceasing, which once you laughed
at as fit only for the dull, the formal, the sour, the poor-spirited,
or the aged, will be approved by your own experience, as it is
even now by your reason and conscience. Oh, that you could
be brought to give one serious hour to religion, in anticipation of
that long eternity where you *must* be serious ! True, you may
laugh now, but there is no vain merriment on the other side of
the grave. The devils, though they repent not, tremble. *You*
will be among those unwilling serious ones then, if you are mad
enough to be gay and careless now ; if you are mad enough to
laugh, jest, and scoff your poor moment now on earth, which is
short enough to prepare for eternity in, without your making it
shorter by wasting your youth in sin. Could you but see who
it is that suggests to you all your lighter thoughts, which you
put instead of divine communion, the shock would make you
serious, even if it did not make you religious. Could you see,
what God sees, those snares and pitfalls which the devil is
placing about your path ; could you see that all your idle
thoughts which you cherish, which seem so bright and pleasant,
so much pleasanter than religious thoughts, are inspired by that
Ancient Seducer of Mankind, the Author of Evil, who stands at
your side while you deride religion, serious indeed himself while
he makes you laugh, not able to laugh at his own jests, while he
carries you dancing forward to perdition,—doubtless you would
tremble, even as he does while he tempts you. But this you
cannot possibly see, you cannot break your delusion, except by
first taking God's word in this matter on trust. You cannot see
the unseen world at once. They who ever speak with God in
their hearts, are in turn taught by Him in all knowledge ; but
they who refuse to act upon the light which God gave them by
nature, at length come to lose it altogether, and are given up to
a reprobate mind.

May God save us all from such wilful sin, old as well as
young, and enlighten us one and all in His saving knowledge,
and give us the will and the power to serve Him !

SERMON L.

(SUNDAYS AFTER TRINITY.)

Curiosity a Temptation to Sin.

" Enter not into the path of the wicked, and go not in the way of evil men. Avoid it, pass not by it, turn from it, and pass away."—PROVERBS iv. 14, 15.

ONE chief cause of the wickedness which is everywhere seen in the world, and in which, alas! each of us has more or less his share, is our curiosity to have some fellowship with darkness, some experience of sin, to know what the pleasures of sin are like. I believe it is even thought unmanly by many persons (though they may not like to say so in plain words), unmanly and a thing to be ashamed of, to have no knowledge of sin by experience, as if it argued a strange seclusion from the world, a childish ignorance of life, a simpleness and narrowness of mind, and a superstitious, slavish fear. Not to know sin by experience brings upon a man the laughter and jests of his companions : nor is it wonderful this should be the case in the descendants of that guilty pair to whom Satan in the beginning held out admittance into a strange world of knowledge and enjoyment, as the reward of disobedience to God's commandment. "When the woman saw that the tree was good for food, and that it was pleasant to the eyes, and a tree to be desired to make one wise, she took of the fruit thereof, and did eat, and gave also unto her husband with her, and he did eat." [1] A discontent with the abundance of blessings which were given, because something was withheld, was the sin of our first parents : in like manner, a wanton roving after things forbidden, a curiosity to know what it was to be as

[1] Gen. iii. 6.

the heathen, was one chief source of the idolatries of the Jews; and we at this day inherit with them a like nature from Adam.

I say, curiosity strangely moves us to disobedience, in order that we may have experience of the pleasure of disobedience. Thus we "rejoice in our youth, and let our heart cheer us in the days of our youth, and walk in the ways of our heart, and in the sight of our eyes." [1] And we thus intrude into things forbidden, in various ways; in reading what we should not read, in hearing what we should not hear, in seeing what we should not see, in going into company whither we should not go, in presumptuous reasonings and arguings when we should have faith, in acting as if we were our own masters where we should obey. We indulge our reason, we indulge our passions, we indulge our ambition, our vanity, our love of power; we throw ourselves into the society of bad, worldly, or careless men; and all the while we think that, after having acquired this miserable knowledge of good and evil, we can return to our duty, and continue where we left off: merely going aside a moment to shake ourselves, as Samson did, and with an ignorance like his, that our true heavenly strength is departed from us.

Now this delusion arises from Satan's craft, the father of lies, who knows well that if he can get us once to sin, he can easily make us sin twice and thrice, till at length we are taken captive at his will. [2] He sees that curiosity is man's great and first snare, as it was in Paradise; and he knows that, if he can but force a way into his heart by this chief and exciting temptation, those temptations of other kinds, which follow in life, will easily prevail over us; and, on the other hand, that if we resist the beginnings of sin, there is every prospect through God's grace that we shall continue in a religious way. His plan of action then lies plain before him—to tempt us violently, while the world is new to us, and our hopes and feelings are eager and restless. Hence is seen the Divine wisdom, as well as the merciful consideration, of the advice contained in so many parts of Scripture, as in the text, "Enter not into the path of the wicked, and go not into the way of evil men. Avoid it, pass not by it, turn from it, and pass away."

Let us, then, now for a few moments give our minds to the consideration of this plain truth, which we have heard so often that for that very reason we are not unlikely to forget it—that the great thing in religion is to set off well; to resist the beginnings of sin, to flee temptation, to avoid the company of the

---

[1] Eccles. xi. 9.   [2] 2 Tim. ii. 26.

wicked. "Enter not into the path of the wicked. . . . Avoid
it, pass not by it, turn from it, and pass away."

1. And for this reason, first of all, because it is hardly possible
to delay our flight without rendering flight impossible. When I
say, resist the beginnings of evil, I do not mean the first act
merely, but the rising thought of evil. Whatever the temptation
may be, there may be no time to wait and gaze, without being
caught. Woe to us if Satan (so to say) sees us first; for, as in
the case of some beast of prey, for him to see us is to master us.
Directly we are made aware of the temptation, we shall, if we
are wise, turn our backs upon it, without waiting to think and
reason about it; we shall engage our mind in other thoughts.
There are temptations when this advice is especially necessary;
but under all it is highly seasonable.

2. For consider, in the next place, what must in all cases be
the consequence of allowing evil thoughts to be present to us,
though we do not actually admit them into our hearts. This,
namely,—we shall make ourselves familiar with them. Now our
great security against sin lies in being shocked at it. Eve gazed
and reflected when she should have fled. It is sometimes said,
"Second thoughts are best:" this is true in many cases; but
there are times when it is very false, and when, on the contrary,
first thoughts are best. For sin is like the serpent which seduced
our first parents. We know that some serpents have the power
of what is called "fascinating." Their eye has the power of subduing—nay, in a strange way, of alluring—their victim, who is reduced to utter helplessness, cannot flee away, nay, rather is obliged
to approach, and (as it were) deliver himself up to them; till in
their own time they seize and devour him. What a dreadful
figure this is of the power of sin and the devil over our hearts!
At first our conscience tells us, in a plain straightforward way,
what is right and what is wrong; but when we trifle with this
warning, our reason becomes perverted, and comes in aid of our
wishes, and deceives us to our ruin. Then we begin to find that
there are arguments available in behalf of bad deeds, and we
listen to these till we come to think them true; and then, if
perchance better thoughts return, and we make some feeble effort
to get at the truth really and sincerely, we find our minds by that
time so bewildered that we do not know right from wrong.

Thus, for instance, every one is shocked at cursing and swear-
ing when he first hears it; and at first he cannot help even
showing that he is shocked; that is, he looks grave and downcast,
and feels uncomfortable. But when he has once got accustomed

to such profane talking, and been laughed out of his strictness, and has begun to think it manly, and has been persuaded to join in it, then he soon learns to defend it.   He says he means no harm by it; that it does no one any harm; that it is only so many words, and that everybody uses them.   Here is an instance in which disobedience to what we know to be right makes us blind.

Again, this same confusion frequently happens in the case of temptations from the world.   We fear worldly loss or discredit; or we hope some advantage; and we feel tempted to act so as to secure, at any rate, the worldly good, or to avoid the evil.   Now in all such cases of conduct there is no end of arguing about right or wrong, if we once begin; there are numberless ways of acting, each of which may be speciously defended by argument, but plain, pure-hearted common sense, generally speaking, at the very first sight decides the question for us without argument; but if we do not listen promptly to this secret monitor, its light goes out at once, and we are left to the mercy of mere conjecture, and grope about with but second-best guides.   Then seeming arguments in favour of deceit and evil compliance with the world's wishes, or of disgraceful indolence, urge us, and either prevail, or at least so confuse us, that we do not know how to act.   Alas! in ancient days it happened in this way, that Christians who were brought before their heathen persecutors for punishment, because they were Christians, sometimes came short of the crown of martyrdom, "having loved this present world,"[1] and so lost their way in the mazes of Satan's crafty arguments.

Temptations to unbelief may also be mentioned here.   Speculating wantonly on sacred subjects, and jesting about them, offend us at first; and we turn away: but if in an evil hour we are seduced by the cleverness or wit of a writer or speaker, to listen to his impieties, who can say where we shall stop?   Can we save ourselves from the infection of his profaneness? we cannot hope to do so.   And when we come to a better mind (if by God's grace this be afterwards granted to us), what will be our state? like the state of men who have undergone some dreadful illness, which changes the constitution of the body.   That ready and clear perception of right and wrong, which before directed us, will have disappeared, as beauty of person, or keenness of eyesight in bodily disorders; and when we begin to try to make up our minds which way lies the course of duty on particular trials, we shall bring enfeebled, unsteady powers to the examination;

[1] 2 Tim. iv. 10.

and when we move to act, our limbs (as it were) will move the contrary way, and we shall do wrong when we wish to do right.

3. But there is another wretched effect of sinning once which sometimes takes place ;—not only the sinning that once itself, but being so seduced by it, as forthwith to continue in the commission of it ever afterwards, without seeking for arguments to meet our conscience withal ; from a mere brutish, headstrong, infatuate greediness after its bad pleasures. There are beasts of prey which are said to abstain from blood till they taste it, but once tasting it, ever seek it : and, in like manner, there is a sort of thirst for sin which is born with us, but which grace quenches, and which is thus kept under *till* we, by our own act, rouse it again ; and which, when once aroused, never can be allayed. We sin, while we confess the wages of sin to be death.

4. Sometimes, I say, this is the immediate effect of a first transgression ; and if not the immediate effect, yet it is always the tendency and the end of sinning at length, viz. to enslave us to it. Temptation is very powerful, it is true, when it comes first ; but, then, its power lies in its own novelty ; and, on the other hand, there is power in the heart itself, divinely given, to resist it ; but when we have long indulged sin, the mind has become sinful in its habit and character, and the Spirit of God having departed, it has no principle within it of strength sufficient to save it from spiritual death. What being can change its own nature? that would be almost ceasing to be itself : fire cannot cease to burn ; the leopard changes not its spots, and ceases not to rend and devour ; and the soul which has often sinned cannot help sinning ; but in this respect awfully differing from the condition of the senseless elements or brute animals,—that its present state is all its own fault ; that it might have hindered it, and will have one day to answer for not having hindered it.

Thus, easy as it is to avoid sin first of all, at length it is (humanly speaking) impossible. "Enter not into its path," saith the wise man ; the two paths of right and wrong start from the same point, and at first are separated by a very small difference, so easy (comparatively) is it to choose the right instead of the wrong way : but wait awhile, and pursue the road leading to destruction, and you will find the distance between the two has widened beyond measurement, and that between them a great gulf has been sunk, so that you cannot pass from the one to the other, though you desire it ever so earnestly.[1]

Now to what do considerations such as these lead us, but to

[1] Luke xvi. 26.

our Lord's simple and comprehensive precept, which is the same
as Solomon's, but more impressively and solemnly urged on us
by the manner and time of His giving it? "Watch and pray,
lest ye enter into temptation." To enter not the path of the
wicked, to avoid it, and pass by it, what is this but the exercise
of *watching*? Therefore He insists upon it so much, knowing
that in it our safety lies. But now, on the other hand, consider
how many are there among us who can be said to watch and
pray? Is not the utmost we do to offer on Sunday some kind
of prayer in church to God ; or sometimes some short prayer
morning and evening in the week ; and then go into the world
with the same incaution and forgetfulness as if we had never
entertained a serious thought? We go through the business of
the day, quite forgetting, to any practical purpose, that all
business has snares in it, and therefore needs caution. Let
us ask ourselves this question, "How often do we think of
Satan in the course of the day as our great tempter?" Yet
surely he does not cease to be active because we do not think of
him ; and surely, too, his powers and devices were revealed to us
by Almighty God for the very purpose, that being not ignorant
of them, we might watch against them. Who among us will not
confess, that many is the time that he has mixed with the world,
forgetting who the god of this world is? or rather, are not a
great many of us living in habitual forgetfulness that this world
is a scene of trial ; that is, that this is its *chief* character, that
all its employments, its pleasures, its occurrences, even the most
innocent, the most acceptable to God, and the most truly profitable in themselves, are all the while so handled by Satan as
may be the most conducive to our ruin, if he can possibly contrive
it? There is nothing gloomy or superstitious in this, as the
plain words of Scripture will abundantly prove to every inquirer.
We are told "that the devil, our adversary, as a roaring lion
walketh about, seeking whom he may devour;"[1] and therefore
are warned to "be sober, be vigilant." And assuredly our true
comfort lies, not in disguising the truth from ourselves, but in
knowing something more than this;—that though Satan is
against us, God is for us ; that greater is He that is in us, than
he that is in the world ;[2] and that He in every temptation will
make a way for us to escape, that we may be able to bear it.[3]

God does His part most surely ; and Satan too does his part :
we alone are unconcerned. Heaven and hell are at war for us
and against us, yet we trifle, and let life go on at random.

[1] 1 Pet. v. 8.   [2] 1 John iv. 4.   [3] 1 Cor. x. 13.

Heaven and hell are before us as our own future abode, one or other of them; yet our own interest moves us no more than God's mercy. We treat sin, not as an enemy to be feared, abhorred, and shunned, but as a misfortune and a weakness; we do not pity and shun sinful men, but we enter into their path so far as to keep company with them; and next, being tempted to copy them, we fall almost without an effort.

Be not you thus deceived and overcome, my brethren, by an evil heart of unbelief. Make up your minds to take God for your portion, and pray to Him for grace to enable you so to do. Avoid the great evils of leisure, avoid the snare of having time on your hands. Avoid all bad thoughts, all corrupt or irreligious books, avoid all bad company: let nothing seduce you into it. Though you may be laughed at for your strictness; though you may lose thereby amusements which you would like to partake of; though you may thereby be ignorant of much which others know, and may appear to disadvantage when they are talking together; though you appear behind the rest of the world; though you be called a coward, or a child, or narrow-minded, or superstitious; whatever insulting words be applied to you, fear not, falter not, fail not; stand firm, quit you like men; be strong. They think that in the devil's service there are secrets worthy our inquiry, which you share not: yes, there are secrets, and such that it is a shame even to speak of them; and in like manner you have a secret which they have not, and which far surpasses theirs. "The secret of the Lord is with them that fear Him." Those who obey God and follow Christ have secret gains, so great, that as well might we say heaven were like hell, as that these are like the gain which sinners have. They have a secret gift given them by their Lord and Saviour in proportion to their faith and love. They cannot describe it to others; they have not possession of it all at once; they cannot have the enjoyment of it at this or that time when they will. It comes and goes according to the will of the Giver. It is given but in small measure to those who begin God's service. It is not given at all to those who follow Him with a divided heart. To those who love the world, and yet are in a certain sense religious, and are well contented with such a religious state, to them it is not given. But those who give themselves up to their Lord and Saviour, those who surrender themselves soul and body, those who honestly say, "I am Thine, new-make me, do with me what Thou wilt," who say so not once or twice merely, or in a transport, but calmly and habitually; these are they who gain the

Lord's secret gift, even the "white stone, and in the stone a new name written which no man knoweth, saving he that receiveth it."[1] Sinners think that they know all that religion has to give, and over and above that, they know the pleasures of sin too. No, they do not, cannot, never will know the secret gift of God till they repent and amend. They never will know what it is to see God till they obey; nay, though they are to see Him at the last day, even that will be no true sight of Him, for the sight of that Holy One will then impart no comfort, no joy to them. They never will know the blessedness which He has to give. They do know the satisfaction of sinning, such as it is; and, alas! if they go on as they are going, they will know not only what sin is, but what hell is. But they never will know that great secret which is hid in the Father and in the Son.

Let us not then be seduced by the Tempter and his promises. He can show us no good. He has no good to give us. Rather let us listen to the gracious words of our Maker and Redeemer "Call unto Me, and I will answer thee, and show thee great and mighty things, which thou knowest not."[2]

[1] Rev. ii. 17. [2] Jer. xxxiii. 3.

SERMON LI.

(SUNDAYS AFTER TRINITY.)

Miracles no Remedy for Unbelief.

*" And the Lord said unto Moses, How long will this people provoke Me ?
and how long will it be ere they believe Me, for all the signs which I
have showed among them ? "*—NUM. xiv. 11.

NOTHING, I suppose, is more surprising to us at first reading
than the history of God's chosen people ; nay, on second
and third reading, and on every reading, till we learn to view it
as God views it. It seems strange, indeed, to most persons, that
the Israelites should have acted as they did, age after age, in
spite of the miracles which were vouchsafed to them. The laws
of nature were suspended again and again before their eyes ; the
most marvellous signs were wrought at the word of God's
prophets, and for their deliverance ; yet they did not obey their
great Benefactor at all better than men nowadays who have not
these advantages, as we commonly consider them. Age after age
God visited them by Angels, by inspired messengers ; age after
age they sinned. At last He sent His well-beloved Son ; and
He wrought miracles before them still more abundant, wonderful,
and beneficent than any before Him. What was the effect upon
them of His coming ? St. John tells us, " Then gathered the
chief priests and the Pharisees a council, and said, What do we ?
for this Man doeth many miracles. . . . . Then from that day
forth they took counsel together for to put Him to death." [1]

In matter of fact, then, whatever be the reason, nothing is
gained by miracles, nothing comes of miracles, as regards our
religious views, principles, and habits. Hard as it is to believe,
miracles certainly do not make men better ; the history of Israel

[1] John xi. 47, 53.

proves it. And the only mode of escaping this conclusion, to which some persons feel a great repugnance, is to fancy that the Israelites were much worse than other nations, which accordingly has been maintained. It has often been said that they were stiff-necked and hard-hearted beyond the rest of the world. Now, even supposing, for argument's sake, I should grant that they were so, this would not sufficiently account for the strange circumstance under consideration; for this people was not moved at all. It is not a question of more or less : surely they must have been altogether distinct from other men, destitute of the feelings and opinions of other men, nay, hardly partakers of human nature, if other men would, as a matter of course, have been moved by those miracles which had no influence whatever upon them. That there *are*, indeed, men in the world who would have been moved, and would have obeyed in consequence, I do not deny ; such were to be found among the Israelites also ; but I am speaking of men in general; and I say, that if the Israelites had a common nature with us, surely that insensibility which they exhibited on the whole, must be just what we should exhibit on the whole under the same circumstances.

It confirms this view of the subject to observe, that the children of Israel *are* like other men in all points of their conduct, save this insensibility, which other men have not had the opportunity to show as they had. There is no difference between their conduct and ours in point of *fact;* the difference is entirely in the external discipline to which God subjected them. Whether or not miracles ought to have influenced them in a way in which God's dealings in Providence do not influence us, so far is clear, that looking into their modes of living and of thought, we find a nature just like our own, not better indeed, but in no respect worse. Those evil tempers which the people displayed in the desert, their greediness, selfishness, murmuring, caprice, waywardness, fickleness, ingratitude, jealousy, suspiciousness, obstinacy, unbelief, all these are seen in the uneducated multitude nowadays, according to its opportunity of displaying them.

The pride of Dathan and the presumption of Korah are still instanced in our higher ranks and among educated persons. Saul, Ahithophel, Joab, and Absalom have had their parallels all over the world. I say there is nothing unlike the rest of mankind in the character or conduct of the chosen people ; the difference solely is in God's dealings with them. They *act* as other men ; it is their religion which is not as that of other men ; it is miraculous : and the question is, how it comes to pass, their

2 E

religion being different, their conduct is the same? and there are two ways of answering it; either by saying that they were worse than other men, and were not influenced by miracles when others would have been influenced (as many persons are apt to think), or (what I conceive to be the true reason) that, after all, the difference between miracle and no miracle is not so great in any case, in the case of any people, as to secure the success or account for the failure of religious truth. It was not that the Israelites were much more hard-hearted than other people, but that a miraculous religion is not much more influential than other religions.

For I repeat, though it be granted that the Israelites were much worse than others, still that will not account for the fact that miracles made no impression whatever upon them. However sensual and obstinate they may be supposed to have been in natural character, yet if it be true that a miracle has a necessary effect upon the human mind, it must be considered to have had some effect on their conduct for good or bad; if it had not a good effect, at least it must have had a bad; whereas their miracles left them very much the same in outward appearance as men are nowadays, who neglect such warnings as are now sent them, neither much more lawless and corrupt than they, nor the reverse. The point is, that while they were so hardened, as it appears to us, in their conduct towards their Lord and Governor, they were not much worse than other men in social life and personal behaviour. It is a rule that if men are extravagantly irreligious, profane, blasphemous, infidel, they are equally excessive and monstrous in other respects; whereas the Jews were like the Eastern nations around them, with this one peculiarity, that they had rejected direct and clear miraculous evidence, and the others had not. It seems then, I say, to follow, that, guilty as were the Jews in disobeying Almighty God, and blind as they became from shutting their eyes to the light, they were not much more guilty than others may be in disobeying Him; that it is almost as great a sin to reject His service in the case of those who do not see miracles, as in the case of those who do; that the sight of miracles is not the way in which men come to believe and obey, nor the absence of them an excuse for not believing and obeying.

Now let me say something in explanation of this, at first sight, startling truth, that miracles on the whole would not make men in general more obedient or holy than they are, though they were generally displayed. It has sometimes been said by unbelievers,

"If the Gospel were written on the sun, I would believe it." Unbelievers have said so by way of excusing themselves for not believing it, as it actually comes to them ; and I dare say some of us, my brethren, have before now uttered the same sentiment in our hearts, either in moments of temptation, or when under the upbraidings of conscience for sin committed. Now let us consider, why do we think so ?

I ask, why should the sight of a miracle make you better than you are ? Do you doubt at all the being and power of God ? No. Do you doubt what you ought to *do ?* No. Do you doubt at all that the rain, for instance, and sunshine, come from Him ? or that the fresh life of each year, as it comes, is His work, and that all nature bursts into beauty and richness at His bidding ? You do not doubt it at all. Nor do you doubt, on the other hand, that it is your duty to obey Him who made the world and who made you. And yet, with the knowledge of all this, you find you cannot prevail upon yourselves to do what you know you should do. Knowledge is not what you want to make you obedient. You have knowledge enough already. Now what truth would a miracle convey to you which you do not learn from the works of God around you ? What would it teach you concerning God which you do not already believe with out having seen it ?

But, you will say, a miracle would startle you ; true : but would not the startling pass away ? could you be startled for ever ? And what sort of a religion is that which consists in a state of fright and disturbance ? Are you not continually startled by the accidents of life ? You see, you hear things suddenly, which bring before your minds the thoughts of God and judgment ; calamities befall you which for the time sober you. Startling is not conversion any more than knowledge is practice.

But you urge, that perhaps that startling might issue in amendment of life ; that it might be the beginning of a new course, though it passed away itself ; that a miracle would not indeed convert you, but it would be the first step towards thorough conversion ; that it would be the turning-point in your life, and would suddenly force your path into the right direction, and that in this way shocks and startlings, and all the agitation of the passions and affections, are really the means of conversion, though conversion be something more than they. This is very true : sudden emotions—fear, hope, gratitude, and the like, all do produce such effects sometimes ; but why is a miracle necessary to produce such effects ? Other things startle us besides miracles :

we have a number of accidents sent us by God to startle us.
He has not left us without warnings, though He has not given us
miracles ; and if we are not moved and converted by those which
come upon us, the probability is, that, like the Jews, we should
not be converted by miracles.

Yes, you say ; but if one came from the dead, if you saw the
spirit of some departed friend you knew on earth : what then?
What would it tell you that you do not know now? Do you now
in your sober reason doubt the reality of the unseen world? not at
all; only you cannot get yourself to act as if it *were* real. Would
such a sight produce this effect? you think it would. Now I
will grant this on one supposition. Do the startling accidents
which happen to you now produce *any* lasting effect upon you?
Do they lead you to *any habits* of religion? If they do produce
some effect, then I will grant to you that such a strange visitation, as you have supposed, would produce a greater effect; but
if the events of life which now happen to you produce *no* lasting
effect on you, and this I fear is the case, then too sure I am
that a miracle too would produce no lasting effect on you,
though of course it would startle you more at the time. I say,
I fear that what happens to you, as it is, produces no lasting
effect on you. I mean, that the warnings which you really have
do not bring you to any habitual and regular religiousness; they
may make you a little more afraid of this or that sin, or of this
or that particular indulgence of it; but they do not tend at all
to make you break with the world, and convert you to God. If
they did make you take up religion in earnest, though in ever so
poor a way, then I will grant that miracles would make you
more in earnest. If God's *ordinary* warnings moved you, His
extraordinary would move you more. It is quite true, that a
serious mind would be made more serious by seeing a miracle,
but this gives no ground for saying, that minds which are *not*
serious, careless, worldly, self-indulgent persons, who are made
not at all better by the warnings which *are* given them, would
be made serious by those miraculous warnings which are not
given.

Of course it might so happen in this or that particular case,
—just as the same person is moved by one warning, not by
another ; not moved by a warning to-day, moved by a warning
to-morrow; but I am sure, taking men as we find them, miracles
would leave them, as far as their conduct is concerned, very
much as they are. They would be very much startled and
impressed at first, but the impression would wear away. And

thus our Saviour's words would come true of all those multitudes who have the Bible to read, and know what they ought to do, but do it not: "If they hear not Moses and the prophets," He says, "neither will they be persuaded though one rose from the dead." Do we never recollect times when we have said, "We shall never forget this; it will be a warning all through our lives"? have we never implored God's forgiveness with the most eager promises of amendment? have we never felt as if we were brought quite into a new world, in gratitude and joy? Yet was the result what we had expected? We cannot anticipate more from miracles than before now we have anticipated from warnings, which came to nought.

And now, what *is* the real reason why we do not seek God with all our hearts, and devote ourselves to His service, if the absence of miracles be not the reason, as most assuredly it is not? What was it that made the Israelites disobedient, who *had* miracles? St. Paul informs us, and exhorts *us* in consequence. "Harden not your hearts, *as* in the provocation, in the day of temptation in the wilderness . . . . take heed . . . . lest there be in any of *you*" (as there was among the Jews) "an evil heart of unbelief in departing from the Living God." Moses had been commissioned to say the same thing at the very time: "Oh that there were such an heart in them, that they would fear Me, and keep My commandments always!" We cannot serve God, because we want the will and the heart to serve Him. We like anything better than religion, as the Jews before us. The Jews liked this world; they liked mirth and feasting. "The people sat down to eat and to drink, and rose up to play;" so do we. They liked glitter and show, and the world's fashions. "Give us a king like the nations," they said to Samuel; so do we. They wished to be let alone; they liked ease; they liked their own way; they disliked to make war against the natural impulses and leanings of their own minds; they disliked to attend to the state of their souls, to have to treat themselves as spiritually sick and infirm, to watch, and rule, and chasten, and refrain, and change themselves; and so do we. They disliked to think of God, and to observe and attend His ordinances, and to reverence Him; they called it a weariness to frequent His courts; and they found this or that false worship more pleasant, satisfactory, congenial to their feelings, than the service of the Judge of quick and dead; and so do we: and therefore we disobey God as they did,—not that we have not miracles; for they actually had them, and it made no difference. We act as they did, though they had miracles, and we have not; because there is one cause of it *common* both to them and us—heartlessness in religious matters, an evil heart of unbelief; both they and we disobey and disbelieve, because we do not love.

But this is not all; in another respect we are really far more favoured than they were; they had outward miracles; we too have miracles, but they are not outward but inward. Ours are not miracles of evidence, but of power and influence. They are secret, and more wonderful and efficacious because secret. Their miracles were wrought upon external nature; the sun stood still, and the sea parted. Ours are invisible, and are exercised upon the soul. They consist in the sacraments, and they just do that veɪy thing which the Jewish miracles did not. They really touch the heart, though we so often resist their influence. If then we sin, as, alas! we do, if we do not love God more than the Jews did, if we have no heart for those "good things which pass men's understanding," we are not more excusable than they, but less so. For the supernatural works which God showed to them were wrought outwardly, not inwardly, and did not influence the will; they did but convey warnings; but the supernatural works which He does towards us are in the heart, and impart grace; and if we disobey, we are not disobeying His command only, but resisting His presence.

This is our state; and perhaps so it is that, as the Israelites for forty years hardened their hearts in the wilderness, in spite of the manna and the quails, and the water from the rock, so we for a course of years have been hardening ours in spite of the spiritual gifts which are the portion of Christians. Instead of listening to the voice of conscience, instead of availing ourselves of the aid of heavenly grace, we have gone on year after year with the vain dream of turning to God some future day. Childhood and boyhood are past; youth, perhaps middle age, perhaps old age is come; and now we find that we cannot "love the thing which God commandeth, and desire that which He doth promise;" and then, instead of laying the blame where it is due, on ourselves, for having hardened ourselves against the influences of grace, we complain that enough has not been done for us; we complain we have not enough light, enough help, enough inducements; we complain we have not seen miracles. Alas! how exactly are God's words fulfilled in us, which He deigned to speak to His former people : "O inhabitants of Jerusalem, and men of Judah, judge, I pray you, betwixt Me and My vineyard. What could have been done more to My vineyard that I have

not done in it? wherefore, when I looked that it should bring
forth grapes, brought it forth wild grapes?"[1]

Let us then put aside vain excuses; and, instead of looking
for outward events to change our course of life, be sure of this,
that if our course of life is to be changed, it must be from
within. God's grace moves us from within, so does our own
will. External circumstances have no real power over us. If
we do not love God, it is because we have not wished to love
Him, tried to love Him, prayed to love Him. We have not
borne the idea and the wish in our mind day by day, we have
not had it before us in the little matters of the day, we have
not lamented that we loved Him not, we have been too indolent,
sluggish, carnal, to attempt to love Him in little things, and
begin at the beginning; we have shrunk from the effort of moving from within; we have been like persons who cannot get
themselves to rise in the morning; and we have desired and
waited for a thing impossible,—to be changed once and for all,
all at once, by some great excitement from without, or some
great event, or some special season; something or other we go
on expecting, which is to change us without our having the
trouble to change ourselves. We covet some miraculous warning,
or we complain that we are not in happier circumstances, that we
have so many cares, or so few religious privileges; or we look
forward for a time when religion will come easy to us as a matter
of course. This we used to look out for as boys; we used to
think there was time enough yet to think of religion, and that
it was a natural thing, that it came without trouble or effort,
for men to be religious as life went on; we fancied that all old
persons must be religious; and now even, as grown men, we
have not put off this deceit; but, instead of giving our hearts to
God, we are waiting, with Felix, for a convenient season.

Let us rouse ourselves, and act as reasonable men, before it is
too late; let us understand, as a first truth in religion, that *love*
of heaven is the only *way* to heaven. Sight will not move us;
else why did Judas persist in covetousness in the very presence
of Christ? why did Balaam, whose "eyes were opened," remain
with a closed heart? why did Satan fall, when he was a bright
Archangel? Nor will reason subdue us; else why was the
Gospel, in the beginning, "to the Greeks foolishness"? Nor
will excited feelings convert us; for there is one who "heareth
the word, and anon with joy receiveth it;" yet "hath no root
in himself," and "dureth" only "for a while." Nor will self-

[1] Isa. v. 3, 4.

interest prevail with us; or the rich man would have been more prudent, whose "ground brought forth plentifully," and would have recollected that "that night his soul" might be "required of him." Let us understand that nothing but the love of God can make us believe in Him or obey Him; and let us pray Him, who has "prepared for them that love Him such good things as pass man's understanding, to pour into our hearts such love towards Him, that we, loving Him above all things, may obtain His promises, which exceed all that we can desire."

SERMON LII.

(SUNDAYS AFTER TRINITY.)

Jeremiah, a Lesson for the Disappointed.

" Be not afraid of their faces: for I am with thee to deliver thee, saith the Lord."—JER. i. 8.

THE prophets were ever ungratefully treated by the Israelites; they were resisted, their warnings neglected, their good services forgotten. But there was this difference between the earlier and the later prophets; the earlier lived and died in honour among their people,—in outward honour; though hated and thwarted by the wicked, they were exalted to high places, and ruled in the congregation. Moses, for instance, was in trouble from his people all his life long, but to the end he was their lawgiver and judge. Samuel, too, even though rejected, was still held in reverence; and when he died, "all the Israelites were gathered together and lamented him, and buried him in his house at Ramah."[1] David died on a royal throne. But in the latter times, the prophets were not only feared and hated by the enemies of God, but cast out of the vineyard. As the time approached for the coming of the true Prophet of the Church, the Son of God, they resembled Him in their earthly fortunes more and more; and as He was to suffer, so did they. Moses was a ruler, Jeremiah was an outcast: Samuel was buried in peace, John the Baptist was beheaded. In St. Paul's words, they "had trial of cruel mockings and scourgings, yea, moreover, of bonds and imprisonment. They were stoned; they were sawn asunder, were tempted, were slain with the sword; they wandered about in sheepskins and goatskins, being destitute, afflicted, tormented; of whom the world was not worthy; they

[1] 1 Sam. xxv. 1.

wandered in deserts, and in mountains, and in dens and caves of the earth." [1]

Of these, Elijah, who lived in the wilderness, and the hundred prophets whom Obadiah fed by fifty in a cave, are examples of the wanderers. And Micaiah, who was appointed the bread of affliction and the water of affliction by an idolatrous king, is the specimen of those who "had trial of bonds and imprisonment." Of those who were sawn asunder and slain with the sword, Isaiah is the chief, who, as tradition goes, was by order of Manasseh, the son of Hezekiah, sawn asunder with a wooden saw. And of those who were stoned, none is more famous than Zechariah, the son of Jehoiada, "who was slain between the temple and the altar." [2] But of all the persecuted prophets Jeremiah is the most eminent; *i.e.* we know more of his history, of his imprisonments, his wanderings, and his afflictions. He may be taken as a representative of the prophets; and hence it is that he is an especial type of our Lord and Saviour. All the prophets were types of the Great Prophet whose way they were preparing; they tended towards and spoke of Christ. In their sufferings they foreshadowed His priesthood, and in their teaching His prophetical office, and in their miracles His royal power. The history of Jeremiah, then, as being drawn out in Scripture more circumstantially than that of the other prophets, is the most exact type of Christ among them; that is, next to David, who, of course, was the nearest resemblance to Him of all, as a sufferer, an inspired teacher, and a king. Jeremiah comes next to David; I do not say in dignity and privilege, for it was Elijah who was taken up to heaven, and appeared at the Transfiguration; nor in inspiration, for to Isaiah one should assign the higher evangelical gifts; but in typifying Him who came and wept over Jerusalem, and then was tortured and put to death by those He wept over. And hence, when our Lord came, while some thought Him Elijah, and others John the Baptist risen from the dead, there were others who thought Him Jeremiah. Of Jeremiah, then, I will now speak, as a specimen of all those prophets whom St. Paul sets before us as examples of faith, and St. James as examples of patience.

Jeremiah's ministry may be summed up in three words, good hope, labour, disappointment.

It was his privilege to be called to his sacred office from his earliest years. Like Samuel, the first prophet, he was of the tribe of Levi, dedicated from his birth to religious services, and

---

[1] Heb. xi. 36-38.   [2] Matt. xxiii. 35.

favoured with the constant presence and grace of God. " Before I formed thee . . . . I knew thee,"[1] says the word of the Lord to him when He gave him his commission, " and before thou camest out of the womb I sanctified thee, and I ordained thee a prophet unto the nations." This commission was given the year after Josiah began his reformation. Jeremiah returned for answer, " Ah! Lord God! behold, I cannot speak; for I am a child." He felt the arduousness of a prophet's office; the firmness and intrepidity which were required to speak the words of God. " But the Lord said unto him, Say not I am a child; for thou shalt go to all that I shall send thee, and whatsoever I command thee thou shalt speak. Be not afraid of their faces, for I am with thee to deliver thee, saith the Lord. Then the Lord put forth His hand and touched my mouth, and said unto me, Behold I have put My words in thy mouth."

No prophet commenced his labours with greater encouragement than Jeremiah. A king had succeeded to the throne who was bringing back the times of the man after God's own heart. There had not been a son of David so zealous as Josiah since David himself. The king, too, was young, at most twenty years of age, in the beginning of his reformation. What might not be effected in a course of years, however corrupt and degraded was the existing state of his people? So Jeremiah might think. It must be recollected, too, that religious obedience was under the Jewish covenant awarded with temporal prosperity. There seemed, then, every reason for Jeremiah at first to suppose that bright fortunes were in store for the Church. Josiah was the very king whose birth was foretold by name above three hundred years before, when Jeroboam established idolatry; who was the promised avenger of God's covenant, " the repairer of the breach, the restorer of paths to dwell in."[2] Israel (the ten tribes) having gone into captivity, schism had come to its end; the kings of the house of David again ruled over the whole extent of the promised land; idolatry was destroyed by Josiah in all the cities. Such were the present blessings which the Jewish remnant enjoyed. At first sight, then, it seemed reasonable to anticipate further and permanent improvement. Every one begins with being sanguine; doubtless then, as now, many labourers in God's husbandry entered on their office with more lively hopes than their after-fortunes warranted. Whether or not, however, such hope of success encouraged Jeremiah's first exertions, very soon, in his case, this cheerful prospect was overcast, and he was left to

---

[1] Jer. i. 5.   [2] Isa. lviii. 12.

labour in the dark. Huldah's message to the king, on his finding the Book of the Law in the temple, fixed the coming fortunes
of Judah. Huldah foretold a woe,—an early removal of the
good Josiah to his rest, as a mercy to him, and to the nation, who
were unworthy of him, a fierce destruction. This prophecy was
delivered five years after Jeremiah entered upon his office; he
ministered in all forty years before the captivity; so early in his
course were his hopes cut away.

But even though Huldah's message be supposed not to reach
him, still he was doubtless soon undeceived as to any hopes he
might entertain, whether, by the express word of God informing
him, or by the actual hardened state of sin in which the nation
lay. Soon, surely, were his hopes destroyed, and his mind sobered
into a more blessed and noble temper,—resignation.

I call resignation a more blessed frame of mind than sanguine
hope of present success, because it is the truer, and the more
consistent with our fallen state of being, and the more improving
to our hearts; and because it is that for which the most eminent
servants of God have been conspicuous. To expect great effects
from our exertions for religious objects is natural indeed, and
innocent, but it arises from inexperience of the kind of work we
have to do,—to change the heart and will of man. It is a far
nobler frame of mind, to labour, not with the hope of seeing the
fruit of our labour, but for conscience' sake, as a matter of duty;
and again, in faith, trusting good *will* be done, though we see it
not. Look through the Bible, and you will find God's servants,
even though they began with success, end with disappointment;
not that God's purposes or His instruments fail, but that the time
for reaping what we have sown is hereafter, not here; that here
there is no great visible fruit in any one man's lifetime. Moses,
for instance, began with leading the Israelites out of Egypt in
triumph; he ended at the age of an hundred and twenty years,
before his journey was finished and Canaan gained, one among
the offending multitudes who were overthrown in the wilderness.[1]
Samuel's reformations ended in the people's wilfully choosing a
king like the nations around them. Elijah, after his successes,
fled from Jezebel into the wilderness to mourn over his disappointments. Isaiah, after Hezekiah's religious reign, and the
miraculous destruction of Sennacherib's army, fell upon the evil
days of his son Manasseh. Even in the successes of the first
Christian teachers, the Apostles, the same rule is observed. After
all the great works God enabled them to accomplish, they con-

[1] 1 Cor. x. 5.

fessed before their death that what they experienced, and what they saw before them, was reverse and calamity, and that the fruit of their labour would not be seen, till Christ came to open the books and collect His Saints from the four corners of the earth. "Evil men and seducers shall wax worse and worse, deceiving and being deceived,"[1] is the testimony of St. Peter, St. Paul, St. John, and St. Jude.

Now, in the instance of Jeremiah, we have on record that variety and vicissitude of feelings, which this transition from hope to disappointment produces, at least in a sensitive mind. His trials were very great, even in Josiah's reign; but when that pious king's countenance was withdrawn on his early death, he was exposed to persecution from every class of men. At one time we read of the people conspiring against him;[2] at another, of the men of his own city, Anathoth, "seeking his life,"[3] on account of his prophesying in the Lord's Name. At another time he was seized by the priests and the prophets in order to be put to death, from which he was only saved by certain of the princes and elders who were still faithful to the memory of Josiah. Then, again, Pashur, the chief governor of the temple, smote him and tortured him.[5] At another time, the king, Zedekiah, put him in prison.[6] Afterwards, when the army of the Chaldeans had besieged Jerusalem, the Jews accused him of falling away to the enemy,[7] and smote him, and imprisoned him; then they cast him into a dungeon, where he "sunk in the mire," and almost perished from hunger.[8] When Jerusalem had been taken by the enemy, Jeremiah was forcibly carried down to Egypt by men who at first pretended to reverence and consult him.[9] and there he came to his end—it is believed, a violent end. Nebuchadnezzar, the heathen king of Babylon and conqueror of Jerusalem, was one of the few persons who showed him kindness. This great king, who afterwards honoured Daniel, and was at length brought to acknowledge the God of heaven by a severe chastisement, on the taking of the city delivered Jeremiah from prison,[10] and gave charge to the captain of his guard concerning him, to "look well to him, and to do him no harm; but to do unto him even as he should say . . . ." An Ethiopian, another heathen, is also mentioned as delivering him from the dungeon.

Such were his trials: his affliction, fear, despondency, and

[1] 2 Tim. iii. 13. [2] Jer. xviii. 18. [3] Ibid. xi. 21.
[4] Ibid. xxvi. 16, etc. [5] Ibid. xx. 2. [6] Ibid. xxxii. 3.
[7] Ibid. xxxvii. 14. [8] Ibid. xxxviii. 6, 9. [9] Ibid. xlii. xliii.
[10] Ibid. xxxix. 14.

sometimes even restlessness under them are variously expressed; that succession and tide of feelings which most persons undergo before their minds settle into the calm of resignation. At one time he speaks as astonished at his failure: "O Lord, art not Thine eyes upon the truth? Thou hast stricken them, but they have not grieved; Thou hast consumed them, but they have refused to receive correction."[1] Again, "A wonderful and horrible thing is committed in the land; the prophets prophesy falsely, and the priests bear rule by their means; and My people love to have it so."[2] At another time, he expresses his perplexity at the disorder of the world, and the successes of the wicked: "Righteous art Thou, O Lord, when I plead with Thee; yet let me talk with Thee of Thy judgments: wherefore doth the way of the wicked prosper? wherefore are all they happy that deal very treacherously? .... but Thou, O Lord, knowest me; Thou hast seen me, and tried mine heart towards Thee."[3] Then, in turn, his mind frets at the thought of its own anxious labours and perplexities: "Woe is me, my mother, that thou hast borne me a man of strife and a man of contention to the whole earth! I have neither lent on usury, nor men have lent to me on usury; yet every one of them doth curse me. .... Why is my pain perpetual, and my wound incurable? .... wilt Thou be altogether unto me as a deceiver, and as waters that fail?"[4] These are the sorrows of a gentle and peaceable mind, forced against its will into the troubles of life, and incurring the hatred of those whom it opposes against its nature. This he elsewhere expresses thus: "As for me, I have not .... desired the woeful day" (which he foretold); "Thou knowest: that which came out of my lips was right before Thee. Be not a terror unto me: Thou art my hope in the day of evil."[5] When Pashur put him to torture he was still more agitated, and said, "O Lord, Thou hast deceived me, and I was deceived. Thou art stronger than I, and hast prevailed. I am in derision daily, every one mocketh me. .... Cursed be the day wherein I was born" (here certainly is the language even of impatience), "let not the day wherein my mother bare me be blessed."[6]

However, of such changes of feelings what was the end?— resignation. He elsewhere uses language which expresses that chastened spirit and weaned heart which is the termination of all agitation and anxiety in the case of religious minds. He who at one time could not comfort himself, at another was sent to

---

[1] Jer. v. 3.   [2] Ibid. v. 30, 31.   [3] Ibid. xii. 1-3.
[4] Ibid. xv. 10-18.   [5] Ibid. xvii. 16, 17.   [6] Ibid. xx. 7-14.

comfort a brother ; and, in comforting Baruch, he speaks in that nobler temper of resignation which takes the place of sanguine hope and harassing fear, and betokens calm and clear-sighted faith and inward peace. "Thus saith the Lord the God of Israel unto thee, O Baruch. Thou didst say, Woe is me now, for the Lord hath added grief to my sorrow ; I fainted in my sighing, and I find no rest. . . . . Behold, that which I have built will I break down, and that which I have planted I will pluck up, even this whole land. And seekest thou great things for thyself ? seek them not : for, behold, I will bring evil upon all flesh ; . . . . but thy life will I give unto thee for a prey in all places whither thou goest ; " that is, seek not success, be not impatient, fret not thyself—be content, if, after all thy labours, thou dost but save thyself, without seeing other fruit of them.

And now, my brethren, does what I have been saying apply to all of us, or only to prophets ? It applies to all of us. For all of us live in a world which promises well, but does not fulfil ; and all of us (taking our lives altogether apart from religious prospects) begin with hope, and end with disappointment. Doubtless, there is much difference in our respective trials here, arising from difference of tempers and fortunes. Still it is in our nature to begin life thoughtlessly and joyously ; to seek great things in one way or other ; to have vague notions of good to come ; to love the world, and to believe its promises, and seek satisfaction and happiness from it. And, as it is our nature to hope, so it is our lot, as life proceeds, to encounter disappointment. I know that there are multitudes, in the retired ranks of society, who pass their days without any great varieties of fortune ; though, even in such cases, thinking persons will have much more to say of themselves than at first sight might appear. Still, that disappointment in some shape or other is the lot of man (that is, looking at our prospects apart from the next world) is plain, from the mere fact, if nothing else could be said, that we begin life with health and end it with sickness ; or in other words, that it *comes* to an *end*, for an end is a failure. And even in the quietest walks of life, do not the old feel regret, more or less vividly, that they are not young ? Do not they lament the days gone by, and even with the pleasure of remembrance feel the pain ? And why, except that they think that they have lost something which they once had, whereas, in the beginning of life, they thought of gaining something they had not ? A double disappointment.

Now is it religion that suggests this sad view of things ? No, it is experience; it is the *world's* doing; it is fact, from which we cannot escape, though the Bible said not a word about the perishing nature of all earthly pleasures.

Here then it is that God Himself offers us His aid by His Word, and in His Church. Left to ourselves, we seek good from the world, but cannot find it; in youth we look forward, and in age we look back. It is well we should be persuaded of these things betimes, to gain wisdom and to provide for the evil day. Seek we great things? We must seek them where they really are to be found, and in the way in which they are to be found; we must seek them as He has set them before us, who came into the world to enable us to gain them. We must be willing to give up present hope for future enjoyment, this world for the unseen. The truth is (though it is so difficult for us to admit it heartily), our nature is not at first in a state to enjoy happiness, even if we had it offered to us. We seek for it, and we feel we need it; but (strange though it is to say, still so it is) we are not fitted to be happy. If then at once we rush forward to seek enjoyment, it will be like a child's attempting to walk before his strength is come. If we would gain true bliss we must cease to seek it as an end; we must postpone the prospect of enjoying it. For we are by nature in an unnatural state; we must be changed from what we are when born before we can receive our greatest good. And as in sickness sharp remedies are often used, or irksome treatment, so it is with our souls; we must go through pain, we must practise self-denial, we must curb our wills, and purify our hearts, before we are capable of any lasting solid peace. To attempt to gain happiness, except in this apparently tedious and circuitous way, is a labour lost; it is building on the sand; the foundation will soon give way, though the house looks fair for a time. To be gay and thoughtless, to be self-indulgent and self-willed, is quite out of character with our real state. We must learn to know ourselves, and to have thoughts and feelings becoming ourselves. Impetuous hope and undisciplined mirth ill suit a sinner. Should *he* shrink from low notions of himself, and sharp pain, and mortification of natural wishes, whose guilt called down the Son of God from heaven to die upon the cross for him? May he live in pleasure here, and call this world his home, while he reads in the Gospel of his Saviour's lifelong affliction and disappointment?

It cannot be; let us prepare for suffering and disappointment, which befit us as sinners, and which are necessary for us as saints. Let us not turn away from trial when God brings it on us, or play the coward in the fight of faith. "Watch ye, stand fast in the faith, quit you like men, be strong;"[1] such is St. Paul's exhortation. When affliction overtakes you, remember to accept it as a means of improving your hearts, and pray God for His grace that it may do so. Look disappointment in the face. "Take . . . . the prophets . . . . for an example of suffering affliction, and of patience. Behold, we count them happy who endure." Give not over your attempts to serve God, though you see nothing come of them. Watch and pray, and obey your conscience, though you cannot perceive your own progress in holiness. Go on, and you cannot but go forward; believe it, though you do not see it. Do the duties of your calling, though they are distasteful to you. Educate your children carefully in the good way, though you cannot tell how far God's grace has touched their hearts. Let your light shine before men, and praise God by a consistent life, even though others do not seem to glorify their Father on account of it, or to be benefited by your example. "Cast your bread upon the waters, for you shall find it after many days. . . . . In the morning sow your seed, in the evening withhold not your hand; for you know not whether shall prosper, either this or that; or whether they both shall be alike good."[2] Persevere in the narrow way. The prophets went through sufferings to which ours are mere trifles; violence and craft combined to turn them aside, but they kept right on, and are at rest.

Now, I know full well, that this whole subject is distasteful to many men, who say we ought to be cheerful. "We are bid rejoice, why then do you bid us mourn?" I bid you mourn in order that you may rejoice more perfectly. "Blessed are they that mourn, for they shall be comforted."[3] "They that sow in tears, shall reap in joy." I bid you take up the cross of Christ, that you may wear His crown. Give your hearts to Him, and you will for yourselves solve the difficulty, how Christians can be sorrowful, yet alway rejoicing.[4] You will find that lightness of heart and cheerfulness are quite consistent with that new and heavenly character which He gives us, though to gain it in any good measure, we must for a time be sorrowful, and ever after thoughtful. But I give you fair warning, you must at first take His word on trust; and if you do not, there is no help for it. He says, "Come unto Me, ... and I will give you rest." You must begin on faith : you cannot see at first whither He is lead

---

[1] 1 Cor. xvi. 13.
[3] Matt. v. 4.
[2] Eccles. xi. 1, 6.
[4] 2 Cor. vi. 10.

ing you, and how light will rise out of the darkness. You must begin by denying yourselves your natural wishes,—a painful work; by refraining from sin, by rousing from sloth, by preserving your tongue from insincere words, and your hands from deceitful dealings, and your eyes from beholding vanity; by watching against the first rising of anger, pride, impurity, obstinacy, jealousy; by learning to endure the laugh of irreligious men for Christ's sake; by forcing your minds to follow seriously the words of prayer, though it be difficult to you, and by keeping before you the thought of God all through the day. These things you will be able to do if you do but seek the mighty help of God the Holy Spirit which is given you; and while you follow after them, then, in the prophet's language, "your light shall rise in obscurity, and your darkness shall be as the noonday. And the Lord shall guide you continually, and satisfy your soul in drought: and you shall be like a watered garden, and like a spring of water, whose waters fail not."[1]

[1] Isa. lviii. 10, 11.

SERMON LIII.

(SUNDAYS AFTER TRINITY.)

𝕿𝖍𝖊 𝕾𝖍𝖊𝖕𝖍𝖊𝖗𝖉 𝖔𝖋 𝖔𝖚𝖗 𝕾𝖔𝖚𝖑𝖘.

" I am the good Shepherd: the good Shepherd giveth His life for the sheep."
—JOHN x. 11.

OUR Lord here appropriates to Himself the title under which
He had been foretold by the prophets. "David My servant shall be king over them," says Almighty God by the mouth
of Ezekiel: "and they all shall have one Shepherd." And in
the Book of Zechariah, "Awake, O sword, against My Shepherd,
and against the man that is My fellow, saith the Lord of Hosts;
smite the Shepherd, and the sheep shall be scattered." And in
like manner St. Peter speaks of our returning "to the Shepherd
and Bishop of our souls." [1]

"The good Shepherd giveth His life for the sheep." In those
countries of the East where our Lord appeared, the office of a
shepherd is not only a lowly and simple office, and an office of
trust, as it is with us, but, moreover, an office of great hardship
and of peril. Our flocks are exposed to no enemies, such as our
Lord describes. The shepherd here has no need to prove his
fidelity to the sheep by encounters with fierce beasts of prey.
The hireling shepherd is not tried. But where our Lord dwelt
in the days of His flesh it was otherwise. There it was true
that the good Shepherd giveth His life for the sheep—"but he
that is an hireling, and whose own the sheep are not, seeth the
wolf coming, and leaveth the sheep, and fleeth, and the wolf
catcheth them and scattereth the sheep. The hireling fleeth,
because he is an hireling, and careth not for the sheep."

[1] Ezek. xxxvii. 24. Zech. xiii. 7. 1 Pet. ii. 25.

Our Lord found the sheep scattered ; or, as He had said shortly before, "All that ever came before Me are thieves and robbers ;" and in consequence the sheep had no guide. Such were the priests and rulers of the Jews when Christ came ; so that "when He saw the multitudes He was moved with compassion on them, because they fainted, and were scattered abroad as sheep having no shepherd."[1] Such, in like manner, were the rulers and prophets of Israel in the days of Ahab, when Micaiah, the Lord's prophet, "saw all Israel scattered on the hills, as sheep that have not a shepherd, and the Lord said, These have no Master, let them return every man to his house in peace."[2] Such, too, were the shepherds in the time of Ezekiel, of whom the prophet says, "Woe be to the shepherds of Israel that do feed themselves ! should not the shepherd feed the flocks? . . . . They were scattered, because there is no shepherd : and they became meat to all the beasts of the field, when they were scattered :"[3] and in the time of the Prophet Zechariah, who says, "Woe to the idle shepherd that leaveth the flock !"[4]

So was it all over the world when Christ came in His infinite mercy "to gather in one the children of God that were scattered abroad." And though for a moment, when in the conflict with the enemy the good Shepherd had to lay down His life for the sheep, they were left without a guide (according to the prophecy already quoted, "Smite the Shepherd and the sheep shall be scattered"), yet He soon rose from death to live for ever, according to that other prophecy which said, "He that scattered Israel will gather him, as a shepherd doth his flock."[5] And as He says Himself in the parable before us, "He calleth His own sheep by name and leadeth them out, and goeth before them, and the sheep follow Him, for they know His voice," so, on His resurrection, while Mary wept, He did call her by her name,[6] and she turned herself and knew Him by the ear whom she had not known by the eye. So, too, He said, "Simon, son of Jonas, lovest thou Me?"[7] And He added, "Follow Me." And so again He and His Angel told the women, "Behold He goeth before you into Galilee . . . . go tell My brethren, that they go into Galilee, and there shall they see Me."

From that time the good Shepherd, who took the place of the sheep, and died that they might live for ever, has gone before them : and "they follow the Lamb whithersoever He goeth ;"[8]

[1] Matt. ix. 36.   [2] 1 Kings xxii. 17.   [3] Ezek. xxxiv. 2, 5.
[4] Zech. xi. 17.   [5] Jer. xxxi. 10.   [6] John xx. 16.
[7] John xxi. 15.   [8] Rev. xiv. 4.

going their way forth by the footsteps of the flock, and feeding their kids beside the shepherds' tents.[1]

No earthly images can come up to the awful and gracious truth, that God became the Son of man—that the Word became flesh, and was born of a woman. This ineffable mystery surpasses human words. No titles of earth can Christ give to Himself, ever so lowly or mean, which will fitly show us His condescension. His act and deed is too great even for His own lips to utter it. Yet He delights in the image contained in the text, as conveying to us, in such degree as we can receive it, some notion of the degradation, hardship, and pain which He underwent for our sake.

Hence it was prophesied under this figure by the Prophet Isaiah, "Behold, the Lord God will come with strong hand, and His arm shall rule for Him . . . . He shall feed His flock like a shepherd : He shall gather the lambs with His arm, and carry them in His bosom, and shall gently lead those that are with young."[2] And, again, He promises by the mouth of Ezekiel, "Behold, I, even I, will both search My sheep, and seek them out. As a shepherd seeketh out his flock in the day that he is among his sheep that are scattered ; so will I seek out My sheep, and will deliver them out of all places where they have been scattered in the cloudy and dark day."[3] And the Psalmist says of Him, " The Lord is my Shepherd, therefore can I lack nothing. He shall feed me in a green pasture, and lead me forth beside the waters of comfort."[4] And he addresses Him, " Hear, O Thou Shepherd of Israel, Thou that leadest Joseph like a sheep, show Thyself also, Thou that sittest upon the Cherubims."[5] And He Himself says in a parable, speaking of Himself, " What man of you having a hundred sheep, if he lose one of them, doth not leave the ninety and nine in the wilderness, and go after that which is lost, until he find it ? And when he hath found it, he layeth it on his shoulders, rejoicing."[6]

Observe, my brethren, it is here said that Christ, the Lord of Angels, condescends to lay the lost sheep on His shoulders : in a former passage of the Prophet Isaiah it was said that He should " gather them with His arm, and carry them in His bosom." By carrying them in His bosom is meant the love He bears them, and the fulness of His grace ; by carrying them on His shoulders is signified the security of their dwelling-place ; as of old time it was said of Benjamin, " The beloved of the Lord shall dwell in

---

[1] Cant. i. 8. [2] Isa. xl. 10, 11. [3] Ezek. xxxiv. 11, 12.
[4] Ps. xxiii. 1, 2. [5] Ps. lxxx. 1. [6] Luke xv. 4, 5.

safety by Him . . . . and the Lord shall cover him all the day long, and He shall dwell between His shoulders;"[1] and again, of Israel, "As an eagle stirreth up her nest, fluttereth over her young, spreadeth abroad her wings, taketh them, beareth them on her wings : so the Lord alone did lead him, and there was no strange god with him." And again, in the Prophet Isaiah, "Bel boweth down, Nebo stoopeth ; their idols were upon the beasts and upon the cattle . . . . hearken unto Me, O house of Jacob . . . . which are carried *by Me* from the womb. . . . . Even to your old age I am He, and even to hoary hairs will I carry you ; I have made and I will bear, even I will carry, and will deliver you."[2]   He alone, who "bowed Himself and came down," He alone could do it ; He alone could bear a whole world's weight, the load of a guilty world, the burden of man's sin, the accumulated debt, past, present, and to come ; the sufferings which we owed but could not pay, the wrath of God on the children of Adam ; "in His own body on the tree,"[3] "being made a curse for us,"[4] "the just for the unjust, that He might bring us unto God," "through the Eternal Spirit offering Himself without spot to God, and purging our conscience from dead works to serve the Living God."[5]   Such was the deed of Christ, laying down His life for us : and therefore He is called the Good Shepherd.

And hence, in like manner, from the time of Adam to that of Christ, a shepherd's work has been marked out with special divine favour, as being a shadow of the good Shepherd who was to come.   "Righteous Abel" was "a keeper of sheep," "and in process of time" he "brought of the firstlings of his flock and of the fat thereof.   And the Lord had respect unto Abel and to his offering."[6]   And who were they to whom the Angels first brought the news that a Saviour was born?   "Shepherds abiding in the field, keeping watch over their flock by night."[7]   And what is the description given of the chosen family when they descended into Egypt?   "Thy servants," they say, "are shepherds, both we and also our fathers;"[8] and what, in consequence, was their repute in Egypt, which surely is a figure of the world? "Every shepherd is an abomination unto the Egyptians."[9]

But there are three favoured servants of God in particular, special types of the Saviour to come, men raised from low estate to great honour, in whom it was His will that His pastoral office should be thus literally fulfilled.   And the first is Jacob, the

---

[1] Deut. xxxiii. 12.   [2] Deut. xxxii. 11.   Isa. xlvi. 1-4.   [3] 1 Pet. ii. 24.
[4] Gal. iii. 13.   [5] 1 Pet. iii. 18.   Heb. ix. 14.   [6] Gen. iv. 2, 4.
[7] Luke ii. 8.   [8] Gen. xlvii. 3.   [9] Gen. xlvi. 34.

father of the patriarchs, who appeared before Pharaoh. He became, as Abraham before him, a father of many nations; he "increased exceedingly, and had much cattle, and maid-servants, and men-servants, and camels, and asses,"[1] and he was visited by supernatural favours, and had a new name given him—Israel for Jacob. But at the first he was, as his descendants solemnly confessed year by year, "a Syrian ready to perish;" and what was his employment? the care of sheep; and with what toil and suffering, and for how many years, we learn from his expostulation with his hard master and relative, Laban: "This twenty years have I been with thee," he says; "thy ewes and thy she-goats have not cast their young, and the rams of thy flock have I not eaten. That which was torn of beasts I brought not unto thee; I bare the loss of it; of my hand didst thou require it, whether stolen by day, or stolen by night. Thus I was; in the day the drought consumed me, and the frost by night; and my sleep departed from mine eyes. Thus have I been twenty years in thy house; . . . . and thou hast changed my wages ten times."[2]

Who is more favoured than Jacob, who was exalted to be a Prince with God, and to prevail by intercession? Yet, you see, he is a shepherd, to image to us that mystical and true Shepherd and Bishop of souls who was to come. Yet there is a second and a third as highly favoured in various ways. The second is Moses, who drove away the rival shepherds and helped the daughters of the Priest of Midian to water their flock; and who, while he was keeping the flock of Jethro, his father-in-law, saw the Angel of the Lord in a flame of fire in a bush. And the third is David, the man after God's own heart. He was "the man who was raised up on high, the anointed of the God of Jacob, and the sweet Psalmist of Israel;"[3] but he was found among the sheep. "He took him away from the sheep-folds; as he was following the ewes great with young ones, He took him; that he might feed Jacob His people, and Israel His inheritance. So he fed them with a faithful and true heart, and ruled them prudently with all his power."[4] Samuel came to Jesse, and looked through his seven sons, one by one, but found not him whom God had chosen: "And Samuel said unto Jesse, Are here all thy children? And he said, There remaineth yet the youngest, and, behold, he keepeth the sheep." And when he came "he was ruddy, and withal of a beautiful countenance, and goodly to look to; and the Lord said, Arise, anoint him, for this is he."[5] And again,

[1] Gen. xxx. 43.   [2] Gen. xxxi. 38-41.   [3] 2 Sam. xxiii. 1.
[4] Ps. lxxviii. 71-73.   [5] 1 Sam. xvi. 11, 12.

after he had been in Saul's court, he "went and returned from Saul, to feed his father's sheep at Bethlehem;"[1] and when he came to the army his brother reproached him for "leaving those his few sheep in the wilderness;" and when he was brought before Saul, he gave an account how a lion and a bear "took a lamb out of the flock," and he went after them, and slew them both, and delivered it. Such were the shepherds of old times, men at once of peace and of war; men of simplicity, indeed, "plain men living in tents," "the meekest of men," yet not easy, indolent men, sitting in green meadows, and by cool streams, but men of rough duties, who were under the necessity to suffer, while they had the opportunity to do exploits.

And if such were the figures, how much more was the Truth itself, the good Shepherd, when He came, both guileless and heroic? If shepherds are men of simple lives and obscure fortunes, uncorrupted and unknown in kings' courts and marts of commerce, how much more He who was "the carpenter's Son," who was "meek and lowly of heart," who "did not strive nor cry," who "went about doing good," who "when He was reviled, reviled not again," and who was "despised and rejected of men?" If, on the other hand, they are men of suffering and trial, how much more so He who was "a man of sorrows," and who "laid down His life for the sheep"?

"That which was torn of beasts I brought not unto thee," says Jacob; "I bare the loss of it; of my hand didst thou require it." And has not Christ undertaken the charge of our souls? Has He not made Himself answerable for us whom the devil had rent? Like the good Samaritan, "Take care of him," He says, "and whatsoever thou spendest more, when I come again I will repay thee."[2] Or, as in another parable, under another image: "Lord, let it alone this year also . . . . and if it bear fruit, well; and if not, then after that thou shalt cut it down."[3] "In the day the drought consumed me," says Jacob; and who was He who at midday sat down at that very Jacob's well, tired with His journey, and needing some of that water to quench His thirst, whereof "Jacob drank himself, and his children and his cattle"? Yet whereas He had a living water to impart, which the world knew not of, He preferred, as became the good Shepherd, to offer it to one of those lost sheep whom He came to seek and to save, rather than to take at her hand the water from the well, or to accept the offer of His disciples, when they came with meat from the city, and said, "Master, eat." "The

[1] 1 Sam. xvii. 15, 28, 35-37.   [2] Luke x. 35.   [3] Luke xiii. 8, 9.

frost" consumed me "by night," says Jacob, "and my sleep departed from mine eyes;" and read we not of One whose wont it was to rise a long while before day, and continue in prayer to God? who passed nights in the mountain, or on the sea? who dwelt forty days in the wilderness? who, in the evening and night of His passion, was forlorn in the bleak garden, or stripped and bleeding in the cold judgment hall?

Again: Moses, amid his sheep, saw the vision of God and was told of God's adorable Name; and Christ, the true Shepherd, lived a life of contemplation in the midst of His laborious ministry; He was transfigured on the mountain, and no man knew the Son but the Father, nor the Father but the Son.

Jacob endured, Moses meditated — and David wrought. Jacob endured the frost, and heat, and sleepless nights, and paid the price of the lost sheep; Moses was taken up into the mount for forty days; David fought with the foe, and recovered the prey—he rescued it from the mouth of the lion, and the paw of the bear, and killed the ravenous beasts. Christ, too, not only suffered with Jacob, and was in contemplation with Moses, but fought and conquered with David. David defended his father's sheep at Bethlehem; Christ, born and heralded to the shepherds at Bethlehem, suffered on the Cross in order to conquer. He came "from Edom, with dyed garments from Bozrah;"[1] but He was "glorious in His apparel," for He trod the people "in His anger, and trampled them in His fury, and their blood was sprinkled upon His garments, and He stained all His raiment." Jacob was not as David, nor David as Jacob, nor either of them as Moses; but Christ was all three, as fulfilling all types, the lowly Jacob, the wise Moses, the heroic David, all in one— Priest, Prophet, and King.

My brethren, we say daily, "We are His people, and the sheep of His pasture." Again, we say, "We have erred and strayed from Thy ways, like lost sheep:" let us never forget these truths; let us never forget, on the one hand, that we are sinners; let us never forget, on the other hand, that Christ is our Guide and Guardian. He is "the Way, the Truth, and the Life."[2] He is a light unto our ways, and a lanthorn unto our paths. He is our Shepherd, and the sheep know His voice. If we are His sheep, we shall hear it, recognise it, and obey it. Let us beware of not following when He goes before: "He goes before, and His sheep follow Him, for they know His voice." Let us beware of receiving His grace in vain. When God called

[1] Isa. lxiii. 1-3. [2] John xiv. 6.

Samuel, he answered, "Speak, Lord, for Thy servant heareth."
When Christ called St. Paul, he "was not disobedient to the
heavenly vision." Let us desire to know His voice; let us pray
for the gift of watchful ears and a willing heart. He does not
call all men in one way; He calls us each in His own way. To
St. Peter He said, "Follow thou Me;" of St. John, "If I will
that he tarry till I come, what is that to thee?" Nor is it
always easy to know His voice. St. John knew it, and said, "It
is the Lord," before St. Peter. Samuel did not know it till Eli
told him. St. Paul asked, "Who art Thou, Lord?" We are
bid "try the spirits, whether they be of God." But whatever
difficulty there be in knowing when Christ calls, and whither,
yet at least let us look out for His call. Let us not be content
with ourselves; let us not make our own hearts our home, or this
world our home, or our friends our home; let us look out for a
better country, that is, an heavenly. Let us look out for Him
who alone can guide us to that better country; let us call heaven
our home, and this life a pilgrimage; let us view ourselves, as
sheep in the trackless desert, who, unless they follow the shepherd, will be sure to lose themselves, sure to fall in with the wolf.
We are safe while we keep close to Him, and under His eye;
but if we suffer Satan to gain an advantage over us, woe to us!

Blessed are they who give the flower of their days, and their
strength of soul and body to Him; blessed are they who in their
youth turn to Him who gave His life for them, and would fain
give it to them and implant it in them, that they may live for
ever. Blessed are they who resolve—come good, come evil,
come sunshine, come tempest, come honour, come dishonour—
that He shall be their Lord and Master, their King and God!
They will come to a perfect end, and to peace at the last. They
will, with Jacob, confess Him, ere they die, as "the God that
fed them all their life long unto that day, the Angel which
redeemed them from all evil;"[1] with Moses, that "as is their
day, so shall their strength be;" and with David, that in "the
valley of the shadow of death, they fear no evil, for He is with
them, and that His rod and His staff comfort them;" for "when
they pass through the waters He will be with them, and through
the rivers, they shall not overflow them; when they walk
through the fire, they shall not be burnt, neither shall the flame
kindle upon them, for He is the Lord their God, the Holy One
of Israel, their Saviour."

[1] Gen. xlviii. 15, 16.

SERMON LIV.

(SUNDAYS AFTER TRINITY.)

Doing Glory to God in Pursuits of the World.

" *Whether, therefore, ye eat or drink, or whatsoever ye do, do all to the glory of God.*"—I COR. x. 31.

WHEN persons are convinced that life is short, that it is unequal to any great purpose, that it does not display adequately, or bring to perfection the true Christian, when they feel that the next life is all in all, and that eternity is the only subject that really can claim or can fill their thoughts, then they are apt to undervalue this life altogether, and to forget its real importance. They are apt to wish to spend the time of their sojourning here in a positive separation from active and social duties : yet it should be recollected that the employments of this world, though not themselves heavenly, are, after all, the way to heaven—though not the fruit, are the seed of immortality—and are valuable, though not in themselves, yet for that to which they lead : but it is difficult to realize this. It is difficult to realize both truths at once, and to connect both truths together; steadily to contemplate the life to come, yet to act in this. Those who meditate, are likely to neglect those active duties which are, in fact, incumbent on them, and to dwell upon the thought of God's glory, till they forget to act to His glory. This state of mind is chided in figure in the words of the holy Angels to the Apostles, when they say, " Ye men of Galilee, why stand ye gazing up into heaven ? "[1]

In various ways does the thought of the next world lead men to neglect their duty in this ; and whenever it does so we may be sure that there is something wrong and unchristian, not in

[1] Acts i. 11.

their thinking of the next world, but in their manner of thinking of it. For though the contemplation of God's glory may in certain times and persons allowably interfere with the active employments of life, as in the case of the Apostles when our Saviour ascended, and though such contemplation is even freely allowed or commanded us at certain times of each day; yet that is not a real and true meditation on Christ, but some counterfeit, which makes us dream away our time, or become habitually indolent, or which withdraws us from our existing duties, or unsettles us.

Yet the thought of the world unseen is apt to do so in various ways, and the worst way of all is when we have taken up a notion that it *ought* to do so. And indeed this is a temptation to which persons who desire to be religious are exposed in one shape or another in every age, and in this age as well as in times past. Men come to fancy that to lose taste and patience for the businesses of this life is renouncing the world and becoming spiritually-minded. We will say a person has been thoughtless and irreligious; perhaps openly so; or at least careless about religion; and though innocent of any flagrant sin, yet a follower of his own will and fancy, and unpractised in any regular and consistent course of religion. He has, perhaps, been outwardly respectful to sacred things and persons, but has had no serious thoughts about the next world. He has taken good and evil—religion and the world—as they came, first one and then the other, without much consideration. He has been fond of gaiety and amusements, or he has been deeply interested in some pursuit or other of time and sense,—whether it be his own trade or profession, or some of the studies and employments now popular. He has fallen in with the ways of the company in which he has found himself; has been profane with the profane; then, again, has had for a season religious impressions, which in turn have worn away. Thus he has lived, and something has then occurred really to rouse him and give him what is called a serious turn. Such a person, man or woman, young or old, certainly does need to take a serious turn, does require a change; and no one but must be very glad to hear that a change has taken place, though at the same time there may be changes not much better than the change which happened to him, whose soul, in our Lord's language, was but "swept and garnished;" not really changed in a heavenly way, and having but the semblance of faith and holiness upon it.

Now the cases I am speaking of are somewhat like that which

our Saviour seems to speak of in the passage referred to. When a man has been roused to serious resolutions, the chances are, that he fails to take up with the one and only narrow way which leads to life. The chances are that "then cometh the wicked one," and persuades him to choose some path short of the true one—easier and pleasanter than it. And *this* is the kind of course to which he is often seduced, as we frequently witness it; viz. to feel a sort of dislike and contempt for his ordinary worldly business as something beneath him. He knows he must have what Scripture calls a spiritual mind, and he fancies that to have a spiritual mind it is absolutely necessary to renounce all earnestness or activity in his worldly employments, to profess to take no interest in them, to despise the natural and ordinary pleasures of life, violating the customs of society, adopting a melancholy air and a sad tone of voice, and remaining silent and absent when among his natural friends and relatives, as if saying to himself, "I have much higher thoughts than to engage in all these perishing miserable things;" acting with constraint and difficulty in the things about him; making efforts to turn things which occur to the purpose of what he considers spiritual reflection; using certain Scripture phrases and expressions; delighting to exchange Scripture sentiments with persons whom he meets of his own way of thinking; nay, making visible and audible signs of deep feeling when Scripture or other religious subjects are mentioned, and the like. He thinks he lives out of the world, and out of its engagements, if he shuts (as it were) his eyes, and sits down doing nothing. Altogether he looks upon his worldly occupation simply as a burden and a cross, and considers it all gain to be able to throw it off; and the sooner he can release himself from it, and the oftener, so much the better.

Now I am far from denying that a man's worldly occupation *may* be his cross. Again, I am far from denying that under circumstances it may be right even to retire from the world. But I am speaking of cases when it is a person's duty to remain in his worldly calling, and when he does remain in it, but when he cherishes dissatisfaction with it: whereas what he ought to feel is this,—that *while* in it he is to glorify God, not *out* of it, but *in* it, and *by means* of it, according to the Apostle's direction, "not slothful in business, fervent in spirit, serving the Lord." The Lord Jesus Christ our Saviour is best served, and with the most fervent spirit, when men are not slothful in business, but do their duty in that state of life in which it has pleased God to call them.

Now what leads such a person into this mistake is, that he sees that most men who engage cheerfully and diligently in worldly business, do so from a worldly spirit, from a low carnal love of the world; and so he thinks it is *his* duty, on the contrary, *not* to take a cheerful part in the world's business at all. And it cannot be denied that the greater part of the world is *absorbed* in the world; so much so that I am almost afraid to speak of the duty of being active in our worldly business, lest I should seem to give countenance to that miserable devotion to the things of time and sense, that love of bustle and management, that desire of gain, and that aiming at influence and importance, which abound on all sides. Bad as it is to be languid and indifferent in our secular duties, and to account this religion, yet it is far worse to be the slaves of this world, and to have our hearts in the concerns of this world. I do not know anything more dreadful than a state of mind which is, perhaps, the characteristic of this country, and which the prosperity of this country so miserably fosters. I mean that ambitious spirit, to use a great word, but I know no other word to express my meaning—that low ambition which sets every one on the look-out to succeed and to rise in life, to amass money, to gain power, to depress his rivals, to triumph over his hitherto superiors, to affect a consequence and a gentility which he had not before, to affect to have an opinion on high subjects, to pretend to form a judgment upon sacred things, to choose his religion, to approve and condemn according to his taste, to become a partizan in extensive measures for the supposed temporal benefit of the community, to indulge the vision of great things which are to come, great improvements, great wonders : all things vast, all things new,—this most fearfully earthly and grovelling spirit is likely, alas ! to extend itself more and more among our country-men,—an intense, sleepless, restless, never-wearied, never-satisfied, pursuit of Mammon in one shape or other, to the exclusion of all deep, all holy, all calm, all reverent thoughts. *This* is the spirit in which, more or less (according to their different tempers), men do commonly engage in concerns of this world ; and I repeat it, better, far better, were it to retire from the world altogether than thus to engage in it—better with Elijah to fly to the desert, than to serve Baal and Ashtoreth in Jerusalem.

But the persons I speak of, as despising this world, are far removed from the spirit of Elijah. To flee from the world, or strenuously to resist it, implies an energy and strength of mind which they have not. They do neither one thing nor the other; they neither flee it, nor engage zealously in its concerns; but they remain in the midst of them, doing them in an indolent and negligent way, and think this is to be spiritually-minded; or, as in other cases, they really take an interest in them, and yet speak as if they despised them.

But surely it is possible to "serve the Lord," yet not to be "slothful in business;" not over-devoted to it, but not to retire from it. We may do *all things* whatever we are about to God's glory; we may do all things *heartily,* as to the Lord, and not to man, being both active yet meditative; and now let me give some instances to show what I mean.

1. "Do all to the glory of God," says St. Paul in the text; nay, "whether we eat or drink;" so that it appears nothing is too slight or trivial to glorify Him in. We will suppose then, to take the case mentioned just now; we will suppose a man who has lately had more serious thoughts than he had before, and determines to live more religiously. In consequence of the turn his mind has taken he feels a distaste for his worldly occupation, whether he is in trade, or in any mechanical employment which allows little exercise of mind. He now feels he would rather be in some other business, though in itself his present occupation is quite lawful and pleasing to God. The ill-instructed man will at once get impatient and quit it; or if he does not quit it, at least he will be negligent and indolent in it. But the true penitent will say to himself, "No; if it be an irksome employment, so much the more does it suit *me.* I deserve no better. I do not deserve to be fed even with husks. I am bound to afflict my soul for my past sins. If I were to go in sackcloth and ashes, if I were to live on bread and water, if I were to wash the feet of the poor day by day, it would not be too great an humiliation; and the only reason I do not, is, that I have no call that way, it would look ostentatious. Gladly then will I hail an inconvenience which will try me without any one's knowing it. Far from repining, I will, through God's grace, go cheerfully about what I do not like. ·I will deny myself. I know that with His help what is in itself painful will thus be pleasant as done towards Him. I know well that there is no pain but may be borne comfortably, by the thought of Him, and by His grace, and the strong determination of the will; nay, none but may soothe and solace me. Even the natural taste and smell may be made to like what they naturally dislike; even bitter medicine, which is nauseous to the palate, may by a resolute will become

tolerable. Nay, even sufferings and torture, such as martyrs have borne, have before now been rejoiced in and embraced heartily from love to Christ. I then, a sinner, will take this light inconvenience in a generous way, pleased at the opportunity of disciplining myself, and with self-abasement, as needing a severe penitence. If there be parts in my occupation which I especially dislike, if it requires a good deal of moving about and I wish to be at home, or if it be sedentary and I wish to be in motion, or if it requires rising early and I like to rise late, or if it makes me solitary and I like to be with friends, all this unpleasant part, as far as is consistent with my health, and so that it is not likely to be a snare to me, I will choose by preference. Again, I see my religious views are a hindrance to me. I see persons are suspicious of me. I see that I offend people by my scrupulousness. I see that to get on in life requires far more devotion to my worldly business than I can give consistently with my duty to God, or without its becoming a temptation to me. I know that I ought not, and (please God) I will not, sacrifice my religion to it. My religious seasons and hours shall be my own. I will not countenance any of the worldly dealings and practices, the over-reaching ways, the sordid actions in which others indulge. And if I am thrown back in life thereby, if I make less gains or lose friends, and so come to be despised, and find others rise in the world while I remain where I was, hard though this be to bear, it is an humiliation which becomes me in requital for my sins, and in obedience to God ; and a very slight one it is, merely to be deprived of worldly successes, or rather it is a gain. And this may be the manner in which Almighty God will make an opening for me, if it is His blessed will, to leave my present occupation. But leave it without a call from God, I certainly must not. On the contrary, I will work in it the more diligently, as far as higher duties allow me."

2. A second reason which will animate the Christian will be a desire of letting his light shine before men. He will aim at winning others by his own diligence and activity. He will say to himself, "My parents" or "my master" or "employer shall never say of me, Religion has spoiled him. They shall see me more active and alive than before. I will be punctual and attentive, and adorn the Gospel of God our Saviour. My companions shall never have occasion to laugh at any affectation of religious feeling in me. No; I will affect nothing. In a manly way I will, with God's blessing, do my duty. I will not, as far as I can help, dishonour His service by any strangeness or extrava-

gance of conduct, any unreality of words, any over-softness or constraint of manner; but they shall see that the fear of God only makes those who cherish it more respectable in the world's eyes as well as more heavenly-minded. What a blessed return it will be for God's mercies to me, if I, who am like a brand plucked out of the burning, be allowed, through His great mercy, to recommend that Gospel to others which He has revealed to me, and to recommend it, as on the one hand by my strictness in attending God's ordinances, in discountenancing vice and folly, and by a conscientious walk; so, on the other hand, by all that is of good report in social life, by uprightness, honesty, prudence, and straightforwardness, by good temper, good-nature, and brotherly love!"

3. Thankfulness to Almighty God, nay, and the inward life of the Spirit itself, will be additional principles causing the Christian to labour diligently in his calling. He will see God in all things. He will recollect our Saviour's life. Christ was brought up to a humble trade. When he labours in his own, he will think of his Lord and Master in His. He will recollect that Christ went down to Nazareth and was subject to His parents, that He walked long journeys, that He bore the sun's heat and the storm, and had not where to lay His head. Again, he knows that the Apostles had various employments of this world before their calling; St. Andrew and St. Peter fishers, St. Matthew a tax-gatherer, and St. Paul, even after his calling, still a tent-maker. Accordingly, in whatever comes upon him, he will endeavour to discern and gaze (as it were) on the countenance of his Saviour. He will feel that the true contemplation of that Saviour lies *in* his worldly business; that as Christ is seen in the poor, and in the persecuted, and in children, so is He seen in the employments which He puts upon His chosen, whatever they be; that in attending to his own calling he will be meeting Christ; that if he neglect it, he will not on that account enjoy His presence at all the more, but that while performing it, he will see Christ revealed to his soul amid the ordinary actions of the day, as by a sort of sacrament. Thus he will take his worldly business as a gift from Him, and will love it as such.

4. True humility is another principle which will lead us to desire to glorify God in our worldly employments if possible, instead of resigning them. Christ evidently puts His greater blessings on those whom the world despises. He has bid His followers take the lowest seat. He says that he who would be great must be as the servant of all, that he who humbleth himself shall be exalted; and He Himself washed His disciples' feet.

2 G

Nay, He tells us, that He will gird Himself, and serve them who have watched for Him; an astonishing condescension, which makes us almost dumb with fear and rejoicing. All this has its effect upon the Christian, and he sets about his business with alacrity, and without a moment's delay, delighting to humble himself, and to have the opportunity of putting himself in that condition of life which our Lord especially blessed.

5. Still further, he will use his worldly business as a means of keeping him from vain and unprofitable thoughts. One cause of the heart's devising evil is, that time is given it to do so. The man who has his daily duties, who lays out his time for them hour by hour, is saved a multitude of sins which have not time to get hold upon him. The brooding over insults received, or the longing after some good not granted, or regret at losses which have befallen us, or at the loss of friends by death, or the attacks of impure and shameful thoughts, these are kept off from him who takes care to be diligent and well employed. Leisure is the occasion of all evil. Idleness is the first step in the downward path which leads to hell. If we do not find employment to engage our minds with, Satan will be sure to find his own employment for them. Here we see the difference of motive with which a religious and a worldly-minded man may do the same thing. Suppose a person has had some sad affliction, say a bereavement: men of this world, having no pleasure in religion, not liking to dwell on a loss to them irreparable, in order to drown reflection, betake themselves to worldly pursuits to divert their thoughts and banish gloom. The Christian under the same circumstances does the same thing; but it is from a fear lest he should relax and enfeeble his mind by barren sorrow; from a dread of becoming discontented; from a belief that he is pleasing God better, and is likely to secure his peace more fully, by not losing time; from a feeling that, far from forgetting those whom he has lost by thus acting, he shall only enjoy the thought of them the more really and the more religiously.

6. Lastly, we see what judgment to give in a question sometimes agitated, whether one should retire from our worldly business at the close of life, to give our thoughts more entirely to God. To wish to do so is so natural, that I suppose there is no one who would not wish it. A great many persons are not allowed the privilege, a great many are allowed it through increasing infirmities or extreme old age; but every one, I conceive, if allowed to choose, would think it a privilege to be allowed it, though a great many would find it difficult to determine *when* was the fit time. But let us consider what is the

reason of this so natural a wish. I fear that it is often not a religious wish, often only partially religious. I fear a great number of persons who aim at retiring from the world's business, do so under the notion of their then enjoying themselves somewhat after the manner of the rich man in the Gospel, who said, " Soul, thou hast much goods laid up for many years." If this is the predominant aim of any one, of course I need not say that it is a fatal sin, for Christ Himself has said so. Others there are who are actuated by a mixed feeling; they are aware that they do not give so much time to religion as they ought; they do not live by rule; nay, they are not satisfied with the correctness or uprightness of some of the practices or customs which their way of life requires of them, and they get tired of active business as life goes on, and wish to be at ease. So they look to their last years as a time of retirement, in which they may *both* enjoy themselves *and* prepare for heaven. And thus they satisfy both their conscience and their love of the world. At present religion is irksome to them; but then, as they hope, duty and pleasure will go together. Now, putting aside all other mistakes which such a frame of mind evidences, let it be observed, that if they are at present *not* serving God with all their hearts, but look forward to a time when they shall do so, then it is plain that, when at length they *do* put aside worldly cares and turn to God, if ever they do, that time must necessarily be a time of deep humiliation, if it is to be acceptable to Him, not a comfortable retirement. Who ever heard of a pleasurable, easy, joyous repentance? It is a contradiction in terms. These men, if they do but reflect a moment, must confess that their present mode of life, supposing it be not so strict as it should be, is heaping up tears and groans for their last years, not enjoyment. The longer they live as they do at present, not only the more unlikely is it that they will repent at all; but even if they do, the more bitter, the more painful must their repentance be. The only way to escape suffering for sin hereafter is to suffer for it here. Sorrow here or misery hereafter; they cannot escape one or the other.

Not for any worldly reason, then, not on any presumptuous or unbelieving motive, does the Christian desire leisure and retirement for his last years. Nay, he will be content to do without these blessings, and the highest Christian of all is he whose heart is so stayed on God, that he does not wish or need it; whose heart is so set on things above, that things below as little excite, agitate, unsettle, distress, and seduce him, as they stop the course of nature, as they stop the sun and moon, or change summer and winter. Such were the Apostles, who, as the heavenly bodies, went out "to all lands," full of business, and yet full too of sweet harmony, even to the ends of the earth. Their calling was heavenly, but their work was earthly; they were in labour and trouble till the last; yet consider how calmly St. Paul and St. Peter write in their last days. St. John, on the other hand, was allowed, in a great measure, to retire from the cares of his pastoral charge, and such, I say, will be the natural wish of every religious man, whether his ministry be spiritual or secular; but, not in order to *begin* to fix his mind on God, but merely because, though he may contemplate God as truly and be as holy in heart in active business as in quiet, still it is more becoming and suitable to meet the stroke of death (if it be allowed us) silently, collectedly, solemnly, than in a crowd and a tumult. And hence it is, among other reasons, that we pray in the Litany to be delivered "from *sudden* death."

On the whole, then, what I have said comes to this, that whereas Adam was sentenced to labour as a punishment, Christ has by His coming sanctified it as a means of grace and a sacrifice of thanksgiving, a sacrifice cheerfully to be offered up to the Father in His Name.

It is very easy to speak and teach this, difficult to do it; very difficult to steer between the two evils,—to use this world as not abusing it, to be active and diligent in this world's affairs, yet not for this world's sake, but for God's sake. It requires the greater effort for a minister of Christ to speak of it, for this reason; because he is not called upon in the same sense in which others are to practise the duty. He is not called, as his people are, to the professions, the pursuits, and cares of this world; his work is heavenly, and to it he gives himself wholly. It is a work which, we trust, is not likely to carry him off from God; not only because it is His work, but, what is a more sure reason, because commonly it gains no great thanks from men. However, for this reason it is difficult for Christian ministers to speak about your trial in this matter, my brethren, because it is not theirs. We are tried by the command to live out of the world, and you by the command to live in it.

May God give us grace in our several spheres and stations to do His will and adorn His doctrine; that whether we eat and drink, or fast and pray, labour with our hands or with our minds, journey about or remain at rest, we may glorify Him who has purchased us with His own blood!

EDINBURGH: T. AND A. CONSTABLE,
PRINTERS TO THE QUEEN, AND TO THE UNIVERSITY.